Maroon & Gold

A History of Sun Devil Athletics

Bob Eger

Sports Publishing L.L.C.
www.SportsPublishingLLC.com

Project manager, book design: Erin J. Sands
Book layout: Erin J. Sands and Jennifer Polson
Photo editor: Bob Eger

Photos Courtesy of ASU Media Relations; University Libraries, Department of Archives and Manuscripts; ASU Alumni Association; various private collections.

ISBN: 1-58261-223-4
Library of Congress Catalog Card Number: 00-101408

Printed in the United States.

WWW.SPORTSPUBLISHINGINC.COM

—To Rick—

*He was as tough as a Frank Kush-coached football team
and the only person who could make me laugh as much as Jim Brock.*

Contents

Acknowledgments

Visions of spending a hard-earned retirement sitting on the beach in Mexico, digging in the ice chest for a cold one while perusing the latest edition of *Baseball America*, were dancing through my head when Mark Brand, Arizona State's assistant athletic director for media relations, pitched this book project to me early in the spring of 1998. Oh, well, I thought. The beach isn't going anywhere. And I had kicked around thoughts of such a project for many years.

Little did I know what I was getting into. Having been around the ASU sports scene on pretty-much a daily basis as a newspaper reporter since 1959, I had a good working knowledge of that period, and I thought I had a decent grasp of the school's early history. Every day in the archives, however, was like a treasure hunt as I unearthed one tidbit after another.

There has been a tendency at the university to overlook the early years in virtually all sports except football and basketball. Baseball, for example, generally was believed to have begun with the arrival of Coach Bobby Winkles in 1959. In reality, however, the school had a viable baseball program as early as 1906, when the Normals were champions of the Arizona Territory.

Women's basketball existed on campus before 1900 and the women were playing outside competition and receiving newspaper coverage as early as 1904. Women's sports were a relatively big deal in the early years, and they surged to the forefront in World Wars I and II as the male students left for the battlefronts. Before a resurgence with the arrival of Title IX in the 1970s, women's athletics actually regressed in many respects in the 1950s and 60s. As recently as the 1970-71 school year, the annual budget for all women's sports was just $9,155. The money came from the Associated Students, not the athletic department.

Hopefully, this book will put to rest the myth that ASU's sports history somehow does not match that of some more storied universities. It didn't measure up in the past only because it had never been chronicled in its entirety.

I am much indebted to the two men I consider to be the foremost sports historians in Arizona—Dean Smith and Barry Sollenberger. Smith's Book—*The Sun Devils, Eight Decades of Arizona State Football*, published by the ASU Alumni Association in 1979—is a wonderful read. It provided a starting point for much of my football research. If you enjoy ASU history, Smith also has written a biography of former ASU President Grady Gammage and a book on the history of Tempe. Sollenberger's book—*Bulldog Baseball, From the Dogs to the Devils*—is a fine history of the early days of the diamond sport on the Tempe campus. Sollenberger also deserves credit for a major project to upgrade ASU's men's basketball records in the summer of 1999, and his generous sharing of his photo files is much appreciated. An outstanding history of the school's early years is *The Arizona State University Story*, published in 1960 by Ernest J. Hopkins and Alfred Thomas Jr.

Major thanks go to Brand and his staff in ASU's sports information office. Among those providing help were Doug Tammaro, Aimee Dombrowski, Julie Reuvers, Sean Moore, Ben Alkaly, Will Phillips and Rhonda Lundin. Student intern Andy Wright spent many hours helping to compile the list of athletes in the back of this book.

Rob Spindler and his staff at the University Libraries' Department of Archives and Manuscripts were a tremendous help in making their resources available. Every member of Spindler's staff provided assistance at one time or another. For the better part of two years I spent almost as much time in the archives as I did at home. I'm sure they considered me part of the furniture. Thanks, too, to the staff of the Arizona Department of Library, Archives and Public Records, for their help in my research.

I can't give enough thanks to Susan Clouse Dolbert, President and Executive Director of the ASU Alumni Association, and to *ASU Vision* Editor Charles Billingsley and Associate Editor Bob Jacobsen for their help with the project. They graciously allowed me to move their archives into my home for several months to assist with my research.

Many of the photographs in the book are the work of Chuck Conley, who is entering his sixth decade of photographing ASU athletes and events. Chuck and his vast photo files were invaluable. The work of Ken Akers, Scott Troyanos and others who produced photos for the Media Relations office over the years was much appreciated.

Thanks, also, to Mike Chavez of Ben Franklin Press in Tempe for taking my concept of a cover design and making it happen. Sports Publishing's Mike Pearson provided invaluable help in getting the project up and running and designer Erin Sands put it all together in an easy-to-read format.

Biggest thanks of all go to my wife Linda, who put up with my long days at the library and longer nights at the computer and who offered unceasing encouragement when I couldn't see the light at the end of the tunnel. I'm not sure I would have survived the project without her support.

To my daughter, Diane Vonderscher, and my son, Ron, thanks for your support and patience during this project. You haven't seen much of your dad the past couple of years, but hopefully that will be rectified soon.

My oldest son, Rick, passed away at the age of 31 in June of 1999, midway through the writing of this book. He was a source of inspiration both before and after his passing, though it was difficult working with a heavy heart. In addition to being a loving son, he was my computer guru. The inevitable computer glitches were magnified without Rick there to answer panic calls at 1 a.m. with questions like, "Everything disappeared from my screen—what do I do now?" I'll never forget Rick's elation when he saw the book's cover design just a few days before his death.

Special thanks, too, to my parents, Emil and Winona Eger of Yuma, and my sister, Suzi Morse of Mesa, who had to be content with phone calls instead of visits while this work was in progress. Through my association with ASU, they have become huge Sun Devil fans over the years.

Last, but certainly not least, thanks to all of the ASU coaches, athletes and administrators whose paths have crossed mine over the past 42 years. I can't count all the friendships that have developed from such associations. I was an "old school" guy who probably got closer to the people I covered than is acceptable by modern journalistic standards. Oh well—it worked for me. And I wouldn't trade the experiences and the associations for anything.

I hope you enjoy the book. Forty-two years of my life have gone into its making.

Bob Eger

Foreword

by Frank Kush

I was elated to learn that Bob Eger was writing a history of Arizona State University athletics. The school has been a big part of my life for many years, and over a long period of time I have learned and experienced much of that history myself. I feel fortunate to have arrived at the school when I did—near the middle of the century. Not only was I present for a period of tremendous growth and success in athletics, but I was able to reach back and communicate with some of those who came before me. That knowledge of the school's history and tradition contributed to the way I approached the coaching job.

When I first came to Arizona State as an assistant football coach in 1955, I drove and drove and drove from Georgia, where I had been in the service. I ended up driving right past the college and into Phoenix. A policeman gave me directions, telling me to look for the football stadium by the big turn in Tempe. I proceeded to drive past the school again going in the other direction. I stopped and asked somebody else, and they said, "The stadium is right over there." Sure enough, there was old Goodwin Stadium. I thought to myself, "God Almighty – this is it?" I think it seated about 13,000 at the time and the campus was relatively small. Coming from Michigan State and playing at places like Michigan and Ohio State and Notre Dame, I was shocked at what I saw.

I was really impressed, though, with the athletes that I found in Tempe. I'm talking about people like Bobby Mulgado and Leon Burton and Dave Graybill and Gene Mitcham. I thought they were fantastic athletes—certainly as good as we had at Michigan State. Not too many people were aware of Arizona State College in those days. We played in the Border Conference, which didn't get a lot of recognition. We played against schools like West Texas State and Hardin-Simmons and New Mexico State. They didn't get a lot of recognition either, but they had some remarkable athletes.

When Dan Devine left Arizona State for Missouri and I took over the head coaching job in 1958, we went from Goodwin Stadium to Sun Devil Stadium. It only seated about 30,000 in those days. Everything was minuscule compared to what they have now. The recruiting money was very meager, but we still managed to attract outstanding athletes in every sport. That whole era was what I call the no-recognition era. People like Joe Zuger and Curley Culp could play with anybody in the country, but they didn't get much recognition because we played night games.

All of our sports really began taking off in the 1960s. Bobby Winkles' baseball teams were winning national titles, Ned Wulk had some great basketball teams and Baldy Castillo's track guys were setting all kinds of records. I attribute a lot of that success to our athletic director, Clyde Smith. He hired outstanding coaches who knew what it took to win. I thought it was interesting that he went to the Midwest for most of his people—not California or some other area.

During those early days I came in contact with a number of people from earlier eras—people like Rudy Lavik, Norris Steverson, Joe Selleh and Tom Lillico. They had some great stories about the early days, and they gave me an understanding of the school's history and tradition. The Sun Angels were a great bunch of guys who did a lot for our program. People like Mike Casteel and countless others too numerous to mention lived and died Sun Devil athletics. You could write a book just about those guys.

The person I feel epitomizes the whole program is Bill Kajikawa. He played and coached several sports at Arizona State. Bill, to me, is what Arizona State is all about. I remember him so vividly from when I first arrived. He was the basketball coach. When Ned Wulk came in to coach basketball, I felt Kaji would be a great asset for our football program as the freshman coach. Not only did he do a remarkable job of helping the freshmen settle into college life, he developed lasting relationships with them. And he was a great recruiter for us over in the Hawaiian islands. He's such a great person on top of everything else.

When I was coaching I tried to establish a link to the past and to indoctrinate people into what it means to compete in athletics at Arizona State. The school really does have a great history, though most people aren't aware of it. I tried to perpetuate some of the traditions—like recognizing the intensity of the rivalry with the UofA.

I thought we had pretty good rivalries with Michigan and Notre Dame when I was at Michigan State, but those rivalries were pretty-much confined to athletics. This thing with UofA goes much deeper than athletics. It involves politics and economics and geography.

I still remember the time of the name-change drive. President Gammage and all of the deans and I would go out beating the bushes trying to draw support for the name change from Arizona State College to Arizona State University. The UofA people would follow right in our footsteps, telling the same people that there should be only one university in the state. It's easy to develop an aggressive attitude toward them when you experience something like that.

When I first arrived in Tempe everything was UofA this and UofA that. Anything north of the Gila River represented Phoenix. They didn't like it then and they still don't, and it went back way before the name-change issue.

A book on the entire athletic history of Arizona State is long overdue, and Bob Eger is the perfect person to write it. Bob and I have a friendship and coach-writer relationship that goes back nearly 40 years. I am confident that his background covering ASU sports and his reputation for attention to detail will provide readers with an informative and entertaining look at the school's sports history.

Introduction

During my first year as Director of Athletics at Arizona State University I have had the pleasure of meeting many of the men and women who contributed to the school's sports history. I long had admired the university from afar, but really had only a rudimentary knowledge of its history. Many of these new friendships have given me a taste of its traditions.

I am extremely excited about the future of ASU athletics, and I am looking forward to learning even more about its past. And what a perfect time for the release of the first complete sports history book to showcase Sun Devil athletics as we move into the new millennium.

Bob Eger, author of *Maroon and Gold: a History of Sun Devil Athletics*, has covered Sun Devil sports in various journalistic capacities for parts of six decades spanning more than 40 years. His vast personal knowledge of Sun Devil sports history and his meticulous research have resulted in a book that any fan will be proud to own.

Eger, an award-winning journalist and an ASU alumnus, currently serves as analyst on radio broadcasts of ASU baseball on the Sun Devil Sports Network. In April of 2000 he was named curator of the new ASU Athletics Hall of Fame, which will occupy most of the ground floor of the newly-remodeled athletics building at the south end of Sun Devil Stadium.

His book, which took 3 years to research and write, really was more than 100 years in the making. It will serve as the authority on the entire ASU athletic program, from its infancy in the 1890s through the proud day when it became a university in 1958 to its present-day status among the nation's elite athletic powers. It is the ultimate compilation of Sun Devil athletic history—the perfect reference for longtime Sun Devil faithful or for newcomers who wish to learn about the school's sports history.

I urge you to join me in reading *Maroon and Gold: a History of Sun Devil Athletics*. An appreciation of history is the first step towards building a future of which we all can be proud.

Gene Smith
Director of Athletics
Arizona State University

Maroon & Gold

A History of Sun Devil Athletics

1891-1900

america's time capsule

normal school | m o m e n t

When you gather together students of college age, they invariably will engage in some form of competition. In the early days on the Arizona Territorial Normal School campus in Tempe, such endeavors usually took the form of a friendly game of horseshoes or an impromptu horse race. (No, they didn't have to worry about parking stickers in those days, but pasturing their horses sometimes was a matter of concern.) But on February 14, 1891, there occurred an event that probably seemed insignificant at the time, but now has a place in Arizona State University's athletic lore. A makeshift team from the Normal got together with a team from the Mormon settlement of Stringtown east of Tempe for a baseball game that is the first known athletic event against outside competition in the school's history. The game apparently was played at Stringtown, because the Normals batted first. It was a raw, windy day, but that didn't deter the hitters. Normal scored twice in the top of the first inning with Lee Gray's double the big hit. But Stringtown took that shot and retaliated with six runs in the bottom of the first. Despite the fact that Stringtown had only six players, it managed to build an 18-9 lead before the game was called after five innings because of a dust storm. Edgar Storment, assistant to school president D.A. Reed, was instrumental in the birth of athletics at the Normal in 1891. He helped students set up a baseball diamond at the southwest corner of campus, a site where East Hall later was constructed. Storment, who later would become the school's fourth president, authorized the purchase of some physical education equipment in 1891 and students began organized exercises for the first time.

The school's first football team, which was formed in the fall of 1896 and played its first game in February of 1897. (University Archives)

After practicing through the fall of 1896, coach Fred Irish decided his Normal football team was ready for an outside opponent. There weren't a lot of options, since the six-year-old University of Arizona did not have a team and Flagstaff Normal had not yet been founded. The United States Indian School in Phoenix had two teams, however, and it was decided that the Indians' second team would be a fitting opponent for the first football game in school history on February 28, 1897. The Normals battled gamely, but their lack of experience and game-type conditioning took a toll in a 38-20 loss to the Indians. Coach Fred Irish made only one substitution, sending Oscar Mullen into the game with seven minutes remaining, and accounts of the game suggested that the Normals tired at the end. According to a Tempe News account of the game, the Indians befuddled the Normals with their "famous revolving wedge." The Normals did have their moments, however. A 90-yard touchdown run by Worth Bellamy brought the Normal fans to their feet.

ASU LEGEND

Charles Trumbull Hayden

Clearly, Charles Trumbull Hayden was a man of vision. A native of Connecticut, he taught school in New Jersey and Indiana before going into the trading business and working his way West. He opened a trading post in Santa Fe, New Mexico, in 1848 and moved to Tucson 10 years later. In 1871 he constructed a primitive home and a flour mill at the foot of a butte along the banks of the Salt River in the central part of the Arizona territory. He also began a ferry service across the river and the community of Hayden's Ferry was born. Hayden's Ferry officially became Tempe on May 5, 1879. Hayden, concerned about the lack of qualified teachers in the Arizona territory, devised a plan to establish a territorial normal school. He promoted the candidacy of his business manager, John Armstrong, for a seat in the Territorial Assembly. Once elected, Armstrong managed to push through the Assembly a bill authorizing the Normal School, which was given an initial appropriation of $5,000 upon its approval on March 12, 1885. Governor Frederick A. Tritle named Hayden president of the Normal School Board of Education. Hayden was recognized as the founder of the university in 1951 when Hayden Hall for men was named in his honor. In 1966, Arizona State's library also was named for him. Hayden gave the state more than a university. His son, Carl Hayden, who graduated from the Normal in 1896, went on to become the first congressman from the state of Arizona and later the dean of the U.S. Senate.

Charles Trumbull Hayden founded the Territorial Normal School, now known as Arizona State University. (University Archives)

NORMAL SCHOOL LORE

The *Tempe News* said of Carl Hayden's 1896 graduation address: "The young man displayed a degree of magnetism seldom found in one of his years and which already marks him as a leader among men."

• The Alpha Boarding Club, forerunner to Alpha Hall, the first campus dorm, charged $1.25 a month in rent and $8.50 monthly for meals. To keep horses from running loose, a pasture was fenced and students were charged $1 a month to board their animals.

TEMPE NORMAL NUGGETS

• The *Tempe News* reported in January of 1891: "Exercise is all the rage at the Normal now. Some of the girls took advantage of the workmen's absence the other day to wheel each other around in the wheelbarrow."

• The *Arizona Republican* in March of 1898 offered this report on women's basketball: "Six uniforms are now completed and in use and there is cloth enough procured to make the rest . . . The girls are making the uniforms themselves. As yet it is not certain whether boys will be admitted to the game or not."

normal school | m o m e n t

A long and colorful football rivalry was launched on Thanksgiving Day, 1899, at Carrillo Gardens field in Tucson when the Territorial Normal School of Arizona squared off against the University of Arizona. A crowd of 300 watched the battle for the Territorial Championship Cup. After a scoreless first half, Normal right halfback Charlie Haigler and left halfback Walter Shute scored the game's only touchdowns. In those days, touchdowns were worth five points. The Normals made one of their two conversion kicks to take an 11-0 lead. They shook off a late safety by UA and held on for an 11-2 victory. Little did Normal fans know at the time that their school would not beat Arizona again until 1931. Unlike many meetings in future years, players and fans were on their best behavior. The *Tempe News* account of the game read: "The spectators were enthusiastic and frequently applauded the work of the Normals as well as of the home team. Too much cannot

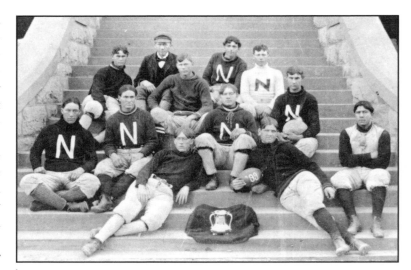

The 1899 Normal football team posed on the steps of Old Main. (University Archives)

be said in praise of the treatment our boys received at the hands of the students, faculty and citizens. The team was met at the train by a delegation of students and were royally entertained at the University dormitory, where after the game they were treated to a genuine Thanksgiving dinner. It is to be hoped that this friendly meeting of the two institutions on the field of manly sport is the forerunner of a lasting friendship between them which will be of material assistance to both, as well as to the interests of athletics in the West."

NORMAL *School* *spotlight*

A description of football in the Arizona Territory in the 1890s from *The Arizona State University Story* by Ernest J. Hopkins and Alfred Thomas Jr.: "The type of football played in the 1890s was as tough a game as man ever played. Those were the days of mass formations—the flying wedge, the revolving wedge, line bucking in close formation, varied by an occasional end run behind three-man interference, three downs to make five yards. Substitutions weren't thought of unless a man was too groggy to stand up. The general effect was that of a railroad collision, but helmets and other modern protection hadn't been developed. The main safeguard was that the field was plowed. Slow as it was by modern standards, it was an exciting game to watch."

LEGEND

Fred Irish

F red Irish is best known as the man who organized the first football team at the Normal School, but he was much more than that. Irish arrived on the Tempe campus in 1896 after completing his undergraduate work at the University of Iowa with Phi Beta Kappa honors. Irish taught all of the science courses offered by the college and immediately set about introducing football to the little community on the banks of the Salt River. Once the football team was up and running, he founded the school's first military training program. His position as commander of the campus cadet corps earned him the nickname "Cap." He also coached women's sports and served as advisor to the student newspaper, *The Normal Student*, and the student yearbook, which had several names in the early years. He coached the school's first seven football teams over a nine-year period before the school dropped football for eight years beginning in 1906. Irish was named registrar of the college in 1925. He served in that capacity until just before his death in 1941. Two prominent campus facilities were named in honor of Irish. Most major athletic events were played at Irish Field prior to the construction of Goodwin Stadium. Irish Hall, a men's residence hall at the south end of campus, was dedicated in his honor in 1940.

Fred Irish coached the first football team at the Normal and served in various capacities for more than 40 years. (ASU Media Relations)

TEMPE NORMAL NUGGET

An 1897 school fight song popular with Normal students:

Marian, my Marian
We will not cower in the dust.
Marian, my Marian
Our splendid team we ever trust.
Marian, my Marian
Remember Haigler's warlike bust,
Remember Walter's warlike thrust,
And all thy redskins in the dust.
Marian, my Marian.

Normal School Lore

N ormal's second building, a three-story brick structure then called Main Building, was dedicated on February 4, 1898. One of the finest feats of architecture in the territory, it later was known as Old Main. The building underwent several transformations over the years. A major project in the late 1990s restored the legendary structure to its former glory and prepared it to serve as the new headquarters of the Alumni Association.

• By the end of the 19th century, the Normal school had turned out more than 100 graduates with teaching credentials, putting a big dent in the Arizona Territory's teacher shortage.

1900-1901

September 8, 1900: A hurricane ravaged Galveston, Texas, killing 6,000 people and causing property damages of $20 million.

November 6, 1900: William McKinley won the presidency for a second term.

January 10, 1901: A well near Beaumont, Texas, brought in oil, the first evidence of oil from that region.

March 3, 1901: The United States Steel Corporation was incorporated in New Jersey.

May 7, 1901: President William McKinley and several members of his cabinet visited Phoenix. It was the first visit ever to a territorial town by a U.S. chief executive.

normal school
moment

Football on the Normal campus was only four years old, but the media already was demanding excellence on the part of the school's gridiron warriors. This somewhat critical review of a game between the Normals and Phoenix Indian School appeared in the *Tempe News* on November 9, 1900: "Saturday's football game between the Normals and Indians resulted in a victory for the latter in a score of 5 to 6. The game was devoid of brilliant work and both teams showed lack of training, which probably will be remedied before the next game." The game drew enough interest for the railroad company to sell excursion tickets so that fans from Tempe could travel to Phoenix for the contest. Coach Fred Irish's team also played two games against Phoenix High School, losing by a 5-0 score in Tempe and winning by an identical score in Phoenix. Though the offense didn't generate a lot of points, the running of halfbacks Charlie Haigler and Walter Shute provided plenty of entertainment for Normal fans.

Decades before serious strength training and dietary supplements became the norm, Normal football star Charlie Haigler did quite well in the muscle department. (University Archives)

Modern college football fans might not have recognized the sport at the turn of the century. The game was played on a field that was 110 yards long and touchdowns were worth five points. The current 100-yard field and six-point touchdown were not implemented until 1912. Field goals were worth five points until 1904 and four points from 1904 through 1909. Teams had three downs to make five yards and a team that scored received the ensuing kickoff. Forward passes were not allowed until 1906, with one exception. One pass was allowed if the ball was thrown at least five yards to the left or right of center. If neither team touched the ball, it went to the defensive team. That rule was in effect until 1910.

LEGEND

Arthur J. Matthews

Arthur J. Matthews was named president of the college on June 7, 1900. He would serve for 30 years and play a major role in the early development of the institution. A robust man who enjoyed outdoor sports himself, he took a hard line against over-emphasis of intercollegiate athletics. Matthews' view was that sports had a significant place in terms of student recreation, but he did not subscribe to the theory, already popular on some campuses, that sports should be a major public event. During Matthews' tenure football was dropped for eight years at the Normal, from 1906 through 1913. There seems no question that under different leadership athletics might have progressed more rapidly on the Tempe campus, but the little school on the banks of the Salt River generally avoided the problems that surfaced at some other schools thanks partly to Matthews' conservative approach. Matthews did play a significant role in the acquisition of 35 acres south of the campus in 1919. Several years later the school's first gymnasium and first football facility that actually could be called a stadium were constructed on that land. Matthews also was instrumental in gaining legislative approval of a four-year Bachelor of Education degree in 1925. Under his leadership, Tempe Normal became Tempe State Teacher's College in 1925.

Arthur J. Matthews was a key figure in the early development of the college. (University Archives)

Normal School Lore

The school, which had operated under as many as four names in its early years, formally adopted the name "Tempe Normal School of Arizona." That would be the official name of the institution until the mid-1920s. The name represented a compromise between two factions. One wanted to call the school Normal School of Arizona and the other was pushing for Tempe Normal.

Though the school has had numerous names and its athletic teams several nicknames over the years, the colors maroon and gold have been a constant since before the turn of the century. A *Tempe News* account of an 1899 game against Phoenix Indian School said "the Normal team had rooters galore, with a waving mass of colors of maroon, old gold and white...."

TEMPE NORMAL NUGGETS

Front-page items from the *Tempe News* of Nov. 2, 1900:

- Carl Hayden and Oscar Keller drove over to Phoenix today.
- Today's exports from Tempe will consist of two cars of hay.
- Fisher G. Bailey this morning returned from his trip to Jerome.
- A number of our people attended the dance at Mesa last night.
- W. A. McGrew pulled out for Silver King with a big load of supplies.
- Dr. Broadway is getting away with most of the prizes at the shooting gallery.

1901-1902

September 6, 1901: President William McKinley was shot as he attended a reception in Buffalo, N.Y. He died of his wounds eight days later.

September 14, 1901: Forty-two-year-old Theodore Roosevelt took the presidential oath of office.

October 16, 1901: In one of his first controversial moves as president, Theodore Roosevelt invited black leader Booker T. Washington to the White House. Many in the South were incensed and reacted with violence against blacks.

May 12, 1902: Nearly 140,000 United Mine Workers went on strike.

May 20, 1902: Four years after the end of the Spanish-American war, Cuban independence was achieved.

tempe normal | moment

Sportswriting at the turn of the century wasn't always impartial. Consider this article in the *Tempe News* of Jan. 17, 1902: "Manager Schureman of the Tempe Normal football team, who has been trying to arrange for a game with the Indian School team, today received word that the Indians would make no date, so it is unlikely the First Normal team will do anything this season. The boys are very much disappointed at not being able to secure a game. They will doubtless have to wait until time has effaced from the memory of the Indians all recollection of the crushing defeats at the hands of the Normals; until the words Haigler, Shute, Sigala, Goodwin, etc. are no longer synonymous of Indian defeat. In refusing to play, the Indians acknowledge the Normal (the) championship for another year." Research fails to uncover those "crushing" defeats referred to by the writer. The Indian School won the 1900 meeting, 6-5. The Normals won, 6-0, in 1899. The Indians won the only other meeting, 38-20, in 1897.

Women's basketball uniforms looked a bit different around the turn of the century than they do now. (University Archives).

Though there was no varsity football team at the Normal in the fall of 1901, the sport still had some visibility. In its 1904 edition recounting the early years of Normal football, the student yearbook, *El Picadello*, said of the 1901 non-season: "The Normal put forward no first team owing to the fact that the material to make a team was exceedingly light and scarce. However, a second, or light team, was organized, which did some very good work." There was one "Big Game" on campus, though it didn't involve a team from the Normal. According to the *Tempe News*: "What promises to be the most exciting game of football ever witnessed in this Valley will take place on the Tempe grounds tomorrow. Chris Sigala, who distinguished himself on the Normal team, has organized an all-Mexican team which he believes will be the champion of the Territory this season. Every man is hardened by constant outdoor exercise and it would be hard to find a sturdier lot of fellows. Tomorrow's game will be with the Mexican team of Phoenix."

LEGEND

Charlie Haigler

How good was Charlie Haigler, the school's first real football hero? It's hard to evaluate Haigler's exploits, because many came against high school opponents, but there's no question he deserves a prominent place among the school's sports legends. Haigler, who was born in Globe but grew up in Tempe, was an electrifying runner who was celebrated in song and had a dormitory named for him 40 years after his Tempe Normal career was over. His athletic ability was in such demand that he played over a six-year span in Tempe, then moved on to Los Angeles where he played four more seasons for University of Southern California, serving as team captain in 1907. Haigler, who was known in his USC days as Cactus Charlie, set weightlifting records at USC that had not been broken by the 1950s. Haigler was one player who legitimately could claim to have brought down the house. In an 1899 game against Phoenix Indian School at a field near St. Francis Xavier Church in Phoenix, he caused such a commotion among spectators that the rickety grandstand collapsed. The *Tempe News* had the following account: "Haigler, with that powerful straight arm, knocked down several large Indians and . . . made a run of fully two-thirds the length of the field, simply running away from all others. This brought the grand stand down, and the entire assemblage surged over to the Normal goal." The *Tempe News* offered this account of Haigler's play in the Normal's 11-2 victory over Arizona in 1899—the first meeting ever between those two rivals: "In the second half, Haigler woke up. He plunged through the line, as one of the spectators remarked, `like a thousand bricks,' and made repeated gains with three and four opponents hanging to him." Team manager E.C. Corbell wrote of Haigler in the 1904 yearbook: "Charles Haigler . . . was no doubt our star man every year that he played. It was a common occurrence to see him run over three men, straight-arm as many more and drag one or two down the field for a touchdown in every game." Haigler earned lifetime passes to athletic events from both Tempe Normal and USC. He was one of a handful of American athletes to carry lifetime passes from two major institutions.

Charlie Haigler, the school's first football star, played the college game for 10 seasons in the days before NCAA regulations. (University Archives)

TEMPE NORMAL LORE

President Arthur J. Matthews secured from the Legislature an appropriation of $13,500 to build the school's first dormitory. The move was unpopular with Tempe residents, who were used to earning extra income from feeding and housing students. Alpha Hall, which opened in October of 1902, was built to house 20 girls, with a dining room in the basement. However, 26 girls managed to squeeze in the first year.

TEMPE NORMAL NUGGET

• This advertisement appeared in the *Tempe News* of Friday, December 6, 1901: "When you meet a person wearing a comfortable-and-at-peace-with-the-world expression, you may make up your mind that that person has on a suit of the elegant underwear that the Arizona Mercantile Company is now selling so cheaply."

1902-1903

November 4, 1902: In congressional elections, the Republicans maintained their Senate majority over Democrats, 57-33.

December 17, 1902: The first radio message was transmitted across the Atlantic.

January 22, 1903: A 99-year lease was signed by the United States and Columbia, giving America sovereignty over a canal zone in Panama.

July 4, 1903: President Roosevelt sent a message around the world and back in 12 minutes through the use of the first Pacific communications cable.

August 8, 1903: Great Britain defeated the United States to capture tennis' Davis Cup.

tempe normal
moment

After a year without football, it took a little urging from the *Tempe News* to prod the school to field a team in 1902. An editorial in the Sept. 20, 1902 issue of the newspaper read: "It seems about time the Normal football team was organized if it expects to be with it with the rest of the teams in the territory. There is an abundance of good material in the school this year to make, with a little practice, a very strong team. Up to last year, the Normal team was considered the best in the Territory, and there is no rea-

The 1902 Normal football team practices on campus. (University Archives)

son why it should not continue to be. The Phoenix High School has already organized and have commenced practicing." Once the team got up and rolling, the Normals proved that scouting had its place in football, even at the turn of the century. Normal Coach Fred Irish and players attended a game between Phoenix High and Phoenix Indian School with notebooks and pens in hand, scribbling numerous notes. It paid off with shutout victories over both of those teams, 39-0 over Phoenix High and 34-0 over Phoenix Indian.

Tempe NORMAL *spotlight*

A women's basketball association was organized on campus, under the direction of Miss Nell White. One published account said the group, "beyond a few weeks of practice, accomplished very little except to arouse interest in the game and prepare the way for more thorough organization." That's exactly what happened, as women's hoops began to enjoy a more prominent place in the school's activity schedule the following year, including receipt of financial assistance from the Board of Education.

Billy Woolf

L ong before there was a Danny White or a Jake Plummer, there was Billy Woolf. There's a common perception that Woolf was the first quarterback in school history, but records indicate that a fellow named Clyde Stewart played the position on the Territorial Normal School's first team, which was organized in the fall of 1896 and first played in February of 1897. Woolf played end. For the next five seasons, however, Woolf was the Normals' QB. If you're counting, you'll note that's six seasons spanning eight years, but nobody was counting back then. Woolf was a student from 1896 through 1899. He managed to play and help coach the team for four seasons covering five years after his college days were over. Though he was a big man on campus both during and after his undergraduate days, Woolf enjoyed greater prominence in later years in the fields of ranching, agriculture, finance and law enforcement. Woolf, popularly known as "Uncle Billy," served as secretary of the Arizona Cattle Growers Association and spent many years as agricultural advisor to Valley National Bank and First National Bank. He served as a Maricopa County Sheriff's officer under Sheriff Carl Hayden and he was a charter member and Captain of Company C of the First Arizona National Guard. While in law enforcement he survived a gunshot wound to the back. When he died in 1964 at the age of 86, the last surviving member school's first football team, he was still actively managing a ranch.

Billy Woolf was a six-year starter in football, five of them at quarterback. (University Archives)

Cost of a round-trip train ticket to attend a "road" game against Phoenix Indian School at East Lake Park in Phoenix: Thirty-five cents.

Monthly cost for comfortable lodging and three meals a day at the men's or women's dormitory at the Normal: $15.

TEMPE NORMAL NUGGETS

• Recruiting news was prominent, even in the early 1900s. One early newspaper account reported the following: "Chester Haigler, brother of the famous ball player Charles, will enter the Normal School this fall. We expect him to come up to Charles as a player as he has the requisites, one being that he weighs 210 pounds." Instead, Chester Haigler ended up following his brother to USC.

• Seven grass tennis courts were laid out on campus, joining two dirt courts that were built during the 1897-98 school year. A tennis club was established in the fall of 1902. The sport was popular, with top players enjoying a certain amount of social status on campus. At this early juncture, however, matches were not played against outside opponents.

Tempe Normal Lore

A popular cheer on the Normal campus in the early 1900s:
"Hi, Ho, Ha! Boom-cis-Bah!
Hi, Ho, Ha! Boom-cis-Bah!
Tempe Normal! Rah, Rah, Rah!"

• Thanks to a trip to California and extensive lobbying by President Arthur J. Matthews, Tempe Normal was granted equal rank with state normal schools in California and with prestigious institutions such as Cal-Berkeley and Stanford. That meant that graduates of the Tempe school could teach in California without passing certification examinations

1903-1904

america's time capsule

tempe normal | moment

The Normal football team wrapped up a 3-0 season and kept its shutout streak intact with a 15-0 victory over Phoenix Indian School at East Lake Park in Phoenix. The Normals had opened the season with a 35-0 victory over Phoenix Indian in Tempe and followed that by blanking Phoenix High School, 18-0. The *Tempe News* called the season finale "one of the hardest fought contests in the history of foot ball in this Valley." The newspaper account said, "The Indians showed a wonderful improvement over their work at the Tempe game." After building a 5-0 first-half lead, the Normals pulled away after intermission. The *News* reported: "The second half, which in times past always netted the Normals good results, was still lucky for the White lads for they went through and around the Indian line for good gains and succeeded in making two more touchdowns, but failed at the goal (conversions) both times." A player referred to only as "Noble" in newspaper accounts was cited for playing hurt. "Noble, the center for the Normals, had a knee badly hurt in the first half, but continued in the game, taking the place of Webb, right tackle, who was also quite seriously hurt," The *News* reported.

Tempe NORMAL *spotlight*

Women's basketball, which had existed in various levels of organization as early as the late 1890s, advanced to the point where it received newspaper coverage in January of 1904. This is *The Arizona Republican's* account of a 14-7 loss to Phoenix High School: "Although victory failed to perch on the Normal banner, the Normal girls are to be congratulated upon their excellent showing in team work. The failure to secure a higher score was due in large measure to ill luck in throwing for goal. A large sized hoodoo seemed to surround the basket and though the ball again and again rolled twice around the edge, it failed to drop inside."

Coach Fred Irish conducts basketball practice for the women's team, which began receiving newspaper coverage. (University Archives)

E. C. Corbell

Around the turn of the century, the team manager enjoyed a prominent role in the football program—at least at Tempe Normal. The job entailed much more than handing out towels and fetching water. A multitude of duties were involved, including scheduling. Normal manager E. C. Corbell served as vice president of the school's Athletic Association, and did much to further public involvement in the program. Corbell was president of the senior class. He was one of just two male students in the 23-member senior group. Here are some of Corbell's thoughts about the early days of Normal football, as written for the 1904 student yearbook: "Since the organization of football in the Normal School in 1896, it has been by far the most popular sport among the students. Many good teams have been put in the field, which have always been supported not only by the faculty and students, but by the entire population of Tempe, who when the team was first organized, contributed very liberally for its support. Every boy in school is loyal to his team, and if he cannot be one of the giants of the gridiron, he is a faithful supporter, always willing to give a willing hand in the training quarters or at the games as a ticket seller, goalkeeper or rooter. The girls attend every game and assist by giving yells and singing football songs to such an extent that the noise of the rooters of the opponents have usually been drowned."

He didn't carry the pigskin, but E. C. Corbell was a big man on campus. (University Archives)

TEMPE NORMAL LORE

This was the program for a big pep rally prior to the season football opener against Phoenix Indian School:
- The Normal Song, by the joint societies.
- Essay, "The importance of athletics in schools," by Annie Priest.
- Address, "History of football," by E. C. Corbell.
- Recitation, "That glorious football game," by Vanessa Wright.
- Address, "A description of a football game in its picturesque features," by E. R. Wilbur.
- Election of a yell leader.
- Practice yells by everybody.

TEMPE NORMAL
NUGGET

- Football team manager E.C. Corbell and the cheerleading corps received due recognition in the 1904 student yearbook. The publication said Corbell "conducted the duties of his position in a businesslike manner that is worthy of the highest praise. And then there were the girls, bless their hearts. How could the boys lose with such encouragement? It has been proven beyond all question that on the foot ball field, as in the gentler walks, the Normal girl is a force that must be reckoned with."

1904-1905

america's time capsule

October 8, 1904: Automobile racing as an organized sport began with the Vanderbilt Cup race on Long Island, New York.

October 27, 1904: The first section of New York City's subway system was opened to the public.

November 8, 1904: Theodore Roosevelt was reelected president of the United States, defeating Alton Parker by nearly two million votes.

April 17, 1905: A New York state law limiting maximum hours for workers was ruled unconstitutional by the U.S. Supreme Court. The high court said the law interfered with the right to free contract.

May 5, 1905: Boston pitcher Cy Young threw major league baseball's first perfect game, retiring 27 consecutive Philadelphia Athletics batters.

tempe normal | moment

The hottest competition for the Normals during the unbeaten (4-0) 1904 football season was between the offense and defense. The offense grew progressively more productive as the season progressed, and the defense came up with four straight shutouts. That extended the Normals' string of shutouts to seven straight over two seasons and 10 in an 11-game span covering four seasons. The season started with a 15-0 victory over Phoenix High school in Tempe, followed by a 24-0 win over Phoenix Indian School on the Normals' home field. Then came a 30-0 romp over Phoenix High before an unruly crowd in Phoenix. The Normals wrapped up the season with a 47-0 whipping of Phoenix Indian in Tempe. They ended up outscoring the opposition 116-0. Halfback Alma Jones captained Coach Fred Irish's club. Also playing prominent roles were halfback Juan Ochoa and end Eugene Shute and brothers Arthur and Bill Woolf.

Tennis was becoming increasingly popular on campus during the early 1900s. (University Archives)

Tempe NORMAL spotlight

The Normal's smashing success on the gridiron left some in Tempe looking down their noses a bit at their football-playing brethren in Phoenix. Following a 24-0 victory over Phoenix Indian School in Tempe, the *Tempe News* reported: " Phoenix has suddenly lost interest in football. The remaining league games should be played at Tempe, where people understand and appreciate the sport." And following a 30-0 whipping of Phoenix High at East Lake Park in Phoenix, the *News* had this to say: "During Saturday's game about a hundred fellows, who from their appearance had stolen their way into the grounds, persisted in going onto the field and on at least two occasions seriously interfered with long end plays by the Normals."

LEGEND

Juan
Ochoa

The term "home-grown product" has been applied to athletes for many decades, but never was it more applicable than in the case of Juan Ochoa. Ochoa was born in 1883 in an adobe house just a long forward pass from what later would become Old Main on the Tempe Normal campus. In 1900 he enrolled at the Normal Training School, which shared the campus with Tempe Normal College, and played five years of varsity football while completing the academic work necessary to complete the eighth grade. In one of his best seasons, 1904, he was not even enrolled in school, though that was relatively common among athletes of those times. Old-timers tell a story of playing one game against Phoenix High School, which had an unusually "mature" player manning a spot in the line. It turns out he was a Phoenix blacksmith, who had a shop near the school, and was talked into playing by members of the Phoenix High team. Ochoa, a halfback, didn't achieve the acclaim of his much-publicized teammate, Charles Haigler, but early reports indicated he was a fine player in his own right. Like Haigler and several other Normal players, he ventured to Los Angeles and played for University of Southern California after his Tempe Normal career was over. According to Haigler's scrapbook, Ochoa was one of USC's top players in 1905. Ochoa later served with Tempe's Company C of the Arizona National Guard, where he engaged in the pursuit of Pancho Villa along the Mexican border near Douglas.

Juan Ochoa was a classic "home grown product" for Tempe Normal's football team. (ASU Archives)

TEMPE NORMAL LORE

A central heating plant to serve all buildings on campus was developed, eliminating the need to feed wood into 17 pot-bellied stoves in various buildings.

• Enrollment in the fall of 1904 soared to 228, moving the Normal ahead of the university in Tucson as the largest educational institution in the territory. The Normal had held that distinction, but had relinquished the honor for a period of five years.

TEMPE NORMAL
NUGGET

• While things were getting rowdy on the gridiron, women's basketball was being conducted with a bit more style and grace. One published account of a 15-8 loss to Phoenix High School concluded with the following: "After the game the Normal basket ball girls entertained the high school players at dinner at the dormitory and later at a hop down town, where the rivals parted at a fitting hour with pleasant memories of the occasion."

1905-1906

September 22, 1905: Willie Anderson won his third consecutive U.S. Open golf tournament.

October 14, 1905: The New York Giants defeated the Philadelphia Athletics to capture Major League Baseball's second World Series.

February 23, 1906: Tommy Burns won the world heavyweight boxing title.

April 7, 1906: The first successful transatlantic wireless transmission was made from New York City to a receiving station in Ireland.

April 18, 1906: A massive earthquake rocked the San Francisco Bay Area, leaving more than 500,000 people homeless.

tempe normal | m o m e n t

A Tempe firm, Hyder Bros., offered an initialed silk handkerchief for each Normal player and a fancy vest to the outstanding player if the Normals beat Prescott High for the territorial baseball championship. The Normals prevailed, and after seeing their opponent off at the train depot, the players descended en masse on the clothier, where each member received his handkerchief. It was left to the umpire, a Mr. Carr, to pick the outstanding player. *The Arizona Republican* reported: "It was a hard question to handle, for all of the members of the team did good work, but Mr. Carr finally by the process of elimination figured it down to four players, Higley, Dykes, Shrigley and Millett. It was left to these four to draw for the prize. In the drawing, Mr. (Art) Millett was the lucky man. With the aid of the balance of the team, the best vest in the house was chosen, put on its new possessor, and Mr. Millett was placed on the shoulders of the other players and carried out on the street where the team gave three cheers for the enterprising firm who had been so liberal with the members."

Art Millett won a new vest as Outstanding Player of territorial baseball championship series. (University Archives)

spotlight

Just one season after outscoring its four opponents by a combined score of 116-0, the Normal football team fell upon hard times. Coach Fred Irish's team lost its opener to Phoenix Indian School, 17-8, then suffered shutouts at the hands of Phoenix High (5-0) and Tempe High (6-0). All three games were played on the Tempe campus. The Bulldogs remained competitive defensively, but the offense suffered from the loss of four stars from the 1904 team—Walter Shute, Juan Ochoa and brothers Bill and Arthur Woolf. Interest in football, which had been at a fever pitch, began to wane as baseball soared in popularity.

LEGEND

Walter Shute

By the 1905 season, Walter Shute's college football career already was behind him, but it certainly was not forgotten. Though his exploits were overshadowed somewhat by those of his legendary backfield running mate, Charlie Haigler, Shute carved out quite a reputation of his own. Shute played left halfback and Haigler right halfback, and between them they represented a formidable one-two punch. It was Shute, not Haigler, who was elected captain of the 1899 team that compiled a 3-0 record and beat Arizona in the first meeting between the two schools. Haigler scored the first touchdown and Shute the second in the Normal's 11-0 victory (touchdowns were worth five points). "Shute played the game well and frequently carried the ball for fine gains. His tackling was also good," the *Tempe News* reported. In appraising the first five teams in school history in the 1904 student yearbook, team manager E. C. Corbell wrote that Shute's "leadership, clear head and courage has never been excelled in the Normal." Shute put that clear head to good use after graduation from the Normal. He obtained a law degree from Northwestern University and was admitted to the bar in Arizona. He was elected district attorney in Gila County and later served as a Superior Court judge. He eventually established a successful law practice in Phoenix.

Walter Shute was the "other half" of a great one-two backfield punch with Charlie Haigler. (University Archives)

TEMPE NORMAL NUGGET

• The baseball team beat Phoenix High, 10-2, to capture the Valley Interscholastic Baseball Championship. The Normals were 2-0 against Phoenix High School and 2-0 against Phoenix Indian School, setting up a match with Prescott High for the territorial championship.

TEMPE NORMAL LORE

The school's first classroom building, initially constructed in 1886, was torn down in 1906 after 20 years of hard use. A new training school building, costing $31,000, was erected on the same spot. It would last until 1928.

1906-1907

america's time capsule

tempe normal | moment

Fred Ayer pitched the first no-hitter in school history, a 7-1 victory over Mesa High. Ayer faced just 29 batters. He struck out 10 and didn't walk or hit anyone, though his teammates committed six errors behind him. Ayer's biggest victory, however, came when he pitched the Normal to a 5-3 win over Arizona in the final game of the season in Tucson, giving the Tempe club the Territorial Championship and a loving cup presented by *The Arizona Republican* newspaper. Arizona won the first game of the two-game series, 10-4. The competition, though spirited, offered none of the hostility that would surface in later years. Here's *The Republican's* account of the Normal's trip to Tucson: "Every member of the party is loud in his or her praise of the treatment all received at the hands of the University men and

The Normal baseball team beat Arizona for the territorial championship. (University Archives)

young ladies. The Normal girls were quartered during their stay with private families in town, the members of the team at one of the best hotels. Everything possible was done for the comfort of the visitors; they were entertained at a dance, at dinners, at a play and all were taken on a tally-ho ride to the Mission. Normal money was no good at all and the University stood every cent of expense while the Normal party was in Tucson. It was fully appreciated too, and if the University baseball team ever comes to Tempe again, these many favors will be repaid with interest."

Tempe NORMAL *spotlight*

Though baseball had been played off and on since 1891 on campus and the 1906 team had gone 5-0 and captured the Valley interscholastic championship and the unofficial territorial crown, 1907 generally is considered the first full season in school history as the schedule expanded to nine games. The Normal negotiated that schedule with a 7-2 record. When word reached campus that the lads from Tempe had won the second game of a season-ending series in Tucson by a 5-3 score, thus claiming the territorial championship, bedlam broke out—at least in the girls' dorm. The *Tempe Normal Student* newspaper reported: "The girls of the dorm celebrated by hailing the first grocery man in sight and clambering into his wagon pell-mell, packed in like sardines in a box. They rode in state about town announcing the victory, counting the score and singing: `Normal forever. Normal forever. Normal forevermore.'"

ASU LEGEND

Fred Ayer

It happens now and then in college sports—an outstanding athlete goes on to a coaching career after his competitive days are over, then moves into athletic administration, perhaps even serving as athletic director. But how about holding all of those positions simultaneously? That was the case with Fred Ayer, who was a star pitcher, baseball coach and athletic director—at the same time. Ayer coached the Normal for five years, from 1907 through 1911. He also was a pitching star all five years, and played first base and third base when he wasn't on the mound. He was named the team's most valuable player in 1909 and was chosen outstanding pitcher in 1907 and 1909. He became the first player in school history to strike out more than 20 batters in a game when he whiffed 22 in a 10-inning game against Evans School in February of 1910. That broke the school record of 18 which he set against Phoenix Union High School in 1909. In 1907, when he coached the Normals to a 7-2 record and the championship of the Arizona Territory, he was the winning pitcher in all seven victories. The biggest was a 5-3 win over Arizona in the season finale in Tucson, which gave the Normals the territorial title. He pitched the first no-hitter in school history against Mesa High in 1907.

Fred Ayer was athletic director, baseball coach and pitching star—all at the same time. (University Archives)

TEMPE NORMAL LORE

Recognizing that the little college on the banks of the Salt River was going to be around for the long haul, the Arizona Legislature gave the Normal School the largest appropriation at that point in the school's history. The college received $60,000 for construction, plus an operating budget of $80,000.

TEMPE NORMAL NUGGETS

• The Normal faculty voted to drop football. *The Arizona Republican* said the action was taken because "many of last year's team have graduated and in the school this season there are but a few who have any knowledge of the game whatsoever and good substantial material is lacking."

• The *Tempe Normal Student's* account of a 7-6 girls basketball loss to Phoenix Indian School: "Our girls certainly looked charming in their new olive drab uniforms with the letters T.N.S. on the blouse. The game was characterized by good will and the absence of any jangle or rough play."

1907-1908

September. 12, 1907: The *Lusitania*, the world's largest steamship, competed its maiden voyage between Ireland and New York.

October 12, 1907: The Chicago Cubs swept the World Series from the Detroit Tigers.

November 16, 1907: Oklahoma became the 46th state in the union.

December 6, 1907: A West Virginia coal mine explosion killed 361 miners.

May 10, 1908: Mother's Day was first celebrated.

tempe normal | moment

With baseball surging into the forefront on campus, it was only fitting the the Normal nine be outfitted properly. Here's what *The Arizona Republican* of March 13, 1908 had to say about the team's much-awaited new uniforms: "The Normal team will be fortified with brand new suits. They put them on for the first time yesterday afternoon to take off the 'hoodoo' usually brought on by new suits. They are maroon, trimmed in black, thoroughly lined, and for material and finish they equal the suits of any of the big colleges." The newspaper concluded: "If suits could win the games would be all the Normal could hope." Unfortunately for the Normals, the

New baseball uniforms were the talk of the campus in the spring of 1908. This photo obviously was taken before they arrived. (University Archives)

magic in the suits wore off quickly. The team won four of its first five games, played Phoenix Indian School to a 3-3 tie, then lost its last seven games to finish 4-8-1. Rival Arizona swept four games from the Normals, though Art Millett hit the first grand slam in school history against UA, which was known simply as the Varsity in those days. UA didn't acquire the Wildcat nickname until 1914. John Mullen was the leading hitter for the Normal with a modest .208 batting average.

Tempe NORMAL *spotlight*

It was becoming clear that the future was gloomy for football, which had the campus buzzing just three years earlier when the Normals outscored four opponents by a combined score of 116-0. In voting to drop the sport in September of 1906, the Normal faculty had cited a lack of potential players on campus. But by the fall of 1907 it was obvious that it went much deeper than that. President Roosevelt threatened to ban the sport after 18 deaths and more than 150 serious injuries were reported during the 1905 season. Respected national institutions such as Stanford, Columbia and Harvard joined the Normal in dropping the sport in 1906. Baseball became the sport of choice in Tempe and women's basketball was beginning to gain in popularity. The football drought lasted until 1914 on the Tempe campus.

LEGEND

John Dykes

John Dykes had a productive athletic career at the Normal, and a lengthy one. He was a starter in football in 1903, 1904 and 1905. When the school dropped football, Dykes became a standout on the baseball team. He was team captain for three seasons in baseball, and he did it as a second baseman in 1907, a catcher in 1908, and an outfielder in 1909. He was named the team's most valuable player in 1907 and 1908. In 1907 he led the team in batting, though his .296 average wouldn't create much of a commotion by modern standards. During his three years as a baseball star, the Normals compiled a combined record of 21-16-1.

John Dykes' football and baseball career at the Normal spanned six school years. (University Archives).

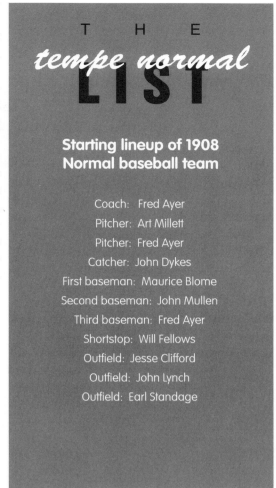

TEMPE NORMAL
NUGGET

This song, popular on campus during the early 1900s, demonstrates the brutality of college football of that time, a major reason the sport was dropped in 1906:

Good-bye mother, I must leave you.
For I hear our Normal call.
To the Gridiron I must hasten.
For they need me there this Fall.
Good-bye mother, do not hold me.
Strap my shinguards into place.
Shove the armor o'er my body.
Tighten up my shoulder brace.
Hark! The enemy advances.
I can here no longer stay.
I must buck the center gladly,
Though a rib or two gives way.
I must get that big six-footer.
I must mash that little fool.
I might die but I'll die happy,
For the honor of the school.

Tempe Normal Lore

Slowly but surely, the home of Tempe Normal was beginning to look more and more like a real college campus. The latest addition was a home for college president Arthur J. Matthews, who had been living in the women's dormitory, Alpha Hall. Construction began during the 1906-07 school year on the structure, which cost $6,250.

1908-1909

america's time capsule

tempe normal
moment

After splitting a pair of games against rival Arizona in Tempe, the Normals had a monumental mission when they visited Tucson for the final two games of the baseball season. They needed a sweep to capture the season series and win the Republican Cup awarded by *The Arizona Republican* newspaper to the territorial champion. The Normals were up to the task. They broke out the bats and thumped UA, 15-8, in the first game in front of a crowd of 450. It was the largest gathering for a game between the Normals and Arizona in the pre World War I era. Another big crowd was on hand the next day as Mayor Henry of Tucson started the festivities by throwing out the first pitch. The Normals won a thriller, 5-4, in 10 innings to capture their third territorial crown in four years. The Normal team that opened the season with consecutive losses to Evans School by scores of 3-0 and 4-3, turned things around with four straight victories and finished with a 10-6 record – the first 10-win season in school history.

The Normals were baseball champions of the Arizona Territory for the third time in four years. (University Archives)

spotlight

The Normal baseball team registered the first extra-inning baseball victory in school history, 3-2 over Phoenix Indian School in 12 innings. The game was played in Tempe. Just five games later the Normals were involved in another extra-inning contest, a 5-4 victory over rival Arizona in 10 innings. That victory, in Tucson, gave the Normal the championship of the Arizona Territory. The 12-inning affair against Phoenix Indian stood alone as a school record for longest game until 1949, when Arizona State College took 12 innings to beat Arizona, 10-9.

LEGEND

John Mullen

Four-hit games are commonplace in modern college baseball, with its aluminum bats and shortage of quality pitching arms. But in the early 1900s, a four-hit game was a big deal. When John Mullen did it against Mesa High in 1910, some of the significance undoubtedly was lost because teammate John Lynch had cranked out five hits earlier the same season against Phoenix Indian School. But it would be three more years before anybody would have another four-hit game for the Normals. A Tempe Normal/Arizona State player would collect four or more hits in a game only 14 times from 1907 through 1948, an average of roughly once every three years. Mullen, a four-year starter for the Normal at shortstop and second base from 1908 through 1911, was the team's leading hitter in as a freshman in 1908 and tied for the honor as a senior in 1911. In that era of dominating pitchers, his numbers were hardly eye catching. His team-leading batting average in 1908 was .208. He and teammate Albert Spikes shared the batting title in 1911 at .255. Mullen was named the team's most valuable player in 1911. He later became president of the school's Alumni Association.

John Mullen twice led the Normals in batting. (University Archives)

TEMPE NORMAL LORE

The continuously-growing campus expanded to 10 buildings with construction of a science building and an auditorium and gymnasium. Estimated construction cost of the science building was $30,500. The auditorium/gymnasium cost an estimated $29,000. The buildings were funded by a Territorial Legislature that was becoming increasingly aware of the needs of the college, which for years had struggled with bare-bones appropriations.

TEMPE NORMAL
NUGGET

• Player-coach Fred Ayer set a school record with 18 strikeouts against Phoenix Union in 1909, but teammate Leo Cuber was Mr. Consistency in the whiff department. Cuber, who played only one season for the Normal, struck out 16 against Phoenix Union, 15 against Phoenix Indian School, 14 against Arizona and 13 in a second outing against Phoenix Indian. His 15-strikeout performance against the Indian School came in a 12-inning game.

1909-1910

February 6, 1910: The Boy Scouts of America organization was chartered by Chicago publisher William Boyce.

March 16, 1910: Auto racer Barney Oldfield set a land speed record of 133 miles per hour.

May 17, 1910: Arizona's most famous hotel, the Adams in Phoenix, was destroyed by fire.

June 19, 1910: Spokane, Washington, became the first city to celebrate Father's Day.

July 4, 1910: Jack Johnson successfully defended his world heavyweight boxing title against Jim Jeffries.

tempe normal moment

With the football program shut down for an eight-year stretch, baseball continued to dominate the sports scene in Tempe. And, as usual, the series against rival Arizona was front and center in the minds of the fans. After three straight seasons in which the Normal played Arizona two games in Tempe and two in Tucson, the teams met three times, all in Tucson, in 1910. That proved to be no problem for the Normals, who won by scores of 4-2, 6-5, and 15-13—the first series sweep against UA in the history of the program. It also gave the Normals five straight victories over Arizona on its home field in a two-year period. If Normal fans had been able to peer into the future, they probably would have rejoiced over that sweep for weeks, because the Normals/Bulldogs/Sun Devils did not win three games in one season against Arizona again until the Bobby Winkles coaching era of the 1960s. The sweep in Tucson gave the Normals their fourth territorial championship in a five-year span. Center fielder John Lynch was the offensive star and Jack Halbert the No. 1 pitcher for the Normals, who finished with a 12-3 record.

Jack Halbert was the pitching star for the Normals, who swept Arizona in Tucson to win their fourth territorial championship in five years. (University Archives)

Tempe NORMAL spotlight

While baseball was soaring in popularity on the Tempe campus, it also was catching fire in the rest of the Salt River Valley. On March 19, 1910, a throng of 1,100 turned out in Mesa to watch the Normals beat Mesa High's Jackrabbits, 8-4. That would stand until 1956 as the largest crowd to watch a Tempe Normal/Arizona State game. The record finally fell in '56 when Arizona State and Arizona drew a crowd of 1,523 for a game in Tucson. By the early 1970s, the Arizona State-Arizona series was off the charts. A 1972 meeting in Phoenix drew 8,716. A 1978 clash in Tucson drew an all-time series record of 10,619.

LEGEND

John Lynch

J ohn Lynch was involved in several "firsts" during his three-year baseball career at Tempe Normal. He was the school's first .300 hitter, batting .333 to lead the team in 1909. He was the school's first .400 hitter with a .414 batting average in 1910. And that was an era when pitchers usually dominated. Lynch was the first Normal player to collect five hits in one game. He did it against Phoenix Indian School in 1910 and the feat wasn't accomplished again until Wade Oliver had a five-hit game against New Mexico in 1948. Lynch, a fleet center fielder, was team captain in 1910. He earned most valuable player honors that season. Lynch's career batting average was .350, which ranks fourth among players in the early era of Arizona State baseball.

John Lynch was one of the school's first baseball hitting stars. (University Archives)

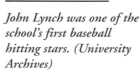

THE tempe normal LIST

Largest crowds in early era baseball (pre-1959)

Crowd	Opponent	Year	Site
1,523	Arizona	1956	Tucson
1,219	Arizona	1958	Tucson
1,158	Arizona	1957	Tucson
1,100	Mesa High	1910	Mesa
887	Arizona	1958	Tucson
822	Arizona	1949	Tucson
750	Arizona	1958	Mesa
600	Arizona	1957	Tucson
600	Arizona	1956	Tucson
561	Arizona	1957	Mesa

TEMPE NORMAL NUGGET

• Jack Halbert set a school record for strikeouts against a college opponent when he whiffed 17 Arizona batters in 1910. The previous record of 14 was set the previous season by Leo Cuber against UA. No. 2 starter Fred Ayer had 22 strikeouts in one game in 1910, but it was against a non-collegiate opponent, Evans School, and the game went 10 innings.

TEMPE NORMAL LORE

P resident William Howard Taft spoke to Tempe residents from the back of a train at the Tempe Depot. He told them he would support Arizona's bid for statehood.

• Arizona's population grew from 122,931 in 1900 to 204,354 in 1910, a rate three times the national growth rate.

1910-1911

November 8, 1910: The Democratic party took control of Congress for the first time in 16 years.

November 14, 1910: The first successful attempt of a naval aircraft launching from the deck of a warship was made off the cruiser *Birmingham*.

March 19, 1911: Theodore Roosevelt Dam on the Salt River was dedicated after seven years of construction, assuring a dependable water supply for central Arizona.

May 11, 1911: The U.S. Supreme Court ordered Standard Oil dissolved because it violated the antitrust law.

May 30, 1911: Ray Harmon won the first Indianapolis 500 auto race.

tempe normal | moment

In October of 1910 the *Tempe Normal Student* predicted great things for the girls' basketball team. The paper said: "The girls have purchased a new basketball and have gone to work in earnest. Judging from the present outlook, this year promises some startling revelations in girls' basketball. New suits have been ordered and the girls expect to so dazzle their opponents with those costumes that they will easily win every game in which they take part." The newspaper wasn't far off. The girls won a pair from University of Arizona (23-20 and 17-16), beat Phoenix Indian School (21-11), Tempe High (47-5), Flagstaff Normal (15-14) and Tucson High (31-7). Their only loss came on the road at Tucson High (16-11), and the *Tempe Normal Student* had plenty of reasons for that setback. "The Normal girls were handicapped in more ways than one," the newspaper reported, "and they are to be congratulated on their splendid efforts. They had never

The girls' basketball team rolled to a 6-1 record, including two wins over Arizona. (University Archives)

played on an indoor court and were not used to a court with no outside lines." Members of the team were Neoma Millett, Lucille Morrison, Hazel Barr, Alma Ellingson, Jennie Weedin and Mary Dunlap.

Tempe NORMAL *spotlight*

The track and field team stole much of the baseball squad's thunder in the spring of 1911, assuming the role of most dominant team on campus. The student annual, *El Picadello*, fairly gushed about the tracksters' exploits. The publication said: "Have we a team? Well, rather! The best in the Territory! The best Arizona has ever produced!" The Normals beat Tempe High School, beat Arizona twice and won a "general event" in which the competition included Tempe High and Phoenix Indian School. *El Picadello* reported: "Practically the only contest in which we were obliged to exert ourselves was the first meet with the University. It was evenly matched from beginning to end, and at no time until the close of the last event could the result be foretold." The Normals captured the final event, the mile relay, to win by a score of 55 to 53. Normal athletes broke seven territorial records in the meet.

Joe Sheldon

When someone talked about the "fastest man in the territory" in the early 1900s, there's a good chance they were talking about some Tombstone gunslinger. Joe Sheldon, however, brought a whole new meaning to the term. Sheldon could flat-out fly. In the spring of 1911 he was the territorial record holder in the 100-yard dash, the 220-yard dash and the quarter-mile run. He also anchored a Tempe Normal mile-relay team that had the fastest time in the territory. His times of 10 1/5 seconds in the 100, 22 3/5 in the 220 and 52 3/5 in the 440 wouldn't cause much of a stir these days, but at the time Sheldon routinely ran off and hid from the competition. His finest moment came on April 15, 1911, in a dual meet against rival Arizona in Tucson. The meet had been nip-and-tuck from the outset and the Normals trailed by three points, 53 to 50 , entering the final event, the mile relay. Sheldon got the baton on the anchor leg virtually even with UA's star sprinter, identified in newspaper accounts only as "Carpenter." Sheldon kicked in the afterburners and left Carpenter in his dust, giving the Normals a 55 to 53 victory. In addition to his exploits on the track, Sheldon had a flair for the gentleman's game, tennis. He teamed with Normal coed Aileen Smith to win the mixed doubles event in the 1911 interscholastic meet.

Joe Sheldon was the fastest man in the Arizona Territory in 1911. (University Archives)

THE tempe normal LIST

Arizona Territory track & field records in 1911

Event	Record Holder	School/Mark
100-yard dash	Sheldon	Tempe Normal 10 1/5 sec.
	Corpstein	Phoenix High 10 1/5 sec.
High jump	Rulo	Indian School 5 ft., 5 1/2 in.
220-yard-dash	Sheldon	Tempe Normal 22 3/5 sec.
High hurdles	Blake	Tempe Normal 16 4/5 sec.
	Strong	U of Arizona 16 4/5 sec.
Hammer throw	Lassen	Tempe High 128 ft., 8 in.
Broad jump	Highfil	U of Arizona 21 ft., 5 in.
Discus	Lassen	Tempe High 110 ft., 10 in.
Quarter mile	Sheldon	Tempe Normal 52 3/5 sec.
Shot put	Dykes	Tempe Normal 43 ft., 6 in.
Low hurdles	Strong	U of Arizona 26 4/5 sec.
Pole vault	Dines	Tempe Normal 10 ft., 3 1/2 in.
Half mile	Stroud	Phoenix High 2 min., 2 sec.
Mile	Haby	Tempe Normal 4 min., 58 sec.
Mile relay		Tempe Normal 3 min., 38 sec.

TEMPE NORMAL LORE

President Teddy Roosevelt spoke to several hundred people March 20, 1911, on the steps of Old Main, one day after dedicating Roosevelt Dam on the Salt River. He predicted that one day as many as 100,000 people might live in the Salt River Valley. Nice call, Teddy, but you erred by about three million on the conservative side.

TEMPE NORMAL NUGGET

• The baseball team struggled to a 4-3 record in a season shortened to seven games because two members of the Salt River Valley League, Mesa High and Phoenix High, dropped out. The school yearbook said the team would have fared much better against a full schedule. According to the yearbook: "Our failure to win the championship this year was not due to an inferior team, but partly to the shortness of the season and the limited number of games played, for our team was the best one in the history of the Normal."

1911-1912

america's time capsule

July 18, 1911: Work began on the first street paving project in the greater Phoenix area. The first segment was on Washington Street between Third and Fifth Avenues in Phoenix.

October 26, 1911: The Philadelphia Athletics won the World Series over the New York Giants.

February 14, 1912: Arizona was admitted to the Union as the 48th state on Valentine's Day. W. P. Hunt was inaugurated as the state's first governor.

April 15, 1912: The British ocean liner *Titanic* struck an iceberg and sank off the coast of Newfoundland, killing some 1,500 people.

July 22, 1912: Decathlete Jim Thorpe was among the American gold medal winners as the Olympic Games came to a close in Stockholm, Sweden.

tempe normal | moment

The baseball team won its first four games and nine of its first 10 en route to a 13-4 record and its second Salt River Valley championship in three years. The 13 victories was the most at that point in school history, topping a 12-3 record in 1910. John Spikes was the Normals' leader in more ways than one. He served as head coach and as team captain. He was voted the team's most valuable player after leading the club in hitting (.407) and compiling a 7-2 pitching record. There was only one college team on the schedule – rival Arizona, which nipped the Normals, 2-1, in a game played in Tempe. The Normals padded their record somewhat by winning all five meetings against neighborhood rival Tempe High. The scores were 2-1, 6-4, 9-2, 11-7 and 12-5. Two of the four losses were to a powerhouse Tucson High club, by scores of 4-3 in Tucson and 8-3 in Tempe.

The baseball team won its second Valley championship in three years. (University Archives)

Tempe NORMAL *spotlight*

Women had been playing basketball at the Normal since before the turn of the century, and with football on the shelf the men decided to get in on the act during the 1911-12 school year. It was the first recorded men's season in school history. School records list a professor, C.W. Adams, as the coach, but published reports at the time indicate the team was organized and coached by one of the players, John Spikes. The student yearbook, *The Fountain*, said: "The Normal boys played splendid games, each one showing clean and manly work on the part of each player. Although allowed to play, no coach was provided, and once again John Spikes came to the front, drilling and encouraging each individual player until our team was the best team in the entire Valley." Joining Spikes on the team were Albert Spikes, Howard Patterson, Fritz Griffin and Horace Griffen. They won their first four games and finished with an 8-2 record.

LEGEND

Albert Spikes

After starring in three sports for southeastern Arizona prep power Douglas High, Albert "Sam" Spikes made athletic history at Tempe Normal. Spikes was a pioneer, playing on the school's first men's basketball team in 1912. His lanky frame served him well at the center position, where he started for three years. He was a four-year starter in baseball, playing first base in 1911 and 1912, shortstop in 1913, and third base in 1914. In 1911 he tied with John Mullen for the team batting lead at .255. He also starred in track and field. His specialty was the discus, an event he won consistently and one in which he eventually became the state record holder. Following graduation, Spikes returned to southeastern Arizona where he became a prominent cattle rancher and cotton farmer in Bowie. Spikes, who also obtained a degree from University of Arizona, served as Superintendent of Schools in Bowie from 1916 through 1945. He spent six years in the Arizona House of Representatives and 16 years in the state Senate. At the time of his death in 1968 at the age of 76, his 22 years in the Legislature was the longest tenure of anyone since statehood. He also was instrumental in the establishment of Cochise College.

Albert Spikes was a mainstay of the Normal basketball, baseball and track and field teams. (University Archives)

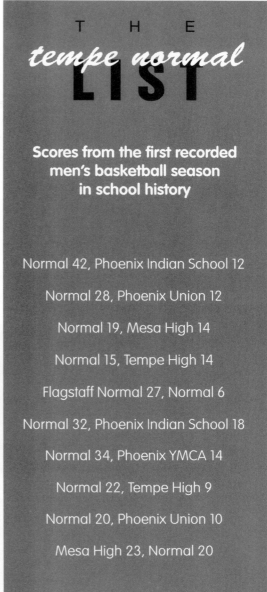

TEMPE NORMAL NUGGET

• One of the big athletic events of the spring was the Salt River Valley track and field meet held at the Fairgrounds in Phoenix. And the feature event of the annual meet was the mile relay, which concluded the meet each year. The prize for winning the relay was a cup, and the Normal relay team took home the hardware in 1912.

TEMPE NORMAL LORE

Tempe had its wild side in the early 1900s, but there also was a moderate element. That was evident when the city voted in prohibition, three years before the rest of Arizona and 11 years before the rest of the nation. Some saloon keepers in Tempe were fined for refusing to close their establishments.

1912-1913

tempe normal
moment

The baseball team fell short of the 13-victory total of the previous season because of a shorter schedule, but posted the longest winning streak and best winning percentage at that point in school history. The Normals won their first 10 games before falling to Phoenix Indian School, 3-2, in the final game of the season. Their 10-1 record produced a winning percentage of .909, which stood as a school record until Coach Jim Brock's first Arizona State team in 1972 finished 64-6 (.914). For the third time in four years the Normals captured the Republican Cup, presented annually by *The Arizona Republican* newspaper to the winner of the Salt River Valley championship. In the next-to-last game of the season the Normals pounded Glendale High, 25-2, setting school records for most runs and largest winning margin. Both marks would stand until the 1921 team whipped Winslow High, 36-6. Coach and Captain John Spikes was the pitching star with a 9-1 record, but the Normals had another little-known pitching weapon. In the one game he pitched, Tom Flannigan struck out 15 Glendale High batters.

Player-coach John Spikes' baseball team set several records while claiming another Salt River Valley title. (University Archives)

Modern athletes don't blink at cross-country travel in jet planes, but the trip from Tempe to Phoenix and back could be an adventure in the early 1900s. The Normal track team, which won a cup for capturing the mile relay at the previous year's Salt River Valley track and field meet in Phoenix, didn't stick around for the final event and a chance at more hardware in 1913. As the mile relay approached, officials tallied the points and discovered that the Normals had accumulated enough points to win the meet without competing in the relay. It was decided to skip the event so team members could get on the road to Tempe before it got dark.

ASU LEGEND

John Spikes

John Spikes certainly fit the role of big man on campus. He was president of the senior class. He starred in baseball, basketball and track and field. If the Normal had fielded a football team at the time, he surely would have played that sport, too. He organized and coached the first men's basketball team in school history in 1912 and served as the school's baseball coach for two seasons while playing for the Normal. During his baseball coaching tenure the Normals had records of 13-4 and 10-1 and captured a pair of Salt River Valley championships. In addition to coaching the baseball team, Spikes was its captain in 1912 and 1913 and was named Most Valuable Player both years. He compiled a 7-2 pitching record in 1912 and followed that with a 9-1 mark in 1913. His 1913 victory total stood as a school record until 1921, when Dale Patterson won 13 games. He tied Fred Ayer's school record by striking out 22 batters in a 12-inning game against Phoenix Indian School in 1913. Spikes struck out 108 batters in 10 games in 1913. That, too, remained a school record until 1921, when Patterson whiffed 165 batters. Did we mention Spikes' bat? He led the team in batting with a .407 average in 1912 and again with a .357 mark in 1913.

Multi-sports star John Spikes was a classic example of the big man on campus. (University Archives)

TEMPE NORMAL NUGGET

- Women's basketball was conducted a bit differently in 1913 than it is today. The official school team was made up entirely of senior players, who won the right to represent the college against outside opposition by compiling an 8-0 record in inter-class competition. Though they dominated on campus, the Normal women lost both of their games against outside competition—4-3 to Flagstaff Normal and 14-9 to Mesa High.

TEMPE NORMAL LORE

After graduate Carl Hayden delivered an inspiring commencement address in 1896, the *Tempe News* predicted greatness for the young man from Tempe. The newspaper was right on target. Hayden was elected Maricopa County Sheriff in 1906 and in 1912 he headed off to Washington, D.C. to become the state's first representative in Congress, where he served with distinction for 57 years.

1913-1914

america's time capsule

tempe normal | moment

After seasons of 13-4 in 1912 and 10-1 in 1913, the baseball team saw its record fall to 7-5 the following season. The Normals clearly missed the leadership of player-coach John Spikes, who had served as team captain the two previous seasons while making important contributions as a hitter and on the mound. Horace Griffen coached the 1914 team, which also was missing its entire starting outfield from 1913. Borrowing a page from Spikes' book, team captain Tom Flannigan led the team in hitting (.314) and also was the team's top pitcher as he divided time between shortstop and the mound. In the biggest game of the year, Flannigan scattered 12 hits as the Normals edged rival Arizona, 4-2, before a lively crowd in Tempe. The *Tempe Normal Student's* report of the game credited the crowd with making a difference. "One of the principal factors in winning the game was the ardent support received from the student body," the newspaper said. "Everybody was there, and they brought their voices along with them . . . Every member of the team is an idol in the eyes of the school and all will receive their share of rooting from this time on."

spotlight

Coach Fred Irish's girls' basketball team bounced back from an off season to record three victories over high school teams from the Salt River Valley, beating Tempe High, Mesa High and Glendale High. In their only game against a collegiate opponent the Normal girls lost a thriller, 14-13, to Flagstaff Normal. Their showing against Flagstaff was a marked improvement over a 14-3 loss to the Lumberjills the previous season. Top players for the Normal were Margurite Stephens, Louisa Rogers, Grace Cordes, Sarah Wilson, Gladys Walker and Ruth Watkins.

The girls' basketball team rebounded from an off season to post a 3-1 record for coach Fred Irish. (University Archives)

ASU LEGEND

Horace Griffen

By a wide margin, Arizona State has sent more players into major league baseball than any other school. Many, like Reggie Jackson, Rick Monday, Bob Horner, and Barry Bonds, are household names. Most modern fans wouldn't recognize the name of Horace Griffen, but he has a special place in the school's baseball history. Griffen, who played the outfield in 1912 and first base in 1913 and 1914, was the first player from the school to sign a contract with a major league club, though he didn't reach the big leagues. Griffen, who also played basketball and served as player-coach during the 1914 baseball season, signed with the Chicago White Sox following the 1914 campaign. He played with Milwaukee and Green Bay in the American Baseball Association before cutting short his professional career to join the armed forces following the start of World War I. After the war, he joined Gen. John J. Pershing's victory marches in New York City and Washington, D.C. He returned to Tempe and resumed his baseball career at the Normal in 1917, something that would not be permitted under today's more stringent rules. He captained the 1917 team and led the club in hitting with a .317 average. In 1956 he made an unsuccessful bid for governor of Arizona.

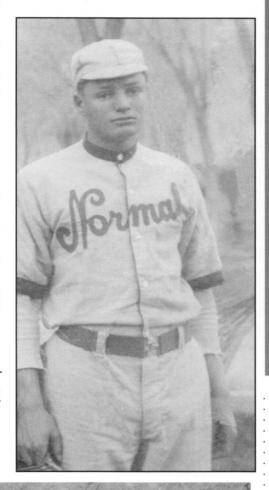

Horace Griffen was the school's first player to sign a professional baseball contract (University Archives)

TEMPE NORMAL NUGGET

• The men's basketball team finished with a 6-5 record, including losses in their only two games against rival Arizona. They won a 27-25 thriller over Flagstaff Normal in the final game of the season to achieve a winning season. Top players included Will Greenberg, Lionel Castle, Ray Fram, Isaac Imes, Aaron McCreary and Albert Spikes.

TEMPE NORMAL LORE

A long-awaited bridge over the Salt River near campus was completed in September of 1913 at a cost of $116,000, facilitating trips to nearby Phoenix.

• Enrollment surged from 264 in 1912 to 365 in 1914 as agricultural courses were added to the curriculum.

1914-1915

January 25, 1915: Alexander Graham Bell placed the first successful transcontinental telephone call from New York City to San Francisco.

February 8, 1915: D.W. Griffith's famous motion picture "Birth of a Nation" opened in Los Angeles.

April 5, 1915: Jess Willard defeated Jack Johnson in 23 rounds to win the world heavyweight boxing title.

April 15, 1915: The water level rose to within nine inches of the top of the great Roosevelt Dam, which had been completed four years earlier on the Salt River in central Arizona.

May 7, 1915: A German submarine sank the British steamship *Lusitania*, killing nearly 1,200 people.

america's time capsule

tempe normal | moment

Football returned to the Normal in the fall of 1914 after an eight-year absence. Athletic Director George Schaeffer appointed himself football coach and managed to round up enough able bodies to field a team. Schaeffer had to do some serious coaching, because only one athlete, team captain Gordon Johnson, had ever played the game. Excitement flared briefly when the team opened with a 12-6 victory over Tempe High, then crushed Glendale High, 72-0, in the first two games on Normal turf. Reality set in when the Normals traveled to Tucson to play Arizona, which romped to a 34-0 victory.

This crew brought football back to the Normal in 1914 after an eight-year absence. (University Archives)

It wasn't easy, but the Normal student yearbook, *The Quindecem*, managed to put a positive spin on that game. The yearbook reported: "The University of Arizona, who by defeating Occidental became champions of the Southwest, was the only team in the state which succeeded in holding our boys scoreless, and they themselves were able to amass but 34 points." After tough losses to Phoenix High (13-9) and Phoenix Indian School (24-6), the Normals closed with victories over the Indians (34-7) and Prescott High (10-7) to finish with a winning record, 4-3. Among the star players were backfield mates Aaron McCreary and Kelly Moeur. Both also were standouts on the baseball and basketball teams.

Tempe NORMAL *spotlight*

As football eased its way back into the limelight on campus, baseball was headed in the other direction. Baseball had been the sport of choice during football's eight-year absence, but the 1915 team was disbanded at midseason after a 2-8 start. The student yearbook said, " . . . we awoke to the fact that many of the fellows who had starred in football, and whom we were counting on in baseball, had for one reason or another, left, till there remained but a shadow of our baseball dream of the first semester. In spite of this, however, T.N.S. turned out a team this year that could not be considered a cipher in any sense of the word. They didn't exactly play championship ball, but nevertheless, it was not like eating lemon pie to beat them."

LEGEND

George Schaeffer

His career coaching record at the Normal includes more losses than victories in football, basketball and baseball, but George Schaeffer was a significant figure in the school's athletic history because he had the fortitude to challenge a strong anti-football lobby and bring the sport back to the college after an absence of eight years. Schaeffer, a former Gettysburg College player who also had attended Penn State, made the trek out West to teach at the Normal and to serve as athletic director. He decided the school was ready to take another crack at football, which had died out following the 1905 season as part of a national groundswell against the sport. President Teddy Roosevelt was among those who opposed football on grounds it was too dangerous. Schaeffer had a small wooden grandstand constructed and set about finding enough husky young men to field a team. The student newspaper called Schaeffer "the gallant young coach who dared to brave the anti-football sentiment and who secured to the athletes of the Normal what has been called the King of American games." Schaeffer's three football teams at the Normal had a combined 7-8 record, though two of those three years produced winning records. His three-year baseball coaching record was 10-19. His two basketball teams were a combined 2-3.

George Schaeffer revived football on the Normal campus. (ASU Media Relations)

TEMPE NORMAL NUGGET

• With many of the top athletes in school gravitating toward football, the men's basketball team played just four games. The Normals beat the Phoenix YMCA, 49-32, and split with Mesa High, winning by a 24-14 score and losing 18-14. A 22-20 loss to Flagstaff Normal in the final game cost them a winning season.

TEMPE NORMAL LORE

Two women's dormitories, North and South Halls, were constructed at a cost of $20,000 each on land purchased from private individuals and the Tempe Land Co. for $6,152. The dorms gave the college the capability of housing more than half of its student body on campus. Another addition to the rapidly-growing campus was an industrial arts building costing $75,000.

1915-1916

america's time capsule

tempe normal moment

Coach George Schaeffer's second football team indicated early that it would be a force, playing favored Arizona tough in a 7-0 season-opening loss in Tucson. The Normals, led by the hard running of Kelly Moeur, then won three straight, beating Phoenix High School, 14-7, and the Phoenix Indian School alumni, 32-0, before smacking Flagstaff Normal, 72-3, on the Lumberjacks' home turf. That tied the school scoring record set in a 72-0 romp over Glendale High the previous season. It would stand as a school mark against college opposition until the Sun Devils drilled Colorado State, 79-7, in 1969. The student yearbook said of the Normal: "Individual stars shone brightly . . . both in the backfield and line. Kelly Moeur, however, was easily the brightest of the constellation." The offense wasn't the whole story for the Normals. They didn't allow more than one touchdown to any of their first four opponents, though Phoenix Indian School managed three scores in a 19-7 victory over the Normal in the season finale.

Action from the Normals' 14-7 football victory over Phoenix High School in 1915. (University Archives)

Tempe NORMAL *spotlight*

A year after the squad was disbanded in midseason, the baseball team shook off a slow start and gave rival Arizona a run for the money in the battle for the state title. The Normals fared well against Phoenix-area high school competition, but lost twice to the Wildcats—3-1 in Tempe and 6-3 in Tucson. Arizona's Asa Porter no-hit the Normals in the Tempe game. Team captain Bob Finch, a catcher, was named Most Valuable Player after leading the team in hitting with a .428 batting average. George Wells was named Outstanding Pitcher – the first of four straight years he would capture that honor. Despite losing its last two games, the team finished with a winning record, 6-5.

Kelly Moeur

One of the most gifted athletes at that point in the school's history, Kelly Moeur starred two years in football and two years in baseball. He undoubtedly would have been a two-year starter in basketball as well, but the school didn't field a team in 1916 so he played just one season. While considering that the students who write in yearbooks are sometimes less than impartial, here's what the Normal's publication had to say about Moeur in the three major sports. Football: "Whenever Kelly got the ball, it always meant a gain, and he had a disconcerting habit of occasionally strolling down the field sixty or seventy yards for a touchdown. Whoever tackled Kelly had to get him right around both shoe tops with both arms around, or Kelly wouldn't wait for him." Basketball: "Kelly Moeur at center was brilliant as usual. He was the best center in the state, and if need arose there were few to exceed him as forward." Baseball: "Hans Wagner the Second, sometimes known as Kelly Moeur, played short. Kelly seldom practiced, rarely being in town long enough to put on a uniform, but he could usually play as good a game without practice as most players can with it."

Kelly Moeur was more than just a football hero on the Tempe Normal campus. (University Archives)

TEMPE NORMAL LORE

With World War I raging, a military company was organized on campus under the direction of Capt. Fred Irish, who had been the school's first football coach. Cadets conducted target shooting and map reading exercises among other training activities. They also performed guard duty. A guard was posted around campus as well as at the cotton gin in downtown Tempe.

TEMPE NORMAL NUGGETS

• The Normal's baseball players had to endure a few snickers when they lost twice—by scores of 9-2 and 5-4—to the Arizona State Hospital, a mental institution. Perhaps there was a residual effect from the previous season, when the Normals committed 26 errors in a 14-4 loss to Evans School. The student newspaper called that game "one continual round of slaughter."

• Early basketball games didn't have all the luxuries that modern fans take for granted—like electronic scoreboards. Consider this newspaper account of a game between the Normals and Phoenix High on the Coyotes' home court: "The game was fast and exciting and neither side had any idea of the score until time was called and the score announced: Phoenix 28, Tempe 26."

1916-1917

November 7, 1916: Woodrow Wilson was reelected president of the United States.

February 3, 1917: The United States severed diplomatic relations with Germany because of increased submarine warfare.

March 2, 1917: The Jones Act made Puerto Rico a U.S. territory.

April 2, 1917: President Wilson requested a declaration of war against Germany.

April 9, 1917: Arizona Gov. Thomas E. Campbell appeared before a mass gathering of Salt River Valley residents and appealed for volunteers to bring the First Arizona Regiment up to quota.

america's time capsule

tempe normal
moment

With U.S. participation in World War I looming, many male students, including some of the school's top athletes, were leaving school to join the armed forces. Coach George Schaeffer, who was responsible for returning football to the Normal in 1914 after an eight-year absence, saw the program dissolve once again. Schaeffer managed to scrape together enough athletes to play a three-game schedule, but the sport's future in Tempe once again was in jeopardy. Not only was it difficult to find enough players to field a team, but opponents were scarce. The Normals lost their only home game, 25-7, to the Phoenix Indian School alumni team. They suffered road losses to Flagstaff Normal, 20-6, and Prescott

With athletes leaving for the war, track and field was one of the few sports still functioning near former levels. (University Archives)

High School, 6-0. Because of the war, there would be no team for the next two years. Basketball also took a hit. The school did not field a team in 1915-16 and played just one game in 1916-17. The 1917 student yearbook, the Saguaro, offered these thoughts about athletics and the War: "May the time come when Normal will again send forth her athletes to the football field and the diamond. But let it not be until her sons and daughters have secured peace, safety and honor for posterity and the nation."

Tempe **NORMAL** *spotlight*

Coach George Schaeffer saw many of his top athletes in football, basketball and baseball leave school for the military. Schaeffer's makeshift baseball team, built around pitcher George Wells, managed just two victories in eight games. Both victories were against Phoenix Indian School, by scores of 2-1 and 3-1. The Normal baseball program contributed 21 players to the war effort. Amazingly, all 21 survived the war and many returned after the conflict to resume their studies and their college athletic careers.

Gordon Goodwin

They didn't play football at Tempe Normal during most of Gordon Goodwin's time there, but that didn't keep him from becoming a three-sport star. Goodwin was a starting forward on the basketball team in 1917, 1918 and 1919. He was captain of the team his senior year. The *Tempe Normal Student* said this of Goodwin at the end of the 1918 season: "Goodwin time and again during the season has won the applause of the crowd by his skillful shooting of goals from various angles of the field." Goodwin also was a starting shortstop on the baseball team for three seasons. He played a vital role on the 1918 team that posted a 6-1 record and won the state championship. When he wasn't on the baseball diamond in the spring, Goodwin was a one-man track team. In the 1919 Salt River Valley Invitational Meet at the Normal School athletic field, he personally scored 25 of his team's 34 1/2 points by winning five events. He earned a loving cup as the meet's best all-around athlete. His victories came in the 100-yard dash (10.2 seconds), pole vault (9 feet, 6 inches), broad jump (19 feet, 2 3/4 inches), discus (94 feet, 9 inches) and 220-yard dash (no time given).

Gordon Goodwin starred in basketball and baseball, but track and field might have been his best sport. (University Archives)

TEMPE NORMAL NUGGET

• First baseman Horace Griffen, who signed a pro baseball contract with the Chicago White Sox in 1914 and played in their minor-league system, returned to school and resumed his college career in the spring of 1917. That would be a no-no under current NCAA rules. Griffen, chosen team captain, led the club with a .317 batting average and was named Most Valuable Player.

TEMPE NORMAL LORE

The vice president of the United States, Thomas R. Marshall, visited campus to give an address. Marshall spoke to Normal students about the importance of having a philosophy of life and of passing along that philosophy as they graduated and entered the teaching profession.

1917-1919

November 3, 1917: U.S. Forces engaged in their first World War I battle in Europe.

December 18, 1917: The U.S. Constitution's 18th amendment was passed, outlawing the manufacture and sale of alcoholic liquors.

August 27, 1918: Two Americans were killed and 29 wounded and an estimated 100 Mexicans killed in a bloody battle in the border city of Nogales, Arizona.

September 19, 1918: Phoenix flier Frank Luke Jr. shot down three German observation balloons, giving him nine such kills in three days on the Lorraine Front.

November 11, 1918: World War I ended on the 11th hour of the 11th day of the 11th month.

tempe normal | moment

Though World War I shut down the football program for two years, basketball made a comeback and the baseball program continued to operate, both under new Coach George Cooper. There was a significant moment in baseball, though it's unlikely anyone knew exactly how important it was at the time. The Normals scored twice in the top of the ninth inning to beat Arizona, 5-3, in the final game of the 1918 season in Tucson, capping a 6-1 season and capturing the state championship. The victory evened the all-time series between the two state rivals at 10 victories each. Hundreds of students turned out to give the team a hero's welcome when it returned to Tempe. There might have been even more of a celebra-

The 1918 baseball team beat rival Arizona to capture the state championship. (University Archives)

tion if Normal fans had known what lay ahead. Arizona would win all three games the next season and begin to pull away in the series. The Wildcats won the next 16 meetings before A-State broke through with a 6-3 victory in 1927. With few talented players remaining in school, the baseball record fell off to 1-8 in 1919. The Normals might have won a second game, except for a bad break in a 1-0 loss in 10 innings at Phoenix High School. A report on the game in the student yearbook said: "(Gordon) Goodwin lined one to center that looked like a homer, but a Ford out in the street happened to be in the way, so he only went to second."

Tempe **NORMAL** *spotlight*

Catcher Bill Robinson scored five runs in the 1918 season opener against Mesa High. Pitcher Mac Nevitt scored four runs in the same game, an 18-2 romp. Nevitt and infielder Fenn "Shake" Harris left school after two games in 1918 to join the service. Robinson's runs-scored mark would stand as a school record until 1948, when it was tied by Ed Manning and Ed Gallardo and topped by Skeets Scanlon, who scored six runs against New Mexico. Scanlon's record was the most ever in the early era of Arizona State baseball. It has been matched three times in the modern era—by Mike Colbern in 1974, Mikel Moreno in 1996 and Andrew Beinbrink in 1999.

ASU LEGEND

George Wells

The Normal baseball team had its ups and downs from 1916 through 1919—actually a lot more downs than ups—but there was one constant. George Wells was out on the mound throwing strikes. Wells didn't always have a lot of support as World War I drained off much of the talent in the program, but he did his part to keep the Normals competitive. Four years in succession he was named the school's outstanding pitcher. His best season was 1918, when he posted a 5-1 record for a 6-1 team that captured the state title with a big victory in the season finale against rival Arizona in Tucson. He set a school record with a 0.99 earned run average and averaged 12.0 strikeouts per game.

Wells produced perhaps his finest effort in the biggest game he pitched. In the 1918 state title game against Arizona, he outdueled UA star Perry Doyle, tying Jack Halbert's school record for most strikeouts against a college opponent with 17. That record of 17 strikeouts would withstand 40 years of challenges throughout the early era of Tempe Normal and Arizona State baseball (pre 1959).

George Wells was named the school's outstanding pitcher four years in succession. (University Archives)

THE tempe normal LIST

Top pitchers' season earned run average in the early and modern eras of Arizona State baseball

Early era (Pre-1959)

ERA	Pitcher	Season
0.99	George Wells	1918
2.28	Gay King	1954
2.70	Jim Sims	1957
3.09	Jim Sims	1958
3.16	Dave Graybill	1957

Modern era (1959-present)

ERA	Pitcher	Season
0.99	Eddie Bane	1972
1.01	Larry Gura	1969
1.14	Gary Gentry	1967
1.35	Skip Hancock	1964
1.39	Jim Otten	1973

TEMPE NORMAL LORE

Tempe Normal sent 106 men into the armed forces. All had trained as members of Capt. Fred Irish's cadet corps. Of that group, 17 returned as commissioned officers and many more as non-commissioned officers.

• Matthews Hall, initially a men's dormitory, was constructed at a cost of $62,000. It was named by its residents in honor of college President Arthur J. Matthews.

TEMPE NORMAL NUGGETS

• This item from the *Tempe Normal Student* of November 5, 1917: "The game which was to have been played between the Tempe Normal and Chandler High basketball teams was called off about one-half hour before the contest was scheduled to start. The reason given was that the High School boys had let their Halowe'en celebration get the better of them."

• How's this for non-support? Normal pitcher George Wells set a school record by averaging 12.3 strikeouts per game in 1919. However, he had a 1-7 record to show for it as the team staggered to a 1-8 finish. How feeble was the Normal offense? Consider that catcher Harold Austin led the team in hitting—with a .190 batting average. That's the lowest average to lead the team in school history.

1919-1920

September 26, 1919: President Woodrow Wilson suffered a stroke during a national tour.

April 20, 1920: The Olympic Games opened in Antwerp, Belgium.

May 14, 1920: The Socialist Party nominated Eugene V. Debs of Indiana for the presidency for the fifth time. Debs was serving a 10-year prison sentence at the time of his nomination.

July 3, 1920: Bill Tilden won the men's singles title at the Wimbledon tennis championships.

July 5, 1920: The Democratic Party nominated Ohio Gov. James Cox for the presidency and Franklin D. Roosevelt of New York for the vice presidency.

america's time capsule

tempe normal moment

After a two-year absence caused by World War I, football made a brief return to the Normal campus in 1919. The results were so discouraging that the sport promptly disappeared again for two more years. That meant the school fielded a team just four times during a 16-year stretch from 1906 through 1921. Coach George Cooper, who came from Pennsylvania to assume the job of athletic director and physical education instructor in 1917, lasted just one year as football coach. With only 60 male students on campus in 1919, most of them a far cry from your classic football types, Cooper had to scramble to put together a team. The results were predictable. The Normals opened the season against a powerhouse Arizona team in Tucson. According to published reports, the Normals were so overmatched that UA Coach Pop McKale pulled his starters early in the second half of a 53-0 romp. The only other game, at Phoenix High School, wasn't much better. The Normals came up on the short end of a 45-3 score.

Crowds flocked to Normal Field in just four of 16 years from 1906 through 1921. (University Archives)

Tempe NORMAL *spotlight*

Second baseman Leo Buck tied Bob Finch's school record with a .428 batting average as the Normals shook off a 1-8 season in 1919 and finished with a 7-3 record in 1920. Finch, a catcher, had set the record in 1916. Buck's big year with the bat earned him Most Valuable Player honors. He also served as team captain. Dale Patterson was the pitching star for the Normals. He was the pitcher of record in all seven of the team's victories and was on the losing end in just one of the three losses. He recorded 80 strikeouts in his eight appearances, the fifth-highest total in the school's early baseball era (1907-1958). The Normals lost two of their first three games, but got their act together and won six of their last seven.

ASU LEGEND

George Cooper

Who knows what kind of a football coaching record George Cooper might have achieved at Tempe Normal if his timing had been a bit different. A graduate of Slippery Rock State Teachers College in Pennsylvania, where he starred in football, Cooper arrived at the Normal in 1917. He had a multitude of assignments, including athletic director, physical education instructor and coach of the football, basketball, baseball and track and field teams. Published reports at the time suggested that his first love was football, but he had little opportunity to show his stuff. His first two years on campus, the Normal did not field a team because World War I had siphoned away most of the top athletes. After a disastrous 0-2 season in 1919, the sport again was dropped for two years. But Cooper proved in other arenas that he could coach. In five seasons as the Normal's baseball coach, his teams won 41 games and lost just 16. His best team was the 1921 club, an offensive juggernaut that rolled up a 17-2 record. Cooper also demonstrated his coaching expertise in basketball. His first team went 14-4 in 1918 and his five teams had a combined record of 43-15. Under his direction the Normals were 11-3 in 1921 and 10-1 in 1922.

George Cooper had dazzling won-lost coaching records in basketball and baseball, but never really had a chance in football. (University Archives)

THE tempe normal LIST

Shutout games in the Arizona State-Arizona football rivalry

Score	Winner	Season
12-0	Arizona	1902
34-0	Arizona	1914
7-0	Arizona	1915
59-0	Arizona	1919
35-0	Arizona	1926
39-0	Arizona	1928
26-0	Arizona	1929
6-0	Arizona	1930
26-0	Arizona	1935
18-0	Arizona	1936
23-0	Arizona	1942
67-0	Arizona	1946
35-0	Arizona	1953
20-0	Arizona State	1956
47-0	Arizona State	1958
31-0	Arizona State	1971
10-0	Arizona	1974

TEMPE NORMAL NUGGET

- The Normals' 59-0 football loss to Arizona was the worst at that point in school history, topping a 34-0 loss to the Wildcats in 1914. It remained the worst loss in the history of the rivalry until Arizona rolled up a 67-0 victory in 1946.

TEMPE NORMAL LORE

It took some serious lobbying, but college President Arthur J. Matthews convinced the school board to purchase 35 acres of land adjoining the campus to the South for $18,000. The acquisition, which represented a substantial financial investment in those days, more than doubled the size of the campus and provided a site for a gymnasium and a football stadium several years later.

1920-1921

america's time capsule

tempe normal moment

With football once again on the shelf because of a lack of available talent, the baseball team stepped up and produced the most productive season at that point in the school's history. Second-year Coach George Cooper's club combined a balanced hitting attack with outstanding pitching as it rolled to a 17-2 record. The previous highest victory total in school history was 13 wins by the 1912 team. The only blemishes on the 1921 record were a 2-1 loss to Phoenix Indian School and a 9-6 loss to rival Arizona in 10 innings. Both games were on the road. Seven members of the starting lineup had batting averages of .360 or higher, topped by a school-record .571 by third baseman Pete Brown. The

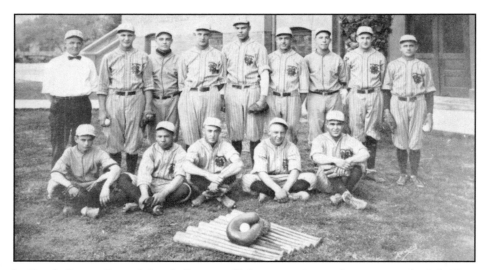

Coach George Cooper's baseball team rolled up a 17-2 record en route to the Salt River Valley championship. (University Archives)

offense really came to life during a late-season swing through northern Arizona. On that three-game trip the Normals blasted Prescott High, 27-15, Winslow High, 36-6, and Flagstaff Normal, 21-6. The 27 runs against Prescott High was a school record, but it lasted just one game. The 36 runs against Winslow High stood as a school record throughout the early era of the school's baseball history, 1907 through 1958. It has been matched once in the modern era, by the 1974 team against Texas-El Paso. Pitcher Dale Patterson, first baseman Brown Capps and outfielder Charles Rollins—signed professional contracts after the season.

Tempe NORMAL *spotlight*

Women's basketball was revived with the arrival of several outstanding high school players on campus in the fall of 1920, though the girls had to twist some arms. The school yearbook, the *Sahuaro*, reported: "Were these girls, so full of pep, going to submit meekly to a year at school without a girls basket ball team? We should say not! 'A basket ball team or bust,' henceforth was our battle cry. With grim determination we marched to Miss (Sally) Hayden and after much persuasion won her consent to the organization of a team. We next mobbed Mr. (Fred) Irish and literally carried him away to the basket ball court, where he was provided with a whistle and given instructions to remove his coat and prepare for action." The girls managed a 3-2 record, with victories over Mesa High, Glendale High, and Winslow High. Members of the team were Polly Milborn, Stella Mae Carson, Lillian Glenn, Alverta Goodwin, Lydia Hopkins, May Watkins, Ada May Etz, and Margaret Seeley.

ASU LEGEND

Dale Patterson

Dale Patterson found his way from the little community of Elfrida in the southeastern corner of Arizona to the Tempe Normal campus on the banks of the Salt River in the central part of the state. It clearly was Elfrida's loss and Tempe Normal's gain. A four-year basketball letterman, he made his biggest mark in baseball. He was an accomplished hitter, batting .482 in 1921, but he was best known for his pitching exploits. He set school records for pitching victories (13-2) and strikeouts (165) in 1921. He didn't just break records, he obliterated them. The previous standards were nine victories and 108 strikeouts by John Spikes in 1913. Patterson's records were not seriously threatened throughout the early era of college baseball in Tempe, stretching through the 1958 season. Not only was Patterson overpowering on the mound, he was a picture of consistency. In March of 1921, he struck out 13 batters four times in succession— against Tempe High, Glendale High, Mesa High and Phoenix Indian School. He averaged 11.0 strikeouts per outing that season. He was one of three Normal players to sign professional contracts at the end of the 1921 season along with first baseman Brown Capps and center fielder Charles Rollins. In addition to his baseball and basketball activities, Patterson also found time to run track.

Dale Patterson was a multi-sport star whose baseball pitching records held up for decades. (University Archives)

TEMPE NORMAL NUGGET

• Before unleashing his baseball team on the rest of the state, Coach George Cooper put together an outstanding basketball outfit. The Normals won their first four games and captured their last three to finish with a 9-2 record. After averaging 36.8 points during their first seven games, the Normals found a lid on the basket in a 20-12 loss to Phoenix Union High. That must have prompted some extra shooting practice, because the Normals closed their season by beating Gilbert High, 55-17, Phoenix College, 55-15, and Flagstaff Normal, 42-13. Cedric Austin, who pitched and played second base for the Normal baseball team, was captain of the basketball team. Others who did double duty between basketball and baseball included Tony Boetto and Dale Patterson.

TEMPE NORMAL LORE

Many downtown Tempe businesses were forced to close their doors as the local economy took a major hit from the postwar depression. A scandal struck the business community when William J. Kingsbury, a Tempe civic leader and president of the Farmer's and Merchant's Bank, was convicted of starting a fire to cover up a $23,500 shortage in the bank's vault. Kingsbury and a cashier were sentenced to prison and the bank went out of business. The economic slowdown was felt on campus, where enrollment stagnated and construction came to a virtual halt.

1921-1922

September 8, 1921: Margaret Gorman of Washington, D.C., won the first Miss America competition.

October 5, 1921: The first radio coverage of the World Series was carried by a wireless station set up at an electrical show in New York and by station WJZ in New Jersey.

November 11, 1921: The "Unknown Soldier" for World War I was buried at Arlington National Cemetery.

February 21, 1922: An explosion on the airship *Roma* killed 34 members of its 45-man crew.

February 27, 1922: The 19th Amendment to the Constitution, providing for women's suffrage, was declared constitutional by the U.S. Supreme Court in a unanimous decision.

tempe normal
moment

The men's basketball team won its first eight games en route to a 10-1 finish that came on the heels of a 9-2 mark the previous season. The only blemish was a 32-30 loss to Gilbert High in a hotly-contested game. Coach George Cooper's Normals won the Class A division in the race for the Salt River Valley championship, and won two of three from Class B champ Gilbert to capture the Valley title. The schedule was less than demanding. The only college opponents were Phoenix College and the University of Arizona freshmen. The Normals beat PC, 30-13, and the UA frosh, 46-18. In an era when a score in the 50s was a big deal, the Normals hit that mark three times. They beat Mesa High, 55-23, Phoenix Indian School, 56-18, and Miami High, 59-30. Among the regulars were Orin Fuller, Pete Brown, Carroll Brown, Harold Clark, Raphael Estrada and John Nix.

The men's basketball team captured the Salt River Valley championship with a 10-1 record. (University Archives)

spotlight

The 1922 baseball team didn't match the gaudy 17-2 record of the 1921 team, thanks partly to a shorter schedule, but it did leave plenty of opposing pitchers shaking their heads in frustration. The Normals compiled a respectable 10-2 record, but the real news was the offensive production. The Normals batted a resounding .392 as a team. The next-highest figure in the early era of Tempe Normal/Arizona State baseball was a .336 mark in 1948. The highest team batting average in the modern era (post 1958) was .356 by the 1981 national championship team and the 1999 club. Shortstop Pete Brown (.511) and pitcher Cedric Austin (.505) led the offensive attack. Brown, who also had a 7-1 pitching record, was named Most Valuable Player.

ASU LEGEND

Pete Brown

One of the top all-around athletes of his time at the Normal, Pete Brown was best known as a veritable hitting machine in baseball. He started as a outfielder in 1919, played third base the next two seasons and moved to shortstop as a senior in 1922. He was the team captain and Most Valuable Player that season, when he led the team with a .511 batting average. Brown's best season, however, was his junior year, when he mashed the ball at a .571 clip, by far the best season average in school history. He played a vital role as the team enjoyed its best season at that point in the school's history with a 17-2 record. Brown also was a three-year starter on the basketball team from 1921 through 1923. He earned All-Valley honors at guard for the 1922 basketball team that captured the Valley championship. He also ran track and played on the 1922 football team when that sport was reinstated at the Normal after a two-year absence.

Pete Brown was a hitting machine in baseball, and also played three other sports. (University Archives)

TEMPE NORMAL NUGGET

• The women's volleyball team, first organized in 1921, began playing games against outside opponents in 1922, going 1-2 in three games. The student yearbook, the *Sahuaro*, said: "Most of the team will be here next year, and if they keep up the good work that they started this year, Tempe Normal School will awake to the fact that volley ball is claiming an active place among the athletic activities of the school."

TEMPE NORMAL LORE

The Golden State Limited train, bound from Chicago to Los Angeles, was held up by masked bandits near the James Train Station eight miles west of Tucson. Express messenger H. Stewart shot and killed one of the eight robbers and wounded another. No passengers were injured and the would-be robbers were routed without obtaining any loot.

1922-1923

america's time capsule

tempe normal
| m o m e n t

Tempe Normal athletic teams acquired a new nickname—Bulldogs—in the fall of 1922. They previously had been known as Normals and Teachers and sometimes Jackrabbits. The name was suggested by a spectator at the season-opening football game which the Normal lost to Mesa High by a 13-6 score. The school newspaper, the *Tempe Normal Student*, got behind the movement in its Nov. 13 edition. The newspaper story read: "Our team was defeated, but not beaten. A team made of the stuff that ours is made of cannot be beaten. It was inexperience and not Mesa that defeated it. Indeed it deserves the name that was given it by a prominent spectator — 'the Bulldogs.' " From that point until they became Sun Devils in 1946, the school's teams were known as Bulldogs. A succession of bulldogs named Pete, adorned in "A" blankets, were prominently displayed at various campus events.

BULLDOG *spotlight*

The men's basketball team shook off a slow start and won three of its last four games to finish with an 8-4 record. The Bulldogs lost twice to rival Arizona, 29-20 and 31-22, but scored a resounding 42-18 victory over Flagstaff Normal in a season-ending tournament. They also whipped Phoenix Indian School, 43-19, to capture the tournament . Guard Orin Fuller and center Harold Clark were named All-State and guard Rafael Estrada was an All-State selection in the junior college division. The women's basketball team was even more impressive, rolling to the state championship with a 14-1 record under new coach Waldo B. Christy, a commerce professor. The women beat the University of Arizona for the first time ever. Captain and center Josephine Moeur was called by the student yearbook "the fastest center in the state."

The men's basketball team rallied for a winning season. (University Archives)

LEGEND

Cedric Austin

N o matter what the athletic endeavor, chances were pretty good in the late teens and early 1920s that Cedric Austin would be in the middle of things. He was a two-year starter in football in 1922 and 1923. He was a four-year starter from 1919 through 1922 in basketball, where he served as team captain. He ran track and even dabbled in tennis. But it was baseball in which Austin, who was nicknamed "Soapy," displayed the most versatility and longevity. In an era where regulations were considerably more lax than they are today, he played five years. He broke in as a second baseman in 1919, played the outfield and served as the No. 2 pitcher in 1920, returned to second base while backing up pitching star Dale Patterson again in 1921, then concentrated on pitching as the No. 1 starter in 1922 and 1923. He was named the team's Most Valuable Pitcher in both of those years. Even when he pitched full-time, Austin didn't lose his batting stroke. His best year with the bat was 1922, when he ripped the ball at a .505 clip. The student yearbook said this about Austin's basketball skills: "He hasn't an equal as a floor man in the state. When he is 'right' he drops them through the draperies with an ease that is appalling."

Cedric "Soapy" Austin was one of the most versatile athletes in school history. (University Archives)

BULLDOG BRIEF

• The baseball team saw its record fall from 10-2 under Coach George Cooper the previous season to 5-5 under new Coach Ernest Willis in 1923. The decline was largely due to a tougher schedule. Arizona, which had not been on the schedule in 1922, appeared four times the following season and won all four games against the newly-named Bulldogs. The Dogs won their last three games against Phoenix Indian School, Tempe High School and the Indian School again to salvage a .500 season. It still was a far cry from the three previous seasons, when the team fashioned a combined 34-7 record under Cooper.

BULLDOG LORE

College President Arthur J. Matthews began a campaign to upgrade the school from a two-year normal school to a four-year teacher's college. The key element of his argument was the fact that most schools in the West were toughening their requirements for teachers from a two-year degree to a four-year course of study, and that Tempe Normal graduates were going to face an increasingly difficult time finding employment. It would take some time, however, to convince the Legislature that a name change was in order.

1923-1924

September 3, 1923: News bulletins from Japan reported that at least 100,000 people perished in the wake of a powerful earthquake and resulting fires.

September 14, 1923: Jack Dempsey retained the world heavyweight boxing crown with a second-round knockout of Luis Angel Firpo, the "Wild Bull of the Pampas."

January 25, 1924: The American team finished fourth in the unofficial team standings as the first Winter Olympics were held in Chamonix, France.

June 30, 1924: The Teapot Dome oil leasing scandal resulted in indictments of several oil company presidents on charges of bribery and conspiracy to defraud the United States.

July 27, 1924: The U.S. won 45 gold medals and finished first in the unofficial team standings at the summer Olympics in Paris, France.

tempe normal
moment

O nly twice at that point in its history—in 1904 and 1914—had Tempe Normal's football team won as many as four games in one season. One of the players on that 1914 team was a young man named Aaron McCreary. In 1923, McCreary returned to the Normal to coach all men's sports and his arrival signaled the revival of the school's football fortunes. With only five returning players from the 0-3-1 team of 1922, McCreary set about rebuilding the program from scratch. The Bulldogs had their ups and downs, but they managed to finish 4-2, matching the victory totals of the 1904 and 1914 teams. The big game was the Thanksgiving Classic tussle at Mesa High. The Normal fans who made the "trip" to Mesa were rewarded with a 24-6 victory as the Bulldogs used their speed to offset the Jackrabbits' superior size. The student yearbook, the *Sahuaro*, carried this account of the game: "Normal displayed a brand of football that was not to be beaten. Although Mesa's team was heavy, our backs made big gains through the line and circled the ends for much yardage. Our fast, tricky plays and accurate passes dazzled the Jackrabbits, and they were unable to do anything to stop us." Among the Bulldogs cited for their outstanding play against Mesa were Kenny Strong, Delbert Goddard, Cedric Austin, Ed Jones and John "Custer" Turner.

Kenny Strong had a big Thanksgiving Day game against Mesa High. (University Archives)

BULLDOG *spotlight*

Though football enjoyed a resurgence on campus, basketball and baseball headed in the other direction. The basketball team lost its first four games—including a 52-17 whipping at the hands of the Miami town team—and struggled to a 3-9 record. The only victories were over the Chandler town team (37-13), Phoenix Indian School (30-28) and Phoenix College (29-22). The Bulldogs lost twice to the University of Arizona varsity and once to the UA freshmen. The baseball team, which had posted a 17-2 record as recently as 1921, suffered its first losing season since 1919, finishing 4-5-1. The Bulldogs were battered in all four games against rival Arizona, losing by scores of 5-0 and 8-4 in Tempe and 16-4 and 14-1 in Tucson. Second baseman Kenny Strong was team captain and earned Most Valuable Player honors. He led the team in batting, though his .235 average wouldn't win many titles these days.

LEGEND

Rafael Estrada

An all-around athlete who starred in football, basketball and baseball, Estrada was one of the first Mexican-American graduates of the Normal at a time when economic conditions made it difficult for minorities to attend college. Estrada, a second baseman, served as team captain in baseball in 1923 and tied with Ken Mullen for the team batting lead at .313. He was named Most Valuable Player. Though he stood only 5-foot-7, Estrada excelled as an end in football, particularly on defense. The student yearbook said: "he was exceptionally good at getting down under punts and very few players ever circled his end for a gain." In baseball, the yearbook said, Estrada was "a good fielder, a crafty general and a speedy runner. His good work with the stick has placed him at the head of batting averages." Estrada, better known as Ralph after his graduation, later obtained a law degree from the University of Arizona and became a prominent civil rights activist. In 1962, he was appointed by President John F. Kennedy as mission director for the Agency for International Development in Nicaragua, a post he held until 1966.

Rafael Estrada went from scrappy football, basketball and baseball star to a U.S. diplomatic post. (ASU Archives)

THE bulldog LIST

Roster of the 1923 football team

(generally considered the one that started the program back to respectability after years of little or no activity)

John Turner

Kenny Strong

Cedric Austin

Delbert Goddard

John Curry

Ed Jones

Bryan Jones

Arthur Way

Loral Dana

Archie Boring

Thelo Motes

Robert Ruse

Theron Palmer

John Goodwin

Mugs Lauffer

Theone Pomeroy

Ellis Johnson

Vernon Friedman

BULLDOG BRIEF

• Baseball had been the talk of campus just a few years earlier, but a sign that times were changing came in the spring of 1924. The season was cut short after 10 games because players indicated they would rather spend their time preparing for an upcoming track and field meet.

BULLDOG LORE

Alumni games are supposed to be times of fellowship and good cheer, but somebody forgot to tell the Bulldogs and an alumni team before their baseball encounter in 1924. The Bulldogs and Bulldog All-Stars were locked in a 4-4 tie in the middle innings when a brawl broke out. When it became evident that the umpires weren't going to be able to restore order, they declared the game a tie. That incident effectively ended the season as players began turning their attention to track and field.

1924-1925

america's time capsule

tempe normal | moment

The Bulldog football team had its first six-win season (6-1-1) at that point in school history as Coach Aaron McCreary continued to build the program after many years of inactivity and struggle. The Bulldogs won their first six games before losing to the Phoenix College alumni, 27-3, and playing a 13-13 tie against the Sherman Indians, a strong touring team. Arizona, which had not been on the schedule since it pounded the Normal 59-0 in 1919, once again was missing. However, Flagstaff Normal returned for the first time since 1916 and fell victim to the Tempe club in a hotly-contested game in Tempe, 20-16. Flagstaff scored first in that game, causing some unrest among Bulldog supporters. The student yearbook reported: "Perhaps it was too much confidence on the part of the play-

Action from the Bulldogs' 20-16 football victory over Flagstaff Normal. (University Archives)

ers that gave Flagstaff the first touchdown. However, as soon as the Bulldogs became aware of their danger, they came back with the same old fight." Though Arizona was not on the schedule, the Bulldogs did play the UA freshman, beating the Wildkittens, 23-13, in Tucson. McCreary's team, much like his 4-2 club of 1923, featured a strong running attack, led by backs Merle Hatch, Earl Pomeroy and Delbert Goddard.

BULLDOG *spotlight*

After 20 years of playing an organized schedule in one form or another, the Normal baseball team finally met a college opponent from out of state. The Bulldogs probably wished they hadn't bothered. Occidental College, a team from the Los Angeles area that reigned as one of the powers of the West Coast, played a pair of games against the Bulldogs during a five-game tour of Arizona in April of 1925. Not only did the Tigers sweep the series by scores of 10-0 and 14-3, the Bulldogs didn't even manage a hit in the first contest. Occidental pitchers Merrill Gregory and Lefty Teachout combined to pitch the third no-hitter ever against the Normal. Arizona pitchers Asa Porter and Chick Morefield had no-hit the Tempe club in 1916 and 1924 respectively.

Aaron McCreary

Aaron McCreary probably would have qualified for "legend" status on his accomplishments as an athlete alone, but he really made his mark in Tempe as a coach. McCreary was a key member of Coach George Schaeffer's 1914 football squad that brought the sport back to the Normal after an absence of eight years. He was a two-year starter in basketball during the 1913-14 and 1914-15 seasons and served as team captain. He also played two years of baseball, manning second base in 1914 and playing catcher in 1915, when he was elected captain. He was named the team's Most Valuable Player in 1915. McCreary went on to earn a bachelor's degree from the University of Arizona,

but he returned to the Normal in 1923 as athletic director and coach of all men's sports. His primary goal was to restore some honor to a football program that for the most part had not even been competitive against local high school teams. His success was immediate. His first team finished 4-2 in 1923 and his second went 6-1-1 – the first six-victory season in school history. Under McCreary, the Bulldogs recorded four straight winning seasons before falling off to 2-3-1 in 1927. His basketball and baseball teams had mixed results during a period of tough economic times, with few funds available for athletics on the Tempe campus.

Aaron McCreary played and coached football, basketball and baseball at the Normal. (University Archives)

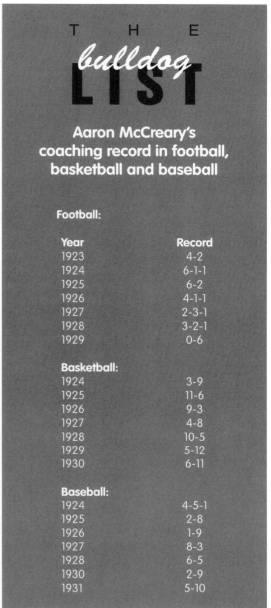

THE bulldog LIST

Aaron McCreary's coaching record in football, basketball and baseball

Football:

Year	Record
1923	4-2
1924	6-1-1
1925	6-2
1926	4-1-1
1927	2-3-1
1928	3-2-1
1929	0-6

Basketball:

Year	Record
1924	3-9
1925	11-6
1926	9-3
1927	4-8
1928	10-5
1929	5-12
1930	6-11

Baseball:

Year	Record
1924	4-5-1
1925	2-8
1926	1-9
1927	8-3
1928	6-5
1930	2-9
1931	5-10

BULLDOG BRIEFS

• The men's basketball team won its first four games, shook off some mid-season problems, and finished strong to post an 11-6 record. The Bulldogs swept Phoenix College (43-14), Flagstaff Normal (43-18) and Eastern Arizona (30-24) to capture a season-ending tournament. Center Lawrence Edwards was an All-State selection.

• The women's baseball—yes, baseball—team played University of Arizona for the first time ever, winning 23-18 in Tempe. UA won a later game, 8-6, in Tucson.

BULLDOG LORE

Tempe Beach, which had been dedicated in July of 1923, began attracting people from all over Arizona for recreational activities and swimming meets as word of the facility spread. The recreation center featured a 175-foot-long swimming pool, which helped locals and visitors alike beat the summer heat for many years.

• The Tempe Board of Trade, which had been active since the early 1890s, changed its name to the Tempe Civic Club and began a campaign to attract new residents and businesses to the city, which had battled hard economic times since the end of World War I.

1925-1926

tempe state teachers college
| m o m e n t

The big news on the campus in the early fall of 1925 was the revival of the football rivalry with Arizona, which had been dormant since the Wildcats destroyed A-State by a score of 59-0 in 1919. Coach Aaron McCreary's team warmed up for the game by trouncing the Sacaton Indians, 55-0, in Tempe and a large following turned out at the train depot to see the Bulldogs board the train for Tucson to do battle with Coach Pop McKale's Cats, who were opening their season. The Bulldogs showed from the start that they had made up some ground in the five years since they had last played the Wildcats. They battled the Cats on even terms through a scoreless first half, then stunned the gathering in Tucson by taking a 3-0 lead late in the third quarter on a 41-yard drop kick field goal by Johnny Riggs.

Deb Goddard skirts end for big yardage in a 55-0 romp over the Sacaton Indians. (University Archives)

The Wildcats' superior depth finally paid off in the fourth quarter, however. They scored twice in the final eight minutes to escape with a 13-3 victory. The Bulldogs had the ball on the UA 1 yard line when time expired.

spotlight

The Bulldog football team recorded a first when it ventured to El Paso, Texas, to play Texas School of Mines in the first out-of-state road game in school history. The Dogs had some momentum after four straight victories, but they found this assignment a bit too tough. The Miners prevailed by a 27-12 score. The game was significant for another reason. It signaled the beginning of the second-longest rivalry in school history behind the one with in-state rival Arizona. Though they did not play each other the following season, the Bulldogs and Miners would meet on an almost-annual basis for many years. The first six meetings in the series were played in El Paso. After four losses and two scoreless ties, the Bulldogs would win the first game played in Tempe, 15-14, in 1932. The teams have met 48 times, with A-State holding a 32-13-3 advantage.

ASU LEGEND

Delbert Goddard

Deb Goddard exhibited both versatility and staying power. (University Archives)

Others may have overshadowed him on the gridiron, the basketball court and the baseball diamond, but few athletes in school history have exhibited the versatility and staying power of Delbert (Deb) Goddard. Perhaps best known as a halfback in football, Goddard lettered four years in that sport (1923-26). He also lettered four years in basketball (1924-27) and four years in baseball (1924-27). Though the baseball team had its ups and downs during his tenure, he played during a significant time in the development of the school's football and basketball programs. During his four years of football, the Bulldogs were 4-2, 6-1-1, 6-2 and 4-1-1. The 1925 yearbook, the *Sahuaro*, said Goddard "was a terror through the line and off tackle. He made constant gains for T.N. He is a beautiful broken field runner and has the pep that put the fight into his team. He is a good punter and passer." The 1926 *Sahuaro* said of Goddard's baseball skills: "Deb covers his territory and takes everything that comes his way. He bats effectively and uses his speed to good advantage in running the bases."

BULLDOG BRIEF

• The basketball team split four games against Arizona en route to a 9-3 record. The only other loss was 42-41 to Phoenix College. All four of the Arizona games were closely contested. The Bulldogs won by scores of 23-18 and 25-19 and lost by scores of 30-24 and 32-21. Two of the Bulldogs' victories were over the Prescott Cowboys (39-15) and the Miami Miners (38-26).

BULLDOG LORE

After three years of hard lobbying by college President Arthur J. Matthews and members of the faculty and the Alumni Association, the Legislature granted Tempe Normal the right to award a four-year Bachelor of Education degree. Previously, only a two-year degree was offered. Along with the change in status came a name change as the school officially became Tempe State Teacher's College.

• For the first time, students painted a "T" on the Tempe butte. That early artwork was the beginning of a custom that has evolved into the painting of an "A," and an annual attempt by University of Arizona students to repaint the letter with their school colors.

1926-1927

**america's
time capsule**

tempe state teachers college
| m o m e n t

Hopefully, the pre-game and post-game festivities provided more action than the school's first homecoming game, a scoreless tie against Phoenix Indian School to wrap up the 1926 season. The tie, on a muddy field, snapped a string of three straight victories for the Bulldogs, who shut out four of the six teams on their schedule while compiling a 4-1-1 record. The student yearbook, the *Sahuaro*, had this to say about the homecoming tie with Phoenix Indian School: "The Indian brass band, accompanied by a concourse of papooses, escorted the braves to Tempe's soft-mud-covered field. When the ball was snapped, Tempe discovered that the mud was too deep and sticky for fast footwork, for which they were noted. Both teams found yardage hard to gain in the mud, but in spite of the hardship, Tempe made steady gains. (Deb) Goddard was playing his best game for T.S.T.C. and succeeded, through heroic efforts, in overcoming many of the difficulties of a slippery field, thus maintaining his standing as the best half-back Tempe has known for a long time." The Bulldogs had a couple of scoring opportunities, but drop-kick field goal attempts by John Riggs missed their mark. The muddy ball hit the cross bar on his first attempt. His second miss came in the final minute of the game as the crowd held its collective breath.

John Riggs missed the mark on a pair of drop-kick field goal attempts with a muddy football in a scoreless homecoming game against Phoenix Indian School. (University Archives)

spotlight

How's this for monotony? The Bulldog basketball team played Arizona four times in succession at midseason and lost all four games. The scores were 27-19, 32-25, 36-29 and 43-25. The Bulldogs also were swept in three games against their neighbors to the north—Northern Arizona Teachers College of Flagstaff. The Lumberjacks won by scores of 31-22, 30-24 in overtime and 36-24. The Bulldogs beat Phoenix College twice and Phoenix Indian school twice in a 4-8 season that followed back-to-back campaigns of 11-6 and 9-3. Starters for the Bulldogs were Bill Griffith at center, Joe Smith and Ernest Simpkins at forward and Doyle Harbison and Johnny Riggs at guard.

ASU LEGEND

Clifford "Droopy" Prather

There was no debating Cliff Prather's talent on the baseball field, where he won Most Valuable Player honors in 1927 and 1928. The only discussion was whether he was more valuable as a pitcher or as a hitter. Prather was the Bulldogs' No. 1 starting pitcher in 1926, '27 and '28. He was named the team's outstanding pitcher in each of those seasons. In 1927, he went 7-1 for a team that had an 8-3 record. Prather often helped win his own games with his bat. He was the team's leading hitter in 1927 (.389) and 1928 (.400). After two years away from the team, Prather returned in 1931 and earned a starting job as an outfielder. Again he led the team in hitting at .338. Perhaps Prather's biggest pitching victory was against rival Arizona in 1927. The school yearbook, the *Sahuaro,* had this account of the game: "The U of A was hurled off their feet by Prather, Tempe pitcher. The team backed Prather like clockwork, and as a result the Bulldogs scored a victory of six to three over the University for the first time since 1911(actually 1918). Prather pitched one of the most brilliant games of the season. Holding the Wildcats down to three runs is no small job, and one which but few pitchers can do."

Clifford "Droopy" Prather was a pitching and hitting star for the Bulldogs. (University Archives)

THE bulldog LIST

Homecoming football record, by decade

Decade	W-L-T
1920s	1-2-1
1930s	5-3-2
1940s	5-1-1
1950s	9-1-0
1960s	9-1-0
1970s	8-2-0
1980s	8-2-0
1990s	8-2-0
2000s	0-1-0

BULLDOG BRIEF

• The Bulldogs more than held their own in the second annual Greenway Track and Field Meet, which was by far the largest event of its kind ever held in Arizona. It attracted athletes from all over Arizona and parts of California. The Bulldogs finished second in the informal class with 35 points, just three behind winner Phoenix Indian School. U of A sprinter John Scott stunned the track and field world by upsetting the "world's fastest human," Charley Paddock of USC, in the 220-yard dash.

BULLDOG LORE

More than 10,000 boxing fans jammed the street in front of *The Arizona Republican* newspaper office in downtown Phoenix to hear a blow-by-blow account of the Dempsey-Tunney heavyweight title fight.

• Jean Smith was elected campus queen. George Bailey and Evelyn Kjellgren had the leads in the YWCA Christmas play, "The Goose Hangs High." Senior class presidents were John H. Barry (first semester) and Allen Riggs (second semester).

1927-1928

america's time capsule

tempe state teachers college
| m o m e n t

The Bulldogs made their first football trip ever to California, where they met a powerful Loyola team. The train trip to Los Angeles was a big adventure, but the powerful Lions were too much for the Bulldogs to handle. The Dogs came up on the short end of a 25-3 score. At least they got on the scoreboard, which was more than they managed in their next two games, a 6-0 loss to Phoenix Indian School and a 19-0 setback at the hands of Northern Arizona Teacher's College, both on the road. After scoring only three points in the first three games, the offense began to roll. And the defense, which had been knocked around a bit in the early going, posted three straight shutouts to end the season. Perhaps scheduling was the problem in a 2-3-1 season. The Bull-dogs played just one home game. They won it, 46-0, over Phoenix College as Tommy McCarty uncorked a school-record 80-yard punt return. The season finale was a study in offensive futility as the Bulldogs and Texas Miners played to a scoreless tie in El Paso.

Tommy McCarty's 80-yard punt return against Phoenix College was a school record. (University Archives)

BULLDOG *spotlight*

The basketball team lost three of four to rival Arizona, but handled local competition without much difficulty. The Bulldogs finished with a 10-5 record—their first double-digit season in victories since they went 10-6 in 1924-25. The Bulldogs were led by senior captain and all-conference performer Joe Smith, who played for three winning teams during his four years as a starter. The Dogs won two of three from Northern Arizona Teachers College, including a 40-25 romp in the first game played in the new gym on the Tempe campus. Though they lost three times to Arizona's Wildcats, their lone victory against the Cats was by a lopsided 47-27 score. The Bulldogs won three of four in the state championship tournament to tie Gila College for the state title. The Dogs were awarded the championship loving cup, not because they were 2-0 against Gila, but because they won a coin toss.

58

Joe Smith

His name might sound like an alias—an attempt to blend in with the surroundings—but there was nothing average about Joe Smith on the athletic field. A three-sport star, he played four years of basketball and baseball and two years of football. Basketball might have been his best sport. He earned All-Valley honors his senior year, when he served as team captain. In his four years of basketball the Bulldogs posted records of 10-6, 9-3, 4-8 and 10-5. The student yearbook said Smith, a forward, "was always the center of the opponents' defense, but was able to loop in the baskets every game." A four-year starter in the outfield, he earned Most Valuable Player honors in 1926, when he captained the baseball team. He led the team in batting that season. Though his average of .266 was modest by modern standards, it was considerably better than Gregg Morrow's team-leading .202 average of the previous season or Kenny Strong's .235 mark of 1924. In an era when home runs were few and far between, Smith slugged two homers in one game against Phoenix Indian School in 1928. That stood as a school record until Vernon Tuckey hit a pair six years later against the Papago Civilian Conservation Corps. Smith's two-homer barrage against Phoenix Indian sparked the Bulldogs to a 32-4 victory—the second-highest run output in the early era of Arizona State baseball.

Joe Smith was one of the most versatile athletes of his era. (University Archives)

BULLDOG BRIEF

• The umpires called off the remainder of a 1928 baseball game between the Bulldogs and an industrial league team, Crane Commercial, in the third inning after a fight broke out in the grandstands on campus. Angry fans were not at all happy over the shortened contest. They retaliated by setting fire to the grandstands, burning them to the ground. The Bulldogs were credited with a 10-8 victory, which allowed them to finish with a winning record, 6-5.

BULLDOG LORE

It was a banner year for athletic facilities on the Tempe State campus. A men's gymnasium was built at a cost of $47,000 on land purchased the previous year just south of the original campus. And a new football field was laid out to the west of the gym, where the Memorial Union now stands. It was named Irish Field in honor of the school's first football coach, Fred Irish, who put together the school's first eight teams beginning in 1897.

1928-1929

november 6, 1928: In a landslide, Republican Herbert Hoover defeated Alfred Smith for the presidency of the United States.

february 14, 1929: The mass murder known as the St. Valentine's Day Massacre took place on Chicago's North Side.

may 16, 1929: "Wings" was selected as the best picture at the first Academy Awards.

june 30, 1929: Bobby Jones won the U.S. Open golf tournament over runner-up Al Espinosa.

july 5, 1929: Helen Wills won the women's singles title at the Wimbledon tennis championship in England for the third consecutive year.

america's time capsule

arizona state teachers college | m o m e n t

The Bulldogs participated in the first night football game in the Southwest against Texas School of Mines at the Miners' not-so-brightly-lit field in El Paso. The game almost halted night football before it had a chance to catch on in the Southwest. Neither team could find the end zone under the murky conditions and the game ended in a 0-0 tie. That game was part of an unusual stretch that saw the Bulldogs play three games in eight days. It all started on a positive note with a 57-0 romp in Tempe over Gila College, which later would become Eastern Arizona Junior College. Then came the scoreless game in El Paso. The obviously weary Bulldogs didn't have much left for their third game in a little more than a week, a 39-0 loss to rival Arizona in Tucson. Coach Aaron McCreary's Bulldogs rebounded from that tortuous stretch to win two of their last three games and finish with a winning record at 3-2-1.

The Bulldogs were no match for the Detroit Tigers in an exhibition game in Phoenix – their first baseball game ever against a Major League team. The Tigers romped, 14-1, behind a three-hitter by one of their best pitchers, Lil Stoner. Arizona State catcher Lattie Coor left a lasting impression on the Tigers, however. Coor, a former Phoenix Union High School standout, threw out three Detroit baserunners attempting to steal second base. Coor's son, Lattie Jr., later would become president of Arizona State University. Lattie Jr. said he was not aware of his father's big day against the Tigers until informed by the author of this book during the fall of 1998.

Lattie Coor Sr. threw out three Detroit Tiger baserunners in a 1929 exhibition game. (B. Sollenberger collection)

LEGEND

Wilburn "Skipper" Dick

You can call him Wilburn. You can call him W.W. You can call him Skipper. Whatever you call him, he played a prominent role in Arizona State athletics in the late 1920s and early 1930s. Dick— we'll call him Skipper—was a starting end on the football team in 1927 and 1928. He was a member of the first A-State team to play a road game in California (at Loyola of Los Angeles in 1927) and participated in the first night football game in the Southwest (at Texas Mines in El Paso in 1928). He also played on the 1928 and 1929 Bulldog basketball teams. After a year away from athletics, he returned to play football in 1930 and 1931 and basketball during the 1930-31 season. It was in baseball, however, that he really made his mark. A starting pitcher who also swung a mean bat, he lettered in baseball in 1931, '32 and '33. The 1932 season was his best. He was named Outstanding Pitcher and Most Valuable Player and led the team in batting at .416. His career batting average for three seasons at A-State was .340. That was the seventh-best career mark in the early era of Arizona State baseball (1907 through 1958). In later years, Dick was better known for his role as an educator and public servant than for his athletic exploits at Arizona State. He served as Superintendent of Public Instruction in Arizona.

W.W. (Skipper) Dick went on to make a name in politics. (ASU Media Relations)

THE bulldog LIST

Members of the 1927 and 1928 football teams who went on to earn recognition in sports, business, education or politics

Player	Later Position/ area of recognition
Wilburn (Skipper) Dick	State Superintendent of Public Instruction
Wallace (Wally) Caywood	Alumni Association executive director
Bill Griffith	Education
Russell (Runt) Goddard	Coaching
Mercier Willard	Coaching
Norris Steverson	Coaching/education
Horace Smitheran	Coaching/athletic administration
John Riggs	Coaching

BULLDOG BRIEF

• The school's first athletic booster club was organized in November of 1928. The group, named the Bulldog Chain Gang, assisted with staging athletic events and helped provide hospitality for visiting teams. The club's first president was multi-sport star Mercier Willard, who was popularly known as "Hot Dog." His official title was Chief Warden.

BULLDOG LORE

A special legislative session changed the school's name from Tempe State Teacher's College to Arizona State Teacher's College at Tempe. The Legislature also authorized the college to upgrade its bachelor of education degree to the more prestigious bachelor of arts in education. Both actions were considered significant milestones in the history of the still-young educational institution.

1929-1930

america's time capsule

arizona state teachers college
| m o m e n t

The football program that enjoyed unprecedented success under Coach Aaron McCreary in the mid 1920s fell on the hardest of times in 1929 as a lack of administrative support finally took its toll. The Bulldogs absorbed a 31-7 whipping at the hands of Texas Mines in the season opener in El Paso, but that was just the start of their miseries. The team did not score again until the closing minutes of the last game of the season, a 21-6 loss to Loyola of Los Angeles in Tempe. In between came shutout losses to the Arizona freshmen (7-0), the Arizona varsity (26-0) and a pair of whitewash jobs at the hands of Flagstaff State, 31-0 and 27-0. That brought to an end a six-year coaching run by McCreary, who had taken a 25-11-4 record into the season. McCreary found it increasingly difficult to compete against opponents whose administrations clearly were more committed to providing resources for athletics.

spotlight

Bob Smith emerged as one of the school's first baseball heroes. Smith, a multi-talented threat who played shortstop and pitched, led the Bulldogs in hitting with a .421 average, highest at the school since Pete Brown batted .511 in 1922. Smith also was named the team's top pitcher. Smith, the team captain in 1930, also won the pitching award in 1929 and 1931. Smith was one of the few bright spots on the Bulldog team, which struggled to a 2-9 record. The only victories were 4-2 over Phoenix Union High School and 5-1 over an industrial league outfit known as Albright's All-Stars. The Bulldogs were 0-4 against rival Arizona, including a humiliating 32-2 loss to the Wildcats in Tucson. Among the other teams that beat the Bulldogs were Arizona Laundry and the Southern Pacific Railroad.

Bob Smith was one of the few bright spots on a 2-9 baseball team. (University Archives)

LEGEND

Horace Smitheran

A four-year starter in football, Smitheran was a hard-nosed fullback who threw the ball successfully on occasion in addition to grinding out the tough yardage up the middle. He played two years for Coach Aaron McCreary, but really flourished in his final two seasons—1930 and 1931—under new Coach Ted Shipkey. Smitheran fit perfectly into Shipkey's wide-open offensive attack, which the young coach had learned while playing for the legendary Pop Warner at Stanford in the mid 1920s. Smitheran's power running was an ideal compliment to the more explosive style of his backfield mate, Norris Steverson. Smitheran was team captain and a key member of the 1931 club that stunned the so-called experts by winning the first Border Conference championship. Smitheran rushed for one touchdown and passed for another as the Bulldogs beat rival Arizona, 19-6, in the 1931 Border Conference title game in Tempe. That victory arguably was the biggest at that point in Arizona State athletic history.

Horace Smitheran was a hard-running fullback for the first Border Conference championship team. (ASU Media Relations).

THE *bulldog* LIST

Football scores in a dismal 1929 season for the Bulldogs

Texas Mines 31, Bulldogs 7

Arizona freshmen 7, Bulldogs 0

Flagstaff State 31, Bulldogs 0

Arizona varsity 26, Bulldogs 0

Flagstaff State 27, Bulldogs 0

Loyola of Los Angeles 21, Bulldogs 6

BULLDOG BRIEF

• The Bulldog baseball team, which absorbed a 14-1 whipping at the hands of the major league Detroit Tigers the previous spring, lowered its sights a bit in the professional ranks. The Bulldogs tackled the Globe Bears of the Arizona-Texas League. The Dogs still didn't win, but the score was a more-respectable 7-2.

BULLDOG LORE

Work began on the original Matthews Library, a $105,000 building that would be the last of 18 structures erected under the presidency of A. J. Matthews who retired at the end of the 1929-30 school year after 30 years in office.

1930-1931

america's time capsule

arizona state teachers college
| m o m e n t

There was one significant "first" in an otherwise undistinguished 3-5-1 football season under first-year coach Ted Shipkey. The Bulldogs played their first night game at home, thanks to eight light poles that were erected just in time for the opener against Gila Junior College. The Bulldogs celebrated the occasion by romping to a 39-0 victory in front of 4,000 fans. Perhaps the most significant game was a 6-0 loss at Arizona early in the season. The Dogs hadn't beaten the Wildcats since their initial meeting in 1899, but this time they at least were competitive. ASTC's student newspaper, *The Collegian*, reported: "An assortment of trick plays, double reverses, spins and lateral passes kept the large crowd on its feet throughout the game. The Bulldogs proved that there was another college power looming up over Arizona." *The Collegian* said Bulldog Russ "Runt" Goddard "was the mainstay of the line. Time after time, he would smear the Wildcat plays before they would reach the line of scrimmage." The Bulldogs found a way to at least partially even the score against their rivals from Tucson, beating up on the UA freshmen, 39-6, later in the season in Tempe. The Bulldogs made a strong bid to close the season with three straight victories, but dropped a 7-6 heartbreaker to Arizona State-Flagstaff in the season finale.

Russ "Runt" Goddard was the defensive star in the Big Game against rival Arizona. (University Archives)

spotlight

Coach Ted Shipkey's basketball team won six of its last seven games to finish 12-6, the second-highest victory total at that point in school history and unquestionably the most impressive campaign since the sport began on campus in 1911-12. The 1917-18 team had finished with a 14-4 record, but that team did not play any college opponents. The student newspaper proclaimed the 1930-31 Bulldogs "Champions of the Southwest." The Bulldogs split four games with rival Arizona and won three of four from rival Flagstaff State. The Dogs cranked up their offense in the final two games of the season, beating New Mexico State by scores of 49-31 and 52-36. Their highest point total prior to those two games was in a 38-20 victory over Arizona. The Bulldogs were a relatively inexperienced team. Center Glen Crabtree was the only returning starter from the 1929-30 club.

Ted Shipkey

After an 0-6 football record in 1929, Arizona State was desperately in need of a winner to guide the program. The Bulldogs got one in Ted Shipkey, who learned his football under the legendary Pop Warner at Stanford from 1924 through 1926. In his three years as a letterman, Shipkey played on teams that compiled a combined 24-3-1 record, played in two Rose Bowls and captured one national championship. An end, Shipkey played all 60 minutes and scored Stanford's only touchdown in the 1925 Rose Bowl game, a 27-10 loss to Coach Knute Rockne's Notre Dame team, featuring the Four Horsemen. Shipkey earned All-America honors in 1926 and capped that season by catching five passes and recovering two fumbles in Stanford's 7-7 Rose Bowl tie with Alabama. Shipkey, who had coached at Sacramento Junior College following his playing career, was the first Arizona State coach to tap the California recruiting market to any great extent. After a 3-5-1 first-year record, Shipkey coached the Bulldogs to a 6-2 mark and the championship of the new Border Conference in 1931. But he was fired after the 1932 season as part of a severe staff cutback forced by the Great Depression.

Former Stanford All-American Ted Shipkey turned around Arizona State's football program during his brief tenure. (ASU Media Relations)

Football record in season openers (by decade)

Decade	Record
Pre-1900s	1-1
1900-1909	3-3
1910-1919	1-3
1920-1929	5-3
1930-1939	4-6
1940-1949	5-1-1
1950-1959	8-1-1
1960-1969	8-2
1970-1979	8-2
1980-1989	8-2
1990-1999	7-3
2000-2001	1--0

BULLDOG LORE

College presidents and athletic administrators met in Tucson in April of 1931 and formed the Border States Intercollegiate Athletic Conference. Initial members were Arizona State Teacher's College at Tempe, University of Arizona, Arizona State Teacher's College at Flagstaff, University of New Mexico and New Mexico A&M. Texas Mines of El Paso would join the conference a short time later.

• Dr. Ralph Swetman began a three-year tour as president of the college. A friend of athletics, he never had an opportunity to implement many of his ideas and programs because of the Great Depression. Growth in athletics, like most facets of the college, was put on hold as everyone tightened their belts and attempted to survive the tough economic times.

BULLDOG BRIEF

• Moving from the junior college football coaching ranks to a major college job would seem to be a no-brainer. But Arizona State Coach Ted Shipkey had to be asking himself if he made the right move after taking his Bulldog club to Sacramento to play Sacramento JC, the team he had coached the previous season. The Bulldogs were only 1-3 at the time, but had been more than respectable in 6-0 and 7-0 road losses to Arizona and New Mexico State the previous two weeks. Sacramento JC showed no mercy on the Bulldogs, however, rolling to a 49-0 victory. Adding injury to insult, star center Mercier Willard suffered a badly broken leg on the game's first play and had to spend several weeks in a Sacramento hospital.

1931-1932

October 25, 1931: The George Washington Bridge, connecting Manhattan with New Jersey across the Hudson River, was opened to traffic.

February 8, 1932: In one of the most famous murder cases in Arizona history, Winnie Ruth Judd was convicted of murdering a friend and shipping her body to California in a trunk. Judd later would make several escapes from the Arizona state mental hospital and would live in freedom until her death of natural causes in 1998.

March 1, 1932: Charles A. Lindbergh Jr., 20-month-old son of the famous aviator, was kidnapped from his home at Hopewell, New Jersey.

July 2, 1932: Franklin Roosevelt accepted the Democratic party's nomination for president and announced his plan for a "new deal."

August 14, 1932: The United States won the unofficial team championship at the Summer Olympic Games in Los Angeles by capturing 16 gold medals.

arizona state teachers college
moment

With the first Border Conference title on the line, football fever reached an unprecedented level in Tempe as rival Arizona visited Irish Field for an October 30 clash under the lights. The grandstands were overflowing and KOY Radio broadcast the game. The Bulldogs scored three times in the first half to put the game away early. The scores came on a two-yard run by Horace Smitheran, and touchdown passes from Smitheran to Landon Hardesty and from Chil Hezmalhalch to Norris Steverson. A third-quarter touchdown by the Wildcats was meaningless as the Bulldogs walked off the field with a convincing 19-6 victory. Local newspapers billed it as the Tempe school's first victory ever in the series, though Tempe Normal won the very first meeting in 1899. Here's what *The Arizona Republic* had to say about the contest: "Arizona's Wildcats aren't wild any more. The Bulldogs of Arizona's teacher's college at Tempe tamed them last night by tenaciously tearing them to bits, scattering fur over the gridiron of Irish Field." Arizona State fans celebrated the victory for days. They probably would have partied longer if they had known their team would not beat Arizona again for 18 years.

Guard Paul "Tuffy" Griffin did much of the dirty work up front for the Bulldogs, who clinched the first Border Conference title with a 19-6 football victory over Arizona. (University Archives)

BULLDOG
spotlight

The baseball team played its most ambitious schedule to date, a 15-game slate under Coach Aaron McCreary. The Bulldogs were 5-10 against a schedule that included several professional clubs. When rival Arizona dropped baseball because of a lack of money, the Wildcats were replaced on the schedule by the traveling Nashville Negro Giants and Arizona Laundry. The Bulldogs registered victories over a couple of professional teams, the Phoenix Senators (9-5) and the Globe Bears (9-6). The Bulldogs were 5-7 at one point, but lost their final three games to the Tempe City Employees (10-6 and 6-2) and the Phoenix Colored Giants (9-0).

ASU
LEGEND

Norris Steverson

Those who encountered Norris Steverson late in his Arizona State career probably remember him as a soft-spoken gymnastics coach. But many years before that he was a terror on the football field—perhaps as fine an all-around back as there was at the school between Charlie Haigler at the turn of the century and Whizzer White in the late 1940s and early 1950s. *The Arizona Republic* of November 1, 1931, said this about Steverson's performance in a 19-6 victory over Arizona: "His speed, his drive and his change of pace in the broken field bewildered the visiting University players. Frequently he would shoot out of a group of half a dozen Arizona tacklers when it seemed certain he was down to add six, eight or 10 yards to gains already recorded. Steverson is probably the best all-around football player in Arizona this year. He is the perfect type of triple-threat man, equally adept at carrying the ball, hurling forward passes or kicking. In the latter two branches he gave as pretty an exhibition as has been seen on an Arizona gridiron in a long time." Even Tucson's *Arizona Daily Star* was effusive in its praise of Steverson. It said: "The irresistible attack of the Bulldogs was built around Norris Steverson, triple-threat halfback, who did most of the ball carrying, kicking and passing. He also turned in the longest run of the day, an 82-yard return of a kickoff." In 1934, Steverson signed a professional contract with the Chicago Bears.

Norris Steverson was a triple-threat halfback for the Bulldogs of the late 1920s and early 1930s. (ASU Media Relations)

BULLDOG BRIEFS

• Three Bulldogs—halfback Norris Steverson, end Skipper Dick and guard Tuffy Griffin—were named to the first All-Border Conference football team. Steverson was selected captain of the All-Conference team.

• Not a single man on the football team weighed 200 pounds. The team's heavyweight was Cecil McCullar, a 197-pound tackle from Superior High School.

• A pecan grove west of North and South Halls was cleared, giving the school's female athletes their first athletic field on which they did not have to dodge trees.

BULLDOG LORE

The Mill Avenue Bridge, which could handle two lanes of traffic in each direction, was completed over the Salt River at a cost of just over $500,000. The structure, 1,577 feet long, replaced a narrow span just downstream.

• A rush of last-minute registrations brought fall enrollment to a record 825, an increase of 224 over the fall figure for 1930. Women made up about 60 percent of the student body.

1932-1933

November 8, 1932: In a landslide victory over Herbert Hoover, Franklin Roosevelt was elected president of the United States.

March 12, 1933: The first fireside chat, a radio address to the entire nation, was delivered by President Roosevelt. His topic was the eminent reopening of the nation's banks.

March 13, 1933: Banks began to reopen across the United States following a prolonged depression.

June 16, 1933: The Banking Act of 1933 was passed by Congress, establishing the Federal Bank Deposit Insurance Corporation.

July 6, 1933: Babe Ruth hit a home run at major league baseball's first All-Star game as the American League defeated the National League, 4-2, at Chicago's Comiskey Park.

arizona state teachers college
| m o m e n t

The 1932 football team was responsible for a couple of historic moments at the beginning and end of the season. The Bulldogs opened the campaign with a 99-0 romp over the Casa Blanca Indians as Cy Morris and Johnny McNeely each scored three touchdowns. That still stands as the highest score and widest victory margin in school history, though the competition was several notches below what the Bulldogs were used to facing. The student newspaper, *The Collegian*, reported: "Line work generally was good, but the attitude of the entire team was one of indifference, probably accounted for by the lack of opposition, which the Indians had promised but failed to supply." The Dogs ended the season with a 43-0 victory over New Mexico in the first meeting ever between the two schools. They would go on to become longtime rivals, playing 28 times over the years. The campus was rocked in May of 1933 when football coach Ted Shipkey was fired as part of massive staff cutbacks necessitated by the Great Depression. Shipkey, a former Stanford All-American, had arrived amid much fanfare three years earlier with hopes of rebuilding a football program that had fallen on hard times. Shipkey produced a Border Conference championship in the first year of that league—1931—though his 1932 team managed only a 4-3-1 record.

The Bulldog Band leads the dedication parade for the Mill Avenue Bridge, which was completed in 1932 and dedicated in May of 1933. (ASU Alumni Association/Tempe Chamber of Commerce/Stan Schirmacher photo)

spotlight

A financial crisis caused by the Great Depression left the school's athletic teams at perhaps their lowest ebb since World War I. The basketball team was 7-10 and lost all four of its meetings with rival Arizona. One of those losses was by one point (30-29). Another was by two points (32-30). Even the baseball team set what then was a school record for losses with a 4-12 finish. There was reason to celebrate, however, when the baseball team ended its season with a 5-1 victory over Arizona in a game played in Tempe. The Wildcats had won the three previous meetings. Even with the financial crunch, athletic officials were interested only in breaking even, not accumulating a surplus. Graduate manager Joe Selleh announced that if gate receipts for a two-game basketball series with Arizona were sufficient to cover expenses for a trip to Las Cruces, New Mexico, it would not be necessary to charge admission for the final two home games.

Joe Selleh

He played on the baseball, golf and tennis teams for three years, but that was only a small part of the contribution that Joe Selleh made to Arizona State athletics. He also coached baseball, golf and tennis, assisted in football, served as graduate manager of athletics, was adviser to the student newspaper, was the school's publicity director and headed the intramural program. In his position as athletics manager, he performed many of the duties of modern-day athletic directors. Following his playing career at A-State, Selleh signed a professional baseball contract with the New York Giants organization. He was only the fifth player at that point in school history to sign a pro contract. After playing for the Phoenix Senators of the Class D Arizona-Texas League, Selleh assumed his coaching duties at ASTC. He coached the Bulldog baseball team for five years, from 1932 through 1936. None of his teams had a winning record, though they came close on occasion. His 1936 club was 8-8 and his 1932 and 1935 teams were 5-7. The goodwill and name recognition generated by Selleh during his athletic exploits served him well during the many years that he owned a sporting goods store in downtown Tempe.

Joe Selleh was a jack-of-all-trades as an athlete, coach and administrator. (University Archives)

THE
bulldog
LIST

Arizona State's baseball coaches and their career records
(listed chronologically)

Coach	Seasons	Record
Fred Ayer	1907-11	37-22-1
John Spikes	1912-13	23-5
Horace Griffen	1914	6-5
George Schaeffer	1915-17	10-19
George Cooper	1918-22	41-16
Ernest Willis	1923	5-5
Aaron McCreary	1924-26, 1928, 1930-31	18-46-1
Leslie Fairbanks	1927, 1929	13-9
Joe Selleh	1932-36	29-44
Earl Pomeroy	1937	4-5
Tom Lillico	1938	7-8
Bill Kajikawa	1940, 1946-50, 1952	50-55
Nick Johnson	1942	4-5-1
Bud Younger	1951	7-15
Jack Machtolff	1952 (co-coach), 1953	11-32-1
Bob White	1954	5-6
Melvin Erickson	1955-58	62-53-1
Bobby Winkles	1959-71	524-173
Jim Brock	1972-1994	1,100-440
Pat Murphy	1995-2000	232-123

BULLDOG BRIEF

• How severe was the apathy towards athletics on the Tempe campus during the Great Depression? Consider that the Lucky 13 Club staged a Wild West dance in April of 1933 to raise money for a baseball trip to Las Cruces, New Mexico, and El Paso, Texas, where the Bulldogs hoped to play the New Mexico Aggies and Texas Mines. Nobody showed up for the dance and the trip was canceled.

BULLDOG LORE

Dr. Ralph Swetman resigned as the school's president after three rocky years of trying to cope with the Great Depression. He had axed 31 of the school's 56 faculty members during that time as the school's legislative appropriation dwindled from $432 per student to $242. Football Coach Ted Shipkey, who had been hired by Swetman, was one of those who lost his job as a result of the cutbacks. The school also failed to re-hire professor Laura Herron, who was beginning to develop a national reputation for her administrative skills as head of the physical education department.

1933-1934

america's time capsule

arizona state teachers college
| m o m e n t

Rudy Lavik, who had made a habit of beating the Bulldogs while head coach at ASTC-Flagstaff, was hired away from the Lumberjacks and given the task of building the Tempe football program to respectability. Lavik's first season was less than a rousing success. The Bulldogs were shut out four times, twice by Lavik's former team, as they struggled to a 3-5 record. The team started the campaign with the longest road trip at that point in school history—a two-week bus excursion to southern California to play Whittier in Pasadena's Rose Bowl and the San Diego Marines, who were liberally stocked with former collegiate stars. The Dogs lost 27-0 to Whittier and 26-0 to the Marines. Two-thirds of the team's victories came from the state of New Mexico—26-13 over New Mexico in Albuquerque and 19-7 over New Mexico State in Tempe. The other victory was 21-7 over Fresno State in a game played at Phoenix High School's stadium in an attempt to boost attendance and meet an unusually hefty $750 guarantee to the visiting team. The Arizona game also was played in Phoenix, where it drew a crowd of 6,000. Ticket prices were $1, 75 cents and 50 cents.

The prospect of larger crowds led the Bulldogs to move two home football games to Phoenix in 1933. (University Archives)

spotlight

Six Bulldog freshman football players slipped into Flagstaff and swiped Arizona State-Flagstaff's prized copper ax. Word of the theft spread quickly, however, and the six were apprehended on the highway back to Tempe. They were returned to Flagstaff to face "charges." Their punishment? Their heads were shaved and painted the Flagstaff school's colors, blue and gold, by Lumberjacks supporters. First-year coach Rudy Lavik, who had coached the previous six years at Flagstaff, found some humor in the situation. Author Dean Smith, in his book on Arizona State football history, said Lavik remarked on their return to Tempe: "I can sympathize with these boys. I lost a lot of hair in Flagstaff myself."

ASU LEGEND

Rudy Lavik

They called him the Wily Norseman, and though he never achieved eye-catching results in his coaching endeavors, he clearly had a major impact in the growth of Arizona State's athletic program. Such coaching legends as Frank Kush and Bill Kajikawa credit Lavik with setting an example of how to train hard and compete in an honorable way. Lavik, born in North Dakota of Norwegian stock, came to Arizona in 1927 to take a coaching and teaching position at Arizona State Teachers College in Flagstaff. While there he coached football, basketball and track, served as athletic director and head of the physical education department and taught some 12 to 14 hours a week. When ASC-Flagstaff President Grady Gammage left that school for the same position in Tempe in 1933, he brought along Lavik to resurrect a struggling athletic department as athletic director and coach of several sports. Lavik was not a proponent of hard-core recruiting, which undoubtedly hurt his won-lost records. His eight Arizona State basketball teams were 72-83 and his five football teams were 13-26-3. But his teams always played hard and within the rules. Lavik continued to teach physical education and preach the merits of physical fitness long after his coaching career was over. He was a familiar figure on his daily run on campus, even into his 70s, and his quick wit made him a popular banquet speaker.

Rudy Lavik served as a role model for many Arizona State coaches through the years. (ASU Media Relations)

BULLDOG BRIEFS

• The national money crunch caused by the great depression resulted in some bargain rates for those seeking an education. Student fees at Arizona State Teachers College at Tempe during the 1933-34 school year were $20 per year for residents and $32 for out-of-state students. Lodging and three meals a day cost $21.50 per month. Even at those prices, most students had part-time jobs to help make ends meet.

• Forward Earl Caplinger set a school basketball scoring record with 30 points in a 50-44 victory over New Mexico State at Las Cruces, New Mexico.

BULLDOG LORE

Dr. Grady Gammage was wooed away from Arizona State Teachers College in Flagstaff to became president of ASTC-Tempe. Gammage would serve more than 26 years and lead the school through its most significant period of growth. He was instrumental in the battle to attain university status. Many observers feel he was the single most influential person in the school's history.

• Plans were announced to pave College Ave. between Lemon and 8th streets in the first step in a CWA project to extend paving to the ASTC campus.

1934-1935

america's time capsule

arizona state teachers college
| m o m e n t

A 14-6 road victory over San Diego State in the final game of the season gave the Bulldogs a 4-3-1 record—the only winning season in Rudy Lavik's five-year tour as head coach. Perhaps the biggest victories, however, were a pair over Arizona State Teacher's College at Flagstaff, which had blanked the Bulldogs twice the previous season—Lavik's first in Tempe after following university president Grady Gammage from northern Arizona to the banks of the Salt River. Because of the move of Gammage and Lavik and because Arizona's Wildcats were routinely pounding the Bulldogs, the Lumberjacks replaced the Cats as A-State's No. 1 rival for a few years in the early 1930s. The Bulldogs and Lumberjacks played twice a year from 1929 through 1936. The Bulldogs handled the Axers fairly easily in their first 1934 meeting in Flagstaff, winning by a 21-0 score. The Axers came to Tempe with revenge on their minds in the next-to-last game of the season. The Bulldogs were somewhat beat up after a 32-6 loss to Arizona in Tucson the previous week, but they managed to hang on for a 6-0 victory over the Lumberjacks and keep alive their hopes for a winning season. Fullback Bill Baxter and end Clarence Sexton were named to the All-Border Conference first team.

Baseball was the diamond game of choice for ASTC's women before softball became popular in the late 1930s. (University Archives)

spotlight

Athletic travel in the early 1930s wasn't quite what it is today. Some players, in fact, had to improvise if they hoped to see action in road games. This account from the October 4, 1934, *Phoenix Gazette* describes how far some Bulldog reserves went in an attempt to be a part of the action when Arizona State played at Loyola of Los Angeles: "Several members of the Arizona Teacher's College varsity football squad were hitch-hiking to Los Angeles today, determined to get into Friday night's contest against the Loyola Lions. The college bus, which is carrying the main contingent, could accommodate only 30 players, so several reserves cast their duffel bags on the bus and started (walking) down the highway."

ASU LEGEND

Bill Baxter

In an era when most of the players were of the home-grown variety, Bill Baxter was an exception. Baxter, a halfback who played for four seasons under coaches Ted Shipkey and Rudy Lavik, hailed from far-off Indiana. As a freshman in 1931, Baxter played halfback in an explosive backfield that also included Norris Steverson and Horace Smitheran. Baxter, who eventually grew into the fullback position, went on to earn All-Border Conference honors in 1933 and 1934. Following his Arizona State career, Baxter signed a professional contract in 1935 with the Hollywood Braves of the Pacific Coast Pro Football League. Baxter and guard Russ Goddard, who also signed with the Braves, were the second and third A-State football players to sign pro contracts. Steverson had signed the previous year with the Chicago Bears.

Bill Baxter came all the way from Indiana to star for the Bulldogs.

BULLDOG LORE

A survey of 31 teacher's colleges around the nation ranked Arizona State last in terms of expenditures per student by the institution. The study showed the Tempe school with an average expenditure of $165 per student. The high was $496 and the median was $253 among the 31 schools surveyed nationally. ASTC officials called it a crisis situation.

BULLDOG BRIEF

• Coach Rudy Lavik was an early trend setter in terms of telling it like it is. Asked about prospects for his 1934-35 basketball team, Lavik told the student newspaper, *The Collegian*: "Our position looks no better than last year's, and look at the past season's record." Lavik was right on. The 1933-34 team went 9-11. The 1934-35 club finished 8-11.

1935-1936

September 8, 1935: Powerful Louisiana politician Huey Long was assassinated in the corridor of the state capitol in Baton Rouge.

November 9, 1935: The Committee for Industrial Organization (CIO) was established by John L. Lewis.

February 16, 1936: The U.S. won two gold medals and placed fifth in the unofficial team standings behind Norway, Germany, Sweden and Finland at the Winter Olympics in Germany.

June 12, 1936: Kansas Gov. Alf Landon and Col. Frank Knox of Illinois were nominated at the Republican National Convention as the party's candidates for president and vice president.

August 16, 1936: The Summer Olympic Games, featuring American track and field star Jesse Owens, came to a close in Berlin, Germany.

arizona state teachers college
moment

Boxing became an official sport at ASTC in 1929, and by the mid 1930s it had evolved into one of the most popular sports on campus. In 1936, a three-way match in Tempe involving ASTC-Tempe, ASTC-Flagstaff and University of Arizona drew the largest crowd ever to witness an indoor athletic event at that point in the school's history. The student newspaper, *The Collegian*, called the two-night affair "the greatest intercollegiate boxing show ever held in the Salt River Valley." The match was conducted under AAU regulations, which permitted no cheering while the fight was in progress but allowed fans to sound off between rounds. Bobby Hilburn at 125 pounds, Ralph Graham at 145, and Rex Hansell at 155 won Arizona Intercollegiate titles for ASTC at that event. At the Border Conference championships later that season in Tucson, Bulldogs Travis Bellsmith at 155 pounds and Chuck Hart at 170 captured individual crowns.

By the mid 1930s, boxing had become one of the most popular sports on the ASTC campus. (University Archives)

spotlight

Joe Island became the school's first black baseball player in the spring of 1936. Island had starred previously at Carver High in Phoenix. Island was a starter in the outfield for coach Joe Selleh's club, which posted an 8-8 record against a schedule that included an ambitious road slate. Island later played 10 seasons with the Phoenix Broncos, an all-black semi-pro team. The Bulldogs played their final nine games on the road, including stops in some out-of-the-way places. Their travels included two games against the Nogales town team, two against the Yuma town team, three against a team from Hermosillo, Sonora, and two against the Ajo town team. Though hometown umpiring sometimes was less than impartial in those days, the Bulldogs managed a 5-4 record in those games.

LEGEND

Tom Lillico

If ever there was a take-charge guy in Bulldog athletics of the 1930s, it was Tom Lillico. A versatile athlete who won his share of honors, he made perhaps his biggest contribution off the field in an administrative capacity. Lillico lettered three years in football (1931 through 1933), three years in basketball (1932 through 1934) and four years in baseball (1931 through 1934). He made the All-Border Conference second team in basketball as a guard in 1934, but his best sport probably was baseball. A first baseman, he was team captain and Most Valuable Player in 1934, when he led the club in hitting with a .454 average. That was the third-highest mark in school history at the time. He coached the baseball team to a 7-8 record in 1938. Only twice from 1923 through 1947 did the Bulldogs win more games (8-3 in 1927 and 8-8 in 1936). Lillico became the backbone of the athletic department in his role as graduate manager. He scheduled games, supervised the budget, handled staging and recruited athletes. He caused a major rift with rival Arizona when he snatched former high school football stars Wayne Pitts, Walt Ruth and Rex Hopper off the UA campus. He also recruited Emerson Harvey, the school's first black football player. Lillico later served as president of the Alumni Association.

Tom Lillico served the college well in several capacities. (ASU Media Relations)

BULLDOG LORE

A building boom engulfed the campus after years of little activity because of the Great Depression. Construction was started in the spring of 1936 on a new football stadium on the south end of campus. A library, dining hall and a dormitory, West Hall, also were constructed. Sidewalks were built throughout Tempe, helping the community move away from the image of a dusty frontier town.

THE bulldog LIST

Arizona State's best finishes in the Border Conference basketball race

Finish	Year	Conf. Record	Coach
1st	1958	8-2	Ned Wulk
1st	1962	10-0	Ned Wulk
1st (tie)	1959	7-3	Ned Wulk
1st (tie)	1961	9-1	Ned Wulk
2nd	1936	11-7	Earl Pomeroy
2nd (tie)	1953	10-4	Bill Kajikawa
2nd (tie)	1960	7-3	Ned Wulk
3rd	1938	9-9	Earl Pomeroy
3rd	1939	11-11	Earl Pomeroy
3rd	1942	10-6	Rudy Lavik
3rd	1948	9-7	Rudy Lavik
3rd (tie)	1955	8-4	Bill Kajikawa

BULLDOG BRIEF

• Coach Earl Pomeroy's basketball team lost its first nine games, but then staged an amazing turn-around to finish 12-14. The Bulldogs, who won 10 of 12 during one stretch, were 11-7 in Border Conference play and finished second in the league after previous finishes of fifth and sixth. It would be 16 years before the Bulldogs would finish as high as second again. Arizona State competed in the Border Conference through the 1961-62 season, but matched that total of 11 conference victories only one more time, when they went 11-11 under Pomery in 1938-39. They won 12 games in an AAU league in the war year of 1944. One of the Bulldogs' victories was 50-45 over the Harlem Globetrotters, who didn't bring along their own opposition in those days.

1936-1937

america's time capsule

arizona state teachers college

moment

A sparkling new football facility, Goodwin Stadium, opened on the south end of campus. The facility, which replaced Irish Field, was named for Garfield Goodwin, a Tempe businessman who played on the school's first territorial football championship team in 1899 and later was a member of the college's Board of Education. It was built by a young contractor named Del Webb, who would go on to earn worldwide acclaim in the building industry. The stadium cost $87,000 to build. It provided seating for 5,000 on the west side with additional temporary seating along the east sideline. One of the "amenities" of the new stadium was a grass playing field. Normal Field, which

Goodwin Stadium, with initial permanent seating of 5,000, opened to much fanfare in the fall of 1936. (ASU Alumni Association)

served the college from 1897 through 1926, had a plowed dirt playing surface. Irish Field, home of the Bulldogs from 1927 through 1935, wasn't much better. Goodwin Stadium had lights for night games and a running track and pits for track and field competition. The college's industrial arts department was housed under the grandstand. A later addition eventually would house a men's dormitory. Seating capacity was boosted to 9,500 in 1940 and 15,000 in 1941.

BULLDOG *spotlight*

Kenneth (Spider) Heywood, Melvin Owens, Worth Phelps, Earl Jones and Harold Clemence were dubbed the "Iron Men" after they played an entire basketball game against Arizona. The Bulldogs opened the season with four straight games against their rivals from Tucson, losing three of the four. The Bulldogs' lone victory over the Wildcats was by a resounding 45-27 score and one of the three losses was by just one point, 37-36. The Bulldogs struggled early, losing six of their first eight games, but played .500 ball from that point to finish 8-12. They were sixth in the Border Conference with a 7-11 league mark. Phelps, a forward, was named to the All-Border Conference first team. Heywood, a forward, earned honorable mention honors.

LEGEND

Harold "Schoolboy" Clemence

Considered one of A-State's top recruiting catches of the 1930s, Harold Clemence came to Tempe from Globe High School with outstanding all-around basketball skills and one of the most lively pitching arms central Arizona had ever seen. A three-year starter in hoops, Clemence was co-captain of the basketball team in 1937 and 1938. But his best sport was baseball. He was A-State's No. 1 starting pitcher in 1936, 1937 and 1938, earning Outstanding Pitcher honors all three years. He was team captain in 1938. Though none of those teams had a winning record, Clemence was outstanding on the mound. Perhaps his best outing was a 4-3 victory over Arizona in 1936. That was the Bulldogs' only victory in five games against the Wildcats that season. Though he didn't put up impressive victory or strikeout totals, Clemence did not go unnoticed by the professional baseball scouts. He signed a pro contract with the Boston Red Sox following the 1938 season. He was the seventh Arizona State player and the second pitcher at that point in the school's history to sign a pro contract.

Harold Clemence starred in basketball and baseball for the Bulldogs and later signed a professional baseball contract. (University Archives)

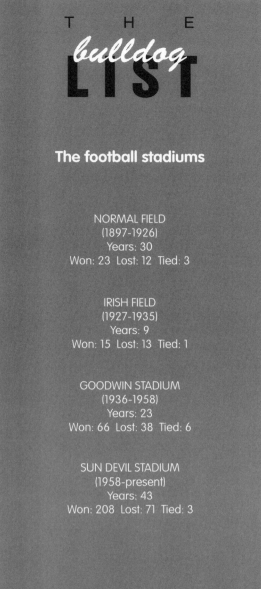

THE bulldog LIST

The football stadiums

NORMAL FIELD
(1897-1926)
Years: 30
Won: 23 Lost: 12 Tied: 3

IRISH FIELD
(1927-1935)
Years: 9
Won: 15 Lost: 13 Tied: 1

GOODWIN STADIUM
(1936-1958)
Years: 23
Won: 66 Lost: 38 Tied: 6

SUN DEVIL STADIUM
(1958-present)
Years: 43
Won: 208 Lost: 71 Tied: 3

BULLDOG LORE

Arizona State continued to make strides academically as well as athletically. The school made a significant breakthrough when the 1937 Legislature gave permission for the college to offer its first graduate degree—a Master of Arts in education. That upgrade became critical when the 1936 Legislature ruled that graduates who only held Bachelor's degrees could not teach in the state's high schools.

BULLDOG BRIEFS

• Bulldog pitching ace Harold "Schoolboy" Clemence was beating rival Arizona in a March game when baseball Coach Earl Pomeroy informed him that his mother had died. Arizona rallied to win the game, but the student newspaper said Clemence "stayed on the mound in a courageous attempt to defeat the Cats."

• Star running back Howard Hooten, popularly known as the "Buckeye Flash," was killed in a logging camp accident near Pondosa, Oregon, in July of 1937. Hooten, around whom the offense was built in 1936, had dropped out of school after a broken leg suffered against New Mexico State had ended his season early.

1937-1938

america's time capsule

arizona state teachers college
moment

The 1937-38 school year was one of mixed emotion for those close to the Arizona State football program. Coach Rudy Lavik was a much-admired man of high principles who refused to subscribe to the aggressive and sometimes seamy tactics that were taking place in college football. But his low-key approach wasn't working at Arizona State. In five years at ASTC his teams had records of 3-5, 4-3-1, 2-5-1, 4-5 and 0-8-1. After much soul searching, college president Grady Gammage, who had brought Lavik with him from ASTC-Flagstaff in 1933, removed Lavik as football coach after the 1937 season. Lavik retained his title of athletic director. Prior to Lavik's final season, Gammage hired Tom Lillico, a former Bulldog sports star, as graduate manager of athletics and charged him with recruiting the best athletes possible to the school. And after Lavik's winless season, Gammage hired a high-visibility coach, Dixie Howell, to head the Bulldog program. Howell was a former star quarterback at Alabama, known for his touchdown passes to the legendary Don Hutson, and was one of the most-recognizable names in college football. Gammage's decision to shoot for the big-time has been hailed by historians as one of the most significant in the school's athletic history.

College President Grady Gammage demonstrated his commitment to winning by hiring high-visibility football Coach Dixie Howell. (ASU Alumni Association)

spotlight

Bulldog guard Earl Jones was named to the All-Border Conference basketball team along with four members of the undefeated conference champion New Mexico State Aggies. Jones was 12th in the conference in scoring for Coach Earl Pomeroy's club, which was 11-12 overall but finished third in the league standings with a 9-9 mark in conference play. Joining Jones in the Bulldogs' starting lineup were forwards Harold Clemence and Dwight Peterson, center Worth Phelps and guard Melvin Owens. There was one bright spot—actually four bright spots—for the Bulldogs in an otherwise lackluster season. They won all four meetings with rival Arizona by scores of 52-41, 37-34, 49-31 and 44-38. That reversed a trend that had seen Arizona sweep all four games in 1931-32 and 1932-33 and win three of four from the Bulldogs the next four seasons.

LEGEND

Emerson Harvey

Emerson Harvey thought his athletic career was over after two years at Sacramento Junior College in California. There simply wasn't a demand for black athletes in the major colleges in the late 1930s. But Arizona State football recruiter Tom Lillico found Harvey working at a drugstore in San Francisco, and talked him into becoming Arizona State's first black football player. Baseball player Joe Island had become the school's first black athlete two years earlier. Harvey quickly earned a spot as a blocking back and defensive end on Coach Rudy Lavik's team. Harvey played a major role in breaking the color barrier in the Southwest. Several college teams from Texas had not faced a black athlete until they played the Bulldogs and Harvey. A quiet, unassuming young man with a great sense of humor, Harvey put up with racial slurs from Bulldogs opponents. He also helped break down racial barriers on the ASTC campus, where black students could not live in dormitories or eat in the dining hall or other dining establishments. Harvey was concerned about his A-State career when former Alabama star Dixie Howell was hired as head coach in 1938.

Would a coach from the deep South feel the same as Lavik about Harvey? "Dixie Howell was completely fair with me," Harvey told historian Dean Smith in a 1972 interview. "He was a great coach, and a good friend." Harvey needed only 1 1/2 years to obtain his degree from ASTC. He spent many years as an industrial arts teacher and coach in Phoenix inner-city schools.

Emerson Harvey, Arizona State's first black football player, helped break the color barrier throughout the Southwest. (ASU Alumni Association)

Arizona State's All-Border Conference first-team selections in basketball

Player	Season
Worth Phelps, c	1936-37
Earl Jones, g	1937-38
Gerald Jones, g	1941-42
Verl Heap, f	1947-48
Wade Oliver, c	1949-50
Roy Coppinger, g	1951-52, 1952-53
Dave Graybill, f	1954-55
Jim Newman, g	19957-58
Paul Howard, g	1958-59, 1959-60
Larry Armstrong, g	1960-61, 1961-62
Joe Caldwell, f	1961-62-
Jerry Hahn, f	1961-62

BULLDOG BRIEF

• Pete the bulldog, ASTC's official mascot, got all the ink, but he wasn't the only canine cavorting on the college's athletic fields in the 1930s and 1940s. During the 1935-36 school year a wire-haired terrier named Suzi became the mascot of the school's women's teams. Suzi stayed on the job for 14 years, sitting in on women's P.E. classes, hanging out at athletic events and journeying along on school-sponsored hiking and camping trips. She often showed up in pictures of women's teams.

BULLDOG LORE

Three of the state's top high school football players—Walt Ruth, Wayne Pitts and Rex Hopper—were lured away from the campus of rival Arizona by ASTC recruiter Tom Lillico during the summer of 1937, causing Arizona athletic officials to cancel the gridiron series between the two schools, until the players in question had graduated.

1938-1939

america's time capsule

arizona state teachers college
moment

The football team was only 3-6 under new coach Dixie Howell and his "Alabama style" attack, but new interest in the sport was apparent on campus. After road losses to San Jose State and New Mexico, the Bulldogs opened their home season with a 13-0 victory over Cal Poly-San Luis Obispo, spurring considerable talk in the community about the new-look Bull-

Dig those uniforms! New Coach Dixie Howell's first team was only 3-6, but the Bulldogs certainly were nattily attired. (ASU Media Relations)

dogs. Pat Downey's account of the game in the Arizona State alumni bulletin read: "The Dogs showed a completely changed style of offensive football as they nosed out the losing jinx for the first time in 13 starts. Wide end sweeps accounted for most of the 221 yards gained against the Mustangs, although 12 completed passes netted 52 yards." The Bulldogs were winless in Border Conference play as they struggled to learn Howell's offense, which was described in various media reports as the Notre Dame Box. Perhaps the Bulldogs should have scheduled more teams from California. In addition to their victory over Cal Poly, the Dogs beat California-Santa Barbara, 10-0, and Whittier, 21-0.

spotlight

The Bulldogs won the first three games of their four-game basketball series against Arizona, stretching their winning streak over the Wildcats to seven straight over two seasons. All four games of the series were hotly contested, with the Bulldogs winning by scores of 36-33, 40-36 and 50-43 before the Wildcats salvaged some respect with a 48-44 victory in the final meeting. The Bulldogs won their final game, 51-42 over New Mexico, to finish with a 13-13 record. They were third in the Border Conference with an 11-11 league mark. Guard Earl Jones, the only returning starter from the 1937-38 club, was an All-Border Conference second-team selection. Coach Clare Van Hoorebeke's freshman team rolled up a 28-5 record. Van Hoorebeck, a former Bulldog athletic star, would later go on to a highly successful coaching career at Anaheim High School in California.

Dixie
Howell

The early stages of football fever began stirring on the Arizona State campus in 1938 with the arrival of Millard (Dixie) Howell. Howell, the All-America quarterback of Alabama's 1935 Rose Bowl team, was one of the most recognizable names in college football. His appointment as Arizona State's head coach gave the Bulldog program an instant dash of credibility. Some of Howell's offensive innovations had folks in the Arizona desert buzzing, but when his four-year A-State coaching career ended with his departure in March of 1942 to serve his country in World War II, his most significant stamp on the program had to do with defense. Of the 27 games his Bulldog teams won or tied, 16 were shutouts. His 1939 team, which compiled an 8-2-1 record, shut out six opponents and held three others to just one touchdown. Howell has been called one of the top defensive strategists in the history of college football. Howell's four-year record at Arizona State was 23-15-4. His biggest contribution was to put the Bulldogs in a post-season bowl game for the first time in school history. His 1939 and 1940 teams both played in the Sun Bowl in El Paso, Texas.

Dixie Howell's appointment as football coach gave Arizona State's program instant credibility. (ASU Media Relations)

Dixie Howell's coaching record at Arizona State

Season	Record	Big Game
1938	3-6	Beat Cal Poly SLO, 13-0
1939	8-2-1	Tied Catholic U in Sun Bowl, 0-0
1940	7-2-2	Lost to Case Western Reserve in Sun Bowl, 26-13
1941	5-5-1	Lost to Arizona, 20-7

BULLDOG BRIEF

• Baseball was dropped as a varsity sport just one year after the Bulldogs had gone 7-8 against a schedule that was heavy on road games. In explaining the move, graduate manager Tom Lillico said: "There will be no baseball this year because of a lack of necessary finances to carry on in the proper way." Lillico and college president Grady Gammage expressed hope that the sport would return with adequate funding in the spring of 1940.

BULLDOG LORE

The Moeur Activity Building, which housed women's athletics and many other activities, was completed in 1939. It was constructed of adobe bricks made from dirt excavated from the building's basement. Federal funds, private gifts and volunteer labor helped the project to completion.
• The increase of enrollment to approximately 1,200 students necessitated the leasing of the Olive Hotel on Mill Ave. for use as a men's dormitory.

1939-1940

america's time capsule

arizona state teachers college
| m o m e n t

Zero was the magic number for the Bulldog football team under second-year coach Dixie Howell. The Bulldogs shutout their first five opponents—the only time in school history that has happened. It also was the number of the day when the Bulldogs played favored Catholic University of Washington, D.C., to a scoreless tie in the school's first New Year's Day bowl game, the Sun Bowl in El Paso. A throng of Bulldog supporters traveled to El Paso by train to cheer on their favorite team, which dominated the Eastern powerhouse Cardinals in most statistical categories. The Bulldogs won the total offense battle, 233 yards to 133, and had 11 first downs to four for Catholic U. Arizona State had three scoring opportunities inside the Cardinals' 15-yard line, but fumbles and interceptions stopped each drive. The highlight of an 8-2 regular season was a 28-6 victory over New Mexico in the Border Conference title game. New Mexico Coach Ted Shipkey, who was fired by Arizona State in 1933, had vowed that no Tempe team would ever beat one of his New Mexico clubs.

Coach Dixie Howell's 1939 Border Conference football champs. (University Archives)

spotlight

An intense series against rival Arizona highlighted an 8-13 basketball season. Emotions in basketball ran particularly high since the two schools did not play in football. Arizona officials refused to play the Bulldogs in football for several years after a recruiting flap over three in-state players. The hoops series saw Arizona win three of four, though all four games were hotly contested. The Wildcats twice won by one field goal and the Bulldogs' lone victory was by two points, 39-37. Arizona's other victory was by a more comfortable 11-point margin. Gerald "Wimpy" Jones picked up where his older brother Earl left off the previous season for the Bulldogs. The school yearbook said Jones "starred many times with high-scoring honors and smart floor play." Jones didn't earn All-Conference honors, but his running mate at guard, Bud Arnett, was named to the All-Border Conference second team.

LEGEND

Wayne "Ripper" Pitts

But for a bit of arm-twisting by ASTC graduate manager Tom Lillico, the name of Wayne "Ripper" Pitts might be listed among University of Arizona football greats. Pitts, a Glendale High School star, was on the UA campus in the summer of 1937 preparing for his freshman season when Lillico paid a social call. Lillico convinced Pitts and a pair of former Glendale High teammates, Walt Ruth and Rex Hopper, to become Bulldogs, not Wildcats. Pitts & Co. promptly led the Arizona State freshmen to a victory over Arizona's Wildkittens. They would not get an opportunity to inflict any damage on the Wildcats at the varsity level, because UA officials severed football relations with A-State until the trio had graduated. No problem for Pitts, a hard-running fullback who found plenty of opponents to punish during the next three years, two of which resulted in bowl appearances. Pitts enjoyed his best season in 1939, when he earned All Border Conference honors and was named to the Little All-America second team. That was the highest honor by an Arizona State football player at that point in the school's history. Halfback Norris Steverson was an Associated Press honorable-mention selection in 1931. Pitts also was elected Homecoming King—as a write-in candidate.

Fullback Wayne "Ripper" Pitts was a Little All-America selection in 1939. (ASU Media Relations)

BULLDOG BRIEF

• Four members of ASTC's Border Conference championship football club were named to the All-Conference team. Fullback Wayne "Ripper" Pitts, halfback Joe Hernandez and guards Al Sanserino and Noble "Rusty" Riggs earned first-team honors. On the national level, Pitts was named to the Little All-America second team. Pitts earned recognition from the Eastern media by playing all 60 minutes against Catholic U. in the Sun Bowl.

BULLDOG LORE

Pete I, the Bulldog mascot, died at the end of the 1938-39 school year and was buried beneath an olive tree on campus. *The Alumni Bulletin* reported: "Behind him he left a son molded in the character of the father. Pete II is taking up his father's functions and will march Homecoming with the college band. Pete I is dead. Long live Pete II."

1940-1941

September 16, 1940: Congress passed the Selective Service Act, requiring all men between the age of 20 and 36 to register for the armed services.

November 5, 1940: Franklin Roosevelt defeated Republican Wendell Willkie for a second term as president.

December 8, 1940: The Chicago Bears crushed the Washington Redskins, 73-0, in the NFL championship game.

June 22, 1941: Germany invaded the U.S.S.R.

July 17, 1941: Joe DiMaggio's incredible baseball hitting streak of 56 consecutive games was ended by the Cleveland Indians.

america's time capsule

arizona state teachers college
| m o m e n t

W est Coast power Gonzaga University, generally considered the toughest opponent Arizona State had ever played at that point in its football history, came to Tempe brimming with confidence and favored by 10 points over the Bulldogs, who were 5-1-1 through their first seven games. Fans were treated to a classic battle in this clash of teams with Bulldogs as their mascots. A-State drew first blood when Hascall Henshaw scored on

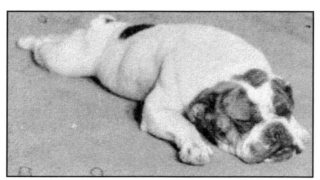

When Pete I (above) passed away in 1939, he was buried under an olive tree on campus and his son, Pete II (right), took the title of Arizona State Teachers College mascot into the 1940s. (ASU Alumni Association)

a double reverse just before halftime. Gonzaga battled back to tie the game in the third quarter. A pass interception deep in Gonzaga territory cost A-State a possible score in the fourth quarter. A few minutes later, Bob Lackey missed a field goal attempt that could have given ASTC the victory. The teams finished in a 7-7 tie—a result that did much to enhance Arizona State's football reputation.

BULLDOG
spotlight

The Bulldogs won their second straight Border Conference football title under third-year coach Dixie Howell, thanks partly to an assist from former A-State coach Ted Shipkey and his New Mexico Lobos. The Bulldogs still weren't playing Arizona because of a recruiting incident involving the two schools in 1937 though they were involved in a spirited race with the Wildcats for the conference crown right down to the final week of the season. In that final week the Bulldogs needed a win over North Dakota in Tempe plus an upset victory by New Mexico over Arizona to capture the conference crown and earn a second straight trip to El Paso's Sun Bowl. The Bulldogs breezed past North Dakota, 30-12, but many fans, armed with relatively new toys called portable radios, were paying more attention to the UA-New Mexico game in Tucson. The Tempe crowd went wild as Shipkey's Lobos prevailed by a 13-12 score. That put the Bulldogs into the Sun Bowl, where they suffered a 26-13 loss to Case Western Reserve of Cleveland.

ASU
LEGEND

Hascall Henshaw

He weighed roughly 140 pounds dripping wet. When his asthma flared up, he sometimes had to head for the bench to catch his breath. Alongside his bruising backfield running mate, Wayne "Ripper" Pitts, he looked totally out of place on a football field. But then Hascall Henshaw would take a handoff from quarterback Walt Ruth and the magic would unfold. Henshaw had a nickname of his own—the "Tombstone Terror." Despite decades of assaults from wave after wave of talented running backs, Henshaw still enjoys a prominent place in Arizona State's football record book. His 91-yard kickoff return against Cal Poly-San Luis Obispo in 1939 remains the sixth-longest in school history. But the play that elevated Henshaw into legendary status occurred against Case Western Reserve in the 1941 Sun Bowl in El Paso, Texas. His 94-yard scamper from scrimmage is the fourth-longest in school history and remains the longest run by an Arizona State player in a bowl game. Such plays rarely were caught on film in those days, but this run was. It generally is considered one of the most famous photographs in A-State sports history. Henshaw, who earned All-Border Conference honors in 1940, was a successful football coach and athletic director at Tempe High. He also served as principal at Griffith Elementary School in Phoenix. He was elected president of the Alumni Association in 1955.

Hascall Henshaw's 94-yard run in the Sun Bowl is one of the most famous in A-State football history. (ASU Media Relations)

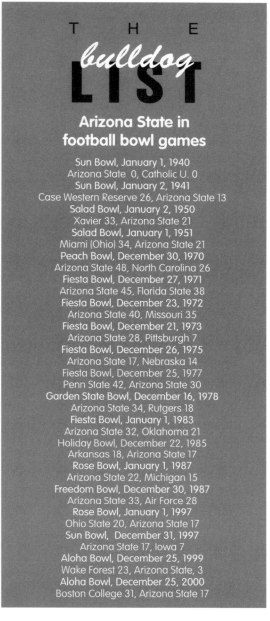

THE bulldog LIST

Arizona State in football bowl games

Sun Bowl, January 1, 1940
Arizona State 0, Catholic U. 0
Sun Bowl, January 2, 1941
Case Western Reserve 26, Arizona State 13
Salad Bowl, January 2, 1950
Xavier 33, Arizona State 21
Salad Bowl, January 1, 1951
Miami (Ohio) 34, Arizona State 21
Peach Bowl, December 30, 1970
Arizona State 48, North Carolina 26
Fiesta Bowl, December 27, 1971
Arizona State 45, Florida State 38
Fiesta Bowl, December 23, 1972
Arizona State 40, Missouri 35
Fiesta Bowl, December 21, 1973
Arizona State 28, Pittsburgh 7
Fiesta Bowl, December 26, 1975
Arizona State 17, Nebraska 14
Fiesta Bowl, December 25, 1977
Penn State 42, Arizona State 30
Garden State Bowl, December 16, 1978
Arizona State 34, Rutgers 18
Fiesta Bowl, January 1, 1983
Arizona State 32, Oklahoma 21
Holiday Bowl, December 22, 1985
Arkansas 18, Arizona State 17
Rose Bowl, January 1, 1987
Arizona State 22, Michigan 15
Freedom Bowl, December 30, 1987
Arizona State 33, Air Force 28
Rose Bowl, January 1, 1997
Ohio State 20, Arizona State 17
Sun Bowl, December 31, 1997
Arizona State 17, Iowa 7
Aloha Bowl, December 25, 1999
Wake Forest 23, Arizona State, 3
Aloha Bowl, December 25, 2000
Boston College 31, Arizona State 17

BULLDOG BRIEF

• In what the student yearbook called "the most classic scheduling boner of the year," New Mexico's Lobos and some scouts from the University of Arizona showed up a day early for a basketball game between the Bulldogs and Lobos in Tempe. "The Lobos players got a good night's rest," the ASTC yearbook said. "Coach (Rudy) Lavik began finding out who was responsible for the blunder and the University of Arizona scouts bought a hamburger, a cup of coffee and a return ticket to Tucson on the next train."

BULLDOG LORE

The college sported a new fight song, written by noted band leader Fred Waring. It was titled, "March on, Arizona State."

• Work began on Haigler Hall, a combination men's dormitory and seating addition to the east side of Goodwin Stadium. Named after the school's first football hero, Charlie Haigler, the $95,000 structure boosted seating capacity from 4,500 to 9,500.

1941-1942

america's time capsule

arizona state teachers college
| m o m e n t

A much-awaited moment in Arizona State football arrived when Arizona's Wildcats re-appeared on the Bulldogs' schedule after a three-year absence. Arizona officials had canceled the series in protest after A-State recruiter Tom Lillico "stole" prime recruits Wayne "Ripper" Pitts, Walt "Cowboy" Ruth and Rex Hopper off the Tucson campus in the summer of 1937. Officials of the Tucson school said they would not play the Dogs until the three former Glendale stars had concluded their college careers at A-State. The Bulldogs fell behind quickly in the contest in Tempe, trailing by a 13-0 score at the half. Arizona State battled back into contention on a 39-yard touchdown pass from Bernie Vitek to Bob Lackey in the third quarter, but the Wildcats put it away with a fourth-quarter touchdown to win, 20-7. The Bulldogs rebounded from that loss to win three of their last five games, including a 33-0 romp over their other in-state rival, ASTC/Flagstaff, and finished with a 5-5-1 record.

Walt Ruth was one of three Bulldogs in the center of a controversy that resulted in suspension of the Arizona State-Arizona football rivalry for three years. (ASU Media Relations)

BULLDOG *spotlight*

Coach Rudy Lavik's basketball team was able to stay focused enough during the wartime atmosphere to post a 10-10 record, only its second non-losing season since the 1933 club went 13-12. The 1939 team also finished .500 at 13-13. Because of the wartime conditions the Bulldogs couldn't find any nonconference opponents. All of their games were against Border Conference foes. A thrilling 42-41 victory over Arizona enabled the Bulldogs to split with their rivals from Tucson. The Wildcats had won the earlier contest by 14 points, 59-45. The Bulldogs were 9-5 with six games to play, but lost five of their last six. Their hopes for a winning season evaporated in a heartbreaking 44-42 loss to Arizona State Teachers College at Flagstaff in the final game of the season. Center Gerald "Wimpy" Jones was a first-team All-Borer Conference selection. Forward Chester McNabb was named to the all-conference second team. Other members of the starting lineup were forward Nick Johnson and guards Gale Mortensen and Tom O'Neil.

LEGEND

Al Onofrio

I n recent years, the talent-rich Los Angeles area has produced a steady stream of football players for the Arizona State program, but it still was somewhat of a rarity when Al Onofrio found his way from the West Coast to Tempe in 1941. A talented running back, Onofrio perhaps was best known as a punter. His punting average of 45.6 yards in 1942 stood as a school record until 1998, when Stephen Baker nosed him out of first place with a 45.7-yard average. Onofrio's average of 48.0 for 10 punts against University of San Francisco in 1942 still stands as a school record for best single-game average for a punter attempting nine or more punts. There was no football at A-State from 1943 through 1945 because of World War II. When the sport resumed in 1946, Onofrio was a member of head coach Steve Coutchie's staff as backfield coach. Onofrio served in the same capacity from 1947 through 1950 under coach Ed Doherty. He coached the freshmen in 1955 and the varsity ends in 1956 and 1957 under coach Dan Devine. Onofrio later succeeded Devine as head coach at Missouri. Onofrio also coached Arizona State's golf team from 1954 through 1957. Under his direction in 1957, the Sun Devils won the Border Conference title and made their first appearance ever at the NCAA tournament, finishing fifth.

Al Onofrio was a star punter who later coached football and golf at Arizona State. (ASU Media Relations)

BULLDOG LORE

The fate of athletics at Arizona State was the subject of much debate in March of 1942 with World War II occupying everyone's thoughts and young men leaving school to join the armed forces. Football coach Dixie Howell and his chief recruiter, Tom Lillico, resigned to join the Navy. After much soul-searching, college president Grady Gammage decided that the school would field a football team in 1942.

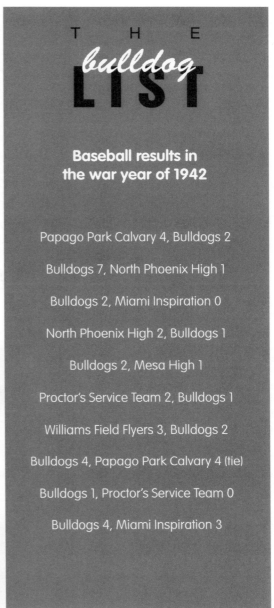

THE bulldog LIST

Baseball results in the war year of 1942

Papago Park Calvary 4, Bulldogs 2

Bulldogs 7, North Phoenix High 1

Bulldogs 2, Miami Inspiration 0

North Phoenix High 2, Bulldogs 1

Bulldogs 2, Mesa High 1

Proctor's Service Team 2, Bulldogs 1

Williams Field Flyers 3, Bulldogs 2

Bulldogs 4, Papago Park Calvary 4 (tie)

Bulldogs 1, Proctor's Service Team 0

Bulldogs 4, Miami Inspiration 3

BULLDOG BRIEF

• With World War II raging, it wasn't easy to field a baseball team. The college, in fact, didn't sponsor one. Player-coach Nick Johnson raised funds and got Curry Home Appliances to provide uniforms and equipment. At least two of the players, Bill Kajikawa and Don Cantrell, weren't even in school, though it was no big deal since the team played no college opponents. Cantrell, a multi-talented star from Casa Grande, started all 10 games in the outfield or on the mound. Cantrell signed a professional contract with the New York Giants after the season. Second baseman Norm Stapley signed with the Brooklyn Dodgers. Stapley, a former Mesa High star, later joined the Navy. He was killed in November of 1943 when the aircraft carrier *Liscome Bay*, on which he served, was torpedoed

1942-1944

November 15, 1942: The U.S. scored a major victory in a naval engagement off Guadacanal, preventing Japanese reinforcements from reaching the island.

December 1, 1942: Nationwide gasoline rationing went into effect.

May 1, 1943: Count Fleet, with jockey Johnny Longden, won the 69th annual Kentucky Derby.

September 8, 1943: Italy surrendered unconditionally to the Allied powers. German troops there fought on.

June 6, 1944: More than 4,000 ships, 3,000 planes and four million Allied troops began the Normandy invasion.

arizona state teachers college
m o m e n t

With players leaving to join the war effort, the Bulldogs attempted to play a football schedule in 1942 under coach Hillman Walker, who had been Dixie Howell's assistant. Howell had resigned the previous spring to enlist in the Navy. The Bulldogs were shut out five times in a 2-8 season and fewer than 20 players remained at the end of the campaign. Fresno State canceled its game in Tempe for financial reasons and the Bulldogs forfeited a game at Hardin-Simmons because they couldn't afford to make the trip. Among the losses were a 40-0 shutout at the hands of the Santa Ana, California, Air Force Base and a 13-0 blanking by the Albuquerque Air Force Base. Because of the war, the school did not field a team the next three years.

Coach Hillman Walker fielded a football team in the war year of 1942, but the depleted Bulldogs were overmatched in most of their games. (ASU Media Relations)

spotlight

Arizona State didn't field baseball teams in 1943, 1944 and 1945 because of the war, but the basketball team did play a 19-game schedule in 1942-43. The Bulldogs posted a 10-9 record under Coach Rudy Lavik against a makeshift schedule, their first winning season since 1933. The Dogs played Arizona State/Flagstaff five times, winning four, and won once in four tries against Arizona. They split two games with New Mexico and lost to Texas Tech. The rest of the schedule was filled by such teams as Marstons, Williams Field and the San Diego Marines. The Bulldogs were 12-2 in 1943-44, though all the games were against local military teams.

BULLDOG LORE

World War II caused enrollment to shrink from 1,300 in 1940 to less than 700 in 1942, but the college received an economic boost in January of 1943 when president Grady Gammage worked out a contract to house a group of Army Air Corps cadets in a pre-flight training program. The money helped keep the college afloat during hard economic times.

1944-1946

america's time capsule

April 12, 1945: President Franklin Roosevelt, who had been reelected to a record fourth term the previous November, died in Warm Springs, Georgia, at the age of 63. He was succeeded by Harry S. Truman.

May 8, 1945: Germany unconditionally surrendered, ending the European phase of World War II.

August 6, 1945: The city of Hiroshima, Japan, was destroyed by the first atomic bomb to be used in war. Nine days later the Japanese surrendered to the Allies.

February 15, 1946: Scientists developed the world's first digital computer in Philadelphia.

July 2, 1946: African-Americans voted for the first time in Mississippi primaries.

arizona state teachers college
m o m e n t

Though the school didn't field a football team in 1944 or 1945, the basketball team played an abbreviated 14-game schedule in 1944-45 and a full 28-game slate in 1945-46. The 1944-45 Bulldogs split four games against Arizona, winning by scores of 53-44 and 46-41 and losing a pair of thrillers, 39-36 and 39-37. The Dogs lost three of four to a local city-league team, O.B. Marstons. The 1945-46 schedule, which produced a 12-16 record, featured a mix of college opponents and military and industrial-league teams. The Bulldogs were 0-4 against Arizona and 0-3 against New Mexico. They had better luck against their rivals from the North, Arizona State/Flagstaff's Lumberjacks. They won three of four from the Jacks, though all were hotly contested. The Bulldogs' victories were by scores of 39-36, 45-41 and 28-27. The lone Lumberjack victory was 36-31. One local team—the Funk Jewlers—had the Bulldogs' number. The Jewlers beat the Dogs four straight times. The Bulldogs lost 10 of their first 11 games, but rebounded to win six of seven at one stretch to finish respectably. The normal starting lineup consisted of Bob Chastain at center, Joe Goodman and Gale Mortensen at the forwards and Norman Ray and Verl Heap at the guards.

With no football on campus because of World War II, basketball soared in popularity in the mid 1940s. (ASU Alumni Association)

spotlight

Baseball resumed in the spring of 1946 after a three-year absence The Bulldogs were 6-6 under coach Bill Kajikawa, who had coached the team to a 5-9 record in 1940. Catcher Lester "Truck" Dayton was the team's leading hitter with a .388 average. Clyde Dougherty was named most valuable pitcher. Most of the opposition came from Phoenix-area military bases. The Bulldogs were 2-0 against the Litchfield Naval Air Station, 1-1 against Luke Air Force Base and 1-3 against the Williams Field Flyers. The Dogs had more success against high school teams, going 2-0 against Mesa High and winning their only encounter against North Phoenix High.

BULLDOG LORE

After a long and bitter battle, the Legislature passed a bill dropping "teachers" from the school's name, making it Arizona State College at Tempe. However, the Legislature refused to grant the school's request to offer Bachelor of Arts and Bachelor of Science degrees in non-teaching fields, referring the matter to the Arizona Board of Regents. A year later, in May of 1946, the Regents ended a wait of many years by granting ASC permission to award those degrees.

1946-1947

america's time capsule

arizona state college
moment

Coach Steve Coutchie was hired away from Mesa High, where he had coached for 18 years, to attempt to rebuild the school's football program after a three-year hiatus because of World War II. In only his second game, Coutchie's team suffered one of the most embarrassing losses in the school's football history. In retrospect, however, it also was one of the most significant. Arizona's Wildcats, coached by Mike Casteel, pummeled the Bulldogs by a 67-0 score in Tucson. Two games later, A-State was destroyed by Nevada-Reno, 74-2. Those lopsided losses caused considerable grumbling among ASC alumni and fans, and college president Grady Gammage vowed that they would not be repeated. Coutchie resigned after a 2-7-2 season and a search was begun for someone who could lead the school into a position of football prominence. Meanwhile, members of the Phoenix Thunderbirds civic group joined with the old Bulldog boosters and other support groups with the intent of upgrading ASC athletics. They called themselves the Sun Angels, a name suggested by group member M. O. Best, a prominent vegetable grower. The organization suggested that the school's athletic teams be called Sun Devils, and the name was adopted by an 816-196 vote of the student body on November 8. A Sun Devil mascot—currently known as Sparky—was created by Walt Disney Productions.

Steve Coutchie's lone season as football coach was not successful, but it was historic. (ASU Media Relations)

spotlight

The baseball team had an 8-8 record under coach Bill Kajikawa. The low point was a 21-6 loss to rival Arizona, which swept the four-game series. There were some plusses, however. Third baseman Joe Anaya batted .404 and shortstop and Most Valuable Player Herb Boetto signed a professional contract with the New York Giants. Jay Miller was named the team's most valuable pitcher. Bob Morris, the No. 2 starter on the pitching staff, pitched a one-hitter in a 5-1 victory over the Litchfield Naval Air Base team. It was only the second one-hitter at that point in school history.

LEGEND

Jim Montgomery

There weren't a lot of highlights for the Bull-dogs during the 1946 football season as the program was rebuilt from scratch after a three-year break for World War II. What few there were often involved Jim Montgomery. Montgomery, generally considered the first in a long line of outstanding pass receivers at Arizona State, led the NCAA with 32 receptions that season. His statistics probably were helped by the fact that the Bull-dogs, who didn't become the Sun Devils until a November 8 student body election, often found themselves on the short end of lopsided scores and had to resort to a passing attack in an attempt to be competitive. The following year, as team captain under new head coach Ed Doherty, he played a vital leadership role as the Sun Devils began to turn the corner toward respectability with a 4-7 record. He was an All Border Conference selection in 1946 and 1947. He was Arizona State's only representative on the all-conference team both of those years. He also was the first post-WW II player from Arizona State to be drafted by a professional football team. He signed with the Pittsburgh Steelers. He uncorked a 90-yard punt against New Mexico in 1946. It still stands as the longest punt in school history.

Jim Montgomery was first in a long line of great pass receivers at Arizona State. (ASU Alumni Association)

SUN DEVIL STAT

• The Sun Devils celebrated their new nickname by ending Arizona's 13-year domination of the Border Conference track and field championships. Al Van Hazel and Joe Batiste finished first and third in the final event, the javelin, to give the Devils the title with 49 1/2 points to 45 5/6 for Texas Tech and 39 5/6 for Arizona. Arizona State athletes won six individual events at the meet in Albuquerque.

Sun Devil Lore

Enrollment skyrocketed from 500 the previous September to 2,200 as servicemen returned home from World War II. "Victory Village" was constructed at the south end of campus, where Gammage Center for the Performing Arts now stands. The village provided housing for married students.

1947-1948

arizona state college
m o m e n t

Rudy Lavik, who coached various sports for 15 years at Arizona State, wrapped up his coaching career in style. His Sun Devil basketball team survived a rocky start to earn the first post-season appearance in school history, a spot in the NAIA championship in Kansas City. The Devils certainly didn't look like a contender for national honors in the early going. After a 54-47 victory over Pepperdine in their opener, they lost six of their next seven games. They shook off that 2-6 start and won nine of their next 11. Their 9-7 record in league games placed them third in the Border Conference and was good enough to earn them a bid to the NAIA tourney. They were involved in a couple of thrillers in Kansas City, beating Northeast Missouri, 68-66, in the first round before being eliminated by Mankato State, 54-

Members of the first Arizona State basketball team to make a post-season appearance. (Barry Sollenberger collection)

53. The Devils finished 13-11 overall, their first winning record since the 1942-43 club finished 11-7. Forward Verl Heap led the Border Conference in scoring and was named to the All-Conference first team. Other starters on that historic team were forward Chesley Cook, center Ed Long and guards Carl Heath and Charles Beall.

spotlight

Ed Doherty, 29, a former Boston College quarterback who had been an assistant coach at BC and Notre Dame, was hired to try to turn around a football program that had fallen on hard times. Doherty brought fellow BC teammate Bill Quinn with him as his top assistant. Several players from New England showed up on the Tempe campus, and once they got over the culture shock they began to contribute. The personable Doherty also began attracting in-state talent, most notably Mesa high school star Wilford "Whizzer" White. Doherty's first team got off to a promising start with four victories in its first six games, but the Sun Devils lost their last five to finish 4-7. The Sun Devils had Arizona on the ropes before the Wildcats rallied for a 26-13 victory.

LEGEND

Verl Heap

A product of St. John's High School, Verl Heap saw his Arizona State athletic career interrupted by World War II following his freshman season in 1942-43. He left school and joined the Air Force, where he served as a B-17 and B-29 pilot. He managed to work in some basketball, leading two different service teams in scoring. He returned to A-State in 1945 and began to build a reputation as one of the top players in school history. An All-Border Conference honorable mention selection as a freshman, he earned second-team honors as a junior and first-team acclaim as a senior upon his return. He led the conference in scoring and was named the league's outstanding player in 1948. As a senior in the spring of 1948, he played a major role as the Sun Devils won a spot in the NAIA national championships in Kansas City. He was named outstanding player in the tournament as the Sun Devils split two games, then became one of the first two Arizonans to sign a professional basketball contract. He later spent one year as an assistant coach at Arizona State before returning to St. John's, where he compiled a 560-158 coaching record in 30 seasons.

Verl Heap led the Border Conference in scoring and was named the league's MVP in 1948. (ASU Alumni Association)

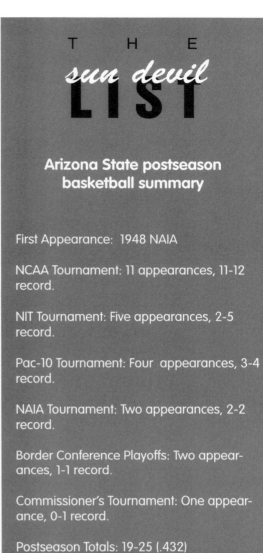
Sun Devil Lore

A new cinder track, considered one of the finest in the nation, was unveiled at Goodwin Stadium in time for an ambitious track and field schedule. Coach Don Kinzle had the cinders imported from the Prescott area. Kinzle's theme for the facility was "Where Champions are Born." Many records were set over the years on the track, which turned out to be lightning fast. When USC visited in March of 1948, Trojan sprint star Mel Patton, who was not scheduled to participate, took one look at the track and elected to run the 100-yard dash, which he won.

SUN DEVIL STAT

• Arizona State's faculty athletic representative, Chuck Southern, was elected to a National Collegiate Athletic Association vice presidency. Southern's election was considered a major breakthrough for the college in terms of advancing the school's name recognition in national circles. ASC also struck a blow for racial equality when it issued a declaration that it would not play any school that would not allow the Sun Devils' black athletes to participate. The declaration was triggered when Texas Mines refused to allow ASC players Morrison Warren and George Diggs to play in the 1947 game in El Paso. For years, ASC had to leave its black athletes behind when it played Texas schools on the road. The Sun Devils dropped Texas Mines and West Texas State from their schedule and refused to schedule Texas Tech until those schools dropped their color barrier in 1951.

1948-1949

November 2, 1948: In a major political upset, Harry Truman defeated Thomas Dewey for the U.S. presidency.

December 15, 1948: Former State Department official Alger Hiss was indicted by a federal grand jury on two counts of perjury.

April 4, 1949: NATO was formed when the North Atlantic Treaty was signed in Washington, D.C.

April 20, 1949: The discovery of cortisone, a hormone promised to bring relief to sufferers of rheumatoid arthritis, was announced.

June 22, 1949: Ezzard Charles defeated "Jersey Joe" Walcott to become the new world heavyweight boxing champion .

arizona state college
| m o m e n t

About 5,000 fans from the Valley followed the Sun Devils to Tucson for the big game against rival Arizona. They made themselves heard among the throng of 16,200, and the Sun Devils made some noise on the field with Coach Ed Doherty's new offensive set. Unfortunately, however, they didn't make enough noise, falling to the Wildcats by a 33-21 score. The Sun Devils trailed 19-7 at the half and second-half touchdowns by Garner Barnett of Bisbee and Mark Markichevich of Globe kept them in the thick of things before the Wildcats pulled away at the end. Though the Sun Devils finished an undistinguished 5-5 in Doherty's first year, a couple of elements attracted some national attention for the team. One was Doherty's offensive tinkering, which resulted in the forerunner of the now-popular "I" formation. The other was the barefoot kicking of Mesa's Bobby Fuller, fairly common now but then a novelty in college football.

Coach Ed Doherty, left, is considered by many the inventor of the now-popular "I" formation. Staff members, left to right, are Bill Quinn, Wendell Patterson, Al Onofrio and Bill Kajikawa. (ASU Alumni Association)

Last-place Arizona State battled first-place Arizona to the wire before losing a 63-60 basketball decision to the Wildcats at Bear Down Gym in Tucson. Center Ed Long scored 19 points and forward Wade Oliver 14 for the Sun Devils. It was the Wildcats' 50th straight home-court victory. Clearly, they were a force on their home floor long before Lute Olson and McKale Center. The Devils earlier had lost a 45-44 heartbreaker to the Cats in Tempe. The Sun Devils also lost a pair of close games to Arizona State College at Flagsataff, 50-45 and 47-44 as they finished 12-16 overall and 4-12 in the Border Conference under first-year coach Bill Kajikawa.

LEGEND

Ed Doherty

Arizona State got an infusion of eastern blood and some innovative football ideas when Ed Doherty was hired in February of 1947 as the school's 11th football coach. Doherty, a former Boston College quarterback and an assistant to the legendary coach Frank Leahy at BC and Notre Dame, had been nicknamed "The Brain" during his playing days. Doherty brought former teammate Bill Quinn with him as chief assistant coach and it wasn't long before several players from New England were wearing the Maroon and Gold. Doherty recruited all-everything high school halfback Wilford "Whizzer" White from Mesa plus such other talented in-state runners as Glendale's Manuel Aja, Bisbee's Garner Barnett and Globe's Mark Markichevich. Doherty didn't stick around long. He never did in his lengthy coaching career. But his teams progressed from 4-7 to 5-5 to 7-3 to 9-2 in his four years as the Sun Devils' head coach. While at ASU Doherty tinkered with the traditional T-formation, moving White from left halfback to a position directly behind the fullback.

"What we did was to invent the "I" formation without realizing it," Doherty once told author Dean Smith. "Using that formation we became one of the nation's leading offensive teams." Doherty is the only person ever to serve as head football coach at both Arizona State and Arizona. He coached the Wildcats in 1957 (1-8-1) and 1958 (3-7). Doherty also made college coaching stops at Rhode Island, Xavier and Holy Cross and served as an assistant with the Philadelphia Eagles. He closed out his coaching career where he was most comfortable, in the high school ranks. He led Phoenix St. Mary's to state titles in 1967 and 1968 and finished second in 1969. He coached Tucson Salpointe to a second-place finish in 1981.

Innovative Coach Ed Doherty turned around a struggling Arizona State football program. (ASU Media Relations)

SUN DEVIL STATS

• Arizona State forward Wade Oliver, the "Buckeye Buckaroo," ranked second nationally in free throw shooting with 104 out of 124 for 83.9 percent.

• The Sun Devil track team won the Border Conference title for the third straight year, rolling up 55 points to 43 for runner-up Arizona at the conference meet in Albuquerque. Individual winners for the Devils were Bob Sieben in the half mile, Don Hildreth in the low hurdles, George Diggs in the broad jump and Bill Miller in the javelin.

SUN DEVIL LORE

Dixie Dees Gammage, first wife of Arizona State president Grady Gammage, died after a long illness. The Gammages had been married 35 years. Mrs. Gammage had served as hostess for many college events before her illness forced her to curtail such activities.

• A new three-story science building opened on campus. It was 20 years in planning and cost $509,000 to construct plus $75,000 for equipment.

1949-1950

america's time capsule

arizona state college
| m o m e n t

After 18 years and 11 consecutive futile attempts, the Sun Devils finally registered a football victory over their rivals from Tucson, Arizona's Wildcats. Though they rolled into the game with five victories in their first six contests and were leading the nation in total offense, the Sun Devils still were underdogs for their midseason meeting with the Wildcats in Tempe. History surely had something to do with that. Arizona held a whopping 20-2 advantage in the all-time series between the two schools. An overflow crowd of 15,000—published reports suggested at least twice that many tickets were requested—jammed into Goodwin Stadium. The Sun Devils emerged from a tense first half with a 7-0 lead thanks to a 3-yard touchdown run by Hank Rich. A-State blew it open in the second half on another TD run by Rich, scoring dashes of 10 and 12 yards by Whizzer White and a quarterback sneak by Cecil Coleman. When it was all over the Sun Devils were proud owners of a 34-7 victory and the series against the Wildcats had become a legitimate rivalry again. The Sun Devils went on to finish the regular season 7-2 before losing to Xavier University of Cincinnati, 33-21, in the Salad Bowl in Montgomery Stadium in Phoenix. With out a doubt, however, the highlight of the season was that resounding victory over Arizona.

ASC led the nation in total offense for much of the season thanks, in part to these four backs. From left: Charles Beall, Mark Markichevich, Cecil Coleman, Whizzer White. (ASU Alumni Association)

SUN DEVIL *spotlight*

Coach Donn Kinzle's track team cruised to its fourth straight Border Conference title, accumulating 83 points to 27 for runner-up Arizona in the conference meet at Goodwin Stadium. Six conference records were broken in the meet, three by the Sun Devils. New standards were set by Bill Miller in the javelin (216-9), Fred Olsson in the 880 (1:56.1) and the mile relay team of Truett McCullah, Olsson, Tom Matteson and Whizzer White, which knocked a full second off the conference mark with a time of 3:19.4.

LEGEND

Cecil Coleman

Explosive halfback Wilford "Whizzer" White grabbed most of the headlines, but the man who ran Coach Ed Doherty's innovative "Lazy T" formation and got the ball into White's hands was a talented quarterback named Cecil Coleman. One publication called him a "dazzling quarterback." A four-year starter from 1946 through 1949, he didn't pass often by current standards. In his most productive year, 1948, he averaged just 14 passing attempts per game. He completed 58 percent of his passes that season for 838 yards and nine touchdowns. The Sun Devils improved every season with Coleman at QB, from 2-7-2 to 4-7 to 5-5 to 7-3. He piloted the Devils to a berth against Xavier of Ohio in the Salad Bowl his senior season. Following his graduation from Arizona State, Coleman landed one of the state's most prestigious high school coaching jobs, at North High School in Phoenix. During a successful six-year stint at North, he obtained his master's degree from Arizona State. After one year as head coach at Long Beach City College in California, he returned to his alma mater to join the staff of coach Dan Devine. He coached one year under Devine and one under Frank Kush before moving on to further his career as a coach and athletic administrator at Fresno State and Illinois.

Cecil Coleman starred at quarterback, then went on to a successful coaching and administrative career. (ASU Alumni Association)

SUN DEVIL STAT

• Senon "Baldy" Castillo, a former three-sport star at Phoenix Union High School who was studying for his masters degree at Arizona State, was named an assistant basketball and track coach. Castillo had served as freshman track coach the previous spring.

Sun Devil Lore

Mike Casteel, former head football coach at Arizona for eight years, was named executive director of the Sun Angel Foundation.

The price for season tickets to Arizona State's seven-game home football season, including games against rivals Arizona and Arizona State/Flagstaff, was $15.60. That worked out to $2.23 per game, a savings of 20 percent over tickets bought at the gate.

1950-1951

america's time capsule

arizona state college
m o m e n t

Manuel Aja runs for big yardage in 47-13 drubbing of rival Arizona. (ASU Alumni Association)

Arizona's Wildcats were expecting some razzle-dazzle from rival Arizona State in the annual Big Game in Tucson because ASC coach Ed Doherty was famous for pulling an occasional rabbit out of the hat. Instead, the Sun Devils unleashed a devastating display of power football as they demolished the Wildcats, 47-13, in front of 27,000 fans, the largest crowd to watch a football game at that point in the state's history. Pounding away at the middle of UA's defensive line, the Sun Devils scored four times in the first half and won going away. ASC's star halfback, Whizzer White, scored on runs of 57 and one yards, but spent much of the contest as a decoy, opening the door for Manuel Aja, Mark Markichevich and Marvin Wahlin to have big games. The Sun Devil attack was directed in flawless fashion by Harold Self, a junior quarterback from Casa Grande who was pushed into starting duty when regular QB Bob Hendricks was sidelined by an injury. Doherty stunned ASC fans when he annnounced five days after the game that he was resigning because of a "lack of security" caused by a state rule limiting coaches to one-year contracts. The Sun Devils finished 9-2 after a 34-21 loss to Miami of Ohio in the Salad Bowl.

spotlight

Led by the exploits of javelin star Bill Miller, coach Don Kinzle's track and field team continued its emergence as a national power. Miller set a national collegiate record with a toss of 237 feet, 10 inches on May 19th. Miller showed his versatility at the national decathlon competition in Santa Barbara, California, in July when he set a national decathlon record in the high jump at 6 feet, 7 7/8 inches. Miller, who stood only 5-9 1/2, leaped nearly a foot over his height. Miller and teammate Whizzer White finished fourth and sixth respectively at the national decathlon competition. The Sun Devils produced 12 Border Conference individual champions. Merle Wackerbarth won both sprints and anchored the winning mile relay team. Don Hildreth captured both hurdles events.

LEGEND

Roy Coppinger

Roy Coppinger later built a reputation as a highly-successful high school baseball coach, but hoops was his primary game at Arizona State. A versatile performer capable of playing both guard and forward, he was the first player in school history to earn All-Border Conference recognition three straight years. He was a second-team all-conference selection as a sophomore in 1950-51, when he averaged 11.5 points a game, second on the team to center Lester Dean (12.0). Though listed as a forward on Arizona State's roster, he was named to the All-Border Conference first team as a guard in 1951-52. He repeated as a first-team all-conference selection in 1952-53, when he averaged 12.2 points per game while leading the Sun Devils to a 13-12 record, their only winning season during a 10-year stretch. He played a vital role as the Devils shook off a 1-10 start and won 12 of their last 14 games, including a 75-73 thriller over rival Arizona. Coppinger also played two years of varsity baseball, sharing starting catching duties in 1951 and 1952.

Roy Coppinger was the first Arizona State basketball player to earn All-Border Conference honors three straight years. (Barry Sollenberger collection.)

THE sun devil LIST

Arizona State football players who led the nation in a single-season statistical category

Season	Player	Category	No.
1950	Whizzer White	Rushing	1,502 yds
1950	Whizzer White	All Purpose Yds	2,065 yds
1950	Bobby Fuller	PATs	48
1950	Henry Rich	Interceptions	12
1957	Leon Burton	Rushing	1,126 yds
1957	Leon Burton	Scoring	96 pts
1957	Bobby Mulgado	Punt returns	19.1 avg
1961	Joe Zuger	Interceptions	11
1961	Joe Zuger	Punting	42.1 avg
1961	Seth Miller	Interceptions	11
1970	Steve Holden	Punt returns	19.2 avg
1974	Mike Haynes	Interceptions	10
1980	Mike Richardson	Interceptions (tie)	8
1983	Luis Zendejas	Field goals	28

SUN DEVIL STATS

- Ladd Kwiatkowski batted .358 to lead the Sun Devil baseball team in hitting. Kwiatkowski would later go on to star as 'Ladmo' on the popular "Wallace and Ladmo" television series in Phoenix.
- The Sun Devil football team led the nation in total offense (470.4 yards per game) and rushing (347 ypg).
- Henry Rich set a national collegiate record with 12 interceptions and Bob Fuller established a national mark with 48 points after touchdowns. Whizzer White led the nation in rushing with 1,502 yards and all-purpose yardage (2,065).

SUN DEVIL LORE

Charles A. Stauffer, Class of 1901, former publisher of *The Arizona Republic* and *Phoenix Gazette*, was named to head the campaign to raise funds for a new $750,000 student union. The goal was $350,000 to supplement a $400,000 bond issue authorized by the Legislature.
- An expanded and reorganized library, named in honor of former college president Arthur J. Matthews, was opened on campus. It was made possible by a $525,000 legislative grant. A highlight was a $125,000 art collection donated by an anonymous Phoenix art lover.

1951-1952

**america's
time capsule**

arizona state college
m o m e n t

There were a couple of significant moments in the Sun Devils' 6-3-1 football season, and one negative post-season development that tarnished the reputation of the budding football power and ultimately cost coach Larry Siemering his job. After a season-opening 33-27 road victory over Utah State, the Sun Devils traveled all the way to Fayetteville, Arkansas, for an intersectional matchup with Arkansas. It was Arizona State's first meeting against a national power, and the fact that it came on the Razorbacks' turf made it an even more imposing assignment. The fired-up Sun Devils stunned the Razorbacks by building a halftime lead, but the hosts used their superior depth to rally for a 30-13 victory. The Sun Devils enjoyed their finest moment in a 61-14 romp over rival Arizona in Tempe, a score that still stands as the most points scored by the Sun Devils against the Wildcats. ASC's explosive backfield set an NCAA record when four backs—Duane Morrison, Bob Tarwater, Buzz Welker and Harley Cooper—each rushed for more than 100 yards. Shortly after the season, however, it was revealed that a Sun Devil player, Edward Andrew Matesic, actually was Joseph Thomas Matesic, who had played the previous season at Indiana and was ineligible under NCAA regulations. Adding to the embarrassment was the fact that Matesic had earned All Border Conference honors at tackle. University president Grady Gammage immediately relieved Siemering of his athletic director's duties. Siemering resigned as football coach in March of 1952.

Larry Siemering's squad scored more points against Arizona than any other Arizona State team, but he resigned in the wake of a scandal. (ASU Media Relations)

The Sun Devils had so much fun pounding Arizona in football, that they decided to do the same in basketball. They put some gloss on an otherwise undistinguished 8-16 season by outscoring the Wildcats, 87-59, in the final game of the season. It was the biggest winning margin at that point in the history of the rivalry and remains the second-highest margin ever for the Devils over the Cats. It broke an 11-year winless streak against UA. With the victory, coach Bill Kajikawa's team finished in a fourth-place tie with Arizona in the Border Conference race with a 6-8 league record. The Sun Devils played most of their schedule on the road because of construction work on their new gym. Their few "home" games were played on neutral courts.

LEGEND
Donn Kinzle

Donn Kinzle will always be remembered as the man who put Arizona State track and field on the map. A star hurdler who was ranked third nationally in 1938, Kinzle graduated from A-State in 1942. He returned as track coach in 1946 after serving with the Royal Canadian Air Force in World War II. It didn't take Kinzle long to begin building a powerhouse. His 1947 team won the Border Conference championship, beginning a string of five straight conference titles. Kinzle also served as executive manager and director of athletics from 1949 through 1951, a period when the football team began to attract national attention under coach Ed Doherty. Among the many outstanding athletes recruited by Kinzle was Bill Miller, who set a national collegiate javelin record. Kinzle also was responsible for the installation of a lightning-quick cinder track in Goodwin Stadium that became the site of many records.

Donn Kinzle put track and field on the map at Arizona State. (ASU Alumni Association)

THE sun devil LIST

Largest margins of victory over Arizona in basketball

Margin	Year	Score
29	1971	112-83
28	1952	87-59
26	1982	82-56
25	1980	97-72
23	1959	85-62
20	1928	47-27
19	1963	73-54
19	1961	94-75
18	1981	83-65
18	1955	92-74
18	1938	49-31
18	1937	45-27
18	1931	38-20

SUN DEVIL STAT

• Former star running back Wilford "Whizzer" White ended several weeks of deliberation by signing a professional football contract with the Chicago Bears of the National Football League in July of 1951. White, who led the nation in rushing with 1,502 yards in 1950, had been weighing several offers, including one from Edmonton, Alberta, in Canada. Published reports put White's salary at $10,000. White also was selected to play for the College All-Stars against the pro champion Cleveland Browns in the annual College All-Star game in Chicago.

Sun Devil Lore

Construction began on campus for a new physical education building and armory with a seating capacity of 6,500 for basketball. The building was to house offices for both the physical education and military science departments and provide classroom space. ASC's alumni magazine, *The Arizona Statesman*, said the old gym, just west of the new building, was "long the butt of wheezy jokes suggesting it was build by the Spanish Conquistadores."

1952-1953

September 23, 1952: Rocky Marciano won his 43rd consecutive bout, beating "Jersey Joe" Walcott for the world heavyweight boxing title.

November 4, 1952: Dwight Eisenhower defeated Illinois Gov. Adlai Stevenson for the presidency of the United States.

January 2, 1953: Wisconsin Sen. Joseph McCarthy, known for his charges of communist infiltration in various organizations, was accused by a Senate subcommittee of "motivation by self-interest."

March 18, 1953: Baseball's Boston Braves moved to Milwaukee, Wisconsin.

May 4, 1953: Author Ernest Hemmingway was awarded a Pulitzer Prize for his book *The Old Man and the Sea.*

arizona state college
m o m e n t

Clyde B. Smith arrived at Arizona State prior to the 1952 season with two objectives—continuing the on-field success achieved under coach Ed Doherty in the post-WW II years, and cleaning up the mess that resulted in the forced resignation of coach Larry Siemering following the 1951 campaign. Smith's very first game was a rousing success. The Sun Devils traveled to Abilene, Texas, to battle Hardin-Simmons, which had won all eleven of the prior meetings between the two schools, most by overwhelming margins. Smith unleashed a powerful weapon—John Henry Johnson—a much-heralded running back from St. Mary's College in California. Johnson carried the ball just seven times, but he accumulated 106 yards and scored on runs of five and 33 yards from scrimmage and a 63-yard punt return as the Sun Devils romped to a 27-6 victory. For some still-unknown reason, Smith stuck Johnson at safety the rest of the season as Marvin Wahlan (11 touchdowns), and Dick Curran (870 rushing yards, 8.1-yard average) handled most of the ball-carrying duties. Johnson, a second-round pick of the Pittsburgh Steelers in 1953, went on to earn a spot in the NFL Hall of Fame after a brilliant 13-year pro career that produced 6,577 rushing yards and 48 touchdowns. The Sun Devils finished 6-3, including a 30-28 victory over Arizona in Tucson, and captured the Border Conference championship. A late interception by Johnson in the end zone preserved the victory in Tucson.

John Henry Johnson played just one season at Arizona State, but he had a major impact on the two biggest football victories of 1952. (ASU Alumni Association)

It was a basketball season to remember for coach Bill Kajikawa's Sun Devils, who won nine of their last 11 games to finish 13-12 overall and tied with Texas Tech for third place in the Border Conference with a 9-5 league record. The Devils whipped New Mexico Western, 68-51, in the District 7 Playoffs in Silver City, New Mexico, to earn a spot in the National Association for Intercollegiate Athletics championships in Kansas City. They beat East Tennessee State, 81-79, in the first round before losing to Nebraska Wesleyan, 83-71. Another highlight was a thrilling 75-73 victory over rival Arizona in a game played in Mesa because of construction of ASC's new gymnasium. The new gym was dedicated February 24 with an 80-76 victory over Texas Tech.

LEGEND

John Jankans

Much has been made over the years of football coach Frank Kush's Pennsylvania recruiting ties. Kush repeatedly tapped the coal mines and steel mills of his native state for a special breed of athlete—one who could stand up to his tough brand of coaching. But several years before Kush, coach Clyde B. Smith found a gem by the name of John Jankans in Reading, Pennsylvania. A slight foot deformity did not keep Jankans from having an immediate impact on the Sun Devil program. Not only did he earn a starting job as a freshman, he won All-Border Conference honors as the Devils captured the league title. He went on to earn All-Conference recognition for four straight seasons. He's the only ASU football player in history to earn first-team All-Conference honors for four consecutive years and the only player in the history of the Border Conference to earn such acclaim. Jankans was chosen to play in the East-West Shrine game. In a *Life* magazine article titled "Future stars who have done great deeds on small campuses," the legendary Frank Leahy wrote of Jankans: "You hardly ever see in college football a man moving with all the characteristics of a real pro. John Jankans of Arizona State College at Tempe is one." Jankans was drafted in the 11th round by the Chicago Bears of the NFL, but he signed as a free agent with Vancouver, B.C, of the Canadian League.

John Jankans is the only four-time, All-Conference first-team football selection in school history. (ASU Alumni Association)

SUN DEVIL STAT

• Senon "Baldy" Castillo, a former Phoenix Union and Phoenix College athletic star, was named track coach. Castillo had served as an assistant track and basketball coach at ASC. Castillo's first Sun Devil team recaptured the Border Conference championship that had eluded A-State in 1952, giving the Devils six conference titles in seven years. ASC won 10 of the 15 events in the conference meet to outscore Arizona, 79 2/3 to 53 1/2.

SUN DEVIL LORE

Old Main, the second-oldest building on campus, was remodeled at a cost of $165,000—more than three times the cost of the original structure. The project added three classrooms and eight offices to the building. The remodeled structure was minus some of its most prominent features, including the front steps, the stairwell and the balcony. The balcony had been condemned.

1953-1954

america's time capsule

July 27, 1953: More than 100 Arizona peace officers seized virtually every man, woman and child in a raid on the historically polygamous village of Short Creek in the isolated strip country north of the Grand Canyon.

December 16, 1953: A new airplane speed record was achieved by U.S. Air Force Major Charles E. Young, who flew a Bell X-1A rocket-powered plane more than 1,600 mph.

February 23, 1954: Inoculation of school children against polio began for the first time. Phoenix and Tucson were selected as the Arizona areas in which the newly-developed Salk polio vaccine would be tested.

March 1, 1954: An explosion of a hydrogen bomb in the Marshall Islands exceeded all estimates of its power.

May 17, 1954: The U.S. Supreme Court declared racial segregation in public schools to be unconstitutional.

arizona state college
m o m e n t

With the cloud of NCAA probation hanging over the school and the football, basketball and baseball teams struggling through losing seasons, coach Baldy Castillo's track and field team maintained its supremacy in the Border Conference. The Sun Devils, fueled by a strong group of distance runners, rolled up 75 points to 64 2/3 for runner-up Arizona in the conference meet at University Stadium in Tucson. Freshman Dale Winder and sophomore Ted Kiene started the meet with a one-two finish in the mile run, giving the Devils a 10-point lead they never relinquished. Royd Shumway won the 880 in a meet-record time of 1:53.9 and anchored the Sun Devils' record-breaking mile relay team. The title was the second in as many years for Castillo and the seventh in eight years for the Devils. The track team's performance was the source of great pride on campus after the football team finished 4-5-1, the basketball team 5-18 and the baseball team 5-6.

Royd Shumway anchors the Sun Devils' winning mile relay team at the Border Conference Championships in Tucson. (ASU Alumni Association)

A group of athletes known as the "Valiant Volunteers" rescued baseball, which had been dropped by the school as an officially-sanctioned sport for what the administration called a lack of interest. Once students Gay King, Lloyd Fernandez and Phil Keyes organized the team and 30 players tried out for the squad, athletic director Dr. Donald R. Van Petten, found $1,000 to fund the team and named assistant football coach Bob White to coach the group. Eventually, Van Petten announced that baseball would be restored as a full-time sport in 1955. Sophomore shortstop Tom Futch hit three doubles in a game against Williams Air Force Base, tying Charles Dains' school record, which had stood since 1915. Futch, the team captain, batted a resounding .429 to earn Most Valuable Player honors.

ASU LEGEND

Dr. Donald R. Van Petten

Dr. D. R. Van Petten was happily employed as a professor of political science at Arizona State College in the winter of 1951-52 when the campus suddenly became embroiled in turmoil. A Phoenix newspaper revealed that an ASC football player had participated under an assumed name, and NCAA investigators uncovered other irregularities. Football coach Larry Siemering resigned under fire after just one season and athletic director Donn Kinzle also submitted his resignation. University president Grady Gammage, looking for stability as he attempted to restore integrity to the program, turned to Van Petten, who took the job reluctantly. Van Petten carried the double load of teaching and running the athletic department. A quiet man who worked tirelessly to restore order to the athletic program while encouraging healthy growth, Van Petten often was praised by Gammage for his loyalty to the college. Van Petten's appointment initially was for two years, but Gammage talked him into a third year. Under Van Petten's guidance, ASC's two-year NCAA probation was ended six months ahead of schedule. The NCAA said it shortened the sentence because of Van Petten's "corrective action and sound administration." Football coach Clyde B. Smith was named athletic director in December of 1954 and Michigan State backfield coach Dan Devine was hired as head football coach. Van Petten returned to the classroom on a full-time basis after making his mark in Sun Devil sports history.

Dr. Donald R. Van Petten brought stability to the athletic program during times of turmoil. (ASU Media Relations)

SUN DEVIL STAT

• Arizona State was placed on two years' probation by the NCAA for violations the governing body said occurred from 1950 through 1952. Among the violations was the use of a football player who played under an assumed name. The NCAA also said there was evidence that Sun Angel Foundation funds were used to aid athletes from the fall of 1949 through the fall of 1951 without being contributed to and administered by the college.

SUN DEVIL LORE

The school year began with a new academic structure, which had been approved by the Arizona Board of Regents after heated debate the previous May. It provided for ASC's first college, the College of Liberal Arts, with a dean overseeing 14 departments. It also provided for a College of Education, with its own dean. The reorganization was bitterly opposed by University of Arizona factions on the Regents, who feared it would set the stage for ASC to attain university status.

1954-1955

america's time capsule

arizona state college
moment

Basketball coach Bill Kajikawa was named Border Conference Coach of the Year after one of the most miraculous turnarounds in school history. The Sun Devils took a hit before the season started when two stars of the 1953-54 team—center Willard Nobley and forward Dick Daugherty—left school to join the U.S. Army. The Devils staggered out of the blocks, losing 10 of their first 11 games. Almost everyone consigned them to the conference cellar. But the Devils had other ideas. They caught fire down the stretch, winning their last five games to finish 10-14 overall. They ended up tied for third in the conference with an 8-4 league record. The highlight of the season was a pair of victories over rival Arizona—92-74 in Tempe and a 104-103 overtime thriller in the final game of the season in Tucson. It was the first time since the 1944-45 season they had beaten the Wildcats twice in one season. Forward Dave Graybill, who led the Sun Devils with a 17.7 scoring average, earned first-team All-Border Conference honors. Guard Jack Perkins (11.0) was a second-team selection and center Don Weischedel (15.9) was an honorable-mention choice.

Forward Dave Graybill earned All-Conference honors and coach Bill Kajikawa was Coach of the Year in the Border Conference. (ASU Alumni Association)

spotlight

Football coach Clyde Smith had outstanding senior leadership on his club—just not enough of it. Four of the five seniors on the team were named to the Border Conference All-Star team that was assembled to play an All-Star squad from the Skyline Conference in the eighth annnual Salad Bowl game in Phoenix on New Year's Day. Representing the Sun Devils, who lost their last three games to finish 5-5, were quarterback Dick Mackey, halfback Jim Bilton, fullback Jay Smith and tackle Bob Luthcke. Tackle John Jankans, a junior, was the team's only official All-Conference first-team selection. He wasn't eligible for the bowl game, which was restricted to seniors only.

LEGEND

Benny Garcia

L ong before Penn State was known as Linebacker U in college football, Arizona State built a reputation as Javelin U in college track and field circles. Bill Miller in the late 1940s and early 1950s, Benny Garcia in the mid 1950s, Frank Covelli in the early 1960s and Mark Murro in the late 1960s and early 1970s were world-class performers in that event. Garcia, who improved upon Miller's marks, then saw Covelli and Murro surpass his best efforts, was a picture of consistency for Coach Baldy Castillo's teams. Four straight years, from 1953 through 1956, Garcia captured the Border Conference javelin crown, improving from a toss of 213 feet, 1 inch in the conference meet as a freshman to 236-1 as a senior. Garcia broke Miller's school record and uncorked the best throw in the nation by a collegian in 1956 with a toss of 242-7. He fell just three feet short of Les Bitner's national collegiate record. Garcia brought some national recognition to ASC when he won the prestigious Drake Relays in 1955 with a throw of 221-11. He competed in the preliminaries for the 1956 U.S. Olympic Team.

Ben Garcia won four straight Border Conference javelin titles for the Sun Devils. (ASU Alumni Association)

SUN DEVIL STAT

• Night baseball has been a way of life for many years in Tempe, but it wasn't until March 25, 1955, that the Sun Devils played their first night game. Dave Graybill made it a memorable occasion with three home runs and six runs batted in during an 11-2 romp over Wyoming. Graybill was the only player to hit three homers in one game during the early era of Arizona State baseball, from 1907 through 1958. His feat has been matched six times during the modern era.

Sun Devil Lore

C ontinuing a reorganization it began in the spring of 1953, the Arizona Board of Regents gave Arizona State permission to create four colleges—Liberal Arts, Education, Business Administration and Applied Arts and Sciences. The measure passed, 5-4, in a heated session as the University of Arizona faction again voiced loud opposition. The Regents deferred action on renaming the institution.

1955-1956

September 21, 1955: Rocky Marciano defeated Archie Moore to retain the world heavyweight boxing title.

October 4, 1955: The Brooklyn Dodgers beat their cross-town rivals, the New York Yankees, in Game Seven of the World Series.

November 25, 1955: Racial segregation on interstate trains and busses was banned by the Interstate Commerce Commission.

February 6, 1956: The University of Alabama's first black student, Autherine Lucy, was suspended, ending three days of campus violence.

April 19, 1956: American actress Grace Kelly married Prince Rainier of Monaco.

arizona state college
m o m e n t

Gene Mitcham gains a big hunk of yardage against Arizona in the annual Big Game. (ASU Alumni Association)

The annual Big Game was even bigger than usual when Arizona's Wildcats visited Goodwin Stadium in Tempe in the next-to-last game of the football season. The Sun Devils took a 7-1-1 record into the game, needing a victory to clinch the Border Conference championship in coach Dan Devine's first season. Arizona coach Warren Woodson's Wildcats were only 4-4-1 entering the game, but they had played a tough schedule and were coming off consecutive lopsided victories over Montana and New Mexico. Sun Devil fans were confident of victory, but Devine cautioned before the game that the Wildcats had considerably more experience than his Devils. Arizona drew first blood in the opening quarter when star running back Art Luppino galloped 20 yards for a touchdown. Luppino's conversion kick gave the Wildcats a 7-0 lead. ASC halfback Bobby Mulgado scored on a one-yard plunge off tackle in the second quarter, but Mulgado's extra point kick sailed four feet wide to the right and Arizona held a precarious 7-6 lead. That's the way it ended as the defenses took charge in the second half. It was the only conference loss for the Sun Devils, who lost the title to Texas Tech. Wingback Gene Mitcham was cited as ASC's outstanding player for his running, pass receiving and stellar defensive play against the Wildcats. The Sun Devils took out their frustrations the following week in a 39-6 romp over Hawaii in Honolulu. Devine was named Border Conference Coach of the Year.

Folks on campus had been buzzing about Leon Burton, a speedy halfback from Flint, Michigan, who had exhibited some elusiveness during the early part of the 1955 football season. The "Flint Flier" turned a lot of heads when he scored five touchdowns the third game of the season against the San Diego Naval Training Center. In the Border Conference opener against Hardin-Simmons at Goodwin Stadium, Burton turned the buzz into a roar. Burton carried the ball only six times against the Cowboys, but he accumulated an amazing 243 yards, an unbelievable average of 40.5 yards per carry. He uncorked scoring runs of 90, 79 and 67 yards as the Sun Devils put up the highest score ever by a Border Conference opponent against Hardin-Simmons, 69-14. Burton's 243 yards rushing was a school record until Ben Malone ran for 250 yards against Oregon State in 1973. It remains the second-best performance in school history.

ASU LEGEND

Tom Futch

He accomplished more on the baseball diamond than in any other sport, but Tom Futch first had a major impact on Arizona State athletics on the basketball court. As a freshman in the 1952-53 season, Futch played a vital role off the bench as the Sun Devils won nine of their final 11 games to earn a post-season play-off berth. Futch, a flashy guard, was not your typical freshman. He was 22 years old and had four years of high-level service ball behind him when he enrolled at A-State. ASC's Alumni magazine, *The Arizona Statesman*, said Futch "amazed cage fans all over the conference with his blind dribbling and ball handling ability." One of his finest freshman moments came in a Border Conference game against Hardin-Simmons. With the Cowboys fouling in an attempt to get possession, Futch made 14 free throws in the fourth quarter as the Sun Devils won, 78-70.

Futch started the next three seasons, earning All-Conference second-team honors with a 12.3-point scoring average in 1955-56. He also played one year of varsity football in 1955. Baseball, however, was his best sport. He captained the team for four straight years, as a shortstop in 1953 and 1954, an outfielder in 1955 and a third baseman in 1956. He was named Most Valuable Player in '53, '54 and '56 and led the team in hitting as a freshman (.364) and sophomore (.429). He set school records for career doubles (17), triples (8) and home runs (17) in the early era of A-State baseball (pre-1959). He signed a pro contract with the Detroit Tigers following his senior season.

Three-sport athlete Tom Futch was a three-time MVP for the Sun Devil baseball team. (Barry Sollenberger collection)

SUN DEVIL STAT

• Coach Al Onofrio's golf team had the best season ever at that point in the school's history, going 11-3 with a second-place finish in the Border Conference championships. Two of the victories were against members of the prestigious Pacific Coast Conference, UCLA and USC. Top members of the team were Duff Lawrence, Jim Bernard, Stan Hobert, Russell French, Allan French and Hervey Simmons.

Sun Devil Lore

A new $1.3 million student union was opened on February 25, 1956, almost 1 1/2 years after the start of construction. Funds for the building came from a legislative appropriation and from an ambitious fund-raising campaign directed by alumni secretary Jim Creasman. Several prominent Arizonans participated in the drive.

• University president Grady Gammage announced that he had placed a new football stadium at the top of his list of building requests for the college.

1956-1957

arizona state college
m o m e n t

Sun Devil players carry coach Dan Devine off the field following a 20-0 victory over Arizona in Tucson. (ASU Alumni Association)

It took 57 years and 30 meetings, but the Sun Devils finally achieved the ultimate in their football rivalry with Arizona. They shut out the Wildcats, 20-0, in Tucson, after having been a shutout victim 13 times in their first 30 games against the Cats. The Sun Devils won their first seven games, but suffered a 28-0 whipping at the hands of Texas Western the week before the Big Game in Tucson. There was plenty of built-up frustration among the Devils, who had rolled up 404 yards against the Miners and had penetrated the Texas Western 30 yard line eight times without scoring. Most observers figured the Devils would need some trickery to score against the Wildcats, who had a rock-solid defensive line. Instead, the Devils ran right at the Cats, as center Gino Della Libera, guards Ken Kerr and Tom Ford, tackles Bart Jankans and Mike Stanhoff and ends Charlie Mackey and Clancy Osborne opened big holes for quarterback Dave Graybill, halfback Bobby Mulgado and wingback Gene Mitcham, who each scored a touchdown. "Nobody expected us to base our strategy on hitting through the middle, so we did just that," said coach Dan Devine, who was carried off the field by his players following the game. The Sun Devils beat Pacific, 19-6, the following week to cap off a 9-1 season. Devine was named Arizona Coach of the Year by the Phoenix Press Box Association.

spotlight

Coach Al Onofrio's team won the school's second Border Conference golf championship and first since 1935. The Sun Devils made a splash in their first appearance at the NCAA championships with a fifth-place national finish as Duff Lawrence became Arizona State's first golf All-American. ASC's golf resurgence was one of several signs that the tide was beginning to turn after many years of playing second-fiddle to Arizona in all the spring sports except track and field. In addition to beating UA three times in golf, the Devils won the second game of a baseball double header in Mesa, 4-3, to snap a losing streak against the Wildcats that dated back to 1948 and covered 31 straight losses. The Devils even got a break of sorts when favored UA didn't show up for a tennis match in Tempe, even though the match was listed on UA's schedule.

LEGEND

Dave Graybill

In the never-ending debate about who was the greatest all-around athlete in Arizona State's long and colorful history, Dave Graybill's name usually surfaces. He didn't generate the headlines of more-publicized teammates in football and baseball, and his basketball exploits came on teams that had losing records, but it's unlikely any athlete in school history played as prominent a role in three sports at the same time. While teammates Bobby Mulgado and Leon Burton generated most of the attention, Graybill's steady quarterbacking was a major reason the Sun Devils finished 8-2-1 and 9-1 in Coach Dan Devine's first two seasons. Graybill still holds the school career record for best pass completion percentage (.583). In basketball, Graybill led the Devils in scoring as a junior forward (17.7) and as a senior guard (15.0). He was an All-Border Conference first-team selection his junior year. A pitcher/third baseman/outfielder, he led the Sun Devils in batting in 1955 (.369), 1956 (.444) and 1957 (.400) and was the team's leading pitcher with a 7-3 record and 3.16 ERA in 1957. His .392 career batting average was the second highest in the early era (pre 1959) of Arizona State baseball and he was the only player during that 50-year period to hit three home runs in one game. Graybill signed a professional baseball contract with the New York Giants in 1957. He later became a national handball champion. His son, Dave Jr., had a 10-0 pitching record for the 1984 Sun Devil team that finished fourth at the College World Series.

Dave Graybill was one of the most productive three-sport stars in Arizona State athletic history. (ASU Media Relations)

THE sun devil LIST

Highest career pass completion percentage in football

Pct.	Comp-Att	Seasons	Comp-Att
.583	Dave Graybill	1953-56	(130-233)
.582	Todd Hohns	1982-83	(384-660)
.579	Jeff Van Raaphorst	1984-86	(503-868)
.575	John Hangartner	1955-58	(157-273)
.574	Paul Justin	1987-90	(287-500)

SUN DEVIL STAT

• Ned Wulk, who coached Xavier of Ohio to two straight NIT quarterfinal finishes, was named head basketball coach. Wulk succeeded Bill Kajikawa, who resigned at the end of the 1956-57 season. Kajikawa had coached for nine years while carrying a full teaching load. Upon his hiring, Wulk said: "My first goal at Arizona State will be to win a Border Conference championship, and my second goal is to fill those 5,000 seats in the gymnasium."

Sun Devil Lore

Prior to the 1956-57 school year the Arizona Board of Regents approved Arizona State's request to add a school of engineering. At a later meeting, the Regents authorized 10 new master's programs. The school of engineering request was bitterly opposed by University of Arizona supporters on the board, but ASC president Grady Gammage told the Regents that a major electronics corporation had pledged to build a factory in the Phoenix area if ASC offered undergraduate and graduate degrees in engineering. The company later was identified as General Electric, which did build a plant.

1957-1958

September 25, 1957: President Eisenhower sent 1,000 Army paratroopers to Little Rock, Arkansas, to enforce desegregation of Central High School.

October 4, 1957: The Soviet Union launched *Sputnik I*, the first Earth satellite.

October 10, 1957: The Milwaukee Braves beat the New York Yankees in Game 7 of the 54th World Series.

January 31, 1958: *Explorer I*, the first U.S. Earth satellite, was launched from Cape Canaveral, Florida.

March 25, 1958: Sugar Ray Robinson regained the world middleweight boxing title for an unprecedented fifth time, defeating Carmen Basilio.

arizona state college
m o m e n t

As long as folks talk about Arizona State football, the debate will go on about whether the 1957 season was the greatest in the school's history, but there seems little doubt it was the most significant. When the Sun Devils crushed Arizona, 47-7, to wrap up a perfect 10-0 campaign, the celebrations went on for days. And the aftermath was felt a year later at the polls when a measure to change the name of the school to Arizona State University passed by a 2-to-1 margin. Many observers felt the euphoria generated by coach Dan Devine's football squad played a major role in the name-change vote. Quarterback John Hangartner's pinpoint passing and halfback Leon Burton's slashing runs paved the way as the Sun Devils whipped the Wildcats for the second straight year. The Sun Devils finished with their highest national ranking at that point in school history—11th by Associated Press and 13th by United Press International. ASU and Auburn were the only unbeaten, untied major college teams in the nation. Burton led the nation in rushing, setting an NCAA record of 9.62 yards per carry on the way to 1,126 yards. Burton and teammate Bobby Mulgado finished one-two nationally in scoring with 96 and 93 points respectively. The Sun Devils led the nation in scoring (39.7 points per game) and rushing (444.9 yards per game). After the Sun Devils walloped the West's top independent team, College of the Pacific, by a 41-0 score in the next-to-last game, Pacific coach Jack (Moose) Myers said, "Arizona State could have won the Pacific Coast Conference championship with ease."

John Hangartner threw a school-record 14 touchdown passes as the Sun Devils rolled to an unbeaten season. (ASU Media Relations)

SUN DEVIL *spotlight*

When he took the Arizona State basketball coaching job the previous spring, Ned Wulk promised excitement and a Border Conference title. Wulk delivered. The Sun Devils started slowly against a tough schedule that featured the likes of Stanford, Southern California, San Jose State, Pepperdine and Santa Clara, but they closed with nine victories in their last 12 games to finish 13-13. More important, they had an 8-2 Border Conference record, capturing the school's first conference title in Wulk's initial try. They had tried unsuccessfully for 22 years to win the league championship prior to Wulk's arrival. It didn't take long for Wulk's run-and-gun attack to produce points in record numbers. The Devils scored a school record 108 points in the sixth game of the season against Loyola of Los Angeles and hit 107 points against New Mexico Highlands four games later.

ASU LEGEND

Dan Devine

W hen Clyde B. Smith resigned as football coach following the 1954 season and moved to the athletic director's chair, he set out to find a young coaching talent who could take the program to the next level. He found just the ticket in Dan Devine, who had produced an enviable coaching record in the Michigan high school ranks before serving as Biggie Munn's backfield coach at Michigan State. It took Devine a while to get acclimated to the desert landscape, but it didn't take him long to put his imprint on the Arizona State program. His first team produced an 8-2-1 record, losing a 7-6 heartbreaker to rival Arizona in Tucson. His second team went 9-1 and shut out the Wildcats for the first time in school history, 20-0. His third team finished 10-0, crushed Arizona, 47-7, achieved a ranking of 11th nationally and led the nation in rushing and scoring. But little Arizona State, which still hadn't attained university status, didn't have the resources to hold a coach of Devine's obvious talents. He was hired away by Missouri, and later went on to coach fabled Notre Dame and the National Football League's Green Bay Packers. However, Tempe was Devine's favorite stop along the way. At the conclusion of his coaching career, he returned as executive director of the Sun Angel Foundation support group. He remains a strong supporter of ASU athletics.

Dan Devine put Arizona State football on the national map in the 1950s. (ASU Media Relations)

Arizona State's unbeaten football seasons

Season	Record	Coach
1899	3-0	Fred Irish
1903	3-0	Fred Irish
1904	4-0	Fred Irish
1957	10-0	Dan Devine
1970	11-0	Frank Kush
1975	12-0	Frank Kush

SUN DEVIL STATS

• Four Sun Devil pitchers combined for the second no-hitter in school history. Roger Kudron, Don White, John Chavez and Joe Sims teamed up for the gem in a 15-0 victory over Luke Air Force Base.

• Alex Henderson, A-State's sensational sophomore distance runner from Sydney, Australia, set American records in both the two-mile and three-mile runs. Henderson's time of 8:46.3 at the NCAA Championships in Berkeley, California, was the fastest two-mile ever run in the United States. It slashed 11 seconds off the NCAA mark. At the national AAU meet in Bakersfield, California, he beat a tough international field by 30 yards in the three-mile at 13:37.1, smashing the American mark of 13:55.

Sun Devil Lore

D an Devine's resignation to accept the head coaching job at Missouri opened the door for his 28-year-old line coach, Frank Kush, to launch one of the most successful coaching careers in college football history. Kush, who initially indicated he would accompany Devine to Missouri, was paid $10,000 for his initial season at Arizona State. Kush, a former Michigan State All-American, had served as Devine's line coach in all three of Devine's seasons at A-State.

1958-1959

america's time capsule

arizona state college
| m o m e n t

A decade-long dream came to fruition on October 4, 1958, when Sun Devil Stadium opened for business on the north end of campus. College officials had hoped the $1 million stadium, which seated 30,450, would be ready for the September 20 season opener against Hawaii, but construction delays pushed the occasion back two weeks. It was not what you would call a perfect opening. Many in the crowd of 27,000 were tied up in a giant traffic jam and missed the kickoff. A steady rain dampened spirits, and the Sun Devils compounded matters by struggling badly to beat a heavy underdog, West Texas State, 16-13. The occasion was more festive at the official dedication prior to the homecoming game against Texas Western on November 8. Mrs. Lynn Laney, whose husband was a member of the Arizona Board of Regents and chairman of the stadium site selection committee, made it official by breaking against the goal posts a bottle of water collected from Arizona rivers. Laney, a Tempe Normal student at the time, was among those who petitioned the college's administration for improved athletic facilities in 1899. The Sun Devils celebrated the occasion by blanking the Miners, 27-0, a nice tune-up for a 47-0 whipping they would apply to Arizona the next week in Tucson. The Devils won their last five games to finish 7-3 under first-year coach Frank Kush.

Sun Devil Stadium, capacity 30,450, as it looked in the final stages of construction in 1958. (ASU Alumni Association)

No sooner had he made Arizona State basketball a force to be reckoned with than coach Ned Wulk had to start all over again. Wulk lost four of the five starters from the team that won the school's first Border Conference title in 1957-58. Only junior forward Albert Nealey returned. Wulk brought in six junior college players, but he still had to combat a lack of height. Only 6-foot-6 center Billy Pryor was taller than 6-4. The Devils took some early lumps, losing to Wichita State, Tulsa and Houston on a tough road trip, but they then won eight straight and 16 of 17 en route to a 17-9 season that ended with a 78-57 loss to New Mexico State in a Border Conference playoff game at Las Cruces, New Mexico. Nealey (17.7 ppg) led the team in scoring, followed by a pair of junior college transfers at guard, Paul Denham (16.4) and Paul Howard (14.8).

ASU LEGENDS

Leon Burton

I f statistics—and the people who saw him run—are to be believed, Leon Burton was the most explosive runner in the history of Sun Devil football. His 34 rushing touchdowns are one clue. Only Woody Green (39) had more. But the real eye-opener is Burton's average of 8.0 yards per carry for his entire college career—far and away the best in school history. He led the nation in rushing with 1,126 yards as a junior in 1957 and his average of 9.6 yards per carry that year established an NCAA record. He also led the nation in scoring that season with 96 points. If he had been the featured back, he undoubtedly would hold every major school rushing record, but he shared the pigskin with fellow running back Bobby Mulgado for three of his four years.

Leon Burton led the nation in rushing in 1957. (ASU Media Relations)

Bobby Mulgado

H e wrapped up his ASC career in the fall of 1957, but they were still talking about Bobby Mulgado's all-around skills in 1958 and for many years to come. One of just three Sun Devils to have his jersey retired, Mulgado was a classic triple-threat back who starred on both offense and defense. In addition to accumulating 2,003 rushing yards and scoring 21 rushing touchdowns from 1954 through 1957, Mulgado was the team's punter and place kicker. He averaged 19.1 yards on 14 punt returns in 1957, and two of his returns went for touchdowns. He also intercepted six passes in 1957 and returned them a total of 113 yards. He scored 93 points that season, second nationally to teammate Leon Burton's 96. Mulgado also could throw and catch. He was perhaps the most complete football player in school history.

Bobby Mulgado was a classic triple-threat back. (ASU Media Relations)

SUN DEVIL LORE

A rizona State College became Arizona State University in a public vote on the November 1958 general election ballot. The controversial measure, which had been opposed vigorously by University of Arizona supporters, passed by a 2-1 margin after a tireless campaign by A-State backers. It was the first time in American history that a university had been named in a public vote.

SUN DEVIL STAT

• A new era of Arizona State baseball began when athletic director Clyde B. Smith hired Bobby Winkles to run the program and pledged to provide improved administrative support. Winkles, a former infielder in the Chicago White Sox farm system, was provided a new diamond east of Goodwin Stadium. Winkles' first team, which did not have a conference affiliation, compiled a 28-18 record as second baseman John Regoli batted .356 and shortstop Benny Ruiz hit .352.

1959-1960

america's time capsule

arizona state university | m o m e n t

Nolan Jones scored 100 points for the 10-1 Sun Devils. (ASU Media Relations)

Defense was the key as second-year coach Frank Kush's football team rolled to a 10-1 record and captured the Border Conference title with a 5-0 league mark. The Sun Devils held their last five opponents to single-digit scoring, including a 15-9 victory over Arizona. The UA game drew an overflow crowd of 32,300 to Sun Devil Stadium, which been opened just the previous season. It was the largest crowd ever assembled for any event at that point in Arizona history. The encouraging sign for Sun Devil fans was the fact that Kush did it with a sophomore-dominated lineup after the loss of many offensive stars from the 1958 club. "We had no great football players," Kush said at the end of the season. "There were no Leon Burtons, Bob Mulgados, Clancy Osbornes or John Hangartners. But every man gave all he had, and we had quite a season." The only blemish was a 24-15 loss to San Jose State in the fifth game of the season. The Sun Devils fell behind, 21-0, in that game, but scored 15 straight points in the third and fourth quarters to make it a contest. Sophomores Joe Zuger (44.8-yard average) and Nolan Jones (100 points) were among the national leaders all season in punting and scoring.

spotlight

It was a fairly insignificant blip in the long and productive career of Joanne Gunderson, but it was an important moment in the history of the Arizona State women's golf program. In the spring of 1960, Gunderson, better known these days as Joanne Carner, captured the national collegiate championship. She was ASU's first national medalist in men's or women's golf. Gunderson already had won the U.S. Amateur title in 1957. She would win it again in the summer of 1960 and again in 1962, 1966 and 1968 before embarking on a long and productive professional career. She also played on four consecutive U.S. Curtis Cup teams from 1958 through 1964. Gundy, as she was affectionately known, started the ball rolling for coach Betty Graham. Soon ASU was turning out candidates for national honors on a regular basis in women's college golf.

LEGEND

Jesse Bradford

Picture a modern-day college football tackle running the hurdles in track. It's not a pretty thought. It's debatable whether the football player or the hurdles would suffer the most damage. Now consider the legend of Jesse Bradford, certainly one of the most unique athletes ever to compete at Arizona State. Bradford was an All-Border Conference first-team selection as a tackle in 1959 and as a guard in 1960. Bradford also ran track. When an offensive tackle dabbles in track and field, he invariably competes in the shot put or the discus. Not Bradford. He was a hurdler, and a good one. He won the Border Conference 220-yard hurdles title with a time of 23.6 in the spring of 1959. But there's a catch. Bradford wasn't built like the 320-pound tackles of today. "He probably weighed 210," said his coach, Frank Kush. And Bradford wasn't really a tackle. "We called him a tackle because we played an unbalanced line," Kush said. "He really was more of a pulling guard. With our style of offense in those days, we liked to have linemen who could run. He definitely could run."

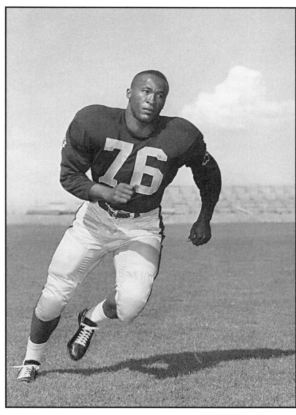

Jesse Bradford was an unlikely hurdles champ. (ASU Media Relations)

SUN DEVIL STAT

• The Sun Devils began making their mark nationally in baseball and basketball under young coaches Bobby Winkles and Ned Wulk. Winkles' baseball team compiled a 32-13 record and cracked the national rankings for the first time in school history, finishing seventh in the final *Collegiate Baseball* rankings. Wulk ran his record against Arizona to 6-0 with his third straight sweep as smooth forward Al Nealey and the explosive guard duo of Larry Armstrong and Paul Howard led the Sun Devils to a 16-7 record and second-place tie in the Border Conference at 7-3.

Sun Devil Lore

University president Grady Gammage died of a heart attack in December of 1959, ending 26 1/2 years on the job. Gammage presided over the school during its greatest period of growth and generally is considered to have been the most influential individual in its development. It was his leadership that played a major role in its designation as a university in 1958.

SUPER LEGENDS

Much thought and research went into the preparation of this Super Legends section. I approached the work with the full realization that readers might not agree with all of the selections and omissions. I wish to emphasize that these selections, as well as the yearly Legends, are strictly the opinion of the author, though I did consult with trusted colleagues from more than 40 years of media associations. I'm sure that if you asked 20 longtime observers of ASU athletics to submit such a list, none would be identical.

The primary emphasis was to recognize coaches and athletes who had significant achievements while at Arizona State, and who had a major impact on the athletic program and the institution. Some went on to greatness in professional athletics. Some did not. But all played a major role in building the athletic program that stands today among the nation's elite.

Among the examples of highly-visible athletes not included in this section are baseball players Reggie Jackson and Barry Bonds. Jackson, a member of Major League Baseball's Hall of Fame, played only one year of baseball and one year of football at ASU. Bonds, a future Hall of Famer, was "only" a second-team All-America selection while at ASU. Charley Taylor was voted into the National Football League Hall of Fame after a brilliant career which saw him retire as the NFL's all-time leading pass receiver. But Taylor, who was surrounded by tremendous talent at ASU, never led the Sun Devils in rushing or receiving.

The era and the sport involved were also factored into the choices for athletes and coaches for this special section. Charlie Haigler, who starred in football more than 100 years ago, perhaps dominated like no other player in school history, but most of his games were against high school teams. Haigler, who played six years at Tempe Normal and four more at University of Southern California, truly was a man among boys. How would he have fared against major college competition? The record of Margaret Klann, who collected 16 national team titles in 21 seasons as archery coach, is remarkable. But where does archery fit into the grand scheme of things?

If the Super Legends section informs, entertains and sparks some debate, then it has served its purpose. There should be no debate, however, over the selection of Bill Kajikawa as Mr. Sun Devil. This one is a slam dunk. In terms of longevity, versatility, congeniality and the honorable way he approached his many duties during five decades at Arizona State, he stands alone. If Bill Kajikawa is not what ASU athletics is all about, he is what it should strive to be all about. All Super Legends photos are courtesy of ASU Media Relations.

Bob Eger

SUPER LEGEND

Senon "Baldy" Castillo

After serving an apprenticeship as an assistant track and basketball coach at Arizona State, Senon "Baldy" Castillo was more than ready to take over the track and field program prior to the 1953 season. An outstanding athlete at Phoenix Union High School and Phoenix College, Castillo assumed a program that already was in good shape, and built it from a regional power to a national force during his 27 years on the job. Castillo, a master recruiter, modestly declines credit for building the program. "Donn Kinzle is the guy who really got it rolling," Castillo said. "He went up to Prescott and brought in cinders for the track, and he recruited some good athletes. I just kept it going." After winning five straight Border Conference championships from 1947 through 1951, Kinzle's last team came up short in 1952. Castillo quickly got the Sun Devils back on track, winning 10 of the 15 events in the 1953 conference meet to capture the league title going away in his first year as head coach. With NCAA probation hanging over the school and the football, basketball and baseball teams struggling through losing seasons, Castillo's crew won its second straight Border Conference crown in 1954, outscoring runner-up Arizona 75 to 64 2/3 on the Wildcats' own track. Castillo's cindermen were heroes on a campus starved for a winner. Castillo recruited throughout the world, and his cast of national and international stars made track and field a hot item in Tempe. Crowds of more than 5,000 turned out for dual meets in the 1960s at Goodwin Stadium on the south end of campus. During his 27-year career from 1953 through 1979, Castillo coached 13 Olympians, 34 All-Americans and 10 NCAA champions. The highlight was the 1977 team that pulled a stunning upset to capture the NCAA team championship at Champaign, Illinois. Aside from the NCAA championship, what stood out in Castillo's career? "We always had good javelin throwers," Castillo said. "Each one was different. Bill Miller, who was one of Kinzle's guys, was like a ballet dancer coming down the lane. Benny Garcia was a good student of it, but he also had power. It just went on and on with guys like Glenn Winningham, Frank Covelli and Mark Murro." Castillo said he got a special kick out of coaching the 1963 mile relay team of Mike Barrick, Henry Carr, Ron Freeman and Ulis Williams, which set a world record of 3:04.5 at the Mount San Antonio Relays in Walnut, California. "That group was fun to coach," he said. "They were extremely talented, but they also worked very hard. And what a great bunch of personalities." Though Castillo's laid-back style was in direct contrast to his tough-as-nails approach, former ASU football coach Frank Kush, one of Castillo's contemporaries, said he admired Castillo's work. "Baldy always had great athletes," Kush said. "They seemed to gravitate to him. He wasn't a demanding coach, but he was very good at helping each athlete develop at his own pace. He knew what had to be done and he did it." Castillo was inducted into the U.S. Track & Field Federation Hall of Fame in December of 2000.

SENON "BALDY" CASTILLO MADE ARIZONA STATE A NATIONAL FORCE IN TRACK AND FIELD. HE COACHED 13 OLYMPIANS, 34 ALL-AMERICANS AND 10 NCAA CHAMPIONS AND LED THE SUN DEVILS TO THE NCAA TEAM TITLE IN 1977.

SUPER LEGEND

Ned Wulk

Ned Wulk made a couple of promises when he arrived at Arizona State from Xavier University of Cincinnati prior to the 1957-58 season: He would make the team a contender in the Border Conference, where the Sun Devils never had won a title since joining the league in 1932. And he would put fans into Sun Devil Gym with his up-tempo brand of basketball. It didn't take Wulk long to deliver. His first team was a modest 13-13 overall, but the Sun Devils finished 8-2 in the Border Conference to capture their first crown. That earned them a spot in the NCAA tournament, where they lost a 72-68 decision to Idaho State in a first-round game in Berkeley, California. But Wulk was just getting started, and the fans began packing the gym. During the next four seasons, before the Border Conference was disbanded, the Sun Devils would win or tie for three league championships and finish second once. They would make a post-season appearance in each of those four years. A move to the Western Athletic Conference—a rugged basketball circuit—proved to be no immediate problem. Wulk's first WAC club went 26-3 overall and 9-1 in league play to capture the conference title. The Sun Devils, who achieved a No. 3 national ranking at one point that season, won a pair of NCAA tournament games before being eliminated by Oregon State one game shy of reaching the Final Four. By the time Wulk's career ended following the 1982 season, the milestones were many. He accumulated a 406-272 record and .599 winning percentage in 25 years as ASU's head coach. When he passed the 400-victory milestone he was one of just four active coaches to win 400 games at the same school. Wulk guided the Sun Devils to 17 winning seasons and nine NCAA Tournament appearances plus two berths in the National Invitational Tournament. His teams were one victory away from a Final Four appearance on three occasions—1961, 1963 and 1975. Wulk was considered an innovator in terms of developing a structured fast-break offense and a full-court zone press on defense. He was widely sought after as a clinic speaker during the height of his career. Amazingly, Wulk was asked to resign in 1982, just one year removed from a 24-4 season and second-place finish (16-2) in the Pac-10. The highly-unpopular move, by an official no longer with the university, remains a topic of discussion among ASU basketball faithful. Wulk, who still attends games regularly and remains a strong supporter of the program, was honored in March of 1999 when the floor of Wells Fargo Arena, formerly the University Activity Center, was named Ned Wulk Court. "I'm overwhelmed," said Wulk, who played a major role in designing ASU's basketball facility and had a 94-24 home record there. "The building means a lot to me. I spent an awful lot of time working on this thing." Wulk also was the architect of the greatest teams in school history, though he said it's impossible to choose his favorite from the 1962-63 team (26-3), the 1974-75 team (25-4) and the 1980-81 club (24-4). "Those are the three that stand out," he said. "They all were different and they all were good. It's hard to compare them because the game changed over the years in terms of the size of the players and everything else."

NED WULK PUT ASU BASKETBALL ON THE MAP DURING A 25-YEAR CAREER THAT SAW HIS TEAMS WIN 406 GAMES AND MAKE NINE NCAA TOURNAMENT APPEARANCES. ASU'S BASKETBALL COURT WAS NAMED IN HIS HONOR IN 1999.

SUPER LEGEND

Frank Kush

Anyone associated with college athletics will tell you that football, and the revene it generates, is the engine that drives most college sports programs. And the man who propelled Arizona State football into the national limelight was a tough coal-miner's son from Pennsylvania named Frank Kush. ASU football already was enjoying success when Kush took over the head coaching job from Dan Devine at the age of 28 in December of 1957. Kush, quite likely the most visible figure in the state's sports history, nurtured the program for 22 years and put his personal stamp on the product. His teams played hard-nosed, physical football and they rarely, if ever, faced an opponent that was better conditioned. "I was coached that way in high school and at Michigan State," said Kush, who was an All-America guard at 175 pounds for the Spartans. "The biggest thing I learned along the way was the importance of fundamentals, and the progress that players could make if they had good coaches." That formula worked beautifully at ASU. When Kush left in the midst of a raging controversy midway through the 1978 season, his teams had compiled a record of 176-54-1, a winning percentage of .764. Nineteen of his 22 teams had winning records and 18 of them won at least seven games. Perhaps most important to ASU fans, Kush's teams won 16 of 21 meetings against rival Arizona, including nine straight from 1965 through 1973. After more than a decade in which ASU had virtually no chance to play in a bowl game because of a lack of recognition, he produced seven bowl teams, six of which were victorious. His 1970 team went 11-0, including a 48-16 Peach Bowl victory over North Carolina that produced the first Top-10 ranking in school history, No. 6 in the final Associated Press poll. Kush's 1975 team capped a 12-0 season with a 17-14 Fiesta Bowl victory over Nebraska that propelled the Sun Devils to a No. 2 national ranking. Kush produced 38 All-Americans and sent 128 players into professional football, 10 of them first-round draft picks. Kush, a member of the College Football Hall of Fame, said he never viewed ASU as a stepping stone to more lucrative opportunities. "I felt very comfortable coaching college football," he said. "The greatest gratification that I got out of it was the satisfaction of seeing players develop socially, academically and athletically—to see kids from a tough background mature into good citizens." It all came crashing down for Kush prior to the third game of the 1978 season when he was dismissed by Athletic Director Fred Miller in the wake of accusations that he struck a player during a game the previous season. It took nearly two decades for emotionsto settle enough for ASU to honor Kush by naming the Sun Devil Stadium playing field in his honor in September of 1996. Kush, who coached the Baltimore Colts of the NFL, the Hamilton Tiger-Cats of the Canadian Football League and the Arizona entry in the United States Football League after leaving ASU, lives in Tempe and was hired in July of 2000 as a special assistant to the Athletic Director. If he were coaching today, would his tough-guy approach still work? "There's no question in my mind that it would," Kush said. "I put on a clinic every year in Alaska, and I do the same things I've always done. If a kid gets me mad, I get all over his butt."

QUITE LIKELY THE MOST VISIBLE FIGURE IN THE HISTORY OF ARIZONA SPORTS, FRANK KUSH BUILT A DYNASTY IN HIS 22 SEASONS AS HEAD FOOTBALL COACH AT ARIZONA STATE. HE IS A MEMBER OF THE COLLEGE FOOTBALL HALL OF FAME.

SUPER LEGEND

Bobby Winkles

In the summer of 1958, Bobby Winkles, a slick-fielding, light-hitting middle infielder in the Chicago White Sox farm system, decided to make a career move. "I was hitting about .230 in Triple-A and Louie Aparicio was playing shortstop and Nellie Fox was playing second base for the White Sox," Winkles recalls. "They're both in the Hall of Fame." Winkles, who had a master's degree from the University of Colorado, decided it was time to launch his coaching career. He heard of an opening at Arizona State, and got word to athletic director Clyde B. Smith that he was interested. Smith, on his way to go trout fishing, called him from Globe and offered him the job for an annual salary of $6,000. Winkles informed Smith that he made $8,700 in Triple-A baseball and supplemented his income by playing winter ball in Venezuela. Winkles said Smith replied: "Bobby, I'm going to Cibecue to fish. They might be biting. I'll give you $6,200." Winkles took it. That was it. No formal interview. A brief phone conversation with Smith and Winkles packed up his wife, Ellie, and baby daughter and hit the highway from Indianapolis to Tempe. "We were coming down old Route 66 from Indianapolis and I saw a sign that said Arizona State College," Winkles recalled. "I walked onto the football field, where they were having practice, and said, 'Hey, I need to see Clyde Smith. I'm your new baseball coach.' They said, 'Son, you're about 125 miles too far north.' Once he found the right campus—in Tempe, not Flagstaff—Winkles was in for another surprise. He mentioned to Smith that he hadn't spotted a baseball field. "Oh, I forgot to tell you—you've got to build one," Smith said. The field, on the south end of campus, was finished just one week before the 1959 season opener. Armed with 20 tuition waivers, which included fees and books but not room and board, Winkles began rebuilding a program that had been disbanded briefly just a few years earlier. That program has produced five national championships—three under Winkles and two under Jim Brock—and sent more players to the major leagues than any other in college baseball. Winkles' first order of business was to end Arizona's domination in the in-state rivalry. His second was to get the Sun Devils into post-season competition. He did both, beating the Wildcats with regularity and advancing to the College World Series for the first time in 1964. Under his guidance, the Sun Devils won national titles in 1965, 1967 and 1969. Winkles coached the Devils for 13 seasons before leaving prior to the 1972 campaign to accept a coaching position with the California Angels. That led to major league managerial positions with the Angels and Oakland Athletics. In addition to compiling a 524-173 coaching record, Winkles turned out a succession of superstars, including Reggie Jackson, Rick Monday and Sal Bando. His many accomplishments earned him selection into the American Baseball Coaches Hall of Fame. The playing field at Packard Stadium was named Bobby Winkles Field in March of 2001.

BOBBY WINKLES LAUNCHED THE MODERN ERA OF BASEBALL AT ARIZONA STATE IN 1959. BEFORE HE LEFT FOR A MAJOR LEAGUE COACHING POSITION PRIOR TO THE 1972 SEASON, HIS SUN DEVILS HAD CAPTURED THREE NATIONAL CHAMPIONSHIPS AND HAD PRODUCED A SUCCESSION OF MAJOR LEAGUE STARS.

SUPER LEGEND

Jim Brock

Jim Brock stepped into a no-win situation when he replaced a local legend, Bobby Winkles, as Arizona State's baseball coach prior to the 1972 season. But Brock won. And won. And won. When his brilliant career came to an untimely end at the end of the 1994 season, he had won 1,100 games, the seventh-highest total by an NCAA Division I coach at that point in history. Brock's Sun Devil teams won national titles in 1977 and 1981. His teams won 13 NCAA regional or district championships and finished third or better 10 times at the College World Series. Four times he was named national coach of the year—by the NCAA in 1977 and 1981, *The Sporting News* in 1984 and *Baseball America* in 1988. He is the only coach ever to win national championships at three major levels—American Legion, Junior College and NCAA Division I. During his 23 years at Arizona State, Brock sent 175 players into professional baseball—an average of almost eight per year. Brock's volatile nature was exceeded only by his limitless sense of humor. He undoubtedly was the most-quoted coach in college baseball during much of his tenure. He was still firing one-liners late in the 1994 season, as he battled the colon and liver cancer that would take his life one day after the conclusion of the College World Series. Though his strength was waning, Brock didn't miss a conference game that season. He led his team through a tough regional tournament at Knoxville, Tennessee, and was in the dugout when the Sun Devils beat Miami, 4-0, in their Series opener. Speaking in little more than a whisper, he gave his team an inspirational pep talk after a scoreless first inning when he sensed that the Sun Devils were flat. "You can make an assumption that you'll be up because it's the College World Series," Brock said. "But you spend so much emotion in the final game of the regional that you sometimes have to find a way to regain that emotion." On his way to Rosenblatt Stadium for the second game of the Series, Brock's condition worsened. The Sun Devils lost to Oklahoma, 4-3, in 11 innings. Brock was airlifted from Omaha to a Mesa hospital shortly before game No. 3. His Sun Devils slammed five home runs to eliminate top-seeded Miami, 9-5, and present him with his 1,100th coaching victory. Oklahoma later eliminated ASU from the series and went on to capture the title. One day later, Brock died at the age of 57. Even Brock's fiercest competitors were lavish in their praise upon his passing. "He was one of the legends of our coaching group," Arizona coach Jerry Kindall said. "We had to take a competitive stance on the field, but first and foremost he was a friend." Stanford coach Mark Marquess called Brock "probably the greatest competitor I've ever faced." One of Brock's most intense rivals, USC coach Mike Gillespie, said: "I was continually amazed at who he was, what he was and what he accomplished. Not only was he a tough, tough coach—his teams were good every year—but he was a notable spokesperson for college baseball." Brock was inducted posthumously into the College Baseball Hall of Fame in January of 1995.

JIM BROCK REPLACED A LEGEND—BOBBY WINKLES—THEN BECAME ONE HIMSELF, WINNING TWO NATIONAL CHAMPIONSHIPS AND FOUR NATIONAL COACH OF THE YEAR AWARDS IN HIS 23 YEARS AS ARIZONA STATE'S HEAD BASEBALL COACH. HIS TEAMS FINISHED THIRD OR BETTER 10 TIMES AT THE COLLEGE WORLD SERIES.

SUPER LEGEND

Wilford "Whizzer" White

The year was 1947. World War II was in the history books. It was a time for rebuilding throughout America, including college athletic programs that had been decimated by the flood of young men and women from the campuses to engage in more urgent pursuits. Arizona State College was no exception. The Bulldogs, who would become the Sun Devils in November of 1946, did not field football teams from 1943 through 1945. When they resumed the sport, the results were not good. ASC was 2-7-2 in 1946 under coach Steve Coutchie, who resigned after the season. University president Grady Gammage hired a highly-regarded young coach named Ed Doherty, who had been an assistant to the legendary Frank Leahy at Boston College and Notre Dame. One of Doherty's first missions was to recruit an explosive running back named Wilford White from nearby Mesa. It was not a slam dunk, though there wasn't much danger of losing White to rival Arizona. White had watched Arizona administer a 67-0 whipping to ASC in the second game of the 1946 season, and he wasn't impressed by the fact that the Wildcats' starters were still in the game in the closing moments. "At that point I decided that I wasn't going to Arizona," White recalls, "though I still hadn't decided on Arizona State." The University of Southern California was hot in pursuit of White, but the big competition was from Tennessee. "The General, Bob Neyland, was their coach," White said. "I went back there to visit and they sent one of their coaches to camp at my house. They offered me all kinds of nice things, including a car. But I kept thinking, 'it's just six miles down the road to Arizona State.' I didn't want to go far away from home because I had never been away from home." White's decision to stay at home was a turning point in Arizona State's athletic fortunes. His electric style put people in the stands, and the Sun Devils improved from 4-7 to 5-5 to 7-3 to 9-2 in his four years there. He rushed for 539 yards as a sophomore, 935 as a junior and a nation-leading 1,502 yards as a senior. His 1,502 rushing yards, 22 touchdowns and 136 points in 1950 still stand as school records. White, who sometimes traversed 40 yards to gain 15, was a perfect fit for the offensive schemes of Doherty, who was nicknamed "The Brain." "We ran what we called the Lazy-T Formation, but it really was the I Formation," White said. "Doherty really was ahead of his time with his innovations. We just thought they were kooky ideas of his at the time. Later on we realized what an innovator he was." White said he particularly enjoyed lopsided victories over Arizona (34-7 and 47-13) his junior and senior seasons, but his most impressive performance was in a 48-21 victory over Idaho in the final regular-season game of the 1950 season. He accounted for seven touchdowns, five rushing, in that game. "That was a big game because Idaho was in the Pacific Coast Conference then," White said. "They called time out and took me out of the game near the end. It was a great day, but a sad time. They got a picture of me sitting on the bench boo-hooing at the end."

WILFORD "WHIZZER" WHITE'S EXCITING STYLE WAS JUST THE TICKET FOR ARIZONA STATE AS IT ATTEMPTED TO REBUILD ITS FOOTBALL FORTUNES AFTER WORLD WAR II. HE LED THE NATION IN RUSHING WITH 1,502 YARDS IN 1950 AND SET SCHOOL SINGLE-SEASON RUSHING AND SCORING RECORDS THAT STILL STAND.

SUPER LEGEND

Joe Caldwell

Some other players have come along to put up bigger numbers, but none have had the impact on Arizona State's basketball program that Jumpin' Joe Caldwell did in the early 1960s. Originally bound for UCLA, Caldwell was literally kidnapped from a dormitory in Los Angeles by ASU assistant basketball coach Fanny Markham, assistant football coach Gene Felker and booster Jose-Maria Burruel and driven to Tempe. "When we were driving, I thought, 'Hell, if somebody wants you so bad that they'll go through all that stuff, maybe that's where I should be,'" Caldwell would say many years later. Caldwell arrived at ASU at a time when the Sun Devils were just starting to attract some attention under innovative head coach Ned Wulk. After starring on a legendary freshman team in 1960-61, Caldwell was the marquee player as the Sun Devils posted records of 23-4, 26-3 and 16-11 the next three seasons and made three straight NCAA tournament appearances. Caldwell is the only player in ASU history to earn first-team All-Conference honors on three occasions—in the Border Conference in 1962 and the Western Athletic Conference in 1963 and 1964. Granted, Caldwell wasn't the whole show. He was surrounded by such talented teammates as Tony Cerkvenik, Art Becker, Dennis Dairman, Gary Senitza and Raul Disarufino. But Caldwell clearly was on center stage. His emotional, charismatic style, his spectacular leaping ability and his knack for shutting down the other team's star player made the 6-foot-5 forward from John C. Freemont High in Los Angeles a huge crowd favorite. "Joe did things that simply weren't being done by other players," Wulk said. "He clearly was ahead of his time." Fans crowded into Sun Devil Gym well before tipoff with hopes that Caldwell would treat them to one of his breathtaking reverse dunks during warm-ups. Caldwell played a starring role for the U.S. team that captured the gold medal in the 1964 Tokyo Olympics. The Detroit Pistons of the National Basketball Association made Caldwell the No. 2 pick of the 1964 draft. The Pistons traded him to the then St. Louis Hawks the following season, and he blossomed into a full-fledged NBA star after the Hawks moved to Atlanta. His most productive season was the 1969-70 campaign, when he averaged 21.1 points, 4.9 rebounds and 3.5 assists for the Hawks. In 1970, Caldwell signed a contract believed to be the richest in all of professional sports at the time with the Carolina Cougars of the fledgling American Basketball Association. He has been involved in a decades-long legal battle over money he claims was owed him from his ABA days. A Phoenix-area resident since the end of his playing career, Caldwell returned to school and obtained his degree from ASU in 1997.

JUMPIN' JOE CALDWELL'S SPECTACULAR LEAPING ABILITY AND CHARISMATIC STYLE HELPED PUT ASU BASKETBALL ON THE MAP IN THE EARLY 1960s. HE WENT ON TO STAR IN THE OLYMPICS AND IN THE NATIONAL BASKETBALL ASSOCIATION AND AMERICAN BASKETBALL ASSOCIATION.

Henry Carr

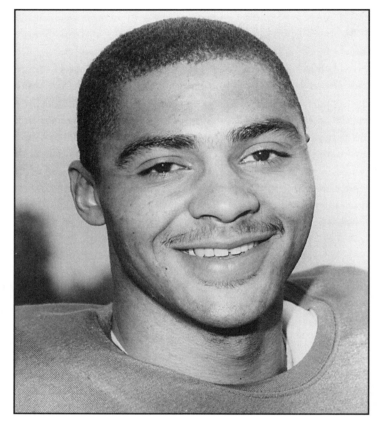

Henry Carr came to Arizona State on a football scholarship, and he went on to play in the National Football League. But it was through track and field that he gave the university more international exposure than money could buy. Billed as the fastest man in the world during his prime, he still is considered by many longtime observers of ASU sports to be the most gifted athlete ever to wear the Maroon and Gold. Carr, who was voted into the National Track and Field Hall of Fame in December of 1997, arrived at ASU almost by accident. Iowa football coach Forrest Evashevski had stashed Carr at a junior college in Iowa, but then found himself unable to offer Carr a scholarship. Evashevski didn't want to compete against Carr in the Big Ten, so he called his old buddy, Arizona State football coach Frank Kush, and asked if Kush could use a halfback who ran like the wind. "I'd never seen Henry play, but I took Evy's word," Kush said. "I flew back to Iowa and went to the junior college and ended up bringing Henry back with me." Though Carr had his moments both as a halfback and defensive back at ASU, the real beneficiary of his talent was Sun Devil track coach Baldy Castillo. "He was just amazing," Castillo said. "Everybody was worried about his start. I worried about it too, for about a week. But after I found out how he could run, I quit being concerned." During the first week of the outdoor season in Carr's initial year at ASU, 1963, he ripped off a time of 20.4 seconds at Goodwin Stadium's old cinder track, knocking one-tenth of a second off the world record for 220 yards around a turn. There was a problem, however—no wind gauge, meaning the record couldn't be submitted for certification. Carr said he recalls Castillo telling him, "Henry, you're just going to have to go out and do it again." No problem. Four days later Carr blistered the 220 in 20.3, knocking two-tenths off the world record. This time, a wind gauge was in place. Later that spring Carr teamed with Mike Barrick, Ron Freeman and Ulis Williams to set a world record of 3:04.5 in the mile relay at the Mount San Antonio Relays in California. That set the track and field world on its ear because of the improbability of assembling four quarter milers on one college campus capable of breaking a relay record typically set by national teams in international competition. In the 1964 Tokyo Olympics, Carr won the individual gold medal in the 200 meters and anchored the 4X400 meter relay team that captured the gold in the world record time of 3:00.7. Castillo, who attended the Olympics, said Carr was a full-fledged international hero in Tokyo. Carr, a three-time All-American in track at Northwestern High in Detroit, now lives in the Detroit suburb of Redford. Though his Olympic memories remain vivid, he said his favorite recollections are of his days at ASU, where he won or tied for three national titles and set world records in three events. "I look back at those Arizona State days very fondly," he said. "We were kids, naïve kids. Those were the innocent days."

HENRY CARR WON OR TIED FOR THREE NATIONAL TITLES AND SET WORLD RECORDS IN THREE EVENTS AT ARIZONA STATE. BILLED AS THE WORLD'S FASTEST HUMAN IN HIS PRIME, HE IS CONSIDERED BY MANY THE MOST GIFTED ATHLETE IN ASU HISTORY.

SUPER LEGEND

Danny White

Danny White had some things to recommend him as he launched his athletic career at Arizona State. First and foremost were the bloodlines. He was the son of legendary Sun Devil running back Wilford "Whizzer" White. And there was a solid and varied high school athletic career at Westwood High in Mesa, where he starred in four sports. But there was little to suggest that he would become the greatest quarterback in ASU football history and go on to play 15 seasons of professional football, 13 with what then was America's Team, the Dallas Cowboys. He was inducted into the National Football Foundation and College Hall of Fame in 1997. And in December of 1999, *The Arizona Republic* named him Arizona's Greatest Athlete of the 20th century. "I was a baseball player," said White, still a part of the Arizona sports scene as coach of the Arizona Rattlers of the Arena Football League. "I wasn't even all-state in high school as a football player. I was all-state in basketball, baseball and track." Arizona State football coach Frank Kush saw promise in White, but there was a problem. "Kush didn't have any scholarships left to give me," White said. "He talked Bobby Winkles into giving me a baseball scholarship." White had given Brigham Young University an oral commitment, but Kush and Winkles teamed up and convinced him to become a Sun Devil. White's first taste of ASU football on the freshman team in 1970 hardly signaled the greatness to come. "We had six freshman quarterbacks and I broke my arm," White said. "I think I started one game." A turning point came during spring practice following White's freshman season. "I threw a pass to the tight end and it hit the ground in front of him," White said. "Kush came over and ripped me across the helmet—I don't know how he didn't break his hand. He said, 'You weak-armed so-and-so—I ought to fire the coach who recruited you.' He didn't hurt me, but he shocked me, and after the shock wore away, anger kind of set in. I became determined to prove to him that he was wrong about me." The next defining moment in White's career came just before the sixth game of the 1971 season at New Mexico. White had been battling Grady Hurst for the starting job, but a shoulder separation had set White back and Kush was undecided all week about who would start against the Lobos. As the opening kickoff was in the air, Kush walked up to White and said, "You're starting." White proceeded to throw six touchdown passes, five in the first half, and a legend was born. Before his ASU career was over he would lead the Sun Devils to records of 11-1, 10-2 and 11-1 and Fiesta Bowl victories over Florida State, Missouri and Pittsburgh. He would set seven NCAA passing records and earn recognition from *Sports Illustrated* as the second-best college quarterback of all time behind BYU's Steve Young. "It almost seems like someone or something was guiding me through all that," White said. "It was a matter of being in the right place at the right time with the right coach and the right people all around me. It seems like the stars just lined up."

DANNY WHITE CAME TO ASU ON A BASEBALL SCHOLARSHIP AND PROCEEDED TO SET THE COLLEGE FOOTBALL WORLD ON ITS EAR. HE SET SEVEN NCAA RECORDS AND LED THE SUN DEVILS TO THREE FIESTA BOWL VICTORIES IN HIS THREE YEARS AS A STARTER, EARNING INDUCTION INTO THE NATIONAL FOOTBALL FOUNDATION AND COLLEGE HALL OF FAME.

SUPER LEGEND

Phil Mickelson

Few individuals in the history of college athletics have dominated their sport like golfer Phil Mickelson during his ASU career in the late 1980s and early 1990s. The Sun Devils knew they were getting a good one when he arrived at ASU from San Diego after a brilliant junior career, but few could have predicted the spectacular success he would enjoy in the collegiate ranks. He won three tournaments and captured the NCAA individual title as a freshman in 1989—one of just five players in history to win the NCAA crown as a frosh. As a sophomore in 1990, he successfully defended his NCAA title, joining Ben Crenshaw as the only golfers to win the NCAAs as a freshman and sophomore. He also won the U.S. Amateur, becoming only the second golfer, along with Jack Nicklaus (1961), to win the NCAA title and U.S. Amateur in the same season. He slipped to a tie for fourth at the 1991 NCAA tourney, but it hardly was a down year for Mickelson. He finished in the top 10 in all 11 tournaments he entered and stunned the pro golf world by winning the Tucson Northern Telecom Open. Only 20, he was just the fourth amateur at the time to have captured a PGA Tour event. He also made the cut at the U.S. Open, Masters and British Open, finishing as the low amateur in the U.S. Open and the Masters. His strong finishes against pro competition fueled speculation that Mickelson might leave school early to join the Tour. That talk had been going on since his freshman year, but true to his word he stayed for four seasons and obtained a psychology degree in 1992. As a senior in 1992 Mickelson became only the second golfer in history to win three NCAA titles. The other was Crenshaw in 1971, '72 and '73. Mickelson destroyed the field at the NCAA tournament in Albuquerque, tying the NCAA record with a 17-under-par performance. He is one of just three players in history to be named a first-team All-American all four years of his college career. He won the Nicklaus Award, based on tournament finishes, three times. He also captured the Haskins Award, voted by college coaches, three times. The Sun Devils finished fifth, first, third and second at the NCAAs during his four years. Though he made pro golf wait, Mickelson wasted little time establishing himself once he joined the Tour. Midway through the 2000 season he had won 16 Tour events and had represented the United States in two Walker Cups, three Ryder Cups, four Presidents Cups and one Dunhill Cup. His best years on the Tour were 1996 and 2000. He won four tournaments and finished second on the money list both years. He was second on the 2001 money list when this book went to press.

PHIL MICKELSON DOMINATED COLLEGE GOLF IN THE LATE 1980s AND EARLY 1990s, WINNING THREE NCAA CHAMPIONSHIPS AND EARNING ALL-AMERICA HONORS FOUR TIMES. HE WON A PGA TOUR EVENT, THE NORTHERN TELECOM OPEN IN TUCSON, AS AN ASU JUNIOR IN 1991.

SUPER LEGEND

Jake Plummer

He arrived at Arizona State as a skinny kid from Boise, Idaho, with a flair for flinging a football but not a lot of glossy credentials in comparison to the so-called big-time quarterback prospects from around the nation. By the time he left, he still was somewhat less than a robust physical specimen, but he had rewritten the school's record books and led the Sun Devils to the doorstep of a national championship. Jake "The Snake" Plummer showed up at a time when the ASU program was in the doldrums. He took some lumps in the early going, enduring seasons of 6-5, 3-8 and 6-5 his first three years in Tempe. But he learned some lessons along the way, and with a supporting cast of talented teammates, lifted the Sun Devils to a magical season in 1996. The Sun Devils served notice that they were something special when they stunned top-ranked Nebraska, 19-0, in the third game of the season before a frenzied crowd in Tempe. They scored improbable victories over Washington (45-42), UCLA (42-34) and Southern California (48-35 in two overtimes) along the way, while rolling up an 11-0 regular-season record. Thanks to some late-game heroics by Plummer, the Sun Devils appeared to have Ohio State beat in the Rose Bowl. Plummer's 11-yard touchdown run with 1:40 to play gave ASU a 17-14 lead. But the Buckeyes drove 65 yards in 12 plays to sore the winning touchdown with 19 seconds remaining and knock the Sun Devils out of the national championship picture. The Sun Devils finished fourth in the final Associated Press rankings. Plummer, who placed third in the Heisman Trophy balloting, received his nickname because of the way he repeatedly slithered out of the grasp of would-be tacklers. Ironically, snakes are far from his favorite thing. "It's kind of funny that they call me 'the snake,'" he said, "I like dogs and cats, but I hate snakes." Plummer, who admitted he sometimes was amazed at watching his escape act on film, said his slender build made such tactics necessary. "I had to become snakelike to stay alive," he said. "Sometimes I watch film after a game and go, 'Wow, how did I get out of that one.'" ASU coach Bruce Snyder often tells the story of how he ruined his best pair of shoes pushing his rental car out of a snowbank in Boise while recruiting Plummer, who also was considering Washington State. "I kept asking myself if I really knew what I was doing, ruining my shoes and getting my clothes wet to chase after this skinny kid, not knowing whether he was any good," Snyder said. Plummer was good, all right. By the time he hung up his cleats and moved on to the Arizona Cardinals of the National Football League, Plummer had established himself as ASU's career leader for passes completed (632), passing yardage (8,827) and touchdown passes (65). He beat Danny White's school record by one in the latter category. In a conference known for prolific passers, Plummer finished third on the Pac-10's all-time list for career touchdown passes and fourth in career passing yards. His third-place finish in the Heisman Trophy balloting was the best ever by an ASU player. Tailback Woody Green finished eighth and White ninth in 1973.

JAKE "THE SNAKE" PLUMMER TOOK SOME LUMPS IN HIS EARLY YEARS, BUT HE EVOLVED INTO A MASTER QUARTERBACK WHO REWROTE ASU'S FOOTBALL RECORD BOOK AND TOOK THE SUN DEVILS TO THE DOORSTEP OF THE NATIONAL CHAMPIONSHIP.

MR. SUN DEVIL
Bill Kajikawa

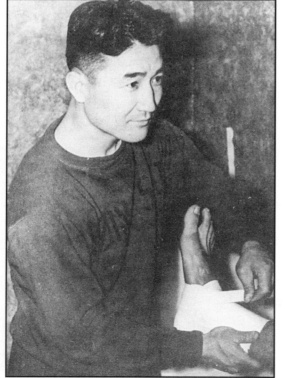

He was a gifted athlete, but you won't find him on any All-America teams. He had a passion for coaching and teaching, but his won-lost records weren't particularly eye-catching. But when it came time to pinpoint one individual as the centerpiece for this book—Mister Sun Devil—it was no contest. The selection of Bill Kajikawa is beyond debate. Legendary football coach Frank Kush, in his succinct style, perhaps puts it best: "Bill Kajikawa epitomizes what Sun Devil athletics is all about."

Kajikawa, the son of a barber, was born in Oxnard, California, and moved to Phoenix with his family in 1929. He immediately launched an outstanding athletic career at Phoenix Union High School. He still remembers how he was "recruited" to Arizona State Teacher's College in the summer of 1933. "One day, after we had graduated from high school, a few of us were hanging around in downtown Phoenix—about First Street and Washington—just kind of looking around for a job, but there weren't any jobs," Kajikawa said. "Vern Tuckey, the student body president at Arizona State, and Tuffy Griffin, the football captain, came by and asked us if we would like to go to school. We said, 'Yes, that sounds like a nice opportunity,' so that's how we got started. They brought me to campus to get registered. The fellow on the athletic board said, 'You're kind of small, aren't you? I'm afraid you're going to get hurt.' I said, 'Well, I'll take my chances.'"

Kajikawa, a 140-pound halfback, played three years of varsity football and three years of baseball before launching a coaching career that would span five decades. "I played basketball my freshman year, but I was kind of short and I realized that they had other boys who could play better," Kajikawa said. The college environment was much different than it is today. "There were no free rides in those days," Kajikawa said. "We were given a scholarship, but we had to work for it. We worked an average of three hours a day. During that period I think just about every student had some kind of job. It was during the depression and very few parents had the resources to send their children to school. Some of the people who were picking cantaloupes in the morning were paid about 10 or 15 cents an hour. If you worked 10 hours, that was $1.50. It's a relative thing. Gasoline, for instance, was about 5 cents a gallon." Kajikawa said his work experience was varied. "I had various jobs, sweeping the streets on campus, watering the fields, dusting the books and the tables in the library. At one time I was a carpenter's helper. I also worked with the plumbers, threading pipes. Another time I was assigned to Bob Svob, who was in charge of the gardens on campus."

Upon graduation from Arizona State in 1937, Kajikawa began coaching the freshman football team, a position he would hold under nine coaches. He also coached varsity basketball from 1948 to 1957 and served as baseball coach at various times for seven seasons between 1940 and 1952. During World War II, Kajikawa interrupted his coaching career to serve with distinction in the U.S. Army's 442nd Regimental Combat Team, 522nd Field Artillery Battalion, in Italy, France and Germany. His outfit, manned entirely by Japanese Americans, was the Army's most decorated combat unit.

Kajikawa said football was his favorite sport. "My big joy was working with the freshman teams," he said. "We had a new crop every year. Many would get homesick. Most were high school stars, and you had to temper that. My wife, Margaret, helped in many ways. We used to have boys over to the house, which you can't do now." His favorite era? "Good times, of course, are related to winning," he said. "That made the Kush era very enjoyable. It was nice to see the program grow and receive first regional, then national, recognition." Kush said Kajikawa was the backbone of the football program. "To me, he was the father of Sun Devil football," Kush said. "The guy was fantastic with our kids. He had a great rapport with them. He made them feel like they were home. He would help them deal with their homesickness and all the other problems that freshmen have. He was one of the great assets of our program."

The man who has impacted the lives of hundreds of Arizona State athletes said he learned much of his coaching and life-skills philosophy from former ASC football and basketball coach Rudy Lavik. "I have to give Coach Lavik a lot of credit," he said. "He sort of tutored me along in the early days. He had very high standards. I've tried to be like him. He was very instrumental in me joining the staff, and he helped me along the way."

Kajikawa received his bachelor's degree from Arizona State in 1937 and his master's in 1948. He was awarded an honorary doctor of laws degree in 1989. He was inducted into the Arizona Basketball Hall of Fame in 1968 and the ASU Hall of Distinction in 1982. He has received countless honors for community service. His daughter, Dr. Christine K. Wilkinson, is Vice President for Student Affairs at ASU. She served as interim athletic director in 1995-96 and in the spring of 2000. In 1995, ASU's football practice field was named The Bill Kajikawa Practice Facility in his honor. "I consider that a special honor," he said. "It means so much more when your own school honors you. You might receive an honor elsewhere, but when your own school recognizes you, it's special, special, special."

BILL KAJIKAWA'S PLAYING AND COACHING CAREER AT ARIZONA STATE SPANNED FIVE DECADES. FORMER FOOTBALL COACH FRANK KUSH SAYS KAJIKAWA "EPITOMIZES WHAT SUN DEVIL ATHLETICS IS ALL ABOUT."

SUPER LEGEND

Joanne Gunderson

The name Joanne Gunderson might not ring a bell with the modern Arizona State sports fan, particularly one who has come aboard the Sun Devil bandwagon in recent years. But, along with diver Patsy Willard, the former ASU golf star was a pioneer in terms of bringing national and international recognition to the school's female sports programs. For the past three decades Gunderson has been a cornerstone of the Ladies Professional Golf Tour under her married name, Joanne Carner. She is affectionately known as Big Mama on the LPGA Tour, but she was best known as The Great Gundy in her amateur days. It all started for Gunderson at the age of 10 in her hometown of Kirkland, Washington. She won the first major tournament she entered—the Washington State Championship—at the age of 14. She won the Western Juniors at the age of 16 and the National Juniors at 17. When she came to ASU to play for coach Betty Graham in 1957, she was the first woman in the United States to receive a golf scholarship. She more than earned her scholarship money, capturing the women's National Collegiate Championship in 1960, starting a string of successes by ASU women's golfers that continues to this day. Carner totally dominated women's amateur golf in the 1960s. She won a record five U.S. Amateur titles and was ranked the top female amateur in the U. S. five years by *Golf Digest*. She played on four U.S. Curtis Cup teams. She is the only woman to have won the USGA Girls Junior, U.S. Women's Amateur and U.S. Women's Open championships. Though her ASU career ended in 1961, she did not turn professional until 1970. She won an LPGA event—the Burdine's Invitational—as an amateur in 1969. No amateur has won an LPGA event since. She turned pro in 1970 and promptly earned LPGA Rookie of the Year honors. She has won 42 LPGA events and has captured the Vare Trophy for low scoring average five times. She has won three LPGA Player of the Year awards. She was inducted into the LPGA Hall of Fame in 1982 and the World Golf Hall of Fame in 1985. She is the oldest woman to win an LPGA event, at the age of 46 in 1985. A popular speaker because of her legendary sense of humor, Gundy has had a variety of interests over the years. Her college coach, Graham, said in a 1961 interview: "Even though she was a physical education major, Gundy minored in art—and she was darn good at it, too." For many years, fishing has been a passion. She lives in Palm Beach, Florida, and still plays about 10 PGA events a year.

FOR THREE DECADES, JOANNE GUNDERSON HAS BEEN KNOWN AS BIG MAMA ON THE LPGA TOUR UNDER HER MARRIED NAME OF CARNER. BEFORE THAT SHE DOMINATED WOMEN'S AMATEUR GOLF AS THE GREAT GUNDY. THE FIRST WOMAN IN THE UNITED STATES TO RECEIVE A GOLF SCHOLARSHIP, SHE WON A NATIONAL COLLEGIATE CHAMPIONSHIP AT ASU IN 1960 AND CAPTURED FIVE U.S. AMATEUR TITLES.

SUPER LEGEND

Patsy Willard

Women's athletics were starving for recognition at Arizona State in the early 1960s. Joanne Gunderson was beginning to make a splash in women's amateur golf circles and coach Anne Pittman's tennis team, still nearly a decade away from becoming a national powerhouse, was garnering some regional attention. That was about it, however, until Patsy Willard came along in 1960. Willard didn't make much of a splash—avoiding one was a major objective of her sport, diving. Willard, of Mesa, gave ASU instant visibility, not only nationally but internationally. Suddenly, wire service stories about diving competitions from around the nation were beginning, "Arizona State coed Patsy Willard." Though Arizona State began competing in women's swimming at the intercollegiate level on a limited basis in 1958, diving was not included in the team competition in those early years. Therefore, you won't find Willard's picture among members of the women's swim teams of the early 1960s. But she competed as a Sun Devil in national and international events. She and Gunderson stand out as the first two female athletes to bring exposure to the school at a time when their male counterparts were attracting almost all of the attention. Willard's first big international showing came in the 1960 Rome Olympics, where she placed fourth in the three-meter springboard competition. When she returned to school for the 1960 fall semester, her timetable called for two months of rest to recover from the intense Olympic and pre-Olympic competition. Her down time lasted about one week. "I got restless," she told this writer at the time. "I just couldn't keep away from it." She immediately resumed her rigorous workout schedule, which kept her busy three to four hours a day, seven days a week. Willard's dedication paid off with a bronze medal at the 1964 Tokyo Olympics. Meanwhile, she was dominating her sport at the national level. A four-time All-American at ASU from 1961 through 1964, she was the first ASU competitor, male or female, to achieve such recognition. She captured eight national championships on the one and three-meter springboards and platform boards. Willard, later known by her married name of Heckel, was a charter inductee into Arizona State's Sports Hall of Fame in 1975.

PATSY WILLARD CAME ALONG AT A TIME WHEN ARIZONA STATE'S FEMALE ATHLETES WERE RECEIVING VERY LITTLE NATIONAL RECOGNITION. SHE HELPED CHANGE THAT, CAPTURING EIGHT NATIONAL TITLES AND EARNING ALL-AMERICA HONORS FOUR TIMES WHILE COMPETING IN TWO OLYMPICS.

SUPER LEGEND

Kym Hampton

Most sports produce lively debate on the subject of the greatest player in school history. When it comes to women's basketball at Arizona State, it's no contest. Kym Hampton simply blows away the competition. A four-time All-Conference and two-time consensus All-American selection, Hampton is the only player in school history—male or female—to score more than 2,000 points and grab more than 1,000 rebounds in a career. Her totals of 2,361 points and 1,415 rebounds from 1981 through 1984 have never been challenged seriously. She is 691 points and 592 rebounds ahead of the runner-up in those two categories. She saved some of her best efforts for the Sun Devils' biggest games. On February 16 of 1982 she scored 20 points and grabbed 17 rebounds as the Sun Devils knocked off undefeated and second-ranked Southern California, 53-51, in Tempe. She scored the winning basket with 16 seconds remaining, then snared a rebound to preserve the victory. In her final game as a Sun Devil in 1984, she erupted for 44 points against rival Arizona. When she stepped off the court that night she held 49 school records, 25 of which still stood 15 years later. Her 44 points against Arizona remains a school record. She also holds the single-game rebound mark of 28. Entering the 1999-2000 season she still ranked ninth on the all-time NCAA career rebounding list. She averaged 19.7 points and 11.8 rebounds during her career. In addition to her offensive skills, Hampton was a defensive presence. Her school career record of 178 blocked shots is 79 more than second-place Fran Ciak. During Hampton's ASU career the Sun Devils had a record of 86-37 (.705) and competed in post-season tournaments three consecutive years—the National Invitation Tournament in 1981 and the NCAA tournament in 1982 and 1983. She led ASU to a national finish of 11th in 1983. After concluding her ASU career, Hampton played 12 seasons overseas. Upon formation of the Women's National Basketball Association in 1997, she returned to the United States, where she played three seasons for the New York Liberty. She was a starter on the New York club that reached the WNBA finals in 1997 and 1999. She retired from professional basketball following the 1999 season to concentrate on a promising singing career. Hampton was inducted into the ASU Sports Hall of Fame in 1989.

A FOUR-TIME ALL-CONFERENCE AND TWO-TIME CONSENSUS ALL-AMERICAN SELECTION, KYM HAMPTON IS THE ONLY PLAYER IN SCHOOL HISTORY—MALE OR FEMALE—TO SCORE MORE THAN 2,000 POINTS AND GRAB MORE THAN 1,000 REBOUNDS IN A CAREER. SHE SET 49 SCHOOL RECORDS.

SUPER LEGEND

Tammy Webb

A gifted athlete who could jump out of the gym, Tammy Webb played a major role in putting Arizona State women's volleyball on the map. Webb was a two-time All-American for the Sun Devils at a time when the program was just beginning to gain national exposure in the mid-1980s. She set school career records for kills and block solos and still ranks high in several single-season and career statistical categories. Her 196 block solos remain a career record by a wide margin and her 1,679 career kills rank second on the school's all-time list. In her junior season, 1985, she set a school record that still stands with 83 block solos. As a senior in 1986 she led the Sun Devils to a 27-7 record and a spot in the NCAA regionals in their first year of Pac-10 competition. In 1995, a panel of media and university representatives named her ASU's Athlete of the Decade for the first 10 years of Pac-10 women's competition. Though clearly worthy of Super Legend status for her ASU accomplishments alone, Webb, then known by her married name of Liley, really made her mark on the national and international scenes. She was captain of the U.S. National Team from 1993 through 1996 and was named Female Volleyball Athlete of the Year in 1993 by the United States Olympic Committee. She played in three Olympics—1988, 1992 and 1996. Her finest Olympic moment might have been in the 1992 Games in Barcelona. She made a major contribution with several kills and an ace as the United States beat Brazil in three games to capture the Bronze Medal. Just one day earlier the U.S. had lost a tough five-game semifinal match to Cuba. Webb-Liley also starred on the Pro Beach Volleyball Tour, earning all-league recognition in 1994. When informed in 1995 of her selection as ASU's Female Athlete of the Decade, Webb told *Arizona Republic* reporter Jeff Metcalfe: "What an honor. You know, at some point my memory always returns to ASU. What happened there is the reason I'm here today." At the time, she was preparing for the 1996 Olympics in Atlanta.

TAMMY WEBB WAS A TWO-TIME ALL-AMERICAN WHO SET SEVERAL SCHOOL RECORDS AND HELPED ASU WOMEN'S VOLLEYBALL EARN NATIONAL RECOGNITION IN THE MID-1980S. SHE WENT ON TO STAR INTERNATIONALLY AS A THREE-TIME OLYMPIAN AND CAPTAIN OF THE U.S. NATIONAL TEAM.

Maicel Malone

Arizona State has turned out its share of outstanding female track and field stars. Gea Johnson in the heptathlon, Lynda Tolbert in the hurdles, discus and shot put stars Leslie Deniz and Ria Stalman and high jumper Coleen Rienstra immediately come to mind. But when it comes down to counting hardware in the trophy case, none of them can match Maicel Malone. All Malone did during her brilliant ASU career was win six NCAA individual and relay titles and accumulate 10 All-America awards. Her specialty was the 400 meters, which she dominated (both indoors and outdoors) in the late 1980s and early 1990s. She set numerous school records, and her school marks at 200 and 400 meters both indoors and outdoors still stand. In an era when champions often come and go quickly, Malone was the nation's dominant 400-meter runner throughout the decade of the 1990s. She was the U.S. champion in that event in 1990, 1996 and 1999. Her dream of capturing an Olympic gold medal became reality on the next-to-last day of the 1996 Olympics in Atlanta when she ran a leg on the winning U.S. 4X400-meter relay team. She also won a gold medal in the 4X400 relay at the 1993 World Championships. Malone's best non-relay time at 400 meters as a Sun Devil was 50.33 seconds. Her personal best in that event is 50.05. In her gold-medal-winning performance at the 1993 World Championships she turned in a 49.4-second relay split. Her time of 51.05 while winning the 1991 NCAA indoor title was an American, collegiate and NCAA meet record. In that same meet she anchored a 4X400-meter Sun Devil relay team that set another American record with a time of 3:32.46. Her pregnancy kept her from earning a spot on the U.S. team for the 1992 Olympics in Barcelona, but she made up for it four years later in Atlanta. Malone, then known by her married name of Wallace, included her then 3-year-old son, Jaylyn, in her victory celebration with teammates after capturing the 4X400 relay gold medal.

MAICEL MALONE WON SIX NCAA TITLES AND 10 ALL-AMERICA AWARDS DURING HER BRILLIANT TRACK AND FIELD CAREER AT ASU. SHE DOMINATED THE 400 METERS NATIONALLY THROUGHOUT THE 1990S AND EARNED A GOLD MEDAL AT THE 1996 ATLANTA OLYMPICS.

SUPER LEGEND
Nina Murphy

World-class athletes and national championships were far from Nina Murphy's mind when she arrived on the Tempe Normal campus in 1924 as a women's basketball coach and part-time physical education teacher. Her mission: instill among the young women on campus her philosophy of mental, spiritual and physical fitness. Murphy and Sally Hayden, sister of U.S. Senator Carl Hayden, were the only women on the physical education faculty at the time. They conducted classes in the basement of the old auditorium. Murphy earned the grand sum of $15 per month. For 45 years, Murphy impacted the lives of the school's female athletes. When she retired in 1969, she had served longer than any active member of the faculty. Murphy's contributions over the years were many. In 1927, she initiated a women's intramural program on campus and organized the school's first Women's Athletic Association. In 1930, she played a major role in the formation of the Arizona Association of Health, Physical Education and Recreation. In 1934, she was named head of the women's physical education department, a position she held until 1964, when she resigned to devote more time to teaching. The women's physical education department endured cramped quarters for many years as limited funds for campus construction were channeled into other areas. The program began to take off in 1939, however, when it moved to the B. B. Moeur Activity Building. In 1962 it moved again, sharing a space with male athletes in the men's physical education building. After 43 years of waiting, a dream came true for Murphy in January of 1967 when a sparkling new women's physical education building was dedicated along with an athletic field for female athletes. It truly could be called The House that Nina Built. Murphy, however, wasn't about bricks and mortar. She was a people person, who earned tremendous respect from her students. That was reflected in the large number of former students who kept in touch over the years, and who never failed to seek out Murphy and pay their respects upon returning to campus. Anne Pittman, who built Arizona State's tennis program into a position of national prominence, said Murphy's contributions to women's athletics can't be overstated. "She understood that women had a right to compete," Pittman said. "If you worked for her and were willing to create a program that was competitive, she backed it." Pittman said Murphy was about competing more than winning and losing. Now, world-class female athletes and national women's championships are not unusual at ASU. Their roots can be traced back to the foundation established by Murphy starting more than three-quarters of a century ago.

THE FOUNDATION FOR ONE OF THE NATION'S STRONGEST WOMEN'S SPORTS PROGRAMS WAS LAID BY NINA MURPHY, WHO INFLUENCED THE LIVES OF ARIZONA STATE'S FEMALE ATHLETES FOR 45 YEARS. SHE EARNED ONLY $15 PER MONTH WHEN SHE LAUNCHED HER CAREER AT THE SCHOOL IN 1924.

Anne Pittman

The record is hazy when it comes to making an accounting of how many tennis matches Anne Pittman coached at Arizona State. During the early part of her tenure, funds for the program came from the Associated Students and not from the athletic department, so it technically had club status. Her status as a Super Legend, however, is not open to debate. Various athletic department records list her tenure as 30 or 31 years. She says it was 34 years. "I came in 1952 and left in 1986," she said. "What do you get when you subtract 52 from 86?" No matter what figure you use, Pittman's tenure was the longest of any head coach in Arizona State athletic history, far outdistancing the 27 years of track and field coach Baldy Castillo, who is No. 2 on the longevity list. Longevity is one thing. Success is another. Pittman can claim both. Her teams consistently were among the nation's best. She coached the Sun Devils to national championships in 1971, 1972 and 1974. Her 1974 team was 22-0 in team competition, won two of three invitational tournaments and captured the Western Athletic Conference championship en route to the national title. Her 1976 team set a school record with 31 victories. Her teams were 338-71 in collegiate dual competition and her career winning percentage of .826 is the best of any ASU coach in any sport. And she did it with very little administrative support. "We had a budget of maybe $200 or $300 for the year," she said of her early years. "I paid the travel expenses myself. I personally spent maybe $2,000 a year, not counting wear and tear on a '52 Plymouth and three other cars, including an old International that lasted 25 years. The first time we even got shoes was the year we went to Kalamazoo, Michigan, for the nationals, which would be 1974. Up until that time the P.E. department provided balls, the kids furnished their own racquets and clothes and I took care of the travel." Another ASU coaching Super Legend, Frank Kush, said he is a big Pittman fan. "I could write a book on Anne Pittman," Kush said. "Anne was a great asset not only for tennis but for our entire athletic program. She was a great fundamentalist and teacher. We used to put some of our football players in her square dance and folk dance classes to improve their footwork and quickness. They told me that dance class was tougher than football practice." An outstanding amateur player in Texas prior to her arrival at ASU, Pittman retained a recruiting pipeline to Texas for many years. She remained an outstanding player well past her retirement from coaching, winning national doubles titles in seniors competition in 1989 and 1991.

DESPITE A LIMITED BUDGET, ANNE PITTMAN PUT ARIZONA STATE ON THE MAP IN WOMEN'S TENNIS, COACHING THE SUN DEVILS TO NATIONAL TEAM TITLES IN 1971, 1972 AND 1974. DURING HER TENURE, THE LONGEST OF ANY COACH IN ASU HISTORY, SHE SAW THE SPORT PROGRESS FROM CLUB STATUS TO PERENNIAL NATIONAL POWERHOUSE.

Mona Plummer

She came along at a time when women's sports at Arizona State were struggling for recognition on their own campus, not to mention garnering a bit of regional or national notice. Mona Plummer took care of that. When she left after 22 years of coaching the women's swimming team, she had made ASU a national powerhouse in that sport. More important, she had touched hundreds of lives. Though she worked her charges hard, Plummer, with her thick-as-syrup Alabama accent, was like a big sister to her swimmers, keeping tabs on their progress in school and staying current with their social lives. Despite a limited budget and shortage of scholarships, Plummer tutored nine Olympians and more than 40 All-Americans between 1957 and 1979. Her Sun Devils won eight national championships. "She was the premier swimming coach during her era and her success helped all other women's sports at Arizona State University prosper," said ASU associate athletic director Herman Frazier. Arizona State's swimming and diving complex, which opened in July of 1981, was named The Mona Plummer Aquatic Center in honor of Plummer on March 1, 1985. Just 16 days later she died after a long bout with cancer. Plummer coached the U.S. swim team in the 1973 World University Games in Moscow and was a member of the U.S. coaching staff at the 1979 Pan American Games. From 1977 to 1980 she served on the U.S. Olympic Committee. Plummer was named assistant athletic director in 1975 and was promoted to associate athletic director in 1977. In proposing the dedication of the aquatic center to Plummer in 1985, ASU President J.R. Nelson said, "Through her service as head coach, as associate professor of physical education and as associate athletic director, she has brought pride and distinction to the university." Plummer's teams won six national championships from 1967 through 1974, missing the title only in 1969 and 1972. Her Devils also won national crowns in 1977 and 1978. The 1977 team finished 141 points ahead of runner-up Stanford. Plummer was inducted into the ASU Sports Hall of Fame in October of 1984. In June of 1985 she was inducted posthumously into the Hall of Fame of the National Association of Collegiate Directors of Athletics.

MONA PLUMMER COACHED NINE OLYMPIANS AND MORE THAN 40 ALL-AMERICANS AND LED THE SUN DEVILS TO EIGHT NATIONAL TEAM CHAMPIONSHIPS DURING HER 22-YEAR CAREER AS ARIZONA STATE'S WOMEN'S SWIMMING COACH.

Baseball was the diamond sport of choice for Arizona State's female athletes in the 1920s and early 1930s, evolving into softball in the mid-30s. From that point through the late 1960s, softball was somewhat of a hit-or-miss proposition. In some years it was a bigger deal at the intramural rather than the intercollegiate level. Arizona State sometimes fielded a team in Phoenix-area industrial leagues. Often the primary collegiate competition came during the annual sports days—a multi-sport festival involving ASC-Tempe, ASC-Flagstaff and University of Arizona, with out-of-state schools sometimes participating. Then along came Mary Littlewood, and the face of ASU softball would change forever. Littlewood first fielded a team in 1967, compiling a 5-1 record. No records are available for the next two seasons—even Littlewood couldn't find them for a book she wrote on the subject—but she began to get the Sun Devil program rolling with a 10-2 record in 1970. Littlewood's 1971 team compiled a 12-2 record and made its first appearance in the College World Series, finishing fourth. In 1972 the Sun Devils were 13-2 and reached the pinnacle of women's softball, winning the national championship. Following their College World Series victory the Sun Devils met a team from Japan in a series billed as being for the mythical world championship. ASU won, four games to one. In 1973 the Devils rolled up a perfect 13-0 record and won their second consecutive national title. Those back-to-back national crowns remain the only two in ASU softball history. Before retiring following the 1989 season, Littlewood compiled a record of 502 wins and 228 losses. In addition to her two national titles, she sent nine teams to the College World Series and 13 into post-season play. She coached six All-Americans. In her book, *ASU Softball, the Littlewood Years*, Littlewood wrote: "I am grateful to have been a part of ASU softball. The sense of keen competition and warm camaraderie shared by our teams has been a unique experience that I shall treasure forever." Littlewood was not just a one-sport coach. She coached volleyball from 1965 through 1974 and women's basketball from 1967 through 1974. Her volleyball coaching record was 59-14 and her basketball record was 49-18. In addition to coaching the Sun Devils to the national softball championships in 1972 and 1973, she took her volleyball team to the nationals with a 21-0 record. "Before Title IX, coaches would handle two or three sports, have no scholarships, and the girls wore the same uniforms for all three sports," Littlewood said prior to her resignation as softball coach in 1989. Littlewood coached more than 40 all-conference athletes in the three sports. Her contributions have earned her a spot in ASU's prestigious Hall of Distinction.

MARY LITTLEWOOD COACHED THREE SPORTS AT ASU, BUT SOFTBALL WAS HER FORTE. SHE SENT 13 TEAMS INTO POST-SEASON COMPETITION WITH NINE OF THEM REACHING THE COLLEGE WORLD SERIES. HER SUN DEVILS WON BACK-TO-BACK NATIONAL TITLES IN 1972 AND 1973.

Linda Vollstedt

S he has been called the John Wooden of women's golf coaches. An LPGA award has been named in her honor. Clearly, Linda Vollstedt is in a league of her own. Wooden, of course, was the fabled UCLA basketball coach whose teams captured 10 NCAA titles. He coached the Bruins for 16 years before winning his first national crown. Vollstedt, a former ASU player, spent 10 years building a solid foundation after taking over the ASU program prior to the 1980-81 season. Her teams recorded six top-10 finishes from 1981 through 1989 before finally breaking through to win the national championship in 1990. That started an unbelievable string that saw Vollstedt's Sun Devils collect six national titles in the 1990s, despite a women's national golf landscape that becomes increasingly competitive each season. Though several other programs keep taking their best shots, ASU has won twice as many national titles as any other school. Players gravitate to Tempe from all over the world to play under Vollestdt, who is a Class-A member of the LPGA teaching division, the highest standard for LPGA or PGA golf teachers. During her ASU tenure, Vollstedt has coached 41 All-Americans, 12 conference medalists, 71 all-conference honorees, nine U.S. Curtis Cup team members, six U.S. Public Links winners, four U.S. Amateur champions and four NCAA individual titlists. She has sent 15 players into the professional ranks. A member of the ASU women's golf team from 1964 through 1968, Vollstedt earned her bachelor of arts degree in education in 1969 and her master's in golf education in 1971. She coached the Phoenix Alhambra High team from 1970 through 1980, winning two state championships and finishing second twice. "I was never really that good," Vollstedt said of her ASU playing career. "I shot in the high 70s." She suffered two broken thumbs in an auto accident, effectively ending her playing career and sending her into coaching, which she said, "was actually the direction I needed to move." Vollstedt has been named National Coach of the Year five times by *Golf Week*—in 1989, 1993, 1994, 1995 and 1997—and three times by the National Golf Coaches Association—1993 through 1995. After first winning the national title in 1990, the Devils strung together national crowns in 1993, 1994 and 1995 and put titles back-to-back in 1997 and 1998. Vollstedt said her 1995 team dominated like no other. "We went undefeated the whole year," she said. "We won 10 tournaments, finished first in the conference and nationals and tied for first in the regional." Vollstedt has built a reputation for instilling lifetime principles in her players in addition to honing their golf skills. Vollstedt resigned as women's gold coach in June of 2001 and assumed a new position involving the marketing and promotion of the men's and women's programs.

LINDA VOLLSTEDT COACHED THE SUN DEVIL WOMEN'S GOLF TEAM TO SIX NATIONAL CHAMPIONSHIPS DURING THE 1990S. SHE HAS COACHED 41 ALL-AMERICANS AND FOUR NCAA INDIVIDUAL CHAMPIONS WHILE BEING NAMED NATIONAL COACH OF THE YEAR FIVE TIMES.

1960-1961

america's time capsule

arizona state university
| m o m e n t

The basketball team shook off a slow start and finished with a 23-6 record, tying New Mexico State for first place in the Border Conference at 9-1. The Sun Devils beat the Aggies, 86-72, in a playoff game in Tempe to win a spot in the NCAA tournament. The Devils beat Seattle, 72-70, and Southern California, 86-71, in regional games at Portland, Oregon, before Utah knocked them out of the tournament, 88-80. The Devils won 18 of 19 games during one stretch and fans were coming out of the woodwork to pack tiny Sun Devil Gym. A record crowd of 5,800 overflowed the gym on Feb. 4 to watch the Devils whip rival Arizona, 94-78. An estimated 1,500 fans were turned away because there was no place to put them. The Sun Devils featured a balanced attack headed by guard Larry Armstrong (19.9 ppg). The other starters were forwards Ollie Payne (15.4) and Tony Cerkvenik (13.3), center Jerry Hahn (13.1) and guard Raul Disarufino (7.7). Meanwhile, Coach Francis "Fanny" Markham's sensational freshman team was rolling up a 17-1 record and outscoring the opposition by an average score of 107-68.

Guard Larry Armstrong led the Sun Devils in scoring. (ASU Media Relations)

spotlight

The Sun Devils began to branch out from a scheduling standpoint in football, playing a Pacific Coast Conference team—Washington State—and a team from the Southeastern part of the country, North Carolina State. Both of those teams visited Sun Devil Stadium and both found out that Southwestern hospitality wasn't all it was cracked up to be. Coach Frank Kush's Devils nipped the Cougars, 24-21, and managed another three-point victory over the Wolfpack, 25-22. Meanwhile, athletic director Clyde B. Smith was working to get the Sun Devils exposure in other parts of the country. Smith announced that the Sun Devils would play a home-and-home series against Wisconsin of the Big Ten beginning in 1967 at Madison, Wisconsin.

ASU LEGEND

Mal & Mel Spence

Coach Baldy Castillo couldn't always tell them apart, but there was no mistaking the contribution made by Jamaican twins Mal and Mel Spence to Castillo's track team. Mal won Border Conference 440-yard titles in 1958, 1959 and 1961 and captured the 880-yard run in 1958 and 1960. He earned All-America honors with a fourth-place finish in the 440 at the 1959 NCAA championships. Mel also gained All-America recognition with a fifth-place finish in the 880 at the 1959 NCAA meet. Both ran legs on ASU's mile relay teams that won the event three times at the Border Conference championships. Opponents surely thought they were seeing double when one brother would conclude his relay leg only to give way to an identical twin with a fresh set of legs. But as big as the Spence twins were on campus, they were much bigger in their native Jamaica. Both brothers competed for Jamaica's 1956, 1960 and 1964 Olympic teams and starred in the Pan American Games in 1959 and 1963. In 1961 they were honored by Jamaican premier Norman Manley for their contributions to that country's international track and field effort. A plaque from ASU citing their contributions as athletes, student leaders and scholars was presented at the same ceremony.

Mal (left) and Mel Spence were international track and field stars. (ASU Media Relations)

SUN DEVIL LORE

Dr. G. Homer Durham was inducted as the university's 10th president in ceremonies on campus March 11, 1961. Dr. H.D. Richardson had served as acting president for six months following the death of Grady Gammage. One of Durham's first acts was a proposal that a new auditorium, designed by Frank Loyd Wright and scheduled to be constructed along the Apache Boulevard-Mill Avenue curve, be named after Gammage.

SUN DEVIL STATS

• The baseball team finished 36-13 under third-year Coach Bobby Winkles and earned a final ranking of 11th by *Collegiate Baseball.* Shortstop Roger Tomlinson was named to the NCAA District 6 first team. Tomlinson signed a professional contract with the San Francisco Giants at the end of ASU's season.

• It was quite a school year for coach Fanny Markham. After watching his freshman basketball team put up unbelievable numbers, he coached the golf team to a 28-3-1 record in dual matches. The Sun Devils won the Border Conference title and finished second at the nationals.

• Halfback Nolan Jones, fullback Clay Freeney, center Fred Rhodes, tackle George Flint and guards Jesse Bradford and Dick Locke earned All-Border Conference football honors.

1961-1962

america's time capsule

arizona state university | m o m e n t

The Sun Devils used a blend of experience and an infusion of talent from the most exciting freshman team in school history to fashion a 23-4 basketball season. The trademark of this team was its ability to score. The Sun Devils topped the 100-point mark seven times—a school record that still stands. The Sun Devils' 130-65 victory over Pasadena College established a single-game scoring mark that has been challenged several times but never topped. The Sun Devils led the nation in average winning margin with a whopping 22.5-point figure. As they did the previous season, the Devils lost three straight road games early in the season—this time to Indiana, Minnesota and Utah—before going on a roll that saw them win 18 straight games. That streak came to an end in the first round of the NCAA tournament when they dropped a 78-73 decision to Utah State at Corvallis, Oregon. Forwards Joe Caldwell and Jerry Hahn and guard Larry Armstrong were named to the All-Border Conference first team. Forward Tony Cerkvenik was a second-team selection as a center. Armstrong was named to the Helms Foundation's All-America third team.

Jerry Hahn was an All-Border Conference first-team selection. (ASU Media Relations)

SUN DEVIL *spotlight*

The name Arizona State was beginning to become synonymous with excellence in women's golf in the early 1960s. Joanne Gunderson had put the Sun Devils on the map in 1960 when she won the National Intercollegiate Championship and earned a spot on the U.S. Curtis Cup team. Among the other high-visibility trophies to her credit while at ASU were the Western Amateur, the Trans-Mississippi and the Tucker Intercollegiate. Then, two years later, along came Carol Sorenson to capture the National Intercollegiate and join Gunderson on the 1962 Curtis Cup team. Gunderson was ASU's first female golf All-American in 1960. Sorenson was the second in 1962.

ASU LEGEND

Tony Cerkvenik

He stood only 6-foot-4 and jumped perhaps high enough to clear a telephone directory, but Tony Cerkvenik was the most prolific rebounder ever to play basketball at Arizona State. His career rebound total of 1,022 and career rebound average of 12.3 have never been challenged seriously during the past four decades. He also holds the school record for most rebounds in a season (415), though his school mark for most rebounds in a game (26), which he shared with Art Becker, was broken by Mark Landsberger, who had 27 against San Diego State in December of 1976. How did Cerkvenik do it? Intelligence and toughness. The former Marine simply would not let anyone invade his territory under the basket. His coach, Ned Wulk, said Cerkvenik was the key to ASU's success in the early 1960s. "Cerkvenik was always a cut above everyone else, even though he never scored that much," Wulk said. "All he did was win. He was 72-13 in the three years that he played." Cerkvenik, a Phoenix-area businessman and a prominent basketball booster after his playing days were over, died November 19, 1996, of injuries suffered in an auto accident.

Tony Cerkvenik's rebounding records have stood for four decades. (ASU Media Relations)

Sun Devil Lore

Formation of a new athletic league—the Western Athletic Conference—was announced, with play scheduled to begin with the 1962-63 school year. The conference included Arizona State and Arizona of the Border Conference plus four members of the Skyline Conference—Utah, Brigham Young, New Mexico and Wyoming.

SUN DEVIL STATS

• Frank Kush became the winningest football coach in school history just five games into his fourth season. A 24-23 victory over Oregon State gave Kush his 28th victory. His record stood at 31-9 after the Sun Devils finished 7-3 and captured the Border Conference title in their last year in the league. Dan Devine, 27-3 in three seasons, previously had the most victories.

• The baseball team beat Arizona in Tucson for the first time in 30 years, winning a May double header by scores of 5-1 and 20-7 to earn a split of the six-game season series.

• A crowd of 40,100—largest ever to see a sporting event in Arizona—watched the Sun Devils drop a 22-13 football decision to Arizona in Tempe.

1962-1963

**america's
time capsule**

arizona state university
m o m e n t

Will there ever be another ASU basketball season like the 1962-63 campaign? A lot of balls have gone through the hoop in the last four decades, but no Sun Devil team has been able to dislodge that bunch for the honor of best team in school history. The Sun Devils were 26-3 and achieved a No. 3 national ranking. And rather than fading with time, the legend continues to grow. The first sign that this team was something special came during a brutal intersectional road trip that began with victories over Kansas (71-62) and Kansas State (77-72) before a 92-90 loss to Wichita State in overtime. The Devils shook off that loss and won their next 10 before an 88-81 loss to Wyoming at Laramie. Then came 11 straight wins before the season ended with an 83-65 loss to Oregon State in the third round of the NCAA tournament at Provo, Utah. The Devils won the Western Athletic Conference title with a 9-1 league mark in their first year of competition in the new league. Forward Joe Caldwell (19.7) and center Art Becker (19.1) led a balanced scoring attack. Forward Tony Cerkvenik averaged 11.9 points and joined Caldwell and Becker to give the Sun Devils three double-figure rebounders. Becker averaged 11.2, Caldwell 10.8 and Cerkvenik 10.8. Dennis Dairman (12.5 points) was the shooting guard and Gary Senitza handled the playmaking and contributed 9.5 points per game. Caldwell and Cerkvenik shared team MVP honors and Becker received honorable mention All-America honors from Associated Press.

Art Becker was the second-leading scorer and top rebounder on the most successful basketball team in ASU history. (ASU Media Relations)

spotlight

Behind quarterback John Jacobs and a couple of pretty fair backs named Charley Taylor and Tony Lorick, the Sun Devils led the nation in total offense (384.4 yards per game) and ranked second in scoring (30.4). Yet when the season had ended the Devils were shaking their heads about what might have been. Their 7-2-1 record was nothing to be ashamed of, yet only seven points separated the Devils from a perfect season. They played Washington State to a 24-24 tie, lost a 15-14 heartbreaker to a tough West Texas State club and dropped the season finale to rival Arizona in Tucson by a 20-17 score. Lorick, who played halfback, led the team in rushing with 704 yards and a 6.7-yard average. Taylor led the team in scoring with eight touchdowns from his wingback position.

LEGEND

Charley Taylor

Nobody was quite sure exactly what position best suited Charley Taylor when the gangly youngster arrived at ASU from Grand Prairie, Texas, in the fall of 1960. But when you watched him hurdle tacklers as a member of the freshman team, you knew he had to have the football in his hands. With the likes of Tony Lorick and Gene Foster already manning the halfback positions, coach Frank Kush installed Taylor at wingback. With athletes playing both offense and defense in those days, and with a wealth of talent around him, Taylor didn't put up big numbers at ASU. He never led his team in rushing or receiving. But all the while the pro scouts were drooling. The Washington Redskins made him a first-round selection in the spring of 1964 and the rest is history. Taylor was named Most Valuable Player of the 1964 College-Pro All Star Game and went on to win 1964 Rookie of the Year honors while catching a NFL rookie record 53 passes for the Redskins. He became the first NFL rookie since 1943 to finish in the top 10 in rushing (sixth) and receiving (eighth). He played in the Pro Bowl his first four seasons and led the NFL in receiving in 1966 and 1967. When he retired after a brilliant career, he was the NFL's all-time leading receiver with 649 catches. In 1984, Taylor became the first ASU player to be inducted into the NFL Hall of Fame.

Charley Taylor went from ASU to NFL Rookie of the Year. (ASU Media Relations)

SUN DEVIL STAT

• Tony Cerkvenik grabbed 26 rebounds in a basketball game against Arizona March 4 in Tucson, tying the school record set the previous season by Art Becker against Brigham Young University. Cerkvenik and Becker would share the record until Dec. 3, 1976, when Mark Landsberger snared 27 caroms against San Diego State to establish a record that still stands.

Sun Devil Lore

ASU athletic teams began competing in the new Western Athletic Conference in all sports but football. The football team played just two games against WAC foes, two shy of the required number.

• The Arizona Board of Regents approved $3.3 million for a new library and $1.1 million for a 60,000-square foot language and literature building.

Junior Carol Hopkins was named to the All-America women's intercollegiate archery team.

The men's gymnastics team finished second in the Western Athletic Conference championship meet.

The men's golf team placed third in the WAC championship tournament.

Sun Devil basketball fans breathed a sigh of relief in June when coach Ned Wulk turned down an offer to coach the Cincinnati Royals of the National Basketball Association.

arizona state university
m o m e n t

With all the major sports at ASU making a significant push for national recognition, track and field more than held its own. Coach Baldy Castillo's troops made one big splash after another in the spring of 1963. The Sun Devils set 12 school records and romped to a lopsided victory in the first Western Athletic Conference championships, but that was small potatoes when you examine the big picture. The Devils also broke three world records and won three NCAA individual titles while finishing fourth in the team competition—the highest finish ever by a team from Arizona. Henry Carr, the sensational sophomore from Detroit, equaled or bettered the listed world record for the 220-yard dash around a turn on five occasions. The listed record was 20.5 seconds. Carr's best was 20.3. Sophomore Ulis Williams twice bested the listed world record in the 440-yard dash with a 45.6 clocking and the mile relay team of Mike Barrick, Ron Freeman, Carr and Williams ran 3:04.5, breaking the world record of 3:05.6. At the NCAA championships in Albuquerque, Carr won the 220 in 20.5, Williams the 440 in 45.8 and Frank Covelli the javelin with a toss of 257-8 1/2.

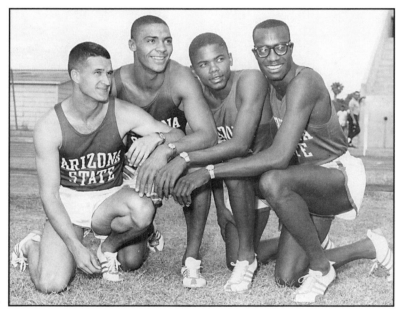

ASU's world-record-setting mile relay team of (left to right) Mike Barrick, Henry Carr, Ron Freeman and Ulis Williams. (ASU Media Relations)

SUN DEVIL *spotlight*

Coach Bobby Winkles' baseball team set seven school season records while compiling a 34-13 won-lost mark. The Sun Devils finished second to Arizona in their first year of Western Athletic Conference competition. The biggest assault on the record books came from pitcher Sterling Slaughter, who more than doubled the school strikeout record with 154, tops in the nation. The old mark was 74. Slaughter also set school marks for victories (11-2) and innings pitched (109). Other individual school marks were set by pitcher Sam Cook for winning percentage (9-1, .900) and John Ruedy in the stolen base department with 25. Team records were set for strikeouts by the pitching staff (402) and earned run average (2.59). Shortstop Luis Lagunas led the Sun Devils in batting (.331), doubles (10), triples (7) and RBIs (36).

LEGEND

Ulis Williams

One of the most celebrated recruits ever landed by ASU track and field coach Baldy Castillo, Ulis Williams spent much of his Sun Devil career in the shadow of teammate Henry Carr, whose constant assaults of the world record book grabbed most of the headlines. But Williams was a world-class athlete in his own right. The spring of 1963 was a busy one for the sophomore speedster from Los Angeles. He captured the NCAA 440-yard dash title with a time of 45.8 seconds and ran the anchor leg on the mile relay team that blazed to a world-record time of 3:04.5 at the Mount San Antonio Relays in Walnut, California, smashing the mark of 3:05.6 set by a United States all-star quartet. During the spring season Williams twice bested the listed world record of 45.7 seconds in the 440, but his accomplishment was overshadowed by the fact that one of those instances (45.6 in the WAC championship meet in Tempe) was in a losing effort to New Mexico star Adolph Plummer, whose unbelievable 44.9 clocking stunned the track and field world. Williams avenged that defeat by running 45.6 again the next week to beat Plummer at the Compton Relays in California. At the 1964 Tokyo Olympics, Williams teamed with Carr, Ollan Cassell and Mike Larrabee to win a gold medal in the 4X400-meter relay in a world-record time of 3:00.7. In 1996, Williams was named president of Compton College in California.

Ulis Williams went from world-class quarter miler to college president. (ASU Alumni Association)

SUN DEVIL STAT

- He stood only 5-foot-10 and weighed just 160 pounds, but senior right-hander Sterling Slaughter could muscle up and throw the ball past college hitters with the best of them. In a game against Colorado State on March 18 in Tempe, Slaughter set a school record that still stands when he whiffed 22. A lot of great pitchers have taken a shot at that mark, but the closest anyone has come was 21 strikeouts by Eddie Bane against LaVerne in April of 1972.

Sun Devil Lore

A major construction boom was changing the face of the campus. Among the largest projects were the Grady Gammage Auditorium, Palo Verde East women's dormitory, 10 new fraternity houses on Alpha Drive and a three-story addition to the engineering center. Gammage Auditorium would earn a reputation over the years as one of the West's finest facilities for the performing arts.

1963-1964

america's
time capsule

October 2, 1963: Pitcher Sandy Koufax of the Los Angeles Dodgers set a World Series record by striking out 15 New York Yankees in the opening game.

November 22, 1963: President John F. Kennedy was killed by an assassin's bullet in Dallas, Texas.

November 24, 1963: Lee Harvey Oswald was shot and killed by Jack Ruby while in the custody of the Dallas police.

February 25, 1964: Challenger Cassius Clay defeated Sonny Liston for the world heavyweight boxing title.

July 2, 1964: The Civil Rights Act of 1964 was signed by President Lyndon Johnson.

arizona state university
moment

The defining moment of the 1963 football season just might have occurred in the dead of the night, across campus from the bright lights and cheering crowd in Sun Devil Stadium. Coach Frank Kush was not a happy camper after the Sun Devils suffered a 33-13 loss to underdog Wichita State in the season opener. After the Devils bussed across campus to their Goodwin Stadium locker room, Kush decided his troops needed some work on fundamentals— immediately. Kush conducted a post-game scrimmage on the practice field until he felt his team's attitude had been properly adjusted. The Devils responded in spectacular fashion. They won their remaining eight games and finished with a national ranking of 13th in the final United Press International poll. A star-studded offensive cast that included running backs Tony Lorick, Charley Taylor and Gene Foster and receivers Jerry Smith and Herman "Ham-Handed" Harrison finished the season ranked fifth nationally in total offense. The Devils capped off the season by smashing rival Arizona, 35-6, in front of a record crowd of 41,000 in Sun Devil Stadium. Lorick scored three touchdowns as ASU snapped a string of three straight losses to the Wildcats.

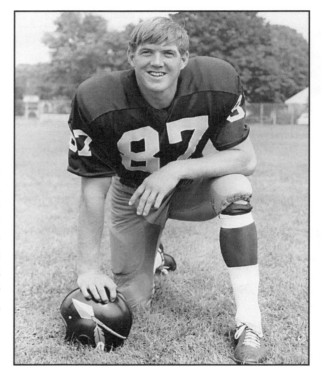

Jerry Smith was one of the stars of an 8-1 football season. (Washington Redskins)

Seniors Joe Caldwell, Art Becker and Gary Senitza led the way as the basketball team borrowed the football team's script, winning 10 of its last 11 regular-season games to tie New Mexico for the Western Athletic Conference title. The Sun Devils earned a spot in the NCAA tournament, where they suffered a 92-90 loss to Utah State in the first round. Both meetings with rival Arizona were classics. The Devils won 68-67 in Tucson, then captured a share of the conference title with a 72-69 victory over the Wildcats in the regular-season finale in Tempe. Caldwell set school records for points in a season (589), season scoring average (21.8) and career scoring (1,518 points). He went on to earn a spot on the U.S. Olympic team that won the gold medal in Tokyo in 1964.

Quarterback Ryan Kealy (8) and offensive lineman Victor Leyva (75) had productive Sun Devil careers. (Scott Troyanos/ASU Media Relations)

Tight end Todd Heap moved on to the NFL after three banner seasons. (Scott Troyanos/ ASU Media Relations)

Outside linebacker Adam Archuleta was Pac-10 Defensive Player of the Year. (ASU Media Relations)

Lefty Jon Switzer was a three-year pitching star. (ASU Media Relations)

Second baseman Brooks Conrad sparkled with glove and bat. (ASU Media Relations)

Amanda Burbridge was co-National Player of the Year in 2000. (ASU Media Relations)

Steve Blackford finished third nationally at 165 pounds.
(ASU Media Relations)

Jon Tunstall captained the 2000 swim team, which finished 10th nationally.
(ASU Media Relations)

Carolyn Adel was a four-time All-American. (ASU Media Relations)

Elizabeth McNabb twice won first-team All-America honors in the floor exercise. (ASU Media Relations)

Sprint star Marcus Brunson set an NCAA 60-meter indoor record in his first race as a Sun Devil. (Media Relations)

Rachel Holt was a first-team All-Pac-10 selection. (Media Relations)

Stacey Tullock was a soccer All-American in each of her first three years as a Sun Devil. (ASU Media Relations)

Alton Mason brought senior leadership to the 2000-01Sun Devils.
(Scott Troyanos/Media Relations)

LEGEND

Tony Lorick

He wasn't quite as flashy as his more celebrated backfield mate, Charley Taylor, but there's probably no player in his era who made a bigger contribution to Sun Devil football than Tony Lorick. Lorick led the team in rushing with 704 yards as a halfback in 1962 and 805 yards as a fullback in 1963 and played a mean linebacker in that time of two-way football. He averaged 6.7 yards rushing as a junior and 7.7 as a senior. He also led the team in scoring and total offense in his final season. The only thing that kept Lorick from being a two-time 1,000-yard rusher was a wealth of offensive talent in the program at the time. Lorick shared the ball-carrying duties with the likes of Taylor, Gene Foster and Larry Todd and rarely had more than 10 or 12 carries per game. Following his senior season, Lorick's teammates voted him the recipient of the Sun Angel Award, presented annually to the player who has contributed most in terms of leadership, team spirit and athletic ability. Lorick played in the 1964 College All-Star game and was drafted in the first round by the American Football League's Oakland Raiders and the second round by the National Football League's Baltimore Colts. He signed with Baltimore and played four seasons with the Colts. He was third in the 1964 NFL Rookie of the Year balloting.

Tony Lorick was a standout on the star-studded football teams of the early 1960s. (ASU Media Relations)

SUN DEVIL STATS

• Coach Bobby Winkles' baseball team compiled a 44-7 record, won the Western Athletic Conference title with an 11-1 league mark, captured the District 7 title with two wins over Air Force and made its first appearance ever at the College World Series in Omaha, Nebraska. The Sun Devils lost to Missouri, 7-0, beat Mississippi, 5-0, then were eliminated by Maine, 4-2, to finish in a sixth-place tie.

• Seattle outscored the Sun Devils, 100-96, to snap ASU's streak of 52 consecutive basketball victories at Sun Devil Gym.

Sun Devil Lore

Ground was broken in January on two additions to a rapidly-changing campus skyline—a six-story language and literature building west of Old Main and an industrial design and technology building at the corner of 8th Street and College Ave.

• The Varsity Inn, a popular student hangout since the 1920s, was razed to make way for a parking lot. The coffee shop at 8th Street and College Ave. had seen four name changes at the university and had spawned many romances and lifetime friendships.

1964-1965

September 12, 1964: Vonda Kay Van Dyke, a senior education major at Arizona State, was named Miss America in ceremonies at Atlantic City, N.J. Another ASU coed, Jane Nelson, Miss New Mexico, was one of the 10 finalists.

September 27, 1964: The Warren Commission on the assassination of President John Kennedy reported that there was no conspiracy and that Lee Harvey Oswald alone was responsible for the shooting.

November 3, 1964: Lyndon Johnson defeated Arizona Sen. Barry Goldwater for the United States presidency.

March 8, 1965: The first United States combat forces landed in South Vietnam to guard the U.S. Air Force base at Da Nang.

June 5, 1965: Astronaut Edward White successfully completed a 20-minute walk in space, the first by an American.

**america's
time capsule**

arizona state university
m o m e n t

The Sun Devils made an early exit in their first trip to the College World Series in 1964, losing twice in three games. It didn't take them long to get the hang of the Omaha Experience, however. In their second trip to Omaha in 1965 they won it all, producing the school's first NCAA team title in any sport. The Devils breezed past Lafayette (14-1), St. Louis (13-3), Ohio State (9-4) and St. Louis again (6-2) before suffering a 7-2 loss to Ohio State. That set up a rubber game between the Sun Devils and Buckeyes for the national title. ASU got a clutch relief pitching job by Doug Nurnberg in the championship game. Nurnberg entered the game with the bases loaded and nobody out in the seventh inning and did not allow a run. He also worked out of a ninth-inning jam to preserve a 2-1 victory. Rick Monday provided ASU's first run with a solo home run in the first inning. The game-winner scored in the sixth when Sal Bando raced home from third on a sacrifice fly by Luis Lagunas. Bando, who set a Series record with 12 hits and tied another mark by scoring 10 runs, was named Most Valuable Player. Bando drove in three runs in the Series opener and had five RBIs in the second game.

Sal Bando was named College World Series Most Valuable Player. (ASU Alumni Association)

Four ASU athletes accounted for four gold medals and one bronze at the 1964 Tokyo Olympics as the school's athletic reputation spread beyond the national level and became international in scope. Henry Carr won the 200-meter dash and anchored the world-record-setting 1,600-meter relay team. Ulis Williams also earned a gold by running a leg on the 1,600-meter relay squad. Carr and Williams were teammates on the 1963 ASU mile-relay team that set a world record. Joe Caldwell scored 14 points as the U.S. beat Russia for the gold medal in basketball. Patsy Willard finished third in the three-meter diving competition.

LEGEND
Rick Monday

H e had a picture-perfect swing and he played center field with a fluid grace rarely seen in college baseball. Some will remember Rick Monday most for those physical traits. Others will remember him more as a pioneer for all of the "firsts" that he brought to Arizona State's baseball program. Monday was the first of the school's 13 College Players of the Year. He earned the honor after batting .359 with 11 home runs in 1965. His 11 home runs was a school record at the time, though it was eclipsed the next season by Reggie Jackson, who slugged 15 homers. Monday also played a prominent role as the Sun Devils captured their first national title at the 1965 College World Series. He homered in each of the Devils' two victories over Ohio State, including a solo shot in the 2-1 championship game victory. Monday, a sophomore, was the first player chosen in major league baseball's initial amateur draft in 1965.

He went to the Kansas City Athletics. He's one of three ASU players who have been taken with the first pick of the draft. The others are Floyd Bannister in 1976 and Bob Horner in 1978.

Rick Monday accomplished more than his share of "firsts" at ASU. (ASU Media Relations)

SUN DEVIL STATS

• ASU golfer Carol Sorenson beat Bridgit Jackson of Great Britain to become just the fifth Yankee ever to win the British Women's Amateur Golf Championship.

• Seniors Mary Ann Wahl and Carolyn Maxwell and junior Judy Severance were named to the four-member All-America archery team selected by the National Collegiate Archery Coaches' Association.

• ASU's wrestling team placed sixth at the NCAA championships in just its second appearance at the nationals. The Sun Devils had finished 35th the previous year.

Sun Devil Lore

G rady Gammage Memorial Auditorium, designed by noted architect Frank Lloyd Wright, was opened at the southwest end of campus, thrusting ASU to the forefront among cultural centers in the West.

• ASU's College Bowl team returned from the national competition in New York with a 4-1 record and $6,000 in scholarship money. It was the school's first venture into national academic competition and it greatly enhanced the university's national reputation in liberal arts.

1965-1966

arizona state university
m o m e n t

The Sun Devils lost four of their first five football games, but rallied to win their last five and finish 6-4. The Devils clinched a winning record with a 14-6 victory over rival Arizona in the final game, but the season highlight might have been a stunning 7-6 Homecoming victory over 14-point favorite Washington State, which came to Tempe with a 7-1 record and a shot at the Rose Bowl. The Devils and Cougars battled through three scoreless quarters before ASU's Rick Davis kicked a 31-yard field goal to give the Sun Devils a 3-0 lead with 6:39 to play. The Cougars were offside on the play, however, and ASU coach Frank Kush gave back the only three points of the game for a first down at the WSU 9 yard line. Quarterback John Goodman then passed to Ken Dyer for a touchdown and Davis made the conversion kick for a 7-0 lead. That play made the difference when WSU scored a late touchdown. The Cougars passed for an apparent two-point conversion, but the play was disallowed because they took too much time.

Ken Dyer's TD catch gave the Sun Devils 7-6 upset victory over Washington State. (ASU Media Relations)

SUN DEVIL *spotlight*

Strongman Jon Cole shattered the school record in the discus when he uncorked a heave of 199 feet, five inches early in March. In April, he set a school mark in the shot put with a toss of 61 feet, 3 1/4 inches. He later improved that to 61-11 1/2. Cole's discus record stood until 1982, when Gary Williky topped it with a toss of 203-6. Cole still ranks second on the school's all-time discus list. His best in the shot ranks sixth in school history. Cole in the discus, Ron Freeman II in the 440-yard dash and Dick Rambo in the pole vault won individual titles at the Western Athletic Conference track and field championships. Cole's winning discus throw was 180 feet even, Freeman's time in the 440 was 46.9 seconds and Rambo's winning vault was 15 feet, 7 inches.

ASU LEGEND

Reggie Jackson

H e came to school on a football scholarship, and he showed considerable ability in that sport when he cracked the starting lineup at cornerback as a sophomore in 1965. But Reggie Jackson was a baseball player first and foremost, and it didn't take him long to establish that fact in the spring of 1966. In his only year of baseball at ASU, Jackson batted .327 with 15 home runs and 65 RBIs for a Sun Devil club that finished 41-11 but failed to qualify for the College World Series. Jackson was a first-team All-American and was named National Player of the Year by *The Sporting News*. He was the second player chosen in the 1966 draft, by the Kansas City Athletics, who had drafted ASU's Rick Monday No. 1 in 1965. Jackson went on to become ASU's most famous baseball letterman, slugging 548 home runs and playing on five World Series champions during a 20-year major league career. He was inducted into the Baseball Hall of Fame during his first year of eligibility in 1993. Jackson was not included in the elite list of Super Legends in this book because he played just one season at ASU. Accomplishments while at ASU were more heavily weighed than post-ASU feats while selecting Super Legends.

Major League Hall of Famer Reggie Jackson came to ASU on a football scholarship. (ASU Media Relations)

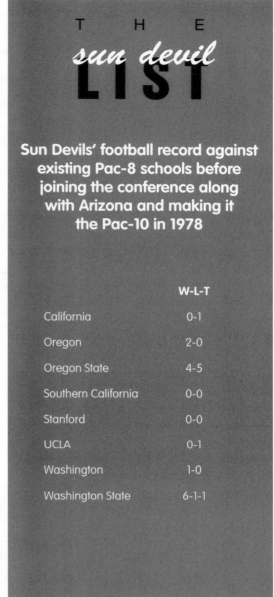

T H E *sun devil* LIST

Sun Devils' football record against existing Pac-8 schools before joining the conference along with Arizona and making it the Pac-10 in 1978

	W-L-T
California	0-1
Oregon	2-0
Oregon State	4-5
Southern California	0-0
Stanford	0-0
UCLA	0-1
Washington	1-0
Washington State	6-1-1

SUN DEVIL LORE

C hristine Kajikawa, daughter of legendary A-State athlete and coach Bill Kajikawa, was named Outstanding Senior Woman. Under her married name of Wilkinson, she would go on to serve the university in several important administrative positions, including stints as interim athletic director in 1995-96 and the spring of 2000.

• Northwestern University professor Willard H. Pedrick was named founding dean of ASU's new College of Law, scheduled to open in 1967.

SUN DEVIL STAT

• Larry Kentera, a four-year football letterman at Arizona State from 1947 through 1950, joined the staff of football coach Frank Kush. Kentera, a former prep standout in Globe, had served for seven years as head coach at San Joaquin Delta Junior College in Stockton, California. Kentera, who was assigned to coach the ends, replaced Dick Corrick on Kush's staff. Corrick left ASU to become offensive line coach at the University of California.

1966-1967

america's time capsule

arizona state university
m o m e n t

Catcher Ron Davini was named Outstanding Player of the College World Series as ASU won its second national title. (ASU Media Relations)

Who said it's easier the second time around? The Sun Devil baseball team, which captured its first national title at the 1965 College World Series, nabbed Title No. 2 in 1967, but not before overcoming some long odds. The Sun Devils lost four of their first five Western Athletic Conference games, and had to go 15 innings to beat rival Arizona in a WAC Southern Division playoff game. They battled their way to Omaha for the third time in four years by beating Brigham Young for the WAC title and Air Force in the District 7 playoffs. The Devils won their first three games in Omaha, 7-2 over Oklahoma State, 8-1 over Boston College and 5-3 over top-ranked Stanford. With no margin for error after a 3-0 loss to Houston, the Sun Devils beat Stanford again, 4-3 in 14 innings, to earn a rematch with Houston in the championship game. After the dramatic victory over Stanford, the title game was a breeze. Tom Burgess struck out 15, Larry Linville, Scott Reid and Ralph Carpenter each drove in two runs and the Cougars self-destructed with six errors as the Devils romped, 11-2. ASU catcher Ron Davini, who became a fan favorite with his hustling style, was named Outstanding Player of the Series. Davini was joined on the All-Tournament team by pitcher Gary Gentry, right fielder Reed, third baseman Dave Grangaard and shortstop Jack Lind.

SUN DEVIL *spotlight*

In a game still considered by many the greatest in school baseball history, the 11th-ranked Sun Devils beat ninth-ranked Arizona, 3-2 in 15 innings before a crowd of 8,314 at Phoenix Municipal Stadium. Gary Gentry, who had shut out the Wildcats, 3-0, in the final regular-season series, took the mound for the Sun Devils in the one-game Western Athletic Conference Southern Division playoff on two days' rest. The Wildcats scored one run in the first inning and another in the fifth and the Devils tied it with single runs in the fifth and sixth. Four hours and 17 minutes after it began, the game ended on Jack Lind's RBI double to right field, scoring Randy Bobb from second base. Gentry, gulping sugar pills between innings, pitched all 15 innings, scattering nine hits, walking five and striking out 18. He threw 208 pitches.

LEGEND

Bernie Wrightson

ASU's swimming and diving program was in its infancy in the mid-1960s. Swimming coach Walt Schlueter and diving coach Dick Smith faced the difficult job of building the program from the ground up beginning in 1963. It wasn't long, however, before Smith had a world-class diving star, Bernie Wrightson. Patsy Willard had been grabbing headlines in the women's diving ranks even before the official formation of swimming and diving teams at ASU, and Wrightson soon followed suit in the men's competition. He became ASU's first male national diving champion in 1966 when he captured the NCAA 1-meter title. Two years later he went international, earning a spot on the U.S. Olympic team coached by Smith. Wrightson was up to the ultimate challenge in diving. He won the three-meter springboard gold medal at the 1968 Mexico City Olympics. Wrightson was the first ASU diver to win both an NCAA championship and an Olympic gold medal. He won a total of nine national championships and captured the Pan Am Games gold medal in 1967. He was a charter inductee into the ASU Sports Hall of Fame in 1975.

Bernie Wrightson was the first ASU diver to win an NCAA championship and an Olympic gold medal. (ASU Media Relations)

Sun Devil Lore

The new women's physical education building opened in the fall of 1966 and was officially dedicated in January of 1967. It featured two gymnasiums, a large dance hall, an all-purpose activity room and several classrooms. Women's athletics previously had been housed in a variety of buildings, including the B.B. Moeur Activity building from 1939 to 1962.

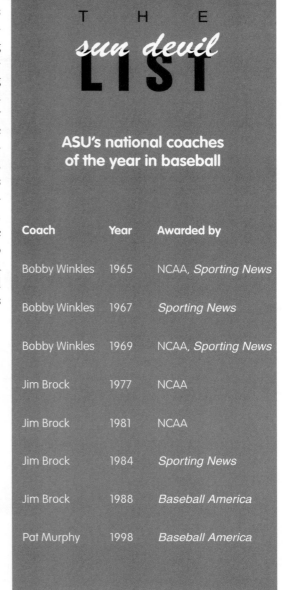

SUN DEVIL STATS

• Heavyweight Curley Culp became Arizona State's first NCAA wrestling champion as the Sun Devils recorded their second Top Ten finish in three years. Culp, a junior, used a leg-trip move called the "Curley Special" to pin Dom Corollo of Adams State in 51 seconds in the national championship match. Culp's performance led the Sun Devils to a No. 8 national finish. They had placed sixth in 1965.

• Sun Devil baseball Coach Bobby Winkles was named National Coach of the Year for the second time in three years by *The Sporting News*.

1967-1968

arizona state university
m o m e n t

Max Anderson rushed for 220 yards as the Sun Devils surprised Wisconsin. (ASU Media Relations)

It was a game of tremendous importance for a budding football program that was trying to attract national attention. Not only was Arizona State playing a Big Ten opponent for the first time, the Sun Devils were doing it in the heart of Big Ten territory. Wisconsin's Badgers provided the opposition in legendary Camp Randall Stadium. More than 500 ASU partisans from around the Midwest poured into Madison to watch the Sun Devils square off against the Badgers, who hadn't lost a home opener in 19 years. Ironically, that loss was at the hands of an Indiana team coached by Clyde Smith, who accompanied the Sun Devils to Madison in his role of athletic director. The Sun Devils' credentials coming into that game were nothing to strike fear in the hearts of the Badgers. The Devils had won their home opener over San Jose State, 27-16, but had lost their second game to Oregon State, 27-21. But coach Frank Kush had his Devils primed for this game. They cruised to a 42-16 victory as fullback Max Anderson rushed for 220 yards. It was part of a glorious day for Arizona football. On the same Saturday afternoon, Arizona's Wildcats were upsetting Ohio State, 14-7, at Columbus. The victory over Wisconsin served as a springboard for the Devils, who won four straight games before suffering a 15-13 loss to Wyoming in a game with Sugar Bowl implications. Anderson set a school record with a 99-yard run from scrimmage against Wyoming. The Devils finished 8-2 after a 47-7 romp over Arizona in the season finale, but were not deemed worthy of a bowl invitation.

The women's swimming team, undefeated in dual meets over a four-year span, dominated the National Intercollegiate Swimming and Diving Championships in Detroit. The Sun Devils overwhelmed the rest of the field, rolling up 160 points to 48 for second-place Michigan. The Sun Devils accumulated 23 gold medals and set eight records. Some 300 competitors from 25 schools participated in the championships. Kendis Moore, a freshman from Phoenix, set national collegiate records while winning the 50-yard backstroke, 100-yard backstroke and 100-yard butterfly. Moore was the first collegian in history to win three events at the nationals. Lyn Krivanich, a sophomore from El Paso, Texas, set a national mark while capturing the 200-yard freestyle.

ASU LEGEND

Curley Culp

The sports information staff used to have a devil of a time getting Curley Culp to look ferocious when he posed for publicity photos, but when he set foot on the football field or the wrestling mat he was an absolute terror. Culp came out of Yuma Union High School without a lot of fanfare, but by the time his ASU athletic career was over he was one of the most decorated athletes at that point in the school's history. From his middle guard position on defense he made it virtually impossible for opponents to run up the middle. *Time Magazine* and *The Sporting News* named him a first-team All-American in 1967. He was perhaps even more impressive as a wrestler, often disposing of his heavyweight opponents in a matter of seconds. A four-time Western Athletic Conference champion, he became the first individual national champion in school history as a junior in 1967, pinning Dom Corollo of Adams State in just 51 seconds. Culp had an 84-9-4 record in four years as a Sun Devil. He was 45-0 in his final two seasons. Culp went on to become an All-Pro defensive tackle with the Kansas City Chiefs and Houston Oilers. He was a charter inductee into the ASU Sports Hall of Fame in 1975.

Curley Culp displays some wrestling hardware. (ASU Media Relations)

SUN DEVIL STAT

• Two of the Sun Devils' all-time track and field greats saw their school records broken during the 1968 spring season. Jerry Bright broke Henry Carr's school record for 200 meters with a time of 20.29 and Ron Freeman II eclipsed Ulis Williams' school mark at 400 meters with a time of 44.41. Freeman, the second Ron Freeman to compete at ASU in the 1960s, went on to capture a gold medal in the 4X400-meter relay and a bronze medal in the 400 meters in the 1968 Olympics.

Sun Devil Lore

A new 15-story women's dormitory—Manaznita Hall—opened north of University Drive and east of the Palo Verde Halls. It provided housing for about 1,000 coeds.

• U. S. Supreme Court Chief Justice Earl Warren and U.S. Secretary of Labor W. Willard Wirtz presented addresses during dedication ceremonies for the John S. Armstrong College of Law Building in February.

1968-1969

america's time capsule

arizona state university
m o m e n t

The Sun Devils' quest for a third national baseball championship didn't exactly get off to a rousing start at the College World Series in Omaha. The Devils ran into Texas freshman pitching sensation Burt Hooton in the first round and managed only four hits as the Longhorns prevailed by a 4-0 score. Things didn't get any easier in the second round, when ASU had to go 11 innings to nip UCLA, 2-1, in an elimination game. Lerrin LaGrow pitched all 11 innings for the Sun Devils, who scored the winning run on an error by Bruin pitcher Jim York in the 11th. Game No. 3 was no picnic either. The Devils scored in just one inning against Massachusetts, but they got four in that frame to win by a 4-2 score behind the pitching of Craig Swan and Larry Gura. From that point on, the Devils cruised. They whipped Tulsa, 11-3, and beat New York University, 4-1, to earn a spot in the championship game against Tulsa. The title game was no contest. Gura, appearing in his fourth tournament game, pitched a complete-game six-hitter, walking none and striking out 10, as the Devils romped, 10-1. Billy Cotton and John Dolinsek hit home runs for ASU. Dolinsek was named Most Valuable Player of the Series.

College World Series MVP John Dolinsek, left, congratulates teammate Paul Ray Powell after a CWS home run. (ASU Media Relations)

Sun Devil *spotlight*

The 1968 ASU-Arizona football game in Tucson was not among the most dramatic in school history, but it might have been one of the most significant. The Sun Devils were 7-2 and Arizona 8-1 entering the contest and the Sun Bowl in El Paso, Texas, had indicated it would take the winner. But UA Coach Darrell Mudra issued a successful take-us-or-leave-us ultimatum to bowl officials before the game. The Sun Devils and their fans were incensed. The fired-up Sun Devils struck early on a couple of long touchdown runs by Art Malone and went on to pound the Wildcats, 30-7, in a game that came to be known as the Ultimatum Bowl. ASU stayed home for the holidays while Arizona was embarrassed by Auburn, 35-10, in the Sun Bowl. The circumstances provided the spark for creation of the Fiesta Bowl, which debuted in 1971.

ASU LEGEND

Art Malone

Art Malone never met a linebacker he couldn't flatten. At least that was the way the hard-running back from Eloy approached the game of football. As a sophomore in 1967, Malone played halfback, but he moved into the fullback spot the next two seasons with devastating results. As a junior in 1968, Malone put together arguably the most productive season ever by an ASU running back. He gained 1,431 yards on 235 carries, a whopping 6.1-yard average, and rushed for 15 touchdowns. And he did it in just 10 games. The only running back in ASU history to gain more yards in a single season was Whizzer White with 1,502 yards in 1950. White, who scored 17 touchdowns rushing, played 11 games. Malone had 14 games of 100 yards or more in his ASU career. He twice cracked the 200-yard barrier in 1968, rushing for 239 yards on 29 carries against New Mexico and gaining 200 yards on just 19 carries against Utah. A two-time All-Western Athletic Conference selection, Malone was WAC Player of the Year in 1968. He played in the East-West Shrine game and the College All-Star game following his senior season. A second-round pick of the Atlanta Falcons, Malone played six years professionally with the Falcons and Philadelphia Eagles. He served for 22 years on the ASU athletic staff, including 12 as Senior Program Coordinator. His duties included responsibility for the upkeep of Sun Devil Stadium, Packard Stadium, Sun Angel Track Stadium and the Whiteman Tennis Center.

Hard-running Art Malone was WAC player of the Year in 1968. (ASU Media Relations)

THE sun devil LIST

ASU's consensus All-Americans in football

Year	Player
1968	Ron Pritchard
1972	Woody Green
1973	Woody Green
1975	Mike Haynes
1977	John Jefferson
1978	Al Harris
1981	Mike Richardson
1982	Mike Richardson
1983	Luis Zendejas
1984	David Fulcher
1985	David Fulcher
1986	Danny Villa
1987	Randall McDaniel
1996	Juan Roque

SUN DEVIL STATS

• Jane Bastanchury Booth won the AIAW women's golf title, becoming the third national collegiate champ at that point in ASU history along with Joanne Gunderson (1960) and Carol Sorenson (1962).

• With sophomore Kendis Moore of Phoenix again leading the way, the women's swimming team won its second straight national championship and went undefeated in dual meets for the fifth straight year.

• Roger Detter set a school record in basketball with 36 consecutive free throws made over 13 games, breaking the mark of 35 set by Art Becker in 1963.

• Bill Lenoir, a three-time All-American at rival Arizona, was named tennis coach at ASU.

Sun Devil Lore

Fueled by the Vietnam war, student unrest and activism was present on the ASU campus. The school escaped the violence that hit many campuses, but there was enough activity to cause some state legislators to propose slashing ASU's budget.

• A new 80,000-square-foot Business Administration building was dedicated. The structure featured 20 classrooms, three seminar rooms, a computer laboratory, a library and numerous faculty offices.

LEGEND

Ron Pritchard

Ron Pritchard had an uncanny knack for finding the shortest distance between his linebacking position and the opposing ball carrier. And when he got there, Pritchard usually arrived in a bad mood. A three-year starter from 1966 through 1968, Pritchard at times appeared to be a man among boys. During his tenure, the Sun Devils were struggling for national recognition. Despite consecutive 8-2 seasons in '67 and '68, the best the Devils could do at the polls was a 20th ranking by UPI in '67 and a 23rd ranking the following year. They were snubbed by the nation's bowl committees both seasons. The lack of recognition for the Devils made it even more impressive when Pritchard earned first-team All-America honors from *Time Magazine*, *The Sporting News* and NEA. He was a second-team pick by AP and UPI. By earning first-team recognition from three of the five agencies, he became the first consensus All-American in ASU history. He was selected for the East-West Shrine Game, the Senior Bowl, the Hula Bowl, the Coaches All-America game and the College All-Star game. He won the Spaulding Award as the outstanding defensive player in the East-West Shrine Game. A first-round pick of the Houston Oilers in 1969, he went on to enjoy a productive professional career.

Ron Pritchard was ASU's first consensus All-American in football. (ASU Media Relations)

LEGEND

Paul Ray Powell

Like Art and Ben Malone, Paul Ray Powell was a product of the central Arizona cotton farming town of Eloy. A starting safety on the football team in 1967 and 1968, he also handled place-kicking duties. He led the nation in kick scoring in 1968. Most of Powell's recognition came in baseball, however. In 1969 Powell, an outfielder, led the Sun Devils in batting (.366), home runs (11) and RBIs (73) and earned first-team All-America honors. He was named College Player of the Year by *The Sporting News*. His .366 batting average tied the school record set by John Regoli in 1960. Powell played a major role as the Sun Devils captured their third national championship at the College World Series in Omaha. His two-run homer against Tulsa in a fourth-round game helped propel the Sun Devils to an 11-3 victory. He was named to the All-CWS team. Powell was a first-round pick by the Minnesota Twins in the 1969 June draft, the seventh player drafted overall. He reached the major leagues with the Twins in 1971 and also spent two seasons in the majors with the Los Angeles Dodgers in 1973 and 1975.

Paul Ray Powell earned national honors in football and baseball. (ASU Media Relations)

LEGEND

Larry Gura

He had to bide his time for two years on talented ASU pitching staffs that featured the likes of Gary Gentry, Tom Burgess, Jeff Pentland and Joe Arnold, but when Larry Gura's turn came, he was ready. In 1969, Gura put together a season that old-timers still talk about in college baseball circles. Gura set an NCAA single-season record for victories with a 19-2 record as the Sun Devils rolled to their third national championship in five years. Gura established a school record with a sparkling 1.01 ERA and struck out 196 batters in 169 innings. Eddie Bane came along in 1972 to break Gura's school ERA record with a 0.99 mark, but Gura's figure remains second-best in school history. Gura made four pitching appearances—two as a starter and two in relief—as the Sun Devils shook off a first-round loss to Texas to capture the national title. He went the distance in the championship game, allowing six hits and no walks and striking out 10 in a 10-1 romp over Tulsa. Gura pitched for the Chicago Cubs, New York Yankees and Kansas City Royals during a 16-year major league career.

Larry Gura set an NCAA record with 19 pitching victories in 1969. (ASU Media Relations)

LEGEND

Mark Murro

Arizona State has had a succession of outstanding javelin throwers over the years. Bill Miller in the early 1950s, Ben Garcia in the mid-1950s, and NCAA champion Frank Covelli in the early 1960s all were world-class competitors. But the Sun Devils never had a javelin star like Mark Murro, before or since. Coach Baldy Castillo knew he was getting a good one when he recruited Murro, who set national high school and junior college records and earned a spot on the U. S. Olympic team before entering ASU. He finished ninth at the Mexico City Olympics in 1968. Upon arrival at ASU, Murro took care of business on the local front, winning Western Athletic Conference titles in 1969, 1970 and 1971. His toss of 292-8 as a sophomore in the 1969 WAC championships established NCAA and American records. In 1970, he became the first American to hurl the spear 300 feet with a throw of 300 feet even.

Mark Murro was the first American to hurl the javelin 300 feet. (ASU Media Relations)

1969-1970

america's time capsule

September 22, 1969: Willie Mays of the San Francisco Giants hit his 600th career home run, joining the legendary Babe Ruth as the only two players to reach that lofty plateau.

November 16, 1969: More than 450 Vietnam villagers were slain by a U.S. infantry unit in what would be known as the My Lai massacre.

March 18, 1970: The first major postal workers' strike began in the United States.

April 29, 1970: U.S. and South Vietnamese troops invaded Cambodia.

May 4, 1970: Four Kent State University students were killed by National Guard troops during an anti-war demonstration.

arizona state university
m o m e n t

David Buchanan was part of a potent backfield punch. (ASU Media Relations)

For the first time in the then eight-year history of the Western Athletic Conference, the Sun Devils were the league's football champions. It was particularly sweet for the Devils, because they clinched it in front of a sellout crowd at Sun Devil Stadium with a 38-24 thrashing of their arch rival, Arizona, in the final game of the season. Optimism began building when the Devils smoked Minnesota of the Big Ten, 48-26, in the season opener in Tempe. But serious doubts set in when early-season losses to Oregon State (30-7) and Utah (24-23) left the Devils with a 2-2 record after four games. Then the high-powered offense began putting up big numbers with "Spaghetti Joe" Spagnola at quarterback and Art Malone and David Buchanan manning the running back spots. ASU won its final six games, averaging 47 points a game over that stretch, to finish 8-2 for the third straight season. And for the third straight year the nation's bowl committees snubbed the Sun Devils. El Paso's Sun Bowl, which succumbed to a University of Arizona power play the previous year, again mysteriously overlooked the Devils. The Sun Bowl committee, still stinging from a wave of criticism in the Phoenix area, picked a 5-4-1 Georgia team for one of its berths as momentum continued to build for a bowl game, to be called the Fiesta Bowl, in Sun Devil Stadium.

spotlight

Arizona State continued to be a prominent name in women's amateur golf circles when Cathy Gaughan-Mant earned medalist honors at the 1970 AIAW tournament. She became the school's fourth national champion, following the footsteps of Joanne Gunderson-Carner (1960), Carol Sorenson (1962) and Jane Bastanchury-Booth (1969). Meanwhile, Bastanchury continued to dominate after concluding her senior season at ASU. After leaving ASU, Bastanchury won her third consecutive Broadmoor Women's Invitational in Colorado Springs and was the No. 1 selection for the U.S. Curtis Cup team. She also would play on the 1972 and 1974 Curtis Cup teams. Bastanchury-Booth's daughter, Kellee Booth, would become an ASU golf star in the 1990s.

ASU LEGEND

Lenny Randle

He wasn't a big, strong guy who lugged the football 25 times a game and he wasn't a slugging star who belted the baseball out of sight, but just about anyone who saw Lenny Randle in action would agree he was one of the most exciting athletes to play either sport at ASU. Speed was the name of Randle's game, and he used it to earn a spot in ASU's Sports Hall of Fame. Randle returned two punts and a kickoff for touchdowns in 1968 and ran back three punts for scores the following season. He still holds eight school records in various punt return categories and eight more in combined punt and kickoff return categories. He stole four bases in one baseball game against Cal Poly-San Luis Obispo in March of 1969, a school record that since has been tied several times. In 1970, he led the Sun Devils in batting with a .335 average. Randle played 12 years of major league baseball with the Washington Senators, Texas Rangers, New York Mets and Seattle Mariners.

Speedy Lenny Randle starred in football and baseball. (ASU Media Relations)

Sun Devil Lore

G. Homer Durham, ASU's president since 1960, resigned to become Utah's first state commissioner of higher education. Dr. Harry K. Newburn was named acting president. The Arizona Board of Regents removed the word "acting" from Newburn's title five months later.

THE *sun devil* LIST

ASU against Big Ten teams in football

Illinois:
ASU won, 21-7, in 1987; ASU won, 21-16, in 1988

Iowa:
ASU won, 17-7, (Sun Bowl) in 1997

Michigan:
ASU won, 22-15, (Rose Bowl) in 1987

Michigan State:
MSU won, 12-3, in 1985; ASU won, 20-17, in 1986

Minnesota:
ASU won, 48-26, in 1969

Northwestern:
ASU won, 35-3, in 1977; ASU won, 56-14, in 1978

Ohio State:
Ohio State won, 38-21, in 1980; Ohio State won, 20-17, (Rose Bowl) in 1997

Penn State:
Penn State won, 42-30, (Fiesta Bowl) in 1977

Wisconsin:
ASU won, 42-16, in 1967; ASU won, 55-7, in 1968

SUN DEVIL STATS

- The Sun Devils set school and Western Athletic Conference football attendance records by drawing 266,269 fans, an average of 44,378 for six home games.

- Mark Murro became the first American to throw the javelin 300 feet with a toss of 300 feet even and Chuck LaBenz set school records in the 1,500 meters (3:40.7) and mile run (3:56.9). LaBenz is the only sub four-minute miler in school history.

- Guard Seabern Hill set a school basketball scoring record, averaging 22.8 points per game. It stood until the 1999-2000 season, when Eddie House averaged 23.0.

1970-1971

america's time capsule

arizona state university
m o m e n t

The Sun Devils hadn't been to a football bowl game since the 1951 Salad Bowl in Phoenix and it appeared they might get shut out again in 1970 despite an unbeaten regular season. Finally, the Peach Bowl in Atlanta agreed to match the Sun Devils against North Carolina, though ASU had to buy its way in by purchasing 10,000 tickets. About 2,000 fans followed the Devils to Atlanta. Other ASU supporters purchased the remaining 8,000 tickets and donated them to servicemen and underprivileged children in the Atlanta area. The conditions definitely were not favorable to the Sun Devils. A week of rain in Atlanta turned into a raging snow storm during the second half of the Peach Bowl, but the Devils seemed to relish the miserable conditions. The running of NCAA rushing leader Don McCauley gave the Tar Heels a 26-21 halftime lead, but the Sun Devils refused to fold. Monroe Eley scored on runs of 8 and 5 yards, Steve Holden had a 13-yard

The Sun Devils rallied for a 48-26 Peach Bowl victory over North Carolina in an Atlanta snow storm. (ASU Media Relations)

scoring run and Bob Thomas plunged over from two yards out as the Devils outscored the Tar Heels 27-0 in the second half and walked away with a resounding 48-26 victory. Eley, who rushed for 173 yards, was named the game's top offensive player. Defensive end Junior Ah You was named the defensive MVP. The victory elevated the Sun Devils to sixth in the final Associated Press poll and signaled ASU's arrival on the national gridiron scene.

SUN DEVIL *spotlight*

The Sun Devils claimed the first of the three national women's team tennis championships they would win under coach Anne Pittman, and they did it in convincing fashion. Pam Richmond Champagne, who had been a finalist in the 1969 USTA collegiate championships, broke through to win the national crown in 1971. She did it by beating her ASU teammate, Margaret "Peggy" Michel, 6-1, 6-2, in the championship match. Champagne then teamed with Michel to capture the doubles championship as ASU rolled to the national team title.

LEGEND

Joe Spagnola

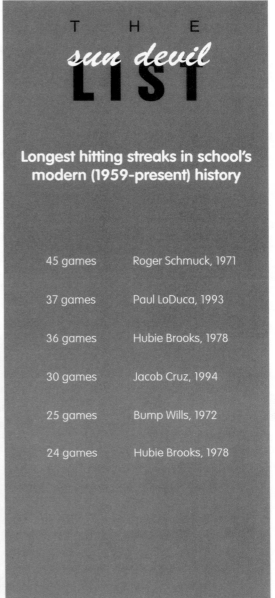

The New York Jets had "Broadway Joe" Namath. In the Arizona desert, one of the heroes of Arizona State's rise to national football prominence was a guy named "Spaghetti Joe" Spagnola. He came up a little short of the standards that cause the pulse of professional scouts to quicken, but he could flat-out win college football games. Coach Frank Kush liked his spunk and style enough to make him the starter at quarterback as a sophomore in 1968 and Spagnola rewarded Kush with three years of outstanding productivity. With Spagnola at the helm, the Sun Devils went 8-2 in '68 and '69 before breaking through with an 11-0 run in 1970, climaxed by a 48-26 Peach Bowl victory over North Carolina. Granted, the supporting cast was impressive in all of those years, but Spagnola was the catalyst for a team that averaged 38.8 points and 463 yards per game during his tenure. His propensity for throwing almost as many interceptions (28) as TD passes (35) during his ASU career sometimes had Kush tearing his hair, but that was overshadowed by Spagnola's ability to put his team in the victory column. His best year was his last, when he completed 92 of 205 passes for 1,991 yards and 18 touchdowns with 14 interceptions.

Longest hitting streaks in school's modern (1959-present) history

45 games	Roger Schmuck, 1971
37 games	Paul LoDuca, 1993
36 games	Hubie Brooks, 1978
30 games	Jacob Cruz, 1994
25 games	Bump Wills, 1972
24 games	Hubie Brooks, 1978

QB Joe Spagnola led the Sun Devils to an unbeaten season in 1970. (ASU Media Relations)

SUN DEVIL STATS

• The unbeaten Sun Devil football team, which attained a No. 6 ranking in the final Associated Press Poll, led the nation in total offense with 514.5 yards per game during the regular season.

• Junior college transfer Paul Stovall averaged 16.3 points per game as the Sun Devils shook off a 4-22 record the previous season to finish 16-10 in basketball.

• Sun Devil shortstop Al Bannister set an NCAA record for most triples in one season with 13.

SUN DEVIL LORE

John W. Schwada, chancellor at the University of Missouri since 1964, was named as the 12th president of the university, effective July 1, 1971.

• A new memorial union— twice the size of the previous building—was opened after a two-year closure for remodeling.

• Fred Miller, former athletic director at Cal State Long Beach, was named to replace Clyde B. Smith, who resigned as athletic director.

LEGEND

Clyde B. Smith

His conservative style sometimes was a source of consternation for ASU fans who wanted a more aggressive approach, but Clyde B. Smith clearly was the right man for the job during most of his tenure as Arizona State's athletic director. After three largely undistinguished years as head football coach (6-3, 4-5-1, 5-5) Smith was named AD and chairman of the physical education department in 1955. He oversaw the most dynamic period of athletic growth at the school before stepping down in 1971. He was present when the school began to build a national football reputation under coach Dan Devine in the late 1950s and he made three of the most important hires in the school's athletic history—football coach Frank Kush, basketball coach Ned Wulk and baseball coach Bobby Winkles. Above all, Smith ran a clean program. Growth might have been more rapid without Smith hauling back on the reins, but he made sure the program grew in an orderly fashion and stayed within the rules. "We were all frustrated at times because we didn't have a lot of resources," Kush said, "But Smitty did the best he could. Some people felt he wasn't very progressive, and he wouldn't play the political games, but he laid down a strong foundation." Wulk said Smith "was always characterized as being conservative and not very forward-looking, but the whole program took off when he was there. The whole basis of that program as it sits there today can be traced back to him. He's never been given much credit for that."

Athletic director Clyde B. Smith brought stability to the program. (ASU Media Relations)

LEGEND

Kendis Moore Drake

Some athletes arrive unheralded on a college campus and gradually develop into stars. That definitely wasn't the case with swimmer Kendis Moore, who set a world record in the 200-meter butterfly in 1965 — two years before she enrolled at ASU. Moore was one of the key figures in ASU's drive to the pinnacle of women's college swimming in the late 1960s and early 1970s. The Sun Devils won the national championship six times in eight years from 1967 through 1974. Moore, a member of the 1968 U.S. Olympic team, finished fourth in the 100-meter Olympic backstroke. A year earlier she won the 200-meter butterfly and swam on the winning 400-meter medley relay team in the Pan American Games. She enjoyed her finest ASU moment in the 1968 national collegiate championships, where she became the first woman ever to capture three collegiate individual titles in one year. She won the 50-yard backstroke, the 100-yard backstroke and the 100-yard butterfly. She repeated her title in the 100-yard butterfly at the 1969 national championships. She was elected to the ASU Sports Hall of Fame in 1977.

Kendis Moore Drake won three national swim titles in one year. (ASU Media Relations)

LEGEND

J.D. Hill

He came along at a time when ASU was brimming with athletic talent, and J.D. Hill was one of the most gifted of them all. A multi-talented athlete, Hill starred for the Sun Devil football team, was a standout sprinter on the track and field team and even took a fling at baseball. Hill was a solid receiver in 1967 and 1968, though he took a back seat to Ken Dyer and Fair Hooker in those two seasons. After sitting out the 1969 season while in coach Frank Kush's doghouse, he came back with a vengeance. He caught 61 passes for 1,009 yards and 11 touchdowns—all school records at the time—for the unbeaten and sixth-ranked 1970 Sun Devils. His 67-yard scoring pass reception from quarterback Joe Spagnola was one of the highlights of ASU's 48-26 Peach Bowl victory over North Carolina. He was named a first-team All-American by *The Sporting News* and *Time* magazine and was a first-round draft pick of the Buffalo Bills. Some of Hill's most legendary feats came on the track. Perhaps the most notable was his victory in the 100-yard dash at the 1968 Western Athletic Conference track and field championships at Laramie, Wyoming. On a typically cold and blustery Laramie day, Hill won in a wind-aided time of 9.3 seconds . . . in his sweats.

J.D. Hill was a gifted all-around athlete. (ASU Media Relations)

LEGEND

Roger Schmuck

They still were using wooden bats in college baseball back in 1971. And in those days, before most of the top high school pitchers were lured away by the big bucks dangled by professional baseball, the college game was liberally sprinkled with quality pitching arms. They often played games in two hours or less, not the 3 1/2 hours of recent seasons, as pitchers dominated. Factor in all of the above, plus the fact that Sun Devil first baseman Roger Schmuck was batting .167 when he showed up at the ballpark on March 8, and what took place over the next two-plus months was absolutely amazing. All Schmuck did was put together a 45-game hitting streak, which stood for 10 years as an NCAA record. Schmuck hit safely in every game from March 8 to May 14, batting a resounding .477 with 10 home runs and 66 RBIs during that stretch. His slugging percentage was in the stratosphere at .829. The streak finally ended when Schmuck went 0-for-4 against UTEP pitcher Mark Bombard. Schmuck's .434 batting average stood as an ASU single-season record until 1993, when Paul LoDuca bumped him into second place by hitting .446. Schmuck's hitting streak withstood an assault by LoDuca, who fell eight games short at 37. Schmuck, who played the outfield for the Sun Devils in 1970 and batted .321, earned first-team All-America honors at first base in '71. He later served briefly as pitching coach at ASU before a lengthy and successful career as head coach at Mesa Community College.

Roger Schmuck's 45-game hitting streak was an NCAA record. (ASU Media Relations)

1971-1972

america's time capsule

arizona state university
|m o m e n t

After years of being snubbed by bowl selection committees and having to buy their way into the Peach Bowl in 1970, the Sun Devils finally arrived as a regular fixture on the national bowl scene with the 1971 Fiesta Bowl, which was played in their own Sun Devil Stadium. Longtime fans still talk about that first game nearly 30 years later. The Sun Devils hooked up in a shoot-out with Florida State, a school that, like ASU, was just beginning to break through as a member of college football's elite. The crowd of 51,098 was the largest ever to watch a bowl game's initial attraction. Florida State quarterback Gary Huff put on a passing clinic, completing 25 of 46 passes for 347 yards and two touchdowns to earn the Outstanding Offensive Player award. Huff and the Seminoles came up short, however, against ASU's balanced attack. Sophomore quarterback Danny White completed 15 of 30 for 250 yards and two TDs, and Woody Green carried 24 times for 101 yards and three scores. Green's two-yard touchdown burst with 34 seconds to play gave ASU a 45-38 victory. Steve Holden provided two big plays for the Sun Devils, catching a 55-yard touchdown pass from White in the second quarter and returning a punt 68 yards for a touchdown to give ASU a seven-point lead in the fourth quarter. ASU defensive end Junior Ah You was named the game's Outstanding Defensive Player. The Sun Devils finished 11-1 with rankings of sixth by United Press International and eighth by the Associated Press.

Two big plays by Steve Holden helped the Sun Devils win the inaugural Fiesta Bowl in a shoot-out against Florida State. (ASU Media Relations)

spotlight

Bobby Winkles, who had built ASU into one of the top powers in college baseball, resigned on January. 1 to accept a coaching position with the California Angels. Winkles, who began his ASU coaching career in 1959, compiled a record of 524-173 and won national championships in 1965, 1967 and 1969. Hired to replace Winkles was Jim Brock, a 1958 ASU graduate who had compiled a 163-80 record in six seasons as head coach at Mesa Community College. Brock's 1970 and 1971 Mesa clubs had won national titles. He was named national junior college Coach of the Year after both of those seasons. Brock's first ASU team went 64-6 overall and 18-0 in the Western Athletic Conference and reached the championship game of the College World Series, where the Sun Devils lost, 1-0, to Southern California. Brock won the "Big Stick" National Coach of the Year Award presented by the Adirondack Bat Company.

LEGEND

Alan Bannister

A first-team All-American shortstop in 1971 and 1972, Alan Bannister set an NCAA record for most triples in a season with 13 in 1971. In 1972, he became the first collegiate player ever to get more than 100 hits in a season (101) and he added two more NCAA records—most RBIs (90) and most total bases (177). He batted .376 in 1971 and .380 in 1972. Bannister, however, brought more to the game than his bat. He is the shortstop on ASU's all-time defensive team. In 1994, the publication *Baseball America* selected an all-time college team. Bannister was the shortstop on that team. He was one of four Sun Devils on that team—twice as many as any other school. The others were second baseman Bob Horner and pitchers Eddie Bane and Floyd Bannister. Alan Bannister went on to play major league baseball for the Philadelphia Phillies, Chicago White Sox, New York Yankees and Kansas City Royals.

Shortstop Alan Bannister set three NCAA baseball records. (ASU Media Relations)

SUN DEVIL LORE

After more than a year of controversy, students, faculty staff and alumni voted 11,122 to 3,142 to retain the 27-year-old Sun Devil emblem that was designed by Disney Studios.

• Women's athletics at ASU received a boost when the school became a charter member of the Association for Intercollegiate Athletics for Women (AIAW). There was one major difference between the AIAW and the men's governing body, the NCAA. The AIAW did not allow recruiting. "The athletes must come to us. We can't go after them the way they can in men's sports," said Dr. Dorothy Deach, chairman of the ASU women's PE department.

THE sun devil LIST

Longest football winning streaks in ASU history

21 games	1969-70-71
13 games	1956-57-58
13 games	1974-75
12 games	1963-64
12 games	1972-73
11 games	1959-60
11 games	1981-82
11 games	1996

SUN DEVIL STATS

• The women's softball team won its first national championship, then beat a team from Japan, four games, to one, to claim the mythical world championship.

• The Sun Devil basketball team, led by forward Paul Stovall, enjoyed its best season in nine years, finishing with an 18-8 record and knocking off three nationally-ranked teams—third-ranked USC, seventh-ranked BYU and 13th-ranked Houston.

• A 24-18 loss to Oregon State in the fifth game of the season snapped the longest football winning streak in school history, 21 games over three seasons.

• John Fort was named ASU's first men's tennis All-American.

• Howard Twitty earned first-team All-America honors as the men's golf team placed fifth at the NCAA tournament.

LEGENDS

Margaret "Peggy" Michel
&
Pam Richmond Champagne

Peggy Michel and Pam Richmond Champagne were central figures in Arizona State's rise to national prominence in women's college tennis under coach Anne Pittman in the late 1960s and early 1970s. They teamed up to lead the Sun Devils to the first of their three national titles in 1971. Richmond was a finalist at the 1969 USTA collegiate singles championships, then captured the crown two years later. She did it by defeating her ASU teammate, Michel, 6-1, 6-2, in the championship match. The two then teamed up to win the collegiate doubles title. They returned in 1972 and successfully defended their doubles crown as the Sun Devils won their second straight national collegiate team championship. Michel went on to international success when she teamed with Australia's Evonne Goolagong to win the 1974 Wimbledon doubles title. Michel and Richmond Champagne are members of ASU's Sports Hall of Fame. Michel was a charter inductee in 1975.

Peggy Michel (left) and Pam Richmond Champagne hold their national doubles championship trophy. (Anne Pittman collection)

LEGEND

Junior Ah You

Arizona State's football teams of the early 1970s were best known for their high-powered offenses, but during the same period there was some quality defensive work being done. One of the chief practitioners was a lightning-quick defensive end from Hawaii named Junior Ah You. During Ah You's three years as a starter the Sun Devils posted records of 8-2, 11-0 and 11-1. Opposing offensive tackles undoubtedly lost plenty of sleep trying to figure out ways to block Ah You, who was a regular visitor to opponents' backfields. He became famous for the "Hawaiian Punch," which simply was a colorful way of describing the act of depositing an opposing quarterback on his backside. Ah You was a three-time All Western Athletic Conference first-team selection. He was named Outstanding Defensive Player of the Sun Devils' 1970 Peach Bowl victory over North Carolina and their 1971 Fiesta Bowl victory over Florida State. Following the 1971 seasons he was named to United Press International's All-America second team and earned honorable mention All-America honors from Associated Press. He went on to play professional football in Canada.

Junior Ah You authored the "Hawaiian Punch." (ASU Media Relations)

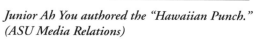

ASU LEGEND

Paula Miller Noel

A charter inductee into ASU's Sports Hall of Fame in 1975, Paula Miller Noel was one of the first true stars of a sport that began formal competition at ASU in 1967. She was named Most Valuable Player of the 1972 Women's College World Series as the Sun Devils won the first of two consecutive national championships. She was named to the All-College World Series team in each of her three appearances there in 1971, 1972 and 1973. She was a National American Softball Association first-team All-America selection in 1974 after having won second-team honors the previous season. Her 0.27 earned run average in 1973 still ranks third-best on ASU's all-time list.

Paula Noel was MVP of the 1972 softball College World Series. (ASU Media Relations)

ASU LEGEND

Steve Lieberman

His sport, archery, didn't get a lot of recognition, but Steve Lieberman achieved some milestones that rank among the most impressive in ASU sports history. Lieberman was the first male ASU athlete to win All-America honors four straight years. He accomplished that feat from 1971 through 1974. He was the United States Intercollegiate champion in 1971, 1972 and 1974. He was the World Field champion in 1973 and was named United States Male Archery Athlete of the Year in 1974. His accomplishments earned him induction into the ASU Sports Hall of Fame as a charter member in 1975.

Archery standout Steve Lieberman was a four-time All-American. (Chuck Conley/ASU Media Relations)

1972-1973

November 7, 1972: The Republican Party enjoyed its biggest landslide victory with the re-election of President Richard Nixon.

December 18, 1972: Paris peace negotiations reached an impasse and full-scale bombing of North Vietnam was resumed by American pilots.

January 22, 1973: An agreement to end the war in Vietnam was signed in Paris by representatives of the United States and North and South Vietnam.

June 9, 1973: Secretariat, called by many the greatest racehorse ever, won the Belmont Stakes and became the ninth Triple Crown winner.

July 16, 1973: The existence of the Watergate tapes was revealed.

arizona state university | m o m e n t

The Sun Devils received so much critical acclaim for their 45-38 victory over Florida State in the inaugural Fiesta Bowl in 1971 that they decided to stage an encore in the 1972 Fiesta. This time the opponent was Missouri and the score was 49-35. The previous year the Sun Devils scored the winning touchdown on a one-yard run by Woody Green with 34 seconds left. They put away Missouri a bit earlier, though it took three fourth-quarter touchdowns to do it. Green waltzed to Outstanding Offensive Player honors, gaining 202 yards on 25 carries and scoring on runs of two, 12, 17 and 21 yards. Green wasn't the whole story by any means. His backfield running mate, Brent McClanahan, gained 171 yards on 26 carries and scored one touchdown. Quarterback Danny White had a typically productive day, completing 13 of 23 passes for 266 yards and two touchdowns. Wide receiver Ed Beverly was on the other end of both scoring passes—a 34-yarder and a 53-yarder. The Sun Devils gained more yards than any team in the history of post-season bowl games—718. It was the third bowl victory in as many years for the Sun Devils, who had gone from 1951 to 1970 without a bowl appearance.

Ed Beverly caught two long touchdown passes in the Sun Devils' 49-35 Fiesta Bowl victory over Missouri. (ASU Media Relations)

SUN DEVIL *spotlight*

The basketball team lost two of three games on a tough early-season road trip to Creighton, Loyola of Chicago and Cincinnati, but the Sun Devils gradually built momentum as the season progressed. They beat rival Arizona in a pair of hotly-contested games, 63-60 in Tempe and 110-105 in Tucson, and captured their third Western Athletic Conference title with road victories over Wyoming and Colorado State in the final week of the regular season. They beat Oklahoma City, 103-78, in a first-round NCAA tournament game in Logan, Utah, but were eliminated by UCLA, 98-81, in the West Regional in Los Angeles. The Sun Devils, who finished 19-9 overall and 10-4 in the WAC, featured a balanced attack led by guards Mike Contreras (16.7 points per game) and Jim Owens (13.2). The front line was made up of center Ron (Rock) Kennedy (10.2) and forwards Ken Gray (8.9) and Mark Wasley (7.8).

ASU LEGEND

Woody Green

Who was the greatest running back in Arizona State football history? Old-timers will tell you nobody was more exciting than Whizzer White, who put on a weekly show from 1947 through 1950 and captured the NCAA rushing title his senior year. Others will point out that nobody can match the 8.0 rushing average of Leon Burton, who played from 1955 through 1958 and led the nation in rushing in 1957. And turn-of-the century newspaper accounts suggest that Charlie Haigler must have been something to behold. If you look at the overall numbers, however, Woody Green stands alone at the head of the pack. In three seasons from 1971 through 1973 the speedster from Portland, Oregon, posted spectacular and amazingly consistent rushing totals. As a sophomore in 1971 he rushed for 1,310 yards and 12 touchdowns. He followed that with 1,565 yards and 16 touchdowns as a junior and 1,313 yards and 12 TDs as a senior. His total of 4,188 yards blows away his closest challenger on ASU's career rushing list, Freddie Williams, who needed four years to amass 3,424 yards. Green's 39 career rushing touchdowns puts him No. 1 in that category. Burton is second with 34. Green had 21 games of 100 or more yards rushing, four more than Williams.

Sun Devils' top football seasons in team scoring and total offense. Bowl game statistics are included

Scoring

Year	Average
1972	46.83
1973	43.25
1968	41.40
1957	39.70
1996	39.25

Total offense

Year	Average
1973	555.1
1972	533.3
1970	508.7
1996	478.1
1950	470.4

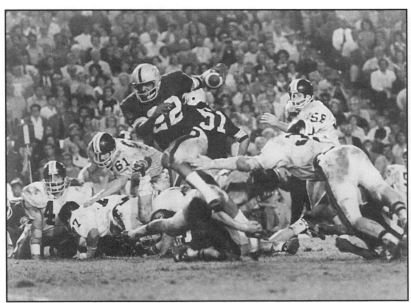

Woody Green rushed for a school-record 4,188 yards and 39 touchdowns in three seasons. (ASU Media Relations)

Sun Devil Lore

Removal of two campus landmarks, North and South Halls, was approved by the Arizona Board of Regents.

• ASU's new Tartan running track, an ultra-modern surface built by public subscription, was opened for student and public use.

SUN DEVIL STAT

• The Sun Devil football team led the nation in scoring (46.4 points per game) and total offense (516.5 yards) and finished third in rushing offense. Those figures do not include their 49-point, 718-yard performance against Missouri in the Fiesta Bowl. Bowl statistics are not included for national ranking purposes.

Arizona State's Maurice Peoples won the NCAA 440-yard dash title, upsetting favorite Benny Brown of UCLA.

ASU coaches Mona Plummer (swimming) and Anne Pittman (women's tennis) were named head coaches of the U.S. national teams for competition at the World University Games in Moscow.

ASU golfer Mary Bea Porter earned first-team All-America honors.

The women's archery team captured its fifth straight national collegiate title.

arizona state university ———
| m o m e n t

Arizona State pitchers have recorded eight no-hitters over the years, but one stands heads and shoulders above the rest. On March 2, 1973, left-hander Eddie Bane tossed the only perfect game in school history against Cal-State Northridge. A little luck usually is involved in a perfecto, but Bane left little to chance. He struck out 19 batters as the Sun Devils won in a breeze, 9-0. Bane said he knew early that he had good stuff. "I came back to the dugout in the middle innings and told our guys they didn't need to be scoring all those runs, because the other guys weren't going to get anything," Bane recalled many years later. Bane warmed up for his 1973 heroics by pitching a two-hitter against New Mexico in May of 1971 and another two-hitter against Chapman in March of 1972. Bane's 19 strikeouts wasn't his career high at ASU. He had 19 on two other occasions and 21 against LaVerne on April 1, 1972. That game lasted 14 innings.

———

Eddie Bane pitched the only perfect game in ASU baseball history against Cal State-Northridge (ASU Media Relations)

The baseball team, under second-year coach Jim Brock, reached the national title game for the second year in a row. And for the second straight year, the Sun Devils lost a one-run decision to USC in the championship game. This time the score was 4-3. The Trojans jumped out to a 4-0 lead after three innings and held off the Devils. Dick Harris singled home a run and Clay Westlake had an RBI double in the fourth inning and Gary Atwell scored on a wild pitch in the sixth, but that was the extent of ASU's scoring. The Sun Devils finished 59-8 overall. They won the Western Athletic Conference title with a 16-1 league mark after a perfect 18-0 conference record the previous season. Westlake (.382) was the team's leading hitter. The Sun Devils' pitching rotation of Eddie Bane (15-1), Jim Otten (15-1) and Dale Slocum (13-2) was dominant all season.

LEGEND

Eddie Bane

Back in the days before mind-boggling signing bonuses for top draft choices, college baseball had its share of big, strong flame throwers on the pitching mound. Eddie Bane wasn't one of them. A diminutive left-hander, Bane definitely didn't fit the mold of a prime pitching prospect. In Bane's case, it didn't matter. Not only was he the top college pitcher of his time, but one of the very best of all time. In 1994, the publication *Baseball America* selected an all-time college team. Bane was one of the five pitchers named to the team, along with Floyd Bannister, who began pitching at ASU in 1974, the year after Bane wrapped up his brilliant career and moved directly from the ASU campus to the major leagues with the Minnesota Twins. Bane's big pitch was a nasty curve ball that allowed him to consistently overmatch college hitters. In addition to the only perfect game in ASU baseball history, he pitched a pair of two-hitters. He struck out 21 batters in a 14-inning outing against LaVerne in 1972 and had three 19-strikeout games to his credit. His 0.99 ERA in 1972 still stands as a school record. A picture of consistency, he was 11-2, 14-1 and 15-1 in three seasons at ASU. One of his finest moments came against Oklahoma in the 1972 College World Series. He pitched a three hitter, walked two and struck out an NCAA tournament record 17 in a 1-0 victory over the Sooners.

Pitcher Eddie Bane went from ASU straight to the big leagues in 1973. (ASU Media Relations)

SUN DEVIL STAT

• Coach Mary Littlewood's women's softball team won its second straight national title at the College World Series. It capped off a perfect 13-0 season and established the Sun Devils as the nation's premier program. They had finished fourth nationally in 1970 before winning back-to-back national crowns.

Sun Devil Lore

ASU grads Guthrie and Peter Packard donated more than half the funds necessary for a new baseball stadium to be named after their father, Wickenburg resident William Guthrie Packard. The $450,000 gift was the largest individual contribution in ASU's history at the time. Packard Stadium would become a showplace among college baseball facilities.

1973-1974

arizona state university
moment

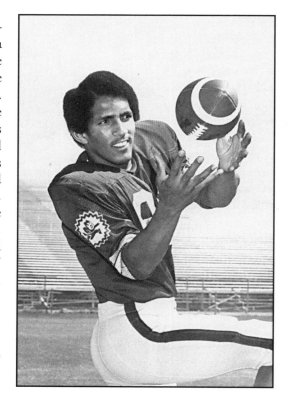

After winning scoring derbies over Florida State and Missouri in the first two Fiesta Bowls, the Sun Devils had a more conventional outing against Pittsburgh in Fiesta Bowl III. The afternoon started on a dismal note for ASU when quarterback Danny White fumbled on the first snap of the game and Pitt recovered on the Sun Devil 12. Two plays later Pitt freshman All-American Tony Dorsett scored from three yards out and the Panthers had a 7-0 lead. They were not heard from again, as the Sun Devils erupted for three touchdowns and a field goal in the final 16:29 to break open a close game and win 28-7. Dorsett got his 100 yards rushing, but it took 30 carries to do it. Meanwhile, ASU's Woody Green gained 131 yards on 25 carries including scoring runs of three, 23 and one yards. Green's big day gave him totals of 434 yards and 10 touchdowns in three Fiesta Bowl games. Those records still stand and likely never will be broken. ASU wide receiver Greg Hudson, who caught eight passes for 186 yards and one touchdown, was named the game's Outstanding Offensive Player. ASU cornerback Mike Haynes, who intercepted two passes and recovered a fumble, was named Outstanding Defensive Player.

Greg Hudson was named Outstanding Offensive Player of the Fiesta Bowl. (ASU Media Relations)

SUN DEVIL *spotlight*

Bobby Douglas, captain of the 1970 U.S. Olympic wrestling team, became ASU's first black head coach when he was named to head the wrestling program. Douglas replaced John Wadas, who moved to an administrative position. It didn't take Douglas long to began turning around the program, which had finished seventh in the Western Athletic Conference the two years prior to his arrival. His 1974-75 team would finish fifth and his 1975-76 team would win the conference title. Douglas would remain at ASU for 18 seasons, winning nine conference championships and claiming the national title in 1987-88.

LEGEND

Ben Malone

Initially, he was best-known as Art Malone's little brother, but it didn't take Ben Malone long to establish an identity of his own. First it was as a blocking fullback for rushing star Woody Green, whose career paralleled his at ASU, but Malone eventually matured into a dangerous runner in his own right. With a lightning-quick start from his up-back position, Malone often was into the secondary before opposing defenses knew what had happened. And his bow-legged gait made him difficult to tackle in the open field. When his ASU career was over, he had averaged more yards per carry (6.4) than his more-celebrated brother Art (4.7). He also averaged more than Green (6.2) or the legendary Wilford "Whizzer" White (6.3). Though he played a significant role in three ASU bowl victories and helped the Sun Devils beat rival Arizona three times, his finest moment might have come on an unfamiliar artificial turf surface in a driving rain and bitter cold on October 27 of 1973 at Portland, Oregon. He gained 250 yards in a 44-14 victory over Oregon State—a single-game rushing record that still stands. And he did it on just 24 carries—an amazing 10.4 yards per carry. As a senior in 1973 Malone joined the 1,000-yard club with 1,186 yards on 191 carries and led the Sun Devils with 15 touchdowns. He was part of a backfield that became the first in NCAA history to have all four members account for 1,000 yards. In addition to Malone, Green rushed for 1,313, quarterback Danny White passed for 2,878 and wingback Morris Owens had 1,076 receiving yards on 50 catches.

Ben Malone's 250 rushing yards against Oregon State still stands as a school record. (ASU Media Relations)

THE sun devil LIST

ASU's all-time single-game rushing leaders

Player	Year	Opponent	Yards
Ben Malone	1973	Oregon State	250
Leon Burton	1955	Hardin-Simmons	243
Art Malone	1968	New Mexico	239
Wilford White	1950	Brigham Young	236
Wilford White	1950	Northern Arizona	232
Darryl Clack	1983	Wichita State	221
Max Anderson	1967	Wisconsin	220
Freddie Williams	1974	Texas-El Paso	216
J. R. Redmond	1998	Southern California	214
Mario Bates	1992	Washington State	214
Woody Green	1971	Utah	214
Wilford White	1950	Utah State	214

SUN DEVIL STAT

- Carol Jurn and Steve Lieberman each earned All-America honors for the fourth time as ASU won the men's and mixed competition and finished second in women's at the national archery finals. It was the second national men's championship for the Sun Devils, who would go on to dominate the sport in both men's and women's competition.

SUN DEVIL LORE

The new University Activity Center, a jewel in the rapidly-expanding athletic complex on the north end of campus, opened in April, too late for the 1973-74 basketball season, but in time for commencement exercises. In addition to providing a home for indoor sports, it housed the school's athletic offices. It also provided a venue for concerts and other activities.

The basketball team finished 18-9, losing to Toledo, 81-74, in the first round of the Commissioner's Invitational Tournament in Toledo, Ohio.

The men's gymnastics team placed second at the NCAA championships in University Park, Pennsylvania. Four Sun Devils—Gary Alexander, L.J. Larsen, Rick Curtis and Greg Bian—earned All-America honors.

The women's golf team finished fourth at the national championship tournament.

The women's volleyball team went 21-0 in its first year of competition under coach Mary Littlewood and finished with a #15 national ranking.

arizona state university
| m o m e n t

Coach Anne Pittman's women's tennis team captured its third national title in four years, beating 61 other schools at the U.S. Lawn Tennis Association's National Women's Collegiate Tennis Championship in Kalamazoo, Michigan. The Sun Devils were led by twins Claire and Kay Schmoyer, who won six matches and reached the semi-finals in doubles. Because of the size of the 245-player field the Schmoyers were forced to play one match at midnight. The Devils didn't have any finalists, but were able to outdistance the rest of the field because of their superior depth. Unseeded Sue Boyle and Bee Kilgore reached the doubles quarterfinals. Isa Ortiz earned 4 1/2 points by winning two matches in championship singles play and three in the consolation bracket. The Sun Devils were 22-0 in dual matches during the regular season, won two of the three invitational tournaments they entered and won the Western Athletic Conference and Western Collegiate Tennis Conference titles. In regular-season individual matches the Sun Devils were 188-5. The

Twins Claire and Kay Schmoyer led the Sun Devils to their third national tennis title in four years. (ASU Media Relations)

team played 27 events from California to Texas during a season that stretched from September to May, and did it on a budget of less than $4,000. Pittman and her players paid their own way to the national championships.

The women's swimming team won its sixth national title in an eight-year stretch under coach Mona Plummer, scoring 242 points to 164 for runner-up Miami in the championship meet hosted by Penn State. Sophomores Libby Tullis and Sally Tuttle led the Sun Devils, who placed 12 swimmers on the All-America team. Tullis won the 100-yard backstroke and swam on the winning 200-freestyle and 400-medley relay teams. Tuttle won the 100-yard freestyle and swam on the winning 200-medley relay and 400-medley relay teams. Tullis' time of 59.74 seconds in the 100-yard backstroke and Tuttle's 53.3 in the 100-yard freestyle were meet records.

LEGEND

Bob Breunig

Arizona State's football program had just about everything you could think of during its climb to national prominence in the late 1960s and early 1970s except for a home-grown defensive hero. Bob Breunig solved that problem. Breunig, a prep football All-American and state wrestling champion at Alhambra High in Phoenix, wasted little time making an impact at ASU. He earned a starting job as a sophomore and proceeded to lead the Sun Devils in tackles with 91 while earning All-Western Athletic Conference first-team honors. He had 19 tackles in one game against Air Force his sophomore season.

He led the Sun Devils in tackles again as a junior with 117 and as a senior with 145, earning All-Conference honors both seasons. He recovered three fumbles and intercepted three passes as a senior. His big senior season earned him first-team All-America honors from the Football Coaches of America, *The Sporting News* and *Time* magazine. Associated Press and United Press International selected him to their All-America second teams. He was only the third ASU defensive player to earn first-team All-America honors at that point in the school's history. Nose guard Curley Culp made the *Time* and *Sporting News* teams in 1967 and linebacker Ron Pritchard was a consensus choice in 1968. Breunig was selected for the East-West Shrine Game and Hula Bowl following the 1974 season and was a third-round pick of the Dallas Cowboys in the 1975 draft. He was a standout for many seasons with the Cowboys.

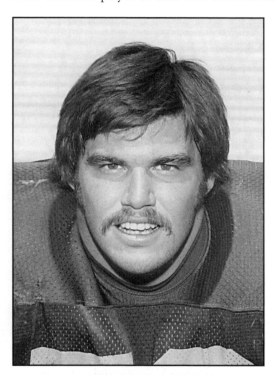

Bob Breunig was a home-grown football defensive hero. (ASU Media Relations)

SUN DEVIL STAT

• Bump Wills set a modern era school record by hitting three home runs in one baseball game March 20 against Cal State-Fullerton. Wills' record lasted 10 years before it was matched in 1984 by Oddibe McDowell against Stanford. Since then, Todd Brown (1985), Ted Dyson (1986), Mike Kelly (twice in 1990) and Jim Austin (1991) have joined the three-homer club.

Sun Devil Lore

ASU's sparkling new baseball facility, Packard Stadium, opened amid much fanfare midway through the 1974 season. The ceremonial first pitch was thrown out by William Guthrie Packard, for whom the stadium was named. More than half of the construction cost was provided through a $450,000 gift by Packard's sons, ASU alumni Peter and Guthrie Packard.

1974-1975

america's time capsule

arizona state university
m o m e n t

The Sun Devils rode coach Ned Wulk's three-guard lineup to a 25-4 basketball record, their best since the 1962-63 team went 26-3 and a mark that still stands as second-best in school history. They started the season by winning their first nine games. The streak was snapped by Oregon, 80-76, in the Far West Classic in Portland, Oregon. The Sun Devils shook off that loss and won their next six games, giving them 15 victories in their first 16 games. Road losses to Colorado State (91-80) and Texas El Paso (75-70) were the only blemishes in a 12-2 Western Athletic Conference season. They won a thriller over Arizona, 83-81, on the Wildcats' home court, then outscored the Wildcats 107-92 in Tempe. A 97-94 victory over Alabama in the first round of the NCAA tournament in Tempe earned the Devils a spot in the West Regional in Portland. They won an 84-81 decision over Nevada-Las Vegas in Portland but were eliminated by eventual national champion UCLA, 89-75. All five starters earned All-Conference recognition. Guard Lionel Hollins (16.7 ppg) was a first team selection, guard Rudy White (14.3) was a second-team choice and honorable mention honors went to center Scott Lloyd (12.0), guard Mike Moon (10.1) and forward Jack Schrader (9.8). Hollins, who had showcased his skills in the Portland area twice during the season, was a first-round choice of the Portland Trailblazers, the No. 5 pick overall, in the NBA draft. White went in the third round to Houston.

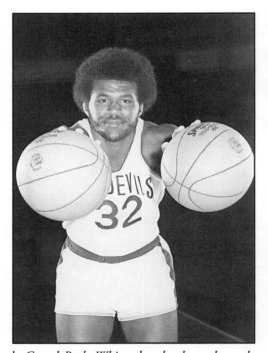

Guard Rudy White played a key role as the basketball team rolled to a 25-4 record. (ASU Media Relations)

SUN DEVIL *spotlight*

Coach Jim Brock's baseball team won more than 60 games for the second time in four years (61-13), but again the Sun Devils came up short at the College World Series in Omaha, Nebraska. The Sun Devils breezed through the Western Athletic Conference at 16-2, won a regional tournament in Tempe and won their first two games in Omaha. The Devils, who had lost to University of Southern California in the championship game in 1972 and 1973, again fell victim to a school with the initials USC. This time it was University of South Carolina that beat ASU by scores of 6-3 and 4-1, relegating the Devils to third place. ASU had broken open a scoreless semifinal game on Jerry Maddox' two-out triple in the eighth inning, but South Carolina erupted for four runs in the top of the ninth. Maddox, who batted .365 and belted a school-record 20 home runs, won the Lefty Gomez Plate as College Player of the Year.

ASU
LEGEND

Lionel Hollins

When the Sun Devils moved into the Activity Center for the 1974-75 season, they needed a showcase player with talents befitting the sparkling new building. Fortunately, they had one in guard Lionel Hollins, who already had made a name for himself the previous year as the Devils played their final campaign in Sun Devil Gym. Hollins, who played high school ball at Rancho High in Las Vegas, transferred to ASU prior to the 1973-74 season from Dixie College in St. George, Utah, where he had earned JC All-America honors. Hollins was named the team's most valuable player as a junior after leading the Sun Devils in scoring at 17.3. Though his scoring average dipped to 16.7 on a balanced ASU club in 1974-75, Hollins was even better as a senior. He set a then school record with 149 assists and was the catalyst as the Sun Devils went 14-0 in their new arena and finished with national rankings of seventh by United Press International and eighth by the Associated Press. Hollins participated in three post-season all-star events—the Pizza Hut Classic, the East-West game and the Aloha Classic. *The Sporting News* and *Basketball Weekly* named him to their All-America first teams. He remains the only ASU player in history to earn first-team All-America honors. The Portland Trailblazers made him the fifth pick in the first round of the NBA draft. The only ASU players ever drafted higher were Joe Caldwell, the No. 2 pick by Detroit in 1964 and Byron Scott, No. 4 by San Diego in 1983.

Lionel Hollins is the only first-team basketball All-American in school history. (Media Relations)

THE sun devil LIST

Arizona State's basketball All-Americans

Player	Year	Organization
Eddie House	2000	AP (hm)
Mario Bennett	1995	AP (hm)
Stevin Smith	1993	AP (hm)
Trent Edwards	1989	AP (hm)
Steve Beck	1987	AP (hm)
Paul Williams	1983	*Sporting News* (hm), *Street & Smith's* (hm)
Byron Scott	1983	AP (2nd team), *Sporting News* (hm), *Street & Smith's* (hm)
Lafayette Lever	1982	AP (2nd team), *Street & Smith's* (hm)
Alton Lister	1981	AP (hm), *Street & Smith's* (hm)
Byron Scott	1981	*Street & Smith's* (hm)
Lafayette Lever	1981	*Street & Smith's* (hm)
Mark Landsberger	1977	*Sporting News* (hm)
Scott Lloyd	1975	*Street & Smith's* (hm)
Lionel Hollins	1975	*Sporting News* (1st team), *Basketball Weekly* (1st team), *Street & Smith's* (hm)
Joe Caldwell	1964	*Sporting News* (hm)
Art Becker	1963	AP (hm)
Larry Armstrong	1961	Helms Foundation (3rd team)

SUN DEVIL STATS

• The women's golf team captured the 1975 AIAW national title in Tucson by a comfortable 23 strokes under first-year coach Judy Whitehouse.

• Coach Marty Pincus' men's tennis team went 21-3 and won its first WAC championship.

• Miami built a big first-day lead and held on to edge ASU in the AIAW national women's collegiate swimming championships in Tempe.

SUN DEVIL LORE

The Western Athletic Conference President's Council ruled that no member institution could provide facilities for pro sports, with possible expulsion from the conference a potential penalty for violators.

• Plans were announced for a new $300,000 tennis complex, to be called the Whiteman Center. Athletic Director Fred Miller said more than half the construction costs were donated by Jack Whiteman and the Whiteman Foundation. The Sun Devil Club also was a major contributor to the facility, which Miller said would be "as fine an intercollegiate complex as there will be in the nation."

1975-1976

america's time capsule

arizona state university
m o m e n t

The biggest football victory in Arizona State history? That debate has raged for years. The 1970 Peach Bowl victory over North Carolina and 1987 Rose Bowl triumph over Michigan certainly are strong candidates. But if you put it to a vote of longtime fans, the likely winner would be the Sun Devils' 17-14 victory over Nebraska in the 1975 Fiesta Bowl. The Sun Devils were unbeaten at 11-0, but they still were the underdogs against the once-beaten Cornhuskers, who were co-champions of the Big Eight. There were undercurrents that the Huskers and some of their fans weren't particularly excited about playing a team from the lowly Western Athletic Conference in a fledgling bowl game that was big on hospitality but short on tradition. The Huskers led, 7-6, after a tense first half, then drove 91 yards on the opening possession of the second half to take a 14-6 lead. But Fred Mortensen, subbing for an injured Dennis Sproul at quarterback, hit John Jefferson with a 10-yard touchdown pass, then passed to Larry Mucker for a two-point conversion to tie the game. With 4:50 remaining, Danny Kush, son of coach Frank Kush, kicked a 29-yard field goal and ASU's defense held on for the victory. Jefferson, who caught eight passes for 113 yards, was named the game's Outstanding Offensive Player. ASU linebacker Larry Gordon was named Outstanding Defensive Player. The victory propelled ASU to No. 2 in the final Associated Press and United Press International rankings.

A fourth-quarter field goal by Danny Kush (left) and Fred Mortensen's clutch passing gave ASU a 17-14 Fiesta Bowl victory over Nebraska in a game many feel was the biggest in the school's football history. (ASU Media Relations)

SUN DEVIL *spotlight*

By almost any standard, it was a monster baseball season, but it also has been called the most frustrating in ASU history. The Sun Devils (65-10) set a school record for victories and breezed through the Western Athletic Conference with a 17-1 mark. The team, considered by many the best hitting club in NCAA history, batted .344 and set NCAA records for hits, doubles, home runs and RBIs. The Sun Devils beat Arizona six times in as many tries during the regular season, and rallied for two runs in the 10th inning to nip the Wildcats again in the opening game of the College World Series. They lost their second game, 2-1, as Eastern Michigan's Bob Owchinko beat Floyd Bannister in a battle of the nation's top two college pitchers. After lopsided victories over Washington State (9-3) and Maine (7-0) the Devils squared off against Arizona for the eighth time that season. This time Arizona won, 5-1. ASU finished third and UA went on to beat Eastern Michigan for the national title.

ASU LEGENDS

Mike Haynes

O nce he survived the initial tug-of-war, Mike Haynes was off and running to an outstanding football career at ASU. That tug-of-war was between offensive coordinator Don Baker and defensive coordinator Larry Kentera, who both wanted Haynes on their side of the field. Head coach Frank Kush made the ultimate decision, choosing defense. Not only did Haynes have a brilliant ASU career at cornerback, he went on to become a perennial all-pro in the National Football League. He was inducted into the NFL Hall of Fame in 1997, joining former Sun Devils John Henry Johnson and Charley Taylor. In his senior season, 1975, Haynes became the third player at that point in ASU history to earn consensus All-America honors. Haynes led the nation in interceptions with 11 as a junior in 1974. He was just the second player in ASU history to return a punt, kickoff and interception for a touchdown. His 97-yard scoring kickoff return against North Carolina State in 1974 is the third-longest in ASU history.

Floyd Bannister

F loyd Bannister didn't leave much room for improvement with his junior season, in which he compiled a 15-4 record and 1.66 ERA and led the nation with 217 strikeouts. Among his victories were a one-hit, 14-strikeout performance against defending national champion Southern California and a two-hit, 17-strikeout outing against rival Arizona. But darned if Bannister wasn't even better the next year, when he tied former ASU star Larry Gura's NCAA record for victories at 19-2 and again led the nation in strikeouts with 213. His 186 innings pitched and 17 complete games still stand as ASU school records. Bannister won the Lefty Gomez Plate award as the nation's outstanding amateur baseball player. He also earned Player of the Year honors from *The Sporting News*. The Houston Astros made him the No. 1 pick in the 1976 June draft.

Sun Devil Lore

A Sports Hall of Fame was established to honor ASU's outstanding athletes, coaches and administrators of the past. The initial group of inductees included 20 athletes.

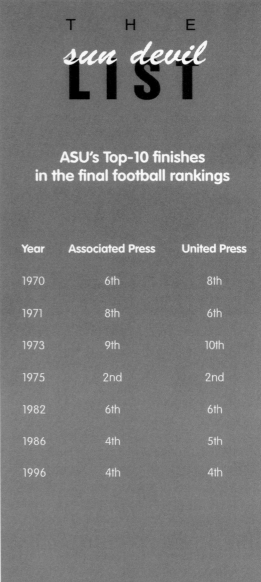

THE sun devil LIST

ASU's Top-10 finishes in the final football rankings

Year	Associated Press	United Press
1970	6th	8th
1971	8th	6th
1973	9th	10th
1975	2nd	2nd
1982	6th	6th
1986	4th	5th
1996	4th	4th

SUN DEVIL STATS

- Football coach Frank Kush was named Coach of the Year by the Walter Camp Foundation.
- The women's archery team won its sixth national title for retiring coach Margaret Klann.
- The women's badminton team won its second straight national AIAW national crown.
- ASU's women placed fourth at the softball College World Series in Omaha.
- The men's gymnastics team won the WAC title and finished sixth at the NCAA meet.

1976-1977

america's time capsule

arizona state university | m o m e n t

The Sun Devils weren't among the favorites when they headed off to Champaign, Illinois, for the NCAA track and field championships. After all, they had finished only third in the Western Athletic Conference meet, and the field at the nationals figured to be even tougher. But coach Baldy Castillo figured all along that the bigger the meet, the better the Sun Devils' chances because a handful of national-caliber athletes might offset a lack of depth. Castillo was right on target. His Sun Devils stunned the track and field world by walking off with the NCAA team title for the only time in school history. Herman Frazier won the 400-meter dash in 45.51 seconds and Kile Arney captured the high jump with a leap of seven feet, six inches. The Sun Devils had three second-place finishes, by Tony Darden in the 200 meters and by the 400-meter and 1,600-meter relay teams. Other critical performances were a third in the pole vault by Ralph Haynie and a fifth in the 400-meter intermediate hurdles by Rick Walker. The Sun Devils celebrated by giving Castillo a bath in the steeplechase water hazard. "It's the most enjoyable bath I ever took," Castillo said. "This has to be my happiest moment in track. You couldn't ask for a better bunch of kids. They really worked for this."

Kile Arney's high jump victory helped lead the Sun Devils to the NCAA track and field title. (ASU Media Relations)

SUN DEVIL *spotlight*

The track and field team didn't confine all of its handiwork to the NCAA championships during the 1977 season. The Sun Devils broke one world record, tied another and established two NCAA marks during the most productive season in school history. The 800-meter relay team of Gary Burl, Tony Darden, Gerald Burl and Herman Frazier ran 1:21.4, knocking one tenth of a second off the world mark of 1:21.5 set by the 1972 Italian national team. That same foursome tied the world mark for 880 yards with a time of 1:21.7. The team of Clifton McKenzie, Gerald Burl, Darden and Frazier broke the NCAA records for the mile and 1,600-meter relays with times of 3:02.8 and 3:01.9 respectively. The 1,600-meter record of 3:03.5 had been set by the same ASU quartet a year earlier.

LEGEND

Herman Frazier

Few individuals in ASU sports history can approach the long-term impact that Herman Frazier has had on the school's athletic department. His first major contribution was capturing the Western Athletic Conference 440-yard dash title as a sophomore in 1975. He would repeat as champ at 400 meters the next two seasons. As his career progressed he would set a world record at 500 meters indoors, run on several world and NCAA-record relay teams and capture the NCAA 400-meter title while leading the Sun Devils to the national team championship in 1977. He brought international recognition to ASU in the 1976 Olympics, where he won a gold medal as a member of the 4X400-meter relay team and captured a bronze in the individual 400 meters. He also was a member of the 1980 U.S. Olympic team. Frazier's contribution to ASU athletics didn't end when he hung up his spikes. He has held several important positions in the school's athletic department. He was named senior associate director of athletics in the summer of 1997. Frazier has held numerous national and international positions involving amateur athletics. Among the his many titles were chairman of the NCAA track and field committee, vice president of USA Track and Field, vice president of the U.S. Olympic committee, assistant chief de mission for the U.S. Olympic team at the Atlanta Olympics, president of the 1999 Fiesta Bowl and chief de mission for the 1999 Pan American Games. On August 22, 2000, Frazier was named Athletic Director at Alabama-Birmingham.

Herman Frazier's contributions to ASU athletics didn't stop when he hung up his spikes. (ASU Media Relations)

THE sun devil LIST

ASU's individual national champions at NCAA men's track and field championships

Year	Champion	Event	Time/Dis.
1996	Pal Arne Fagernes	javelin	259-8
1994	Nick Hysong	pole vault	18-8.25
1990	Shane Collins	shot put	66-3.25
1981	Dwayne Evans	200 meters	20.20
1977	Herman Frazier	400 meters	45.51
1977	Kyle Arney	high jump	7-6
1976	(Cliff Mckenzie, Rick Walker Carl McCullough, Herm Frazier)	4X100-meter relay	3:03.49
1973	Maurice Peoples	440 yards	45.0
1969	Mark Murro	javelin	265-9
1964	Ulis Williams	440 yards	45.9
1963	Henry Carr	220 yards	20.5
1963	Frank Covelli	javelin	257-8.5
1963	Ulis Williams	440 yards	45.8
1959	Alex Henderson	2 miles	8:46.8

SUN DEVIL STAT

• Mark Landsberger grabbed 27 rebounds in a basketball game against San Diego State, breaking the school record of 26 shared by Art Becker (1962) and Tony Cerkvenik (1963). Landsberger went on to average 14.4 rebounds for the season, eclipsing the mark of 14.3 set by Cerkvenik in 1961. Landsberger's 14.4 average still stands as the best single-season average in school history.

Sun Devil Lore

Clyde B. Smith, head football coach from 1952-54 and athletic director from 1955-71, died following a heart attack at the age of 70. "Smitty" helped bring the program back to the straight and narrow following a 1951 football recruiting scandal and was at the helm during the period when ASU teams surged into positions of national prominence on several fronts.

1
9
7
6
–
1
9
7
7

<u>H I G H L I G H T S</u>

ASU began to make its presence felt on the women's track and field scene, winning the Intermountain Conference title and sending seven athletes to the national championships. Dana Collins became the school's first individual national champ with a victory in the pentathlon.

The women's archery team won its fourth straight national title and eighth in the nine years since the inception of the National Archery Association.

The women's softball team went 25-4 overall and 8-0 in the Intermountain Conference and finished fourth at the College World Series in Omaha, Nebraska.

The men's tennis team was 25-4 and the women's team 19-2. The men finished second in the Western Athletic Conference and the women second in the Intermountain Conference.

Men's golf placed second in the WAC tournament.

arizona state university
|m o m e n t

After several near misses, the Sun Devils presented coach Jim Brock with his first national baseball championship and the fourth in school history. The Devils won a thriller, 2-1, over South Carolina in the College World Series championship game as Chris Bando's seventh-inning home run broke a 1-1 tie and walk-on Jerry Vasquez pitched a five-hit complete game. Vasquez, who said he had a tired arm as evidenced by 13 fly-ball outs, somehow found the strength to retire the last nine batters he faced. He struck out just three, but two were in the ninth inning. It was ironic that Bando scored the winning run on his own home run. In 1965, his older brother, Sal, scored the winning run in the championship game as the Sun Devils won their second national title. ASU second baseman Bob Horner, who batted .444 in the tournament with two home runs and nine RBIs, was named the Series Most Valuable Player. Horner was joined on

Chris Bando's home run gave the Sun Devils a 2-1 victory over South Carolina in the College World Series championship game. (ASU Media Relations)

the all-tournament team by third baseman Brandt Humphry, shortstop Mike Henderson, first baseman Chris Nyman, designated hitter Jamie Allen and Vasquez. The victory gave Brock the distinction of being the only coach to win national titles at three levels—American Legion, junior college and major college. The Sun Devils finished with a 57-12 overall record. They won the Western Athletic Conference title with a 15-3 league mark.

A rating of women's athletics based on national finishes in 10 sports for the 1976-77 school year ranked ASU No. 1 nationally by an overwhelming margin. The Sun Devils accumulated 199 points—more than double the totals for runner-up Southern California (92) and third-place UCLA (91). ASU's point total got a big boost from the women's swimming team, which captured the AIAW championship in Providence, Rhode Island. The Sun Devils totally dominated that meet, finishing 141 points ahead of runner-up Stanford. Melissa Belote, who captured three gold medals at the 1972 Munich Olympics, won three events at the AIAW meet. She won the 200-yard and 400-yard individual medleys and the 200-yard backstroke. "We went beyond our own expectations in winning by so many points," coach Mona Plummer said.

ASU LEGEND

John Jefferson

He caught more passes than any other player in Arizona State history, yet it was one grab that sets John Jefferson aside from a talented collection of receivers who have performed for the Sun Devils over the years. The play was so big it still is referred to as "The Catch" a quarter of a century later. It remains the most talked-about play in a long and colorful ASU-Arizona rivalry and probably in Sun Devil football history. The play came just before the half of the 1975 ASU-UA game in Tempe with the 9-1 Wildcats leading the 10-0 Sun Devils, 14-3, and a Fiesta Bowl berth against Nebraska awaiting the winner. Jefferson laid out horizontally to make a spectacular grab of an 8-yard pass from quarterback Dennis Sproul, pulling the Sun Devils to within four points. They rallied to win, 24-21, and their subsequent 17-14 Fiesta Bowl victory over Nebraska earned them their highest ranking ever, No. 2 in both news service polls. Jefferson's career, however, involved much more than one catch. He led ASU in receiving for four straight years from 1974 through 1977 and his 188 career receptions still stands as a school record by a wide margin over runner-up Eric Guliford (164). A consensus All-American in 1977, he was a first-round pick of the San Diego Chargers in the 1978 NFL draft.

"The Catch" was the best of many great pass receptions by John Jefferson. (ASU Media Relations)

THE sun devil LIST

ASU'S 50-win baseball seasons

Record	Year	Coach	Final Ranking
65-10	1976	Jim Brock	1st
64-6	1972	Jim Brock	1st
61-13	1975	Jim Brock	3rd
60-13	1988	Jim Brock	1st
59-8	1973	Jim Brock	1st
58-15	1982	Jim Brock	9th
57-12	1977	Jim Brock	1st
56-11	1969	Bobby Winkles	2nd
56-12	1978	Jim Brock	2nd
55-13	1981	Jim Brock	1st
55-20	1984	Jim Brock	1st
54-8	1965	Bobby Winkles	1st
53-12	1967	Bobby Winkles	4th
52-16	1990	Jim Brock	5th
50-13	1971	Bobby Winkles	18th

(Note: *Collegiate Baseball* rankings through 1980; *Baseball America* rankings after 1980.)

SUN DEVIL STAT

• Julie Pyne became the sixth ASU woman golfer to win first-team All-America honors as the Sun Devils captured their third straight Intermountain Conference championship. The Sun Devils finished third against a national field at the Betsy Rawls Invitational and fourth at the AIAW championships. It was their third straight top-five finish at the nationals.

Sun Devil Lore

The Arizona Board of Regents authorized Arizona State and Arizona to accept an offer from the Pac-8 Conference, making it the Pac-10. It climaxed several years of expansion talk, but wasn't unanimously hailed on the ASU campus. Football coach Frank Kush, for one, opposed the move. "The people over there have looked down their noses at us for years," Kush said. "Now all of a sudden they want us."

1977-1978

arizona state university | m o m e n t

The Sun Devils' bid for a sixth straight bowl victory came up short as Penn State used a powerful ground attack to register a 42-30 victory over A-State in Fiesta Bowl VII. A blocked punt produced one Penn State touchdown and a fumble recovery set up another as the Nittany Lions constructed a 14-0 first-quarter lead and never looked back. The Sun Devils narrowed the score to 17-14 at the half on Dennis Sproul touchdown passes of 11 yards to Arthur Lane and 13 yards to Ron Washington, but Penn State built the lead to 31-14 in the second half. ASU pulled to within striking distance at 34-28 at one point in the fourth quarter, but the Lions put it away on a three-yard touchdown run by Matt Suhey. ASU's final two points were scored on a safety. Sproul, who completed 23 of 47 passes for 336 yards and three touchdowns, was named the game's outstanding offensive player. Penn State's Matt Millen was named defensive player of the game. The Nittany Lions rolled up 268 yards on the ground to 90 for the Sun Devils.

Dennis Sproul's 336 passing yards weren't enough to offset Penn State's ground game in Fiesta Bowl VII. (ASU Media Relations)

SUN DEVIL *spotlight*

The Sun Devils rode the big bats of Bob Horner, Hubie Brooks and Chris Bando into the finals of the College World Series, but lost to their nemesis, top-ranked Southern California, 10-3. The Sun Devils needed to beat the Trojans twice to win the title, but USC scored three runs in the second inning and eventually built a 10-0 lead. The Sun Devils scored three runs in the eighth inning on doubles by Bando and Jamie Allen. It was ASU's fourth appearance in the title game in coach Jim Brock's first seven years on the job. The Sun Devils beat South Carolina for the 1977 crown, but lost to Southern California in 1972, 1973 and 1978. The Devils finished 56-12 with a No. 2 national ranking.

LEGEND

Bob Horner

The words "Apollo" and "liftoff" may conjure up thoughts of the space program for some, but for longtime baseball fans in Arizona they have an entirely different meaning. Glendale's Apollo High produced Bob Horner, the greatest home run hitter in ASU baseball history and one of the top college players of all time. Consider these numbers: A .389 batting average. The national leader in home runs (22), RBIs (87), hits (102) and total bases (191). Pretty impressive, right? Well, those were Horner's *sophomore* statistics at ASU. As a junior, when he won the Golden Spikes award as the nation's top college player and was named College Player of the Year by *The Sporting News*, Horner batted .412 with 25 home runs and 100 RBIs. A lot of talented hitters have taken shots at Horner's 25 home runs over the years, but it stood as a school record until surpassed by Mitch Jones in 2000. Horner holds the school record for career home runs with 56, well ahead of Mike Kelly (46) and Barry Bonds (45). In addition to his batting exploits, Horner set what then was a school record for best fielding percentage by a second baseman (.976) in 1977. He won the Outstanding Player Award at the 1977 College World Series. His accomplishments earned him a spot on the all-time college all-star team selected by the publication *Baseball America* in 1994. The Atlanta Braves made Horner the No. 1 pick of the June 1978 draft.

Bob Horner is ASU's all-time leading home run hitter. (ASU Media Relations)

THE sun devil LIST

ASU's first-round draft picks in baseball

Player	Year	Pro Team	Overall Pick
Rick Monday	1965	Athletics	1
Reggie Jackson	1966	Athletics	2
Paul Ray Powell	1969	Twins	7
Eddie Bane	1973	Twins	11
Floyd Bannister	1976	Astros	1
Ken Landreaux	1976	Angels	6
Bob Horner	1978	Braves	1
Hubie Brooks	1978	Mets	3
Mike Sodders	1981	Twins	11
Oddibe McDowell	1984	Rangers	12
Barry Bonds	1985	Pirates	6
Anthony Manahan	1990	Mariners	38*
Mike Kelly	1992	Braves	2
Sean Lowe	1992	Cardinals	15
Todd Steverson	1992	Blue Jays	25
Marc Barcelo	1993	Twins	33*
Antone Williamson	1994	Brewers	4
Jacob Cruz	1994	Giants	32*
Ryan Bradley	1997	Yankees	40*
Dan McKinley	1997	Giants	49*
Ryan Mills	1998	Twins	6

*Sandwich pick between first and second rounds

SUN DEVIL STATS

- ASU ranked third nationally in the Knoxville, Tennessee, *Journal's* ranking of men's athletic programs. The newspaper's mathematical formula showed UCLA with 97 1/2 points, Southern California with 89 and ASU with 63 1/2.
- The Sun Devils continued their success in women's athletics, winning their customary national titles in swimming, badminton and archery and capturing Intermountain Conference championships in track and tennis.
- The men crashed the party in archery and badminton, joining the ASU women as national champs in those two sports for the first time ever.
- Celeste Wilkinson set a school record that still stands with a javelin toss of 186-8.
- Julie Pyne won first-team All-America honors in women's golf for the second straight year.

Sun Devil Lore

An 8,000-seat addition to Sun Devil Stadium boosted its capacity to 58,000 for the 1977 season, but it was only a part of a massive rebuilding program. The following year, capacity would jump all the way to 70,491. Funds for the two-phase program came from the sale of revenue bonds and a donation of $2.5 million by the Sun Angel Foundation. The two-phase addition more than doubled the 30,000-seat capacity of the original stadium, which opened in October of 1958.

1978-1979

September 15, 1978: Muhammad Ali regained the heavyweight boxing title with a 15-round decision over Leon Spinks.

November 18, 1978: More than 900 people, including 211 children, were found dead in Guyana. Jim Jones, leader of a religious sect, led the group in a mass suicide by poison.

January, 1979: Heavy rains turned the normally dry Salt River bed near the ASU campus into a raging torrent and played havoc with Valley traffic. Authorities estimated that 419,000 man-hours were lost daily during the height of the delays.

March 26, 1979: Michigan State, led by Magic Johnson, beat Indiana State and Larry Bird in the NCAA basketball championship game at Salt Lake City.

March 28, 1979: Three Mile Island, near Harrisburg, Pennsylvania, was the site of a near nuclear disaster.

arizona state university
moment

Sun Devil fans weren't quite sure what to expect when Southern California's second-ranked Trojans came to town for ASU's first conference home game as a member of the Pac-10. Just three weeks earlier the Devils had been blown out at Washington State, 51-26, in their their first Pac-10 game ever. They had rebounded to trounce Texas-El Paso and Northwestern, but those schools were small fish compared to the mighty Trojans, who were playing ASU for the first time. ASU fans need not have worried. The fired-up Devils, fueled by a fanatical state-record crowd of 71,138 in newly-expanded Sun Devil Stadium, performed brilliantly. Quarterback Mark Malone passed for 167 yards and one touchdown and ran for 139 yards and another score and ASU's defense held the Trojans' star tailback, Charles White, to 59 yards on 18 carries as the Sun Devils breezed to a 20-7 victory. Just before the end of the first quarter ASU defensive end Bob Kohrs recovered a Trojan fumble at the USC 30-yard line. Three plays later Steve Hicks kicked a 40-yard field goal that proved to be the only scoring of the first half. A one-yard touchdown run by Malone and a 16-yard scoring pass from Malone to John Mistler in the third quarter gave ASU a 17-0 lead. The Devils made it 20-0 on a 28-yard field goal by Hicks early in the fourth period. The Trojans went on to finish 12-1, beat Michigan in the Rose Bowl and share the national championship with Alabama. All 22 starters from that USC team ended up playing in the NFL.

Quarterback Mark Malone led the Sun Devils to an upset victory over second-ranked Southern California. (ASU Media Relations)

After five Fiesta Bowl appearances in the first seven years of that bowl's existence, the Sun Devils ventured all the way to East Rutherford, New Jersey, to play Rutgers in the inaugural Garden State Bowl. The Devils fell behind, 10-0, late in the second quarter, but a 26-yard touchdown pass from Mark Malone to Robert Weathers narrowed the margin to 10-7 at the half. ASU dominated the second half, scoring 21 straight points to take command and roll to a 34-18 victory. Malone completed 13 of 31 passes for 268 yards and had a hand in all five ASU touchdowns—passing for three and running for two. ASU receiver John Mistler, who caught seven passes for 148 yards and one touchdown, was named Most Valuable Player.

ASU LEGEND

Al Harris

A l Harris was one of the few ASU players who had the distinction of terrorizing opposing quarterbacks in two conferences. A star defensive end, he earned first-team All-Western Athletic Conference honors in 1977, then repeated the achievement the next season when the Sun Devils joined the Pac-10. But Harris' honors went far beyond the conference level. He was the sixth consensus All-American in school history, and the first to be accorded unanimous All-American acclaim. That's the ultimate—even better than consensus. He did it in 1978 by making the All-America first teams selected by the Associated Press, United Press International, Football Coaches, *The Sporting News*, Football Writers and the Walter Camp Foundation. Harris led the Sun Devils with 46 unassisted tackles in 1978 and set two school record that still stand with 19 quarterback sacks for 160 yards in minus yardage. He also recorded 21 pass rush harassments and deflected six passes. The Chicago Bears made Harris the ninth pick of the first round of the 1979 NFL draft. Harris was inducted into ASU's Sports Hall of Fame in October of 1981.

Defensive end Al Harris was ASU's first unanimous All-American in football. (ASU Media Relations)

SUN DEVIL STAT

• The Sun Devil basketball team had a modest 16-14 season, but it did leave a lasting impression in the school record book. For one game, on February 10, 1979 against Oregon State, the Sun Devils were on fire like no team in school history. They shot an amazing .756 from the floor against the Beavers, making 34 of 45 shots. Just one week earlier the Devils had warmed up for the occasion by shooting a school record .673 (35 of 52) against California. Those two performances, within one week, still rank first and fourth on the school's all-time list. That ASU team shot .482 for the season—more than respectable but only eighth-best on the school's all-time list.

Sun Devil Lore

A spring shakeup of major proportions in the athletic department saw track coach Baldy Castillo reassigned to new duties just two years after his team won the NCAA championship. Golf coach George Boutell and baseball pitching coach Roger Schmuck resigned and tennis coach Marty Pincus was fired within a few days. Boutell was rehired seven weeks later.

1979-1980

america's time capsule

arizona state university
m o m e n t

In perhaps the most dramatic and emotion-charged moment in Arizona State athletic history, football coaching legend Frank Kush announced just before a home game against Washington that he had been fired. Kush then coached the Sun Devils to a 12-7 upset victory over the Huskies and was carried off the field by his players. Kush, who built ASU into a position of national prominence during his 23 years as head coach, said he was fired by athletic director Fred Miller because Miller did not believe his denial of charges that he struck punter Kevin Rutledge. Rutledge had filed a $1.1 million lawsuit against Kush, Miller and the university, alleging that Kush had hit him following a bad punt. Rutledge also charged that Kush and assistant coach Bill Masgill had harassed him into quitting the team and giving up his scholarship. In a formal statement, Miller said, in part, " . . . if we cannot have integrity in athletics or in higher education, then why are we in this profession?" Kush and Miller each

Coach Frank Kush is carried from the field following a 12-7 upset of Washington, just hours after Kush announced he had been fired. (Chuck Conley/ASU Media Relations)

held three news conferences during the next few days as charges and counter-charges flew back and forth. Public support for Kush was substantial, though certainly not unanimous. At one point, Sun Angel Foundation president Harry Rosenzweig called for Kush's reinstatement and Miller's dismissal and withdrew pledged funding for several projects, including a university golf course. The Sun Devils were 3-2 in the five games coached by Kush that season. They were 3-4 in the final seven games coached by interim head coach Bob Owens.

SUN DEVIL *spotlight*

Coach Ned Wulk's basketball team, projected for sixth place in the Pac-10, finished second behind powerful Oregon State and reached the second round of the NCAA tournament. The Sun Devils breezed to a 99-71 first-round victory over Loyola Marymount in Tempe before falling to Ohio State, 89-75, in the second round. The Sun Devils finished 22-7 overall, beat rival Arizona twice and set a school record for team field goal percentage at 51.7. The team featured outstanding scoring balance, and all five starters went on to play in the National Basketball Association. They were forwards Kurt Nimphius (16.6 points per game) and Sam Williams (12.4), center Alton Lister (12.0) and guards Byron Scott (13.6) and Lafayette (Fat) Lever (11.6).

LEGEND

Fred Miller

His final days at Arizona State weren't pretty, but the athletic legacy left behind by Dr. Fred Miller could be considered downright beautiful. Miller was fired in January of 1980 in the wake of the controversial dismissal of football coach Frank Kush and the disclosure of improprieties in the ASU athletic department. But much was accomplished during Miller's 8 1/2-year tenure as athletic director. Miller always will be known as the bricks-and-mortar guy at ASU. An engaging, personable sort, he was a master fund-raiser. During his stay at ASU, the school's athletic facilities surged to the forefront on the national scene. Sun Devil Stadium was expanded to more than 70,000 seats and the $8.5 million, 14,733-seat Activity Center, 8,000-seat Packard Baseball Stadium, 5,000-seat Sun Angel Track Stadium and 2,000-seat Whiteman Tennis Center were constructed. No state funds were used for the football expansion or the baseball, track and tennis facilities. As part of his "plan without end," Miller also laid the groundwork for what later would become the Karsten Golf Course and the Mona Plummer Aquatic Center. As early as the mid-1970s he envisioned permanent water in the Salt River and an ASU crew team—a vision that has taken more than a quarter century to fulfill. Miller wasn't all about buildings, however. Sun Devil teams won 24 conference championships during his tenure. In 1977 alone, ASU teams captured national championships in baseball, track and field, women's swimming and women's archery.

Fred Miller ran the athletic department during its greatest building boom. (ASU Media Relations)

SUN DEVIL LORE

Joe Kearney, athletic director at Michigan State, was hired by University president John Schwada to replace Fred Miller, who was fired by Schwada. Kearney, in turn, hired MSU's Darryl Rogers as head football coach.

• Eight football players who received academic credit for work they did not do were declared ineligible by the university on November 16 and the Pac-10 ruled that ASU must forfeit its three conference victories to that point.

SUN DEVIL STATS

• Mark Malone set an NCAA record for longest run by a quarterback with a 98-yard scoring scamper against Utah State.

• Coach Bobby Douglas' wrestlers had their best-ever showing to that point in school history with a fifth-place finish at the NCAA championships.

• Coleen Rienstra won the high jump and Ria Stalman finished second in the discus as ASU placed sixth in the AIAW national women's track and field championships.

• The men's and women's archery teams won national championships as Tom Stevenson and Carol Clark captured individual honors.

1980-1981

america's time capsule

arizona state university
| m o m e n t

The Sun Devils launched their 1981 baseball season with a slogan: "Omaha and Fun in '81." Boy, did they have fun. Not only did they make it to Omaha, Nebraska, site of the College World Series, but they had just about all the fun you could imagine while capturing their fifth national championship and the second for coach Jim Brock. This wasn't a Cinderella story. The Sun Devils breezed through the Pac-10 Southern Division with a 26-4 record and took a No. 1 ranking into the CWS. The Devils won their first two games in Omaha, but suffered an 11-10 loss to Oklahoma State in their third game, despite seven RBIs by Stan Holmes. That reduced their margin of error to zero, but that proved to be no problem. They eliminated South Carolina and Texas to earn a championship showdown with Oklahoma State, which had suffered a loss to Texas two days earlier. ASU starting pitcher Kendall Carter, who had beaten Texas earlier to improve his record to a nation-leading 19-1, didn't have his usual stuff against the Cowboys, who touched him for two first-inning runs. Brock went to his bullpen for relief ace Kevin Dukes, who allowed a bloop single in the second inning and a double in the ninth and nothing in between. Meanwhile, the Devils accumulated 13 hits to win comfortably, 7-4. Holmes, who drove in 17 runs to smash the Series record of 11 set by ASU's Bob Horner in 1978, was named the CWS Most Valuable Player.

College World Series MVP Stan Holmes embraces the Sun Devils' national championship trophy. (ASU Media Relations)

spotlight

Arizona State's football season under first-year coach Darryl Rogers didn't produce a lot of magical moments—until the very end. The Sun Devils, who took a 6-4 record into their final game against rival Arizona in Tucson, spanked the Wildcats by a 44-7 score. It was the sixth-most lopsided ASU victory in the history of the series. The Sun Devils led 14-0 after one quarter and 31-0 at the half and never looked back. The defense played a major role in the victory. Linebacker Vernon Maxwell blocked a punt and recovered it in the end zone for ASU's second touchdown. The Sun Devils' third TD came on a 35-yard interception return by safety Mike Richardson. Maxwell had a monster game with 16 tackles, three for minus yardage, a quarterback sack and a fumble recovery in addition to his blocked punt for a touchdown.

LEGENDS

Gail Amundrud & Cheryl Gibson

ASU was blessed in the late 1970s and early 1980s with several female athletes who not only won national championships, but won them in bunches. Two of the most productive were swimmers Gail Amundrud and Cheryl Gibson, who earned international acclaim for their native Canada before enrolling at ASU. Gibson was a silver medalist in the 1976 Olympic Games. As Sun Devils, Amundrud won eight national titles and Gibson six from 1978 through 1981. Amundrud won the 100-yard and 200-yard freestyle crowns in 1978 and repeated in both events in 1979. She also swam on four national championship relay teams. Gibson won individual titles in the 200-yard backstroke in 1978 and 1981 and also won the 400 yard individual medley in '81. She also swam on national championship relay teams in 1978, 1979 and 1981.

Gail Amundrud (ASU Media Relations)

Cheryl Gibson (ASU Media Relations)

Coleen Rienstra & Ria Stalman

While Amundrud and Gibson were churning up the water in the swimming pool, Coleen Rienstra Sommer and Ria Stalman were were making their marks in track and field. Under her maiden name, Rienstra won the national outdoor high jump title in 1980 with a leap of 6 feet even. Perhaps even more significant, however, was her mark of 6-4 to set a collegiate record. In 1981 she captured the national indoor title at 6-3 3/4, then defended her outdoor crown with a jump of 6-1 1/4. Stalman won the national collegiate championship in the discus in 1979 and 1981 and finished second in 1980. Her greatest moment came three years later, however, when competing for her native Netherlands, she won the gold medal at the 1984 Summer Olympics.

Coleen Rienstra

Ria Stalman

Sun Devil Lore

Joe Kearney resigned after less than six months as athletic director to become commissioner of the Western Athletic Conference. Texas Tech AD Dick Tamburo, a former assistant football coach at ASU, was named to replace Kearney.

• The NCAA placed ASU on two years probation in football for improper academic credits and irregularities in the sale of football tickets.

• A new $3 million swimming and diving complex, with seating for 2,000 spectators, opened on the north end of campus.

THE sun devil LIST

ASU's national baseball titles

Year	Coach	Title game results
1965	Bobby Winkles	ASU 2, Ohio State 1
1967	Bobby Winkles	ASU 11, Houston 2
1969	Bobby Winkles	ASU 10, Tulsa 1
1977	Jim Brock	ASU 2, South Carolina 1
1981	Jim Brock	ASU 7, Oklahoma State 4

SUN DEVIL STATS

• Sun Devil third baseman Mike Sodders was named College Player of the Year by *Baseball America*.

• Golfer Dan Forsman was Pac-10 Player of the Year.

• The Sun Devils won their customary national titles in men's, women's and mixed archery and women's badminton. They finished second nationally in men's badminton, fourth in men's track and women's swimming, fifth in men's golf and eighth in women's track, where Coleen Rienstra won the high jump and Ria Stalman captured the discus.

1981-1982

america's time capsule

arizona state university
m o m e n t

There figured to be some yards gained and some points scored when Arizona State and Stanford teed it up on October 24, 1981, at Stanford. The Sun Devils, led by quarterback Mike Pagel, had put up 52 points in their opener against Utah and were coming off a 45-10 victory over California. Stanford was led by a preseason All-America quarterback named John Elway. Hardly anyone, however, could have anticipated what transpired on that afternoon. When the dust had cleared the Sun Devils were a 62-36 winner and the teams had combined to set five NCAA and 10 Pac-10 Conference records. An unbelievable 23 ASU school records fell by the wayside. Pagel, who later would beat out Elway for first-team all-conference honors, hooked up in a dandy dual with the Stanford star. Elway's third touchdown pass of the game gave Stanford a 24-17 lead in the second quarter, but a hand injury forced Elway to the sidelines for the rest of the game. With Elway gone, the Sun Devils scored the next 38 points on five touchdown passes by Pagel and a Luis Zendejas field goal. Pagel completed 26 of 34 passes for 466 yards and seven touchdowns. He personally broke four Pac-10 records and seven school marks. His performance earned him national offensive player-of-the-week honors from *Sports Illustrated*.

ASU quarterback Mike Pagel outgunned Stanford star John Elway in a 62-36 Sun Devil romp. (ASU Media Relations)

spotlight

Quarterback Mike Pagel didn't use up all of his magic in that wild seven-touchdown victory over Stanford. A crowd of 69,714—largest of the season at Sun Devil Stadium—showed up for the season finale against Arizona despite soggy conditions created by a day of rain. ASU's fans were hoping for some more magic from Pagel, and they weren't disappointed. After Arizona grabbed a 6-0 lead in the second quarter, Pagel threw three touchdown passes in the same period to send the Sun Devils on their way to a 24-13 victory. His TD tosses were 44 yards to Jerry Bell and 20 and 35 yards to Bernard Henry. Pagel's 20-yarder to Henry was his 28th of the season, breaking the Pac-10 single-season record.

LEGEND

Fat Lever

Lafayette "Fat" Lever had a lot of great moments in his ASU basketball career, but none better than February 20, 1982, against Arizona at the University Activity Center. Many longtime followers of the sport still consider it the greatest all-around game in school history. Lever set what then was a school record with 38 points and tied the school mark for free throws with 16 in 18 attempts. He also led both teams in rebounding (13), steals (7) and assists (6). And the fact that it came in an 82-56 rout of arch rival Arizona made it that much sweeter. "It's probably the greatest accumulation of statistics in ASU history," coach Ned Wulk said at the time. It would be difficult to contest that statement today. Lever was named to the Associated Press All-America second team at the conclusion of the season. At that point in ASU's history he was only the second player to receive such a high honor. Lionel Hollins had been a member of *The Sporting News'* All-America first team in 1975. The Portland Trail Blazers made Lever the 11th pick in the first round of the 1982 NBA draft. Lever, a product of Pueblo High School in Tucson, was the fourth Sun Devil in history, and the first from an Arizona high school, to be drafted in the first round.

Fat Lever had perhaps the greatest all-around game in ASU basketball history in rout of rival Arizona. (Media Relations)

SUN DEVIL LORE

J. Russell Nelson became the 13th president of ASU.

• The largest home crowd in ASU baseball history, 9,387, turned out to watch the Sun Devils beat Arizona, 9-5, at Packard Stadium.

• Two days after his team upset fourth-ranked Oregon State in the season finale, head basketball coach Ned Wulk was relieved of his duties by athletic director Dick Tamburo. Wulk's record in 25 years at ASU was 406-272.

SUN DEVIL STAT

• It was a big year for school records in track and field. Gary Williky set school marks in the shot put (68 feet, 2 1/2 inches) and discus (203-6) and Deon Mayfield established a new standard in the triple jump with a leap of 54-10 3/4. All three records still stand. LaMonte King set a school indoor record at 55 meters with a time of 6.17 seconds. It, too, has not been surpassed.

1982-1983

america's time capsule

arizona state university | m o m e n t

The Sun Devils could have earned their first trip to the Rose Bowl by beating Washington in Tempe, but the two-time defending Pac-10 champion Huskies prevailed by a 17-13 score in front of the largest crowd to witness an athletic event at that point in the state's history, 72,021. When Washington State knocked off the Huskies the following week, the Sun Devils got a new life. This time Arizona's Wildcats spoiled the party with a 28-18 victory over the Devils in Tucson. That put the Sun Devils into the Fiesta Bowl, where they took out their frustration on Oklahoma, 32-21. The Devils won it by outscoring the Sooners 14-0 in the fourth quarter on a one-yard run by Alvin Moore and a 52-yard touchdown pass from Todd Hons to Ron Brown. ASU's defense forced five turnovers and Luis Zendejas booted three field goals, including a Fiesta Bowl record 54-yarder. Sooners' freshman running back Marcus Dupree chugged to a Fiesta Bowl record 239 yards on 17 carries before leaving the game in the third quarter with a pulled hamstring. Dupree was named Outstanding Offensive Player. ASU defensive end Jim Jeffcoat won Outstanding Defensive Player honors. Hons passed for 329 yards.

Defensive end Jim Jeffcoat was named Outstanding Defensive Player of ASU's 32-21 Fiesta Bowl victory over Oklahoma. (Chuck Conley/ASU Media Relations)

SUN DEVIL *spotlight*

Jim Carter became ASU's first NCAA men's golf champion, winning a four-way playoff at the San Joaquin Course in Fresno, California. Carter finished four days of regulation play with a two-under-par score of 287. That tied him with Doug Harper of Fresno State, Scott Verplank of Oklahoma State and Paul Thomas of Texas. Carter captured the title with a par on the first hole of a four-man sudden-death playoff. Carter's performance earned him first-team All-America honors—the eighth time a Sun Devil had been so honored at that point in the school's history. Despite Carter's heroics, the Sun Devils did not show up in the team standings. For the first time in 22 years, they did not qualify a team for the NCAA championships. They had finished third in 1982 and fifth in 1981.

ASU LEGENDS

Barry Bonds

If you consider his post-ASU career, Barry Bonds clearly would be in the elite Super Legend category, but the primary objective of this book is to acknowledge athletes for their accomplishments while wearing the Maroon and Gold. Not that Bonds had a bad career at ASU. He was named to the All-College World Series team as a freshman in 1983 and was a second-team All-American as a junior in 1985. His 23 home runs that year tied him with Oddibe McDowell for the second-best total at that point in ASU history, topped only by Bob Horner's 25 dingers in 1978. Bonds would have earned more recognition at ASU, but he was overshadowed for two years by McDowell, who was College Player of the Year in 1984. The Pittsburgh Pirates thought enough of Bonds to make him the sixth pick in the first round of the 1985 draft. A brilliant professional career should earn him a spot in Major League Baseball's Hall of Fame.

Barry Bonds
(ASU Media Relations)

Byron Scott

Byron Scott didn't waste any time making an impression at ASU. As a freshman, he was named Pac-10 Rookie of the Year. By the time he wrapped up his career as a Sun Devil he would be the leading scorer in school history with 1,572 points, though that mark since has been eclipsed by Stevin Smith (1,673), Ron Riley (1,834), Jeremy Veal (1,984) and Eddie House (2,044). Scott led the Pac-10 in scoring during the 1982-83 season with a 21.6 point average. He was the only Sun Devil to accomplish that feat until Veal in 1997-98, and House in 1999-2000. Scott was named to the Associated Press All-America second team following the 1982-83 season. He is one of just three Sun Devil basketball players in history to be named to a major All-America first or second team. The fourth pick of the 1983 draft by San Diego—the second-highest pick of any ASU player ever—Scott spent most of a lengthy pro career with the Los Angeles Lakers.

Byron Scott
(Chuck Conley/ASU Media Relations)

Sun Devil Lore

Arizona State received the biggest equipment gift in its history, a $2 million computer system donated by IBM Corp. to ASU's engineering excellence program. Given normal depreciation in the computer industry, it's probably worth $29.95 today.

THE sun devil LIST

ASU's national champions in women's track & field (outdoors)

Year	Athlete	Event
1991	(Toinette Holmes, Shanequa Campbell, Dana Jones, Maicel Malone)	4X400m relay
1990	Gia Johnson	Heptathlon
1990	Maicel Malone	400m
1990	Lynda Tolbert	100m hurdles
1988	Lynda Tolbert	100m hurdles
1988	(Lynda Tolbert, Maicel Malone, Tamika Foster, Jacinta Bartholomew)	4X400m relay
1983	Leslie Deniz	Discus
1981	Ria Stalman	Discus
1981	Coleen Reinstra	High jump
1980	Coleen Reinstra	High jump
1979	(Kathey Crawford, Freida Cobbs, Brenda Calhoun, Val Boyer)	4X400m relay
1978	(Kathey Crawford, Denise Waddy, Brenda Calhoun, Val Boyer)	4X400m relay
1977	Dana Collins	Penthalon

SUN DEVIL STATS

• Paul Williams set a school basketball single-game scoring record with 45 points against the University of Southern California.

• Leslie Deniz broke the U.S. women's discus record, then topped her own national mark three times. Her best of 213 feet, 1 inch still stands as a school record. She also set a school record that still stands with a toss of 55-10 1/2 in the shot put.

• The baseball team finished third at the College World Series, women's gymnastics was second at the nationals and men's swimming was seventh. Archery enjoyed its third sweep in four years—first in men's, women's and mixed. In badminton, the men finished first and the women second at the nationals.

1983-1984

america's time capsule

arizona state university | m o m e n t

ASU's Luis Zendejas entered the NCAA record book, but his brother, Max, won the game for Arizona. (ASU Media Relations)

The Zendejas brothers shared the spotlight as Arizona nipped Arizona State, 17-15, in front of 70,033 fans at Sun Devil Stadium in one of the most dramatic finishes in their long and colorful football rivalry. ASU's Luis Zendejas broke two NCAA records and tied another, but his brother, Max, kicked a 45-yard field goal as time expired to win it for the Wildcats. Luis Zendejas, a junior, kicked field goals of 33, 23 and 36 yards, giving him 28 for the season and tying the single-season NCAA record set by West Virginia's Paul Woodside. He also set NCAA records for most points scored by kicking in a season (112) and three seasons (295). A 21-yard touchdown pass from Todd Hons to Mike Crawford gave ASU its first lead of the game, 15-14, with 13:18 to play. The Sun Devils got the ball at their own 20 yard line with 5:38 to play and a chance to run out the clock, but they went three plays and out. The Wildcats took over at their 37 with 4:44 on the clock and drove to the ASU 28, where they called time out to on third and one with three seconds remaining to set up Max Zendejas' heroics. It was Arizona's second straight victory in the series, the first time they had beaten the Sun Devils in consecutive years since 1961 and 1962.

spotlight

The Sun Devils finished fourth at the College World Series in Omaha, Nebraska, but nobody finished ahead of outfielder Oddibe McDowell when it came time to select the college player of the year. McDowell won the Golden Spikes Award, which goes to the nation's outstanding college player. He also captured the player of the year award presented by the publication *Baseball America*. McDowell had a monster year for the Sun Devils, who finished 55-20 overall and won the Pac-10 Southern Division with a 23-7 league mark. He climaxed the year with a legendary home run against Oklahoma State at the College World Series. The blast, off pitcher John Duval, disappeared into the night beyond the right field fence. Legend has it the ball ended up in the Henry Dorley Zoo across the street from Rosenblatt Stadium. Such a feat is physically impossible, but it has made for a good story over the years.

ASU LEGENDS

Heather Farr

Heather Farr won her share of honors during an outstanding golf career at Arizona State, but it was her courageous bout with cancer in the years that followed that gripped not only her many followers in Arizona but the entire international golf community. A first-team All-American in 1984 and second-team selection in 1985, Farr won the 1984 U.S. Public Links Championship and was low amateur in the 1983 U.S. Open. She played on the 1984 Curtis Cup and World Amateur teams. After a promising beginning on the LPGA tour, she bravely battled cancer for four years until the disease took her life in November of 1993. A tribute in her honor was erected in the Karsten Golf Course clubhouse on campus in 1994 and the Sun Angel Foundation created an endowment in her name to support women's golf at ASU.

Heather Farr
(Chuck Conley/ASU
Media Relations)

Oddibe McDowell

He stood only five-foot-nine and weighed just 160 pounds, but Oddibe McDowell was living proof that good things do, indeed, come in small packages. A former high school and junior college star in south Florida, McDowell was drafted three times before he arrived at ASU amid much fanfare prior to the 1983 season. He more than lived up to his reputation, batting .352 with seven home runs, 50 RBIs and 36 stolen bases in 39 attempts as a junior before putting together a tremendous season that won him the national Player of the Year award from *Baseball America* and the Golden Spikes Player of the Year award in 1984. As a senior, McDowell batted .405 with 23 homers and 75 RBIs. He swiped 36 bases for the second straight year.

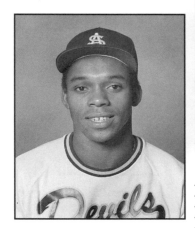

Oddibe McDowell
(ASU Media Relations)

THE sun devil LIST

ASU-UofA football games decided by three points or less

Year	Score	Site
1995	Arizona 31, ASU 28	Tempe
1994	Arizona 28, ASU 27	Tucson
1992	ASU 7, Arizona 6	Tucson
1987	ASU 24, Arizona 24	Tempe
1985	Arizona 16, ASU 13	Tempe
1983	Arizona 17, ASU 15	Tempe
1979	Arizona 27, ASU 24	Tempe
1978	ASU 18, Arizona 17	Tucson
1975	ASU 24, Arizona 21	Tempe
1966	ASU 20, Arizona 17	Tucson
1962	Arizona 20, ASU 17	Tucson
1955	Arizona 7, ASC 6	Tempe
1952	ASC 20, Arizona 18	Tucson

SUN DEVIL STATS

- Lynn Nelson set women's school records at 3,000, 5,000 and 10,000 meters in track. Her 3,000-meter time of 9:09.76 and her 5,000-meter mark of 15:58.57 still stand as school marks.
- Heather Farr and Tina Tombs earned first-team All-America honors as the Sun Devils finished second at the NCAA women's golf championships.
- The men's 4X800-meter relay team of Pete Richardson, Eddie Davis, Treg Scott and Michael Stahr set an American record of 7:08.96 at the Sun Angel Classic track and field meet in Tempe.
- Assistant archery coach Rick McKinney, a former ASU archery standout, was named Sportsman of the Year by the U.S. Olympic Committee.
- The Sun Devils had a clean sweep in archery and badminton, winning men's women's and mixed national team titles in both sports.

Sun Devil Lore

The Arizona Legislature approved a $2 million expenditure to begin work on a branch campus in west Phoenix.

- A $13 million engineering research center opened on campus.

1984-1985

america's time capsule

arizona state university
| m o m e n t

Once again the ASU-Arizona football rivalry went down to the final moments, and once again the Wildcats prevailed, this time by a 16-10 score in Tucson. The Sun Devils, trailing by six points, appeared to have a golden opportunity when they blocked a punt at their own 43 yard line with 3:07 remaining. Sophomore quarterback Jeff Van Rapphorst quickly moved the Devils to a first down at the UA 27 yard line, converting a fourth-and-four situation along the way. But on second and five at the Arizona 22, blitzing linebacker Steve Boadway hit Van Raaphorst as he attempted to pass and the ball fell into the arms of Arizona's Craig Vesling, who was lying on the ground nearby. Arizona ran out the final 1:25. The loss cost the Sun Devils a winning season. They finished 5-6, the first losing campaign in coach Darryl Rogers' five years at ASU. Rogers left after the season to become head coach of the NFL's Detroit Lions. John Cooper was hired from Tulsa to replace Rogers.

Darryl Rogers left ASU to coach the Detroit Lions after a loss to UA cost the Sun Devils a winning season. (ASU Media Relations)

SUN DEVIL *spotlight*

Arizona State was well-represented at the Olympic Games in Los Angeles. Former ASU student Gina Hemphill, granddaughter of past Olympic great Jesse Owens, carried the Olympic torch into the LA Coliseum. An ASU tandem finished one-two in the women's discus with former Sun Devil Ria Stalman of the Netherlands capturing the gold medal and senior Leslie Deniz winning the silver. Former ASU track and football star Ron Brown won a gold medal in the 4X100-meter relay after finishing fourth in the 100 meters. Rick McKinney won a silver medal in archery and former baseball star Oddibe McDowell won a silver in baseball, which was classed as a demonstration sport. Wrestling coach Bobby Douglas was an assistant on the U.S. team that was one of the Olympics' big success stories with a collection of gold medals. Several ASU swimmers starred for other countries. Neil Cochran and Paul Easter teamed with former Sun Devil Andy Astbury to win a silver medal for Great Britain in the 4X200-meter relay.

LEGEND

Luis Zendejas

By the time he had wrapped up his ASU career at the conclusion of the 1984 football season, Luis Zendejas had totally rewritten the NCAA record book's kicking section. He was the proud owner of 11 individual records and shared one more. Zendejas' biggest record wasn't exclusively for kickers. It was the NCAA scoring mark of 356 points held by former University of Pittsburgh running back Tony Dorsett. Zendejas took aim on Dorsett's mark at the beginning of the 1984 season and steadily narrowed the gap. He virtually assured himself of the record in the ninth game of the season when he kicked three field goals and five conversions in a 44-10 romp over Oregon to pull to within one point of Dorsett. He broke the record in a 45-14 victory over Colorado State the following week with a second-quarter conversion kick. He finished with 368 points, 12 more than Dorsett's record. Zendejas' scoring mark later was broken, but four of his NCAA records still stood entering the 2000 season. The most prestigious of those is for the most times kicking three or more field goals in one game in a career. Zendejas did it 13 times. Zendejas' junior season was his most productive. He led the nation with 28 field goals in 37 attempts and made 28 of 29 conversions. Not only did Zendejas have an accurate leg, but a strong one. The seven longest field goals in ASU history all were off of his foot, including a school-record 55-yarder against Oregon State in 1982.

Luis Zendejas owned or shared 12 NCAA kicking records by the time he left ASU. (Chuck Conley/ASU Media Relations)

THE sun devil LIST

School's all-time leaders in points scored in football

Points	Player	Years
380	Luis Zendejas	1981-84
327	Wilford White	1947-50
296	Nolan Jones	1958-61
288	Woody Green	1971-73
256	Leon Burton	1955-58

Note: Bowl statistics count toward school records but not NCAA marks.

SUN DEVIL STATS

• Danielle Ammaccapane won ASU's fifth national women's collegiate individual golf title and the first in 15 years.

• Eddie Urbano, a senior from Tucson, became ASU's first NCAA wrestling champion since Curley Culp in 1967 when he captured the 150-pound title. In a space of three days during the regular season the Sun Devil wrestling team upset second-ranked Oklahoma State and third-ranked Iowa State to vault from ninth to third in the national rankings.

• ASU's top-ten national finishes: Second in women's gymnastics, third in women's golf, fourth in men's gymnastics and sixth in wrestling. The archers swept national honors in men's, women's and mixed. Badminton was No. 1 in men and mixed and No. 2 in women's.

Sun Devil Lore

Legendary swimming coach Mona Plummer died on March 17 after a long illness. The aquatic center was named in her honor.

• A 1 1/2-year centennial celebration, which included more than 300 events, drew to a close on campus. It marked the 100th anniversary of legislation creating the Arizona Territorial Normal School in Tempe.

1985-1986

america's time capsule

arizona state university
m o m e n t

The men's gymnastics team was only third in the Pac-10 championships, but the Sun Devils put it all together to capture the school's first NCAA title and earn National Coach of the Year honors for coach Don Robinson. "I've had to wait 18 years for this moment," said Robinson, who had guided the Sun Devils to second-place national finishes in 1974 and 1978. "I can't believe it's finally here. All the kids were just great. We won this as a team, and I'm proud of them all." It was a controversial finish for the Sun Devils, who beat powerhouse Nebraska, host of the national tournament, on a technicality. ASU and Nebraska initially tied at 283.9 points. ASU was awarded the team title after Nebraska Coach Francis Allen submitted his fourth protest of the meet and had it disallowed. Under NCAA rules, if a coach's fourth protest is disallowed, 0.3 points is deducted from his team's score. That left Nebraska with 283.6 points. Dan Hayden won the high bar with a 9.85 score and captured the parallel bars with a 9.8. His twin brother Dennis scored valuable points with a 9.8 on the high bar and a 9.7 on the parallel bars. Jerry Burrell scored 9.8 in the floor exercise to tie UCLA's Brian Ginsberg for first place. The Sun Devils captured eight All-American awards, led by Dan Hayden with four.

The men's gymnastic team captured its first NCAA championship after a couple of second-place finishes. (Chuck Conley/ASU Media Relations)

Sun Devil spotlight

The unranked Sun Devils, under first-year coach John Cooper, almost pulled off an upset of 14th-ranked Arkansas in San Diego's Holiday Bowl, but Kendall Trainor kicked a 37-yard field goal with 21 seconds remaining to give the Razorbacks an 18-17 victory. The Sun Devils made a valiant attempt to pull it out at the end after Darryl Clack's 37-yard kickoff return gave them good field position. A 21-yard pass from Jeff Van Raaphorst to Aaron Cox gave the Sun Devils a first down at the Arkansas 42 with nine seconds remaining. After an incomplete pass, Kent Bostrom's 59-yard field goal attempt was short by about eight yards. Bostrom had kicked a 47 yarder in the first quarter. The loss left the Sun Devils with an 8-4 record.

ASU LEGEND

David Fulcher

David Fulcher's ASU football career began amid some uncertainty and ended prematurely, but in between the Sun Devils had themselves one heck of a football player. On national letter-of-intent day in 1982, both the Sun Devils and Arizona's Wildcats reported Fulcher as a member of their recruiting class. That's because he told both ASU assistant coach Willie Shaw and UA assistant Willie Peete that he was coming to their school. But when Shaw showed up at the ASU football office with a signed letter late in the day, the Sun Devils knew they had won the battle. They won a lot of battles with Fulcher, a hard-hitting safety who caught everyone's attention with 20 tackles against UCLA as a freshman. At 6-foot-3, 228 pounds, Fulcher was even bigger and better than the prototype safety. He had 110 tackles as a freshman, 100 as a sophomore and 76 with six interceptions and six pass deflections as a junior. A second-team All-American (*Sporting News*) as a freshman, he was a consensus All-American the next two years. He joined Woody Green (1972-73) and Mike Richardson (1981-82) as the only two-time consensus All-Americans in school history. He probably could have three-peated, but he chose to by-pass his senior season to make himself available for the NFL draft. He was a third-round pick of the Cincinnati Bengals and went on to have an outstanding NFL career.

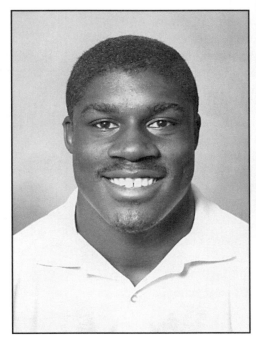

David Fulcher was a two-time consensus All-American in football. (ASU Media Relations)

THE sun devil LIST

Longest pass plays in ASU football history

Yards	Players/Opponent	Year
95	Jeff Van Raaphorst to Aaron Cox/ USC	1985
95	Fred Mortenson to John Jefferson/ TCU	1975
93	Dennis Sproul to Larry Mucker/ California	1976
91	Dennis Sproul to John Jefferson/ Utah	1977
90	Jeff Krohn to Richard Williams/ Oregon	2000
87	Danny White to Alonzo Emery/ Washington St.	1973
85	Larry Todd to Tony Lorick/ Wichita St.	1962

Note: All of the plays above resulted in a touchdown

SUN DEVIL STATS

• It was announced that ASU's women athletes would begin competing in a new women's Pac-10 Conference beginning with the 1986-87 school year. The Sun Devil women had been competing in the Pac-West Conference with Arizona, Stanford, USC and UCLA.

• ASU combined its men's and women's track and field programs under one head coach and elevated the joint program to major sports status after a disappointing spring season that saw the men score just one point and the women five at the NCAA championships. Clyde Duncan was named head coach of the dual programs.

• Sophomore golfer Danielle Ammaccapane was named Arizona Amateur Athlete of the Year by the Phoenix Press Box Association for winning the NCAA title and National Public Links in 1985.

SUN DEVIL LORE

Charles Harris was named athletic director and charged with restoring order to a once-proud athletic program that had become embroiled in turmoil.

• Basketball coach Bob Weinhauer was informed in July that his contract would not be renewed. Steve Patterson was named interim head coach after a five-week search.

• ASU received deed to 29.4 acres of U.S. Forest Service land adjacent to Camp Tontozona which it planned to use to expand and upgrade the mountain retreat.

1986-1987

america's time capsule

arizona state university
m o m e n t

After years of waiting and several close calls, the Sun Devils finally made it to Pasadena for the fabled granddaddy of them all, the Rose Bowl. And they didn't disappoint the thousands of fans who trekked across the desert to watch them play Big Ten champ Michigan. The Sun Devils spotted the Wolverines an early 15-3 lead, then roared back with 19 unanswered points to register a 22-15 victory in John Cooper's second season as head coach. The Devils began whittling into Michigan's lead with Kent Bostrom's second field goal of the game, a 17 yarder, in the second quarter. A four-yard touchdown pass from Jeff Van Raaphorst to Bruce Hill narrowed the margin to 15-13 at the half. The Sun Devils took the second-half kickoff and drove 80 yards in 12 plays for the go-ahead touchdown, a one-yard pass from Van Raaphorst to Hill in the back of the end zone. In the fourth quarter, Bostrom's third field goal of the game nailed down the victory as ASU's defense held the Wolverines to four first downs and minus five yards rushing after intermission. An interception by safety Robby Boyd late in the fourth quarter put the game on ice for the Sun Devils. Hill's two touchdown catches and Bostrom's three field goals tied Rose Bowl records. The Sun Devils finished 10-1-1 with a No. 4 ranking in the final Associated Press poll, second-best in school history to the unbeaten 1975 team's No. 2 ranking.

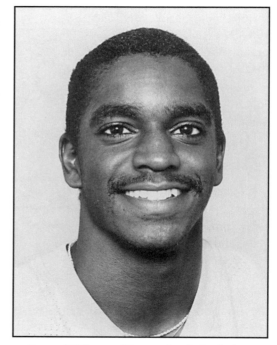

Bruce Hill's two TD catches helped the Sun Devils beat Michigan in the Rose Bowl. (ASU Media Relations)

SUN DEVIL *spotlight*

The ASU athletic program, which battled through considerable turmoil in the late 1970s and early 1980s, began making its presence felt once again on the national scene. ASU had the third most successful overall program in the nation according to the annual rankings compiled by the *Knoxville Journal* in Tennessee. The men ranked fifth and the women seventh. Top 10 finishes by ASU teams in 1986-87: Football, 4th; women's gymnastics, 5th; baseball, 7th; women's swimming, 7th; wrestling, 9th; men's swimming, 10th. As usual, ASU dominated archery and badminton, sweeping national honors in men's, women's and mixed competition in both sports.

LEGENDS

Billy Mayfair

Nobody was bigger in amateur golf circles in 1986 and 1987 than Billy Mayfair, a home-grown product of Camelback High School in Phoenix. Mayfair became the first golfer ever to win both the U.S. Public Links (1986) and the U.S. Amateur. (1987). A four-time All-American, he won first-team All-America honors in 1987 and 1988. He was the Pac-10 Player of the Year in 1987. He won a spot on the U. S. Walker Cup team in 1987, the first player from Arizona in 18 years to participate on the team. Mayfair captured individual honors in the Pacific Coast Amateur tournament in 1987 and 1988 and the Pacific Northwest GA Amateur the same two years. He has gone on to enjoy a successful career on the PGA Tour.

Billy Mayfair
(Ken Akers/ASU Media Relations)

Jeff Van Raaphorst

ASU quarterback Jeff Van Raaphorst didn't make the All-Pac-10 team in 1986. He didn't even earn honorable-mention honors. He wasn't selected in the NFL draft. All Van Raaphorst did was win. He took the Sun Devils to a 10-1-1 record and No. 4 national ranking, thanks to a 22-15 Rose Bowl victory over Michigan. Before that game, Michigan quarterback Jim Harbaugh drew most of the attention, but it was Van Raaphorst who was named the game's Most Valuable Player on offense after completing 16 of 30 passes for 193 yards and two touchdowns. Van Raaphorst still holds the school record for most pass completions in one game—38. He did it twice, against Florida State as a sophomore in 1984 and against Arizona as a senior in 1986. His 532 passing yards in the Florida State game was a school record until Paul Justin threw for 534 yards against Washington State in 1989.

Jeff Van Raaphorst
(Chuck Conley/ASU Media Relations)

THE sun devil LIST

ASU single-game passing records

Most Passes Attempted

63	Paul Justin (Houston, 1990)
59	Jeff Van Raaphorst (Florida State, 1994)
56	Ryan Kealy (Arizona, 1998)
55	Jeff Van Raaphorst (Arizona, 1986)
49	Mike Pagel (Ohio State, 1980)
48	Danny White (Utah, 1973)
48	Todd Hons (Arizona, 1982)
48	Bret Powers (UCLA, 1991)

Most Passes Completed

38	Jeff Van Raaphorst (Florida State, 1984)
38	Jeff Van Raaphorst (Arizona, 1986)
34	Paul Justin (Houston, 1990)
33	Ryan Kealy (Arizona, 1998)
33	Paul Justin (Washington State, 1989)
29	Todd Hons (Washington State, 1983)
28	Mark Malone (UCLA, 1979)
28	Bret Powers (UCLA, 1991)

Most Passing Yards

534	Paul Justin (Washington State, 1989)
532	Jeff Van Raaphorst (Florida State, 1984)
511	Ryan Kealy (Arizona, 1998)
474	Paul Justin (Houston, 1990)
466	Mike Pagel (Stanford, 1981)
437	Jeff Van Raaphorst (Arizona, 1986)

SUN DEVIL STAT

• Volleyball coach Debbie Brown was named Pac-10 Coach of the Year after her team finished 27-7 and earned an NCAA tournament berth in their first year in the Pac-10. The Devils were third in the Pac-10 with a 13-3 conference mark. Tammy Webb earned first-team All-America honors and Regina Stahl second-team acclaim from the American Volleyball Coaches Association.

Sun Devil Lore

The 1987 Pulitzer Prize in poetry was awarded to ASU English professor Rita Dove. She won the award for a collection of poems titled *Thomas and Beulah*, published by the Carnegie-Mellon University Press. It was based on the life of her maternal grandparents, who moved from the South to Akron, Ohio, where they lived from the turn of the century to the mid 1960s. The collection of 44 poems took six years to write.

1987-1988

america's time capsule

arizona state university
moment

For years, ASU's wrestling team had been on the outside looking in as Iowa and Iowa State took turns capturing the NCAA championship. The Sun Devils had five top-10 finishes the previous nine years, but the best they could manage was a fifth-place showing in 1980. Then came the breakthrough. Coach Bobby Douglas' team came from well off the pace to win the title with a tremendous showing on the final day of the NCAA tournament at Ames, Iowa. The Devils were in fourth place, 10 1/2 points behind Iowa, entering the consolation finals, but they mounted a major rally and became the first team in 10 years to win the national crown without an individual champion. It was the first time in 14 years that a school other than Iowa or Iowa State had won the national title. The Sun Devils accumulated 93 points to 85 1/2 for runner-up Iowa and 83 3/4 for defending champion Iowa State. ASU's top finisher was Mike Davies, who lost to Ohio State's Mark

Mike Davies played a big role as the Sun Devils captured their first NCAA wrestling title. (Ken Akers/ASU Media Relations)

Coleman, 5-0, in the 190-pound championship match. The Devils got third-place finishes from Chip Park at 126 pounds, Dan St. John at 158 pounds and Jim Gressley at 167 pounds. Tommy Ortiz was fourth at 142 pounds, Rod Severn fifth in the heavyweight division and Zeke Jones sixth at 118 pounds.

SUN DEVIL *spotlight*

There was a lot of huddling going on during the football team's visit to southern California for its Freedom Bowl matchup with Air Force, and not all of it was on the field. At the team's Costa Mesa, California, hotel, fans and media gathered in small groups to digest rumors that head coach John Cooper was about to leave for greener pastures. Sure enough, after the Sun Devils beat Air Force, 33-28, for their fourth bowl victory in their last five tries, Cooper announced he was leaving ASU to become head coach at Ohio State. Cooper was 25-9-1 with three bowl appearances in three seasons at ASU. His defensive coordinator, Larry Marmie, was named to succeed him as head coach. The bowl game? ASU got 272 passing yards from Daniel Ford and 93 rushing yards from Darryl Harris. The Devils took command with a 24-point second quarter and held off a late charge by the Falcons.

LEGENDS

Randall McDaniel

The 1984 football season produced only five victories, but it will be remembered for a position switch that was perhaps as significant as any in school history. During an open week early in the season, coach Darryl Rogers took a tight end with so-so hands and quick feet and moved him to guard. That player, former Agua Fria High School star Randall McDaniel, became one of the finest offensive guards ever to play the game at any level. By the time his ASU career was over, McDaniel had played a major role in Rose Bowl and Freedom Bowl victories and had earned Consensus All-America honors as a senior in 1987. He's one of just three ASU offensive linemen to win such acclaim along with Danny Villa in 1986 and Juan Roque in 1996. But McDaniel's best days were ahead of him. A first-round pick of the Minnesota Vikings, he went on to earn selection to the Pro Bowl for 11 straight seasons beginning in 1990.

Randall McDaniel
(ASU Media Relations)

Dan St. John

Though it doesn't grab a lot of headlines, ASU's wrestling program has produced more than its share of nationally and internationally prominent competitors. Perhaps the best of the best was Dan St. John, who played a key role with a third-place finish in ASU's only national NCAA team championship in 1988, then won national individual crowns at 158 pounds in 1989 and 167 pounds in 1990. St. John won more matches (147) and more dual matches (71) than any other wrestler in ASU history. His school record 49 consecutive victories from 1988 through 1990 smashed the mark of 41 first set by Buzz Hayes in 1963-64 and matched by Curley Culp in 1967-68. He twice won 21 matches in a season (21-0-0 in 1988-89, 21-0-1 in 1989-90). Only Zeke Jones, who was 22-0-0 in 1989-90) has won more.

Dan St. John
(ASU Media Relations)

THE sun devil LIST

Most career victories by ASU wrestlers

Wins	Wrestler	Years
147	Dan St. John	(1986-90)
136	Mike Davies	(1983-88)
135	Steve Blackford	(1997-2001)
134	Zeke Jones	(1986-90)
127	Dan Severn	(1977-81)
118	Thom Ortiz	(1986-90)
117	Dave Severn	(1975-79)
115	Ray Miller	(1990-93)
113	Markus Mollica	(1993-96)
105	Eddie Urbano	(1982-85)
104	Glenn McMinn	(1964-67)
104	Jim Gressley	(1984-89)
103	Rod Severn	(1985-88)
103	Shawn Charles	(1990-93)
102	Buzz Hayes	(1962-65)

SUN DEVIL STATS

• ASU's Pearl Sinn became the first woman golfer ever to win the U.S. Amateur and U.S. Public Links tournaments in the same year.

• Sun Devil wrestling coach Bobby Douglas was elected to the National Wrestling Hall of Fame.

• The baseball team put on one of its greatest stretch drives ever, winning 23 straight and 32 of 33 to capture the Pac-10 Southern Division title over defending national champion Stanford. The Cardinal beat the Sun Devils, however, in the national championship game at the College World Series.

Sun Devil Lore

Pope John Paul II wrapped up a busy day in the Phoenix area with an evening mass at jam-packed Sun Devil Stadium. The Pontiff compared the Phoenix Bird to the risen Christ. The ASU appearance followed addresses at St. Mary's Basilica and Veteran's Memorial Coliseum and a parade down Central Avenue witnessed by 100,000.

• The Karsten Solheim family donated $2 million toward the construction of a new $6.5 million golf course on campus. University president J. Russell Nelson said it was the largest monetary gift ever committed to ASU.

1988-1989

November 8, 1988: Vice President George Bush defeated Massachusetts Gov. Michael Dukakis in the presidential election.

January 2, 1989: Notre Dame clinched the national college football championship with a 34-21 Fiesta Bowl victory over West Virginia in Sun Devil Stadium.

January 22, 1989: Joe Montana passed for a record 357 yards as the San Francisco 49ers won their third Super Bowl title under coach Bill Walsh, 20-16 over the Cincinnati Bengals.

March 24, 1989: The oil tanker *Exxon Valdez* struck a reef in Prince William Sound, Alaska, leaking more than a million barrels of crude oil into the water.

August 10, 1989: President Bush nominated Army General Colin Powell to be chairman of the Joint Chiefs of Staff. Powell became the first African-American to hold the nation's highest military post.

arizona state university
| m o m e n t

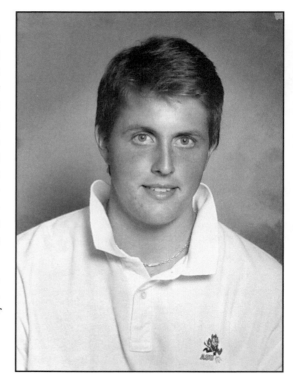

Sun Devil freshman Phil Mickelson wasted little time stamping his name in the record books. The left-hander from San Diego became the second ASU male golfer to win an NCAA individual title when he outdistanced the field at the NCAA championships at Oak Tree Country Club in Edmond, Oklahoma. ASU's Jim Carter won the NCAA crown in 1983. Mickelson, who turned 19 a few days after winning the tournament, was the youngest player and the first left-hander ever to win the NCAA title. He was the fourth freshman in history to capture the crown. Mickelson's first-place points led ASU to a fifth-place finish in the tournament. The Sun Devils finished 23 strokes behind champion Oklahoma. After just one season, Mickelson already was fielding questions about the possibility of leaving school early to join the PGA Tour. "I've kind of set myself on a four-year plan, to graduate in four years," he said. "I'm really in no hurry (to join the Tour)."

Freshman Phil Mickelson became the youngest player ever to win the NCAA golf tournament. (ASU Media Relations)

ASU shocked the college basketball world by hiring Michigan basketball coach Bill Frieder on the eve of the NCAA tournament. Michigan officials would not let Frieder coach in the tournament and assistant coach Steve Fisher led the Wolverines to the national title. Frieder replaced Steve Patterson, who resigned in February, just before concluding his fourth season as ASU's head coach. Assistant coach Bob Schermerhorn finished the season as interim head coach. Frieder's Michigan teams had won 24 or more games in five of the six previous years. He took over an ASU program that hadn't had a winning season since 1981-82. Frieder signed a four-year contract at ASU. His total package was estimated at $300,000. He took a pay cut to leave Michigan for what he called "a career move."

LEGEND

Lynda Tolbert

Hurdles didn't represent obstacles to Lynda Tolbert, just stepping stones to victories. And before her ASU career was over, she was one of the most decorated track and field stars in the school's history. Tolbert won the 1988 and 1989 NCAA outdoor 100-meter hurdles titles and captured the 1990 NCAA indoor 55-meter hurdles crown. She also ran on the winning 4X100-meter relay team at the 1988 NCAA championships. *Track and Field News* ranked her the No. 1 American hurdler and No. 5 in the world for the 1989 season. She still holds the collegiate record for the indoor 60-meter hurdles. An eight-time All-American at ASU, Tolbert went on to finish fourth in the 100-meter hurdles at the 1992 Olympics.

Lynda Tolbert was an eight-time All-American and a collegiate record-holder in the hurdles. (ASU Media Relations)

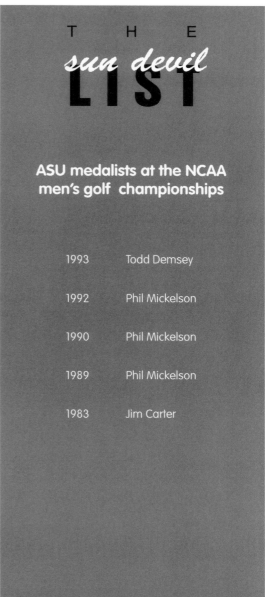
SUN DEVIL STATS

• For the second time in three years, ASU was ranked third nationally in the *Knoxville Journal's* combined ratings of men's and women's athletic programs. The Sun Devils were fifth in men's sports and fourth in women's. Top 10 national finishes were recorded by wrestling (second), men's golf (fifth), women's golf (tie for sixth), women's gymnastics (tie for seventh) and women's swimming (eighth). ASU teams swept national titles in men's women's and mixed archery and badminton for the third straight year and fourth in the last five.

• Jody Newman became ASU's 10th national individual champion in men's gymnastics when he won the floor exercise at the NCAA championships in Lincoln, Nebraska.

Sun Devil Lore

ASU's athletic facilities moved into the upper echelon nationally with the addition of a $9 million, seven-story athletic building at the south end of Sun Devil Stadium. The building housed coaches' and athletic administrative offices, a football locker room, strength training and sports medicine facilities, academic support services, a ticket office and team shop.

1989-1990

**america's
time capsule**

arizona state university
m o m e n t

Everything fell into place for the Sun Devil men's and women's golf teams early in the summer of 1990. After several near misses, both the men and women captured NCAA team championships, making ASU the first school in NCAA history to win the big prize in both men's and women's college golf in the same year. It was only the fifth time in NCAA history that men's and women's teams from the same sport had won national crowns in the same year in any sport. The previous best finish for ASU's men was third in 1969, 1977, 1978 and 1982. The women had won a national AIAW title in 1975, but their best finish at the NCAA tournament was second in 1984 and 1988. The men rallied from 11 strokes back to win on the final day at the Innsbrook Golf Resort in Tarpon Springs, Florida, as sophomore Phil Mickelson successfully defended his 1989 individual title and became the first golfer ever to win medalist honors as a freshman and a sophomore. The women used a balanced attack to win the women's title by 16 strokes over Pac-10 rival UCLA. Brandy Burton, Missy Farr, Tricia Konz and Amy Fruhwirth all had their moments for the Sun Devils. Burton, the pre-tournament favorite, finished in a tie for eighth.

The women's golf team joined the men to make NCAA history by winning national titles in the same year. (Scott Photography/ASU Media Relations)

SUN DEVIL *spotlight*

Sophomore Shane Collins became the first ASU male athlete in 13 years to win a field event at the NCAA championships when he captured the 1990 shot put title with a toss of 66 feet, 3 and 3/4 inches. ASU's last previous field event winner was Kyle Arney in the high jump in 1977. Collins' toss was the second-best in school history behind Gary Williky's heave of 68 feet, 2 1/2 inches in 1982. Collins also starred in football for the Sun Devils. He started all 11 games as a freshman in 1988 and went on to earn All Pac-10 honors as a senior in 1991. He was a second-round pick of the Washington Redskins in the 1992 NFL draft.

ASU LEGEND

Mike Kelly

The debates probably will never subside over who was the best baseball player in ASU history, but there is little question about who was the most decorated. Outfielder Mike Kelly captured four national player-of-the year awards as a sophomore in 1990. He is the only Sun Devil ever to be cited as player of the year by more than two agencies. Kelly received the award from *Baseball America*, *Collegiate Baseball* and *The Sporting News* as well as the Bob Smith Award selected by the National Collegiate Baseball Writers Association. As a junior in 1991 he won the Golden Spikes player of the year award. He's the only Sun Devil in history to be named national player of the year in more than one season. He also is the only three-time All American in ASU baseball history. He was named national Freshman of the Year by *Collegiate Baseball* in 1989—the first ASU player ever to win that honor. Kelly's best year was his sophomore season, when he batted .376 with 21 home runs, 83 runs scored and 82 RBIs. He also swiped 20 bases in 22 tries and played spectacularly in center field. The Atlanta Braves made him the second pick of the June 1991 Major League draft.

Baseball star Mike Kelly won four National Player of the Year awards as a sophomore. (ASU Media Relations)

SUN DEVIL STATS

- ASU juniors Joel Finnigan and David Lomicky teamed up to win the U.S. Amateur tennis doubles title. It was only the third time they had played together as a doubles team.
- Sophomore outfielder Tommy Adams set school and Pac-10 Southern Division records by driving in nine runs against Nevada-Las Vegas. And he did it in the first four innings with two three-run homers and a three-run double.
- Junior Gea Johnson set eight school and stadium records while overwhelming the field in the heptathlon competition at the ASU Track and Field Invitational. She won all seven heptathlon events.
- ASU—along with Texas—was one of just two schools with men's and women's programs in the top five nationally in rankings compiled by the newspaper *USA Today*. ASU was ranked fourth in men's sports and fifth in women's.

Sun Devil Lore

Arizona State's golf teams got a tremendous boost and the Tempe landscape was enhanced substantially when the Karsten Golf Course opened for business on the northeast end of the campus in September of 1989.

- Lattie Coor became ASU's 15th president on January 2, 1990.

1990-1991

**america's
time capsule**

arizona state university
| m o m e n t

Arizona State got the big-name coach it wanted when it hired Bill Frieder away from national basketball powerhouse Michigan. His mission? Turn around a program that had fallen on hard times. His credentials suggested he could get the job done, but the swiftness with which he accomplished the task was stunning. In just his second season as ASU's head coach, Frieder and the Sun Devils found themselves smack in the middle of March Madness. A 19-9 regular-season record and third-place finish in the Pac-10 earned ASU a spot in the NCAA tournament for the first time since the 1980-81 season. The 1980-81 club was 24-3 in the regular season and ranked second nationally, but it lost to Kansas in the first round of the NCAA tourney. Frieder's club made it to the second round, beating Rutgers, 79-76, at the Omni in Atlanta, Georgia. In the second round, the Sun Devils repeatedly cracked the vaunted full-court press of second-ranked Arkansas before fatigue set in and the Razorbacks eliminated the Sun Devils, 97-90. Frieder said ASU's lack of depth made the difference, and he promised to address that deficiency. The Devils got 58 points from freshmen Jamal Faulkner (29), Dwayne Fontana (18) and Stevin Smith (11) against Arkansas.

Bill Frieder's second ASU basketball team earned a spot in the NCAA tournament. (ASU Media Relations)

Maicel Malone set school records at 200 meters and 400 meters outdoors and established American, collegiate and NCAA meet records at 51.05 seconds in winning the NCAA indoor 400-meter title. Malone also anchored the ASU 4X400 relay team which established an American indoor record of 3:32.46 while winning the event at the same meet. Her teammates on the 4X400 relay team were Shanequa Campbell, Toinette Holmes and Dana Jones. Malone's time of 22.91 in the 200 meters outdoors broke the school mark of 23.36 set by Val Boyer in 1980. Her time of 50.33 in the 400 meters smashed the school standard of 52.30 set the previous spring by Holmes.

ASU LEGEND

Bobby Douglas

When Bobby Douglas took over the ASU wrestling program prior to the 1974-75 season, there was a mountain of work to be done. The Sun Devils had made just one appearance in the NCAA tournament the previous five years—a 23rd-place finish in 1972. Under Douglas, a former world-class wrestler himself, the progress was steady. The Devils finished 34th in Douglas' first year, 21st in 1976 and 11th in 1977. They cracked the Top 10 with an eighth-place finish in 1979 and improved to fifth in 1980. After four straight Top-10 finishes in the mid-1980s, they broke through to capture the school's only NCAA title in 1988. They followed that with a pair of second-place national finishes. Along the way the Sun Devils won seven straight Pac-10 titles from 1985 through 1991. Douglas accomplished all of that with a budget far less than that of the traditional national wrestling powers. While building ASU's program, Douglas continued to earn international acclaim. He was on the coaching staff of five straight U.S. Olympic wrestling teams and was head coach of the U.S. team for the 1992 games in Barcelona, Spain. He was elected to the National Wrestling Hall of Fame and the NAIA Wrestling Hall of Fame.

Bobby Douglas built the wrestling program into a national power. (ASU Media Relations)

SUN DEVIL **STATS**

- Wrestling coach Bobby Douglas was named head coach of the U.S. Olympic team for the 1992 Games in Barcelona.

- ASU's archery and badminton teams achieved their customary sweeps of men's, women's and mixed titles in national collegiate competition. ASU finished third in men's golf, third in women's tennis, ninth in men's tennis, ninth in men's swimming and ninth in women's gymnastics.

Sun Devil Lore

The ASU marching band received the Sudler Intercollegiate Marching Band Trophy, which goes annually to the college or university band judged to have the highest musical standards and most innovative routines. The trophy competition, which is voted on by NCAA schools, is managed by the John Philip Sousa Foundation. ASU band director Robert Fleming called it "the Heisman Trophy of bands."

1991-1992

September 9, 1991: Heavyweight boxing champion Mike Tyson was indicted on rape charges by a Marion County, Indiana, grand jury.

November 7, 1991: Professional basketball star Magic Johnson retired after announcing that he had tested positive for the HIV virus.

December 25, 1991: Mikhail Gorbachev resigned his position as leader of the Soviet Union.

May 1, 1992: President George Bush ordered federal troops to riot-torn Los Angeles to quell unrest triggered when a jury acquitted four policemen charged with beating Rodney King.

May 22, 1992: More than 50 million television viewers tuned in to watch Johnny Carson's final appearance on "The Tonight Show."

arizona state university
moment

The Sun Devils crushed Arizona, 37-14, to salvage a 6-5 football season, but it wasn't enough to save coach Larry Marmie's job. One day after the annual football banquet, at which Marmie's status wasn't addressed, athletic director Charles Harris announced that Marmie's contract would not be renewed. ASU's victory ended a nine-year winless streak against the Wildcats—eight losses and one tie. Fans stormed the field after the game and tore down the Sun Devil Stadium goal posts. Tucson native Mario Bates, in his first start, gained 161 yards on 35 carries. Bates outgained the entire UA team, which managed only 155 yards of total offense. ASU's defense picked off four Arizona passes, two by safety Adam Brass. Eric Guliford scored two touchdowns for the Sun Devils on a 24-yard pass from Bret Powers and a 68-yard punt return. Marmie, who was elevated to the head coaching job from defensive coordinator after John Cooper left for Ohio State following the 1987 season, compiled a four-year record of 22-21-1. His teams posted records of 6-5, 6-4-1, 4-7 and 6-5. During that time, home attendance dropped from an average of 70,717 in 1988 to 55,715 in 1991. In January of 1992, ASU hired Bruce Snyder away from California as its new head coach.

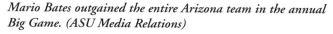

Mario Bates outgained the entire Arizona team in the annual Big Game. (ASU Media Relations)

The women's basketball team, picked to finish last in the Pac-10, won nine of its last 11 league games to finish fifth and earn a spot in the NCAA tournament for the first time since the 1982-83 season. The Sun Devils had the misfortune of playing DePaul in a first-round game on its home floor and suffered a heartbreaking 67-65 loss after building a seven-point lead in the second half. Point guard Ryneldi Becenti was named to the All Pac-10 first team. Coach Maura McHugh's Devils finished 20-9 overall and 11-7 in conference play. It was ASU's first 20-victory season since coach Juliene Simpson's 1982-83 club finished 23-7 and it was the school's first winning season in six years.

ASU LEGEND

Sheri Rhodes

Sheri Rhodes' exploits might not have been the most visible in ASU athletic history, but they certainly were the most successful. A three-time All-American in archery, she went on to coach the Sun Devils to almost total domination of the national scene in that sport. From 1977 until the sport was disbanded in 1993, Rhodes' teams won 46 of a possible 51 national championships in men's, women's and mixed archery. Rhodes coached well over 100 All-Americans during that time. Granted, Rhodes had some built-in advantages. ASU is believed to be the only school in the nation to have offered archery scholarships during part of that period. The few schools that did fund the sport did so on a limited basis. Shortly before it was dropped as a varsity sport at the end of the 1993 season, archery had a modest budget of $20,500 exclusive of coaches' salaries. It offered tuition waivers and books, but not room and board, for six male and six female athletes. But though Rhodes had some resources not enjoyed at other institutions, there was no questioning her credentials on the national and international level. She was named to coach the 1988 U.S. Olympic team. Half of the six members of that team were former ASU archers—Rick McKinney, Jay Barrs and Debra Ochs.

Sheri Rhodes dominated as a competitor and a coach in archery. (ASU Media Relations)

SUN DEVIL STATS

• Phil Mickelson wrapped up his brilliant college golf career by winning the NCAA individual title for the third time in four years. He joined Ben Crenshaw of Texas (1971-73) as the only three-time winner in NCAA history. Mickelson won first-team All-America honors for the fourth time and captured his third straight Pac-10 Player of the Year award.

• Another three-peat came from track star Maciel Malone, who made history when she won her third NCAA indoor 400-meter title at the championship meet in Indianapolis, where she starred in high school at North Central State High.

SUN DEVIL LORE

Cuts in state funding and a drop in tuition revenue forced ASU officials to lay off employees for the first time in 10 years and to cut classes and eliminate unfilled positions. About 200 classes were eliminated.

• For the second year in a row enrollment on the main campus dropped as enrollment continued to grow on the ASU West campus.

1992-1993

america's time capsule

November 3, 1992: Democrat Bill Clinton won the presidential election over incumbent George Bush and independent candidate Ross Perot.

December 8, 1992: The first United Nations-authorized troops landed in Somalia to assist the starving populace.

February 26, 1993: New York City's World Trade Center was bombed by terrorists.

April 19, 1993: Nearly 100 people perished in a fire that ended the 51-day standoff of David Koresh's Branch Davidians against federal agents in Waco, Texas.

June 20, 1993: The Chicago Bulls beat the Phoenix Suns, 99-98, to win their third consecutive NBA championship.

arizona state university
| m o m e n t

The Sun Devils continued their rise to national prominence in both men's and women's golf. The women won their second NCAA team championship of the 1990s and Todd Demsey won NCAA men's medalist honors—the fourth time in a five-year stretch that an ASU player had captured the top individual honor. The women dominated college golf from the outset during the 1992-93 season, finishing first or second in all but one of their tournaments. At the NCAA championships the Devils started slowly, but gradually moved up the leader board with a balanced attack. A tremendous back nine on the final day enabled the Sun Devils to win by two shots over Texas. All five members of the ASU lineup earned major post-season awards. Wendy Ward was a first-team All American and Emilee Klein a second-team All American. Tracy Cone and Linda Ericsson earned All-Regional honors and Ulrika von Heijne was an Academic All-American. Demsey's NCAA title in Lexington, Kentucky, helped lead the ASU men to a sixth-place national finish. Demsey earned a spot on the 1993 U.S. Walker Cup team, where he won all three of his matches.

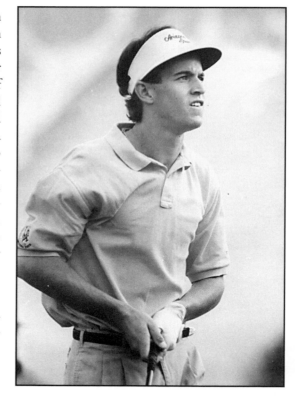

Todd Demsey won the NCAA men's individual golf title and ASU's women captured the team crown. (ASU Media Relations)

Markus Mollica became the first ASU freshman to win an NCAA wrestling title when he captured the 158-pound crown in 1993, but he had to share the spotlight with a couple of more experienced teammates. Ray Miller and Shawn Charles earned their share of headlines when they became the school's first four-time All-Americans. Miller won the national title at 167 pounds to cap a perfect 28-0 season and finish his ASU career with a 115-25-1 record. In four years at the nationals Miller finished fifth, fourth, second and first. Charles was national runner-up at 126 pounds for the second straight year as he finished with a 28-2 record. The Sun Devils placed fourth in the team competition.

ASU
LEGEND

Paul
LoDuca

He was one of the littlest Sun Devils at 5-foot-10, but Paul LoDuca wielded the biggest bat in college baseball in 1993. LoDuca set school records with 129 hits and a .446 batting average and his 37-game hitting streak was the longest in the nation that season. His heroics earned him National Player of the Year honors from *The Sporting News*. LoDuca's hitting streak was second-longest in school history behind Roger Schmuck's 45-game streak in 1971, which stood for 10 years as an NCAA record. LoDuca's offensive production didn't surprise anyone who had followed his baseball career. He had batted .441 and .470 his final two years at Apollo High in Glendale and .449 and .461 in two years at Glendale Community College.

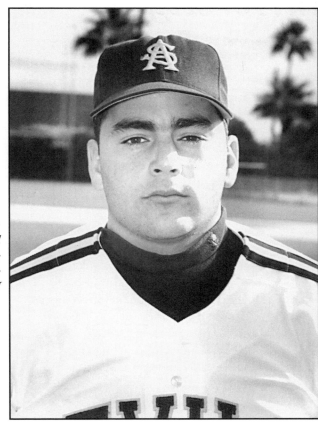

Small in stature, Paul LoDuca wielded the biggest bat in college baseball in 1993. (ASU Media Relations)

SUN DEVIL STATS

• Three of ASU's most successful sports from a competitive standpoint fell victim to the budget ax when athletic director Charles Harris announced that men's gymnastics and men's and women's archery and badminton would be dropped at the end of the school year.
• More than 20 present and former Sun Devils participated in the 1992 summer Olympics in Barcelona.
• Archery and badminton enjoyed their customary sweeps of men's, women's and mixed titles in their final year of competition. It was the third straight sweep in those two sports and the seventh in eight years.
• The 1992-93 basketball team contributed two players, Wun Versher and James Bacon, to the world-famous Harlem Globetrotters.

SUN DEVIL LORE

A rash of incidents over a short period of time prompted ASU president Lattie Coor to form a four-man team, headed by athletic director Charles Harris, to study and revamp the university's system for dealing with student-athlete misconduct.

1993-1994

america's time capsule

arizona state university
moment

Jim Brock's Sun Devils battled valiantly in an attempt to win one last national title for their dying coach. (ASU Media Relations)

It was perhaps the most gripping story in American sports in 1994. As Arizona State baseball coach Jim Brock battled for his life, his team fought valiantly to present him with one last coaching milestone—his third national championship. Neither Brock nor his Sun Devils won their battle, but that did not diminish the impact of his tale of courage. In the summer of 1993, shortly after his return to Tempe from the College World Series, Brock learned that he had cancer of the colon and liver. He had surgery in July of 1993 to remove 80 percent of his liver and several inches of his colon. Despite his weakened condition from weekly chemotherapy treatments, he returned to coach the 1994 season. Though his condition deteriorated as the season progressed, he did not miss a conference game. He coached his team to victory in the Mideast Regional in the stifling heat and humidity of Knoxville, Tennessee, and went to Omaha, Nebraska, ahead of his team to conserve energy for the Series. The Sun Devils responded to a second-inning pep talk by Brock and beat Miami, 4-0, in their Series opener. He was too ill to attend game No. 2, a 4-3 loss to Oklahoma. He was airlifted home to a Mesa hospital prior to game No. 3. With Brock's lucky chair sitting empty in the dugout, his Sun Devils blasted five home runs and eliminated top-seeded Miami, 9-5, for Brock's 1,100th career coaching victory. Oklahoma eliminated ASU and went on to beat Georgia Tech for the national title. Brock died one day later at the age of 57.

SUN DEVIL *spotlight*

The women's golf team did something that no team had done before—win three national championships in one decade. Playing in the wind and rain with a wind chill in the low 40s, the Sun Devils pulled away from rival Southern California on the final day to win the NCAA title by 16 strokes at West Linn, Oregon. Emilee Klein captured medalist honors and teammate Wendy Ward was just two strokes behind. Those two earned first-team All-America honors along with Heather Bowie. Tracy Cone was a second-team selection. It was a tremendous turnaround for the Devils, who had a disappointing third-place finish in the NCAA West Regional at Albuquerque, New Mexico.

ASU LEGEND

Don Robinson

One of just two men's gymnastics coaches in school history, Don Robinson took over the program from Norris Steverson in 1969 and coached the team until the university dropped the sport at the end of the 1993 season. The apex of Robinson's career came in the 1985-86 season, when the Sun Devils captured the only NCAA championship in school history. The Sun Devils had come close with a fourth-place finish in 1984-85. A tireless worker who fought continually to earn recognition for his sport, Robinson battled unsuccessfully to save the team in the early 1990s when it appeared it would fall victim to the budget ax after NCAA participation fell from 64 schools to 35 over a three-year period. A minimum of 50 schools was required for a sport to receive NCAA certification. In 1992, Robinson was told he must raise a $2.5 million endowment to keep the sport alive. He was unable to raise the funds and the sport was dropped along with archery and badminton.

Don Robinson put ASU men's gymnastics on the map during his 25-year coaching career. (ASU Media Relations)

SUN DEVIL STATS

• The first support group committed totally to advancing the cause of women's athletics at ASU—the Wings of Gold—was formed during the spring semester.

• Don Bocchi, who spent nine seasons as an ASU assistant football coach, was named executive director of the Sun Angel Foundation support group.

• Women's golf (No. 1) and baseball (third-place tie) were the only teams to crack the top five nationally, but several other Sun Devil teams had top-10 finishes. Wrestling was tied for eighth, men's golf tied for ninth, women's gymnastics 10th, women's tennis 10th and women's track tied for 10th.

SUN DEVIL LORE

ASU joined the ranks of top research institutions in the nation when it earned the designation "Research University I" from the Carnegie Foundation for the Advancement of Teaching. ASU was one of 71 public universities among a field of 3,597 to earn the designation.

1994-1995

america's time capsule

arizona state university | m o m e n t

Coach Bill Frieder's basketball team jumped into the national rankings early in the season by winning the Maui Invitational with victories over Texas A&M, 13th-ranked Michigan and seventh-ranked Maryland. That propelled the Sun Devils to 12th in the Associated Press rankings and they did not fall out of the Top 20 the rest of the season. They were third in the Pac-10 with a 12-6 conference mark and finished 24-9 overall— their best record in 14 years. Among the regular-season highlights were two thrilling victories over rival Arizona—53-52 in Tempe and 103-98 in double overtime in Tucson. In both games Arizona had the higher national ranking. The Sun Devils won their first two games in the NCAA tournament, beating Ball State, 81-66, and Manhattan, 64-54, at Memphis, Tennessee, before losing to second-ranked Kentucky, 97-73, at Birmingham, Alabama. Center Mario Bennett led the Sun Devils in scoring with an 18.7-point average. Bennett became the sixth first-round NBA draft pick in school history when the Phoenix Suns selected him as the 27th overall pick in the first round.

Mario Bennett helped lead the Sun Devil basketball team to its best record in 14 years, 24-9. (ASU Media Relations)

The women's golf team won a record third consecutive national title after dominating the sport from start to finish during the collegiate season. The Sun Devils grabbed the first-day lead in the NCAA Championships at the Landfall Club in Wilmington, North Carolina, and rolled to a 26-stroke victory over runner-up San Jose State. Kristel Mourgue d'Algue, a Sun Devil senior from France, captured medalist honors. It was the seventh individual national championship in school history and the second in as many years. Emilee Klein was the 1994 winner. ASU's Wendy Ward tied with San Jose State's Vibeke Stensrud for runner-up honors. Mourgue d'Algue, Ward, Kellee Booth and Heather Bowie earned first-team All-America honors. The Sun Devils won all seven regular-season tournaments they entered plus the Pac-10 championships. The only hint of a blemish on their record was a tie with San Jose State for first at the NCAA West Regional in Tucson.

LEGEND

Christine Garner

One of the most versatile female athletes ever to compete at ASU, Christine Garner earned second-team All-Pac-10 honors in softball as a freshman. As a senior, she averaged 8.4 points per game for the women's basketball team—second-best on the club. She was the team's leading rebounder with a 6.7 average. But those two sports were only sidelights for Garner, who starred for the volleyball team for four seasons. She led the team in kills for four straight years to pass U.S. National Team captain Tammy Webb as the school's career kills leader. She was third all-time in the Pac-10 in kills with 1,871. In 1993 her kills average of 4.71 ranked sixth nationally. She led the Sun Devils to Sweet 16 appearances as a junior and senior and played for the U.S. National Team from January to May of 1995. A three-time All-Pac-10 selection, Garner was a second-team All-American in 1995. She won a silver medal at the 1994 Goodwill Games. She joined the ASU volleyball coaching staff in the summer of 2000.

Christine Garner was one of the most versatile athletes ever at ASU. (ASU Media Relations)

THE sun devil LIST

ASU volleyball career kills leaders

Kills	Player
1,871	Christine Garner (1992-1995)
1,679	Tammy Webb (1983-1986)
1,597	Amanda Burbridge (1997-2000)
1,517	Christy Nore (1985-1988)
1,392	Valentina Vega (1982-1983, 1985-1986)
1,296	Lisa Stuck (1980-1983)
1,260	Mindy Gowell (1987-1991)
1,185	Terri Cox (1994-1997)
1,077	Sue Nord (1986-1989)
1,032	Tracey Barberie (1984-1987)
1,031	Leanne Schuster (1991-1994)

SUN DEVIL STATS

- Wrestler Markus Mollica won the NCAA individual title at 167 pounds. It was his second national title.
- Coach Pat Murphy's first ASU baseball team finished 34-21 overall and fourth in the Pac-10 Southern Division at 13-17, but was not selected for postseason competition.
- The men's golf and wrestling teams both checked in with No. 4 national finishes. The women's tennis team finished ninth.

Sun Devil Lore

University House, where ASU presidents had lived since it was constructed in 1961, was converted to offices. President Lattie Coor had to receive university permission to vacate the 5,350-square-foot structure, which often was used for entertaining at university-sponsored events. Coor's contract specified that he live there. The university planned to continue using University House for entertaining as well as office space.

1995-1996

September 6, 1995: Baltimore Orioles shortstop Cal Ripken Jr. played his 2,131st consecutive game before a sold-out crowd at Oriole Park in Camden Yards, breaking the record set by baseball legend Lou Gehrig in 1939.

October 3, 1995: The "Trial of the Century" came to an end in Los Angeles when the jury, sequestered for 266 days, deliberated less than four hours and found O.J. Simpson not guilty of double murder in the death of his ex-wife and a friend.

April 3, 1996: Federal agents seized the home of Theodore Kaczynski, thought to be the notorious Unabomber, who had been sought for more than 17 years in connection with a series of mail bombs that killed three and injured more than 20.

July 17, 1996: TWA Flight 800, traveling from New York City to Paris, exploded and crashed into the Atlantic Ocean off the coast of Long Island, killing all 230 people aboard.

arizona state university
| m o m e n t

Sun Devil golf coach Randy Lein didn't have a Tiger in his tank, but his team had enough gas to outlast fast-closing Nevada-Las Vegas and capture the NCAA men's championship at the Honors Course in Ooltewah, Tennessee, near Chattanooga. It was the second men's title for ASU, which won its first crown in 1990. The Sun Devils took a five-stroke lead over UNLV into the final day. The Rebels shot the best round on the last day, but the Devils held on for a three-stroke victory. Much of the attention was focused on Stanford star Tiger Woods, who managed to capture the individual title by four shots over Arizona's Rory Sabbatini despite a final-round 80. ASU's Darren Angel was tied for third, six strokes behind Woods, after a 76 on the last day left him at 291. Other ASU scores included Pat Perez at 298, Scott Johnson at 300, Joey Snyder at 301 and Chris Hanell at 305. Angel and Snyder earned honorable-mention All-America honors. Hanell was an academic All-American.

Darren Angel played a major role as the men's golf team won its second NCAA championship. (Scott Troyanos/ASU Media Relations)

Sun Devil Stadium was the focus of the football world and Tempe merchants were beside themselves with glee as fans streamed into the area for an unprecedented stretch of football-related activity. First, there was the Tostitos Fiesta Bowl, matching Florida and Nebraska for college football's national championship. That was followed less than a month later by the Valley's first Super Bowl, matching the Dallas Cowboys and Pittsburgh Steelers. All the while, the university and Sun Devil Stadium basked in an overwhelming wave of publicity. For the record, top-ranked Nebraska claimed the national crown by rushing for an NCAA bowl game record 524 yards and crushing second-ranked Florida, 62-24. Dallas rewarded its legions of Valley fans with a 27-17 Super Bowl victory over Pittsburgh.

ASU LEGEND

Markus Mollica

Markus Mollica made the college wrestling world sit up and take notice in 1993 when he capped a 31-3 season by winning the national title at 158 pounds. Mollica was only a freshman—the first ASU wrestler ever to capture a national crown as a frosh. Mollica went back to the nationals as a sophomore and finished fifth at 158 pounds. In 1995, Mollica moved up to 167 pounds and won his second national championship. He joined Dan St. John (1989-90) as the only Sun Devils ever to win two NCAA individual titles. Mollica recorded his fourth consecutive top-five finish at the nationals in 1996, when he placed fourth at 167 pounds. That made him a four-time All-American—one of just three in ASU history. The others were Shawn Charles and Ray Miller, who both competed from 1990 through 1993. During Mollica's four years the Sun Devils finished fourth, eighth, fourth and 10th at the nationals.

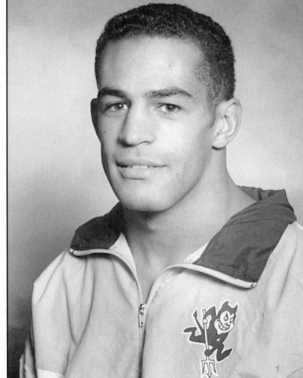

Markus Mollica won two NCAA wrestling titles while earning All-America honors four times. (ASU Media Relations)

SUN DEVIL STATS

• Former Sun Devil football coach Frank Kush was inducted into the College Football Hall of Fame in South Bend, Indiana.

• The women's golf team finished sixth at the NCAA tournament after three straight national titles.

Sun Devil Lore

Christine Wilkinson, vice president for university affairs, was named interim athletic director after the resignation of Charles Harris, who had served for 10 years. Wilkinson, daughter of ASU playing and coaching legend Bill Kajikawa, was widely hailed for unifying the athletic department during the 1995-96 school year, between the administrations of Harris and Kevin White.

1996-1997

america's time capsule

arizona state university
moment

When quarterback Jake "The Snake" Plummer slithered his way to the end zone on an 11-yard run with 1:40 left to give Arizona State a 17-14 lead over Ohio State in the Rose Bowl, thoughts of a national championship danced in the heads of Sun Devil fans. Those thoughts turned out to be premature. The Buckeyes drove 65 yards in 12 plays and scored the winning touchdown with 19 seconds remaining to dash those title aspirations and spoil ASU's hopes of an unbeaten season. Long-time Rose Bowl observers hailed it as one of the most dramatic games in the colorful history of the granddaddy of them all. It was the most-watched college bowl game of the season, earning a full television rating point more than the Sugar Bowl showdown between Florida and Florida State. Plummer, who earlier finished third in the Heisman Trophy balloting, wrapped up his college career by completing 19 of 35 passes for 201 yards and one touchdown, a 25-yarder to Ricky Boyer to tie the game at seven-all in the second quarter. Linebacker Derek Smith was the defensive star for the Sun Devils, recording 18 tackles, getting two quarterback sacks and deflecting a pass. With the loss, the Sun Devils (11-1) finished fourth in the final Associated Press and United Press International rankings.

Jake Plummer is off and running in the Rose Bowl thriller against Ohio State. (Scott Troyanos/ASU Media Relations)

SUN DEVIL *spotlight*

In a football season filled with magical moments, one stood out above the rest. On September 21, Nebraska's top-ranked Cornhuskers visited Sun Devil Stadium, where they had crushed Florida, 62-24, in the Tostitos Fiesta Bowl just 263 days earlier to win their second straight national championship. The Huskers seemingly had little reason to be concerned. They had dismantled the Sun Devils, 77-28, the previous year in Lincoln. But this night belonged to the Sun Devils. Some 200 former players turned out for ceremonies naming the playing field for former ASU coach Frank Kush, and they witnessed one of the most stunning victories in school history. The Sun Devils won, 19-0, as Jake Plummer threw a 25-yard scoring pass to Keith Poole, Robert Nycz kicked two field goals and ASU's defense recorded three safeties. The victory vaulted the Sun Devils from 17th to sixth in the Associated Press rankings.

Derrick Rodgers

He only spent a year on the ASU campus—hardly long enough to learn the names of all his football teammates. But Derrick Rodgers made an impression that will last for years. Rodgers, who played trumpet in the band, not football, in high school, arrived from Riverside, California, Community College without a lot of fanfare. Though undersized for a defensive end at 212 pounds, it didn't take him long to make his presence felt. In his first game, against Washington, he had seven tackles, three for minus yardage, three quarterback hurries and a sack. He also forced a fumble that led to an ASU touchdown. He went on to lead the Pac-10 in tackles for a loss with 23 and finish tied for second with 12 sacks. He made several All-America teams and clearly was a leader of the defensive unit that led the Pac-10 in every major defensive category.

*Derrick Rodgers
(ASU Media Relations)*

John Spini

He's still chasing that elusive national championship, but women's gymnastics coach John Spini has achieved just about every other major milestone during his 20-year ASU coaching career. Spini's teams have finished second at the national championships on four occasions and have recorded 15 Top Ten finishes. His career winning percentage of .745 (254-87-1) is tops among all ASU coaches. It didn't take Spini long to begin making his mark at ASU. His first team in 1981 finished fifth nationally and his first seven teams finished no lower than fifth at the nationals. Spini was named WCAA Coach of the Year in 1982 and 1983 and was cited from 1994 through 1996 as Pac-10 Coach of the Year. During his tenure, Spini-coach gymnasts have amassed 70 All-America awards and produced nine NCAA individual championships.

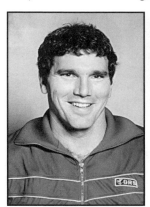

John Spini

THE sun devil LIST

Top 10 national finishes by the women's gymnastics team

Finish	Year	Coach
2nd	1997	John Spini
2nd	1986	John Spini
2nd	1985	John Spini
2nd	1983	John Spini
4th	1999	John Spini
4th	1984	John Spini
5th	1987	John Spini
5th	1982	John Spini
5th	1981	John Spini
6th	1998	John Spini
6th	1976	Monique Sublette
7th	1992	John Spini
7th (t)	1989	John Spini
7th	1978	Marie Bilski
7th	1977	Marie Bilski
8th	1988	John Spini
9th	1991	John Spini
9th	1980	Marie Bilski
10th	1994	John Spini

SUN DEVIL STATS

- The women's gymnastics team matched its best showing ever at the national championship meet with a second-place finish. It was the Sun Devils' highest finish since a second-place showing in 1986.

- Women's soccer debuted as a varsity sport at ASU with a 3-0 victory over Cal State Northridge. The Sun Devils were 4-11-1 under coach Terri Patraw as 10 freshmen played regularly and the top two goalkeepers missed most of the season.

Sun Devil Lore

Plans were announced to restore Old Main to its original appearance and make it the headquarters of the Alumni Association. The building, originally constructed in 1898, has been a campus centerpiece in various forms over the decades. It was the second building constructed on campus and at three stories was the tallest building in the Salt River Valley at the time. It also was the first to be wired for electric lighting.

The men's golf team tied for fifth nationally—its third straight top-five finish and 10th straight in the top 10.

The women's tennis team finished seventh at the nationals.

Coach Pat Murphy's baseball team reached the finals of the Atlantic Regional tournament in Miami but lost twice to host Miami on the final day. The Sun Devils finished the season with a No. 11 national ranking.

The men's swimming team placed 11th at the NCAA meet.

arizona state university ———
|m o m e n t

Can you say dynasty? That's what was brewing on the national women's collegiate golf scene after Arizona State won its fourth national title in five years and its fifth of the 1990s. The Sun Devils served notice early in the season that they would be a factor at the nationals, though defending national champion Arizona was favored to repeat. The Devils won the *Golf World*/Palmetto Dunes Collegiate and edged the Wildcats by one stroke at the NCAA West Regional. They recorded four runner-up finishes and did not finish lower than fourth in 10 tournaments. Junior Kellee Booth and sophomore Tui Selvaratnam led the Devils at the nationals. Booth tied for fifth and Selvaratnam shot a course record and career-low 67 on the third day of competition and went on to finish in a seventh-place tie. Junior Jeanne-Marie Busuttil and sophomore Keri Cornelius tied for 25th. Booth and Busuttil earned second-team All-America honors. ASU began the final day of play tied with San Jose State, but nipped the Spartans by two strokes on the final day. Sun Devil coach Linda Vollstedt was named national coach of the year for the fifth time by *GolfWeek*.

Coach Linda Vollstedt's golf team captured its fourth national title in five years and fifth of the 1990s. (Scott Photography/ASU Media Relations)

SUN DEVIL *spotlight*

Kevin White took over as athletic director in June of 1996 and began implementing an ambitious plan to eliminate a budget deficit and restore ASU to a spot among the nation's college sports powers. White praised the work done by interim athletic director Christine Wilkinson during the year between Charles Harris' resignation and the beginning of White's administration. "I don't know how anyone could have made the transition better," White said. "Christine has a keen instinct. She's somebody who obviously has a great deal of credibility on our campus as well as nationally." White, known as a master fund raiser during five years as athletic director at Tulane and five years before that at Maine, said solving the financial problems in ASU's athletic department would be a major priority.

LEGEND

Juan Roque

When quarterback Jake Plummer re-wrote ASU's record passing records, a number of factors other than Plummer's strong right arm were involved. One of the biggest—literally—was the guy who protected Plummer's backside—left tackle Juan Roque. The Sun Devils knew they were getting a good one when they beat out Southern California for the services of Roque, considered by many the top offensive line prospect in California after an outstanding career at Ontario High. But they had no idea how good. As he matured into a 6-foot-8, 313-pound giant, Roque began dominating opposing defensive ends. An outstanding student, Roque already had obtained a history degree before his senior season rolled around. He could have left school for the NFL draft after three seasons, but elected to return for a season that unfolded as one of the greatest in school history. When they began handing out post-season awards, Roque won more than his share. He was a consensus All-American—the only one on that star-studded Sun Devil Rose Bowl team. He's one of three ASU offensive linemen to win consensus All-America honors along with Danny Villa in 1986 and Randall McDaniel in 1987. The Detroit Lions picked Roque in the second round of the 1997 NFL draft.

Juan Roque was quarterback Jake Plummer's bodyguard. (ASU Media Relations)

SUN DEVIL STAT

• Former baseball coach Bobby Winkles was inducted into the American Baseball Coaches Association Hall of Fame in January. Winkles built the ASU program into a position of national prominence while compiling a record of 524-173 from 1959 through 1971. His teams captured national championships in 1965, 1967 and 1969. Winkles left for a coaching position with the California Angels prior to the 1972 season.

Sun Devil Lore

ASU scientists played major roles in designing instrument packages for a series of Mars missions. Among the campus groups involved were the geology department and the department of physics and astronomy.

• The first class to graduate from the new ASU East campus—120 students from the School of Technology and the School of Agribusiness and Resource Management—were honored at a convocation ceremony in December.

1997-1998

america's time capsule

arizona state university
m o m e n t

Timing is everything in college baseball, and the Sun Devils got hot at the right time. After a 12-game conference winning streak gave them an 18-11 record and third-place finish in the tough Pac-10 Southern Division, the Sun Devils stormed through the Midwest Regional in Wichita, Kansas, to earn their 18th appearance in the College World Series and their first under fourth-year coach Pat Murphy. The Devils were seeded sixth at the Series, but they beat third-seeded Florida State, 11-10, second-seeded Miami, 9-3, and seventh-seeded Long Beach State, 14-4, to earn a spot in the championship game against their old Six-Pac rival, Southern California. The Trojans won by the football score of 21-14, in one of the wildest title games in Series history. The score of that game in front of a national television audience called attention to what many perceived to be a problem in college baseball—souped-up aluminum bats. By the start of the 1999 season the NCAA had legislation in place requiring a less-lively bat. The Sun Devils finished with a No. 2 national ranking by *Baseball America*. ASU left fielder Willie Bloomquist won the Six-Pac batting title at .414 and earned second-team All-America honors from *USA Today/Baseball Weekly*.

Willie Bloomquist won the Pac-10 Southern Division batting title as the Sun Devils reached the national championship game. (ASU Media Relations)

spotlight

It was supposed to be a rebuilding year for the ASU football team, but that didn't keep the Sun Devils from rolling up a 9-3 record, including a 17-7 Sun Bowl victory over Iowa. It was the Sun Devils' 17th bowl appearance and their second straight, following a Rose Bowl loss to Ohio State. The Sun Devils went into the Sun Bowl game without starting quarterback Ryan Kealy, who suffered a knee injury in the regular-season finale against Arizona. But backup quarterback Steve Campbell played an error-free game and tailback Michael Martin won Most Valuable Player honors and took the heat off Campbell with 169 yards on 27 carries. It was a particularly satisfying finish for Martin, a senior, who missed the Rose Bowl game because of a neck injury. During the season sixth-year coach Bruce Snyder became the second-winningest coach in ASU history behind the legendary Frank Kush.

LEGEND

Jeremy Veal

ASU's basketball team seemed to generate more news off the court than it did between the lines during much of Jeremy Veal's time in Tempe, but that didn't keep the sweet-shooting guard from San Dimas, California, from etching his name in the record books while steering clear of all the extracurricular activity. Veal finished his ASU career as the school's all-time scoring leader with 1,984 points, breaking the mark of 1,834 set by Ron Riley from 1992 through 1996. Veal averaged 23.5 minutes as a freshman and became a starter for good the final four games of his freshman season. He averaged 7.4 points per game that season, and followed that with averages of 18.9 as a sophomore, 18.7 as a junior and 20.8 as a senior. His senior scoring average was tops in the Pac-10, making him just the second Sun Devil in history to accomplish that feat. Byron Scott led the league in 1982-83 at 21.6. Veal earned honorable mention All-America honors from the Associated Press as a senior and was a two-time All-Pac-10 selection. He's one of just four Sun Devils to win all-conference honors on two occasions.

Jeremy Veal finished his ASU basketball career as the school's all-time scoring leader. (ASU Media Relations)

Sun Devil Lore

The State Historic Preservation Office awarded the largest grant in its history, $233,000, to the renovation of the university's oldest remaining building, Old Main. Constructed in 1898, the structure was the second building on campus.

SUN DEVIL STAT

• It was a tumultuous year for the Sun Devil basketball team, which was picked to finish last in the Pac-10 in a preseason media poll. Coach Bill Frieder resigned under fire prior to the start of the season after allegations that former ASU players Stevin "Hedake" Smith and Isaac Burton were involved in a 1994 point-shaving scheme. The pair later pleaded guilty. Assistant coach Don Newman was given the title of interim coach for one season. Under Newman, the Sun Devils finished 18-14 overall and tied for fifth in the Pac-10 at 8-10. They earned a spot in the National Invitational Tournament, where they lost at Hawaii, 90-73, in the first round. Guard Ahlon Lewis led the nation in assists (9.19 per game) and broke the Pac-10 record with 294. On April 7, Rob Evans, head coach at Mississippi the past six years, was named head coach.

1997-1998 H I G H L I G H T S

ASU recorded its second-best finish in the Sears Cup competition for all-around athletic excellence. The Sun Devils ranked 12th nationally.

The men's golf team placed fifth at the NCAA championships, its fourth straight top-5 finish.

Women's tennis had another big year, tying for second in the Pac-10 and finishing in a ninth-place tie at the NCAAs. It was the ninth time in the last 10 years that ASU had advanced to the round of 16.

The women's gymnastics team placed third in the Pac-10 and sixth at the NCAA championships.

Men's swimming placed 10th nationally, one spot higher than the previous season.

arizona state university
moment

The beat—and the beatings—went on for the women's golf team. The Sun Devils claimed their second straight national championship and fifth in the last six years. This time it wasn't close. The Sun Devils crushed second-place Florida by 18 strokes in the NCAA tournament at the University Ridge Golf Course in Madison, Wisconsin. It was the Sun Devils' sixth NCAA title—twice as many as any other school. All occurred in the 1990s. Freshman Grace Park and senior Kellee Booth led the Devils at the nationals. Park finished third and Booth fourth. Park and Booth earned first-team All-America honors. Park ranked first and Booth third in the MasterCard Collegiate Rankings. Junior Tui Selvaratnam ranked 29th, senior Jeanne-Marie Busuttil 34th and junior Keri Cornelius 47th. Park won the 1998 Rolex/Eleanor Dudley Collegiate Player of the Year Award. Booth won the Marilyn Smith Award and the Honda Award. Along the road to the nationals Park captured the Fall Preview tournament and the West Regional title. Booth won the PING/ASU Invitational.

The women's golf team captured its sixth national title by a comfortable margin of 18 strokes. (ASU Media Relations)

SUN DEVIL *spotlight*

At 202 pounds, Pat Tillman was supposed to be too small to play linebacker in a big-time program like ASU's. But when you add in all the hardware he collected his senior season, his weight probably doubled. Tillman was named Pac-10 Defensive Player of the Year and won first-team All-America honors from *The Sporting News* and was a second-team selection by the Associated Press. An outstanding student, Tillman also scored big with corporate America. He was a GTE first-team Academic All-American and Honda Scholar Athlete of the Year. Tillman led the Sun Devils with 93 tackles, including 15 for a total of 60 yards in losses. He intercepted three passes, recovered a fumble and blocked a kick.

ASU LEGEND

Kellee Booth

She won only one tournament during her four years at Arizona State—the PING/ASU Invitational as a senior—yet there is no question that Kellee Booth ranks among the best players ever in the nation's premier women's golf program. Booth was a picture of consistency in her ASU career. She had eight top-10 finishes in 11 events as a freshman in 1994-95 and capped off the season by finishing 14th at the NCAA championships. That would be the only time she failed to crack the top 10 at the nationals. She finished second as a sophomore, fifth as a junior and fourth as a senior. She was a first-team All-American as a freshman, sophomore and senior and a second-team selection as a junior. She was a major contributor to three national championship teams. A three-time academic All-American, Booth had a 3.55 GPA in business management. She was a finalist for NCAA Woman of the Year in 1998. Her mother, Jane Bastanchury-Booth, was the third ASU player to win a national title (AIAW) in 1969. They are the only mother/daughter combination to have earned spots on the Curtis Cup team. Jane made the team in 1970, 1972 and 1974 and Kellee was selected in 1996.

Kellee Booth was a perennial Top-10 finisher at the NCAA women's golf tournament. (ASU Media Relations)

THE sun devil LIST

Top National Finishes by the Women's Golf Team

Finish	Year	Coach
1st	1998	Linda Vollstedt
1st	1997	Linda Vollstedt
1st	1995	Linda Vollstedt
1st	1994	Linda Vollstedt
1st	1993	Linda Vollsted
1st	1990	Linda Vollstedt
1st	1975 (AIAW)	Judy Whitehouse
2nd	1999	Linda Vollstedt
2nd (t)	1988	Linda Vollstedt
2nd	1984	Linda Vollstedt
3rd	1985	Linda Vollstedt
3rd	1980 (AIAW)	Linda Vollstedt
3rd	1976 (AIAW)	Judy Whitehouse
4th	1986	Linda Vollstedt
4th	1977 (AIAW)	Judy Whitehouse

SUN DEVIL LORE

ASU lost two prominent members of its rich history. Kathryn Gammage, second wife of former university president Grady Gammage, died December 25, 1997, at the age of 82. She retired in 1992 after 31 years in the development office. Alfred Thomas died November 20, 1997. He spent 19 years as faculty athletic representative (1953-72) and also served as registrar, director of admissions and archivist.

SUN DEVIL STAT

• In only its second year of competition, the women's soccer team made great strides. After a 4-11-1 record in their inaugural season, the Sun Devils finished 11-7-1 overall and fifth in the Pac-10 with a 5-3-1 conference mark. The Devils won seven of their first nine matches, including a 2-1 victory over rival Arizona in Tucson. The Devils also beat 19th-ranked Southern California, 3-2, handing the Trojans their first loss ever in the Los Angeles Coliseum. ASU outscored its opponents 24-9 in the first half. Freshmen Antoinette Marjanovic (nine goals, seven assists) and Jaclyn Clark (10 goals, five assists) tied for fifth in the Pac-10 in scoring with 25 points each.

1998-1999

america's time capsule

arizona state university
m o m e n t

It was a day of mixed emotions as sophomore Grace Park captured the NCAA women's golf championship, but Mother Nature and a controversial rule combined to keep the Sun Devils from winning their third straight national title and seventh in the 1990s. Park, who announced a few days after the tournament that she was leaving school to turn professional, was awarded the individual crown after high winds, hail and lightning halted the national tournament with six holes to play at the Tulsa Country Club in Oklahoma. Park's 1-under-par total of 212 was one stroke better than Candy Hammerman of Duke. Because of the weather, the tournament was called by the NCAA Women's Golf Committee and third-round leader Duke declared the winner. Fast-closing ASU, which had started the day eight strokes behind Duke, had closed to within two shots of the Blue Devils when play was halted. The aborted final round was played on a Saturday. The teams were unable to finish play on Sunday because of the "Brigham Young Rule," which prohibits play on Sunday. However, BYU was not in the tournament. In women's NCAA golf, all 19 teams play 72 holes. Had the field been cut to the top 12 teams as in men's play, the tournament would have been over when the storm struck.

Grace Park won the NCAA women's golf individual title, but the Sun Devils came up two strokes short in team play. (Scott Troyanos/ASU Media Relations)

SUN DEVIL *spotlight*

Freshman Kirsten Voak stamped her name in the record books when she threw consecutive no-hitters in the National Invitational Softball Tournament at Sunnyvale, California. Voak came within one walk of a perfect game as the Sun Devils beat Loyola Marymount, 17-0, in five innings. She followed that performance with another no-hit, one-walk game as the Devils beat Arkansas, 5-0, in seven innings. Voak's pitching played a major role as the Sun Devils earned a spot in the College World Series for the first time since 1987. Voak compiled a 24-14 record and was named Most Outstanding Player of the Region 6 Tournament after going 4-0 with an 0.69 ERA and 45 strikeouts in 30 innings. The Sun Devils were ousted in two games at the College World Series in Oklahoma City, losing 4-1 to Washington and 2-0 to California, a pair of rivals from the nation's toughest conference, the Pac-10.

LEGEND

Andrew Beinbrink

A 14th-round pick of the Boston Red Sox out of high school in San Diego, Andrew Beinbrink came to Arizona State with a reasonable amount of fanfare. But few would have imagined at the time that he would leave school four years later as the most prolific run producer in ASU and Pac-10 history. Beinbrink, who played third base most of his ASU career, drove in 283 runs to obliterate the school career RBI record of 250 set by Clay Westlake from 1973 through 1976, before the Sun Devils joined the Pac-10. He also shattered the Pac-10 record of 220 RBIs set by Stanford's Paul Carey from 1987 through 1990. Beinbrink also scored 245 runs in his ASU career, breaking the school record of 236 set just one year earlier by Mikel Moreno. It was an upset of sorts that Beinbrink was even around ASU for his senior season. He was drafted in the 10th round by the Colorado Rockies following his junior year and it was widely assumed he would sign a professional contract. In fact, his scholarship money was allocated to incoming recruits. But teammate Willie Bloomquist relinquished his scholarship, enabling Beinbrink to return and continue his assault on the record books. Beinbrink had a monster senior season, batting .402 with a team-leading 14 home runs and a conference-leading 85 RBIs. He earned All-Conference honors for the third straight year.

Andrew Beinbrink was an RBI machine for the Sun Devil baseball team. (ASU Media Relations)

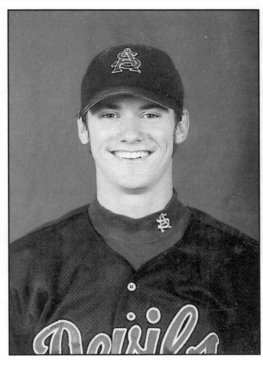

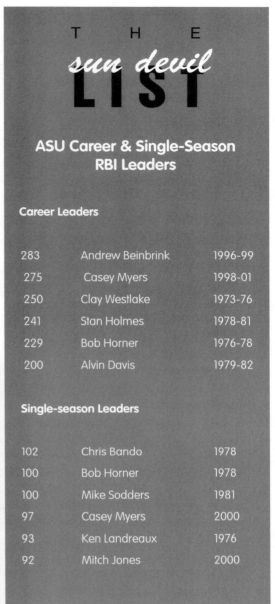
SUN DEVIL STATS

• Sophomore Marcus Brunson, in his first race for ASU after transferring from Wyoming, broke the NCAA 60-meter indoor record with a time of 6.46 seconds at the Flagstaff Invitational. Brunson, son of former ASU football player Mike Brunson, broke the mark of 6.50 set by Lee McRae of Pittsburgh in 1987.

• Paul Casey, a sophomore from Surrey, England, shot the first score of 60 in NCAA history to lead the Sun Devils to their fifth consecutive Pac-10 men's golf title at the Broadmoor Golf Club in Seattle. The previous NCAA record low round was a 61 by Stanford's Tiger Woods in the final round of the 1996 Pac-10 championships.

• Dwight Phillips, a junior transfer from Kentucky, set a school and Pac-10 record of 26-10 in the long jump at the Pac-10 championships in Tempe. The old school mark of 26-8 was set by Kenny Frazier in 1984.

SUN DEVIL LORE

Spring enrollment was down by 433 students from the previous spring's record 46,069. Officials said the drop was in the senior and freshman classes. Seniors were graduating sooner because of a reduction of required credit hours from 126 to 120. Freshman numbers dropped because of tougher admission requirements. Spring enrollment typically is lower than fall because of December graduations. ASU's main-campus enrollment ranked third nationally behind University of Texas and Ohio State.

1999-2000

August 17, 1999: A strong earthquake struck Turkey, killing more than 14,000 people and injuring at least 35,000 more.

September 18, 1999: Hurricane Floyd, reduced to a tropical storm as it moved up the eastern United States, left 34 dead and thousands homeless.

November 18, 1999: Eleven Texas A&M students and one recent graduate were killed and 27 injured in the collapse of a 40-foot tower of logs being assembled for the traditional bonfire rally prior to the A&M-Texas football game.

December 19, 1999: More than 5,000 people were killed, 6,000 were missing and 150,000 left homeless in Venezuela's worst natural disaster of the century, massive floods and mudslides that followed torrential rains.

January 1, 2000: The much-awaited turn of the century arrived with considerable celebration around the world but with little of the violence or massive computer glitches that had been predicted.

arizona state university
m o m e n t

On his final collegiate visit to his hometown San Francisco Bay area, Sun Devil guard Eddie House put on a show that will be talked about for decades. House, who had set a school single-game record of 46 points December 16 against San Diego State, obliterated that mark with 61 points in a 111-108 double-overtime victory over California January 8 in Berkeley. It tied the Pac-10 record set in 1967 by UCLA's Lew Alcindor, who later became Kareem Abdul-Jabbar. It was sweet revenge for House, who grew up as a Golden Bear fan but never got a recruiting call from Cal's coaches. "I took that personally," House said. House had the Midas touch against the Bears, hitting 18 of 30 shots, including 7 of 10 from three-point range. He made 18 of his 19 free throw attempts. House personally outscored 55 Division I teams on January 8. His performance marked only the fifth time since 1978 that a player scored more than 60 points in a game involving two Division I teams. The NCAA record for a game involving two Division I teams was 72 points, set by Kevin Bradshaw of U.S. International against Loyola Marymount in 1991. Bradshaw took 59 shots in that game, compared to House's 30.

Eddie House set a school scoring record and tied the Pac-10 mark with 61 points against California. (ASU Media Relations)

The law of supply and demand has not been good to the Sun Devils in their football series against rival Arizona during the past two decades. The demand for victories has far exceeded the supply. Entering their November 27 meeting at Sun Devil Stadium, the Sun Devils had lost two straight in the series and had won just three times in the past 17 meetings. This time, however, the Sun Devils took care of business. The Devils outscored the Wildcats 28-13 after intermission and walked away with a 42-27 victory and an Aloha Bowl invitation. It was a costly victory for A-State, which lost quarterback Ryan Kealy to a torn ACL in his right knee during the fourth quarter. Before going down, Kealy completed 14 of 22 passes for 287 yards and two touchdowns, including a 28-yarder to tight end Todd Heap midway through the third quarter to give the Devils a 28-14 lead.

LEGENDS

J. R. Redmond

Entering his senior season, J.R. Redmond needed a banner year to leap from out of a pack of quality running backs to spot among Arizona State's all-time rushing leaders. Redmond literally took the ball and ran with it. The speedy senior from Carson, California, rushed for 1,174 yards and 12 touchdowns and caught 15 passes for 100 yards and another score to take his place among the Sun Devils greats. Redmond, who blended speed, elusiveness and power, finished his ASU career with 3,223 rushing yards, placing him third on the school's all-time list behind Woody Green (4,188) and Freddie Williams (3,424). Redmond also was an accomplished punt and kickoff return man throughout his ASU career, and even played a few downs in the secondary as a senior. His versatility earned him first-team All-Pac-10 honors as an all-purpose performer his senior season. He was second-team pick as a running back.

J.R. Redmond
(Scott Troyanos/ASU Media Relations)

Eddie House

First and foremost, Eddie House considers himself a point guard—a guy whose primary objective is to distribute the basketball to the scorers. Well, you could have fooled the players who tried to guard him during the 1999-2000 season. House went on a season-long scoring spree that still had Pac-10 hoops followers shaking their heads long after the campaign was over. House became the first player in Pac-10 history with four 40-point games in one season. He scored 61 against California, 46 against San Diego State, 42 against Penn State and 40 against UCLA. He had eight games of 30 points or more as he set school records for points (736) and points per game (23.0). But he also posted numbers that back up his claim that he ultimately will find his niche at the point as he moves on to the professional ranks. He led the Sun Devils in assists (111) and steals (74).

Eddie House
(ASU Media Relations)

SUN DEVIL STAT

• ASU wrapped up the best cross country season in school history with two top 15 finishes at the NCAA championships at Bloomington, Indiana. The women finished 11th in their second NCAA appearance, improving 11 positions from the previous year. The men placed 14th in their first NCAA championship appearance.

Sun Devil Lore

ASU lost one of the most influential and popular figures in its long and colorful history when James Creasman died on August 25 at the age of 85. Creasman, often referred to as "Mr. ASU," served as executive secretary of the Alumni Association from 1947 through 1967 and held the position of director of university relations from 1967 through 1984. He spearheaded the school's successful name-change campaign in 1958. He was perhaps most visible as the voice of ASU's marching band at halftime of football games.

The Sun Devil women's tennis team finished its season with a 15-8 record and a No. 9 national ranking. The Sun Devils advanced to the quarterfinals of the NCAA championships for the first time snce 1997.

Sun Devil freshman Miriam Nagl earned first-team All-America honors and was named National Freshman of the Year by the National Golf Coaches Association. The Sun Devils finished 11th at the NCAA championships in Sunriver, Oregon.

The wrestling team finished in a tie for 16th place at the NCAA championships, as juniors Quinn Foster (149 pounds) and Steve Blackford (165) earned All-America honors.

The men's track and field team finished in a tie for 17th place at the NCAA outdoor championships in Durham, North Carolina, its highest finish in 17 years. The women placed 38th.

arizona state university
moment

Despite supercharged aluminum bats, diluted pitching talent and bigger, stronger athletes honed by improved training methods, one ASU baseball record had stood untouched since 1978. Barry Bonds had tried. Oddibe McDowell and Mike Kelly had tried, but nobody could dislodge the 25 home runs slugged by Bob Horner. Then along came Jones. Mitch Jones, a senior outfielder/first baseman from Orem, Utah, pulled into a tie with Horner in the 46th game of the season with a monster shot against Oklahoma at Bricktown Ballpark in Oklahoma City April 25. Nine games later, Jones broke the record with a three-run shot in the seventh inning of a 24-10 victory over rival Arizona in Tucson. The Sun Devils led that game just 10-9 at the time, but Jones' blast propelled them into a three-way tie with Stanford and UCLA for the Pac-10 championship. Jones hit for the cycle in that game with two singles, a double and a triple in addition to his home

Mitch Jones set a school single-season record with 27 home runs. (ASU Media Relations)

run. He got the tough part—the triple—in his last at bat. He drove in six runs in that game and stole a base for good measure. Jones added to his record with his 27th four-bagger in the first inning of a first-round NCAA playoff victory over Miami of Ohio in Packard Stadium.

A preseason poll of Pac-10 baseball coaches predicted a sixth place finish for the Sun Devils, but they put together a season to remember, forging a tie with Stanford and UCLA for the Pac-10 championship. The Sun Devils earned the automatic NCAA qualifying spot by virtue of wining two of three games over both the Cardinal and Bruins. The NCAA rewarded the Sun Devils with a host berth for an NCAA regional tournament and the Devils took a No. 4 national ranking *(Baseball America)* into the regional. They appeared to be sitting pretty after beating Miami of Ohio and Texas in their first two games, but they lost twice to the Longhorns on the final day of the tournament. That earned Texas a Super Regional host berth against Penn State and ended ASU's season at 44-15. The Sun Devils were 17-7 in Pac-10 play. Left fielder Mitch Jones and catcher Casey Myers were finalists for National Player of the Year.

LEGENDS

Casey Myers

His numbers were impressive, but Casey Myers' contribution to Arizona State's baseball team went far beyond statistics as he earned Pac-10 Player of the Year honors. "I can't imagine another player in the country who did more for his team than Casey did for us," ASU coach Pat Murphy said. "He was like having another coach on the field." Myers, a junior catcher, batted .412—the 10th-best figure in school history—and drove in 97 runs—the fourth-best total ever at ASU and just five behind Chris Brando's school record. He slugged 18 home runs, four more than his freshman and sophomore totals combined. In an era when most pitches are called from the bench, Myers called virtually all of the Sun Devils' pitches from behind the plate. Murphy said Myers' pitch calling and handling of an unheralded pitching staff was a major reason ASU developed into a national contender.

Casey Myers
ASU Media Relations)

Paul Casey

His bid for the NCAA championship came up short when he failed to qualify for the final two rounds, but Paul Casey still managed to plaster his name all over the record books. Casey, a junior from Surrey, England, captured his third consecutive Pac-10 individual championship with a record-setting 265 at the Pac-10 Championships at ASU's Karsten Golf Course as the Sun Devils won their sixth straight conference crown. Casey's total of 23 strokes under par smashed the old conference tourney mark of 18 under par, set by Stanford's Tiger Woods in 1996. Casey's second-round 72 at the NCAA championships gave him a 69.87 stroke average for the year, breaking Phil Mickelson's school record of 69.95. Mickelson established that standard as a senior in 1991-92.

Paul Casey
ASU Media Relations)

Sun Devil Lore

Arizona State ranked 12th nationally among 381 participating schools in terms of the number of National Merit Scholars in its freshman class according to a report by the National Merit Corp. ASU had 132 Merit Scholars among its first-year class, just one less than the prestigious Massachusetts Institute of Technology. Harvard was the leader with 394.

• Gene Smith, athletic director at Iowa State since 1993, was named AD at Arizona State on July 27, 2000. Smith was chosen after a lengthy search to replace Kevin White, who resigned in March to become AD at Notre Dame.

THE sun devil LIST

Most home runs in a season by a Sun Devil baseball player

Home Runs

No.	Player	Season
27	Mitch Jones	2000
25	Bob Horner	1978
23	Barry Bonds	1985
23	Oddibe McDowell	1984
22	Bob Horner	1977
22	Mike Sodders	1981
21	Scott Shores	1994
21	Mike Kelly	1990
21	Tony Mattia	1987

SUN DEVIL STAT

• Kirsten Voak (30-11) broke her own school records for pitching victories and strikeouts (316) as the Sun Devil softball team earned a host role in the NCAA tournament. The Sun Devils (43-19) were eliminated in the Region 5 tournament by Alabama, spoiling their bid for back-to-back College World Series appearances for the first time since the NCAA began administering the championships in 1982. The Sun Devils' 43 victories tied for the most in school history. ASU was ranked fifth nationally entering the Regional.

2000-2001

america's time capsule

arizona state university
m o m e n t

It wasn't the most successful football season in Arizona State history, but it certainly was one of the most bizarre. Just nine days before the regular-season finale against rival Arizona in Tucson, Athletic Director Gene Smith announced that head coach Bruce Snyder was being terminated. Smith said Snyder would be allowed to coach the team against the Wildcats and in a bowl game, if the Sun Devils should receive an invitation. Snyder's troops responded by whipping the Wildcats, 30-17, in front of 54,297 fans at Arizona Stadium to earn a spot in the Aloha Bowl. The Sun Devils dug into their bag of tricks, including a 13-yard scoring run by kicker Mike Barth on a fake field goal. Just one week later Smith announced the hiring of Boise State coach Dirk Koetter as ASU's new head coach. Koetter was 25-10 in three seasons at Boise State. In his final game, Snyder's Sun Devils suffered a 31-17 loss to Boston College in the Aloha Bowl as starting quarterback Jeff Krohn suffered a shoulder injury late in the first half. Snyder, who was named National Coach of the Year by 15 agencies following an 11-1 1996 season, finished his ASU career with a 58-45 record in nine seasons.

Dirk Koetter replaced Bruce Snyder as head football coach. (ASU Media Relations).

SUN DEVIL *spotlight*

Sunday, March 11, 2001, is a day Arizona State women's basketball Coach Charli Turner Thorne will not soon forget. She learned that her team had earned a spot in the NCAA Tournament – ASU's first since 1992. Hours later she gave birth to her second son, Liam, whose pending arrival resulted in a physician accompanying Turner Thorne on one late-season road trip. The Sun Devils, picked well down in the conference standings in most preseason projections, surprised the experts by tying Washington and Stanford for the title. The Sun Devils lost to Louisiana State, 83-66, in their first-round NCAA game in West Lafayette, Ind. Junior center Melody Johnson scored a career-high 25 points for the Sun Devils, who finished with a 20-11 record.

ASU LEGENDS

Adam Archuleta

If ever there was a rags-to-riches story in ASU athletics history, it is the tale of linebacker Adam Archuleta. Archuleta walked on as an undersized linebacker in the fall of 1996 from Chandler High School, where he had won honorable-mention All-State honors, but failed to attract the attention of major-college recruiters. By the time he left, Archuleta was the most-decorated member of the team. He played in every game as a redshirt freshman in 1997, but only in a backup role. He won a starting job in 1998, ranking third in the Pac-10 with 18 tackles for loss. He led the conference in that category with 21 as a junior, when he recorded 111 total tackles. He was named Pac-10 Defensive Player of the Year as a senior in 2000 after recording 127 tackles. He had 15 tackles for loss, four sacks, five pass deflections, four fumble recoveries, three forced fumbles and one interception.

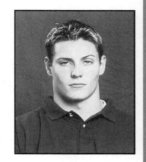

Adam Archuleta went from walk-on to stardom. (ASU Media Relations)

Amanda Burbridge

She entered Arizona State as "one of the 15 most favored volleyball recruits in the nation" in the estimation of *Student Sports* magazine, and Amanda Burbridge certainly didn't disappoint. A product of Scottsdale Chaparral High, Burbridge achieved a ranking among the school's all-time greats by the time she wrapped up her Sun Devil career in the fall of 2000. *VolleyCentral.com* named her National co-Player of the Year at the conclusion of her senior season. In her final campaign she set an ASU single-season record with 599 kills. She finished with 1,597 career kills – the third-best total in school history. In October, she broke the school match kills record on consecutive nights with 39 and 38 respectively against Washington and Washington State. She also earned Academic All-America third-team honors with a 3.43 GPA in Sociology while leading the Sun Devils to an 18-12 record and their 13th appearance in the NCAA Tournament.

Volleyball star Amanda Burbridge was co-National Player of the Year. (ASU Media Relations)

Sun Devil Lore

Intel's chief executive officer, Craig Barrett, and his wife, Barbara, gave a $10 million endowment to ASU's Honors College. It was the largest contribution ever made to ASU and the largest personal bequest to an honors program in the nation.

Ground was broken early in the spring of 2001 for a major addition to the intercollegiate athletics building—a project that promised to return ASU's athletics support facilities to the forefront nationally. A highlight of the project was a new ASU Sports Hall of Fame, tentatively scheduled to open in the early fall of 2002.

THE sun devil LIST

Results of a 2001 internet poll which asked the question: Which male/female athlete had the biggest impact on ASU's sports history? Voters were asked to consider the athletes' ASU career only.

Male Athlete	Sport	Pct. of Vote
Jake Plummer	Football	38.2
Danny White	Football/Baseball	26.6
Phil Mickelson	Golf	11.8
Whizzer White	Football/Track	7.1
Mike Haynes	Football/Track	4.8
Bob Horner	Football	3.8
Curley Culp	Football/Wrestling	3.7
Joe Caldwell	Basketball/Track	1.6
Dave Graybill	Football/Basketball/Baseball	1.4
Henry Carr	Track/Football	1.0

Female Athlete	Sport	Pct of Vote
Heather Farr	Golf	42.6
Christine Garner	Volleyball/Softball/Basketball	21.4
Joanne Gunderson	Golf	7.7
Kym Hampton	Basketball	7.4
Maicel Malone	Track	7.4
Lynda Tolbert	Track	4.6
Tammy Webb	Volleyball	3.6
Paula Miller Noel	Softball	2.6
Kendis Moore	Swimming	1.8
Patsy Willard	Diving	0.9

SUN DEVIL STAT

• Golfer Jeff Quinney captured the U.S. Amateur title prior to heading into his senior season.

• Lisa Aguilera finished fifth at the NCAA Women's Cross Country Championships, leading the Sun Devils to a best-ever sixth-place team finish.

• The late Jim Brock, a four-time national college baseball coach of the year, was inducted posthumously into the Arizona Sports Hall of Fame.

• Suzie Gaw, Arizona State's career home run leader with 16 from 1979 through 1982, was elected to the Amateur Softball Association National Softball Hall of Fame.

These four coaches are knocking at the door of legend status. Each has had a significant impact on his/her program—achieving positions of national prominence with prospects for an even brighter future.

Women's tennis coach Sheila McInerney led her team to 15 NCAA tournament appearances in her first 16 seasons at ASU, and her 2001 team was ranked 14th and headed toward another NCAA tourney as this book went to press in the spring of 2001. McInerney's Sun Devils reached the NCAA quarterfinals five times between 1992 and 2000. She was named Wilson/ITA National Coach of the Year in 1997.

Pat Murphy, a highly-successful coach at Notre Dame, was named to replace the late Jim Brock prior to the 1995 season, and has kept alive ASU's rich baseball tradition. His first six ASU teams averaged 39 victories and his 1998 club reached the championship game of the College World Series. That performance earned Murphy National Coach of the Year recognition from *Baseball America*. He was named Pac-10 Coach of the Year in 2000 when his club, picked to finish sixth, ended up with a share of the conference title.

SHEILA McINERNEY
Led her team to 15 NCAA tournament appearances in her first 16 seasons at ASU.

Charli Turner Thorne took over a dismal women's basketball program prior to the 1996-97 season and has turned the Sun Devils into a national presence. Each of her five teams has improved from the previous season. Her fourth team earned a bid to the Women's National Invitational Tournament—ASU's first post-season berth since 1992. Her 2000-01 club finished 20-10 overall and captured a share of the Pac-10 title, earning Turner Thorne Pac-10 Conference Coach-of-the-Year honors.

Linda Wells, who completed her 12th year as ASU's women's softball coach in 2001, is one of the most prominent and successful coaches in NCAA history, ranking eighth in career victories with 767 late in the 2001 season. Prior to the 2001 campaign, Wells had coached 52 all-conference players during her tenure at ASU – an average of nearly five per season. Her 2001 club, ranked eighth nationally at midseason, was headed towards its ninth NCAA Regional appearance in 12 seasons.

PAT MURPHY
His first six ASU teams averaged 39 victories and his 1998 club reached the championship game of the College World Series.

CHARLI TURNER THORNE
Finished 20-10 overall and captured a share of the Pac-10 title, earning Pac-10 Conference Coach-of-the-Year honors.

LINDA WELLS
Ranked eighth in NCAA career victories with 767 late in the 2001 season.

LEGENDS WITHIN THEIR REALM

Archery coach Margaret Klann and badminton coach Merle Packer certainly achieved legendary status among their peers during lengthy coaching careers at ASU. They were not included in the Super Legends section because the quality of competition in their sports was not as rigorous as in other sports. Many schools did not have archery and badminton teams during the period when ASU dominated those sports. Still, there is no denying that Klann and Packer produced teams that simply ran off and hid from the competition year after year.

Klann began building the ASU archery program in 1955 when the head of the women's physical education program, Nina Murphy, presented her with a $100 budget to get things underway. Klann invested some of the funds in a dual meet against San Bernardino Valley College of California and the ASU program was born. Klann coached the Sun Devils for 21 years, capturing 16 national team titles and producing seven individual champions. She coached 43 All-Americans. Klann, who retired after the 1976 season, was known as "Miss Archery, USA". She was nominated for U.S. archery coach in 1972 and 1976. Klann has been inducted into ASU's Hall of Distinction, which honors former coaches and administrators.

Packer began coaching the ASU badminton team in 1967. By the time she retired following the 1984 season, her teams had won 13 national team championships and produced 56 All-Americans. Her first All-American was Kirstie Kaiser in 1968. During one 10-year stretch between 1975 and 1984 she coached at least two All-Americans in every season. Two of her pupils, Sue Annis Kellogg (1970-72) and Carrie Morrison (1976-79), have been inducted into ASU's Sports Hall of Fame. Packer is a member of ASU's Hall of Distinction.

MARGARET KLANN
Won 16 national archery team championships in 21 years.

MERLE PACKER
Produced 13 national team titles and coached 56 All-Americans.

KEY TO VARSITY ATHLETES LIST

This list, compiled from old yearbooks, newspapers and athletic department records, is more than a compilation of letter winners. Because criteria for awarding varsity letters varied dramatically from year to year and sport to sport, the author felt a comprehensive list should include all athletes who participated at the varsity level against outside competition, regardless of whether they were awarded an official varsity letter. This is by far the most complete list ever compiled involving Arizona State's male and female athletes. It dates back to the 1890s and includes several sports in which the Sun Devils currently do not compete. Most official athletic department records go back no more than 40 or 50 years, so the compilation of this list was a lengthy and tedious undertaking. Prior to the 1940s, standout athletes in intramural competition often were given equal billing to varsity athletes in student yearbooks, and sometimes in newspaper stories. Those athletes were not included in this list unless they also competed against other schools. As with any list of this magnitude, errors and omissions may occur. If you discover an inaccuracy or omission, please contact the ASU Sports Information office so that its records can be updated. Female athletes are listed by their maiden names.

KEY TO ABBREVIATIONS

bb – baseball
box – boxing
fb – football
marc – men's archery
mbm – men's badminton
mbk – men's basketball
mcc – men's cross country
mgo – men's golf
mgy – men's gymnastics
msw – men's swimming & diving
mtn – men's tennis
mtr – men's track & field
wre – wrestling
rif – rifle (coed)
warc – women's archery
wbm – women's badminton
wbb – women's baseball
wbk – women's basketball
wcc – women's cross country
wfh – women's field hockey
wgo – women's golf
wgy – women's gymnastics
wsoc – women's soccer
wsb – women's softball
wsw – women's swimming & diving
wtn – women's tennis
wtf – women's touch football
wtr – women's track & field
wvb – women's volleyball

* All of the photos in this section are courtesy of the Media Relations Office, Department of Intercollegiate Athletics, Arizona State University.

VARSITY ATHLETES LIST

A

Aaron, Curtis	ftb	1979
Abado, Reema	wsw	1985
Abal, Pablo	msw	1997, 98, 99, 2000
Abbey, Jennifer	wsw	1998
Abbott, Brian	mgo	1986
Abelardo, Arebalo	mcc	1973
Abele, Peter	msw	1981, 82, 83, 84
Abolos, Sandra	warc	1977
Abono, Cecil	ftb	1965, 66, 67
Abounader, Slibe	mtn	1947
Abraham, Cheryl	wsb	1982
Abrahams, Mary	wsb	1947
Frances	wfh	1947
Abramsen, Susan	wtr	1991
Abranovic, Alan	wre	1963
Acker, Becky	wgy	1998, 99, 2000, 01
Acker, Sharon	wtr	1979, 81
Ackerley, Chad	ftb	1991, 92, 93
Acosta, Ruben	mtn	1956
Acuff, Dan	bb	1962
Acuff, Guy	ftb	1936, 37
Acuff, Lillian	wbk	1939, 40
	wbm	1940
	wsb	1940
Acuff, Norma	wbk	1934
	wfh	1933
Adams, Bob	ftb	1931
Adams, Craig	mtr	1999
Adams, Derrick	mbm	1979, 80, 81, 82
Adams, Ellis	bb	1915
	ftb	1915
	mtr	1914
Adams, Grant	mtn	1986, 87
Adams, Harlan	mtr	1952, 54
Adams, John	bb	1970, 71
Adams, John	mgo	1975, 76
Adams, Judi	warc	1981, 82
Adams, Leland	ftb	1988, 89
	mtr	1988, 89, 90
Adams, Lorieann	wcc	1994, 95
	wtr	1994, 95
Adams, Melba Jo	wsb	1950
	wtn	1949
	wvb	1950
Adams, Sarah	wsw	1997, 98, 99, 2000
Adams, Skip	msw	1964
Adams, Steve	ftb	1942
Adams, Tommy	bb	1989, 90, 91
Adams, Vince	ftb	1985
Addidale, Kenneth	mtr	1948
Addington, Jim	mcc	1957, 59
	mtr	1958
Adel, Carolyn	wsw	1997, 98, 99, 2000
Adler, Bob	mtr	1975, 76, 77
Adleta, Ashley	wgo	1993, 94
Adolph, Julie	wsb	1999
Adrian, Donella	wsw	1998
Aepli, Betty	wfh	1938
	wgo	1938, 39
Aepli, Mary	wbb	1943
	wbk	1943, 44, 45

	wbm	1945
	wfh	1943
	wsb	1943
	wtf	1943, 45
	wtn	1942, 43
	wvv	1943, 44, 45
Agbebaku, Victor	mtr	1992, 93
Agostinelli, Joe	mcc	1998, 99
	mtr	1999, 2000
Aguayo, Roy	mtr	1974, 75
Aguilar, Louie	msw	1977, 78, 79
Aguilar, Tony	ftb	1999, 2000
Aguilera, Lisa	wcc	1998, 99, 2000
	wtr	2000, 01
Aguirre, Mike	fb	1998, 99, 2000
Ah You, Junior	ftb	1969, 70, 71
Ahern, Jeff	bb	1978, 79, 80, 81
Aho, Lorraine	wsw	1968, 69
Ahr, Leslie	wbk	1980, 81
Aiken, Cathy	wbk	1979, 80
Aiken, Nancy	wbk	1979
	wtr	1979, 80
Aiker, Wiley	ftb	1937, 38, 39
Aistin, Wayne	rif	1950
Aitken, Jim	ftb	1950, 51, 52
Aja, Manuel	ftb	1947, 48, 49, 50
Aker, Wily	mtr	1937, 38, 39
Akers, Libby	wgo	1984, 85, 86, 87
Akinremi, Christy	wtr	1993, 94
Akinremi, Omolade	wtr	1993, 94, 95
Akinremi, Omotayo	wtr	1993, 94, 95
Akpan, Ime	wtr	1992, 93
Alapa, Clifton	ftb	1973, 74, 76
Albarracin, Eric	wre	1993, 94, 95
Albers, Roberta	wgo	1969
Albert, Jen	wbk	2001
Alberts, Bill	bb	1971
Albon, Cole	mgy	1992, 93
Albrecht, Steve	msw	1985, 86
Albrick, Ed	bb	1949
	ftb	1948
Albright, Kelly	wsw	1981
Alden, Scott	ftb	1973, 74, 75
Aldridge, Jim	mcc	1955
	mtr	1957
Alego, Barbara	wgo	1948
Alejandrino, Philip	wre	1999, 2000
Alesci, Tony	bb	1963, 64, 65
Alevras, Christian	mcc	1995
	mtr	1996
Alexander, "Schoolboy"	bb	1910
Alexander, Cecil	ftb	1922
	mbk	1923
Alexander, Dave	bb	1989
Alexander, Gary	mgy	1972, 73, 74, 75
Alexander, Gary	mgy	1987
Alexander, Jamie	wbb	1921
Alexander, Jeff	wre	1999, 2000, 01
Alexander, Jerry	mcc	1974
	mtr	1975
Alexander, Kenny	bb	1990
Alexander, Kris	mcc	1998, 99, 2000
	mtr	2000, 01
Alexander, Mickey	wvb	1950
Alexander, Ray	ftb	1973, 74

Alford, B.J.	ftb	1994
Alford, Bob	ftb	1950, 51, 52
Alfred, Chasta	wtr	2001
Allan	mtr	1923
Allan, Bill	wre	1974
Allen	mtr	1934
Allen	wbb	1923
Allen, Anabelle	wbm	1941
	wsb	1940, 41
	wfh	1941, 42, 43
Allen, Barbara	wvb	1923
Allen, Becky	wcc	1982
	wtr	1982, 83
Allen, Bob	mgo	1977
Allen, Dick	ftb	1947, 48
Allen, Doug	ftb	1981, 82, 83, 84
Allen, Eric	ftb	1984, 85, 86, 87
Allen, Helen	warc	1972
Allen, Jackie	wtn	1952
Allen, Jamie	bb	1977, 78, 79
Allen, Jean	wsb	1943
	wtn	1943
	wvb	1943
Allen, John "Bat"	mbk	1925, 26
	ftb	1924, 25
Allen, John	ftb	1951, 52, 53, 56
Allen, Justin	mbk	2000
Allen, Loren	ftb	1924, 25, 27, 28
	mbk	1926
Allen, Margorie	wsb	1943
	wtf	1943
	wbk	1942, 43
	wfh	1942, 43
	wvb	1942, 43
Allen, Monique	wvb	1991, 92, 93, 94
Allen, Paul	ftb	1941
Allen, Rodney	bb	2001
Allen, Sarah	wbk	2000
Allen, Shirleen	wtn	1949, 50, 51
Allen, Tom	ftb	1978, 79

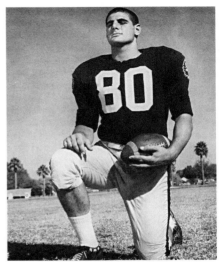

An ASU football award is named in honor of the late Cecil Abono, who played in the mid-1960s.

Golfer Danielle Ammaccapane was a three-time All-American and NCAA medalist in 1985 before launching her professional career.

Four-year basketball letterman Jay Arnote later had a successful coaching career.

248

Name	Sport	Years
Arollo, Elizabeth	wtr	2000, 01
Arons, Curt	ftb	1983, 84
Aronsohn, Liz	wbm	1987, 88, 89, 90
Arredondo, Dan	ftb	1953, 54, 55, 56
	mtr	1955
Arredondo, Joe	mgy	1961
Arrigoni, Dawn	wcc	1987, 88, 89, 90
	wtr	1988, 89, 90, 91
Arrozqui, Mike	ftb	1969, 70
Arslanian, Cliff	msw	1989, 90
Arthur-Akropfi, A.	mtr	1998
Artis, Carlos	ftb	1993
	mbk	1993, 94
Arvin, Joan	wsb	1970
Arviso, Catherine	wvb	1967
Arvizu, Al	bb	1937, 38
Ashcroft, George	bb	1907
Ashe, Bob	box	1933
	bb	1933, 34, 35
	mbk	1934, 35
Ashley, Ralph	wre	1975
Ashton, Margaret	wcc	1981
Askins, Elizabeth	wbk	1924
Asmuth, Paul	msw	1978, 79, 80
Astbury, Andy	msw	1980, 81, 82, 83
Atencio, Cynthia	wcc	1999, 2000
	wtr	2000
Atkins, Brian	msw	2000
Atkins, Lisa	wgy	1978, 79, 80, 81
Atkinson, Karl	mtr	2001
Attaway, Greg	mbk	1984
Atwell, Gary	bb	1970, 71, 72, 73
Atzet, Jon	msw	1986
Audi, Raja	mtr	2001
Aumas, Francois	mtr	1974, 75, 76, 77
Aune, Keith	wre	1966
Ausrum, Clara	wsb	1943
Austin Isaac	mbk	1990, 91
Austin, Alex	mbk	1986, 87, 89, 90
Austin, Cedric	bb	1919, 20, 21, 22, 23
	ftb	1922, 23
	mbk	1919, 20, 21, 22, 23, 24
	mtr	1923
Austin, Harold	bb	1917, 18, 19
	mbk	1919
	mtr	1919
Austin, Jim	bb	1989, 90, 91
Austin, Lawrence	ftb	1914
Austin, Wilfred	mtr	1919
	bb	1919, 20, 21, 22
	mbk	1919, 20
Avant, Greg	mgo	1987
Avery, Mary	rif	1963
Avila, Irma	wbk	1980, 81
Axelson, Vince	mgo	1985, 86, 87
Axelsson, Ann	wsw	1983, 84
Axton, Milt	msw	1967, 68, 69
Ayer, Fred	bb	1907, 08, 09, 10, 11
	ftb	1905
Ayers, Graham	msw	1983
Azevedo, Ana Catrina	wsw	1992, 93
Azevedo, Matt	wre	1997, 98
Azlan, Betsy	wtn	1949

B

Name	Sport	Years
Baca, Joanie	wtr	2001
Baccus, Bob	ftb	1940
Bachert, Jeanie	wgy	1966
Back, Thelton	mtr	1953

Name	Sport	Years
Bacon, Barry	ftb	1992, 93
Bacon, James	mbk	1993, 94, 95
Bagge, Jocelyn	wsw	1993
Baggott, Rob	mtn	1982, 83
Bagley, Brian	marc	1985, 86, 87, 88
Baham, Sarah	wsw	1999, 2000, 01
Bailey, Cope	marc	1985, 86, 87, 88
Bailey, Eileen	wtn	1969, 70, 71
Bailey, Frank	mbk	1966, 67, 68
	mtr	1965, 66
Bailey, Mason	msw	1985, 86, 87
Bailey, Renee	wvb	1975
Baily, Carol	wtn	1970, 71, 72
Bain, Greg	mgy	1973, 74
Bain, Peggy	wvb	1948
Bair, Darryl	mgy	1967, 68, 69
Baird, Jeff	msw	1978
Bairos, Gary	wre	1982, 84, 85, 86
Baiz, Victor	wre	1973
Bakalos-Gonzales, Sergio	mtr	1996
Baker, Anne	wbk	1912, 13
Baker, Anthony	ftb	1978, 80, 81
Baker, Danny	wre	1972
Baker, Darryl	msw	1991
Baker, Don	mgy	1977, 78, 80, 81
Baker, Doug	bb	1982
Baker, James	ftb	1971, 72, 73
Baker, Jennifer	wtn	2001
Baker, Joann	wsw	1980, 81
Baker, Jon	ftb	1993, 94
	mtr	1993, 94, 95
Baker, Rob	mbk	1970
Baker, Roger	rif	1959, 60, 61
Baker, Stephen	ftb	1998, 99
Baker, Ted	bb	1936
Baklarz, Johnny	ftb	1941, 42
Balbiers, Jeannine	wtn	1979, 81, 82, 83
Balcom, Bruce	mgo	1966
Baldenegro, Julie	wsb	2000
Baldock, Suzy	wgy	1987, 88, 89, 90
Bale, Doug	msw	1989
Bales, David	mgo	1985, 86
Balian, Mike	ftb	1993, 94
Ball, Barb	wgy	1979, 80
Ball, Beverly	wtn	1964
Ball, John	mcc	1998, 99
	mtr	1999, 2000
Ball, Lori	wbm	1979, 80, 81, 82
Ball, Lucy	wtn	1955
Ball, Mike	ftb	1933, 34, 35
Ball, Wayne	bb	1990, 91
Ballard, Deke	ftb	1972, 73
Ballou, Heather	warc	1992, 93
Balsamo, Tony	ftb	1947, 48, 49, 50
Balshor, John	ftb	1939, 40, 41
Balsz, Mary Louise	wbb	1943
	wgo	1942
	wsb	1943
Baltazar, Yvette	wsb	1986, 87, 88, 89
Ban, Mark	bb	1982
Bando, Chris	bb	1975, 76, 77, 78
Bando, Sal	bb	1964, 65
Bane, Eddie	bb	1971, 72, 73
Bane, Jaymie	bb	1997
Baniewicz, Don	bb	1957, 58
Bank, Ronnie	msw	1966, 69
Bankhead, Harold	mtr	1948
Banks, Andy	mtn	1985, 86
Banks, Darrell	ftb	1989, 90
Banks, Tyrone	wre	1996
Bannister, Alan	bb	1970, 71, 72
Bannister, Floyd	bb	1974, 75, 76
Bantom, Dawn	wbk	1989, 90
Baraban, Bill	mgo	1974

Name	Sport	Years
Barbara, Jennifer	wsoc	1996
Barbarick, Henry	ftb	1948, 49
Barber, Alice	wtn	1927
	wvb	1927
Barber, John	mtr	1970
Barber, Larry	mgo	1992, 93, 94, 95
Barber, Richard	mgo	1994, 95
Barberie, Tracey	wvb	1984, 85, 86, 87
Barbour, Lois	wtn	1938
Barbour, Louise	wsb	1938
Barcelo, Marc	bb	1993
Barclay, Bill	mgy	1980, 81, 82, 83
Barclay, Don	bb	1947
Barclay, Janelle	wtn	1980
Barclay, Scott	mgy	1973, 74, 75, 76
Bardis, George	mtr	1978
Barefoot	mtr	1931, 32
Barela, Ronnie	mtr	1978, 79, 80
Barge, Brian	ftb	1978
Barinaga, Tyna	wbm	1966, 67, 68
	wvb	1967
Barkas, Bob	mtr	1961
Barker, David	wre	1993, 94
Barkley, Hugh	bb	1907
Barkley, Ina	wgo	1941
	wsb	1940
Barkley, Ted	ftb	1946
Barlia, David	mtr	1984, 85, 86, 88
Barlow, Anne	wtn	1977
Barlow, Glenn	mbk	1949, 50
Barmettlor, K.	wsw	1963
Barnard, Jeff	msw	1974, 75, 76
Barnard, Matt	mcc	1982
	mtr	1981, 83
Barnes, Al	bb	1948
Barnes, Bob	wre	1983, 84, 85
Barnes, Debbie	wgy	1978, 79, 80
Barnes, Mike	ftb	1995, 96
Barnett, Chad	mcc	2000
	mtr	1999, 2000, 01
Barnett, Garner	ftb	1947, 48, 49
Barnett, John	mgy	1984
Barnett, Mike	mgo	1971, 73, 74
Barney, James	bb	1926, 27, 28
	ftb	1926, 27
Barney, Matt	mbk	1977
	mtr	1977
Barnson, Roger	bb	1958, 59, 60, 61
Barr, Bette	wsw	1962
Barr, Betty	wsb	1972
	wvb	1973
Barr, Dave	bb	1988
Barr, Hazel	wbk	1911
Barr, Lafayette	rif	1956
Barratta, M.	wsw	1963
Barrell, Shannon	mcc	1967
Barrett, Bill	mcc	1969
Barrett, Chad	mcc	2000
	mtr	1999, 2000, 01
Barrett, Kim	wcc	1994, 95, 96
	wtr	1995, 96
Barrett, Marty	bb	1979
Barrick, Mike	mtr	1960, 61, 62, 63
Barrington, Marjorie	warc	1952
Barrios, Teresa	wcc	1987, 88, 89
	wtr	1985, 86, 88, 89
Barron, Grace	wtn	1951, 52
Barron, Robert	rif	1953
Barrs, Jay	marc	1983, 84
Barry, John	ftb	1915, 16
Barry, Maryanne	wtr	1983, 84
Barry, Matt	msw	1998, 99, 2000
Barry, Pat	ftb	1973
Barryhill, Larry	mcc	1964, 65
Bartel, Leah	wsb	1995, 96, 97

After starring at ASU in 1986-87, Mike Benjamin went on to a major league baseball career with the Giants, Phillies, Red Sox and Pirates.

Name	Sport	Years
Bartelt, Page	wtn	1993, 94
Barth, Mike	ftb	1999, 2000
Barthel, Dave	ftb	1976, 78
Bartholomew, Clare	bb	1956
	mgo	1956
Bartholomew, Jacinta	wtr	1987, 88, 89
Bartholomew, Mike	bb	1959
	ftb	1958, 59, 60
Bartholomew, Scott	marc	1989, 90, 91
Bartlett, George	bb	1936, 37
	box	1936
Bartley, Jackie	wgy	1976, 77
Barton, Dayton	bb	1978
Barton, Gene	mtr	1966
Barton, Jason	mtr	2001
Barton, Rodney	mbm	1982, 83, 84
Bartunek, Nancy	warc	1977, 78, 79
Baruch, Matt	mgy	1990, 91, 92, 93
Bass, Bill	msw	1988, 89, 91, 92
Bastanchury, Jane	wgo	1969, 70
Bastien, Holly	wgy	1976
Bateman, Bud	mcc	1955
Bateman, Tim	mgo	1971
Bates, Clifton	mtn	1958
Bates, Kendrick	ftb	1997, 98, 99
Bates, Lorraine	warc	1944
Bates, Mario	ftb	1991, 93
Bates, Solomon	ftb	1999, 2000
Batiste, Joe	mtr	1947, 48
Batiste, Mike	mbk	1997, 98, 99
Baton, Bruce	msw	1968
Battle, Albrey	ftb	1995, 96, 97, 98
Battle, Greg	ftb	1982, 83, 84, 85
Battle, Terry	ftb	1994, 95, 96
Bauer, August	bb	1916
Bauer, Chris	warc	1967, 68, 69
Bauer, Duke	msw	1980, 81, 82, 83
Baughn, Brent	msw	1964
Bauman, Bill	mtn	1969
Baumann, Jim	mtn	1983, 84, 85
Baumgarner, Tim	ftb	1976
Baumgartner, Dave	ftb	1996
Baversfield, Max	box	1937
Baxter, Bill	ftb	1931, 32, 33, 34
	mbk	1934
Baxter, Jay	msw	1970
Baxter, Richard	ftb	1916
Baxter, Terri	wsw	1984, 85, 86, 87
Baybrook, Tom	msw	1975
Bayes, D.	mgo	1962
Bayless, Betty Joe	wbk	1943, 44, 45
	wtf	1943, 45
	wtn	1945
Baylis, Rob	msw	1982
Beach, Erica	wsb	1999, 2000, 01
Beach, Sandy	wcc	1980, 81, 82, 83
	wtr	1981, 82, 83, 84
Beakley, John	mbk	1944, 45
Beal, James	ftb	1999, 2000
Beall, Charles	mbk	1948, 49, 50
	ftb	1947, 48, 49
Beals, Bryan	bb	1985, 86
Beals, Colin	mtr	1949
Bear, Richard	ftb	1985, 86
Beard, Danny	ftb	1955
Beardslee, Pat	wre	1958
Bearman, Tom	mtn	1971, 72
Beasley, Chris	bb	1983, 84
	mbk	1983, 84
Beasley, Jack	mtr	1957
Beasom, Jeff	mgy	1980, 81, 82, 83
Beaty, Annette	wtr	1976, 77
Beauchamp, Ed	bb	1947
Beaudine, April	warc	1992, 93
Beaudry, Pete	wsw	1969, 70, 71, 72
Beaugureau, Betsey	wsw	1959
Beaver, Jerry	mtn	1951, 52
Becenti, Ryneldi	wbk	1992, 93
Beck, Edna	wvb	1924
Beck, Ruthie	wtn	1960
Beck, Stanley	rif	1950
Beck, Steve	mbk	1984, 85, 86, 87
Beck, Thelton	rif	1950
Becker, Art	mbk	1962, 63, 64
Becker, Mark	mbk	1987, 88, 89, 90
Becker, Tracy	wtn	1986
Beckers, Lucille	wbk	1922
Bedewi, Paul	mgy	1990, 91, 92, 93
Bednar, Joanne	warc	1979
Beechum, Gabe	mtr	1992, 93
Begay, Alvina	wcc	2000
Begg, Sidney	wtn	1972
Begley, Marie	wbm	1941
	wfh	1941
	wsb	1940
Behn, Eva	wbk	1912, 13
Behr, Pat	wvb	1967
Beinbrink, Andrew	bb	1996, 97, 98, 99
Belcher, Chuck	mcc	1989, 90, 91, 92
	mtr	1990, 91, 92, 93
Belcher, Linda	wsb	1979, 80, 81
Belet, Tina	wvb	1979
Belgum, Nancy	wtn	1976, 77, 78, 79
Belknap, Carroll	mtn	1911
Bell, Ardyce	wbk	1938
Bell, Barbara	wbm	1975
Bell, Barbara	wgo	1959, 60
Bell, Dave	mtr	1972
Bell, Eva	wtn	1969
Bell, Frank	ftb	1953, 55, 56
Bell, Jerry	ftb	1978, 79, 80, 81
Bell, Nancy	wsw	1958, 59
Bellack, John	mgo	1948
Bellamy, Worthy	ftb	1896
Belland, Joe	ftb	1955, 56, 57, 58
Bellion, Clem	mgy	1954
Bellis, Angelo	wre	1981, 83
Bellsmith, Travis	box	1935, 36
Beloat, Bob	mtn	1960
Belote, Melissa	wsw	1976, 77, 78, 79
Belotti, Christine	wgy	1991, 92
Beltran, Elena	wtr	1997, 98
Beltran, Juan	msw	1995, 96, 97, 98
Beltran, Rick	mtr	1966, 67
Belzner, Jackie	wtr	1987, 88
Bemis, Beth	wsw	1983
Bemis, Marjorie	warc	1948
Benavides, Paolo	msw	1999, 2000
Bendetti, Joe	mgo	1986, 87
Benedict, Allen	bb	1960
	ftb	1956, 57, 58, 59
Benedict, Jim	bb	1983
Benedict, Matt	msw	1999
Benedixon, Mollie	wvb	1928
Benesch, Scott	msw	1988, 89, 90, 91
Benham, Lenwood	bb	1946
Benincasa, Robyn	wsw	1985, 86, 87, 88
Benitez, Juan	msw	1981
Benjamin, Mike	bb	1986, 87
Benjamin, Naomi	wfh	1941
Benko, Lesley	wsw	1998
Bennett, Ann	warc	1950
Bennett, Don	mtn	1950, 51
Bennett, Dwight	mtr	1971, 72
Bennett, Frances	wtn	1929
	wvb	1928
Bennett, Gwen	wgo	1969
Bennett, Jennifer	wbk	1998, 99
Bennett, Keith	bb	1985
Bennett, Marilyn	wsw	1961
Bennett, Mario	mbk	1992, 94, 95
Benscoe, Judy	wtn	1955, 56, 57
Benson, Jean	wbk	1942
Benson, Tom	wre	1970, 71
Bentley, Howard	bb	1919
	mbk	1919
Bentley, Jocelyn	wtr	1981
Benton, Grady	ftb	1992, 93
Bera, Rich	msw	1994, 95
Berg, Tina	wvb	1987, 88, 89, 90
Bergan, Karen	wtn	1988, 89, 90, 91
Bergenheier, Michael	marc	1987, 88, 89
Berger, Bill	bb	1970, 71, 73
Berger, Brian	bb	2000
Berger, Carol	wgo	1986, 87, 88
Berger, Curtis	ftb	1993, 94
Berger, Mette	wtr	1984, 85, 86, 87
Berggren, Peter	msw	1983, 84
Bergold, Alan	wre	1967
Berman, Mark	mtn	1951
Bernard, Jim	mgo	1956, 57, 58
Bernard, Steve	msw	1966
Berner, Don	mgo	1949
Berney, Mike	msw	1977
Bernstein, Nate	mtn	1941
Bernstein, Paul	mtn	1980, 81
Bernstein, Sally	wsw	1973, 74
Bernudez, Reyes	wre	1986
Berrian, Tony	mtr	1998, 99, 2000, 01
Berry, Eric	ftb	1988
Berryhill, Larry	mtr	1964, 65, 66, 67
Bertelson, Edward	ftb	1916
Bertoncino, Jim	mgo	1979, 80
Bertsch, Jackie	wgo	1977, 78
Bester, Tesra	wtr	1991, 92
Bethke, Rick	bb	1974, 75
Betoney, Missy	wbk	1985
Betten, Randy	bb	1994, 95
Bettencourt, Amy	wsw	1975, 76, 77, 78
Betts, Rick	marc	1983, 84, 85
Betz, Carrie	wsb	1992, 93
Beuckman, Barbara	wgo	1961, 62
Beuermann, Gayle	wsb	1981
Bever, Mike	wre	1974, 75
Beverly, Ed	ftb	1970, 71, 72
Biang, Brian	ftb	1999, 2000
Bickel, David	mtr	1986, 87, 88

Bickers, Wayne	mtr	1951
Bickford, Kim	wsb	1983, 84
Biddulph, Kemp	mtn	1958
Biegel, Mark	msw	1985, 86, 87, 88
Biesen, Rita	wtn	1969, 70
Bietz, Rich	mgo	1984, 85, 86
Bigbee, Mike	ftb	1972
Bigbie, Ashley	wsw	1997
Bigler, Don	ftb	1959, 60, 61
Bill Stevenson	mtn	1947
Billard, Brenda	wtr	1979
Billie, Irene	wbk	1979
Billingsley, Dan	wre	1983
Billmeier, Sally	wsw	1971
Bilton, James	ftb	1951, 52, 53
Bing, Erroyl	mbk	1975
Binkley, Roger	marc	1969
Biorkman, Carey	mtn	1997
Biorkman, Chris	mtn	1997
Birch, Wendy	wtn	1982
Bird, Maureen	wsw	1998
Biron, Eve-Lyne	wgo	1986, 87, 88
Bishop, Benny	mgy	1963, 64, 65
Bishop, Carla	wbk	1984
Bishop, David	msw	1980
Bishop, Mark	mgy	1992
Bissell, Scott	wre	1975
Bissinger, Don	mbk	1944
Bitzer, Brook	wsoc	1999
Bizik, John	mgo	1988, 89, 90
Bizuneh, Fasil	mcc	1998, 99
	mtr	2000, 01
Bjella, Connie	wsw	1985, 86
Bjork, Stellan	mtn	1975, 76, 77
Bjorn, Alven	mtn	1969, 70
Black, Allen	bb	1981
Black, Bob	ftb	1952
Black, David	msw	1981, 82, 83, 84
Black, Dennis	mtr	1992
Black, John	ftb	1993, 1995
Black, Mike	ftb	1979, 80, 81, 82
Blackford, Steven	wre	1998, 99, 2000, 01
Blackwell, Valerie Ann	wtr	1977
Blagg, Julie	wsoc	1996, 97
Blain, Didgie	wsw	1970, 71, 72
Blain, Sada	wsw	1971, 72
Blaine, Barbara	warc	1947
Blair, Bill	msw	1958, 59
Blair, Kristal	wvb	1997
Blake, Jack	bb	1957, 58
Blake, Jennifer	wvb	1973, 74, 75
Blake, Parley	bb	1909, 10, 11
Blakely, Ed	mcc	1975, 76, 77
	mtr	1976, 77, 78
Blakes, Greg	ftb	1977, 78
Blanco, D.	wbm	1962
Bland, Jennifer	wtn	1980, 81
Blanford, Jim	mgo	1972, 73, 74
Blasius, Diane	wsw	1965
Blasius, Donna	wsw	1965
Blasius, Glen	msw	1966, 67
Blaska, Sarah	wsoc	1996, 97, 98, 99
Blaylock, Jason	msw	1991, 92, 93, 94
Blaze, Bill	marc	1980, 81
Blazina, Frank	mtr	1929
Bleamaster, Les	mcc	1954
Bliss, Tom	msw	1973
Blocher, Courtney	wvb	2000
Blome, Maurice	bb	1907, 08, 09
Bloom, Bobbi	wvb	1988, 89
Bloomquist, Willie	bb	1997, 98, 99
Blount, Howard	ftb	1931
Blount, Ralph	ftb	1905
Bloxham, Steve	msw	1971, 72, 73, 74

Blue, John	bb	1970, 71
Blue, Sally	wtn	1964
Bluell, Craig	msw	1966
Blukis, Gordon	msw	2001
Boals, Sue	wgo	1967, 69
Boardman, Betsy	wbk	2001
Boaz, Don	mgo	1959
Bobb, Randy	bb	1967
Boden, Peter	msw	1985, 86, 87, 88
Boden, Tina	warc	1992, 93
Bodine, Chris	wre	1980, 81, 83, 84
Bodine, Fred	mtr	1947
Bodney, Mike	mgo	1974
Boeller, Barb	wtn	1966
Boetto, Anthony	ftb	1919
Boetto, Herb	bb	1947
Boetto, Tony	bb	1919, 20, 21, 22
	mbk	1918, 19, 20, 21, 22
Bogard, Jim	mtr	1965
Bogert, Ross	mcc	1964
Boggess, Suzy	wvb	1981, 82
Boglione, Bob	mcc	1969, 70
	mtr	1970, 71
Bogus, Frank	wre	1965
Bohay, Gary	wre	1981, 83
Bohl, Jessica	wsoc	1997, 98, 99, 2000
Bojorquez, David	bb	1946, 47
Boldt, Priscilla	wtr	1997
Bolen, Kerry	wre	1976, 77, 78
Boles, Marty	wsb	1974
	wvb	1973, 74, 75
Boles, Zada	wbb	1943
	wsb	1943
	wtf	1943, 45
	wtn	1943, 44, 45
Boling, Tony	mbk	1954
Bolt, Priscilla	wcc	1996
Bolton, Brent	mcc	1995
	mtr	1997
Bolton, Tassie	wsw	1970, 71
Boncore, Steve	bb	1979, 80
Bond, George	mbk	1917
Bond, Jason	bb	1994, 95, 96
Bond, Tyson	mtn	1993
Bonda, Tom	mtn	1970, 71, 72
Bonderud, Fred	ftb	1955
Bonds, Barry	bb	1983, 84, 85
Bondurant, Tom	bb	1973
Bonham, Dave	mgy	1957, 58, 59, 61
Bonham, Kim	wcc	1989
Bonilla, Pete	wre	1989, 90, 91
Bonk-Vasko, Jon	mtr	1997, 98, 99
Bonner, Ron	ftb	1975
Bonnet, Tim	marc	1971
Bonnett, Pam	wvb	1980
Bono, Mindy	wgo	1989, 90, 91
Booker, Phil	ftb	1966, 67
Boom, Merry Ellen	wvb	1986, 87
Boone, Jo Elyn	wvb	1979, 80
Boone, Kathy	wbk	1979
Boopathy, Asok	mbm	1989, 90, 91
Boopathy, Surya	mbm	1992, 93
Booth, Kellee	wgo	1995, 96, 97, 98
Borden, Dick	mtr	1958
	wre	1958
Borg, Sandy	wgo	1975
Borg, Wade	mgo	1972, 73,74
Borger, Brenda	warc	1978, 79, 80, 81
Boring, Archie	ftb	1923
Bosch, Frank	ftb	1914
Bosley, Llona	wtn	1934
Bostock, Frank	mcc	1948
	mtr	1946, 47, 48

George Boutell went from golf star (1965, '66) to golf coach (1976-1986).

	mtn	1946
Bostrom, Kent	ftb	1985, 86, 87
Bosworth, Briggs	mtn	1964, 65, 66, 67
Botkin, Lorene	wbb	1922
Bouck, Gary	ftb	1978, 79
Boudreau, Jim	bb	1981, 82
Boudreaux, Paul	mcc	1985, 86, 88, 89
	mtr	1986, 87
Boulden, Ron	mgy	1955
	bb	1953, 56
Bourassa, Matt	marc	1993
Bourgeois, O'Jay	ftb	1957, 58
Bouse, Betty	warc	1952
Bousquet, Ryan	mcc	2000
Boutell, George	mgo	1965, 66
Bouwer, Annette	wvb	1977, 78
Bowden, Britnee	wgy	1999
Bowen, Frank	bb	1922, 23
	ftb	1922
	mbk	1922, 23
Bowen, John	mbk	1958, 59
Bowen, Katherine	wbb	1943
	wbk	1942, 43, 44, 45
	wfh	1942, 43
	wsb	1943
	wtf	1943
	wvb	1942, 43, 44, 45
Bowen, Keith	ftb	1988
Bowen, Mitchell	mtn	2000, 01
Bowen, Renaye	wtr	1976, 77, 80
Bowen, Velma	wfh	1939, 41, 42
	wsb	1940
Bower, Archie	mtn	1978, 79, 80
Bowers, Mark	mgy	1985, 86, 87
Bowers, Matt	msw	1967
Bowers, Tracy	wcc	1986
	wtr	1987
Bowie, Arthur	bb	1936, 37
Bowie, Heather	wgo	1994, 95
Bowland, Mark	mtr	1989
Bowler, Amy	wvb	1998
Bowles, Mike	ftb	1978, 79
Bowles, Zada	wbk	1943, 44, 45
Bowling, Mike	mbk	1971, 72
Bowman, Mary Ann	wvb	1946
	wbm	1945
Bowyer, Walt	ftb	1979, 80, 81, 82
	mbk	1981
Boyd, Jean	ftb	1991, 93
	mtr	1994
Boyd, Larry	ftb	1991, 92, 93
Boyd, Mark	mtr	1985, 86, 87, 88
Boyd, Robby	ftb	1985, 86, 87, 88
Boyer, Jeff	ftb	1997

Val Boyer anchored NCAA championship 4x100 meter relay teams in 1978 and 1979.

Boyer, John	msw	1965
Boyer, Ricky	ftb	1995, 96, 97
Boyer, Val	wtr	1978, 79, 80, 81
Boyland, Jane	wsw	1981, 82
Boyle, Bill	ftb	1932, 33, 34
Boyle, Dave	msw	1959
Boyle, Georgia Mae	wtn	1940
Boyle, Melissa	wbk	1994, 95, 96, 97
Boyle, Peggy	wsb	1943
Boyle, Susan	wtn	1974, 75, 76
Boynton, Denise	wsw	1996, 97
Braatz, Jerome	bb	1986
Bracamonte, Dick	bb	1953, 54
Brackett, Scott	msw	1983, 84, 85, 86
Brackett, Steve	mcc	1986
	mtr	1989
Bradberry, Jack	bb	1946
Bradford, Jesse	mtr	1961
	ftb	1958, 59, 60, 61
Bradford, Nancy	wfh	1950
Bradley, Jim	mgy	1958
Bradley, Neil	msw	1988
Bradley, Pat	wgo	1972
Bradley, Ryan	bb	1995, 96
Bradley, Wayne	ftb	1972
	mtr	1972, 73
Bradshaw	mtn	1930
Bradshaw, Allison	wtn	1999, 2000
Bradshaw, Nancy	wtn	1947
	wvb	1946
Brady, Forest	bb	1915
	mbk	1915
Brady, Hilbert	bb	1937
	ftb	1937, 38
	mtr	1938, 39
Brady, Jim	ftb	1972
Brady, Rhonda	wtr	1978
Brady, Stephanie	wbk	1993, 94
Brafield, Leslie	wsw	1979
Braga, Devyn	wsb	1998, 99, 2000
Bragg, Henry	msw	1996
Bragg, Samantha	wsw	1995
Braig, Brenda	wtn	1976
Braman, Bill	mbk	1957
Bramlage, Ron	wre	1986
Bramlet, Jim	ftb	1964, 65, 66
Branch, Bruce	ftb	1978, 1980, 81
Branch, David	mgy	1983, 84
Brandes, Debbie	wtn	1976
Brandon, Jim	ftb	1950
Brandt, Christy	wgo	1970, 71

Brandt, Sharon	wbm	1977
Brandt, Thomas	ftb	1914
Branham, Lydia	wsb	1947
	wtn	1945, 46, 47
Brannan, Gabe	msw	1996
Brannen, Bonnie	wsb	1999, 2000, 01
Brannen, Lenny	mgo	1971, 72
Brantley, William	mbk	1967
Brasher, Bob	ftb	1989, 90, 91, 92
Brass, Adam	ftb	1989, 90, 91, 92
Bratkowski, Steve	ftb	1980, 81
Bray, Bill	bb	1940
Braziel, Bob	mtr	1955
Brecher, Al	mtn	1967
Breck, Wayne	mgo	1960, 61
Breckinridge, Jay	ftb	1999, 2000
Breedlove, Carrie	wsb	1995, 96, 97, 98
Breeze, Ron	wre	1978
Brei, Jim	mgy	1983
Breitfeller, Tom	mgo	1982, 83, 84
Brendan, Tully	msw	1996
Brennan, Ed	bb	1980, 81, 82
Brenner, Terry	bb	1969, 70
Bresnahan, Carole	wgy	1983, 84, 85, 86
Bressant, Pierre	mbk	1978, 79, 80, 81
Bretschneider, Roland	msw	1965
Breunig, Bob	ftb	1972, 73, 74
	wre	1972
Brewer, Dee	wsb	1991
Brewer, Leslie	mtn	1925, 26, 29, 30
Brewer, Mark	bb	1980, 81
Brewer, Quincy	mbk	1994, 95, 96, 97
Brewster, Chick	wtn	1944
Brewster, Rex	bb	1956
Brewster, Rex	bb	1975
Brian, Don	wre	1962
Brice, La'Nia	wtr	1992
Bridgeman, Jennifer	wcc	1997, 98, 99, 2000
	wtr	1998, 99, 2000, 01
Bridgeman, Jerry	ftb	1960
Bridges, Gregory	msw	1996
Bridges, Jason	bb	1987
Bridgewater, Bill	mtn	1948, 49
Brigs, Marc	msw	2000, 01
Bright, Jerry	mtr	1967, 68, 69
Brignall, Phil	mgo	1959
Brimhall, Elias	mtr	1926
Brimhall, Lottie	wvb	1927
Brimhall, Stanford	ftb	1936-37
Brinkman, Tina	wgy	1992, 93, 94, 95
Brinkmann, Ann	wbk	1981
Brinkmann, Margie	wbk	1981
Brion, Larry	bb	1961, 62
Brisbin, Geoff	msw	1988, 89, 90, 91
Brisby, Ella Mae	wvb	1967
Bristow, Sue	wsb	1981, 82
Britton, Che	ftb	1997, 98, 99, 2000
Britton, Jenny	wgy	1981, 82
Britton, Rick	mtr	1967
Britts, Jeff	wre	1979
Broadbent	mtn	1923
Brock, Georgene	wtn	1956, 57, 58, 59
Brody, Steve	bb	1989, 90, 91
Brogan, William	bb	1921, 22
	mtr	1921, 22
Bronstein, Paul	wre	1984, 85, 86, 87
Brookbank, Theresa	wsw	1976, 77, 78
Brooks, Bennie	mtr	1934, 35, 36
Brooks, Hubie	bb	1977, 78
Brooks, Mitch	mgy	1980
Broucek, Mark	msw	1980, 81, 82, 83
Broughton, Bob	mcc	1951, 52, 53
	mtr	1952, 53

Broughton, Norma	wbb	1925
	wtn	1924, 25
	wvb	1925
Broughton, Teniqua	wtr	1999, 2000
Broussard, Polly	wsw	1968
Browden, Andrew	mgy	1990
Brown, Adrian	mbk	1989
Brown, Allen	wre	1967
Brown, Bernard	mgo	1934, 35, 36
Brown, Bernard	mtr	1973
Brown, Bill	mcc	1969, 70, 71, 72
	mtr	1970, 71, 72, 73
Brown, C.J.	mtr	1993
Brown, Carrol	ftb	1922
	mbk	1923
Brown, Chad	ftb	1996, 97
Brown, Cornelia	wgo	1938, 39, 40
Brown, Debbie	wtn	1978, 79, 80
Brown, Dickie	ftb	1966, 67, 68
Brown, Dione	wbk	1942
	wfh	1942
	wsb	1942
	wvb	1942
Brown, Don	bb	1980
Brown, Doyle	mtr	1965, 66, 67
Brown, Eric	mgy	1989, 90, 91, 92
Brown, Geoff	mcc	1994
	mtr	1995
Brown, George	bb	1910, 11
Brown, James	mbk	1972, 73, 74
Brown, Jay	wre	1969
Brown, Jim	bb	1967
Brown, Joanne	wgo	1941
Brown, John	ftb	1965
Brown, Joslyn	warc	1982, 83
Brown, Juanita	wvb	1961
Brown, Kent	mgy	1974, 75
Brown, Kristin	wsw	1984, 85, 86, 87
Brown, Loree	wbk	1939
	wfh	1938
Brown, Margie	warc	1951, 52, 53
	wsb	1951
	wtn	1951, 54
Brown, Mark	ftb	1992, 93
Brown, Mhairi	wtn	2000, 01
Brown, Neil	mtr	1989
Brown, Pam	wtr	1985
Brown, Pete	bb	1919, 20, 21, 22
	ftb	1922
	mbk	1921, 22, 23
	mtr	1921, 22

Hubie Brooks batted .432 for the 1978 Sun Devils, then played 14 years for five major league teams.

Brandie Burton earned first-team All-America honors in 1990 before leaving for the LPGA Tour.

C

Callahan, Mitch	ftb	1982, 83
Callicoat, Reid	ftb	1931, 32
	mbk	1932
	mtn	1933, 34
Calnimptewa, Ronnie	wre	1981
Calvert, Sandy	wgo	1975
Calvin, Christy	wtr	1991
Calvin, Otis	wre	1981, 82
Calzia, John	bb	1970
Camerena, DeDe	wsb	1991, 92, 93
Cameron, Chris	mcc	1986
	mtr	1987
Cameron, Jeri	wgy	1980, 81, 82, 83
Camp, Jim	mtr	1983, 84, 85, 86
Campbell, Cheryl	wbk	1980
Campbell, Claire	wsb	1947
	wvb	1946
Campbell, Dodie	wtr	1983, 84, 85, 86
Campbell, Fred	mcc	1948
Campbell, Fredrick	mtr	1992, 93
Campbell, Jack	mtr	1947, 48, 49, 50
Campbell, Judy	wtn	1958, 59
Campbell, Michael	mtr	2000, 01
Campbell, Shanequa	wtr	1991, 92, 93, 94
Campbell, Steve	ftb	1995, 96, 97, 98
Camper, Brian	mbk	1990, 91
Campion, Maura	wsw	1977, 78, 79, 80
Campolo, Dominic	bb	1940
	ftb	1939, 40, 41
Campos, Danny	mgo	1992
Campos, Lisa	wgy	1985
Campos, Theresa	wgy	1982, 83, 84, 85
Camut, Joe	ftb	1956, 57, 59
Candelari, Ricky	bb	1988
Candrian, Carey	wsoc	2000
Cannella, Dave	marc	1976, 77, 78, 79
Cannon, Brad	mgo	1996, 97, 98, 99
Cannon, Jerry	mtr	1953
Canter, Paul	marc	1968
Cantrell, Don	bb	1942
Capers, Marcell	mbk	1993, 95
Caplinger, Earl	bb	1934, 35
	mbk	1934, 35, 36
	mtr	1933
Caplinger, Gerald	bb	1930, 31, 32, 33
Capps, Brown	bb	1919, 20, 21
	mbk	1919
	mtr	1921, 22
Capps, Don	mcc	1956, 59
	mtr	1957
Capsitran, Cynthia	wsb	1978

Kendall Carter, now a Diamondbacks scouting executive, posted a 19-1 pitching record for ASU's 1981 national championship baseball team.

Carbajal, Manuel	ftb	1991
Cardinale, Sal	bb	1993
Cardineau, Yan	msw	1987, 88, 89, 90
Cardon, Tommy	msw	1995, 96
Carey, Ellen	wtn	1958
Carey, George	msw	1964, 65, 66
Carey, Kim	wgy	1976
Carey, Megan	wgy	1999
Carl, Bob	ftb	1976, 77, 78, 79
Carl, Kalene	wbk	1997
Carlino, Mark	mbk	1986, 87, 88
Carlisle, Shelley	wsw	1982
Carlough, Donna	wsw	1971
Carlson, Bruce	bb	1949
Carlson, Craig	mtn	1962, 63
Carlson, Kynny	mtr	1991
Carlton, Rich	bb	1969
Carmen, Teddy	warc	1932
Carmichael, Tom	mbm	1986, 87, 88, 89
Carney	wsb	1941
Carnicelli, Terri	wsb	1989, 90, 91, 92
Carns, Catherine	wbb	1936
	wbk	1937, 38
	wfh	1938
Carothers, Ron	ftb	1967, 68, 69
Carpenter, Andre	mtr	1975
Carpenter, Molly	wgy	1987, 88, 89, 90
Carpenter, Ralph	bb	1966, 67
Carpenter, Stacy	wtr	1991
Carper, Candis	wbk	1992
Carr, Al	bb	1959
	ftb	1955, 56, 57, 58
Carr, Debbie	wsw	1975, 76, 77
Carr, Ed	die	
	mtn	1926, 27, 28
	bb	1926, 27
Carr, Frank	ftb	1980, 82, 83
Carr, Henry	ftb	1963
	mtr	1962, 63, 64
Carrigan, Keith	bb	1985
Carrilo, Adeline	warc	1967, 68
Carroll, Jay	mcc	1986
Carroll, Laurie	wtr	1981
Carroll, Stephen	msw	1991
Carruthers, Taylor	mtr	1930
Carson, Debra	wtr	1977, 78, 79, 80
Carson, Stella Mae	wbk	1921
Carson, Steve	mtr	1980, 81
Carstens, Kristen	wtr	2000
Cart, Julie	wtr	1976, 78, 79, 80
Carter, Bob	ftb	1972
Carter, Ed	mtn	1997, 98, 99, 2000
Carter, Heather	wgy	1987, 88, 89, 90
Carter, Jim	mgo	1982, 83, 84
Carter, Kendall	bb	1981, 82, 83, 84
Carter, Kirk	ftb	1975
Carter, Leslie	rif	1950
Carter, Lorraine	wbm	1940
	wsb	1940
Carter, Mary	wvb	1977, 78, 79, 80
Carter, Matt	msw	1998, 99, 2000
Carter, Michelle	wsw	1995, 96
Carter, Noble	ftb	1899, 1900, 02, 03
Carter, Oliver	wre	1963
Carter, Vincent	wre	1964
Cartledge, Crantz	ftb	1896-97
Cartun, Dave	bb	1963, 64, 65
Carunchio, Dennis	ftb	1957
Carusetta, Andy	mcc	1995, 96, 97
	mtr	1996, 97, 98
Caruthers, Mike	mtn	1978, 79
Carvalho, Cian	wbk	2001
Carver, Lea	wgy	1999, 2000
Carver, Scott	mtr	1976, 77, 78

Carver, Shante	ftb	1990, 91, 92, 93
	mbk	1993
Casale, Joe	mgo	1950
Casarez, Lucy	wsb	1979, 80, 81, 82
	wvb	1978
Case, Libby	wgy	1976, 77, 78, 79
Case, Robert	msw	1985
Casey, Leland	bb	1929, 30
	ftb	1929
	mcc	1929
Casey, Paul	mgo	1998, 99, 2000
Casey, Tim	ftb	1984
Cassidy, David	bb	1986, 87, 88, 89
Cassidy, Jim	marc	1989, 90, 91, 92
Casson, Mike	mcc	1975
Cassuto, Kerry	mgy	1970, 71
Cast, Caroline	wsw	1985, 86, 87
Castalgo, Paul	mgy	1988
Casten, Chad	msw	1993, 94, 95
Castile, Lewis	bb	1912, 13, 14, 15
Castillo, Art	wre	1985
Castillo, Cesar	bb	2001
Castillo, Chris	wre	1993, 94, 95, 96
Castillo, Lito	bb	1956
Castle, Lewis	ftb	1914
Castle, Lionel	mbk	1914, 15
	mtr	1913, 14
Castle, Steve	wre	1974
Castner, Chris	marc	1988, 89, 90, 91
Castro, Juliane	wsb	1993, 94
Catarello, Patrick	wre	1998
Catlett, Ann	wcc	1984
Catlett, Marcia	wgy	1973
Caughlin, Mary	wbk	1919
Cavalliere, Bob	wre	1963, 64
Cavanagh, Geri	wgo	1981, 82, 83
Caveness, Martha Jane	warc	1940, 41
Caywood, Cleo	ftb	1928, 29, 30
Caywood, Wally	bb	1929
	ftb	1927, 28, 29
	mtr	1928, 30
Cazel, Scott	mgy	1981, 82, 83
Celays, Don	bb	1924
Cellars, Charles	mtr	1923
Cercone, Matt	ftb	1997, 98
Cerkvenik, Tony	mbk	1961, 62, 63
Cermak, Jeff	bb	1996, 97
Certo, Tish	wgo	1985, 86
Cesar, JoAnne	wgo	1978, 79
Cesario, Greg	mgo	1984, 85, 86, 87
Cesta, Joe	ftb	1997, 98
Chaboudy, Anna	wtn	1970
Chadwick, Guy	mbm	1979, 80
Chamberlain, Cathy	wsb	2000
Chamberlain, Jeanne	wtn	1927
Chamberlaine, Dorothy	wbb	1921
Chambers, Barb	wsb	1978, 79, 80
Chambers, Steve	ftb	1975, 76, 78
Champeau, Judee	wsw	1964
Chan, Jenny	wbm	1989, 90, 91, 92
Chancy, Chris	mtr	1994
Chandler, Marie	wtn	1947
Chandler, Pam	wtr	1983, 84
Chaney, Lorena	warc	1944
Chapelle, Leroi	mtr	1940
Chapin, Russ	mtn	1950
Chapman, Connie	wsw	1982
Chapman, Evelyn	wfh	1950
Chapman, Mike	mtr	1973, 74, 75
Chapman, Pat	mtr	1978, 79
Chapple, Teri	wtr	1981, 82, 83
Charest, Carolyn	wyy	1966
Charlebois, Jeff	wre	2001
Charlebois, Louis	mgo	1937

Carole Cheuvront was a four-time All-American in archery from 1977 through 1980.

Charles, Bob	mgy	1958
	mtr	1955, 57, 58
Charles, Brian	mtr	1990
Charles, Derrick	ftb	1995
Charles, Parnell	ftb	1991, 93, 94
Charles, Shawn	wre	1990, 91, 92, 93
Charlton, Reggie	mtr	1996, 97
Charroin, Olivier	mgo	2001
Chartrand, Craig	msw	1969, 70
Chase, Bev	warc	1953
Chase, Carl	ftb	1915
	bb	1916
Chastain, Bob	mbk	1946, 47
Chatham, Chester	bb	1929
Chavez, John	bb	1957, 58
Chavez, Rex	bb	1952, 53, 54, 55
Chavira, Adam	wre	2000, 01
Chavira, Juan	mcc	1998, 99
	mtr	2000
Cheatham, Bill	wre	1956
Cheek, Larry	msw	1977
Cheney, Adeline	wtn	1933, 34, 35, 36
Cherry, J. Juan	ftb	1997, 98
Cherry, Michelle	wbk	1991, 92
Cherry, Rich	mtr	1968
Chesley, Horace	bb	1930
Chester, Mary	wsw	1991
Cheuvront, Carole	warc	1977, 78, 79, 80
Cheuvront, Ron	bb	1955
Chew, Jim	mgo	1963, 64, 65, 66
Chewning, Phil	mtr	1973, 74
Childers, Bob	mtn	1937, 38
Childs, Bob	msw	1989
Childs, Jim	mtr	1964, 65
Chipps, Sam	bb	1966, 67
Chmielinski, Ted	bb	1999
Choat, John	bb	1966
Chong, Chae-Ho	bb	1986
Choppa, Shelly	wtr	1991, 92, 93, 94
Chornomud, Dwight	wre	1991
Chowaniec, Mike	ftb	1966, 67, 68
Christensen, Al	mtr	1955
Christensen, Kelly	wgy	1999, 2000
Christenson, Alan	mtr	1952
	ftb	1952
Christian, Nancy	wvb	1990, 91, 92, 93
Christianson, Ebba	wbb	1936
Christianson, Les	mgy	1963, 64, 65, 66
Chuhlantseff, Don	ftb	1988
Chulew, Max	mcc	1976
	mtr	1977

Churchill, Dan	wre	1969
Ciak, Fran	wbk	1987, 88, 89, 90
Cioffi, Pam	wtn	1990, 91, 92, 93
Cislaghi, Guido	bb	1929, 30, 31, 32
	ftb	1930, 31
Clack, Darryl	ftb	1982, 83, 84, 85
	mtr	1983, 85
Clair, Clevon	mtr	1994, 95
Clapham, Clayton	wre	1963
Clapinski, Greg	bb	1993
Clapp, Chauncey	box	1935, 36
Clapp, Frances	wbb	1924, 25
Clapp, Marjorie	wsb	1940
Clard, Janis	wsb	1950
Clark	mtr	1934
Clark, Andy	msw	1985, 86, 87
Clark, Brian	msw	1992
Clark, C.	wsw	1963
Clark, Casey	mtr	2000, 01
Clark, Claudia	wsw	1968, 69, 70
Clark, Deanne	wsb	1977
Clark, Greg	ftb	1984, 85, 86, 87
Clark, Harold	mbk	1922, 23
Clark, Hilary	wvb	1994, 95
Clark, Iggy	bb	1940
Clark, Jaclyn	wsoc	1997, 98, 99, 2000
Clark, Kareem	ftb	1996, 97, 98, 99
Clark, Kevin	marc	1979, 80
Clark, Michael	wre	1998
Clark, Robert	mtr	1939
Clark, Sally	wvb	1980, 81, 82
Clark, Sue	wtn	1964
Clark, Susan	wtn	1978, 79, 80, 81
Clark, Theresa	wbk	1981
Clark, Verdell	wbk	1925
Clark, Wade	bb	1934
	mbk	1934, 35
Clarke, Carolyn	wtn	1967, 69, 70
Clattenburg, Eddie	ftb	1999
Claw, Al	wre	1964
Clay, Machtier	ftb	1999, 2000
Claypatch, Kathy	wgo	1986
Claypool, Scott	ftb	1987, 88
Clayton, Royal	bb	1985, 86
Cleaver, Drew	mtr	1985
Clegg, Amanda	wsw	1997, 98, 99, 2000
Clemence, Harold	bb	1936, 37, 38
	mbk	1936, 37, 38
Clemente, Fran	wbk	1980
Clements, Bob	mtr	1954, 55
Clements, Dudley	bb	1919
Clements, Leonard	mtr	1926, 27
Clements, Norman	ftb	1928, 29, 30, 31
	mbk	1930, 31
Clemmens, Bert	wre	1972
Clevenger, Francis	ftb	1935, 36, 37
Clevenger, Pat	ftb	1964
Clevenger, Ruth	wbk	1943
	wsb	1943
	wtf	1943
	wvb	1942, 43
Clewis, Charles	mtr	1982
Click, Nancy	wtr	1977
Cliff, Leslie	wsw	1977, 78
Clifford, Jesse	bb	1907, 08
Clifford, Pat	mtr	1974, 75
Clinchy, Lisa	wsb	1981, 82, 83
Clinton, Anson	wre	1963
Clough, Dave	mcc	1956, 57, 59
	mtr	1957, 58, 59, 60
Clupper, Mike	ftb	1969, 70, 71
Cnota, Jennifer	wsw	1993, 94, 95, 96
Coats, Carol	wtn	1971
Coats, Linda	wsb	1977, 78

Coats, Rachel	wsw	1991
Cobb, Crystal	wbk	1991, 92, 93, 94
Cobbs, Freida	wtr	1979
Coberly, Jean	wtn	1973
Cochell, Larry	bb	1963
Cochran, Greg	bb	1972, 73, 74, 75
Cochran, Heather	wbm	1983, 84
Cochran, Neil	msw	1984, 85, 86, 87
Coenigs, Dave	wre	1958
Coffin, Edwin	bb	1917
	ftb	1915, 16
Coffin, Linda	wgo	1968
Coffin, S.	wsw	1963
Coffinger, Mike	ftb	1953, 54, 55, 56
Coggins, Milt Jr.	mgo	1953, 54
Cohen, Adam	wre	1982, 84, 85, 86
Cohen, Charlie	mtr	1992, 93, 94, 95
Cohen, Holly	wsoc	1999, 2000
Cohen, Jeremy	mtn	1974, 75, 76, 77
Cohen, Wendy	wgy	1983
Coker, Carrie	wcc	1979, 80, 81
	wtr	1979, 80, 81, 82
Coker, Linda	wvb	1968
Colavin, Michelle	wgy	1988, 89, 90, 91
Colbern, Mike	bb	1974, 75, 76
Cole, Albon	mgy	1991, 92
Cole, Ben	ftb	1928, 29, 31
	bb	1928, 29, 31, 32
Cole, Chris	mtr	1972
Cole, Cindy	wgy	1987
Cole, Emma	wbb	1924
	wbk	1924
Cole, Jon	mtr	1963, 64, 65, 66
Cole, Karen	wsb	1970
	wvb	1968
Cole, Lee	ftb	1994, 95
Cole, Mark	wre	1975
Cole, Roy	mbk	1921
	bb	1921
	ftb	1922
	mtr	1921, 22
Coleburn, Al	mtr	1960, 61
Colella, Sam	ftb	1951
Coleman, Cecil	ftb	1946, 47, 48, 49
Coleman, Daniel	mtr	1992
Coleman, Jack	wre	1964
Coleman, Janice	wgo	1947
Coleman, Phil	ftb	1940, 41
Coley, Gary	wre	1970, 71
Colleary, Ellen	wtr	1980
Colleary, Ellen	wtr	1981

Jon Cole (1963-66) still ranks among the school's all-time discus and shot put leaders, but was perhaps best known for his weightlifting feats.

Dana Collins was a two-time All-American (1977, 1978) in the pentathlon.

Collett, Randy	ftb	1973
Colley, Dannyelle	wsw	1997
Collier, Jack	mtn	1949
Collinge, Jack	bb	1969, 70
Collins, Bob	mtn	1949, 50
Collins, Buddie	mcc	1933
Collins, Chester	wre	1984
Collins, Dana	wtr	1977, 78, 79, 80
Collins, Fred	mgo	1940
Collins, Guy	ftb	1896
Collins, Heather	warc	1991, 92
Collins, Lynn	mbk	1991, 92
Collins, Michael	bb	1996, 97, 98
Collins, Peggy	wtn	1929
Collins, Pinky	wsw	1974
Collins, Roger	ftb	1947
Collins, Sean	wre	1985
Collins, Shane	ftb	1988, 89, 90, 91
	mtr	1989, 90, 91, 92
Collis, Mike	mtr	1976, 77
Colloca, Mike	mtn	1984, 85, 86
Colquitt, Debbie	wsw	1983, 84
Colvard, Mike	mgy	1976, 77
Combs, Janice	wtn	1972, 73
Combs, Freddie	bb	1988
Combs, Leah	wbk	1999, 2000, 01
Comeaux, Darren	ftb	1980, 81
Commerford, Pat	mgy	1971
Comstock, Mike	msw	1982
Conat, Nancy	wtr	1982
Concialdi, Joe	mtn	1974, 75
Condez, Al	wre	1972
Condit, Keith	box	1937
Condon, Bruce	mgo	1972, 73, 74
Cone, Tracy	wgo	1991, 92, 93, 94
Conine, Jason	wre	2000, 01
Conley, Doug	mcc	1969
	mtr	1969, 70, 71
Conlisk, Robert	mbk	1991, 92, 93, 94
Connell, Eric	mgy	1971, 72, 73
Connelly, Lee	wtn	1972
Conner, Ebony	wtr	1996
Conniff, Betty	wbb	1943
Conniff, John	bb	1950
Connolly, Joe	ftb	1969, 69, 70
Connolly, Juele	wsw	1959
Connolly, Robin	wbk	1984, 85, 86
	wvb	1987
Connor, Chad	marc	1990, 91, 92
Connors, Helen	wtr	1978, 79, 80
Conrad, Brooks	bb	1999, 2000, 01
Conroy, Dottie	wsb	1991, 92
Consaul, Ross	msw	1973, 74, 75, 76

Conte, Paola	wtn	1988, 89, 90, 91
Contes, Jim	wre	1972
Conti, Bill	msw	1990, 91, 92
Contreras, Caroline	warc	1930
	wvb	1928
Contreras, Gracie	wbm	1964
Contreras, James	mgo	1985, 86
Contreras, Joaquin	wre	1998
Contreras, Mandy	wsw	1997, 98, 99, 2000
Contreras, Mike	mbk	1971, 72, 73
Conway, Joe	mbk	1918
	ftb	1916, 1919
Cook	mtr	1931
Cook, Arlene	wbm	1940, 41
	wbm	1942
Cook, Chesley	mbk	1947, 48, 50
Cook, Cristi	wbm	1983, 84
Cook, Curt	wre	1974
Cook, Dorothy	warc	1935
Cook, Larry	bb	1966
Cook, Marjorie	wbb	1943
	wbk	1943, 44, 45
	wfh	1943
	wsb	1943
	wtf	1943, 45
	wvb	1943, 44
Cook, Melinda	wsb	1989, 90
Cook, Sam	bb	1961, 62, 63, 64
Cook, Vince	bb	1985
Cooke, Calvin	mgo	1960, 61
Cooke, Dale	mbk	1982
Cooley, Enid	wbk	1919
Coons, Brad	mcc	1984
Cooper, Anson	bb	1932, 33, 34
	ftb	1930, 31, 32, 33
Cooper, Betsy	wtn	1947
Cooper, Bill	box	1937
Cooper, Doug	msw	1958, 59
Cooper, Harley	ftb	1950, 51, 52
	mtr	1952
Cooper, Kelly	wcc	1984
Cooper, Larry	bb	1966
Cooper, Marylou	wgy	1977
Cooper, Matt	ftb	1999, 2000
Cooper, Molly	wgo	1998, 99, 2000, 01
Coor, Lattie	bb	1928, 29
Coparanis, Carol	wtn	1984, 85, 86, 87
Cope, Everett	bb	1958, 59
Copeland, Mike	ftb	1983, 84
Copley, Jacob	msw	1999, 2000, 01
Coppinger, Jim	ftb	1948, 49
Coppinger, Julie	wtn	1993, 94, 95, 96
Coppinger, Roy	bb	1951, 52
	mbk	1950, 51, 52, 53
Coppola, Rich	mbk	1964, 65, 66
Corbell, Louis	bb	1907
Corbell, Paul	bb	1911, 12
	mbk	1912
Corbett, Kim	wsb	1992, 93
Corbin, Jeff	mtn	1968
Corby, John	mtr	1971, 72
Cordell, Kelly	wcc	1989, 90, 91, 92
	wtr	1990, 91, 92, 93
Cordell, Milt	mtn	1955, 56
Cordes, Grace	wbk	1914, 15
Corea, Nancy	wbk	1981
	wvb	1977, 78, 79, 80
Corea, Sue	wvb	1980, 81
Corneal, George	ftb	1965
Cornelius, Bill	mgy	1959, 60, 61, 62
Cornelius, Carol	wvb	1968
Cornelius, Keri	wgo	1996, 97, 98, 99
Cornell, Nick	ftb	1991
Corominas, Mike	bb	1993, 94, 95

Corritore, John	mgy	1980
Cosentino, Dom	ftb	1942, 46, 47
Cosentino, Frank	ftb	1938, 39, 40, 41
Cosner, Barry	mgo	1982, 83, 84
Cosner, Brian	mgo	1979, 80, 81
Cosner, Ron	ftb	1959, 60, 61
Cosnser, Arthur	ftb	1950
Cota, Julia	wsb	1976
Cotarobles, Armando	mtn	1956
Cotter, Sam	bb	1951
Cottingham, Jennifer	wtr	1986, 87
Cottler, Stephanie	wsb	1995
Cotton, Bill	bb	1968, 69
Cotton, Bruce	mgo	1967, 68
Cottrell, Kristina	wtr	1995
Coughlin, Jami	wvb	1998, 99, 2000
Coughran, Wiley	ftb	1899, 1900
Coulson, Candida	wtr	1999, 2000, 01
Coulter, Carolyn	wtr	1984
Countryman, Karla	wsb	1995
Countryman, Shari	wsw	1988, 89, 90, 91
Cours, Ray	ftb	1942
Courtney, Carie	wgy	1995, 96, 97, 98
Covarrubias, Fred	bb	1955
Covelli, Frank	mtr	1962, 63
Cover, Jerry	mtn	1952, 53
Covielo, Dick	bb	1960
Cowan, Anthony	mtr	1986
Cowley, Kelly	wgy	2001
Cowman, Allison	wsw	1984, 85, 86
Cox, Aaron	ftb	1984, 85, 86, 87
Cox, Beverly	wtn	1954
Cox, Dennis	mtr	2001
Cox, Jada	wgy	2001
Cox, J.R.	mcc	2000
Cox, Laddie	mtr	1953, 54, 55
Cox, Larry	mgy	1977
Cox, Mike	mtr	1981, 82
Cox, Norm	mgy	1963, 64, 65, 66
Cox, S.	warc	1963
Cox, Terri	wvb	1994, 95, 96, 97
Cox, Tracy	wsw	1984, 85, 86, 87
Coxe, George.	rif	1961, 62, 63, 64
Coyle, Ken	ftb	1968, 69, 70
Crabtree, Glen	bb	1930
	mbk	1929, 30, 31, 32
Craft, Katie	wsb	1947
Craft, Ken	ftb	1960
Craig, Bill	mbk	1918
	ftb	1919
Craig, Sydney	bb	1916
Crain, Brady	mtr	1979

Frank Covelli captured the NCAA javelin title in 1963.

Crain, Dan	marc	1987, 88, 89
Crandall, Kenny	mbk	1999
Crandall, Lee	mcc	1933
Crane, Mary Lou	wbm	1953
	wtn	1954
Cranford, Opal	wbk	1935
Crawford, Eric	bb	1990, 91
	ftb	1987, 88, 89, 90
Crawford, Jim	bb	1969, 70, 71, 72
Crawford, Kathy	wtr	1978, 79, 80, 81
Crawford, Malchi	ftb	1994, 95, 97
Crawford, Mike	ftb	1983, 84, 85
Crawford, Monroe	mtr	1952
Crawford, Opal	wfh	1935
Crawford, Regis	ftb	1999, 2000
Crawley, Gladys	wbk	1924
Crays, Steve	mtr	1989
Creary, Julie	wsw	1974, 75
Crenshaw, Chauncey	mcc	1980
	mtr	1980, 81, 82, 84
Cribari, Lisa	wsw	1989
Crile, Bruce	wre	1962
Crippen, Eddie	bb	1991
Cripps, Bill	wre	1978, 79 80
Criscione, Candi	wcc	1999, 2000
	wtr	1999, 2000, 01
Crismon	box	1929
Crisp, Rainy	wbk	2000, 01
Critchley, Dan	bb	1909, 10
Critchley, David	mtn	1995, 96
Croft, Jeff	wre	1987
Cronin, Brian	mcc	1991
	mtr	1991, 92
Cronin, Tom	bb	1960
Cronkite, Burton	mbk	1933
Croonquist, Dan	mgo	1978, 79
Cross, JoAnne	wgo	1987
Cross, Julie	wgo	1983, 84, 85
Crossen, Kendra	wsw	1998
Crouse, Hazel	wtn	1924, 25
Crouse, Lucy	wsb	1981, 82
Crow, Jamie	mgo	1981, 82, 83
Crow, Jan	wgo	1967, 68, 69
Crow, Patsy	wtn	1968
Crow, Robert	bb	1925
Crowe, Eric	msw	1996
Crowe, Larry	ftb	1973
Crowley, Mike	msw	1991, 92
Crum, Kevin	mtr	1974
Crumbaker, Ellen	wbm	1947
	wfh	1947
	wsb	1947
	wvb	1946, 47
Crump, Bill	mbk	1954
Crumpton, Chuck	bb	1998, 99
Cruz, Abraham	mbk	1924
Cruz, Albert	bb	1929, 30, 31, 32
Cruz, Jacob	bb	1992, 93, 94
Cruz, Juan	ftb	1972
Cruz, Sylvia	wvb	1976
Cseresnyes, Reka	wtn	1995, 96, 97, 98
Cubbage, Connie	wtn	1956, 57
Cuber, Leo	bb	1909
Cucjen, Romy	bb	1983, 84
Cuda, Tracy	marc	1977, 78, 79, 80
Cuff, Ryan	mbk	1995
Cuie, Ron	ftb	1973
Culbert	mtr	1933
Culbert, Agnes	wbb	1924, 25
	wbk	1924, 25
Culbert, Harry	mcc	1929
	mtr	1927, 28, 30
Culbreath, Kathy	wvb	1990, 92, 93, 94
Culiver, Wayne	mtr	1962

Cullen, Nicole	wsb	2001
Culp, Curley	ftb	1965, 66, 67
	wre	1965, 66, 67, 68
Culpepper, Dwayne	mtr	1987
Cummings, Ruth	wfh	1935
	wtn	1934, 35, 36
Cunningham, Dave	mgo	1988, 89, 90, 91
Cunningham, Dick	mtr	1962
Cunningham, J.	wsw	1972
Cunningham, J.R.	mbk	1995
Cunningham, Rheannon	wsw	1996
Cupchak, Mike	ftb	1959, 60
Cupps, Tom	ftb	1954
	bb	1955
Curnow, Murray	ftb	1902
Currah, Joanne	wsw	1993, 94, 95, 96
Curran, Dick	ftb	1952, 53
Currie, Kimberly	wsw	2001
Currier, Bob	ftb	1973
Curry, Cathy	wgo	1978, 79, 80, 81
Curry, Howard	ftb	1931
Curry, John	bb	1924
	ftb	1923
Curry, Sherry	wsb	1988, 89
Curtis, Gregg	mgy	1988
Curtis, Jim	ftb	1936-37
Curtis, Link	bb	1962
Curtis, Nelson	mtn	1953, 54
Curtis, Rick	mgy	1972, 73, 74, 75
Curtis, Shane	marc	1987
Cusick, Nan	wtn	1976, 77, 78
Cuskie, Katie	wsw	1999, 2000, 01
Cutler, Judy	wtn	1977, 78
Cyskiewicz, Kelly	wgy	1989, 90, 91, 92
Czaplak, Ed	ftb	1950

D

D'Addea, Joan	wsb	1951
D'Ambrosio, Dominic	mcc	1999
D'Angelo, Lou	bb	1991, 92
Dacquisto, Lisa	wsb	1994, 95, 96, 97
	wvb	1995
Dadey, Mary	wbk	1922
Daggy, Micah	wre	1998
Dahl, Emily	wsw	1996
Dahle, Gary	msw	1969, 70
Dailey, Lamont	mtr	1991, 92, 93, 94

Lisa Dacquisto set numerous school records during a brilliant softball career from 1994 through 1997.

Dennis Dairman, who starred on ASU's great basketball teams of the early 1960s, now presides in another kind of court, as a judge.

Dailey, Tania	wcc	1994
	wtr	1994, 95
Dains, Charles	bb	1915
	ftb	1914
Dains, Ray	bb	1914
Dairman, Dennis	mbk	1962, 63, 64, 65
Dalbey, Troy	msw	1990, 91
Dale, Ian	mbk	1992
Dale, Merrilee	wsw	1985
Dalmolin, Al	ftb	1934, 35, 36
	bb	1936, 37
Dalton, Dick	mgy	1970, 71, 72, 73
Dalton, Lynn	mbk	1947, 48, 49
Daly, Fiona	wtr	1996, 97, 98, 99
Dameron, Ellen	wsw	1970, 71
Dameron, Sid	mtr	1946
Dana, Farrell	ftb	1927, 28
Dana, Lorel	ftb	1923, 24
Dander, Jennifer	wcc	1991, 92, 93
	wtr	1993
Dangel, Jodi	wvb	1979
Dani, Peter	mtn	1998
Daniel, Kathy	warc	1980, 81
Daniel, Tom	wre	1957, 58
Daniel, Willie	ftb	1998, 99, 2000
Daniels, Dana	wbk	1984
Daniels, Don	mtn	1959
Daniels, Virgil	ftb	1926
	bb	1927, 28
Dannaker, Phil	mbk	1970
Darden, Tony	mtr	1977, 78
Dare, Jody	wvb	1978
Darnall, Stephanie	wsb	1989
Darnton, Mary	wtn	1969
Daugherty, Dick	mbk	1954
Daugherty, Spike	mgo	1967
Davenport, Bob	ftb	1968, 69, 70
Davenport, Dave	msw	1967
Davenport, J.	wsw	1962
Daves, George Jr.	bb	1955
David, John	mcc	1964
Davidson, Dan	bb	1974, 75
Davidson, Kori	wtn	1992, 93, 94, 95
Davies, Mike	wre	1985, 86, 87, 88
Davila, Dan	wre	1968, 69
Davini, Ron	bb	1967, 68
Davis	mtr	1931

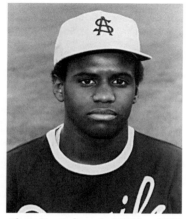

Alvin Davis batted .395 for ASU's 1981 national baseball champs and later starred for the Seattle Mariners.

Davis, Alma	ftb	1899, 1900, 02
Davis, Alvin	bb	1979, 80, 81, 82
Davis, Arlaina	wtr	1998, 99, 2000, 01
Davis, Becky	wsb	1988, 89, 90, 91
Davis, Bennett	ftb	1934, 35, 36
	mtr	1936, 37
Davis, Bill	ftb	1938, 39, 40
Davis, Bob	mbk	1952
Davis, Carl	mtr	1964
Davis, Darryl	mgy	1980
Davis, Derek	mbk	1976, 77, 78, 79
Davis, Derrick	mbk	1999
Davis, Dick	mgo	1963
Davis, Doreisha	wtr	1998, 99
Davis, Duane	mbk	1996
Davis, Eddie	mcc	1981, 82
	mtr	1982, 83, 84, 85
Davis, Henry	mgo	1940
Davis, Jack	rif	1956
Davis, Jake	ftb	1946
Davis, Jim	marc	1969
Davis, John	wre	1963, 64
Davis, John	wre	1979, 80
Davis, Mason	bb	1924
Davis, Pat	wvb	1968
Davis, R. J.	msw	1969
Davis, Ralph	marc	1950
Davis, Regina	wbk	1991, 92
Davis, Richard	ftb	1989
Davis, Rick	ftb	1963, 64, 65
Davis, Roger	ftb	1970, 71
Davis, Susan	wgo	1971
Davis, Troy	ftb	1996, 97, 98
Davis, W.E.	mgo	1956
Davis, Wendell	mtr	1949
Davison, Cynthia	wtr	1977
Davison, Jerone	ftb	1991, 92
Dawson, Bob	mbk	1942
Dawson, Kristina	wsoc	1998
Dawson, Mildred	wbb	1936
Day, Amy	wsb	1992, 93, 94
Day, Chad	bb	1995
Day, Craig	msw	1989
Day, Lori	wsw	1993
Day, Paul	ftb	1983, 84, 85, 86
	mtr	1983
Day, Tom	mbk	1974
Dayton, Lester	bb	1942, 46
Deakman, Josh	bb	1995
Dean, Bill	bb	1951, 52

Dean, Brett	mgo	1989, 90, 91, 92
Dean, Chip	ftb	1975
Dean, Dick	mtn	1958
Dean, Lester	mbk	1951, 52, 53
Dean, Mitch	bb	1976, 77, 78
Dean, Moffat	bb	1912, 13
	mtr	1913
Dean, Norm	wre	1966
Dean, Steve	wre	1981
Deane, Tina	wtr	1977
Deans, Tom	mcc	1951, 52
	mtr	1952, 53
Deardorff, Tom	bb	1982
DeBenon, Charles	bb	1956
DeBono, Paul	ftb	1990
deCathelineau, Susan	wsw	1983, 84
Decker, Debbie	wsw	1976
Decker, Donna	wsw	1981, 82
Decker, Jeff	ftb	1991
DeClerco, Jack	ftb	1928
	bb	1926, 27, 28, 29
DeCree, Toya	wbk	1982
Dedera, Don	marc	1950, 51
Dedrick, Ada	wvb	1961
Dedrick, Doug	ftb	1976, 77
Dedrick, Mark	mgy	1973, 74, 75, 76
DeFrance, Chris	ftb	1977, 78
	mtr	1978, 79
DeFrancesco, Katie	wgo	1991, 92, 93
DeGeneste, Quinten	mtr	1965, 66
DeHart, Bob	mtn	1942
DeHoff, Carolyn	wbk	1987, 88, 89, 90
Deines, Jim	mbk	1982, 83, 84, 85
DeKellis, Tom	ftb	1938, 39
	mtr	1938, 39, 40
DelaCruz, Annette	wsb	1985
Delamater, Connie	wtn	1971
Delbridge, Larry	ftb	1970, 71, 72
Delcarson, Steve	mgy	1977, 78
Delgado, Felipe	msw	1994, 95, 96
Delgado, Robert	msw	1996, 97, 98, 99
Della Libera, Gino	ftb	1955, 56, 57, 58
	mtr	1958
Delnoce, Ryan	ftb	1998, 99, 2000
Delnoce, Todd	bb	1991, 94
Delnoce, Tom	ftb	1967, 68, 69
Delucchi, Dustin	bb	1997, 98, 99
Demarest, Dean	mtr	1980
Demery, Calvin	ftb	1969, 70, 71
Dempster, Kurt	bb	1985, 86, 87
Demsey, Todd	mgo	1992, 93, 94, 95
Denelsbeck, Don	wre	1971, 72, 73
Denesto, Roderick	ftb	1999, 2000
Denham, Paul	bb	1959
	mbk	1959
Denithorne, Debbie	wsw	1989, 90
Deniz, Leslie	wtr	1981, 82, 83
Dennard, Glenn	ftb	1984, 85
Dennard, Ryan	ftb	1999, 2000
Dennis, Bill	mtr	1946, 47
Dennison, Keith	msw	1989, 90, 91, 92
Denny, Kris	wcc	1981, 82, 83, 84
	wtr	1982, 83, 84, 85
Denton, Jim	ftb	1975
Derbis, Al	ftb	1951, 52, 53
Derickson, Jeremy	msw	1994
Dermer, Rod	wre	1966
Derminio, Mike	mgo	2001
Dernovich, Rex	mbk	1962
DeRosa, Rudy	ftb	1948
DeRose, Barry	box	1937
DeRose, J.	rif	1962
DeRousie, Lisa	wbm	1982
Derr, Debbie	wtr	1976, 77, 78

Detter, Roger	bb	1967, 68, 69
	mbk	1967, 68, 69
Dettman, Lenora	wfh	1947
DeVallance, Dennis	mtr	1957, 58
Devaney, Lyndsay	wsw	2001
DeVera, Faye	wtn	1998, 99, 2000, 01
Devereaux, Mike	bb	1984, 85
Devero, Cyndi	wgy	1978
DeVitt, Jared	wre	1991
DeVore, Laura	wsw	1991, 92
Dewar, Joan	wvb	1967, 68
Dewey, Dee	wsw	1964
Dewey, Ian	wre	1994
DeWitt, Dan	mtr	1953
DeWitt, Jane	wgy	1980
DeWitt, Joe	mgo	1934, 35
DeWitt, Paul	mbk	1935, 36, 40
DeWitt, Tom	mgy	1980, 81, 83, 84
Dhein, Tom	mtr	1965, 66
Diaz de Leon, Guillermo	msw	1996, 97, 98, 99
Diaz, Art	mgo	1975, 76, 77, 78
Diaz, Lotcha	wtn	1956
Diaz-Sandi, Licurgo	mgy	1988, 89, 90, 91
DiBrell, Zack	ftb	1975
Dice, John	ftb	1988
Dick, Heidi	wsw	1997, 98
Dick, Ralph	bb	1969
Dick, W.W. "Skipper"	mbk	1928, 29, 31
	ftb	1927, 28, 30, 31
	bb	1931, 32, 33
Dickson, Cindy	wcc	1982, 83
Didech, Gregg	mgy	1977
Diebold, Brian	mgy	1967, 68
Diggs, George	ftb	1947, 48
	mtr	1946, 47, 48, 49
Diggs, George	wre	1962
DiGiambatista, Tom	mgy	1977
Dikos, Greg	bb	1996, 97
Dillard, Rodney	ftb	1985, 86, 87, 88
Diller, Sue	wgy	1980
Dilley, Chuck	ftb	1956
DiNanno, Michelle	wbm	1975, 76
Dirks, Dwaine	mtn	1973
DiSalvo, Fred	bb	1949, 50, 51, 52
Disarufino, Raul	ftb	1960
	mbk	1962, 63
Dise, Ray	mtr	1964, 65
Disney, Scott	mgo	1983, 84
Disque, Jeff	mgy	1977, 78, 79
Ditch, Mike	msw	1975, 76, 77
Dittler, Kevin	wre	1984
Dixon, David	ftb	1990, 91
Dixon, Emilio	ftb	1950
Dixon, John	bb	1938
Dixon, John	msw	1979
Dixon, Pat	wbm	1959
Dixon, Ralph	ftb	1979, 80
Dlabik, Rob	wre	1989, 90, 91
Doane, Mickey	wtr	1983
	wcc	1982, 83
Doble, Eric	bb	1999, 2000, 01
Dobson, Bob	mgo	1947
Dobson, Virginia	wbm	1945
	wbk	1943
	wtf	1943, 45
	wvb	1944, 45
Dock, Kara	wsw	1990
Dodd, Bill	bb	1985
Dodd, Brian	bb	1988, 89
Dodd, Edna	wgo	1938
Dodd, Kyle	mbk	2000, 01
Dodd, Scott	bb	1991
Dodde, Marcia	wfh	1949
Dodds, Bob	mtr	1947, 48, 49, 50

Doery, Lynn	wtr	1977
Dolinsek, John	bb	1968, 69
Dollaghan, Tricia	wsw	1980, 81
Dombrowski, Bob	bb	1985, 86, 87, 89
Domine, Linnie	mtn	1947
Don, Cleve	bb	1949
Donat, Nancy	wcc	1981, 82
	wtr	1983
Donelan, Jeremy	msw	1995
Donithan, Monique	wtr	1978, 79
Donley, Dan	marc	1986, 87, 88, 89
Donnelly, Gary	mtn	1981
Donnelly, Sue	warc	1967, 68
Dorame, Rosie	wbm	1977, 78, 79
Doran, Ed	wre	1973
Doran, Susan	warc	1991, 92, 93
Dorch, Kevin	mtr	1981
Dorf, Rob	mcc	1989
	mtr	1988, 89, 90, 91
Dorsey, Eugene	bb	1917
Doss, Dave	mtr	1936
	box	1935, 36
Doty, Maris	wtr	1998
Doucet, Dave	mtn	1950, 51
Dougherty, Clyde	bb	1946, 48
	ftb	1942, 46
	mtr	1946
Dougherty, John	msw	1975, 76, 77
Douglas	mtr	1919
Douglas, Darcee	wsw	1981
Douglas, David	wre	1999, 2000, 01
Douglas, John	mgy	1983, 84
Douglas, Mike	wre	1996, 97
Douma, Todd	bb	1990
Douthit, Tom	mbk	1968, 69, 70
Douty, Dean	bb	1985
Dowling, Mike	msw	1999, 2000, 01
Downey, Pat	mtr	1937
Downing, Phil	bb	2000
Downs, Glenn	bb	1914, 15
Downs, Marilyn	wfh	1949
	wsb	1947, 49
	wvb	1946, 47
Downs, Tom	rif	1959, 63
Doyle, Bill	mtn	1957
Doyle, Tricia	warc	1979, 80, 81, 82
Dragon, Oscar	ftb	1969, 70, 71
Dragoo, Justin	ftb	1991, 92, 93, 95
Draheim, Tom	wre	1983, 84, 85
Drake, Joe	ftb	1957, 58, 59, 60
Drakulich, Pete	mbk	1939, 40, 41
	mgo	1939, 40, 41
Draper, Bob	msw	1959
Draper, Dick	mtn	1960, 61, 62
Drayton, Nate	mbk	1974, 75, 76
Drenth, Jenny	wtr	1999
Driggs, Blair	msw	1971, 72, 73, 74
Driggs, Judy	wvb	1967
	wgy	1966
	wsb	1967
Driggs, Stuart	msw	1971, 72
Driscoll, Connie	wgo	1969, 70, 71
Driscoll, Dave	mgy	1971, 72, 73
Driscoll, Francis Patrick	ftb	1947
Drumm, Kelly	msw	1986
Drumm, Mike	wre	1962
Drumm, Pat	wre	1962
Drury, Angie	wcc	1979
	wtr	1980
Drusys, Karen	wsw	1971
Drye, Debbie	warc	1972, 73
Dryer, Beverly	wbm	1959
Dryer, Shirlea	warc	1948, 49
	wvb	1948

Dryer, Virgie	warc	1949
Dubendorfer, Eric	wre	1996
Dubey, Nicholas	mtn	2001
DuBois, Don	mgo	1979, 80, 81
DuBois, Lois	wtn	1956, 57, 58, 59
DuBois, Ron	mbk	1997, 98, 99
Dubrul, Wayne	wre	1958
Duca, Paul	wre	1957, 58
Duca, Sam	bb	1952
	ftb	1949, 50, 51
Duckens, Mark	ftb	1987
Duckett, Elyse	wtr	1983
Ducote, Layton	mbk	1955, 56
	bb	1955
Dudek, Tom	ftb	1951
Dudley, Margaret	wvb	1948
Duerbeck, Mary	wcc	1997, 98, 99, 00
	wtr	1998, 99, 2000, 01
Duff, Jeff	mtr	1985
Duffen	mtr	1931
Duffy, Chris	bb	2001
Dugan, Mike	ftb	1982, 83
	mtr	1980, 81, 82
Duganne, Martha	wtr	1976, 77, 78
Duggar, Hester	wbk	1925
Duke, Fred	rif	1957
Duke, Jerry	rif	1953
Dukes, Kevin	bb	1978, 79, 80, 81
Dukes, Pat	bb	1980, 81, 82
Dumsch, Aaron	ftb	1998
Duncan, Clyde Jr.	mtr	1987, 88
Duncan, Donald	mtn	1941
Duncan, Jeff	bb	1999, 2000
Duncan, Tammy	wsb	1989
Dungca, Moses	mgy	1985, 86, 87
Dunhill, Jeff	mgy	1992
Dunlap, Mary	wbk	1911
Dunlop, Julie	wgy	1980
Dunn, Bill	bb	1991, 92, 93
Dunn, Dan	ftb	1964, 65, 66
Dunn, David	mtr	1997
Dunn, Fannie	wsb	1950
Dunn, Jack	ftb	1953
Dunn, James	ftb	1998, 99
Dunn, Joyce	wsb	1938
Durand, Carlita	wsw	1958
Duranovic, Mirza	mtn	2001
Durante, Joe	mgy	1991 92, 93
Durante, Michael	mgy	1991, 92, 93
Durante, Roger	mgy	1991
Dureya, Pam	wsw	1989, 90, 91, 92
Durroh, James	mtr	1980
Durso, John	mtr	1980
Dutton, John	mtr	1969
Duupis, Brenda	wgo	1982, 83
Duvall, Claude	ftb	1932, 33, 34
Dwiggins, Jeremy	marc	1990, 91, 92, 93
Dwyer, Carol	wsw	1999
Dycus, Jim	wre	1965
Dyczewski, Sue	wsw	1986, 87, 88
Dye, Mickey	warc	1984, 85, 86, 87
Dyer, Duffy	bb	1965, 66
Dyer, Frances	wgo	1939
Dyer, Ken	ftb	1965, 66, 67
	mtr	1967
Dyer, Kenneth	bb	1930, 32
Dykes, Frank	ftb	1904
Dykes, John	bb	1930, 32
Dykes, John	ftb	1903, 04, 05
Dykes, Leonard	bb	1910
Dyson, Ted	bb	1983, 84, 86, 87

Duffy Dyer played on ASU's 1965 national championship club. He later spent 13 seasons with four major league teams.

E

Each, Jake	ftb	1998, 99
Eager, Danalu	wtn	1957
Earhart, Harry	mtn	1923
	mtr	1923, 24
Earle, Shannon	wsw	1987, 88
Easley, Floyd	ftb	1986, 88
Easley, J.B.	ftb	1926
Easley, Leanne	wsb	1972, 73, 74, 75
	wvb	1974, 75
Eason, Nijrell	ftb	1999, 2000
Easter, Brian	ftb	1993
Easter, Paul	msw	1984, 85
Easter, Undrekus	mtr	1999, 2000
Eastman, Lea	wtn	1982, 83
Eaton, Bill	mtr	1951
Eaton, Bill	mtr	1970, 71, 72, 73
Eaton, Geoff	mgy	1991, 92
Ebbert, Dave	mcc	1986, 87
	mtr	1987
Eberhard, Ray	ftb	1960
Eberman, Tom	rif	1953
Echenique, Mary Agnes	wtn	1944, 45
Echeveria, Rachael	wfh	1947, 49
	wsb	1949
Eckenstein, Jane	wbk	1940
	wbm	1940
Eckermann, Jarrod	mtn	2001
Eckhardt, Doug	wre	1989, 90
Eckhart, Della	wbb	1922, 23, 25
	wbk	1923
Ecklund, Gloria	wtn	1964, 65
Economides, Steve	mgy	1976, 77, 78, 80
Economy, Agnes	wfh	1942
Edgar, "Schoolboy"	bb	1935
Edgar, Margaret	warc	1933, 34
Edge, Walter	mtr	1961, 62
Edgin, Melba	wfh	1948
	wsb	1947
Edginton, Ryan	bb	2001
Edison, Terri	wvb	1980, 81, 82
Edmiston, Sherman	mtr	1982
Edson, Karen	wtn	1970, 71
Edstrom, Mike	mbm	1992, 93
Edwards, Anthony	mtn	1993
Edwards, Bob	mbk	1967, 68, 69
Edwards, Cyril	mbk	1960
Edwards, Debbie	wbk	1979

Edwards, Ebony	wbk	1998, 99
Edwards, Irene	wsb	1940
Edwards, Lawrence	mbk	1924
Edwards, Leonard	mbk	1923, 24, 25
Edwards, Lionel	mtr	1924
Edwards, Marshall	ftb	1977, 78
Edwards, Mike	ftb	1984, 85
Edwards, Reggie	mtr	1976, 77, 78
Edwards, Trent	mbk	1988, 89
Eerkes, Heather	wsw	1993, 94
Eggeman, Pam	wgy	1979
Eggert, Sharon	wsw	1988
Egloff, Dick	ftb	1965, 66, 67
Ehasz, Norm	ftb	1976
Ehlers, Joe	mcc	1959
Ehmann, Kurt	bb	1991, 92
Ehrenkranz, Corrine	wtn	1976
Eiler, Andrea	wcc	1998, 99
	wtr	2000
Eiler, Byron	bb	1979
Eiler, Dale	bb	1976, 77, 78, 79
Eiler, Larry	bb	1976, 77, 78
Eisenhart, Jack	bb	1916
Eisenhut, Jill	wbk	1979
Eiter, Rob	wre	1986, 87
Ek, Lloyd	wre	1965, 66
Ekstrand, Don	ftb	1970, 71
Elder, Jane	warc	1952, 53
Elder, Mike	mcc	1974, 75, 76, 77
	mtr	1975, 76, 77, 78
Elderick, Jean	warc	1944
Eldridge, Lem	mtr	1962
Eley, Monroe	ftb	1970, 71
Elgin, Keith	wre	1982, 83
Elias, Karl	msw	1983, 84, 85, 86
Elias, Sergio	mtn	1994, 95, 96, 97
Elieff, Nicole	wtr	1996
Eliott, Don	mtn	1962, 63
Elko, Bill	ftb	1979
Ellenoff, Peter	marc	1985, 86, 87
Eller, Jay	mgy	1990, 91, 92, 93
Ellingson, Alma	wbk	1911
Ellingson, George	ftb	1933, 34, 35, 36
Elliott, Barbara	wtn	1951
Elliott, John	mgo	1952, 53, 54
Ellis, Alvin	mbk	1921
Ellis, Brian	mtr	1992, 93, 94, 95
Ellis, Jean	warc	1969
Ellis, Joyce	wsw	1972
Ellis, Kevin	mtr	1986

Monroe Eley scored two touchdowns as ASU capped an unbeaten 1970 football season with a 48-26 Peach Bowl victory over North Carolina.

Ellis, Nancy	wsb	1967
	wtn	1966, 67
Ellison, Kendrick	mbk	1980
Ellsberry, Ashley	wgy	2000, 01
Ellsberry, Wendy	wgy	1996, 97, 98, 99
Ellsworth, Charles	bb	1951
Ellsworth, Ed	ftb	1924, 25
Ellsworth, Faun	wvb	1925
Ellsworth, Louis	mtr	1940, 41
Ellsworth, Maurice	mtr	1940, 41
Ellsworth, Pam	wtr	1978
Elsass, Cindy	warc	1980, 81
Elsberry, V.	rif	1962
Elvin, Cathy	wvb	1979, 80
Elwonger, Stephanie	wsw	1997, 98, 99, 2000
Emerson, Gary	msw	1974
Emery, Alonzo	ftb	1971, 72, 73
	mtr	1971, 72, 73
Emmons, George	mtn	1961
Emmons, Helen	wgo	1938
Enderton, Hebert	ftb	1915
Enderton, Herbert	mbk	1915
Endres, Chris	mgo	1983
Endres, George	ftb	1971, 72, 73
Engel, Adria	wtn	2001
England, Cecil	box	1929
	ftb	1928, 29
England, Roy	mtr	1957
Engle, Gary	msw	1970
Englehart, Lynda	wbk	1979
Engler, Gail	wvb	1968
English, Kevin	mbk	1969, 70, 71
Ennis, Hugh	mbk	1929
	mtr	1928, 29
Enos, Wanda	wbk	1979
Enright, Joe	bb	1921
Ensley, Joy	wbm	1977
Ensley, Nancy	wbm	1975, 76
Entwisle, Jim	mgo	1982, 83
Entz, Marjory	wbb	1925
Erb, Susana	wtr	1978
Erhardt, Ron	ftb	1955, 56, 57, 58
Erhart, Doris	warc	1951
Erickson, Bob	mtn	1967
Erickson, Guy	mtr	1972
Erickson, Jane	wsb	1940
Erickson, Tyler	mgo	2001
Ericson, Anna	wsw	1998, 99, 2000, 01
Ericson, Duwan	msw	1977, 78, 79, 80
Ericsson, Linda	wgo	1993, 94, 95, 96
Eriksson, Magnus	msw	1991
Erlen, Christina	wsw	1987, 88, 89
Ermisch, , Karl	bb	1987
Ernster, Mark	bb	1997, 98, 99
Ervin, Paul	ftb	1974, 75, 76
Ervington, Ben	mcc	1997
	mtr	1998
Escalera, Juan	mcc	1998
	mtr	1999
Escarcega, Kathy	wsb	1984, 85, 86, 87
Escobar, Rafael	mtn	1993
Eskew, Missy	wsb	1992
Eskridge	warc	1930
Eslinger, Jim	ftb	1951
Esmay, Tim	bb	1986, 87
Espinoza	box	1929
Espinoza, George	wre	1975, 76, 77, 78
Espinoza, Joe	mgy	1985, 86, 87, 88
Espinoza, Tamara	wtr	1999, 2000
Esposito, Mike	bb	2000, 01
Esquivel, Marion	wvb	1967
Esses, Renee	wtn	1979
Essig, Clara	wbm	1940

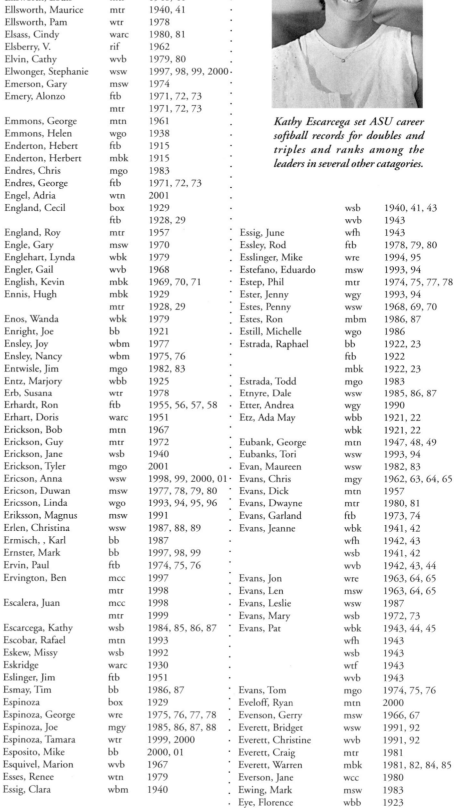

Kathy Escarcega set ASU career softball records for doubles and triples and ranks among the leaders in several other catagories.

	wsb	1940, 41, 43
	wvb	1943
Essig, June	wfh	1943
Essley, Rod	ftb	1978, 79, 80
Esslinger, Mike	wre	1994, 95
Estefano, Eduardo	msw	1993, 94
Estep, Phil	mtr	1974, 75, 77, 78
Ester, Jenny	wgy	1993, 94
Estes, Penny	wsw	1968, 69, 70
Estes, Ron	mbm	1986, 87
Estill, Michelle	wgo	1986
Estrada, Raphael	bb	1922, 23
	ftb	1922
	mbk	1922, 23
Estrada, Todd	mgo	1983
Etnyre, Dale	wsw	1985, 86, 87
Etter, Andrea	wgy	1990
Etz, Ada May	wbb	1921, 22
	wbk	1921, 22
Eubank, George	mtn	1947, 48, 49
Eubanks, Tori	wsw	1993, 94
Evan, Maureen	wsw	1982, 83
Evans, Chris	mgy	1962, 63, 64, 65
Evans, Dick	mtn	1957
Evans, Dwayne	mtr	1980, 81
Evans, Garland	ftb	1973, 74
Evans, Jeanne	wbk	1941, 42
	wfh	1942, 43
	wsb	1941, 42
	wvb	1942, 43, 44
Evans, Jon	wre	1963, 64, 65
Evans, Len	msw	1963, 64, 65
Evans, Leslie	wsw	1987
Evans, Mary	wsb	1972, 73
Evans, Pat	wbk	1943, 44, 45
	wfh	1943
	wsb	1943
	wtf	1943
	wvb	1943
Evans, Tom	mgo	1974, 75, 76
Eveloff, Ryan	mtn	2000
Evenson, Gerry	msw	1966, 67
Everett, Bridget	wsw	1991, 92
Everett, Christine	wvb	1991, 92
Everett, Craig	mtr	1981
Everett, Warren	mbk	1981, 82, 84, 85
Everson, Jane	wcc	1980
Ewing, Mark	msw	1983
Eye, Florence	wbb	1923

Ron Fair set a school single-game pass receiving record with 19 catches against Washington State in 1989.

Sun Devil offensive lineman John Folmer (1963, '64, '65) later became a top executive of El Paso's Sun Bowl.

Ford, Tom	ftb	1955, 56, 57, 58
Foreman, Johnny	mbk	1927
	mtr	1927
Forillo, Gary	bb	1980
Forler, Jim	wre	1966, 67
Forler, Pat	wre	1965
Forman, Pauline	wbk	1919
Forner, Jennifer	wsb	2000, 01
Forney, Lucas	msw	1998
Forrister, Dewey	ftb	1964, 65, 66
Forsman, Dan	mgo	1978, 79, 80, 81
Fort, John	mtn	1971
Forth, Brian	ftb	1997, 98, 99, 2000
Fortune, Carla	wsb	1996, 97
Fosdick, Carl	mgy	1963, 64, 65
Foshie, Josh	mbk	1933
Foster, Bruce	msw	1981, 82, 83, 84
Foster, Clifford	mtr	1938, 39
Foster, Gene	ftb	1962, 63, 64
Foster, Jack	bb	1914, 15
	ftb	1915
Foster, Jeffery	ftb	1994
Foster, Jerry	mtn	1947
Foster, Jim	bb	1971, 72
Foster, Patty	wsw	1959
Foster, Quinn	wre	1998, 99, 2000
Foster, Tamika	wtr	1986, 87, 88, 89
Fougner, Gerald	mcc	1990, 92
	mtr	1992
Fowler, Shane	wsw	1991, 92, 93
Fowler, Ted	bb	1954
Fox, Art	ftb	1936, 37
Fox, Ben	ftb	1999, 2000
Fox, Michael	wre	1986
Fox, Shawn	wre	1991
Foy, Ed	wre	1964
Foy, Jodie	wtr	1996
Fram, Alfred	bb	1917
	mbk	1917
Fram, Katherine	wtn	1941
Fram, Ray	mbk	1913, 14, 15
	mtr	1912, 13, 14
Francis, Clarence	mcc	1933
Francis, Melani	wbk	1993, 94
Franco, Elaine	wtn	1956
Franek, Bob	mcc	1971, 72, 73, 74
	mtr	1972, 73, 74, 75
Frank, Aaron	wre	1989, 90
Frank, Audrey	warc	1953
Frank, Bob	mgy	1971
Frank, Maureen	warc	1984, 85, 86
Frank, Noel	mbk	1960

Frankel	mtr	1941
Franken, Don	mcc	1975, 76
	mtr	1975
Franken, Laura	wtr	1985
Franklin, Ethel	wbk	1918
Franks, Mike	msw	1976, 77
Franks, Monte	ftb	1999
Franquero, Emmanual	bb	1935, 40
Fransom, Elaine	wtn	1958
Frasco, Lori	wgy	1979
Fraser, Kim	bb	1957
Fraunfelder, Herman	bb	1949
Frazier, Ben (Buttons)	ftb	1929, 30
Frazier, Bob	box	1937
Frazier, Herman	mtr	1975, 76, 77
Frazier, Ken	mtr	1983, 84
Frederick, John	msw	1958, 59
Frederick, Mildred	wfh	1938
Freedman, Mitchell	ftb	1995, 96, 97, 98
Freeland, Jim	mtr	1992
Freeland, Katie	wgy	1993, 94, 95, 96
Freeland, Sydney	mcc	1999, 2000
	mtr	2001
Freeman, Art	wre	1956
Freeman, John	mtn	1973, 74
Freeman, Larry	bb	1952
Freeman, Lee	mgy	1972
Freeman, Ron	mtr	1966, 67, 68
Freeman, Ron	mtr	1961, 62, 63
Freeman, Stephanie	wbk	1995, 96, 97, 98
Freeman, Vernon	ftb	1923
Frees, Debbie	wtn	1969, 70
Freeson, Tom	wre	1958
Freestone, Al	ftb	1924, 25, 26
Freestone, Dick	bb	1933
Freestone, Johnnie	mtr	1929
Fregosi, James	msw	1980, 81
Freire, Julio	mcc	1985, 86
	mtr	1986
Freitas, John	bb	1979
French, Allen	mgo	1956
French, Linda	wbm	1985, 86, 87
French, Marty	mbm	1981, 82, 83, 84
French, Mike	msw	1978, 79, 80
French, Paul	bb	1999
French, Russell	mgo	1956
French, Wes	wre	1987
Freney, Clay	ftb	1959, 60, 61
Frerichs Kyle	mtr	2000, 01
Fresh, Pat	ftb	1991
Frew, Jack	ftb	1935,36
Friberg, Michaela	wgo	1998, 99, 2000, 01
Frick	mtr	1931, 33
Frick, Henry Clay	ftb	1932
Frick, Matt	bb	1995
Frick, Mike	mcc	1988, 89, 90
	mtr	1988, 89, 90, 91
Fridich, Pat	ftb	1979
Fridrich, Noelle	wvb	1986, 87, 88, 89
Friedberg, Drew	bb	1998, 99, 2000, 01
Friedman, Adam	wre	1995, 96, 97, 98
Friedman, Mike	marc	1971
Friedrickson, Jo	wsw	1975, 76
Frisch, Alison	wsw	1988
Frisch, Scott	mgo	1988, 89, 90
Fritsch, Betty	wvb	1950
Fritsch, Warner	ftb	1937, 38, 39
Fritz, Larry	bb	1969
Fritzinger, Tina	wbk	1979
Froemming, Dennis	mgo	1970, 71
Frost, Barbara	wfh	1950
Frost, Nick	wre	2000
Fruhwirth, Amy	wgo	1987, 88, 89, 90
Fry, Phillips	mtn	1957

Fry, Vomen	ftb	1932, 33, 34
	mtr	1934
Frye, Barbara	wbk	1942
Frye, Don	wre	1985, 86, 87
Fuchs, Eric	msw	1987, 88, 89, 90
Fuentes, Javier	bb	1995, 96
Fuertsch, Chris	wre	1981
Fuiks, Karen	wsw	1961
Fuiks, Kelly	wgo	1977, 78, 79, 80
Fuina, David	mgo	1992
Fujii, Eri	wsw	1993
Fulcher, David	ftb	1983, 84, 85
Fulghum, Gene	bb	1938
Fullard, Cedric	mtr	1985
Fuller, Bob	ftb	1948, 49, 50
Fuller, Candace	wsw	1991, 92, 93, 94
Fuller, Dan	msw	1986, 87
Fuller, David	msw	1985, 86, 87, 88
Fuller, Larry	mbk	1951
Fuller, Orin	mbk	1922, 23
Fuller, V.	wbk	1945
	wtf	1945
	wvb	1945
Fullford, John	bb	1994, 95
Fulton, Ken	mgo	1963, 64, 66
Fulton, Skyler	fb	2000
Funicello, Jeff	wre	1990, 91, 93, 94
Funk, Glen	marc	1969
Furcini, Jim	mgy	1970, 71, 72, 73
Furrey, Meryl	mgo	1934
	bb	1932, 33, 34
	ftb	1931, 32, 33
Fusco, Carmen	wvb	1997
Futch, Tom	bb	1953, 54, 55, 56
	ftb	1955
	mbk	1953, 54, 55, 56
Fyfe, Glenn	mgy	1981
Fyneface, David	mtr	1979

G

Gaary, Jean	warc	1950, 51
Gabbert, Rose	wvb	1924
Gabbidon, Earl	ftb	1980
Gable, Glen	ftb	1994, 95, 96, 97
Gable, Tim	mgy	1977
Gablin, Dory	wtr	1977
Gabrean, Chuck	msw	1985, 86, 87, 88
Gaddis, Earl	ftb	1982, 83
Gage, Jimmy	mcc	1948
Gagich, Paul	wre	1994, 95
Gagliardi, Joe	msw	1990
Gagnon, Anne	wsw	1979, 80
Gaiowski, Lisa	wtr	1976, 77
Galabinski, Marty	mtr	1983
Galaviz, Tony	mtr	2001
Galbreath, Kevin	ftb	1990, 91, 92
Gale, Jaime	wtr	1981
Galinda, Zack	mcc	1998, 99
Galindo, Anita	warc	1950
	wsb	1951
Galindo, Zack	mtr	2000
Gall, Jennifer	wsb	1998, 99
Gallagher, Jim	mtr	1950
Gallagher, Kathy	wsw	1984
Gallagher, Mike	bb	1965, 66
Gallant, Neal	mgy	1988
Gallardo, Ed	ftb	1968, 69
Gallardo, Eddie	bb	1948, 49, 50
Gallardo, Jorge	wre	1996
Gallimore, Jeff	ftb	1983, 84, 85, 86
Gallivan, Jim	mtr	1984

Mike Gallagher pitched for the Sun Devils in 1965 and 1966, but is better known for his annual Alumni Game hijinx.

Gallivan, John — mtr — 1983
Galloway, Duane — ftb — 1981, 82
Galloway, Randy — msw — 1971
Galvin, Shannon — wsw — 1984
Gambin, Ralph — wre — 1967
Gambino, Chris — mtn — 1990, 91, 92, 93
Gamble, Alex — marc — 1982
Gamble, Fred — marc — 1969
Gamble, Suzie — wgy — 1984
Gamperle, Pete — mcc — 1983
Ganley, Phil — bb — 1952, 55
Gannon, Dianne — wsw — 1964, 65, 66
Gannon, Jim — bb — 1940
 — mtn — 1940, 41
Gannon, Maureen — wsw — 1964, 65
Gannon, Rene — wsw — 1964, 65, 66
Gannon, Richard — mtn — 1939
Gano, Ford — box — 1937
Gant, Bailey — mgo — 1990
Gant, Leon — mtr — 1966
Gapen, Kent — mtr — 1983, 84
Garbarini, Henry — ftb — 1975
Garcia, Ben — mtr — 1953, 54, 55, 56
Garcia, Ernie — ftb — 1954
Garcia, Jerry — wre — 1987, 88
Garcia, Jo — wsb — 1990
Garcia, Joe — ftb — 1940, 41
Garcia, John — mtr — 1977, 78
Garcia, Mark — mtr — 1978, 79
 — wre — 1980
Garcia, Matt — wre — 2001
Garcia, Mike — wre — 1989
Garcia, Sharette — wcc — 1989, 90, 91, 92
 — wtr — 1992, 93
Garcia, Stephen — ftb — 1998, 99
Garden, Jeff — msw — 1967
Gardner, Andy — mtr — 1994, 95, 96
Gardner, Ben — mgy — 1958
Gardner, Debbie — wsw — 1979, 80, 81, 82
Gardner, Hank — mgo — 1982, 83, 84
Gardner, Lennon — wtr — 1988, 89, 90
Gariba, Salaam — mtr — 1993
Garmon, Richard — msw — 1964, 65
Garner, Amy — wsw — 1992, 93, 94, 95
Garner, Brad — mgy — 1991
Garner, Chrisine — wbk — 1997
 — wsb — 1993
 — wvb — 1992, 93, 94, 95
Garrabrants, Steve — bb — 2001
Garre, Dee — wfh — 1950
Garrett — mtr — 1941

Garrett, Chris — ftb — 1985, 86, 87, 88
Garrison, Cliff — ftb — 1925
Garver, Mike — mbk — 1931
 — mtn — 1930, 33
Garwood, Doris — warc — 1932
Garwood, Dorothy — warc — 1932
Gasaway, Jean — wvb — 1979
Gaskell, Bob — ftb — 1963, 64
Gaskins, Ronnesia — wcc — 1995, 96
 — wtr — 1994, 95, 96
Gaspari, Greg — wre — 1981
Gatchell, Martha — wsw — 1967, 68, 69, 70
Gathings, Dave — mcc — 1971
Gaughan, Cathy — wgo — 1969, 70, 71, 72
Gaw, Suzie — wsb — 1979, 80, 81, 82
Gawlitta, Laura — wsw — 1983
Gay, Carol — wtn — 1965, 66, 67, 68
Gayle, Jacqueline — wtr — 1994, 95
Geary, Shannon — wgy — 2000
Gedman, Wayne — ftb — 1953, 54, 55, 56
Geerts, Eric — msw — 1984, 85, 86, 87
Geerts, Scott — msw — 1982, 83, 84, 85
Gehres, Bob — bb — 1950
Gehrke, Jay — bb — 1997, 98
Geiberger, Bryan — mgo — 1996
Geiger, Bryan — mtn — 1991, 92
Geiger, Meredith — wtn — 1991, 92, 93, 94
Geis, Tom — mgo — 1954
Geisendaffer, Ralph — wre — 1974
Geisler, Helen — wtr — 1988
Geist, Gary — mtr — 1973, 74, 75
Geldian, Gerry — ftb — 1973, 74, 75
Gelnett, Donna — warc — 1982, 83
Gemmill, Dave — msw — 1966, 67, 68, 69
Gennicks, Elza — ftb — 1998, 99
Gentry, Gary — bb — 1967
Gentry, Roma — wbb — 1936
 — wbk — 1934, 35, 36, 37
 — wfh — 1935
George, Merilee — wtn — 1972
Gerber, Tom — ftb — 1981, 82, 83, 84
Germaine, Maggie — wgy — 2001
Germani, Marcie — wgy — 1980, 81
Gersten, Mark — mtr — 1985, 86, 87, 88
Gervin, Gee — mbk — 1997
Geske, Neil — mgy — 1979, 80
Getty, Dorothy — wtn — 1950
Getz, Carol — wtn — 1968
Gevorkian, Tsolak — mtn — 1995, 96
Geyer, Gary — mcc — 1982, 83, 84, 85
 — mtr — 1983, 84, 85, 86
Ghaffari, Siv — wre — 1990, 91
Giacoma, Adelaide — wbk — 1941
 — wfh — 1942
 — wsb — 1941
Giacoma, Katherine — wbb — 1936
 — wbk — 1935, 36, 37, 38
 — wfh — 1935, 38
 — wsb — 1938
Giacoma, Madeline — wbk — 1934
Giacoma, Pete — ftb — 1936
Giardino, Kerry — wtn — 1997, 98, 99, 2000
Gibbons, Katie — wbk — 1940
 — wsb — 1940
Gibbons, Walter — ftb — 1946
Gibney, Frank — bb — 1948
Gibson, Charles — mgo — 1972, 73, 74, 75
Gibson, Cheryl — wsw — 1978, 79, 81, 82
Gibson, Jean — wgo — 1938
Gibson, Oscar — ftb — 1940, 41
Giebel, Elise — wtr — 1977
Gieger, Jack — ftb — 1956, 57
Gieseke, Sara — wsw — 1994, 95
Gifffin, Jeanette — wvb — 1924, 25

 — wbb — 1924, 25
 — wtn — 1924
Gifford, Jean — wbb — 1936
 — wtn — 1936
Gilardi, Theresa — wbm — 1970
Gilbert, Bob — mtn — 1953, 54
Gilbert, Cindy — warc — 1981
Gilbert, Jerry — wvb — 1950
Gilbert, L. — rif — 1962, 63
Gilbert, Parke — mtn — 1933
Gilbert, Shawn — bb — 1984
Gilbert, Ted — mbk — 1941
Gilbertson, Cris — wgo — 1966
Gilder, Bob — mgo — 1970, 71, 72, 73
Gilder, Bryan — mgo — 1994, 96, 97, 98
Gilette, Bob — wre — 1975
Gill, Bob — mgy — 1978
Gill, Christine — wsb — 1997, 98, 99
Gill, Darrell — ftb — 1976, 77, 78
Gill, Ruth — wgy — 1999
Gillaspie, Megan — wsoc — 1997, 98, 99, 2000
Gillespie, George — mtn — 1973
Gillespie, Kelly — wsw — 1981, 82, 83, 84
Gillett, Cheryl — wsw — 1984, 85
Gillette, Don — ftb — 1935, 36
Gillette, Ruth — wsb — 1938
Gillie, Pat — bb — 1976, 77
Gilligan, Helen — wsb — 1980
Gillis, Sharon — wsoc — 1996, 97
Gillmore, Ken — rif — 1957
Gillmore, Richard — mcc — 1933
Gillott, Paul — wre — 1977
Gilmore, Tracey — wsw — 1968
Giltner, Mike — mtr — 1980
Gimse, Travis — ftb — 1999
Ginter, Sue — wsw — 1979
Ginther, John — wre — 1986, 87, 88, 89
Giorgianni, Amber — wgy — 2001
Giorsetti, Angela — wgo — 1947
Giorsetti, Joe — bb — 1942
Giorsetti, John — bb — 1940
Giorsetti, Mike — bb — 1937, 37
Gipson, Mike — ftb — 1981
Girard, Jeff — mtr — 1989, 90, 91, 92
Girodo, Tara — wsoc — 1999
Gittens, Willie — ftb — 1979, 80, 81, 82
Given, David — ftb — 1978
Gladish, Erik — wre — 1999, 2000
Glasenapp, Lynn — wsw — 1980
Glasgow, Bonnie — wsw — 1979, 81, 82
Glasgow, Carla — wgo — 1965
Glass, Paul — fb — 2000
Glass, Ronda — wtn — 1981
Glass, Uumoiya — ftb — 1994
 — mtr — 1995, 96, 97
Glazebrook, Pete — bb — 1988
Gledhill, Julie — wbk — 1996, 97
Gleim, Edna — wsb — 1940, 41
Glendening, Marjorie — warc — 1935
Glenn, Bill — bb — 1918
 — mbk — 1918
Glenn, D. — marc — 1963
Glenn, Ebon — mtr — 2001
Glenn, Kirby — mbk — 1972
 — mtn — 1973
Glenn, Larry — wre — 1974
Glenn, Lillian — wbk — 1921, 22
Glenn, Sid — ftb — 1947, 48
Glick, David — bb — 1978
Glider, Rick — mtr — 1970
Glitsos, Gus — bb — 1937, 38
 — mbk — 1938
Glitz, Laura — wtn — 1986, 87, 88, 90
Glover, LeRoy — mcc — 1954

Name	Sport	Years
Gnall, Leilani	wsw	1994, 95, 96, 97
Goar, Lionel	mbk	1951
Gober, Kerwin	msw	1977, 78, 79, 80
Godbold, Geraldine	wtn	1945
Goddard, Delbert	bb	1924, 25, 26, 27
	ftb	1923, 24, 25, 26
	mbk	1924, 25, 26, 27
Goddard, Russell (Runt)	ftb	1927, 29, 30
Godfrey, Marshall	msw	1994, 95, 96
Godward, Pam	wgy	1978, 79, 80, 81
Goedecke, Lisa	wgo	1975
Goering, Sandra	wbk	1980
Goewey, Janet	wgy	1976, 77, 78
Goggin, Sara	wsw	1991, 92, 93, 94
Gold, Barb	wsw	1980, 81
Gold, Bob	mbm	1980, 81, 82
Goldberg, Rich	mbk	1989
Golden, Doris	wtn	1951
Golden, Howard	marc	1972
Goldfarb, Jeff	msw	1975
Goldman, Marilyn	wtn	1976
Goldskewitsch, Vic	mgy	1970, 71, 72, 73
Goldstein, Edward	msw	1996
Goldstein, Joel	mbm	1988, 89, 90
Golich, Dean	wre	1985
Golub, Andrew	mtn	2000
Gomez, LeRoy	wre	1974
Gomez, Raul	mtr	1940, 41, 42
Gomez, Yolanda	warc	1968
Gonia, An	wsw	1966
Gonzales, Carlos	wre	1976
Gonzales, Kathy	wbm	1975, 76
Gonzales, Maria	wbm	1976
Gonzalez, Dave	wre	1990
Gonzalez, Kelly	wre	1989, 90, 91
Gonzalez, Martin	mgy	1978, 80
Good, Sally	wtn	1976
Goodall, Steve	bb	1995
Goodfellow, Bob	ftb	1950
Gooding, Bill	mtn	1968, 69, 70
Gooding, Kristen	wsw	1997, 98
Goodman, Griffin	ftb	1999, 2000
Goodman, Joe	mbk	1946
Goodman, John	ftb	1964, 65, 66
Goodman, Scott	bb	1999
Goodman, Shannon	mtr	1987, 88
Goodrich, Annette	wcc	1979, 80
	wtr	1979, 80
Goodrich, Bert	box	1929
	mtr	1926, 27, 28, 29
Goodwin, Alverta	wbk	1921, 22
Goodwin, Garfield	bb	1934
Goodwin, Garfield	ftb	1896, 98
Goodwin, Glory	wbb	1923
	wvb	1923
Goodwin, Gordon	bb	1917, 18, 19
	fb	1919
	mbk	1917, 18, 19
	mtr	1919
Goodwin, Joe	bb	1946
Goodwin, John	bb	1923, 24
	ftb	1922, 23, 27
Goodwin, Julius	bb	1913
	mtr	1913
	mtr	1913
Goodwin, Mary Ann	wtn	1940
Goodwin, Sadie	wvb	1928
Goodwin, Sheri	wgo	1969
Goodwin, Woodrow	bb	1935
Goor, Joe	mtn	1951
Goorjian, Greg	mbk	1979
Goos, Debbie	wgo	1975
Gordon, Allen	mtn	1973

Name	Sport	Years
Gordon, Larry	ftb	1973, 74, 75
Gorlesky, Erin	wsw	2001
Gorman, Bill	bb	1959, 61, 62
Gorman, Curt	marc	1978, 79
Gorrell, Rob	bb	1991
Gosewisch, Chip	bb	1996, 97, 98, 99
Gosney, Dean	rif	1953
Gosselin, Bill	ftb	1947, 48, 49, 50
Gostele, John	mgo	1970, 71
Gottlieb, Pam	wsw	1995
Gotzian, Debbi	wgo	1975
Gould, Gloria	wgy	1977
Goulette, Fred	ftb	1914
Gowdy, Denise	wtr	1982
Gowell, Mindy	wvb	1988, 89, 90, 91
Grady, Tom	msw	1985, 86, 87, 88
Gragg, Bill	bb	1940
Graham, Don	mgo	1971, 72, 73, 74
Graham, Edna	wvb	1928
Graham, Gary	bb	1961, 62, 63
Graham, John	ftb	1946
Graham, Maryanne	wsw	1974, 75
Graham, Maurice	box	1935
	ftb	1933
Graham, Ralph	box	1935, 36
Graham, Rhett	mgo	1998
Graham, Tom	wre	1980, 83
Grainger, Carly	wsb	2000
Granat, Jim	mgo	1994
Grandstaff, Bob	bb	1984
Grangaard, Dave	bb	1967, 68
Grange, Geoff	mtn	1970, 71, 72
Grannell, Dave	ftb	1973
Grannis, Bradley	mtr	1985
Grant, Allison	wsw	1979, 80, 81, 82
Grant, Eddie	ftb	1986, 87, 88, 89
Grant, Scott	mgy	1978, 79, 80
Grant, Susie	wvb	1961
Granville, Kari	warc	1989
Granville, Kolby	marc	1993
Grasis, Gonzo	bb	2000
Graska, Dave	mgo	1965
Grasmoen, Ed	ftb	1927
	mbk	1928
	mtn	1928
	mtr	1928
Grassl, Karl	ftb	1953, 54, 55, 56
Grassl, Tom	ftb	1955, 56, 57, 58
Grattan, Dewey	mtn	1982, 83, 84
Gravatt, Michele	wsb	1986, 87, 88, 89
Graven, Kevin	ftb	1982, 83, 84
Gravender, Pam	wbk	1979
Graves, John	mtr	1979, 1980, 81, 82
Graves, Leigh	wtn	1982
Graves, Marvin	wre	1964
Gray, Bill	bb	1968
Gray, David	msw	1994
Gray, Edith	wfh	1934, 35
Gray, Fran	msw	1990
Gray, Irene	wsb	1979, 80, 81
Gray, Jim	mgy	1989
Gray, Ken	mbk	1973, 74
Gray, Richard	ftb	1969, 70, 71
Gray, Rick	mtr	1993, 94
Gray, Stuart	wre	1979
Gray, Tom	mgo	1978, 79
Graybill, Dave	bb	1982, 83, 84
Graybill, Dave	bb	1954, 55, 56, 57
	ftb	1953, 54, 55, 56
	mbk	1955, 56, 57
Greathouse, George	ftb	1957
Greaves, Cathy	wsw	1979
	wtr	1977, 78, 79, 80
Greaves, George	ftb	1978

Name	Sport	Years
Green, Bob	ftb	1953
Green, Brad	wre	1986, 89
Green, Cam	msw	1980, 81, 82
Green, Dennis	mcc	1961
Green, Gaston	mcc	1961
	mtr	1961, 62
Green, Gerald	ftb	1998, 99
Green, Jim	msw	1978
Green, John	mtn	1951
Green, Ray	ftb	1939, 40, 41
Green, Steve	wre	1977, 78
Green, Willie	ftb	1981, 83, 84
Green, Woody	ftb	1971, 72, 73
	mtr	1971, 72, 73
Greenburg, Will	mbk	1914
Greene, Duane	mtr	1995
Greene, Kelly	wtr	1981
Greene, Sean	mtr	1987, 88, 89, 90
Greenleaf, Bill	mgo	1967
Greenlee, Chris	mbk	1970
Greenlee, Jim	wre	1973
Greenup, Carla	wvb	1980, 81, 82
Greer	mtr	1941
Greer, David	wre	1963
Greer, Tiffany	wtr	2000, 01
Gregory	mtr	1938
Gregory, Don	rif	1961
Gregory, Milne	ftb	1937
Grelle, L.	mgo	1962
Gressley, Jim	wre	1986, 87, 88, 89
Gressley, Tim	wre	1991
Gretta, Jim	bb	1964, 65, 66
Greves, Richard	msw	1996
Grew, Dana	wsb	1985
Grex, David	mcc	1997, 98, 99
	mtr	1998, 99
Grey, Rick	mcc	1992, 93
Gribler, Travis	bb	1994
Grider, Buzz	ftb	1976
Gridley, Shannon	wbk	1989, 90, 91, 92
Grier, John	ftb	1984
Grieve	wre	1971
Griffee, Kim	wbk	1979, 80, 81
Griffen, Fritz	bb	1912
	mbk	1912
Griffen, Horace	bb	1912, 13, 14, 17
	mbk	1912, 13
	mtr	1913, 14
Griffin, Bill	rif	1957
Griffin, Jeff	marc	1990
Griffin, Paul	bb	1934
	mtr	1931
Griffin, Richard	ftb	1967, 68
Griffin, Toni	wtr	1976, 77
Griffith, Bill	ftb	1926, 27, 28
	mbk	1927
	mtr	1926, 27, 28, 29
Griffith, Geoff	mcc	1980
Griffith, Irene	wbb	1921, 23
	wvb	1923
Griffith, Paul	ftb	1928, 29, 30, 31
Griggs, Ed	mtr	1954, 57, 58
Grijalva, Mike	bb	1996, 97
Grimes, Edwin	mtr	1939
Grimes, Tony	mgo	1981, 82
Grimes, Victor	mgy	1983
Griner	mtr	1934
Griswold, Sean	wre	1989, 90, 91, 92
Gritzner, Fritz	mtr	1957, 58
Groff, Tom	mgy	1990
Groover, Phil	bb	1962
Groppenbacher, David	mcc	1991
Grotlish, Karen	wtn	1968

Eric Guliford ranks second on ASU's all-time pass-receiving list with 164 catches.

Groundwater, John	wre	1999, 2000
Grow, Dan	ftb	1967
Grudzinski, Alicia	wsw	1990
Gruenwald, Gretchen	warc	1950, 51, 52
Guerin, Fort	msw	1990, 91
Guinn, Jeff	ftb	1980
Guinnip, Chris	mcc	1989, 90, 91
	mtr	1990, 91, 92
Guliford, Eric	ftb	1989, 90, 91, 92
Gumpf, John	ftb	1954, 55, 56, 57
Gunderson, Gaute	mtr	1996
Gunderson, Joanne	wgo	1958, 59, 60, 61
Gunning, Tate	bb	1999
Gunthorpe, Osborne	wre	1965
Gunville, Keith	ftb	1949, 50, 51
Gura, Larry	bb	1967, 68, 69
Gurley, Dave	mgo	1969, 70
Gurney, Judy	wsw	1958, 59
Gusich, John	bb	1999, 2000
Gustafson, Roy	msw	1959
Guthrie, Harry	ftb	1927
Guthrie, Paul	ftb	1936
Gutierrez, David	wre	1998
Gutierrez, Frank	wre	1997, 98
Gutierrez, Jon	bb	2001
Gutierrez, Kalani	wtr	1989
Gutierrez, Steve	ftb	1951
Guy, Traci	wtn	1991
Guye, Gregg	mbk	1976, 77
Guzauskas, Adam	msw	1998, 99, 2000
Guzman, Dan	wre	1984
Guzsella, Karin	wbm	1977
Gyetko, Brian	mtn	1988, 89, 90, 91
Gyetko, Len	mtn	1988, 89, 90

H

Haas, Aimee	wtn	1994, 95, 96, 97
Haberman, Tom	ftb	1981
Habey, Romero	bb	1909, 10, 11
Haby, Noralea	wfh	1948, 50
Haby, Romeo	mtn	1911
Hackbarth, Kim	wbk	1987, 88, 89, 90
Hackiewicz, Becky	wsw	1992, 93, 94, 95
Hackleman, Randolph	mtr	1934
	ftb	1932, 34, 35
Hackworth, Carl	ftb	1938
Had, Allison	wcc	1996, 97

	wtr	1997
Haddad, Bruce	mtn	1993
Haddad, Camillo	mtr	1930
Haddock, Bill	bb	1947
Haddock, Bob	bb	1952
Haddock, Glenn	rif	1953
Haddock, Tom	bb	1947, 49, 50
	mbk	1949
Hadlock, John	rif	1957
Hadly, Jim	msw	1981
Hagan, John	wre	1963
Hagely, Theresa	wbk	1915, 16
Hagemeyer, Terri	warc	1976
Haggard, Darrell	mcc	1981
	mtr	1982
Haggerty, Jim	bb	1977, 78, 79
Hahn, Brent	bb	1985
Hahn, Jerry	mbk	1962
Haigler, Charles	ftb	1897, 99, 1900, 1902
Haij, Scott	bb	1995
Haines, Lew	mbk	1943
	ftb	1942
Haines, Lynn	wtn	1962, 63, 64
Hains, Angela	wsw	1999
Hakansson, Pia	wtr	1976, 77
Halack, Jenny	wvb	1987, 88, 89, 90
Halbert, Jackson	bb	1909, 10
Haldas, Lisa	wtn	1987, 88
Hale, Elizabeth	warc	1940
Hale, Lisa	wtr	1991, 92
Hale, Steve	ftb	1973
Hales, Heidi	wtr	1990, 91
Hall, Bob	marc	1968, 69
Hall, Dave	wre	1973, 74
Hall, Gary	mgy	1960, 61
Hall, Karolyn	warc	1969
Hall, Peggy	wbk	1984
Hall, Reedy	ftb	1971, 72, 73
Hall, Rick	mgy	1976, 77, 78, 79
Hall, Russell	rif	1957
Hall, Shari	warc	1953
Hall, Tom	msw	1991, 92, 93, 94
Hall, Trevor	mtr	1974, 75
Hall, Windlan	ftb	1969, 70, 71
Halland, Jon	bb	1990
Hallander, Gary	mgy	1978
Hallberg, S.	wbm	1961, 62
Hallberg, Steve	mgo	1964
Haller, Darrell	rif	1950
Haller, Linda	wgo	1969
Halligan, Lauren	wsw	1990, 91
Hallinan, Chris	mcc	1976
	mtr	1977
Hallman, Lou	ftb	1952
Halpern, Ken	mtr	1970
Halpern, Mike	msw	1969, 70
Halstead, Chuck	wre	2000
Halstead, Jim	mtn	1967, 68, 69
Halter, Susan	wsb	1972
Halverson, Dan	mcc	1954
	mtr	1954
Halvorson, Greg	bb	1996, 97, 98
Hamblin, Lamar	mtr	1941, 42
Hambly, Mabel	wvb	1923, 24
Hamburg, Jason	wre	1991
Hamilton, Brett	marc	1987, 88
Hamilton, Dennis	mbk	1964, 65, 66
Hamilton, Jill	wtn	1987, 88, 89, 90
Hamilton, Kathryn	wgo	1996, 97
Hamilton, Margaret	wbb	1925
	wvb	1925
Hamilton, Nelson	wre	1958
Hamilton, Sandra	wbk	1981, 82

Hamilton, Shawn	mcc	1969
Hamman, Betty	wtn	1955
Hammer, Betty	warc	1952
Hammer, Bill	ftb	1949, 50
Hammer, Noarne	wgy	1966
Hammeren, Eric	msw	1988
Hammergren, Tucker	bb	1988, 89, 90
Hammond, Tim	mtn	1997, 98, 99
Hammontree, Bill	mbk	1950
Hampton, Don	ftb	1960
Hampton, Elizabeth	wbm	1940
	wtn	1938, 39
Hampton, Jim	ftb	1953
Hampton, Kym	wbk	1981, 82, 83, 84
Hancock, Beulah	wsb	1947
	wfh	1947
Hancock, Carol	wtr	1976, 77
Hancock, Earle	mtn	1923
Hancock, Greg	bb	1968
Hancock, Skip	bb	1964
Handel, Kathy	wsb	1967
	wvb	1967
Handler, Gary	mgy	1980
Handley, Jack	bb	1962, 63, 64
Hanell, Chris	mgo	1994, 95, 96, 97
Haney, Jan	wtn	1967
Hangartner, John	ftb	1955, 56, 57, 58
Hanger, Irene	wsb	1940, 41
Hanigsberg, Michele	wgy	1985, 86, 88
Hanley, Paul	wre	1966
Hanlon, Chuck	marc	1983
Hanna, Don	bb	1976
Hanna, Frank	marc	1952, 53
Hanna, George	bb	1959
Hanna, Herbert	ftb	1899, 1900, 02
Hanna, I.	ftb	1916
Hanna, Lucile	wbb	1924, 25
	wbk	1924, 25
Hannifer, Ruthie	wvb	1961
Hansen, Glen	msw	1985
Hansen, Herb	mgy	1973, 74, 75, 76
Hansen, John	msw	1971, 72, 73, 74
Hansen, Ken	bb	1968, 71
Hansen, Lucille	warc	1944, 45, 46, 47
Hansen, Mike	bb	1970, 71
Hansen, Natalie	wsw	1988
Hansen, Rex	box	1935, 36
Hansen, Thomas	msw	1996
Hanson, Charles	bb	1920, 21
Hanten, Dave	mgo	1964, 65, 66, 67
Harberson, Mike	mcc	1986
	mtr	1987
Harbison, Doyle	bb	1927, 28
	ftb	1926
	mbk	1927, 28
Harbison, John	mcc	1964
Hardaway, John	mtn	1949, 50
Hardesty, George	bb	1953, 55
Hardesty, Landen	bb	1932, 34
	ftb	1930, 31, 32, 33
Hardesty, Sue	wtn	1953
Hardwicke, LeRoy	mtn	1942
Hardy, Bruce	ftb	1974, 75, 76, 77
Hardy, Steve	msw	1977, 78
Hardy, Trina	wtr	1982
Harelson, Dorothy	warc	1940, 41
Harelson, Jack	mgo	1935
	mtn	1933, 34, 35
Harelson, Jim	msw	1947
Hargitay, Violetta	wtn	1976
Hargrave, Bob	bb	1951, 52
Hargrays, Courtney	mbk	1995
Hari, Jeff	msw	1985, 86
Harkey, Betty	wtn	1954, 55

Harkin, Dave	mcc	1989, 90, 91
	mtr	1990, 91
Harkins, Leroy	mcc	1959
Harkrader, Tommy	ftb	1989, 90, 91, 92
Harlan, Stan	ftb	1942
Harman, Anita	wsw	1958
Harman, Jake	wre	1996, 97, 98
Harman, Sandy	wsb	1970
Harmer, Mike	wre	1963, 64
Harmon, Bill	bb	1936
Harper, Bill	mcc	1953, 54, 55
	mtr	1955, 56
Harper, Dale	mtr	1946
Harper, Dave	mcc	1954
	mtr	1954
Harper, Elton	ftb	1933, 34
Harper, Emery	ftb	1950, 51
Harper, John	ftb	1955
Harper, Luther	mbk	1964
Harper, Michelle	wtr	1987
Harper, Pam	wtr	1984
Harper, Sandra	wgy	1973
Harper, William	mtr	1953, 54, 55
Harrington, Doug	mtn	1957, 58, 59
Harrington, Earl	mcc	1954
	mtr	1952, 53, 54, 55
Harris, Al	ftb	1975, 76, 77, 78
Harris, Beatrice	wvb	1925
Harris, Betty	wfh	1949
	wsb	1950
Harris, Carl	msw	1966, 67
	msw	1967
Harris, Clay	mgy	1990, 91, 92
Harris, Darek	mtr	1988
Harris, Darryl	ftb	1984, 85, 86, 87
Harris, Dick	bb	1973
Harris, Dulaine	mbk	1964
Harris, Fenn	bb	1916, 18
	ftb	1915
Harris, Floyd	ftb	1964
Harris, Jack	mgy	1966, 67, 68
Harris, Jane	wgo	1985, 86
Harris, Jason	msw	1993, 94, 95, 96
Harris, Jeon	wtn	1949
Harris, John	ftb	1975, 76, 77
Harris, Kelly	wvb	1992, 93
Harris, Ken	bb	1979, 80
Harris, Mike	ftb	1977, 78
Harris, Natalie	wvb	2000
Harris, Phil	mtr	1979
Harris, Ray	msw	1968, 69
Harris, Sam	mtr	1977, 78
Harris, Scott	mgo	1971
Harris, Scott	mgo	1981, 82
Harris, Tony	bb	1986, 87
Harris, Virgie	wtn	1928
Harris, Willie	bb	1969
	mbk	1967, 68, 69
Harrison, Bob	mtr	1965, 66
Harrison, Herman	ftb	1961, 62, 63
	mtr	1961
Harrison, R.J.	bb	1973, 74, 75
Hart, Charles	mtr	1935, 36
	box	1935
Hart, Derrick	mtr	1990, 91
Hart, Mildred	wbk	1912
Hart, Tom	mgy	1979, 80, 81, 82
Harthorne, Elisa	wsoc	1996, 97
Hartin, Debbie	wsw	1977
Harting, Chris	msw	1972, 73
Hartman, Ana Lee	wbk	1919
Hartman, Paul	mgy	1978, 79, 80, 82
Hartranft, Bill	bb	1913, 14, 15

	mtn	1914
Hartsook, Ruth	wbk	1942
	wvb	1942
Hartzell, Becky	wsw	1995, 96
Harvey, Emerson	ftb	1937, 38
Harvey, Eric	ftb	1993
Harvey, Jay	mtn	1971, 72
Harvey, Stacy	ftb	1984, 85, 86, 87
Harwood, Ronnie	mtn	1933, 34, 35
Hasel, Phil	msw	1970, 71, 72
Hashimoto, Grace	wtn	1958
Haskew, Norma	wtn	1956, 57
Hassett, Eden	wcc	1984
	wtr	1985
Hastings, Weldon	bb	1937, 38
	ftb	1936, 37, 38
	mgo	1936, 37, 38, 39
Hatch, Boyd	mbk	1948, 49, 50, 51
Hatch, Genner	ftb	1926
Hatch, Merrill	ftb	1924, 25, 26
	mbk	1925, 26, 27
	mtr	1925, 26
Hatch, Quola	wtn	1957, 58
Hatch, Shaylor	ftb	1999
Hatch, Virginia	wvb	1928
Hatcher, Emma Jean	warc	1933
	wbk	1934
	wfh	1933, 34
Hatcher, Jason	msw	1996
Hatfield, Frank	mcc	1964, 65
Hathaway, Pete	rif	1957
Hatleid, Brian	msw	1996, 97, 98, 2000
Hatley, A.	mtr	1954
Hau, Jenny	wsw	1988
Hauenstein	mtr	1933
Haugland, Linda	wsw	1984, 85
Haulot, Gertrude	wbb	1921, 22
Hause, Jason	mgo	1996, 1998, 99, 2000
Havens, John	mgy	1978, 80
Haverfield, Mike	wre	1981
Haveron, Ernest	wre	1963
Hawes, Turner	ftb	1924, 25
	mtr	1926
Hawk, Tom	bb	1977, 78, 79
Hawken, Doug	mtr	1970, 71
Hawking, Kristin	wcc	1996, 97
	wtr	1997, 98
Hawkins	mtr	1936
Hawkins, Ben	ftb	1963, 64, 65
	mtr	1963, 64
Hawkins, Cheryl	wtn	1979, 80, 81, 82
Hawks, Kathy	wtn	1969, 70
Hawn, Jim	ftb	1980, 81, 82
Haws, Virgil	mbk	1945
Hayden, Dan	mgy	1985, 86, 87
Hayden, Dennis	mgy	1985, 86, 87
Hayden, N	wbm	1962
Hayden, Tim	mcc	1982, 83
	mtr	1983, 84
Hayenga, Bert	mtn	1982, 83
Hayenga, Miriam	wtn	1980
Hayes, Bessie	wbk	1918, 19
Hayes, Burt	mbk	1962, 63, 64
Hayes, Buzz	wre	1962, 63, 64, 65
Hayes, Cassie	wsb	1970, 71, 72
Hayes, Eric	wre	1984, 85
Hayes, Jon	mbk	1989
Hayes, Mark	ftb	1988, 89, 90
Hayes, Mike	mtr	1991
Hayes, Patti	wsb	1975, 76, 77, 78
	wvb	1974, 75, 76, 77
Hayhurst, Harris	mtn	1934
Haynes, Bruce	bb	1969

Ben Hawkins thrilled Sun Devil football fans with his acrobatic catches from 1963 through 1965.

Haynes, Mike	ftb	1972, 73, 74, 75
	mtr	1974, 75
Haynie, Ralph	mtr	1976, 77
Haywood, Walter	mtr	1982, 83
Hazard, Anthony	mtr	1996, 97, 98, 99
Hazel, Alvan	mtr	1947
Hazel, Nick	mgy	1990
Hazelwood, Naomi	wtn	1957
Hazen, Bill	msw	1965
Hazen, Matt	msw	1992
Head, Robbie	mbk	1951
Healy, Carrie	wvb	1978, 79
Heap, Theo	mbk	1949
Heap, Todd	ftb	1998, 99, 2000
	bkb	2000
Heap, Verl	mbk	1943, 46, 47, 48
	mtr	1946
Hearndon, Willie	mbk	1967
	mtr	1966
Heath, Carl	mbk	1947, 48, 49, 50
	mtr	1948
Heath, Jack	mbk	1959

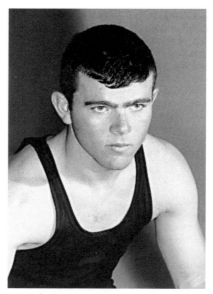

Wrestler Buzz Hayes was a three-time Western Athletic Conference champ at 147 pounds in the early 1960s.

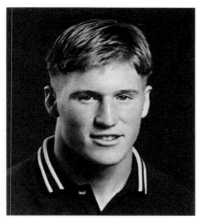

Todd Heap had three banner football seasons and mixed in some time on the hardwoods.

Heather, Mike	msw	1975, 76
Heber, Richard	mtr	1952
Heckel, Joey	wre	1994
Hedenskog, Claire	wsw	2000, 01
Heffelman, Ralph	bb	1919
	ftb	1916
Hefti, Jon	mtr	1974
Hegberg, Jeff	mtr	1990, 91
Hegi, Ernest	mtn	1961
Heiberger, Julie	wsw	1985, 86, 87
Heide, Bruce	mtr	1976, 78, 79, 80
Heidemann, Mike	bb	1994
Heiden, Dick	bb	1962, 63, 64
Heidke, Jeff	msw	1981, 82
Hein, Priscilla	wcc	1998
	wtr	1997, 98, 99
Heinemann, Keith	wre	1974
Heins, Amy	wtn	1973, 74, 75, 76
Heintzelman, Brian	bb	1998
Heiple, Jim	msw	1970
Heiple, Pat	wsw	1967, 70
Heiple, Tina	wsw	1969, 70, 71, 72
Helfand, Eric	bb	1989, 90
Helfin, Tracy	wvb	1993, 94, 95, 96
Helfrich, Jennifer	wvb	1989, 90, 91, 92
Helgen, Dick	mtn	1955
Helgeson, Grant	mtn	1979
Helig, Jim	ftb	1974, 75
Hellam, Duane	ftb	1951, 52, 53
Helland, Gregg	msw	2000, 01
Heller, Jesse	wre	1995
Heller, Rhoda	warc	1967
Helmerson, Clint	mtr	1978, 79
Helms, Pat	warc	1971
Helms, Ted	mtn	1973, 74, 75
Helsel, Byron	bb	1946
Helton, Brenda	wgy	1973
Helton, John	ftb	1966, 67, 68
Heming, Brian	mtn	1960, 61
Hemminger, Robert	ftb	1983
Henderlite, Tony	wfh	1942
Hendershot, Larry	ftb	1966
	mtr	1963, 64, 65, 66
Henderson, Alex	mcc	1957, 59
	mtr	1957, 58, 59, 60
Henderson, Dan	wre	1993
Henderson, Jim	bb	1989, 90, 91, 92
Henderson, Mike	bb	1975, 76, 77
Henderson, W.	mbk	1913
Hendrichson, Jim	msw	1970
Hendricks, Bob	ftb	1950, 52, 53

Hendricks, Don	ftb	1977, 78, 79
Hendricks, Heidi	wsw	1989, 90, 91, 92
Hendrix, Beverly	wtn	1940
Hendrix, Phil	mtr	1981
Hendrix, Rod	msw	1970, 71
Hendrix, Ross	msw	1958
Henley, Howard	mtr	1980, 81, 82, 83
Henley, Linn	wbk	1982, 83
Henne, Jan	wsw	1970, 71, 72
Hennes, Jule	ftb	1922
Henricksson, Ann	wtn	1977, 78
Henry, Bernard	ftb	1978, 79, 80, 81
Henry, Doug	bb	1983, 84, 85
Henshaw, Hascall	ftb	1938, 39, 40
Heppe, Luke	mtr	2000
Herbert, Meredith	wsw	1992, 93, 94
Herbst, Wes	mtr	1977
Herczyk, Ed	bb	1961
Herlitz, Fred	mcc	1983, 84, 85, 86
	mtr	1984, 85, 86, 87
Herman, Mark	mtr	1975, 76
Hermanson, Jon	mtn	1978, 79, 80
Hermanson, Jon	mtr	1973, 74
Hermosillo, Tanya	wsb	1995, 96, 97
Hernandez, Adrian	mtr	1994
Hernandez, Ez	mcc	1998, 99
	mtr	1999
Hernandez, Joe	ftb	1939, 40
	mtr	1940
Hernandez, Tony	mcc	1990, 91
	mtr	1991, 92, 93
Herne, Lars	mgo	1990, 91
Herrada, Mike	bb	1955
Herrera, Johnny	mtr	1942
Herreras, Angela	wcc	1995
	wtr	1996
Herrick, Nancy	wtn	1966, 67
Herring, Brad	msw	1980, 81, 82, 83
Hersh, Scott	mtr	1979, 80
Hershberg, Tim	msw	1978, 79
Hershey, George	mtr	1958, 59, 60
Hershey, Lettie	warc	1944
Hertel, Mary Ann	wtn	1954
Herty, Hal	ftb	1940, 41
Hertz, Mary	wbk	1989
	wtr	1990, 91
Hertzog, Phil	bb	1967
Herz, Bob	mcc	1964
Herzan, Tom	mgo	1977
Hess, Michelle	wgy	1997, 98, 99, 2000
Hess, Rich	wre	1966
Hess, Robert	mtr	1984, 85
Hester, Reggie	mbk	1998

Australian Alex Henderson was NCAA two-mile champion in 1959.

Doug Henry parlayed an outstanding ASU baseball career into 10 years in the major leagues with the Brewers, Mets, Giants, Astros and Royals.

Hester, Tom	mtr	1963, 64, 65
Hewett, Leslie	wtn	1980, 81, 82, 83
Hewitt, Kathy	wgo	1977, 78, 79
Hewlett, Glen	ftb	1947
Hewson, Sam	msw	1978, 79, 80, 81
Heywood	mtr	1933
Heywood, Ken	mbk	1936, 37
	mtr	1936, 37
Hezmalhalch, Bob	ftb	1930, 31
	mtr	1932
Hezmalhalch, Charles	ftb	1931, 32
Hibsman, Laura	wvb	1996, 97, 98, 99
Hickcox, Mary	wgo	1950
Hickernell, Fred	mtn	1951, 52, 53
Hickman, Debbie	wtr	1978
Hickman, John	bb	1953, 54, 55, 56
	ftb	1952, 53, 54, 55
Hickox, Mary	wtn	1928
Hicks, Ben	ftb	1896, 97
Hicks, Chrristine	wbb	1936
Hicks, Hadley	bb	1957, 58
	ftb	1956
Hicks, Mark	ftb	1980, 81, 82
Hicks, Steve	ftb	1977, 78
Hicks, Terry	mbk	1982
Hidalgo, Jaime	mgo	1987
Higgins, Brian	mcc	1987
Higgins, Gary	mbm	1971
Higgins, Ginny	wsw	1978, 79, 80, 81
Higgins, Kevin	bb	1988, 89
Higgins, Martha	wvb	1968
Higgins, Mike	mtr	1970
Highter	mbk	1955
Hightower, Davaren	ftb	1998, 99, 2000
Higley, Tom	ftb	1905
Hilbers, H.L.	mtn	1916
Hilbers, Leonard	bb	1914, 16
Hilburn, Bobby	box	1936, 37, 38
Hildebrandt, Dave	msw	1971
Hildebrandt, Mike	bb	1975, 76, 77
Hildreth, Don	ftb	1947
	mtr	1948, 49, 50, 51
Hildreth, Fen	mtn	1933, 34
Hileman, William	bb	1914
Hill	mtr	1933
Hill, Alonzo	ftb	1961, 62, 63
Hill, Bernard	mtr	1953
Hill, Bob	wre	1974
Hill, Brian	wre	1990
Hill, Bruce	ftb	1983, 84, 85, 86
Hill, Donna	wtn	1976
Hill, Donnie	bb	1981

267

Hill, Gavin	ftb	1990, 92
Hill, J.D.	bb	1968
	ftb	1967, 68, 70
	mtr	1969
Hill, Jack	mtn	1939, 40
Hill, Larry	mcc	1961
Hill, Marjorie	warc	1938
Hill, Mark	msw	2001
Hill, Seabern	mbk	1968, 69, 70
Hill, Sherilyn	wbm	1959
Hill, Wanda	wvb	1927
Hills, Christian	mgo	1993, 94
Hilton, Hillary	wvb	1968
Hinderland, Dave	mtr	1980
Hines, Brendan	bb	1997, 99, 2000
Hines, Hubert	mtr	1925
Hinks, Otto	msw	1998, 99, 2000, 01
Hinshaw, John	bb	1929
Hinton, Casey	box	1929
Hinton, Don	mgy	1980, 81, 82, 83
Hinton, Houston	ftb	1932
Hinton, John	bb	1929, 30, 31, 32
Hinton, Nell	wbb	1936
	wbk	1935
	wfh	1935
Hinton, Phyllis	wfh	1950
Hiramine, Joyce	wtn	1980
Hird, Tom	mgo	1948
Hirmer, Pete	mgo	1963
Hirose, Doris	wtn	1957, 58, 59, 60
Hirota, Joy	wgo	1967, 68
Hirsch, Harvey	marc	1952
Hitchcock, Dan	ftb	1922
Hitchcock, Valerie	wgy	1996
Hitt, Chuck	mtn	1942
Hittle, Jerry	marc	1952, 53
Hix, Bonita	wtn	1965, 66
Hixon, Missy	wsb	1999, 2000, 01
Hladki, Andy	wre	1972, 73
Hlebechuk, Jamie	wsb	1999, 2000
Hoban, Tim	ftb	1969, 70, 72
Hobart, Ann	wvb	1923
Hobart, Teddy	wsw	1958, 59
Hobbs, Charley	ftb	1973, 74
Hobert, Stan	mgo	1956, 57, 58
Hochevar, Jerry	bb	1959, 60
Hodges, Hayden	mtn	2001
Hodges, Jerry	rif	1956, 57
Hodges, Marilyn	wtn	1949, 50
Hodgson, Mark	mtr	1980
Hodgson, Wendy	wgo	1970, 71, 72, 73
Hodur, Heather	wgo	1986, 87, 88, 89
Hoeflich, Meg	wsw	1980, 81, 82, 83
Hoersch, Barb	wsb	1977
Hoffer, Scott	msw	1984, 85, 86, 87
Hoffland, Kim	wtn	1982, 84
Hoffman, Cindy	wsw	1996, 97
Hoffman, Jeff	ftb	1996, 97
Hoffman, Phil	msw	1978
Hoffman, Randy	wre	1979, 80
Hoffmeister, Bobbi	wgo	1975, 76, 77, 78
Hogan, John	ftb	1950
Hogan, Mike	bb	1982
Hogansen, Jim	ftb	1936
Hogrefe, Ken	mgy	1978, 79, 80
Hogue, Ken	mtr	1968
Hohman, Scott	mgy	1986, 87, 88, 89
Hohn, Ed	mtr	1953
Hoke, Judy	wsb	1970, 71, 72, 73
Holbrook, John	mtr	1968, 69, 70, 71
Holcomb	mtr	1927
Holcumb, Dwight	wre	1992, 93, 94
Holdeman, Nelson	bb	1928
Holden, Alice	wbm	1961

Holden, Steve	ftb	1970, 71, 72
	mtr	1970, 71, 72
Holder, Demsey	mbk	1944
Holder, Mae	wbk	1918
Holder, Scott	msw	1990
Holderbach, David	msw	1991, 92, 93, 94
Holderman, Ruth	wbk	1925
Holehan, Lee	mtr	1953, 54, 55, 56
Holiday, Shawn	mbk	1982, 83
Holland, Andre	mtr	1981
Holland, Art	wre	1968, 69
Holland, Charles	mbk	1955, 56
Holland, Dana	wre	2001
Holland, Rob	wre	1989, 90, 91
Holland, Stan	wre	1989, 91
Hollar, John	mtr	1938, 39
Hollaway, Keren	wtn	1979
Hollcraft, Tom	msw	1988
Holleran, Gina	wgy	1995, 96, 97, 98
Holliman, James	mbk	1975, 76, 77
Hollinger, Rick	msw	1967
Hollins, Lionel	mbk	1974, 75
Hollister, Allison	wtr	1977
Holliway, Eric	mbk	1984, 85, 86, 88
Holly, Carroll	mbk	1957, 58, 59
Holly, Chuck	msw	1963, 64, 65
Holly, Lenny	mbk	1996
Holman, Matt	mbk	1996
Holman, Rex	wre	1990, 91
Holmes, Cassandra	wsw	1996
Holmes, Don	mbk	1964, 65
	mcc	1962
Holmes, Mike	msw	1964
Holmes, Sandy	wvb	1961
Holmes, Seneca	wtr	2001
Holmes, Stan	bb	1979, 80, 81
Holmes, Toinette	wtr	1988, 89, 90, 91
Holmes, Tracy	wbm	1985, 86, 87, 88
Holmquist, Gene	wre	1980
Holroyd, Glen	mtn	1974, 75, 76
Holshevnikoff, Jeff	msw	1983, 84
Holt	warc	1930
	wtn	1929
Holt, Agnes	wtn	1939
Holt, Edith	wbk	1924, 25
Holt, Guy	ftb	1916
Holt, Jim	bb	1933, 34, 35
Holt, Ken	mgy	1967, 72
Holt, Rachel	wbk	1997, 98, 99, 2000
Holten, Mike	mtn	1985, 86, 87, 88
Holthus, Tom	wre	1978

Toinette Holmes earned All-America honors in 4x400-meter relay in 1988 and the 400 meters in 1990.

Holton, Ester	wbk	1934
	wfh	1933, 34, 35
Holton, Hazel	wfh	1943
	wtn	1942, 43, 44
Holtzman, Bob	rif	1959, 61, 62, 63
Holway, Mary Beth	wsw	1984
Holzworth, Teri	wtr	1983
Honchell, F.	marc	1963
Honness, Chris	wre	1978
Hons, Todd	ftb	1982, 83
Hood	mtr	1936
Hood, James	ftb	1983
Hood, Stewart	rif	1956
Hooker, Fair	ftb	1966, 67, 68
	mtr	1969
Hooks, Bryan	ftb	1988, 90, 91, 92
Hooper, Nancy	wsw	1977
Hooper, Rex	ftb	1938
Hooten, Howard	ftb	1936
Hooten, Kirk	mtr	1987, 88
Hoover, Darrell	bb	1965
	ftb	1963, 64, 65
Hoover, Don	marc	1950, 51
Hoover, Melvin	ftb	1977, 78, 79, 80
Hopkins, C.	warc	1962, 63
Hopkins, Chris	ftb	1992, 93, 94, 95
Hopkins, Lydia	wbk	1921, 22, 23
	wbb	1921, 22, 23
Hopkins, Stephanie	wtn	1966, 67
	wvb	1967, 68
Hopp, Terry	wgo	1959
	wsw	1959, 61
Hoppe, Steve	ftb	1999
Hopwood, Mike	mbk	1970, 71, 72
Hopwood, Rick	mgo	1971
Horn, Dan	mtr	1974
Horn, Robyn	warc	1984, 85, 86
Hornbeck, Ken	ftb	1966, 67, 68
Horne, Jim	mtn	1952
Horneff, Fran	mtr	1977, 78
Horner, Bob	bb	1976, 77, 78
Horner, Ed	mbk	1942, 43
Hornett, Jill	wtr	1976, 77
Horrocks, Autumn	wgy	1994
Horsley, Cyd	wsw	1972, 74, 75
Horsley, Jeff	mtr	1969
Hort, Ryan	mcc	1995
	mtr	1995, 96, 97
Hosso, Sue	wsb	1976
Houghton, Marsha	wgo	1968, 69
Houk, Laini	wsw	1990
Houle, Laura	wsb	1982, 83, 84, 85
House, Eddie	mbk	1997, 98, 99, 2000
Houseman, Shannon	wcc	1997, 98
	wtr	1998, 99
Houser, John	ftb	1972, 73, 74
Houser, Tiffany	wsw	1996, 97, 98, 99
Houston, Norine	wtr	1979
Hovelman, Bill	bb	1935, 36
Hoverson, Buzzie	ftb	1951
Howard, Bob	mbk	1962, 63
Howard, Bob	mgy	1971, 72
Howard, John	wre	1989
Howard, Jonathan	mbk	2001
Howard, Paul	mbk	1959, 60
Howard, Phil	mtr	1974
Howard-Jones, Patty	wbk	1979
Howe, Dewey	ftb	1915
Howe, Paul	msw	1987, 88, 89, 90
Howell, Chad	ftb	1999
Howell, Evla	wfh	1942
Howell, Todd	FB	2000
Hoyer, Lyda	wgo	1936
Hrovat, Dale	bb	1972, 73, 74

Hubbard, Ashley	wvb	1998, 99, 2000
Huber, Albert	ftb	1928, 29
Huber, Kenneth	ftb	1930
	mtr	1931
Huber, Pearl	wbb	1922, 23
Huber, Ray	mbk	1937
Hubert, Janet	wtr	1978
Hubley, Lawrence	ftb	1988, 89
Huckabee, Ronald	mgo	1975
Hudgens, Bill	ftb	1942
Hudgens, Dave	bb	1975, 76, 77, 78
Hudson, Barb	wsw	1977
Hudson, Debbie	wsw	1973, 74
Hudson, Greg	ftb	1973, 74
Hudson, Hugh	bb	1928, 29
Hudson, Pam	wsw	1975
Huebner, Linda	wtr	1977
Huebsch, Lynda	wsw	1977
Huedepohl, Tim	marc	1991, 92, 93
Huerta, Jim	wre	1965
Huffley, Bernard	ftb	1931
Huffmaster, Trish	wcc	1989, 90, 91
	wtr	1990, 91
Hugh, Betsi	wsw	1990, 91, 92, 93
Hughes, Betty Lou	wvb	1950
Hughes, Darryl	mtr	1974, 75, 76
Hughes, Joe	rif	1950
Hughes, John	wre	1973, 74
Hughes, Mary Fran	wbm	1985, 86, 87
Hughes, Mike	bb	1971, 72
Hughes, Pam	wgy	1973
Hughes, Paul	mbk	1956
Hughes, Ralph	wre	1965
Hughes, Susan	wsb	1976, 77
Hughes, Tom	mbk	1959, 60
Hughes, Zachary	wre	1994
Hugoboom, Cliff	ftb	1947, 48, 49, 50
Huish, Justin	marc	1993
Huish, L.	wsw	1962
Hull, Erin	wsb	1995, 96, 97, 98
Hull, Greg	mtr	1972, 73
Hullman, Dave	mbk	1970, 71, 72
Hulskamp, Tina	wgo	1968
Hummer, George	ftb	1966, 67, 68
Humphrey, Brandt	bb	1975, 76, 77
Hunnerlach, Donna	wcc	1980
	wtr	1980, 81
Hunsaker, Hal	bb	1938
	mtr	1939, 40
Hunt, "Schoolboy"	bb	1920
	mbk	1920
Hunt, Carl	wre	1956
Hunt, Chuck	bb	1966
Hunt, Elaine	wvb	1967
Hunt, Lufkin	mbk	1943
Hunt, Melanie	wgo	2001
Hunter, Broderick	mbk	1975
Hunter, Kathy	wbk	1979
Hunter, T.	rif	1963
Huntoon, Tim	mtr	1989
Hunts, Larry	rif	1953
Huppenthal, Mark	wre	1978, 79,80
Hurato, Anthony Jr.	mtr	2000
Hurbis, Jennifer	wcc	1999, 2000
	wtr	2001
Hurley, Kim	wgy	1989
Hurst, Brandi	wsb	1989, 90
Hurst, Gaynell	wbb	1921, 22
Hurst, Grady	ftb	1970, 71
Hurst, Valeda	wbb	1922
Hurt, Charles	ftb	1935
Hurtado, Anthony Jr.	mcc	1999
Hurtz, Bob	mtr	1965
Hussein, Ahmed	msw	2001

Huston, Scott	bb	1987, 88
Hutchins, Julius	ftb	1977
Hutchinson	ftb	1903
Hutchinson, Paula	wgo	1968
Hutchison, Craig	msw	1997, 98
Hutsell, Jean	wfh	1950
	wsb	1950
Hyatt, Norma Dale	wgo	1947, 48
	wsb	1947, 49
	wtn	1945, 46, 47
Hyde, Doug	wre	1991
Hyde, Merrill	bb	1962, 63, 64
Hyhus, Duke	marc	1952
Hyman, Daniel	wre	1999, 2000, 01
Hymer, Jeff	wre	1975
Hysaw, Courtney	mtr	1998
Hysong, Adra	wtr	1994, 95, 96, 97
Hysong, Nick	mtr	1991, 92, 93, 94

I

Iacovelli, Mark	wre	1978
Iani, Lou	ftb	1950, 51, 52, 53
Id-Deen, Abigi	mtr	2001
Igono, Josiah	ftb	1999, 2000
Igou, Brad	ftb	1977, 78, 79
Ikeda, Danny	bb	1960, 61, 62
Ikeda, Robin	wvb	1991, 92
Iler, Lillian	wfh	1947
Imboden, Auldric	mbk	1943
Imes, Isaas	mbk	1914
Imhauser, Ken	mgy	1990, 91, 92
Imobedn, Glenn	mtr	1948, 50
Impson, Richard	mgy	1966, 67, 68
Ingalis, Davis Everett	ftb	1947
Ingram, Allyson	wtn	1986
Ingram, Linty	bb	1987, 88
Inoue, Karine	wsoc	1997, 98, 99, 2000
Ioane, Junior	ftb	1998, 99
Irvin, Ivory	ftb	1989, 90, 91
Irvine, Ed	bb	1977, 78, 79
Irvine, John	mtr	1981, 82
Irvine, Randy	wre	1964
Irvine, Virginia	wfh	1938
Irwin, Heather	wsoc	1999
Isaac, Leslie	wsw	1972
Isaacson, Bill	mtr	1948
Isabell, Mary Jane	wsw	1959
Isacson, Ethel	wsb	1942

Pitcher Linty Ingram won 17 games for the 1988 baseball team that finished second nationally.

Isbell, M.	wsw	1962
Isham, Dave	mgy	1978, 79, 80
Isham, Steve	mgy	1972, 73, 74, 75
Isiah, Tarre	mbk	1986, 87
Iske, Patti	warc	1977, 78, 79, 80
Island, Joe	bb	1936, 37
Issaccson, Ethel	wbk	1942
	wvb	1942
Ivener, Jeramy	mbk	1999
Iverson, G.	rif	1963
Ives, Jason	msw	1995, 96
Ivy, Archie	ftb	1915, 16
Ivy, Elizabeth	wbk	1918, 19
Iwakiri, Momo	warc	1950

J

Jackel, Paul	wre	1973
Jackson, Charlotte	wtn	1955, 56, 57
Jackson, Courtney	ftb	1996, 97, 98, 99
Jackson, Dannie	mtr	1977, 78, 79, 81
Jackson, Darrell	bb	1974, 75, 76, 77
Jackson, Dwayne	bb	1979
Jackson, Fred	mgy	1955
Jackson, Gary	mbk	1973, 74, 75, 76
Jackson, Henry	bb	1948
Jackson, Jim	bb	1983
Jackson, Jim	wre	1957, 58
Jackson, J.J.	bb	2001
Jackson, John	mgo	1968, 69, 70
Jackson, Kelly	wsb	1982, 83, 84
Jackson, Lenzie	ftb	1995, 96, 97, 98
Jackson, Reggie	bb	1966
	ftb	1965
Jackson, Regina	wtr	1980, 81
Jackson, Rhonda	warc	1976
Jackson, Ricky	mtr	1981
Jackson, Ron	ftb	1959, 60
Jackson, Tami	wvb	1982
Jackson, Tyke	wcc	1995
	wtr	1993, 94, 95, 96
Jackson, Warren	wre	1963
Jacob, Su	wsw	1972
Jacob, Terry	bb	1976
Jacobs, Dick	mtr	1953
Jacobs, George	marc	1952
Jacobs, John	bb	1957, 58, 59, 60
Jacobs, John	ftb	1961, 62, 63
Jacobs, Matt	mtn	1999, 2000
Jacobs, Rich	msw	2001
Jacobson, Bob	mgo	1964
Jacobson, Christian	msw	1998, 99
Jacobson, Gary	mgo	1972, 73, 74, 75
Jacobson, Hank	bb	1952
Jacobson, Kent	bb	1970, 71, 72
Jacobson, Penny	wcc	2000
Jaeger, Winifred	wtn	1923
Jafke, Jim	mgo	1963
Jahn, Mike	wre	1966
James, B.	wtn	1963
James, Brandon	bb	1997
James, Carrie	wsb	1994, 95, 96, 97
James, Karey	wsb	1990, 91
	wsb	1991
James, Lynn	ftb	1987, 88, 89
	mtr	1988, 89, 90
Jameson, Andy	msw	1984, 85, 86, 87
Janco, Nancy	wtn	1975, 76, 77, 78
Jandro, Renee	wsw	1982
Janisse, Bobby	wre	1991
Jankans, Bart	ftb	1954, 55, 56, 57

Jankans, John	ftb	1952, 53, 54, 55
	mtr	1955, 56
Jansen, Darrell	mtr	1961, 62, 63, 64
Janssen, Cynthia	wsw	1994, 95, 96
Jantz, Chris	msw	1988, 89, 90, 91
Jantz, Chris	wgy	1991, 92, 93, 94
Jantzen, Theresa	wbk	1999, 2000
Jaqua, Jeff	mtr	1980
Jaromsak, Paul	rif	1956, 57
Jarrard, Kate	wsw	1987
Jarvis, Kathy	wcc	1987, 88, 89
	wtr	1988, 89
Jarvis, Rich	mbk	1959
Jasper, Brian	mgy	1992, 93
Jaurequi, Mike	mcc	1971
Jay, Howard	msw	1976, 77
Jean-Marie, Ivan	mtr	1995
Jeans, Gary	mcc	1975
Jedick, Josie	wsw	2000, 01
Jeffcoat, Jim	ftb	1979, 80, 81, 82
Jefferies, Jim	mgy	1960, 61
Jefferies, Ron	wre	1980
Jefferson, Jim	bb	1981, 82, 83
Jefferson, John	ftb	1974, 75, 76, 77
Jefferson, Randy	ftb	1986
Jeffrey, Chris	wsw	1993, 94, 95, 96
Jeffrey, Peter	mgy	1992
Jeffries, John	wre	1977, 78
Jeffries, Randy	wre	1974, 75
Jeffries, Tim	wre	1975, 76, 77, 78
Jeisy, Don	mtr	1958, 59, 60, 61
Jenkins, Bob	wre	1977, 78
Jenkins, Everett	ftb	1935, 36
	mbk	1936
Jenkins, Jason	mcc	1991
	mtr	1991, 92
Jenkins, Jayme	wsb	1994, 95, 96, 97
Jenkins, Ralph	ftb	1953
Jennings, Brian	ftb	1997, 98, 99
Jennings, Ivan	mgy	1954, 58, 59
Jensen, Cliff	ftb	1955
Jensen, Garrett	mcc	1999, 2000
	mtr	2000
Jensen, Nick	mtr	1999
Jensen, Paul	rif	1964
Jensen, Ray	rif	1956, 57
Jensen, Tony	wre	1970
Jepsen, Ron	mtr	1963
Jernigan, Harvey	box	1937
Jernigan, Juanima	wgo	1938
Jerome, John	mbk	1988
Jerro, Frozena	wbk	1992, 93
Jeschke, Peter	mtn	1992, 93, 94
Jewell, Ben	mcc	1951, 52
	mtr	1949, 50, 51, 52
Jiminez, Carlos	box	1933
	mcc	1929, 33
	mtr	1930, 32, 33
Jobe, Jed	wre	1998
Jobski, Jerry	mcc	1966, 67, 68, 69
	mtr	1966, 67, 68, 69
Joelson, Greg	ftb	1987, 88
Joffey, Mark	mtn	1974, 75
Joganich, Tim	msw	1982
Jogis, Chris	mbm	1984, 85, 86, 87
Johannesen, Jeff	ftb	1997, 98
Johannsen, Bill	mtr	1973, 74
Johansen, Drew	msw	1990, 91
Johansson, Camilla	wsw	1998, 99
Johansson, Per	mgo	1989, 90
John, Angelo	mcc	1967, 68, 69
John, Jerry	mbk	1955, 56, 57
Johnnson, Steve	mgy	1981, 82
Johns, Joe	mtn	1961

Johnson	mtr	1931, 32
Johnson	mtr	1936
Johnson, Alyce	wtn	1970
Johnson, Alys	wtr	1981, 82
Johnson, Alyssa	wbk	1997
	wsb	1993, 94, 95, 96
Johnson, Barbara	wsw	1969
Johnson, Blake	msw	1977, 78, 79, 80
Johnson, Bobby	ftb	1964, 65
Johnson, Bobby	ftb	1967, 68
Johnson, Brett	ftb	1986, 87
Johnson, Brett	mgo	2001
Johnson, Carl	mtr	1988, 89, 90
Johnson, Chris	mgy	1979, 80, 81
Johnson, Cindy	wsw	1974
Johnson, Don	mgo	1952
Johnson, Ellis	ftb	1923
	mtr	1923
Johnson, Erika	wtr	1996, 98, 99, 2000
Johnson, Gia	wtr	1988, 89, 90, 91
Johnson, Glenn	ftb	1941, 47
Johnson, Gordon	ftb	1914
Johnson, Herb	mtr	1979
Johnson, Hunter	mgo	1994, 95
Johnson, J.	wsw	1962
Johnson, James	bb	1949
Johnson, Jeri	wgy	1976, 77
Johnson, Jessica	wtr	2001
Johnson, Joel	msw	1973, 74
Johnson, Joey	mbk	1988
	mtr	1988
Johnson, John Henry	ftb	1952
	mtr	1953
Johnson, Karyl	wsw	2000, 01
Johnson, Kathy	wbk	1982
Johnson, Ken	ftb	1983
Johnson, Kirk	mgy	1991, 92, 93
Johnson, Kristan	wcc	1984, 85
	wtr	1985
Johnson, Kyle	mgy	1993
Johnson, Kym	wsw	1992, 93
Johnson, LaJuana	wbk	1992
Johnson, Larry	ftb	1995, 96, 97
Johnson, Latoya	wbk	1996, 97
Johnson, Leland	box	1935, 36, 38
Johnson, Melody	wbk	2000, 01
Johnson, Michael	wre	1963
Johnson, Mike	marc	1972
Johnson, Nick	bb	1942, 48
	mbk	1941, 42, 43
Johnson, Nick	ftb	1999

Gia Johnson was the 1990 national heptathlon champion and still holds the school record in that event.

Johnson, P.	wsw	1963
Johnson, Pam	warc	1969
Johnson, Richard	mbk	1996
Johnson, Rick	mtr	1973
Johnson, Rod	msw	1991
Johnson, Ron	mbk	1968, 69, 70
Johnson, Sam	ftb	1972, 73
Johnson, Scott	mgo	1994, 95, 96, 97
Johnson, Skip	mgy	1963, 64, 65, 66
Johnson, Stacey	wbk	1992, 93
Johnson, Steve	ftb	1984, 85
Johnson, Steve	msw	1985, 86
Johnson, Terence	ftb	1987, 88, 89, 90
Johnson, Tiffannie	wvb	1990, 91, 92, 93
Johnson, Tony	ftb	1986, 87, 88
Johnson, Traivon	ftb	1994, 95, 96
Johnson, Ty	bb	1997, 99, 2000, 01
Johnson, Vernon	mbk	1985, 86
Johnson, Viola	wbb	1924, 25
	wbk	1924, 25
	wtn	1924
Johnson, Wendy	wsb	1991, 92, 93, 94
Johnson, Zan	wsw	1985
Johnson-Gates, Tiffany	wvb	1994
Johnston, Bob	mgo	1965
Johnston, Bruce	msw	1969, 70, 71
Johnston, Chris	bb	1981, 82
Johnston, Dick	wre	1968, 69
Johnston, Jacqueline	wbm	1984
Johnston, Larry	wre	1966
Johnston, Tyson	mbk	2001
Johnstone, Craig	wre	1972, 73
Johnstone, Judy	wvb	1976, 77
Joliff, Tricia	wvb	1990
Jolly, Mary	wsb	1975
Jolly, Michelle	warc	1991, 92, 93
Jonassen, Gaylord	bb	1955, 56, 58
Jonatan, Solaiman	mbm	1980, 81, 82, 83
Jones, Chip	msw	1991
Jones, John	bb	1959
Jones, Alma	ftb	1902, 03, 04, 05
Jones, Anthony	ftb	1996, 97
Jones, Bernard	ftb	1986, 87
Jones, Betty	wgo	1947
Jones, Brent	mbk	1980, 82, 83
Jones, Bryan	ftb	1923, 24
Jones, Carl	mtn	1926
Jones, Charley	ftb	1956, 57
Jones, Cheyne	mcc	1999, 2000
	mtr	2000, 01
Jones, Chris	mgo	1994
Jones, D"Angelo	mbk	1998, 99
Jones, Dan	ftb	1979, 80
Jones, Dana	wtr	1988, 89, 90, 91
Jones, Darby	mtr	1969, 70, 71
Jones, Denise	wbm	1990, 91, 92, 93
Jones, Donna	wgo	1973
Jones, Earl	bb	1938
	mbk	1937, 38, 39
Jones, Ed	mtn	1923
	bb	1923, 24
Jones, Emma	wtr	1977
Jones, Evelyn	wbk	1912
Jones, Gerald "Wimpy"	mbk	1940, 41, 42
	mtr	1940, 42
Jones, Gerald	mbk	1963, 64, 65
Jones, Hank	bb	1938
	mbk	1937, 38, 39
Jones, Horace	mtr	1929, 31, 32
Jones, Jack	rif	1959
Jones, Jeremy	bb	1998
Jones, Jim	mcc	1975
Jones, Ken	bb	1978, 79, 80

Jones, Ken	ftb	1957
Jones, Kyran	ftb	1999
Jones, Lauri	wtr	1982, 83
Jones, Leon	ftb	1933, 34
	mtr	1930
Jones, Levi	ftb	1998, 99, 2000
Jones, Lisa	wbk	1987, 88, 89, 90
Jones, Louis	rif	1957
Jones, Mark	ftb	1974, 75, 76, 77
Jones, Marlon	mbk	1990
Jones, Mary Jane	wbm	1940
Jones, Matt	mgo	1999, 2000, 01
Jones, Mike	mtr	1981
Jones, Mike	wre	1991
Jones, Mindi	wgy	1991, 92, 93, 94
Jones, Mitch	bb	1999, 2000
Jones, Nolan	ftb	1958, 59, 60, 61
Jones, Olivia	wbk	1982, 83
Jones, Sam	msw	1977, 78, 79, 80
Jones, Skylar	mcc	1970, 71, 72
	mtr	1971, 72, 73
Jones, Vesta	wbb	1924
	wvb	1924, 25
Jones, Vince	mtr	1998, 99, 2000, 01
Jones, Vincent	mtr	1980
Jones, Virgil	bb	1938
Jones, Walt	mbk	1934, 35
Jones, Walter	mtr	1951, 53, 54
Jones, Waymond	mtr	1968
Jones, Wes	ftb	1926
Jones, Willie	mtr	1981, 82
Jones, Zeke	wre	1987, 88, 89, 90
Jones, Zona	wbk	1937
	wgo	1939
Jonkosky, Kristi	wtn	1988, 89, 90, 91
Jononch, Tom	ftb	1942, 43, 44, 45, 46
Jonsson, Micael	msw	1994, 95
Jordan, Billy	mbk	1982, 83, 84, 84
Jordan, Mary	warc	1980
Jordon, Jewell	wfh	1948
	warc	1948
	wvb	1948
Jorgenson, Gabe	wgo	1947
Joseph, Jeff	ftb	1984, 86, 88
Joseph, Stacy	wsw	1975, 76, 77, 78
Joshua, Roy	mbk	1978, 79
Jost, Bill	mcc	1962
	mtr	1961
Joy	mtr	1933
Joy, Sam	mtr	1954
Jozwiak, Christy	wtr	1982
Juan, Don	mgo	1964, 65
Judd, Shirley	wbk	1945
	wbm	1945, 46, 47
	wtn	1945
	wvb	1945
Judie, Adrienne	wtr	1998, 99, 2000, 01
Julian, Danielle	wgy	1982, 83
Julian, John	ftb	1954, 55
Julian, Max	ftb	1941
Julian, Tom	ftb	1969, 70
Jurgenson, Katie	wsw	2000
Jurn, Carol	warc	1971, 72, 73, 74
Jurva, Charles	mtn	1968
Justin, Paul	ftb	1987, 88, 89, 90

K

Kaaiawahia, Natalie	wtr	1984
Kaday, Todd	wre	1990

Quarterback Paul Justin (1987 through 1990) ranks fourth on ASU's all-time passing yardage and total offense lists.

Kahler, Sara	wsb	2000, 01
Kahn, Amina	wtn	1955
Kaiser, Kirstie	warc	1968, 69
Kajikawa, Bill	bb	1935, 37, 42
	ftb	1934, 35, 36
Kalastro, Mark	ftb	1937, 39, 39
	mtr	1938, 40
Kalis, Todd	ftb	1984, 85, 86, 87
Kallof, Joe	mgo	1959
Kalmbach, Al	msw	1979
Kalnins, Ed	mtr	1981
Kalof, Tom	mgy	1961
Kaloff, Joe	mgo	1960
Kalos, Tom	mgy	1961, 62
Kamaka, Ron	mtr	1984, 85
Kamakaala, Thord	mgy	1989
Kaminski, Sandy	wtn	1959
Kammerer, Pat	wtr	1977, 78
Kamp, Bill	mtr	1950, 51
Kanada, Craig	mgo	1987
Kane, Courtney	warc	1993
Kane, Jim	ftb	1966, 67, 68
Kang, Jimin	wgo	2001
Kanouse, Larry	mtr	1963
Kanter, Dave	mtn	1971, 72, 73, 74
Kaplan, Jason	mcc	1987, 88, 89, 90
	mtr	1989, 90
Kappas, Joe	mgy	1968, 69, 70
Kaput, Majorie	wtr	1976, 77
Karasek, Chris	ftb	1962
Karney, Mike	fb	2000
Karp, Jeff	mtn	1984, 85, 86, 87
Karrels, Kathryn	wtr	1993, 94, 95
Karrels, Rose	wcc	1993, 94, 95
Kartler, Bryce	bb	2000, 01
Kastner, Mark	mtr	1967
Kaszuba, Beata	wsw	1993, 94, 95
Katres, Mike	mgo	1963
Kaufman, J.	wsw	1962
Kaufman, Mary	wtr	1993
Kautz, Julie	wgy	1987
Kavgian, Bob	bb	1960, 61, 62, 63
Kavinsky, Joe	ftb	1953
Kavzlarich, Adolph	ftb	1928
Kawamura, Michael	wre	1997, 98, 99, 2000
Kazor	wre	1971
Kealy, Ryan	ftb	1997, 98, 99
Kearney, John	mbk	1994

Kearns, Doug	msw	1970, 71, 72
Keating, Bob	rif	1963
Kec, Bob	ftb	1962, 63, 64
Kee, Roland	mtn	1951
Keefner, Eric	bb	2001
Keegan, William E.	ftb	1904
Keel, Greg	mgy	1979
Keene, John	wre	1987
Keeney, Veronica	wfh	1950
Keesling, Karen	wgo	1965, 66, 67, 68
Keever, Kim	wgy	1995, 96, 97, 98
Kegans, Scott	ftb	1981, 82
Kegler, Jimmy	mtr	1992, 93
Kehrli, Marty	msw	1976, 77
Kein, Kevin	mcc	1987
	mtr	1987
Keith, Marlow	mtr	1938, 40
	mtn	1940, 41
Keith, Stan	wre	1958
Keith, William	bb	1930
	mcc	1929
Kellams, Christy	wbk	1995, 96
Kellar, John	mtr	1970
Keller, Cheri	wsb	1990, 91, 92, 93
Keller, Dale	ftb	1961, 62
Keller, Todd	wre	1999, 2000
Kellerman, Cassie	wsw	2000
Kelley, Christopher	msw	1982
Kelley, Jeff	msw	1998
Kelley, Jim	ftb	1970
Kellums, Brian	marc	1992
Kelly, Bill	mbk	1947
Kelly, Hugh	bb	1954
Kelly, Jim	wre	1968
Kelly, John	msw	1972
Kelly, Mike	bb	1989, 90, 91
Kelly, Sandy	wsw	1977
Kelly, Seanan	ftb	1998
Kelly, Tom	wre	1962
Kelly, Ty	mcc	1998, 99
	mtr	2000
Kelly, Urit	mbk	1997, 98
Kemp, Jeff	mtr	1979, 81
Kemp, Joe	bb	1986
Kemp, Phil	bb	1956, 57, 58
Kemper, Gerald	msw	1965
Kempton, Glenn	bb	1930
Kendall, Dave	ftb	1995, 96
Kendig, Wally	mtn	1961

Dale Keller endeared himself to Sun Devil football fans with his sliding catch of a two-point conversion pass with a minute to play to give ASU a 24-23 victory over Oregon State in 1961.

Larry Kentera played football for the Sun Devils from 1947-1949 and served on the coaching staff from 1966-1978.

Kendrick, Bill	ftb	1958
Kendrick, Dennis	bb	1971, 72, 73
Kenley, Dave	mtr	1952, 53
Kenly, Gladys	wtn	1955
Kennedy, Bill	mbk	1971, 72
Kennedy, Hiram	mtr	1957
Kennedy, Jim	msw	1981
Kennedy, Kittia	wgy	1978, 79, 80
Kennedy, Mike	ftb	1967, 68, 69
Kennedy, Ron	mbk	1972, 73, 74
Kennedy, Steve	bb	1961
Kenneth, Mike	bb	1973
Kenny, Phil	mgo	1974, 75
Kensenik, G.	rif	1962
Kensett, Carolyn	wtn	1972
Kent, Lew	bb	1983, 84
Kent, Robbie	bb	1995, 96
Kentera, Larry	ftb	1947, 48, 49
Kenyon, B.	rif	1962
Kenyon, Karen	wvb	1961
Keough, Tim	mcc	1975
Keplinger, Ann	wsw	1973
Keppeler, John	msw	1986, 87
Kern, Don	ftb	1982, 83
Kernaghan, Todd	mgo	1988, 89, 90, 91
Kerns, Bill	mbk	1944
Kerns, Doug	msw	1972
Kerr, Jeannette	wgo	1977, 78, 79, 80
Kerr, Ken	ftb	1956, 57, 58
Kerr, Louise	wtn	1950
Kertson, Scott	marc	1981
Keshmiri, Jamy	mtr	1992
Kessel, Lori	wsw	1982
Kessler, Collette	wtn	1977
Kessler, Holly	wtn	1982
Kettering, Carol	wtr	1978
Keyton, James	ftb	1980, 81, 82,83
Kidd, Albert	ftb	1983
Kidd, Mike	msw	1993, 94, 95, 96
Kidney, Charlotte	wbm	1952, 53
	wtn	1954
Kiefer, Karl	ftb	1957, 58, 59
	bb	1958
Kiene, Ted	mcc	1953, 54, 55
	mtr	1953, 54, 55
Kienitz, Fred	msw	1977, 78
Kienitz, Kurt	wre	1974
Kier, Judy	wgo	1959, 60
Kiernan, Joel	mbm	1987, 88, 89, 90

Kiesel, Dave	mgy	1990, 91, 92, 93
Kikut, Aski	ftb	1963
Kilburn, Erin	wsw	1993, 94, 95
Kilby, Ann	warc	1975, 76, 77
Kilby, Bruce	ftb	1970, 71, 72
Kilgo, Rusty	bb	1988, 89
Kilgore, Bea	wtn	1975
Kilgore, Marilynn	wtn	1974
Kilian, Marty	bb	1992
Killingsworth, Jean	wsb	1973, 74
Killingsworth, John R.	ftb	1946, 47
Kilpatrick, Don	mgo	1950, 51
Kilthau, Eddie	mgo	1980, 81
Kim, Mike	mgo	1998
Kimball, Will	ftb	1953, 54
Kincaid, Kacey	wtr	1998
Kincaid, Roberta	wtn	1935
Kindig, Ed	ftb	1972, 73
King, Clarence	ftb	1922
King, Doug	msw	1989, 90, 91, 92
King, Freddie	wre	1984
King, Gay	bb	1954, 55
King, Jack	rif	1961
King, Jim	msw	1966
King, Joan	wtn	1967
King, Kathy	wtn	1979, 80
King, Kaylene	wgy	1981, 82
King, LaMonte	mtr	1981, 82
King, Natalie	wsb	1988, 89
King, Nate	ftb	1981, 82, 83, 84
King, Ozzie	ftb	1946, 47
King, Richard	msw	1965
King, Stephanie	wbk	1984, 85, 86, 87
Kingsrud, Mike	mgo	1983, 84
Kinister, Buck	marc	1952
Kinkaid, Buck	wtn	1929
Kinsey, Mike	mbk	1962
Kinsley, Dawn	wcc	1984
Kinzle, Donn	mtr	1942
Kirby, Craig	mgy	1973, 74, 75, 76
Kirby, Scott	ftb	1985, 86, 87, 88
Kirby, Tim	ftb	1989, 90, 91
Kirby, Virginia	warc	1933, 34
Kirchoff, Lisa	wtr	1994
Kirk, Ian	mgy	1993
Kirkendoll, Thad	wre	1990
Kirkham, Greg	wre	1973, 74, 75
Kirkman, Larry	mtn	1983
Kirkpatrick, Gerald	mtr	1957
Kistler, Harlan	wre	1981
Kistler, Jackson	wre	1981, 82
Kistler, Lindley	wre	1981, 82
Kisto, Tracie	wvb	1986, 87, 88, 89
Kitchen, Kitch	wbk	1999, 2000
Kitterman, Katherine	wfh	1942
	wgo	1942
	wtn	1941
Kjar, Rob	mgy	1993
Kjolstad, Bente	wtn	1977, 78
Kleckner, Dave	mbk	1985, 86
Klein, Dave	mgo	1959
Klein, Emilee	wgo	1993, 94
Klein, Melvin	bb	1947
Klein, Stephanie	wgy	1991, 92, 93, 94
Klein, Sue	wvb	1968
Kleindorfer, Harry	ftb	1953, 54
Kleinman	mcc	1933
	mtr	1933
Kleinman, Heber	bb	1936
	ftb	1932, 33, 34
Kleinman, Jan	bb	1964, 65, 66
Klemonski, Dennis	mtr	1962
Klepacki, John	ftb	1963, 64
Klimchock, Luann	wtn	1989, 90, 91, 92

Kline, Margie	wsw	1970, 71
Kline, Rick	msw	1970
Klinger, Matt	mtn	1999, 2000, 01
Kloner, Amy	wcc	1996
Klusman, Aaron	bb	2001
Kluver, Lisa	wgo	1981, 82
Knappen, Tim	mtr	1971, 72
Knepper, Jeff	mgy	1979, 80, 82, 83
Knez, Brian	msw	1976
Knight, Calvin	wre	1958
Knight, Donnell	mbk	2000, 01
Knight, John	ftb	1983, 84, 85
Knight, Mark	mtr	1992, 93
Knock, Kirk	msw	1984
Knodle, Dan	wre	1977, 78
Knollmiller, Jay	mbk	1994
Knowles, Stuart	msw	1983, 84, 85, 86
Knox, Chris	wre	2000, 01
Knudsen, David	wre	1993
Knudsen, Karl	mbm	1984, 85, 86, 87
Knudson, Gary	ftb	1987, 88
Kobar, Gene	bb	1969, 70, 71
Koch, Barry	bb	1981, 82
Koch, Robert	mcc	1973
Kochanski, Allen	ftb	1984
Kochanski, Mark	ftb	1979, 80
Koech, Thomas	mtr	1991
Koeller, Katie	wsw	1992
Koelsch, Pete	mcc	1959
Koenig, Judie	wsb	1967
Koepke, Rebecca	wvb	1981, 82
Koeppen, John	mtr	1972, 73
Koeth, Joe	wre	1979, 80, 81, 82
Koethler, Steve	mbk	1989
Kohlhaus, Phaedra	wcc	1995, 96
Kohlman	mtr	1933
Kohlmeier, Chris	msw	1974, 75
Kohn, Ken	msw	1983, 84
Kohn, Michael	msw	1981, 82, 83
Kohohaus, Phaedra	wtr	1996
Kohrs, Robert	ftb	1977, 78, 79
Koisdowski, Dick	ftb	1955, 57, 57, 58
Kolb, Chuck	ftb	1963, 64
Kolb, Damien	bb	1996, 97
Kolopus, Tom	wre	1983, 84, 85
Kolstad, Lynn	warc	1969
	wsb	1970
Kolyszko, Jimmy	mbk	1992, 94, 95
Komadina, Annie	wbk	1943
	wfh	1943
	wsb	1943
	wtf	1943
	wvb	1943
Komadina, Frank	ftb	1942
Komadina, Mary	wvb	1944, 45, 46, 47
Komadina, Tony	bb	1973, 74
Kometer, Linda	wsw	1990, 91, 92
Komitzky, Amy	wcc	1987, 88, 89
	wtr	1988, 89, 90
Koning, Bill	bb	1994
Konz, Tricia	wgo	1990, 91, 92, 93
Koontz, Craig	ftb	1999, 2000
Koopman, Amy	wgy	1985
Koos, Bill	mtn	1939
Korb, Kristin	wsb	1995
Kordas, Greg	ftb	1990, 91, 92
Korsten, Bob	mtr	1942
Kortmeyer, Scott	bb	1993
Kosak, Don	mtr	1975
Koshuta, Vic	wre	1975
Kosier, Kyle	ftb	1998, 99, 2000
Kosinski, Patricia	wvb	1974
Koski, Wilbert	ftb	1946
Koss, Cathie	wcc	1985, 86

	wtr	1986, 87
Koss, Stein	ftb	1983, 84, 85, 86
Kostyk, Joe	bb	1956, 57, 58, 59
Kotilainen, Liisa	wbk	1995
Koury, Mike	wre	1969, 70, 71, 72
Kovach, Sarah	wsw	1994, 95
Kovacic, Emilio	mbk	1990
Kovalick, Mike	wre	1976, 77, 79, 80
Kovar, John	msw	1988
Kozlowski, Greg	mtr	1986
Kraemer, Brian	mtr	2000
Kraft, Katie	wfh	1948
	wgo	1948
	wtn	1948
Kraft, Michele	wtn	1982
Krahenbuhl, Tiffany	wbk	1993, 94, 95
Kraloretz, Don	mtr	1988
Kramer, Aaron	bb	1998
Kramer, Frank	ftb	1985
Kramer, Paul	bb	1942
Krantz, Andy	mtn	1980, 81
Krause, Robert	wre	1978
Kravanich, Lynn	wsw	1966, 68
Kravoletz, Don	mtr	1990
Krealy, Ryan	ftb	1997, 98, 99
Kreipl, Shanen	wsb	1992, 93, 94, 95
Kremb, Muriel	warc	1977
Kremer, Kim	wsw	1989
Kremer, Nancy	wsw	1987
Krichmen, Harold	mtn	1956
Kriehn, Jerry	mtn	1964
Krimm, Alex	msw	1996
Kristjansson, Logi	msw	1996
Krofchik, Charles	ftb	1958,59
Krofchik, Mike	ftb	1960, 61, 62
Krohn, Jeff	ftb	2000
Kromka, Tom	bb	1947, 48, 49
Kronberg, Jean	warc	1969
Kruhm, Karla	wsw	1982, 83, 84, 85
Kruljac, Eric	wre	1972
Krumme, Sarah	wcc	1983, 84, 85, 86
	wtr	1984, 85, 86
Kryjewski, Konrad	mtr	1980
Kuahi, Kani	ftb	1977, 78, 79
Kuburz, Bard	ftb	1975,76
Kuchar, Wally	mgo	1970, 71
Kucharski, Todd	mtr	1988, 89
Kudron, Roger	bb	1957, 58, 59, 60
Kuehne, Trip	mgo	1992, 93
Kuester, Alan	msw	1989, 90
Kugleman, Jeff	mtr	1995, 96, 97
Kuhles, Aaron	mbk	1919
Kuhlmey, Kathie	warc	1993
Kuklish, Scott	msw	1971, 72, 73
Kulak, Kerrie	wsoc	1996, 97, 98, 99
Kuperstein, Ken	mtn	1986, 87, 88
Kupiszewski, Steve	msw	1982, 83, 84, 85
Kurcharsky, Bill	mbk	1976, 77, 78, 79
Kurtz, Ginger	wsb	1972
Kurtz, Hal	mgy	1978
Kurtz, Harold	bb	1946
Kush, Dan	ftb	1973, 74, 75, 76
Kush, Dave	bb	1978, 79
Kush, Joe	ftb	1961, 62, 63
Kutsunai, Diane	wsw	1979
Kuyper, Tom	mbk	1980, 81, 82, 83
Kvietkus, Mike	mtr	1975
Kwasny, Rich	bb	1967
Kwiatkowski, Ladd	bb	1951, 52
Kwiatkowski, Shari	wgy	1981, 82, 83, 84
Kyle, Jason	ftb	1993, 94
Kyler, Melannie	wsb	1977, 78
Kysar, Jeff	ftb	1991, 92, 93, 94

LaBass, Eddie	ftb	1947, 48
LaBenz, Chuck	mcc	1967, 68, 69
	mtr	1967, 68, 69, 70
Lacey, Andre	ftb	1990
Lackey, Bob	ftb	1939, 40, 41
Laderer, John	msw	1984, 85, 86, 87
LaDuke, Nathan	ftb	1987, 88, 89, 90
La Fountaine, Babs	wsw	1973
Lagopatis, Panagiotis	msw	1996
LaGrow, Lerrin	bb	1968, 69
Lagunas, Luis	bb	1963, 64, 65
Laib, Megan	wtr	2000, 01
	wcc	2000
Laiho, Mika	mtr	1996, 97, 98
Laipple, Paul	mtr	1972
Lamadric, Xavier	msw	1996
LaManque, John	mtr	1983
Lambdin, Scott	mtn	1988, 89
Lambert, Chandra	wbk	1995
Lambert, Dave	mgy	1963
Lambeth, Jim	ftb	1957, 58, 59, 60
Lambson, Gail	wre	1973
Lambson, Jim	wre	1967, 68, 69, 70

Chuck LaBenz set school records for 1,500 meters and one mile in 1970 that still stand 30 years later.

Lambson, Marshall	ftb	1973
LaMena, Laura	wtr	1987, 88, 89
Land, Derrick	ftb	1991
	mtr	1992
Landa, Mark	mtr	1994, 95, 96
Lander, Cassandra	wbk	1980, 81, 82, 83
Landers, Danny	wre	2000
Landers, Tim	ftb	1988, 89, 90, 91
Landes, Winston	mtr	1970
Landis, Jean	warc	1947
Landmark, Willy	msw	1991
Landreaux, Ken	bb	1974, 75, 76
Landreth, Glenn	ftb	1937, 38
Landry, Mark	msw	1988
Landsberger, Mark	mbk	1977
Lane, Arthur	ftb	1977, 79
Lane, Cammy	wtr	1996
Lane, Carolyn	wtn	1975
Lane, Claudia	wgo	1966, 67
Lane, J.	ftb	1916
Lane, Sammie	warc	1952, 53
Lane, Shannon	wsw	1989
Lane, Temryss	wsoc	2000
Lang, Rechelle	wbk	1998, 99
Langas, Karl	msw	1980

Ken Landreaux was a first-round pick of the Angels in 1976 after batting .408 for the Sun Devils. He played 13 seasons with the Angels, Twins and Dodgers.

Lange, Michael	mbk	1966, 67
	mtr	1965
Langenhuizen, Jennifer	wsb	1998, 99, 2000
Langford, Larry	ftb	1965, 66, 67
Langley, Bill	ftb	1930
Langridge, Mike	ftb	1994, 95
Langston, Justin	ftb	1994, 95
Langston, Mike	ftb	1981, 82
Langston, Sandra	wsb	1994
Lanker, Glen	ftb	1975
Lansdorp, Stephanie	wtn	1995, 96, 97, 98
Lappalinen, Kalevi	mtr	1961
Larkin, Eric	wre	1999, 2000
Larremore, Nancy	wbm	1964
Larsen, Bob	mtn	1946, 47, 48, 49
Larsen, Marty	mgy	1992, 93
Larsen, Mindi	wvb	1995, 96, 97
Larson	mtr	1934
Larson, Doug	ftb	1986, 87, 88
Larson, Erica	wtr	1996, 97, 98
Larson, Jon	msw	1982, 83
Larson, L.J.	mgy	1973, 74, 75, 76
Larson, Mack	mbk	1948, 49
Larson, Patty	wgo	1970
Larson, Sondra	wvb	1986, 87
Larson, Terry	mtr	1975
Larson, Winston	ftb	1931, 32
LaRue	box	1933
	mtr	1932
LaSala, Leo	bb	1979, 80
LaSarge, Dan	msw	1977, 78, 79, 80
Lasher, Kurt	ftb	1989, 90, 91
Laswell, Steve	mbm	1970
Lathrop, Kit	ftb	1976, 77
Lathrop, Scott	msw	1985, 86
Latourette, Verne	mbk	1942, 43
	mtn	1942
Lattin, Dick	mcc	1961
	mtr	1961, 62
Latz, Jeff	msw	1972, 73, 74, 75
Latz, John	msw	1976
Lauderbeck, Mark	mcc	1980
Lauffer, Jake "Mugs"	bb	1924
	ftb	1923
Laughlin, Gene	marc	1953
Laughlin, Kari	wsoc	1996, 97, 98
Laurens, Caroline	wgo	1999, 2000

Laurie, Bill	wre	1964
Laursen, Carl	mtr	1951
Lautenschlager, Janae	wsw	1989, 90, 91
Lauterbach, Mark	mtr	1981
Lavario, M.	mtr	1954
Lavender, Melody	wtr	1976
Lavik, Ruth	wbm	1941
	wsb	1943
	wtn	1942, 43
Law, David	mtr	1974
Law, Dick	ftb	1949
Law, Juanita	wbb	1943
	wbk	1942
	wsb	1943
Lawler, Ellen	wsb	1976, 77
	wvb	1976
Lawler, Mike	marc	1971
Lawrence, Christa	wtr	1996
Lawrence, Duff	mgo	1956, 57, 58, 59
Lawrence, Jeff	mgo	1985, 86
Laws, Arnold	ftb	1989, 90, 91
Lawson, Larry	mcc	1971, 72, 73, 74
	mtr	1972, 73, 74, 75
Laybe, V.	mtn	1946
Lazar, Nate	msw	1988, 92
Lazor, Bobby	mbk	1998, 99
Le Mar, Debra	wsw	1973
Lea, Ron	bb	1963, 64, 65
Leach, Erin	warc	1987, 88
Leafdale, C.	warc	1962
Leak, Nola	wvb	1923
Leaman, Kelly	wsw	1992
Leaphart, Randy	ftb	1995, 96, 97, 98
Leath, Frank	mtr	1952, 53, 54
Leavitt, Jerry	wtn	1976, 77, 78, 79
Leavy, Denise	wcc	1981
	wgy	1980
	wtr	1982, 83, 84
LeBaron, T.	ftb	1928
LeBeau, Dick	mgy	1955, 57, 58, 59
	mgy	1955
LeBlanc, David	msw	1989, 90, 91, 92
Leckey, Chris	mgo	1991
Leddy, Julia	wvb	1999, 2000
Ledesma, Judy	wgo	1969
LeDonne, Dennis	mgo	1980, 81, 82, 83
Lee, Ben	mbm	1985, 86, 87, 88
Lee, Bob	ftb	1964
Lee, Bob	mcc	1947
	mtr	1947, 48, 49, 50
Lee, C.	warc	1963
Lee, David	mgo	1979, 80, 81
Lee, Eddie	mtr	1955
Lee, Gary	mtr	1988, 89
Lee, Howard	mbk	1965
Lee, Jerry	mtr	1952, 54, 55
Lee, Jewell	mtr	1955
Lee, Jim	mtr	1975
Lee, Maurice	mtr	1998, 99, 2000
Lee, Michael	ftb	1977, 78, 80
Lee, Quinn	mcc	1933
Lee, Tim	ftb	1959, 60, 61
Lee, Todd	mtn	1984, 85, 86, 87
Leebrick, Karl C.	ftb	1905
Leech, Anna	wtr	1991, 92
Leek, Rick	ftb	1969
Leeke, Harriet	wbm	1953
	wtn	1953, 54
Leeper, Debie	wbk	1980
Leeper, Jim	mtr	1992, 93
Lees, Arthur	msw	1975
Lefebre, Bob	bb	1960, 61
Lefebvre, Jim	wre	1984, 85, 86
Leffler, Ina	wtn	1961, 62

Legler, Chris	mcc	1999
Lehmberg, Mike	mcc	1978
Lehnert, Emery	rif	1950
Leigh, Heather	wtr	1999, 2000, 01
Leinheiser, Bill	bb	1969, 70
	mbk	1968, 69
Leirvaag, Beda	wsw	1984, 85, 86, 87
Leisy, Don	mgo	1982, 83, 84
Lembi, Damon	bb	1994, 95
LeMena, Laura	wcc	1986, 87
Lemke, Jennifer	wtr	1982, 83
Lemon, Jim	mgo	1990, 91
Lemons, Pascal	bb	1910, 13, 14
	mbk	1913
Leninger, Bob	wre	1972, 73
Lenstrohm, John	mtr	1980, 81, 82, 83
Lentine, Jim	bb	1973, 74
Lenz, Lori	wcc	1981
Leon, Richy	bb	1995, 96, 97, 98
Leonard, Brett	wbk	2000, 01
Leonard, Edd	mtn	1961
Leonard, John	ftb	1999
Leonard, Mike	wre	1965, 66
LePeilbet, Amy	wsoc	2000
Lerma, Bill	box	1935, 36
	mtr	1936, 37
Lerner, Ronnie	mtn	1974, 75, 76, 77
LeSieur, Marika	wgy	1987, 88, 89, 90
Leslie, Reggie	bb	1986
Less, Dan	mgy	1968, 69, 70, 71
Lessig, Mark	mtr	1980
Lester, Shirley	wbm	1949, 50, 51
Lester, Tom	mtn	1948, 50
LeSueur, Bill	mbk	1941
LeSueur, Bob	ftb	1946
LeVan, Pam	wyy	1976
Levens, Amanda	wbk	2000, 01
Lever, Lafayette "Fat"	mbk	1979, 80, 81, 82
Levi, Eugene	mbk	1940
	mtr	1940, 41
Levi, Jim	marc	1993
Levi, Walter	mbk	1942
Levie, Alex	mtn	1983, 84
Levin, David	mbm	1976
Levin, Doug	mbm	1980
Levings, Jane	wsw	1977, 78
Levins, Glenn	mtn	1980
Levy, Stuart	mtr	1952
Levy, Susan	wtn	1970
Lewin, D.J.	mgo	1998, 99
Lewis, Ahlon	mbk	1997, 98
Lewis, Ben	mgy	1983, 84
Lewis, Cary	wre	1963
Lewis, Charles	mcc	1954
Lewis, Cheryl	wtr	1978
Lewis, Emery	mbk	1988, 89, 90, 91
Lewis, Freddie	mbk	1965, 66
Lewis, Gary	mtr	1973
Lewis, Hal	wre	1964, 65
	ftb	1964
Lewis, John	rif	1950
Lewis, Mary	wfh	1938
Lewis, Richard	mtr	1962
Lewis, Robert	mcc	1973
Lewis, Sam	mbk	1947
Lewis, Sammy	ftb	1946, 47, 48
Lewis, Scott	ftb	1978, 79, 80
Lewis, Steve	marc	1979, 80, 81, 82
Lewis, Thelma	wbb	1936
Lewis, Todd	mcc	1987, 88, 89, 91
	mtr	1989, 90, 91, 92
Lewneeb, Rayma	wvb	1950
Leydecker, Randy	wre	1999, 2000

Leyva, Victor	ftb	1997, 98, 99, 2000
	mtr	1998, 2000
Liace, Rocco	wre	1986
Liano, Aurora	wfh	1935
Lichay, Lori	wbm	1988, 89, 90, 91
Lichte, Chuck	wre	1964
Lichter, Neil	msw	1990, 91
Licini, Dave	bb	1999
Liddell, James	mtr	1988, 89
Liden, Tom	mtn	1965
Liebeck, Jered	bb	2000, 01
Lieberman, Laurie	msw	1964
Lieberman, Steve	marc	1971, 72, 73, 74
Liebman, Michael	wre	1996
Liffick, Larry	mtr	1964
Liggett, Becky	warc	1985, 86, 87, 88
Light, Marilyn	warc	1982
Lightner, Elizabeth	wsw	2001
Ligon, Vernon	mgo	1941, 42
Li'i Liu	wbk	2001
Lillico, Tom	bb	1931, 32, 33, 34
	ftb	1931, 32, 33
	mbk	1932, 33, 34
Lilly, Allyson	wsw	1997, 98
Lincoln, John	mcc	1968, 69
Lind, Jack	bb	1966, 67
Lind, Susan	warc	1978, 79, 80
Lindeman, Dave	marc	1976, 77, 78
Lindenau, Wolf von	mtn	1994, 95, 96
Linder, Dawnyell	wtr	1997, 98, 99
Linder, Jennifer	wsw	1988, 89, 90
Lindner, Randy	mbk	1965, 66, 67
	bb	1965
Lindkuist, Lars	msw	1983
Lindley, Ron	mtr	1973, 74, 75
Lindner, Troy	mtr	1997, 98, 99
Lindroos, Carol	mtr	1958, 59, 60, 61
Lindsey, Casey	bb	1977, 78, 79
Lindsey, Delrik	mtr	1999
Lindsey, Frank	ftb	1942
Lindsey, Lee	wsb	1978, 79
Lindstrom, Jack	mbk	1939, 40
Linne, Paul	mgy	1986, 87, 88, 89
Linthicum, Gary	bb	1960, 61, 62
Linville, Larry	bb	1967, 68
Liptak, Pete	wre	1990
Listach, Pat	bb	1988
Lister, Alton	mbk	1979, 80, 81
Lister, Danna	wgy	1992, 93, 94, 95
Lister, Stephanie	wsw	1984, 85, 86, 87
Little, Jim	wre	1956, 57, 58
Littlefield, John	bb	1974
Littleton, Ed	bb	1959, 60, 61
Litvinoff, Larry	mtr	1968, 69, 70, 71
Livingston, Mary	wvb	1961
Livingston, Terry	ftb	1957, 58
Lizarraga, Cory	bb	1999
Lloyd, Scott	mbk	1974, 75, 76
Lobb, Sheri	wvb	1978, 79
Locher, Bill	wre	1973
Locke, Dick	ftb	1959, 60, 61
Locke, Lawrence	ftb	1952
Locke, Roger	ftb	1960, 61, 62
Lockling, Bret	ftb	1916
	bb	1916, 17, 18
	mbk	1917, 18
LoDuca, Paul	bb	1993
Loeffler, Bill	mgo	1976, 77, 78
Loera, Orlando	mtn	1939, 40, 41
Loesch, Jamie	marc	1990, 91, 92, 93
Loesch, Kathy	warc	1993
Lofton, Judy	wgo	1961
Logan, Barbara	wbm	1963
Logan, Jeff	mgy	1974, 75, 76, 77

Logvin, Eric	mtr	2000, 01
Lohmann, Tammy	wsb	1994, 95, 96, 97
Loia, Tony	ftb	1978, 79, 80, 81
Lombardi, Tony	ftb	1980, 81, 82, 84
Lomeli, Mona	wbk	1984, 85, 86, 87
Lomicky, Dave	mtn	1989, 90, 91
Long, Carolyn	wgo	1947
Long, Ed	mbk	1945, 47, 48, 49
Long, Erlinda	wcc	1991
Long, Jim	mgo	1972
Long, Louis	msw	1958
Long, Mary	wgo	1938
Long, Steve	wre	1973
Longenbaugh, Laura	wtn	1950, 51
Longham, J.	wsw	1962
Longstreth, Dave	mtr	1969
Longstreth, Don	mtr	1972
Longstreth, Paul	mcc	1964
	mtr	1965, 66, 67
Lontgton, Bill	msw	1980, 81
Lootens, Brian	bb	1992, 93
Lopez, Eli	mbk	1994, 95
Lopez, George	bb	1983, 84, 85
Lopez, Henry	ftb	1904
Lopez, Jimmy	wre	1999, 2000
Lopez, Joel	wre	1991
Lopez, Lucy	wsw	1984, 85
Lopez, Mike	bb	2000, 01
Lopez, Pete	mtr	2000, 01
Lopker, Brian	ftb	1983, 84
Loraine, Christian Rene	mtr	2001
Loraine, Rene	mtr	1997
Lorenz, Elise	wsoc	1999
Lorenzen, Chris	ftb	1974, 75
Lorick, Tony	ftb	1961, 62, 63
Lorona, Bob	bb	1948, 49, 50, 51
Lorrenz, Erica	wsw	1989
LoSasso, Angie	wsb	1983, 84, 85, 86
Lothe, Tim	wre	1980
Lott, Mady	wvb	1923
Lott, Pat	msw	1965, 66
Lou, Ron	ftb	1970, 71, 72
Loughran, Mike	mbk	1952, 53, 54
Loustalot, Mike	mgo	1983, 84
Lovas, Lee	ftb	1953
Love, Becky	wsw	1971, 72
Love, Sharon	wgo	1958
Lovelace, Ed	mtr	1988, 89, 90, 91
Lovell, Allison	wsw	1995

Lovell, Bobbie	wgo	1958
Lovett, Jerry	bb	1952
Lovett, Mark	ftb	1974, 75, 76
Lovflad, Mike	msw	1984, 85
Lovrich, Pete	bb	1962
Lowe, Jennifer	wsw	1999, 2000, 01
Lowe, Obie	ftb	1966
Lowe, Rameeka	wbk	1994, 96, 97, 98
Lowe, Sean	bb	1992
Lowell, Mary	wgo	1963, 64, 65
Lowery, Phill	bb	1996, 97, 98
Lozier, Karen	wvb	1961
Lubach, Harry	ftb	1948, 49
Lucas, Dan	ftb	1993, 94
Lucas, Martha	wbk	1941
	wsw	1941
Lucero, Jennifer	wvb	1995, 96, 97
Luckett, Lucien	ftb	1941
Luckie, Jackie	warc	1951, 52
Lucy, Frank	bb	1975, 76
Ludden, Bill	ftb	1938, 39
Lueck, Bill	ftb	1963, 64, 65
Lujan, Ramiro	bb	1961
Lukin, Harold	bb	1922, 23
Lumpkin, Joey	ftb	1978, 79, 80
Lumpkin, Ron	ftb	1970, 71, 72
Lund, Kathy	wvb	1961
Lund, Phil	mtr	1965
Lundgaard, Tom	msw	1976, 77, 78, 79
Lundie, Jim	ftb	1954, 55
Lundin, Therese	wsw	1989, 90, 91, 92
Lundstrom, Stefan	mbm	1993
Lunebring, Herman	ftb	1934
	mbk	1935
Lunn, Phil	mcc	1964
Lupton, Kari	wsw	1989
Lusher, Lyle	bb	1933, 35, 36
	ftb	1932, 33, 34
Luth, Leroy	mbk	1967
Luthcke, Bob	ftb	1952, 53, 54
Luther, Jim	mgy	1985
Luxa, Frank	mcc	1957
Lybring, Anders	msw	2000, 01
Lyddon, Fred	bb	1959
Lyen, Carol	warc	1962
Lyford, Ted	mgo	1963, 64, 65
Lyght, Trent	msw	1978, 79, 80, 81
Lyman, Cathy	wsw	1964
Lynch, Debbie	wvb	1985, 86, 87, 88
Lynch, John	bb	1908, 09, 10
Lynch, Patrick	wre	1992, 93, 94, 95
Lynn, Brad	ftb	1942
Lyon, Lisa	wvb	1978, 79
Lyons, Joe	msw	1991, 92
Lysgaard, Jim	bb	1975
Lyttle, Patrick	msw	1998
Lzene, Attila	msw	2000

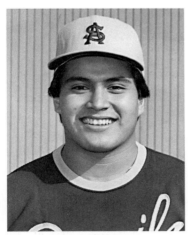

Third baseman George Lopez starred on ASU's 1984 Pac-10 Southern Division championship club and batted .379 the following season.

M

Maas, John	mcc	1977, 79
	mtr	1978, 79
Mabry, Don	wre	1983
Mabry, Syl	bb	1959
MacArthur, Paul	wre	1968
Macchiaroli, Tony	wre	1978
MacDonald, Kelly	wcc	1997, 98, 99
	wtr	1998, 99, 2000, 01
MacDonald, Sally	wsw	1999
MacDonald, Simon	msw	1999, 2000, 01
MacDougal, Tom	bb	1963, 64

MacGillivaray, Kevin	wre	1978
Machado, Rebecca	wsw	1998
Machin, Lisa	wgy	1979
Maciasek, Amy	wcc	1997, 98, 99
	wtr	1998, 99, 2000
Mack, Dudley	bb	1953
Mack, Lindsey	wsoc	1999, 2000
MacKay	mtn	1994
MacKay, Wade	mtr	1982
Mackey, Charlie	ftb	1953, 54, 55, 56
Mackey, Dick	ftb	1951, 52, 53, 54
Mackey, Jeff	mbk	1967, 68, 69
Mackey, Tim	mtr	1986, 87
Mackie, Dan	ftb	1979, 80, 81
MacLennon, Kenneth	ftb	1914, 15
MacMullin, John	msw	1971
MacWilliam, Don	mgy	1980, 81
Madden, Dan	ftb	1982, 83, 84
Madden, Tom	wre	1985
Maddox, Frank	ftb	2000
Maddox, Jerry	bb	1974, 75
Maddy, Jack	bb	1949, 50
Maddy, Rex	bb	1951
Madison, Spencer	bb	1946
Madow, Ronald	wre	1972
Madrid, Michelle	wsb	1990
Madrid, Tanis	bb	1951, 52, 53
Madril, Ruben	bb	1953
	ftb	1953, 54
Maeser, LaPrele	wbb	1923, 24
Magazzeni, Tom	ftb	1983, 84
Maggi, Bob	bb	1966
Maglich, Karen	wsw	1963, 64
	wvb	1961
Magner, Jerry	msw	1981
Mahasse, Cornelius	mtr	1996
Maher, Dan	mcc	1999, 2000
	mtr	2001
Mahl, Lisa	wsb	1987
Mahlstede, Jeff	ftb	1987, 88
Mahoney, Wilma	wbk	1915
Maier, Jeff	ftb	1991
Maier, Lewis	ftb	1914, 15, 16
Maile, Jon	wre	1977, 78, 80
Mailey, Avis	wtr	1976, 77, 78
Majeski, Joe	bb	1986
Majewski, Claudio	msw	1988, 89, 91
Makatura, Buddy	msw	1982
Malanify, Jeff	msw	1978, 79, 80
Malatesta, Patricia	wsw	1999, 2000, 01
Malchak, Michael	msw	1999
Maldanado, Barbara	wbm	1964
Malde, Sanjay	mbm	1984, 85, 86, 87
Malin, Doug	msw	1970
Malone, Art	ftb	1967, 68, 69
Malone, Ben	ftb	1971, 72, 73
Malone, Eddy	bb	1977, 78
Malone, James	ftb	1983
Malone, Maicel	wtr	1989, 90, 91, 92
Malone, Mark	ftb	1977, 78, 79
	mtr	1977
Maloney, Kerry	wsb	1995, 96
Maloney, Mike	ftb	1979, 80
Maltby, Greg	mgy	1981, 82, 83, 84
Manahan, Anthony	bb	1988, 89, 90
Mancuso, Jim	bb	1995
Mandarino, Larry	mtr	1969, 70
Manders, Mark	mgy	1977, 78
Mangili, Paul	msw	1985, 86, 87, 88
Mangini, Rob	mgo	1990, 91, 92, 93
Manha, John	mbm	1989
Manhertz, Sydney	mtr	1974
Manierre, B.	wsw	1963
Manley, John	mtr	1972

Mann, Bennie	bb	1947
Mann, Rich	mtr	1972
Mann, Richard	ftb	1966, 67, 68
Mann, Shari	wgy	1984, 85, 86, 87
Mannelly, Brian	mtr	1992, 93
Manning, Ed	bb	1948, 49
Manning, Jim	mgy	1961
Manning, Ray	mtr	1972, 73
Manning, Ronald	ftb	1952
Mansfield, Ann	wtn	1968
Mansfield, Mark	wre	1987, 88, 89
Mansperger, Dick	ftb	1956, 57
Manthey, Nick	mgo	2001
Mantlo, Jerry	bb	1970, 71, 72
Mants, Riley	wsw	1999, 2000, 01
Manville, Dick	mgy	1958
Manville, Don	mgy	1958, 59
Manville, Tammy	wgy	1978
Manzello, Joseph	wre	1998
Manzo, Isidoro	mgy	1983, 84, 85
Maran, Beth	wtn	1983, 84
Marble, Paul	msw	1973
Marcaccio, Gustavo	mtn	1997, 98, 99
Marcotte, Bill	msw	1980, 81, 82
Marcus, Fred	bb	1946
Mariani, Mike	mtr	1982, 83
Marich, George	bb	1936, 37, 38
	ftb	1937
Marich, Martin	ftb	1940, 41
Marietta, Ron	bb	1996, 97
Marin, Ben	mcc	1959
	mtr	1958
Marino, Ray	bb	1948, 49, 50, 51
Mariucci, Steve	bb	1986, 87
Marjanovic, Antoinette	wsoc	1997, 98, 99, 2000
Markham, Mike	mtr	1966, 67
Markichevich, Mark	ftb	1947, 48, 49, 50
Markland, Amanda	wcc	1997, 98, 99
	wtr	1998, 99
Marks, Terry	mtr	1978
Marley, Rena	wbk	1916, 17, 18, 19
Marmie, Larry Jr.	ftb	1989, 90, 91
Marquez, Alfred	bb	1946
Marquez, Art	bb	1952
Marquez, Monica	wcc	1986, 87
	wtr	1987, 88
Marrs, Bob	mgo	1934
Marsh, Chester	mbk	1921
Marsh, Stan	bb	1950
Marshall, Mike	wre	2000, 01
Marshall, Verling	ftb	1926
Marsiglia, Paula	wsw	1994
Martens, Rudy	mtr	1933
	ftb	1932
Martin, Alice	wtn	1924
Martin, Benny	mcc	1956
Martin, Beth	wcc	1999, 2000
	wtr	2000, 01
Martin, Bill	mtr	1946
Martin, Catherine	wbm	1942
Martin, Cliff	bb	1968
Martin, Corey	msw	1997, 98
Martin, Dave	mgy	1978, 79
Martin, Davie	wre	1981
Martin, Dawn	wtn	1992, 93
Martin, Frederico	msw	2001
Martin, Jason	bb	1985
Martin, Jason	ftb	1990
Martin, Jesse	marc	1967, 68, 69
Martin, Jonah	bb	2000, 01
Martin, Ken	bb	1953
Martin, Kevin	mgo	1970
Martin, Larry	bb	1965, 66
Martin, Lisa	wsb	1985

Martin, Michael	ftb	1995, 96, 97
Martin, Michelle	wtn	1997
Martin, Sean	mtr	1986
Martin, Steve	bb	1989
	ftb	1988
Martinelli, Raymond	mgy	1981
Martinez, Bert	bb	1980, 81, 82, 83
Martinez, Mike	ftb	1974, 75, 76
Martinez, Moses	mgy	1989, 90
Martinez, Nachie	wsw	1982, 83, 84, 85
Martinez, Ray	bb	1959
Martinez, Sandy	warc	1978, 79, 80, 81
Martinez, Tiff	ftb	1923, 33
	mcc	1933
	mtr	1931, 32, 33, 34
Martinez, Walter	bb	1953, 55, 56
Marting, Dan	mtn	1988, 89, 90, 91
Martoccia, Chip	msw	1984, 85, 86
Martori, Art	wre	1963
Martori, Jill	wsw	1989
Martz, Troy	ftb	1992, 93, 94
Masaniai, Danny	fb	2000
Maskrey, Kris	warc	1988, 89, 90, 91
Mason, Alton	mbk	1999, 2000, 01
Mason, Bruce	mgy	1978, 79, 80, 81
Mason, Kathy	warc	1988, 89
Mason, Kevin	mtn	1979, 83
Mason, Mike	mcc	1978
	mtr	1979, 80
	mtr	1980
Mason, Olin	ftb	1939, 40
Mason, Pat	ftb	1989
Mason, Russ	mcc	1978, 79
	mtr	1977, 78, 79
Mason, Terry	mtr	1978
Massa, Julie	wgo	1983, 84, 85, 86
Massarand, Bill	bb	1967, 68, 69
Masson, Cali	wcc	1991
	wtr	1992, 93
Masson, Christie	wcc	1992, 93, 94, 95
	wtr	1992, 93, 94, 95
Mastaler, Rudy	bb	1946
Masterson, John	mtr	1973, 74, 75
Masterson, Vaughn	mtr	1984
Mataali, Rocky	ftb	1974, 75
Matesic, Andy	ftb	1951
Mathers, Mike	wre	1988
Mathers, Rob	wre	1987, 88

*In 1997, Antoinette Marjanovic
became the first ASU soccer player to
earn All-Pac-10 honors.*

Matheson, Ross	mtn	1991, 92
Mathews, Kim	wcc	1986, 87
	wtr	1987
Mathis, Bernard	mtr	1984, 85, 86, 87
Mathis, Kathy	wsw	1970, 71
Matlock, Steve	ftb	1971, 72
Matlock, Tamika	wbk	1994
Matranga, Jeff	bb	1992
Matsik, Mike	bb	1961
Matsumoto, Jane	warc	1969
Matsumoto, Tyrus	bb	1999
Mattern, Jerry	msw	1975, 76
Mattes, Tracy	wtr	1992
Matteson, Tom	mtr	1950, 51
Matthews, Calvin	mgo	1996, 97
Matthews, Harold	mtr	1971
Matthews, Jerry	mbk	1959
Mattia, Tony	bb	1987
Mattice, Kathy	wvb	1967, 68
Mattingly, Mark	mgo	1977, 78, 79
Mattingly, Robyn	wvb	1998, 99
Mattson, Kirstin	wvb	1993, 94, 96, 97
Mattson, Rob	bb	1988, 89
Maucieri, Nick	ftb	1951, 52, 53
Mauck, Ed	ftb	1963, 64
Maupin, Kerry	wgo	1967
Maurer, Leslie	wsw	1980, 81, 82
Mauro, Florence	wsw	2001
Max, Warren	mtr	1930
Maxwell, Vernon	ftb	1979, 80, 81, 82
May, Stephanie	wsb	1987, 88, 89, 90
Mayberry, Germaine	bb	1992
Mayberry, Keith	mtr	1951
Mayer, Barb	wsw	1974
Mayfair, Bill	mgo	1985, 86, 87, 88
Mayfield, Deon	mtr	1981, 82, 83, 84
Maynard, Mike	mcc	1975
Mayr, Kurt	mgo	2000, 01
Maze	wre	1971
Mazur, Scot	ftb	1981, 82
Mazzaglia, Olivia	wtr	1999, 2000, 01
McAbee, Paggy	wsb	1978, 79
McAdam, Paul	mbm	1989, 90
McAlister, Mary	wbk	1939
McAllister, Brad	ftb	1991
McAllister, Mary	wsb	1938
	wbb	1936
	wfh	1938
McArney, Charlene	wgo	1936
McArtor, Jennifer	wsw	1991, 92, 93
McBride, Dave	wre	1985
McBroom, Jack	mtr	1951
McBurney, Jim	mtr	1963, 64, 65
McBurney, Sam	mgo	1941
McBurney, Tim	mtr	1970
McCain, Mike	bb	1978, 79, 80, 81
McCaleb, Bill	bb	1942
McCalister, Bryant	mtr	1988
McCallister, Stan	bb	1953, 54
McCandless, Sherry	wgo	1950, 51
McCann, Bob	mbk	1966, 67
McCann, Jim	ftb	1969, 70
McCann, Patrick	msw	1994, 95, 96
McCarron, Tracy	wsb	1986
McCart, Kathie	warc	1990, 91, 92
McCarthey, Tracy	wtr	1984, 85, 86
McCarthy, Allen	mgo	1963
McCarthy, Phil	mbk	1952
McCartney, Deddrick	ftb	1994, 95
	mtr	1992
McCarty, Charlie	mgy	1959
McCarty, Ossie	ftb	1959, 60, 61
McCarty, Tom	mgy	1960, 61
McCarty, Tommy	mbk	1929, 30, 31

Outfielder Dan McKinley had a monster year for the Sun Devils in 1997, batting .422 with 15 home runs and 32 stolen bases.

Rick McKinney was a four-time All-American archer who made the U.S. Olympic Team in 1976, 1984 and 1988.

McMillan, Roy	mgo	1978, 79, 80, 81	Medlock, Larry	mtr	1962	Middents, Mark	msw	1969
McMinds, Patty	warc	1982, 83, 84	Mee, Hamilton	ftb	1996, 97	Miele, Laura	wbk	1990, 91
McMinn, Glenn	wre	1965, 66, 67	Mee, Mike	mgo	1963	Miers, Craig	mcc	1976, 77
McMinn, Glenn	wre	1986, 87, 88	Meeker	mtr	1938		mtr	1977, 78
McMinn, Rob	wre	1994, 95, 96	Meerdink, Sue	wgo	1961, 62	Mifsud, Tony	mcc	1964
McMinn, Wayne	wre	1990, 91, 92, 93	Mehlhorn, Kim	wvb	2000	Mikles, Lee	mgo	1974, 75, 76, 77
McMullen, Corey	mbk	1982, 83	Meidinger, Dawn	wvb	1985, 86, 87, 88	Mikulas, Lynne	wgo	1989, 90, 91
McNabb, Chester	bb	1940	Meier, Dan	bb	1998	Milazzo, Peter	ftb	1993
	mbk	1940, 41, 42	Meier, Ted	mgo	1972, 73	Milborn, Polly	wbk	1921, 22
McNabb, Elizabeth	wyg	1997, 98, 99, 2000	Meikle, Archie	mgo	1940, 41	Miles, Leslie	wtr	1980
McNally, Eileen	wsb	1975	Meitzler, Al	ftb	1957	Miller, Albert	mtr	1954, 55, 58
McNaughton, Andrew		1988, 89, 90, 91	Melfy, Tricia	wtr	1992, 93, 94	Miller, Alice	wgo	1975, 76, 77, 78
McNaughton, Tom	bb	1983	Melley, Mike	msw	1995, 96	Miller, Alyson	wsw	1997, 98, 99, 2000
McNeely, Johnny	ftb	1932, 33	Meloling, John	marc	1984, 85, 86, 87	Miller, Bill	mtr	1946, 48, 50, 51
McNeely, Sheila	wtr	1986	Mendez, Leslie	wsw	1981	Miller, Bill	mtr	1955
McNeil, Henry	bb	1933, 34	Mendoza, S.	warc	1963	Miller, B.J.	fb	2000
McNeil, Joan	warc	1940	Menezes, Marcelo	msw	1994	Miller, Bob	mtn	1935
	wbb	1943	Menke, Jack	bb	1933	Miller, Cathy	wtr	1983, 84, 85, 86
	wbk	1940, 41, 42		mtn	1933	Miller, Chris	mgy	1989, 90
	wgo	1941	Mercado, Eva	wbm	1967	Miller, Darrow	msw	1965
	wsb	1940, 41, 42, 43		wvb	1967, 68	Miller, Denny	bb	1978
	wtn	1940, 42, 43	Mercer, Art	mtr	1927	Miller, Dick	mtr	1966, 67, 68, 69
	wvb	1942	Merchant, Michelle	wsw	1982, 83, 84, 85	Miller, Donna	wvb	1976
McNeill, Henry	ftb	1929	Meredith, Lisa	wgo	1999, 2000	Miller, Elizabeth	wtn	1951, 52
McNulty, Vera	wbk	1912, 13	Meredith, Tom	wre	1957, 58	Miller, Eugene	mtr	1993
McPeek, Dan	mtr	1963, 64, 65	Meredity, Lisa	wgo	1999, 2000, 01	Miller, Floyd	bb	1922, 23
McPeek, Dick	mtr	1967	Mergerson, Pearl	wbm	1950	Miller, Frank	ftb	1905
McPherron, Pat	mtr	1980	Merkel, Dudley	mgo	1963	Miller, Halbert	ftb	1905
McPherson, Pat	mtr	1978	Mero, Bobbie	wsw	1969	Miller, Hamilton	bb	1916, 17, 18
McQueen, Ali	wtn	1954	Merrell, Colleen	wvb	1974		ftb	1916
McReynolds, Ryan	ftb	1987, 88, 89, 90	Merrick, Jim	bb	1963, 64, 65			
McShane, Terry	wre	1973	Merrill, Boyd	mtr	1931, 32	Miller, J.	mtn	1963
McVay, Rory	msw	1997, 98, 99		mcc	1933	Miller, Jamie	wsw	2000
Mead, Bill	bb	1957, 58	Merrill, Eugene	mgo	1941, 42	Miller, Jay	bb	1947
Mead, Bill	mcc	1973	Merrill, Todd	msw	1987, 88, 89	Miller, Jerry	wre	1974
	mtr	1973, 74	Merson, Susie	wvb	1982	Miller, Jodi	wsb	1987, 88
Mead, Jim	wre	1980	Merten, Kelly	wgo	1981	Miller, Joe	bb	1968, 69
Meade, Bob	mcc	1970	Merten, Lauri	wgo	1979, 80, 81, 82	Miller, John	bb	1960, 61, 62
Meadows, Gavin	msw	2001	Merwald, Lynne	wgo	1975	Miller, K.	mtn	1963
Meaney, Paul	mbk	1964, 65, 66	Merwin, Rick	mtr	1968, 69	Miller, Larry	msw	1974
Mechea, Claude	mtr	1927, 28	Meservey, Yolanda	wtr	2001	Miller, Lemmie	bb	1980, 81
Medchill, Mike	wre	1968	Meskimons, Irving	ftb	1905	Miller, Louise	wbk	1938, 39
Medigovich, Dave	ftb	1946, 47, 48	Mess, Mike	ftb	1968, 69, 70		wfh	1938, 39
Medigovich, Stella	warc	1938	Messias, Rodrigo	msw	1995		wsb	1938
Medina, Cruz	bb	1953, 55	Messick, Josephine	wbb	1924		wtn	1939
Medina, Louie	bb	1984, 85		wvb	1925	Miller, Marshall	mtn	1941, 42
Medley, Pete	wre	1967, 68	Metcalf, Drew	ftb	1987, 88, 89, 90	Miller, Maxine	wgo	1939
Medlin, Fred	mbk	1915	Metcalf, Steve	mgy	1980, 81	Miller, Melanie	wvb	1978
			Metts, Tom	mcc	1973	Miller, Melissa	wsb	1996, 97, 98, 99
				mtr	1973, 74	Miller, Paula	wsb	1971, 72, 73
			Metz, Bryan	wre	1989	Miller, Ray	wre	1990, 91, 92, 93
			Metz, Verdel	wbk	1916, 17, 18	Miller, Rick	msw	1982
			Meyer, Dee	wcc	1979	Millers, Seth	ftb	1967, 68, 69
				wtr	1976, 77	Miller, Steve	mcc	1961
			Meyer, Gertrude	warc	1941		mtr	1962
			Meyer, Greg	mtr	1987, 88	Miller, Ted	ftb	1935
			Meyer, Jill	wtr	1995	Miller, Vanessa	wtn	1983, 84, 85, 86
			Meyer, Jim	ftb	1983, 84	Miller, Voni	wsw	1980, 81
			Meyer, John	ftb	1979, 80, 81	Millet, Wayne	mbk	1933
			Meyer, Klaudia	wtr	1976	Millett, Arthur	bb	1907, 08
			Meyer, Pete	msw	1970	Millett, Earl	mtr	1926
			Meyer, Pete	mtn	1967	Millett, Laree	wfh	1935
			Meza, Henry	ftb	1953	Millett, Neoma	wbk	1911
			Mial, April	wbk	1989	Millies, Kimberly	wgo	1992
			Micela, Joe	wre	1997, 98	Milliron, Jim	ftb	1962, 63
			Miceli, Rob	ftb	2000		wre	1962, 63, 64, 65
			Michael, Steve	bb	1976, 77, 78	Mills, Carolyn	wsw	1985, 86, 87, 88
			Michaels, Dave	msw	1966	Mills, Lucia	wtn	1923
			Michel, Peggy	wtn	1969, 70, 71, 72	Mills, Mike	marc	1971
			Michelena, Cristiano	msw	1992, 93, 94	Mills, Naomi	wtn	1957
			Mickelson, Derek	bb	1994, 95	Mills, Ryan	bb	1996, 97, 98
			Mickelson, Kurt	msw	1974, 75, 76, 77	Mills, Toby	ftb	1990, 91, 92, 93
			Mickelson, Phil	mgo	1989, 90, 91, 92	Milner, Robby	bb	1998, 99, 2000
			Mickelson, Tim	mgo	1997, 98	Mineah, Ralph	ftb	1916
						Miniefield, Kevin	ftb	1989, 90, 91, 92

Now a scout for the Kansas City Royals, Louie Medina belted 17 home runs in 1984 and batted .379 in 1985 for the Sun Devils before moving on to the Cleveland Indians.

Name	Sport	Years
Minitti, Bob	ftb	1960, 61 62
Minor, Blas	bb	1987, 88
Minter, Howard	bb	1921
Minter, Leola	wvb	1925
Mintie, Kathy	wtr	1979
Mirani, Donna	wbk	1988
	wtr	1988
Mirassou, Pam	wtn	1985, 86, 87
Mistler, John	ftb	1978, 79, 80
Mitacek, Frank	ftb	1963, 64
Mitcham, Gene	ftb	1951, 52, 55, 56
Mitchell, Ed	ftb	1955, 56, 57, 58
Mitchell, James	wre	1977, 78
Mitchell, Kenny	ftb	1995, 96, 97, 98
	mtr	1996, 97, 98, 99
Mitchell, Larry	mgo	1947
Mitchell, Nan	warc	1950
Mitchell, Norman	mgo	1948
Mitchell, Sidney	mtr	1979
Mitchell, Tyrone	mbk	1987
Mitchum, K.	box	1929
Mix, Eric	msw	1991, 92, 93, 94
Mixdorf, Cheri	wtn	1976, 77, 78
Mixon, David	msw	1971
Miyagi, Kaoru	wtn	1983, 84
Miyauchi, Diane	wbm	1970, 71
Moe, Dan	msw	1975, 76
Moen, Nancy	wgo	1982, 83, 84, 85
Moeur, Josephine	wbk	1922, 23
Moeur, Kelly	bb	1915, 16
	ftb	1914, 15
	mbk	1915
Moeur, William	bb	1926
Moffatt, Patti	wsw	1970
Molina, Gabe	bb	1996
Molina, Mimi	wgo	1983, 84, 85, 86
Moll, Anna	wtn	1995, 95, 96
Mollica, Marcus	wre	1993, 94, 95, 96
Molloque, Tony	mtr	1937
Molt, Molly	wtn	1977
Monago, Ted	ftb	1992
Monday, Jim	wre	1977
Monday, Mike	wre	1975, 76, 77
Monday, Rick	bb	1965
Monette, Bill	bb	1970
Mong, Larry	bb	1954
Mongini	mtr	1941
Monk, Nayron	mbk	1977
Monarrez, Armando	mtr	2000, 01
Monsen, Annette	wvb	1995
Monson, Michelle	wvb	1989, 90, 92, 93
Mont Pas, Jeff	mtr	1980
Montano, Mateo	mtr	1999
Montesanto, Brian	ftb	2000
Montgomery, Mario	ftb	1981, 82, 83, 84
Montgomery, Charlotte	wgo	1977, 78, 79, 80
Montgomery, Emily	wvb	1925
Montgomery, Florence	wbb	1923, 24
	wvb	1923, 24
Montgomery, George	ftb	1990, 91, 92, 93
Montgomery, Jim	ftb	1946, 47
Montgomery, Wana	wsb	1940
Montoya, Herb	mtr	1958
Montoya, Leo	mcc	1995
Montoya, Leonard	mtr	1996
Montpas, Jeff	mtr	1980
Monttinen, Jarmo	mtr	1998
Moon, Glenn	bb	1978, 79
Moon, Laura	wgy	2001
Moon, Mike	mbk	1973, 74, 75
Mooney, Lynn	wsb	1972, 73
Moore, Alvin	ftb	1978, 79, 81, 82
Moore, Bob	wre	1957, 58
Moore, Bobby	marc	1993
Moore, Brandon	wre	1989
Moore, Burt	mtr	1936, 37
Moore, Clarence	mtr	1951, 52, 54
Moore, Dereck	ftb	1989, 90, 91, 92
	mtr	1989, 90, 91
Moore, Dixie	wgo	1968
Moore, Donna	wvb	1961
Moore, Ervette	wtr	1981, 82
Moore, Greg	mtr	1978, 79, 80, 81
Moore, Holly	wtr	1987
Moore, Jason	ftb	1998, 99, 2000
Moore, Jim	mgy	1979
Moore, Jim	msw	1978
Moore, Judy	wbm	1959
Moore, Kendis	wsw	1969, 70, 71, 72
Moore, Mel	mgo	1954, 55
Moore, Randy	ftb	1973, 74, 75
Moore, Rosiland	wbk	1987, 88
Moosbrugger, Pete	mtr	1981
Morado, Arnulfo	wre	1963
Moraga, Bobby	box	1936
Morales, Ada	wbm	1940
Morales, Frank	bb	1951
Morales, Ida	wsb	1940
Morales, Mike	ftb	1996
Morales, Mike	wre	1972, 73, 74
Morales, Ron	wre	1975
Moran, Cindy	wgy	1980
Moran, Ralph	mbk	1942
Moreland, John	ftb	1978, 79, 80
Morelli, Lauren	wsw	1998, 99, 2000, 01
Moreno, Jose	wre	1997, 98, 99, 2000
Moreno, Julio	wre	1987, 88, 89
Moreno, Mikel	bb	1995, 96, 97, 98
Moreno, Milo	mbk	1956, 57
Moreno, Rogelio	wre	1989, 90, 91
Moreno, Yolanda	wsb	1982, 83, 84, 85
Morgan, Avia	wtr	1995, 96, 97
Morgan, Bill	mtn	1937
Morgan, Gwen	wsw	1971
Morgan, Hal	wre	1994
Morgan, John	mtr	1990
Morgan, Johnny	bb	1931
	mtr	1931
Morgan, Kyle	mcc	1999, 2000
	mtr	2001
Morgan, Lamont	ftb	1995, 96
Morgan, Ruth	wbk	1943, 44, 45
	wfh	1947
	wsb	1947
	wtf	1943, 45
	wvb	1944, 45, 46, 47
Morgan, Shannon	wvb	1993
Morley, Mike	mgo	1966, 67, 68
Morris	mtn	1933, 34
Morris, "Schoolboy"	bb	1909
Morris, Bob	bb	1947
Morris, Bradley	mbk	1952, 53
Morris, Chris	mtr	1992
Morris, Cyrus	mtr	1934
	ftb	1932, 33, 34
Morris, Jackie	warc	1950
Morris, Maggie	wtn	1979
Morris, Richard	msw	1996, 97, 98, 99
Morris, Rick	bb	1985, 86
Morris, Tanya	wbk	1984, 85
Morris, Tricia	wgy	1981, 82
Morrison, Ann	wbm	1977
Morrison, Bob	mgo	1950
Morrison, Bobbie	wgo	1976, 77, 78, 79
Morrison, Carrie	wbm	1976, 77, 78, 79
Morrison, Celeste	wtr	1976
Morrison, Chico	mbk	1960
Morrison, Duane	bb	1952

Carrie Morrison was a four-time All-American in badminton from 1976 through 1979.

Name	Sport	Years
	ftb	1949, 51, 52
	mbk	1951, 52
Morrison, Eileen	wbm	1980, 81, 82, 83
Morrison, Gale	mbk	1941, 42, 43, 46
Morrison, Gertrude	wbb	1922
Morrison, Lucille	wbk	1911
Morrison, Lynn	wsw	1973
Morrow, Ben	mbk	1929
	mtr	1929
Morrow, Beth	warc	1969
Morrow, George	mtr	1924
Morrow, Gregg	mtr	1925
	bb	1924, 25
Morrow, Ruth	wbk	1924
Mortensen, Fred	ftb	1975, 76, 77
Mortensen, Michelle	wvb	1997, 98, 99, 2000
Mortensen, Paul	mtn	1951, 53, 54, 55
Mortenson, Ben	mtr	1946
Mortenson, Lucille	wbk	1915
Mortenson, Susie	wsw	1987, 88, 89, 90
Morton, Pamela	wtr	1986
Mosca, Vince	mtr	2001
Moscote, Rafael	msw	1996
Moses, Glenn	ftb	1928, 29, 30
	bb	1930
	mbk	1929, 30, 31, 32
Moses, Steve	bb	1983
Moses, Steve	marc	1981, 82, 83, 84
Mosher, Brian	msw	1976, 77, 78, 79
Moskau, Paul	bb	1973
Mosley, Donavan	mtr	1996
Mosley, Reggie	bb	1983
Mosley, Shamona	wbk	1988
Moss, Bill	mtn	1975
Moss, Charles	bb	1933, 34
	mgo	1934
Moss, Charles	mtn	1928
Moss, Christine	wvb	1925
Moss, Curtis	mtr	1988
Moss, Eric	ftb	1990, 91
Moss, Speck	ftb	1914
	mtr	1914
Moss, Winona	wbb	1923, 24
	wvb	1923, 24
Motes, Thelo	mbk	1923, 24
	ftb	1923, 24
Mothershed, Cody	mbk	1948
Motiejunas, Algis	mtr	2001
Motreno, Roxanne	wsb	1973, 74
Motschman, Leslie	wsw	1967
Mott, Chris	ftb	1975, 76, 77, 78

Kristel Mourgue d'Algue was the NCAA women's golf champion in 1995.

Mougeot, Bill — mbk — 1933, 34
Mourgue d'Algue, Kristel — wgo — 1994, 95
Mowry, Steve — mcc — 1974
Moxley, Amy — wsoc — 1996, 97
Moyer, Paul — ftb — 1981, 82
Mpwo, Eniak — mtr — 1998
Mucker, Larry — ftb — 1974, 75, 76
Muder, Dan — ftb — 1977
Mueller, Laura — wsw — 1984, 85
Mueske, Daryl — ftb — 1978, 79, 80, 81
Muffley, Bernard — ftb — 1931
Mulder, Dee Dee — wbk — 1988
Muldrow, Marquise — ftb — 1999, 2000
Mulgado, Bobby — ftb — 1954, 55, 56, 57
Mulkins, Marilyn — warc — 1980, 81
Mullen, Bob — ftb — 1924, 25, 27
 — mbk — 1925, 28
Mullen, John — bb — 1909, 09, 10, 11
Mullen, Kenneth — bb — 1922, 23
 — mbk — 1923, 24, 25
 — mtr — 1923
Mullen, Oscar — ftb — 1896
Mullen, Robert — bb — 1925, 28
Mullen, Ted — mtr — 1969
Muller, Louise — wtr — 1976, 77
Mullertz, Camilla — wbk — 1985
Mulligan, Greg — bb — 1967
Mulligan, Jeff — mtr — 1987, 88
Mulligan, Trevor — mtr — 1994
Mullin, Meghan — wsoc — 1996, 97, 98
Mumford, Diana — wtr — 1982
Munger, Sidney — mgy — 1959
Muniz, Manuel — ftb — 1946, 47, 48, 50
Munoz, Jerry — wre — 1974, 76, 77
Munoz, Joe — mtr — 1951
Munson, Miles — mbm — 1983, 84
Muraca, Manny — bb — 1954
Murano, Kevin — mgy — 1991
Murdock, Raechel — warc — 1930
Murphy, Alice — wsw — 1970
Murphy, Casey — wsw — 1997, 98, 99, 2000
Murphy, Jeff — mtn — 1979
Murphy, Jim — ftb — 1963, 64
Murphy, Kyle — ftb — 1994, 95, 96, 97
Murphy, Lesley-Ann — wsb — 1997, 98, 99, 2000
Murphy, Marty — mcc — 1988, 89
Murphy, Nick — ftb — 1999, 2000
Murphy, Richard — ftb — 1995

Murphy, Ryan — mgo — 1994
Murphy, Tom — mtr — 1968
Murray, Don — mtr — 1977
Murray, Leroy — wre — 1985, 86
Murray, Les — mtn — 1941, 42
Murray, Steve — bb — 1984
Murro, Mark — mtr — 1969, 70, 71
Murty, Stacey — wbm — 1990, 91, 92, 93
Musser, Marc — bb — 1967
Mustafa, Isiah — ftb — 1995, 96
Myers, Bill — marc — 1977
Myers, Bill — mgo — 1971, 72
Myers, Casey — bb — 1998, 99, 2000, 01
Myers, Clint — bb — 1971, 72, 73
Myers, Glen — marc — 1950, 51
Myers, Glenn — marc — 1980, 81, 83, 84
Myers, John — mbk — 1964, 65, 66
Mygren, Jacob — mgo — 1996

N

Naddour, Mike — mgy — 1976, 77, 78, 79
Nafziger, Wayne — mgo — 1947
Nagashima, Hiroshi — mtn — 1996, 97, 98, 99
Nagel, Steve — mgy — 1971, 72
Nagl, Miriam — wgo — 2000
Naglich, K. — wsw — 1962
Nahra, Brad — mbk — 2000, 01
Naia, Michele — wgy — 1993, 94, 95, 96
Nall, Bob — marc — 1972, 73, 74
Napolitan, John — mtr — 1999, 2000, 01
Napolitano, Dan — ftb — 1954, 55, 56, 57
Napolitano, Dick — ftb — 1954, 55, 56
Nard, Mona — wsb — 1991, 92, 93, 94
Narrimore, Dan — wre — 1956
Nasby, Jeff — mgy — 1979, 80
Nascimento, Emmanuel — msw — 1989, 90, 91, 92
Nash, Alison — wtn — 1996, 97, 98, 99
Nash, Johnny — mbk — 1977, 79, 80, 81
Nash, Ken — mtr — 1966, 67
Natale, Sue — wtr — 1977
Nations, Dale — mgy — 1955
Nauman, Dick — mtn — 1948
Nava, Ignacio — mtr — 1948
Navarez, Rafael — mcc — 1933
Navarrete, Raul — bb — 1947
Navarro, Pat — wsb — 1975
 — wvb — 1973, 74, 75
Neal, Billy — bb — 1994
Neal, Kim — wgy — 1983, 84, 85, 86
Neal, Lester — mbk — 1992, 93
Neal, Troy — bb — 1959, 60
 — mbk — 1958, 59, 60
Nealey, Al — mbk — 1958, 59, 60
 — mtr — 1957
Near, Dan — wre — 1981, 83
Neatherly, Bill — mtr — 1980
Neeley, Bob — mbk — 1946
Neeley, Linda — wsb — 1984, 85, 86, 87
Neeley, Teri — wsb — 1977, 78
Neely, Aleene — wbk — 1941, 42
 — wsb — 1941, 42
 — wfh — 1942, 43
 — wvb — 1942
Neely, Bob — bb — 1948
Neely, Dick — mbk — 1945
Neely, Theo — wbk — 1939, 40
 — wfh — 1939
 — wsb — 1940
 — wsw — 1967
Neese, Phyllis — wsb — 1967
 — wsw — 1966

 — wvb — 1968
Neff, Zoan — wtn — 1950
Neiburg, J. — mtn — 1963
Neidhoefer, Kristen — wsw — 1989, 90
Neilson, Dave — bb — 1946
Neilson, Roland — mtr — 1946
Nelson, Amy — wbk — 1992
 — wvb — 1990, 91, 92
Nelson, Don — mbk — 1962
Nelson, Dornel — ftb — 1960, 61, 62
Nelson, Fred — bb — 1967, 68
Nelson, James — mgy — 1977, 78, 79, 80
Nelson, Jim — mbk — 1991, 92
Nelson, Jim — mgy — 1963, 64, 65, 66
Nelson, Joyce — wbm — 1950, 51
Nelson, Lisa — wsw — 1981
Nelson, Lucille — wbk — 1915, 16
Nelson, Lynn — wcc — 1981, 82, 83, 84
 — wtr — 1984, 85
Nelson, Matt — ftb — 1993, 94
Nelson, Ricky — bb — 1979, 80, 81
Nelson, Rusell — mbm — 1977, 78, 79
Nelson, Sally — wtn — 1968
Nemecek, Lad — bb — 1962, 63, 64
Nemet, Nancy — wsw — 1983, 85, 86, 87
Nereson, Tina — wsw — 1971
Nesbit, Jim — ftb — 1936, 37
Neu, Chris — msw — 1983
Neumore, David — ftb — 1987, 88
Nevarez — mtr — 1934
Nevitt, Mac — bb — 1918
Nevitt, Maydean — wgo — 1947
 — wfh — 1948
New, Jim — msw — 1979, 80
Newalt, Harvey — msw — 1959
Newhall, Jim — msw — 1972, 73, 74, 75
Newhall, Phyllis — warc — 1950, 51
 — wbm — 1950
Newman, Carol — wvb — 1967
Newman, Don — mgy — 1981
Newman, Jim — mbk — 1957, 58
Newman, Jody — mgy — 1989, 90, 91, 92
Newman, Leaf — wbk — 1998, 99
Newman, Lucas — wre — 1985

Kim Neal was a four-time gymnastics All-American from 1983-1986. She captured national individual titles in the floor exercise (1983) and vault (1986).

O

A three-time tennis All-American from 1984 through 1986, Sheri Norris was the first Sun Devil to compile more than 80 singles victories.

281

Name	Sport	Years
Ordway, Les	mtr	1978
Ore, Elizabeth	wsw	2000, 01
Orn, Mike	msw	1981, 82, 83, 84
Orozco, Mark	mtr	1996
Orr, Don	mcc	1981, 83
	mtr	1982, 84
Orr, Doris	wgo	1940
Orr, Harry	mbk	1963
Orr, Robert	rif	1964
Orsund, Sandra	wtr	2001
Ortega, Carl	wre	1974
Ortega, Ricardo	bb	1934
	box	1935
Ortega, Vic	bb	1937, 38, 40
Ortez, Monica	wbm	1977, 78, 79
Ortiz, Isaabel	wtn	1974, 75, 76
Ortiz, Eddie	wre	1979, 80
Ortiz, Jesus	mtr	1967, 68, 69, 70
Ortiz, Richard	wre	1981, 82
Ortiz, Tommy	wre	1987, 88, 89, 90
Orton, Andrew	msw	1991
Orzell, Dave	ftb	1973, 74
Osborn, Jeff	bb	1968, 69, 70
Osborne, Carolee	wsw	1994, 95
Osborne, Chuck	ftb	1965, 66, 67, 68
Osborne, Clarence	ftb	1954, 55, 56, 57
Osborne, Kes	box	1937
Osborne, McArthur	mtr	1983, 84, 85
Osborne, Nancy	wsw	1988, 89, 90, 91
Osburn, Stephanie	wbk	1985, 86, 87, 88
Oscarson, Jeff	bb	1973, 74
Osiecki, Sandy	ftb	1982, 83
Osterrieth, Alex	mtn	1997, 98, 99, 2000
Osthimer, Clinton	ftb	1952
Otten, Jim	bb	1972, 73
Ottmann, Ashley	wvb	1996, 97, 98
Outlaw, Doug	wre	1977
Overton, Kay	warc	1953
Overton, Kim	warc	1968
Owen, Casey	wsw	1994, 95, 96
Owen, Curtis	wre	2000, 01
Owen, Justin	mtr	2000, 01
Owens, Coart	mtr	1979, 80
Owens, Melvin	mbk	1937, 38
Owens, Morris	ftb	1972, 73, 74
Owens, Pam	wbm	1976, 77, 78, 79
Owens, Tom	mbk	1963
Owers, Eric	mcc	1962, 63, 64, 65
	mtr	1962, 63, 64, 65
Owers, Geoff	mcc	1992, 93, 94
	mtr	1993, 94, 95
Oyler, Nan	wtr	1976
Oziwo, Okeme	mbk	1996, 98, 99

P

Name	Sport	Years
Pa, Patrick	mgy	1986, 87, 88, 89
Pabst, Bill	bb	1935, 36
Pace, Don	ftb	1931, 32, 34, 35
	mbk	1934, 35
Pace, Tom	fb	2000
Pacheco, Jason	bb	1996, 97
Packer, Merle	warc	1947
	wbk	1940
	wbm	1941
	wgo	1941, 47
	wsb	1940, 41
Paddock, Frank	mtr	1959, 60
Paddock, Surretta	wtn	1938, 39, 41
Paddock, Warren	mtr	1933

Name	Sport	Years
Padelford, Bob	bb	1952
Padgett, Kirk	mgo	1972
Padilla, Greg	mgo	1996, 97, 98, 99
Padilla, LeRoy	wre	1965
Padilla, Randy	wre	1968
Padjen, Gary	ftb	1976, 77, 78, 79
Padre, Macario	mbm	1990, 91, 92
Page, George	mtr	1993
Page, Shawn	mcc	1991
	mtr	1992
Page, Susan	warc	1991, 92
Pagel, Mike	bb	1980, 81, 82
	ftb	1978, 79, 80, 81
Pagnetti, Al	ftb	1954, 55, 56
Paige, John	mgo	1967
Pain, Fred	mcc	1954
Paine, Rhonda	wtr	1983, 84
Pair, Trish	wbm	1977
Pairitz, Todd	wre	1982
Palacio, Oscar	mgo	1994, 95, 96, 97
Palenta, Ray	ftb	1946, 48
Palm, Jan Erik	mtn	1975, 76
Palme, Karin	wtn	1998, 99, 2000, 01
Palmer, Amy	wcc	1982
Palmer, Amy	wsw	1992, 93, 94, 95
Palmer, Bob	mgo	1966, 67
Palmer, Dan	mbk	1942
Palmer, Earl	bb	1946
Palmer, Ed	mbk	1967
Palmer, Marvin	ftb	1935, 36, 37
	mbk	1936, 37
Palmer, Theron	ftb	1922
Palmer, Willis	mtr	1957, 58, 59
Palmisano, Leanne	wtn	1982
Palmore, Courtney	ftb	1998, 99
Palumbo, Paul	ftb	1964, 65, 66
	wre	1964
Panek, Ernie	bb	1960, 61
Paplowski, James	ftb	1956
Pappas, Penny	wtr	1977
Papscun, Kimberly	wbk	1988
Paraham, Brigitte	wbk	1979
	wtr	1979, 80, 81, 82
Parent, Mary-Ann	warc	1981, 82, 83, 84
Parham, Joe	ftb	1963
	mtr	1963, 64
Park, Chip	wre	1984, 85, 87, 88
Park, Grace	wgo	1998, 99
Park, James	msw	1996
Park, Jin	mgo	1998, 99, 2000, 01
Parker	mtr	1934
Parker, Andrew	mtr	1986, 87
Parker, Anthony	ftb	1984, 85, 86, 87
Parker, Cheryl	wtr	1978, 79
Parker, Dick	mtr	1935
Parker, James	mtr	1936, 37
Parker, James	mtr	1979
Parker, Jim	wre	1962
Parker, Lesa	wtr	1993, 94
Parkhart, Dorothy	wfh	1935
Parkinson, Mike	bb	1977, 78
Parkman, Elsie	wbb	1924
	wbk	1923, 24
Parks, Billy	msw	1981, 82
Parks, Larry	mbk	1968
Parks, Winona	wtr	1979
Parra, Bob	wre	1978
Parrish, Gene	wre	1966, 67, 68
Parrott, Carroll	ftb	1947
Parry, Bill	bb	1936
	ftb	1934, 35, 36
Parry, Frank	bb	1907
Parsons, Cole	mgy	1984
Parsons, Mary Jo	wtn	1933, 34

Name	Sport	Years
Parsons, Ryan	wre	1992, 93
Parsons, Simon	mtr	1995
Partee, Wayne	wre	1967
Pascale, John	ftb	1914, 15
Paschke, Dan	ftb	1976
Passe, Jason	mgy	1992
Passey, Viola	wbk	1912, 13
Pate, Bob	bb	1975, 76
Pate, Bryan	mtr	1995, 96, 97
Pate, Thomas	bb	1917
	ftb	1916
	mbk	1917
Patella, Nick	ftb	1955, 56
Patoni, Darren	msw	1987
Patoni, Suzanne	wtr	1988, 89, 90
Patrick, Maynard	msw	1996
Patrick, Porry	mtr	1938
Patrone, Dom	ftb	1949, 50, 51
Patschke, Patty	warc	1952, 53
Patterson, Brianna	wsw	2001
Patterson, Dale	ftb	1919
	bb	1920, 21
	mbk	1917, 18, 20, 21
	mtr	1921, 22
Patterson, Dave	mtr	1951
Patterson, Don	ftb	1942
Patterson, Eric	bb	1986
Patterson, Kay	wtr	1979
Patterson, Pat	ftb	1946, 47, 48
Patterson, Pat	wbk	1943
Patterson, Shawn	ftb	1984, 85, 86, 87
Patterson, Virginia	wvb	1944
Patterson, Wendell	ftb	1946, 47, 48
Patti, Leah	wtr	1984, 85
Patton, Jason	mbk	1998, 99
Patton, Steve	wre	1981
Patty, Dave	mgo	1970
Paul, Arthur	ftb	1990, 91
Paul, Bill	mbk	1951, 52, 53
	mgo	1951, 52, 53
Paul, John	mcc	1947, 48
	mtr	1946, 47, 48
Paul, Mary Lee	warc	1949, 50
Paulk, Jeff	ftb	1995, 96, 97, 98
Paulsen, Austin	msw	1998, 99, 2000, 01
Paulsen, Nancy	wsw	1968
Paulson, Jane	wtn	1984
Paulson, Joe	bb	1966, 67, 68
Paulson, Liz	wbk	2000, 01
Pavlich, Bob	ftb	1952
Pavlik, John	bb	1964, 65, 66
Pavlovich, Louis	bb	1942
Payer, Dolph	mcc	1954
	mtr	1955
Payne, Joe	mtr	1947, 48, 49, 50
Payne, Ollie	mbk	1961, 62
Payne, Terry	mtr	1985, 86
Payton, Erika	wsw	1986
Peabody, Chuck	mtr	1952, 53
Peake, Jennah	wsoc	1996
Pearce, Zebulon	ftb	1897
Pearl, Sheila	wtn	1966, 67, 68
Pearson, Connie	wtn	1968
Pearson, Joel	mgy	1966
Pearson, Josh	mtr	1998
Pease, Jess	ftb	1949, 50
Peavler, Kyle	ftb	1993, 94
Pebler, Steve	mtr	1972, 73
Peck, Jamie	wvb	1996, 97, 98, 99
Peckovich, Ralph	ftb	1948
Pederson, Paul	mtn	1964, 66, 67
Peery, Noah	bb	1993, 94
Peisachov, Paulina	wtn	1970
Pelekoudas, Lee	bb	1970, 71, 72

Jeff Pentland was a pitching standout on Sun Devil baseball teams of the mid 1960s. He later returned as hitting coach, and now serves as hitting coach of the Chicago Cubs.

Pelletier, Linda	wsb	1974, 75, 76, 77
Pellicino, Rocky	ftb	1942
Pena, Tony	bb	1990, 91
Penacho, Jay	wre	1990
Pendergast, Tom	bb	1947
Pendergrast, Kelli	wsb	1984
Penn, Chris	wtn	1975, 76
Penn, Frank	wre	1974
Penney, Debbie	wvb	1988, 89, 90, 91
Pennies, Nancy	wtn	1959
Penning, Bruce	mtr	1986, 87, 88, 89
Pennington, Chad	bb	1998, 99, 2000
Pennington, Joe	mgo	1960, 61
Penterman, Les	mtr	1946
Pentland, Jeff	bb	1966, 67, 68
Pentz, Dave	ftb	1968, 69, 70
Peoples, Maurice	mtr	1972, 73
Peper, Robert	mtr	1994, 95, 96
Peppler, Patti	wbk	1984, 85, 86, 87
Peralta, Amelina	wbb	1943
	wbk	1942
	wfh	1942, 43
	wsb	1942, 43
	wtf	1943
	wvb	1942, 43
Peralta, Martin	bb	1987, 88
Percival, Frances	wfh	1947
Percy, Simon	msw	1991, 92, 93, 94
Pereyra, Ana Lucia	wtn	1996, 97, 98, 99
Perez, Bena	wtn	1927
	wvb	1927
Perez, Fernanda	wsw	1980, 81, 82, 83
Perez, Pat	mgo	1995, 96, 97
Perkins, Bruce	ftb	1988, 89
Perkins, Bruce	mbk	1950, 51, 52
Perkins, Jack	mbk	1953, 54, 55
Perkins, John	mtr	1965, 66
Perkins, Kim	mtr	1979
Perkins, Sam	mtr	1972
Peroulis, J.R.	ftb	1999
Perrault, Susan	wgo	1986, 87, 88
Perrino, Phil	ftb	1947, 48, 49, 50
Perrone, Vito	mcc	1980, 81, 82
	mtr	1981
Perry	mtr	1936
Perry, Bill	ftb	1942
Perry, Bob	bb	1948
Perry, Chad	mtr	1991
Perry, George	ftb	1977
Perry, John	ftb	1965

Perry, Kent	bb	1966, 67
Perry, Lloyd	msw	1972
Perry, Mike	rif	1961
Perry, Nella	wgy	1966
Perry, Sally	wtn	1966, 78
Perry, Stan	mtn	1983, 84, 85
Perry, W.	bb	1915
	ftb	1914
Perryman, Mark	wre	1999, 2000
Persinger, Cheryl	wsb	1984, 85, 86, 87
Person, Suzy	wgy	1991, 92, 93, 94
Peru, Reynaldo	ftb	1977, 79, 80, 81
Peschel, Harland	mgo	1963
Peschiera, Mario	mtr	1985, 86
Pesho, Terri	warc	1985
Peters, Amandus	mtr	1930, 33, 34
Peters, Dave	msw	1980
Peters, Frosty	mgo	1934, 35, 36
Peters, Gary	wre	1973, 74
Peters, Gordon	mtr	1972, 73, 74
Peters, Joe	ftb	1978, 79
Peters, Rick	bb	1974, 75, 76, 77
Peters, Roger	mbk	1946
Peters, Sabrina	wcc	1980, 81
Peters, Scott	ftb	1998, 99, 2000
Peterson, Ann	wsw	1968
Peterson, Arnie	ftb	1949, 50
Peterson, Bob	mgo	1979
Peterson, Bob	wre	1962
Peterson, Brian	mgy	1977, 78, 80, 81
Peterson, Clayton	ftb	1940
Peterson, Dwight	bb	1937
	mbk	1937, 38, 39
Peterson, Erin	bb	1965
Peterson, Gary	msw	1966
Peterson, Gary	mtn	1953
Peterson, Greg	wre	1980
Peterson, Howard	bb	1912
	mbk	1912
Peterson, Ida	wbk	1923
Peterson, Jack	mtr	1947, 48, 49, 50
Peterson, Jennifer	wsoc	1998, 99
Peterson, Jessie	wvb	1927
Peterson, Jim	bb	1974, 75, 76
Peterson, Justin	wre	2000, 01
Peterson, Katherine	wtn	1924
Peterson, Mike	msw	1983
Peterson, Pete	bb	1996
Peterson, Reed	mbk	1945, 48, 49
	mtr	1949
Peterson, Rob	ftb	1975, 76
Peterson, Scott	ftb	1979
Peterson, Sue	wgo	1975
Peterson, Tim	ftb	1975, 76, 77
Peters-Stern, Sabrina	wcc	1982
	wtr	1983
Petray, Claire	wtn	1971, 72
Petric, Alex	mgo	1977, 78, 79
Petrie, Carol	wbm	1947
Petrie, Jerry	ftb	1947
Petrulis, Jay	wre	1988, 89, 90
Petta, Vito	ftb	1941
Pettengill, Dave	mtn	1973, 74, 75
Pettijean, Mary Lou	wvb	1967, 68
Pettit, Tom	mtr	1957, 58, 59
Pettorini, Peter	mgy	1992
Petty, Dale	wvb	1967
Petty, Joe	ftb	1970, 71, 72
Pew, Vivian	warc	1936
Pezely, Franco	bb	2000, 01
Pfeuffer, Katrina	wsw	1997, 98, 99, 2000
Pfister, Bob	ftb	1975, 76, 77
Pflugheber, Carol	wsw	1971, 72, 73, 74
Pfuhl, Lisa	wcc	1979, 80, 81, 82
	wtr	1980, 81, 83

Phair, Mike	ftb	1991, 92
Phelps	mtr	1936
Phelps, Jeff	bb	1998, 99, 2000, 01
Phelps, Kelly	warc	1990
Phelps, Ken	bb	1975, 76
Phelps, Rex	ftb	1946
Phelps, W.	ftb	1897
Phelps, Worth	mbk	1936, 37, 38
Phifer, Ron	bb	1958
Phillips, Bill	wre	1958
Phillips, Bunnie	wgo	1971
Phillips, Catherine	wbb	1936
	wbk	1935, 36, 37
	wfh	1935, 38
	wsb	1938
Phillips, Clyde	ftb	1935, 36, 37
	mbk	1936, 37, 38
	mtr	1937, 38, 39
Phillips, Dwight	mtr	1999, 2000
Phillips, J.	mtn	1946
Phillips, Kevin	marc	1977, 78, 79
Phillips, Liz	wsb	1990, 91
Phillips, Mark	mtr	1987, 88
Phillips, Melba	wfh	1949
	wsb	1949
Phillips, Robert	rif	1956
Philopena, Theresa	wtr	1980, 82
Piccinini, Eduardo	msw	1992, 93, 94, 95
Pickard, Tom	mbk	1951, 52
Pickens, Leon	msw	1980, 81
Pickens, Wendell	bb	1934
	ftb	1933, 34
	mbk	1934
Pickering, Linda	wtr	1978, 79, 80
Pidgeon, Lorena	wvb	1961
Piemonte, Ron	msw	1982, 83, 84
Pierantozzi, Donna Jean	wcc	1987
	wtr	1987
Pieratt, Greg	ftb	1999
Pierce, Jeff	mgo	1986
Pierce, Mike	mtr	1962
Pierce, Pam	wvb	1982
Pierce, Tracey	mtr	1984
Pieroni, Paul	mtr	1974
Pierson, Anna Lee	wfh	1934, 35
Pierson, Lyle	ftb	1951, 52, 53
Pies, Ron	mtr	1962
Piesch, Cadie	wsw	1970
Pike, Mike	wre	1975, 76, 77, 78
Pilgrim, Bill	mgy	1968, 69, 70
Pilgrim, Chris	warc	1969
Pillipod, Colleen	wtr	1976, 77
Pina, Frank	bb	1951, 52
Pina, Michael	mgy	1981, 82
Pina, Robert	wre	1978
Pinger, Cynthia	wtn	1979
Pingitore, Mike	bb	1949, 50, 51
Pinkard, Mike	ftb	1999, 2000
Piper, Brian	bb	1979, 80
Piper, Tom	ftb	1951
Pirila, Laila	wtn	1970
Pirtle, Jodie	wsb	1994, 95, 96
Pittman, Tim	wre	1968
Pitts, Gioia	wtr	1991
Pitts, John	ftb	1965-66
Pizzello, Lizz	wsw	1999
Plaisted, Kelly	wvb	1987, 88, 89, 90
Plank, Greg	msw	1997, 98, 99, 2000
Plant, Dan	msw	1980, 81, 82, 83
Plant, Harvey	mgy	1959, 60, 61, 62
	msw	1958, 59
Platt, Chris	mbk	1978
Plavan, Darleen	wfh	1950
	wsb	1949

Plummer, Cameron	msw	1987
Plummer, Jake	ftb	1993, 94, 95, 96
Plummer, Wes	ftb	1966, 67, 68
Plunkett, Mike	bb	1968
Pohle	mtr	1938
Pohle, Shelby	ftb	1937, 38, 40
Pohlmann, David	msw	1991, 92
Pojman, Everett	wre	1964
Polan, Steve	bb	1975
Poland, Ed	mgy	1971
Polete, Bill	bb	1940
Polingyumptewa, Larry	mtr	1973
Pollard, Henry	ftb	1978
Pollard, Jim	mbk	1981, 82, 83
Pollock, Robin	wsw	1990
Poloni, John	bb	1973, 74, 75
Polson, Leif	wre	1998
Pomella, Angie	wsw	1998, 99, 2000
Pomeroy	box	1929
Pomeroy, Adah	wbb	1921, 22
Pomeroy, Earl	ftb	1924, 25
	mtn	1925, 26
	mtr	1926
Pomeroy, Ed	ftb	1951, 52
Pomeroy, Nadine	wfh	1933, 34, 35
	warc	1935
	wbk	1934, 35
Pomeroy, Theron	bb	1924, 25, 26, 27
	ftb	1923, 24, 25, 26
Pomery, Tim	mtr	1990, 91
Ponce, Kathy	wsb	1996, 97, 98, 99
Ponder, Lynnae	wtr	1976, 77
Ponko, Marie	wfh	1939
Pontius, Cathy	wbk	1979
Pool, Doug	mgo	1971, 72
Poole, Keith	ftb	1993, 94, 95, 96
Poole, Sherry	wbk	1984, 87
Poorman, Paul	mbk	1956
Popoff, Alex	bb	1942
Popovec, Mike	bb	1966
Popp, Grant	mcc	1999, 2000
	mtr	2001
Popstra, Katy	wtn	1996, 97, 98, 99
Porambo, Carl	mtr	1984, 85, 86, 87
Porras, Jaime	bb	1995
Porter, Bill	bb	1957, 58
Porter, Georgia	wtn	1944, 45, 46, 47
Porter, Harold	bb	1950, 51, 52
Porter, Joe	mgo	1966, 67

Golfer Mary Bea Porter was a first-team All-American in 1973. At the time, she was only the fifth Sun Devil woman to earn such distinction.

Porter, Mary Bea	wgo	1969, 71, 72, 73
Portley, Maurice	wre	1973
Posovar, Marlin	mtr	1993
Posson, Candy	wsw	1971
Posson, Patty	wsw	1968
Posvar, Marlin	mcc	1993, 1994
Poteet, Claudia	wsw	1970
Potente, Tom	mgy	1983, 84
Pottorff, Nathan	ftb	1942
Poulin, Anne	wsoc	2000
Poulos, Gus	bb	1953
	ftb	1951, 52, 53, 54
Poulson, Nancy	wsw	1965
Powell, Bud	mbk	1932
Powell, Carl	ftb	1953
Powell, Kaye	wsw	1959
Powell, Mike	mtr	1974
Powell, P.	box	1936
Powell, Paul Ray	bb	1968, 69
	ftb	1967, 68
Powell, Ronnie	mtn	1965
Power, Jim	ftb	1896, 97, 98
Powers, Bill	msw	1986, 87
Powers, Billie	marc	1952
Powers, Bret	ftb	1990, 91
Powers, Donny	mgo	1968, 69, 70
Powers, Rick	wre	1980, 81, 82, 83
Prather, Clifford	bb	1926, 27, 28, 31
Prather, Dick	mgo	1957, 58
Prather, John	mcc	1976, 77, 78, 79
	mtr	1978, 79, 80
Prather, Karla	wsb	1967
Pratt, Charles	msw	1971, 72
Pratt, Jonathan	ftb	1999
Pratt, Torey	wtn	1996, 97
Pratt, Trent	bb	1999, 2000
Preciado, Sue	wsb	1975
Prentice, Gary	mtr	1953, 54
Preston, Cas	mtr	1951
Preston, Steve	mcc	1985, 86
	mtr	1986
Preston-Curvey, Kevin	ftb	1989, 90
Prewitt, Chad	mbk	1999, 2000, 01
Price, Cedric	ftb	1973, 74, 75, 76
Price, Christie	wsb	1970
Price, Cody	ftb	1998
Price, John	mgy	1967, 68, 69
Price, Laura	warc	1968
Price, Lillian	wfh	1949, 50
	warc	1948

Price, Marge	wbm	1947
	wgo	1947
Price, Thelma	wtn	1938
Prickett, Alan	wre	1968
Prier, Kristen	wsw	1993, 94
Priest, Lindsay	wvb	1996, 97, 98, 99
Prill, Lisa	wgo	1982, 83
Prince, Lou	bb	1954
Prince, Phillip	mcc	1997, 98, 99, 2000
	mtr	1998, 99, 2000, 01
Prince, Todd	wre	1977, 78
Pritchard, Ron	ftb	1966, 67, 68
Pritchert, Craig	bb	1983
Privetti, Ron	msw	1970
Proby, Bryan	ftb	1993
Proctor, Jim	mbk	1964, 65
Proctor, Tami	wgo	1990, 91, 92, 93
Prohhoroff, Nick	ftb	1942
Prosen, Carol	wtn	1962
Proudfoot, Janee	wsb	1976
Proverzio, Esther	wtn	1960
Province, Fritz	ftb	1954, 55, 56
Provitola, Armando	ftb	1950
Prudhome, Greg	mtn	1990, 91
Pryor, Bill	mbk	1959, 60
Pryor, Buddy	bb	1982
Pryor, Deby	wtr	1980, 81, 82
Pryor, Randy	wre	1980
Psomas, Alex	wre	1985
Puccio, Pete	wre	1977, 78
Puebla, Manuel	mcc	1999
	mtr	2000
Puente, Don	ftb	1952
Pugh, Frances	wsb	1941
Pugh, Kathi	wbk	1979, 80, 81
Pugh, Pauline	wbb	1921, 22, 23
	wbk	1922
Pujalet, Michele	wsw	1976
Purcell, Craig	mtn	1989, 90
Purpura, Frank	mgo	1971
Pursell, R.D.	wre	2000, 01
Purtzer, Paul	mgo	1968, 69, 70
Purtzer, Tom	mgo	1970, 71, 72, 73
Purvis, Glenn	mtr	1973
Puryear, Steve	ftb	1988
Pushkin, Jay	mtr	1976, 77
Putman, Earl	mtr	1951, 52
	ftb	1951
Putzer, Melissa Jo	wbm	1986
Puzz, Matt	msw	1983
Pyle, Virgil	mtr	1926, 27
Pyne, Bob	mtr	1977, 78
Pyon, Jung	bb	1992

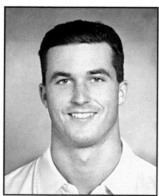

Keith Poole was quarterback Jake Plummer's favorite target as the Sun Devils rolled up an 11-0 regular-season football record in 1996. Poole ranks third on ASU's all-time list for reception yardage.

Tom Purtzer—two-time winner of the Arizona Collegiate tournament—was a second-team All-American in 1973 before launching a lengthy professional golf career.

Q

Quakenbush, Glen	wre	1979, 80
Quas, Jodi	wsw	1988, 89, 90, 91
Quezada, Ramiro	wre	1972, 73
Quigley, Amber	wtr	2001
Quilicy, Al	ftb	1947
Quinney, Jeff	mgo	1998, 99, 2000, 01
Quinones, Mike	marc	1950
Quinonez, Pete	mtr	1981, 82
Quintana, Carol	wsw	1970, 71, 72
Quintanar, Manuel	mcc	1967, 68, 69
	mtr	1967, 68, 69, 70
Quirk, Theresa	wtn	1973
Quy, Dorothy	wgo	1947

R

Raby, Dan	mcc	1978, 79, 80, 81
	mtr	1979, 80, 81, 82
Race, Christy	wcc	1999
	wtr	1999
Radford, Kristen	wtn	2001
Radford, Susan	wcc	1984, 85
	wtr	1985, 86
Radovic, Joe	msw	1991
Radovich, Mark	ftb	1974, 75, 76
Raeder, John	rif	1957
Rafferty, Mark	mcc	1970, 71, 72, 73
	mtr	1971, 72, 73, 74
Raine, Steve	bb	1979
Raines, Bobby	mtr	2001
Rains, Tia	wsw	1990, 91, 92, 93
Rajsich, Gary	bb	1974, 75, 76
Raley, Ken	mbk	1973
Raley, Mike	msw	1993, 94
Raley, Ted	bb	1926
Ramalho, Renato	msw	1992, 93, 94
Rambo, Dick	mtr	1967, 68, 69, 70
Ramenofsky, Marilyn	wsw	1964, 65
Ramirez, Angel	bb	2000, 01
Ramirez, Dan	mtr	1994, 95
Ramirez, David	mgy	1981
Ramirez, J.D.	bb	1985
Ramirez, Mario	bb	1960, 61
Ramos, Rudy	wre	1987
Ramsay, Kaleb	ftb	1998, 99
Ramsay, Korey	ftb	1998, 99
Ramsey, Tom	wre	1973, 74, 75
Ramsey, Viola	warc	1935
	wbk	1934
	wfh	1933, 34, 35
Ran, Amir	mtn	1997, 98, 99
Ranby, Jack	msw	1966, 67
Rance, Christon	ftb	1997, 98, 2000, 01
Rand, Allen	mtr	1966
Randall, Esther	wtn	1929, 30
Randall, Lola Mae	wsb	1950, 51
Randall, Wayne	mtr	1950
Randle, Lenny	bb	1968, 69, 70
	ftb	1968, 69
Randolph, Bob	bb	1979
Rang, Jim	msw	1967, 68, 69
Rang, John	msw	1969, 70, 71
Rankin, Terry	wtr	1976
Rankin, Tom	wre	1980, 81
Rannow, Margaret	warc	1940, 41
Ransom, Lloyd	bb	1987
Raphael, Allen	msw	1959

Jodi Rathbun's name is equally well-distributed throughout both the school's basketball and softball record books. She starred in both sports in the mid 1980s.

Rapp, Bill	msw	1979
Rappaport, Louis	ftb	1938, 39
	mbk	1939
Rashada, Harlen	ftb	1992, 93, 94
Rashoff, Beckky	wgy	1984, 85
Rasmussen, Christian	msw	2001
Rasmussen, Jeff	mtr	1982
Rasmussen, Jeremy	mcc	1999, 2000
	mtr	2000, 01
Raspberry, Brian	mtr	1997, 98, 99
	mtr	1998, 99
Rath, Bob	mbk	1955, 56
Rathbun, Jodi	wbk	1983, 84, 85, 86
	wsb	1985, 86, 87
Rathbun, Marian	wgo	1953
Ratliff, Courtnie	wtr	2000, 01
Ratliff, Earnie	mtr	1947
Rau, Marilyn	wsb	1971, 72
Rauer, Troy	bb	1995
	ftb	1992, 93
Rausch, Steve	ftb	1990, 91, 92
Rawitzer, Kevin	bb	1992, 93
Rawlings, Mike	bb	1973, 74
Rawlins, Bill	bb	1950, 51
Ray, Audeen	wbk	1935
	wbb	1936
	wfh	1935
Ray, Bev	warc	1976
Ray, Bill	mtn	1972
Ray, George	mgo	1949
Ray, Melanie	wgy	1976, 77
Ray, Norman	mbk	1946
Ray, Okley	mbk	1940, 43
Ray, Otis	mbk	1935, 36
	mtr	1935, 36
Rayburn, Jim	wre	1986
Raymond, Mark	mgy	1978
Re, Giannina	wtr	1995
Rea, Clark	bb	1991
Rea, Myrna	warc	1934, 35, 36
	wbk	1934
	wtn	1934
	wfh	1933, 34, 35
Reade, Art	mcc	1962, 63
	mtr	1963, 64, 66
Reader, Larry	mbk	1952
Ready, Jamel	ftb	1997, 98, 99
Reak, Gary	bb	1983
Reakes, Richard	mtn	1962

Rearden, Jim	mcc	1982
Reash, Steve	mbk	1969
Reaves, Larry	ftb	1959, 60, 61
Reay, Mary Lue	wbk	1940, 41, 42
	wgo	1941
	wfh	1941
	wsb	1940, 41, 42
	wtn	1940, 41, 42
	wvb	1942
Rebenar, Margaret	wsb	1976
Reber, Paul	mtn	1993, 94, 95, 96
Recker, Maria	warc	1978, 79
Rector, Randy	bb	1984, 85
Rector, Stephanie	wsb	1996
Redd, Wayne	mtr	1979, 80
Redden, C.	ftb	1896
Redden, Evelyn	wvb	1927
Redden, Lela	wbb	1921
Redden, M.	ftb	1897
Redenius, Eric	ftb	1981
Redfearne, Liz	wgo	1981, 82
Redhage, Shawn	mbk	2000, 01
Redhair, Mike	mbk	1987, 88, 89, 90
Redmond, J.R.	ftb	1996, 97, 98, 99
Redondo, Jeanne	wsb	1993, 94
Redson, Cathy	wsw	1981, 82
Reed, Alan	bb	1962
Reed, Amy	wsw	1985, 86
Reed, Bob	ftb	1949, 50, 51
Reed, Dorothy	warc	1951, 52
Reed, Ken	bb	1971, 72
Reed, Lorena	wgy	1982, 83
Reed, Peter	msw	1971
Reed, Ralph	msw	1970
Reed, Ricky	wre	1977
Reed, Ron	mgo	1963
Reed, Uvonte	mbk	1986, 87
Reedis, Tina	wcc	1984
Reep, Carol	wgo	1975
Rees, Sean	bb	1989, 90, 91
Reese, Donna	wsw	1980
Reeves, Bill	wre	1958
Reeves, Charlotte	wtr	1980
Reeves, Micky	mtr	1990
Reeves, Roloff	bb	1916
	ftb	1915
Regan, Kitty	wbk	1912, 13
Regier, Nancy	wgo	1968, 69
Regoli, John	bb	1958, 59, 60
Reichmuth, Leilahi	wsw	1985, 86, 87, 88
Reichow, Jody	wsb	1976, 77

Hot-hitting infielder John Regoli batted .356 in 1959 and .366 in 1960 to help Coach Bobby Winkles revive ASU's baseball fortunes.

Goalkeeper Erin Reinke helped ASU launch its women's soccer program in 1996. She was named the team's MVP in 1997, her first full season.

Reid, Bob	bb	1958, 59
Reid, Cam	msw	1981, 82, 83
Reid, David	mbk	1963, 64, 65
Reid, Elizabeth	wgy	1997, 98, 99, 2000
Reid, Jason	bb	1990, 91
Reid, Scott	bb	1967
Reidy, Tom	mbm	1990, 91, 92, 93
Reiff, Traci	wvb	1997
Reilly, Ramona	wtn	1935
Reilly, Ryan	ftb	1997, 98, 99
Reiman, Elmer	bb	1931
Reiner, Matt	mgy	1979
Reinke, Erin	wsoc	1996, 97, 98, 99, 2000
Rekiere, Chuck	mgy	1983, 84, 85, 86
Rekiere, Pam	wbm	1987, 88, 89, 90
Relles, Ross	ftb	1938, 39, 40
Rembert, Bob	ftb	1958, 59, 60
Renshaw, John	ftb	1991
Rensmeyer, Jeff	bb	1994
Rensmeyer, Mike	bb	1993
Renzi, Ron	wre	2000, 01
Renzo, Al	mtr	1980
Repak, Matt	mcc	1994, 95, 96, 97
	mtr	1995, 96, 97, 98
Reppert, Jim	mtr	1950, 51, 52
Reuter, Judy	wsw	1972, 73
Revello, Phyllis	wsb	1967
Reverman, Mike	msw	1975
Rey, Jack	mgy	1983
Reyes, Don	wre	1991, 92, 93
Reyes, Juan	mcc	2000
Reynolds, Jason	ftb	1994, 95
Reynolds, Melissa	wsoc	1996, 97, 98
Reynolds, Paul	bb	1992
	ftb	1996, 97
Reynolds, Susanne	wsb	1993, 94
Reynosa, Jim	ftb	1983, 84, 85
Rhee, Dave	mgy	1990, 91
Rhoades, Fred	ftb	1959, 60, 61
Rhoads, Ken	mtr	1984
Rhode, Christian	mgy	1988, 89, 90, 91
Rhodes, Emily	wcc	1991
Rhodes, Eva	wvb	1928
Rhodes, Lisa	wsw	1992, 93, 94, 95
Rhodes, Ola Mae	wgo	1947
Rhoton, Dana	wsb	1950, 51
	wtn	1950, 51, 52

Rhyne, Kendall	ftb	1991, 92, 93, 94
Ribelin, Tom	mbk	1940
Ricca, Jean	warc	1948
	wfh	1947, 49, 50
	wsb	1949, 50
Rice, Becky	wsb	1973, 74
Rice, Derek	wre	1995
Rice, Greg	ftb	1987, 88
	mtr	1988, 89
Rice, Howard	mgy	1954
Rice, Stan	msw	1979, 80
Rice, Wayne	bb	1967
Rich, Henry	bb	1951
	ftb	1950
Rich, Meg	wsw	1990
Richard, Danelle	wvb	1977
Richard, Gerald	mtr	1974, 75
Richard, Sidney	wre	1978, 79
Richard, Thomas	marc	1986, 87
Richards, Jeff	wre	1980, 81
Richards, R.O.	ftb	1899, 1900, 02, 03
Richardson, Bobby	mgo	1988
Richardson, Damien	ftb	1994, 95, 96, 97
Richardson, Glenn	bb	1955, 56
Richardson, Jerry	bb	1961
Richardson, Katherine	wtn	1940, 41
Richardson, Lamar	mbk	1996, 97
Richardson, Marie	wbm	1941
Richardson, Marion	wgo	1941
Richardson, Mike	ftb	1979, 80, 81, 82
Richardson, Pete	mtr	1982, 83, 84
Richardson, Robert	msw	1980, 81, 82, 83
Richart, Mary	wtn	1950
Richey, Mike	ftb	1989, 90, 91, 92
Richman, Elise	wtn	1984, 85, 86, 87
Richmond, Pam	wtn	1970, 71, 72
Ricketts, Jodi	wtn	1976, 77, 78, 79
Riddell, Catherine	wtn	1923
Riddle, Hamilton	msw	1976
Ridgeway, Al	bb	1942
	mbk	1941
	mgo	1941, 42
Rieger, Terry	mcc	1973
Rienstra, Coleen	wtr	1980, 81
Rietow, Dave	msw	1963, 64, 65
Rifenbark, Marti	wtn	1970
Rifkin, Art	bb	1951, 52
Rifkin, Burt	bb	1952
Riggs, Ben	mtr	1961
Riggs, Eddie	bb	1924, 25, 26, 27
Riggs, Gerald	ftb	1978, 79, 80, 81
Riggs, John	box	1933
Riggs, Johnny	bb	1926, 28
	ftb	1925, 26, 27
	mbk	1927, 28
Riggs, Noble	ftb	1937, 38, 39
Riggs, Steve	mcc	1997
Riiser, Ann-Kristin	wsw	1997, 98
Riley, Joe	bb	1952
Riley, Ralph	mgy	1990, 91, 92
Riley, Ron	mbk	1993, 94, 95, 96
Riley, Tom	wre	1981, 82, 83, 84
Ringeisen, Keith	mtr	1994, 95
Rinker, Don	marc	1968, 69
Ripp, Libby	wbk	1986, 87
Ripple, Bob	ftb	1947, 48, 49, 50
Rish, Chip	ftb	1985
	mtr	1986, 87, 88
Risner, Darrell	mbk	1962
Risoli, Ralph	wre	1973
Risquez, Ann Marie	wsb	1994
Rist, Bente	wsw	1987, 88, 89, 90
Ritchey, Shawn	wsb	1979, 80, 81, 82
Ritchie, Charlie	mgo	1972, 73, 74

Ritter, Al	mtn	1964
Ritter, Craig	ftb	1991, 92
Ritter, Mike	ftb	1989, 90, 91
Rivard, Jill	wsoc	1996, 97, 98, 99
Rivas, Oscar	bb	1989
Rivera, Santiago	bb	1993
Riviello, Vinny	wgo	1993, 94, 95, 96
Roach, Barbara	wbk	1942, 43
	wfh	1942
	wvb	1942
Roach, Charley	mtn	1951, 52
Robards, Cherry	wvb	1967
Robb, Terese	wvb	1999
Robbins, Betty	wtn	1966
Roberds, Cherry	wbm	1967, 68
	wsb	1967
Roberson, Jamie	wre	1979, 81
Roberts, "Roach"	bb	1914, 15
Roberts, Beth	wgy	1979, 80
Roberts, Bill	mtr	1955, 56
Roberts, Blair	mtn	1979, 80
Roberts, Dennis	mtn	1994
Roberts, Dennis	wre	1984, 85, 86
Roberts, Jeff	bb	1982, 83, 84, 85
Roberts, Jim	ftb	1982, 83
Roberts, Libby	wtr	1980
Roberts, Marie	warc	1940
	wbk	1942
	wbm	1940, 42
	wfh	1941
	wsb	1940, 41, 42
	wvb	1942
Roberts, Mike	mtr	1971
Roberts, Millie	wsb	1967
	wsw	1967, 68, 69, 70
Roberts, Sue	wsw	1965
Roberts, Val	warc	1968
Roberts, Vida	wbk	1919
Roberts, Wayne	msw	1984, 86
Robertson, Charles	mtr	1934
	mcc	1933
Robertson, Bob	ftb	1990, 91
Robertson, H.	mtr	1954, 55
Robertson, Jerry	mtr	1957, 58
Robertson, Kirk	ftb	1994, 95, 96
Robeson, Greg	mtr	1995, 96, 97
Robinette, Rhonda	wgy	1999, 2000, 01
Robinson, Billy	ftb	1981, 82, 83, 84
Robinson, Brian	mgy	1992
Robinson, Brian	mtr	1982
Robinson, Frank	mtr	1955
Robinson, Frank	mtr	1974
Robinson, Glenn	mtr	1980, 81
Robinson, Harry	ftb	1916
Robinson, John	ftb	1967
Robinson, Ken	mcc	1967, 68, 69
	mtr	1966, 67, 68, 70
Robinson, Kenny	mtr	1983, 84, 85, 86
Robinson, Monique	wtr	1986, 87, 88, 89
Robinson, Stan	ftb	1973, 74, 75, 76
Robinson, William	bb	1917, 18
Robinson, Zelma	wbb	1936
	wbk	1935
	wfh	1935
Robinson-Blanchard, L.	mtr	1997, 98, 99, 2000
Robison, Ted	bb	1965, 66
Robson, Dave	bb	1989, 90, 91, 92
Roby, Helen	wbb	1925
	wbk	1925
	wtn	1924
Rocha, Joe	bb	1988
Roche, Barbara	wbb	1943
	wsb	1943
	wtf	1943

Name	Sport	Years
Rockell, Mary	wsw	1971
Rockwell, Ann	wtn	1964, 65, 66
Rockwell, Eva	wsb	1977
Rockwell, Hank	mbk	1939
	mtr	1938, 39, 40
Rockwell, Harry	ftb	1937, 38
Rockwell, Tammy	wtr	1994, 95
Rodgers, Andrea	wsb	1998, 99, 2000
Rodgers, Andy	mgy	1992
Rodgers, Charlie	rif	1956, 57
Rodgers, Derrick	ftb	1996
Rodgers, Kathy	wsw	1964
Rodiles, Jose	bb	1983, 84
Rodriguez, Ari	mcc	1994, 95, 96, 97
	mtr	1995, 96, 97, 98
Rodriguez, Jim	wre	1987
Rodriguez, John	wre	1958
Rodriguez, Paul	mgy	1959
Rodriguez-Mesa, Ivan	msw	1997, 98
Roe, Helen	wfh	1935
Roe, Milton	rif	1950
Roe, Pargess	ftb	1932
Roedinger, Andy	mtn	1985, 86, 87
Roedinger, Janet	wtn	1971
Rogalla, Anne	wsw	1998, 99, 2000
Rogers, "Schoolboy"	bb	1908
Rogers, Avis	wvb	1924
Rogers, Bill	wre	1963
Rogers, Charlie	mgy	1970
Rogers, Courtney	mtn	1953, 54
Rogers, Diana	wtr	1976
Rogers, Frank	ftb	1951, 52, 53
Rogers, Jamie	wsw	1998
Rogers, Jennifer	wvb	1988, 89, 90, 91
Rogers, Kenny	msw	1977
Rogers, Louisa	wbk	1914, 15
Rogers, Miles	mtn	1998, 99, 2000
Rogers, Pam	wsw	1976, 77, 78, 79
Rogers, Paul	bb	1958
Rogers, Rick	mtr	1979
Rogers, Tedrick	mtr	1996, 97
Rogge, Bud	ftb	1942
Roggenhorst, Jan	wvb	1967, 68
Rojo, Jermiah	mcc	1999
	mtr	1999
Rojo, Jesus	mtn	1989
Rojohn, Jennifer	wtn	1988, 89, 90, 91
Rokita, Bob	ftb	1965, 66, 67
Rokoff, Mike	mtn	1958
Rolf, Carl	marc	1972
Rollins, Charles	bb	1920, 21
	mbk	1920, 21
	mtr	1921, 22
Rollins, Dell	ftb	1926
	mtr	1926
Romanick, Ron	bb	1980
Romanini, Dawn	wgy	1977, 78, 79
Romano, Sabra	wgy	1990
Romero, Felicia	wsb	2001
Romero, Joe	wre	1979, 80
Romero, Zack	ftb	1994, 95, 96, 97
Romine, Jack	msw	1969, 70
Romine, Kevin	bb	1981, 82
Romo, Robert	bb	1916
Ronaldson, Tony	mbk	1992
Roomsburg, Tony	warc	1940, 41
Rooney, John	mgo	1954
Roose, Katie	wcc	1980
Roque, Juan	ftb	1994, 95, 96
Rosado, Billy	wre	1977, 78
Roscoe, Kris	mtr	1995
Rose, Brett	msw	1984, 85, 86, 87
Rose, Elizabeth	wbk	1938, 40
	wfh	1938
	wgo	1938, 39, 40
	wsb	1938, 39, 40
	wtn	1938
Rose, Jim	ftb	1955
Rose, Jim	mtr	1970, 71
Rose, Joe	mtr	1957, 58, 59
Rose, John	mtr	1960, 61, 62, 63
Rose, Tyrone	wre	1975
Roseborough, Ed	ftb	1967, 68
Rosen, Steve	mtn	1963, 64
Rosette, Leo	ftb	1978
Rosetti, Mickey	wre	1975
Ross, Alex	msw	1970
Ross, Bruce	msw	1974, 75, 76, 77
Ross, Heather	wbm	1979, 80, 81, 82
Ross, Sandy	wsw	1961
Ross, William	bb	1954
Rostron, Richard	mtr	1974, 75
Rot, Bradley	mgy	1982, 83, 84, 85
Roth, Bobby	bb	1955, 56
Roth, Dan	mcc	1959
	mtr	1962
Rothchild, Marc	mtn	1991, 92
Rothermund, Don	mtr	1957
Rotolante, Randy	wre	1974, 75
Rounds, Lee	ftb	1955
Rouse, Barney	ftb	1940, 41
Rouse, John	ftb	1934, 35, 36
Rouwenhorst, Jan	wsb	1967
	wbm	1967
Row, Katheryn	wtn	1942, 43
Rowan, Ann	wsb	1988, 89, 90, 91
Rowell, Kelly	wsw	1977, 78
Rowland, Garon	mgy	1993
Rowland, Liz	wgo	1977, 78, 81
Royden, Bert	mtn	1983
Royere, Marita	wsb	1974, 75, 76, 77
Rram, Katherine	wtn	1939
Rubel, Genevieve	wbb	1923
Rubin, Dave	marc	1981, 82, 83, 84
Rubin, Regina	wbm	1981, 82, 83, 84
Rubio, Maria	wvb	1968
Ruck, Leo	ftb	1915
Rucker, Robert	mtr	1988, 89, 90, 91
Rucker, Sandy	wgo	1967, 68
Rudd, Frank	ftb	1916
Rudolph, Dea Ann	wsw	1980
Rudolph, Frank	ftb	1983, 84, 85, 86
Rudolph, S	wbm	1962
Ruedy, John	bb	1963, 64
	mtr	1964
Ruegamer, Grey	ftb	1995, 96, 97, 98
Ruff, Tina	wsb	1994, 95, 96, 97
Ruiz, Benny	bb	1958, 59
Ruiz, Enrique	bb	1999
Rukkila, John	mcc	1969
	mtr	1969
Rumsey, Dan	bb	1986, 87, 88, 89
Runge, Matt	mgo	1967
Runge, Mike	mcc	1975
Runge, Paul	bb	1961, 62
Runion, Howard	wre	1958
Runnquist, Jonas	mgo	1997, 98, 99, 2000
Rupcich, Mike	bb	1970, 71, 72
Ruse, Robert	bb	1923, 24
	ftb	1923
Ruskey, Jason	bb	1994
Rusnak, Ellie	wsw	1979
Russell, Carl	ftb	1974, 75, 76, 77
Russell, Cyrus	ftb	1948
Russell, Kathy	wsw	1967
Russell, Leonard	ftb	1990
Russell, Vernon	mbk	1959
Russo, Pete	wre	1963, 65, 66, 67
Russo, Tony	mgy	1982, 83, 84, 85
Russo, Tony	wre	1964, 65, 66
Russo, Vince	mtn	1995
Rust, Gary	mgy	1977, 78, 79
Rustman, Jay	mgo	1972
Ruston, John	mtr	1961
Rusty, Barbara	wfh	1947
Ruth, Walt	bb	1940
	ftb	1938, 39, 40
Rutila, Kim	wtn	1979
Rutkowski, Paul	mtr	1983
Rutledge, Kevin	ftb	1977, 78
Ryan, Ann	wbk	1979
Ryan, Cal	mbk	1967
Ryan, Dan	mgy	1970, 71
Ryan, Eddie	rif	1957
Ryan, Mickey	ftb	1954, 55
Ryan, Shaughn	mbk	1986, 87
	mtr	1986, 87
Ryan, Steve	mgo	1967, 68
Rybacki, David	mtn	1974, 75, 76
Ryden, Bill	mgy	1980, 81, 83
Ryder, Brian	ftb	1990, 91, 92, 93
Ryer, Dave	mtr	1985, 86
Rylance, George	bb	1937
	mtr	1937
Ryley, Frank	mtr	1951
Ryther, Peggy	wcc	1980, 81, 82
	wtr	1981

S

Name	Sport	Years
Saarman, Paul	mtr	1948
Saba, Norm	ftb	1949
Saban, Bill	mtn	1938, 39
Sabbagh, Tom	bb	1948
Sabin, Helen	wvb	1948
Sabo, Karen	wsoc	1996
Sachs, Doug	mtn	1987, 88
Saenz, Dick	bb	1955
Saenz, Frankie	wre	2000, 01
Sahan, Frank	bb	1918, 19
Sain, John	bb	1971, 72, 73
Sain, Mike	wre	1974
Sain, Tom	bb	1973, 74, 75
Salandra, Nick	wre	1994

Kevin Romine batted .410 in 1981 and .406 in 1982. He's the only player in modern history to string together back-to-back .400 seasons.

Name	Sport	Years
Salas, Leo	wre	1968
Salazar, Philip	wre	1981
Salcedo, Ronni	bb	1982
Salcido, Connie	wtn	1949, 50
Saleaumua, Dan	ftb	1983, 84, 85, 86
Salem, Tim	ftb	1984
Salerno, Fran	wbm	1951, 52
Salinas, Felix	wre	1968, 69
Salsinger, Joe	bb	1948
Salsman, Lisa	wbk	1990, 91, 92, 93
Samilton, Jawell	ftb	1998, 99
Sampson, Mary Claire	wsw	1958
Sampson, Demond	ftb	1991
Samson, Jack	rif	1950
Samuels, Scott	bb	1991, 92
Sancette, Josie	wbk	1941, 42
	wfh	1942
	wsb	1941, 42
	wvb	1942
Sancette, Julie	wbk	1939
	wsb	1938, 39, 40, 41, 42
	wvb	1942
Sanchez, Francisco	msw	1996, 97, 98, 99
Sanchez, J.J.	mgy	1989, 90
Sanchez, Joe	mtn	1955, 56
Sanchez, Marco	wre	1990, 91, 92, 93
Sanchez, Mike	mtr	1971
Sanchez, Vivianne	wsw	1995
Sand, Kristine	wbk	1997, 98, 99, 2000
Sandage	mtr	1914
Sandell, Alan	ftb	1956, 57
Sanders, Eddie	ftb	1977, 78
Sanders, Kirsten	wsw	1993, 94
Sanders, Louise	wbb	1936
	wbk	1935
	wbk	1937, 38
	wsb	1938
Sanders, Mary Ann	wtn	1981
Sanders, Ron	mcc	1964, 65
Sanders, Ronnie	mtr	1958
Sandidge, Staci	wsw	1984
Sandle, Chris	mbk	1985, 86
Sandman, Bridget	wgy	1994, 95, 96, 97
Sandmire, Yvonne	wgy	1976, 77, 78
Sands, Steve	marc	1978
Sandvig, Carol	wtn	1971, 72, 73
Sanford, Craig	mtr	1983
Sanserino, Albert	bb	1940
	ftb	1938, 39, 40
Sanson, Tom	ftb	1951
Santana, Sam	ftb	1992, 93, 94, 95
Santel, Don	mbk	1954
Santeo, Claudine	wbk	1934
Santoro, Dan	wre	1976, 77
Sapolu, Saute	ftb	1985, 86, 87, 88
Sar, John	mcc	1962
Sarfate, Dennis	bb	2000
Sargsian, Sargis	mtn	1994, 95
Sarullo, Fran	wsb	1976
Sasada, Kelly	wsw	1998, 99, 2000, 01
Sattler, Pam	wtn	1968, 69, 70, 71
Sauer, Lainie	wsw	1990
Sauer, LeAnn	wtr	1986
Sauer, Lois	wsb	1951
Saunders, Bill	ftb	1947, 48, 49
Saunders, Dennis	mgo	1974, 75, 76, 77
Saunders, Dick	bb	1957, 58, 59, 60
Saunders, Jim	mgo	1968, 69, 70
Saunders, Lynne	wvb	1973
Saunders, Townsend	wre	1989
Savage, Kay	wvb	1976
Savage, Virgil	ftb	1950, 51, 52
Savinon, Chuck	wre	1972
Savoy, Joan	wgy	1979, 80

Name	Sport	Years
Sawaia, Wade	bb	1942, 46
Sawtell, Rick	msw	1989, 90, 91, 92
Sawyer, Dorothy	wbk	1935
	wfh	1933, 35
	wgo	1933, 34
Sayer, Ted	mtr	1957
Saylor, Clyda Jean	wbb	1943
	wbk	1943, 45
	wfh	1943
	wsb	1943
	wtn	1943
	wtf	1943, 45
	wvb	1943
Sbarbaro, Keith	mgo	1990, 91, 92, 93
Scales	box	1929
Scales, Katy	wbk	1980
Scanlon, Kara	wsw	1990
Scanlon, Walter	bb	1948, 49, 50, 51
Scanlon, William	mtn	1916
Scannell, Mike	mcc	1981, 82, 83, 84
	mtr	1982, 83, 84, 85
Scarano, Charles	mbm	1980, 81, 82, 83
Scarfo, Ron	ftb	1964
Scavo, John	ftb	1964
Schaareman, Wendy	wtr	1993
Schad, Joelle	wtn	1992, 93, 94, 95
Schad, Vernon	mgo	1950, 51, 56
Schaeffer, Glenn	ftb	1934, 35, 36
Schaffer, Janet	warc	1989, 90, 91, 92
Schaldach, Charlene	wtn	1979, 80
Schauer, Cec	wgo	1968
Schaumberg, Elke	wtn	1987
Schechtman, Steve	mgy	1980, 81, 82
Scheetz, Carol	wtr	1976, 77
Schefsky, Steve	bb	1977, 78
Schenke, Tom	mgo	1965
Schertzer, Kara	wtn	1992, 93, 94, 95
Schienbein, Dale	mgo	1985, 86
Schiff, Patti	wtn	1980, 81, 82
Schilens, Mike	mtr	1996
Schilling, Roger	mtr	1980, 82
Schlesinger, Jeff	mtr	1967, 68, 69
Schlink, Pete	bb	1981, 82
Schluchter-Nevez, Scott	wre	1992, 93
Schlueter, Nancy	wsw	1988
Schmelz, Alan	bb	1963, 64, 65
	mbk	1963, 64, 65
Schmidt, Barry	mgy	1976, 77, 78, 79
Schmidt, Czeslo,	ftb	1947, 48, 49
Schmidt, Eric	ftb	1994
Schmidt, Herman	mtr	1955
Schmidt, Jerrilyn	wsw	1986
Schmidt, Steve	mcc	1973
	mtr	1974
Schmidt, Thomas	ftb	1998, 99
Schmitt, Carl	mgy	1992
Schmitt, Char	wsb	1988
Schmitt, Lyn	wgy	1982, 83, 84, 85
Schmitt, Steve	mtr	1973
Schmitz, Carolyn	wtn	1982
Schmitz, Shirley	wfh	1947, 48, 49
	wvb	1946
Schmoyer, Claire	wtn	1972, 73, 74, 75
Schmoyer, Kay	wtn	1972, 73, 74, 75
Schmuck, Roger	bb	1970, 71
Schoeffler, Brian	mcc	1976
	mtr	1977
Schofield, Andy	mtr	1985
Scholz, Kurt	marc	1987
Schone, Paul	marc	1972
Schorr, Bill	bb	1987
Schott, Linda	wgy	1980
Schouten, Jim	mcc	1999
	mtr	1999, 2000

Name	Sport	Years
Schrader, Jack	mbk	1973, 74, 75
Schram, Jack	ftb	1980, 83
Schram, Patty	wgo	1975
Schrantz, Bill	marc	1950, 51
Schreck, Kristi	wtn	1983
Schreiber, Jim	mgo	1971, 72, 73
Schreiner, Karl	mtr	1960, 61
Schreur, Gerhard	mbk	1968, 69, 70
Schrieber, Jared	mtr	1996, 97, 98
Schroeter, Russ	wre	1973
Schroyer, Ryan	bb	2001
Schubert, Don	msw	1982, 83
Schuerman, Bart	mgo	1971
Schuessler, Adrienne	wsw	1988, 89, 90, 91
Schuh, Mike	ftb	1985, 86, 87, 88
Schuler, Ellis	mbk	1931, 32, 33
	bb	1932
	ftb	1931, 32
Schuljak, George	ftb	1951
Schuljak, Jake	ftb	1951
Schulte, Jan	wgo	1970, 71
Schultz, Greg	ftb	1978
Schultz, Lois	wsw	1964
Schultz, Maria	wsw	1982, 83, 84
Schulz, Sam	mtn	1961
Schumacher, Pam	wsb	1983
Schuknecht, Kory	ftb	1972, 73, 74
Schuster, Leanne	wvb	1991, 92, 93, 94
Schutzel, Kurt	mgy	1980
Schwabauer, Lance	wre	1957, 58
Schwabe, Mike	bb	1987
Schwartrzkopf, Kristin	warc	1985, 86, 87
Schwartz, Larry	msw	1970
Schwartzberg, Jerry	ftb	1999
Schwarz, Casey	wcc	1999
	wtr	1999, 2000
Schwarz, Chuck	mcc	1979, 80, 81, 82
	mtr	1979, 80, 82, 83
Schwarz, Mike	mtr	1979, 81, 82, 83
Schweikhart, Herman	bb	1935, 36, 37
Schwimmer, Emily	wsoc	2000
Schwinghamer, Julie	wtr	1984, 85
Scialo, Mike	bb	1990, 91, 92
Scimo, Ralph	marc	1978, 79, 80
Scofield, Mike	rif	1956
Scott, Ardell	ftb	1982, 83
Scott, Art	mbk	1941
Scott, Brandon	mtr	2000
Scott, Brian	mgy	1969, 70, 71, 72
Scott, Byron	mbk	1980, 81, 83
Scott, Carl	mbm	1970
Scott, Charles	bb	1983, 84, 85
Scott, Chester	mcc	1954
	mtr	1954, 55
Scott, Louis	mcc	1964, 65, 66
	mtr	1964, 65, 66, 67
Scott, M.	wtn	1963
Scott, Penny	wtn	1964, 65, 66
Scott, Randy	mgy	1988
Scott, R.L.	wbk	1922
Scott, Robin	warc	1988
Scott, Ron	wre	1972, 73
Scott, Sarah	wgo	1975, 76, 77, 78
Scott, Shanel	wsoc	1998, 99, 2000
Scott, Steve	ftb	1975
Scott, Tedd	bb	1931
Scott, Terry	mtr	1972, 73
Scott, Tony	ftb	1980
Scott, Tony	mtr	1978
Scott, Treg	mcc	1984, 85
	mtr	1983, 84, 85, 86
Scroggins, Erin	mcc	1991, 92, 93, 94
	mtr	1992, 93, 94, 95
Scroggins, Willie	ftb	1975, 76

Seals	mtr	1914
Sebald, Bonnie	wcc	1979
Sedillo, Andrew	wre	1991, 92
Sedlar, Bob	ftb	1952, 53, 54, 55
Seedborg, John	ftb	1961, 62, 63
Seeley, David	msw	1998
Seeley, Margaret	wbk	1921
Seferovich, Pat	wre	1965, 66, 67
Segala, Sophia	wbb	1925
Segalia, Chris	ftb	1899, 1900, 1902
Segar, John	mgy	1968
Segovia, Eloise	wsb	1949
Segulia, Ann	wvb	1946
Seibert, Gib	bb	1980, 81, 82
Seifert, Daniela	wcc	1987, 88, 89
	wtr	1989
Seigwart, Ed	ftb	1975
Seime, Pat	marc	1983
Seivert, Dan	ftb	1953
Seivert, Mike	ftb	1977, 78
Selchow, Harry	bb	1948
Seleine, Julie	wcc	1983, 84
	wtr	1984
Self, Candy	warc	1969
	wsb	1970
Self, Harold	ftb	1949, 50, 51
Seljeskog, Vanessa	wtr	1977
Sell, Henry	mtn	1945
Sellchow, Harry	ftb	1946
Selleh, Joe	bb	1931
Sellers, Charles	mbk	1924
Sellers, James	rif	1953
Sells, Todd	mtr	1984, 85, 86
Selvaratnam, Thuhashini	wgo	1996, 97, 98, 99
Semrad, Al	mgo	1969, 70
Sena, Rachel	wtn	1971
Senini, Edward	msw	1971
Senior, Mark	mtr	1986, 87
Senior, Rosiland	wbk	1989, 90
Senitza, Gary	mbk	1962, 63, 64
Seniuk, Petra	wsb	1978, 79
Senseman, Ed	mbk	1950, 51, 52
Senz, Bob	msw	1982, 83
Sepulveda, Martin	wre	1980, 81, 82
Serginese, Herman	ftb	1966, 67, 68
Serrano, Ed	bb	1984, 85
Serritella, Christy	wsb	1989, 90, 91, 92
Setka, Annie	wfh	1935
Setka, Eva	wfh	1941
Setka, Nellie	wbk	1939
	wfh	1938, 39
	wsb	1938
Setka, Steve	ftb	1936, 37
Settles, Jim	mtn	1981, 82, 83
Severance, Judy	warc	1964, 65, 66, 67
Severn, Dan	wre	1977, 78, 80, 81
Severn, Dave	wre	1976, 77, 79, 80
Severn, Mike	wre	1981, 82, 83, 84
Severn, Rod	wre	1985, 86, 87, 88
Severson, Mark	marc	1978
Sevin, Pete	mcc	1970, 71
	mtr	1970, 71, 72
Sevin, Steve	mcc	1971
Sexauer, Matt	mcc	1997
	mtr	1998
Sexton, Clarence	mtr	1933, 34, 35
	bb	1935
	ftb	1931, 32, 33, 34
Seymour, Gary	wre	1968, 70
Shabe, Jim	mtr	1957
Shad, Vernon	mtn	1950
Shadle, Wendi	wtr	1983
Shafer, Barry	ftb	1934
Shafer, Kirsten	wsw	1994, 95

Judy Severance was the nation's top-ranked women's archer in 1965, 1966 and 1967 and the first archer in the nation to win all-America recognition four times. She was ASU's first four-time All-American in any sport.

Wrestler Dan Severn compiled a 127-11-1 career record, was a three-time conference champ and a two-time All-American.

Shafer, Shane	ftb	1997
Shaffer, Brynn	wsoc	2000
Shafton, Leonard	mtr	1947
Shald, Miranda	wsw	2001
Shaler, Janet	wbm	1970
Shamblee, Jep	ftb	1939, 40
Shamosh, Robert	msw	1991, 92, 93, 94
Shanks, Brian	mgo	1974, 75
Shannon, Dave	mgy	1984, 85
Shapiro, Dave	mcc	1975
Shapiro, Jessica	wsb	1995
Sharkey, Teri	wbk	1983
Sharp, Wayne	wre	1986, 87
Sharpe, Charles	mcc	1998, 99, 2000
	mtr	1999, 2000, 01
Sharpe, Cindy	wsb	1977, 78
	wvb	1976, 77
Shaughnessey, Jim	ftb	1967, 68, 69
	wre	1966
Shaw, David	mbm	1987, 88
Shaw, Greg	msw	1971, 73
Shaw, Jonathan	msw	2001
Shaw, Myra	wsw	1985, 86, 87, 88
Shaw, Randy	marc	1971
Shaw, Rick	ftb	1966, 67
Shawn, Edwin	bb	1933, 34, 36

Shawn, Gwen	wsb	1970
Shea, Kelly	wsw	1999, 2000
Sheaffer, Jon	fb	2000
	bb	2001
Shearin, Bob	msw	1980
Sheedy, Rosalie	wgo	1962, 63
Sheehan, Jeff	msw	1986, 87
Sheff, Dave	mgo	1969, 70, 71
Sheldon, Joe	mtr	1911
Shell, Tanner	mbk	2000
Shelley, Ed	mtr	1946
Shelstad, Gail	wbm	1981
Shelton, Amy	wgy	1997, 98, 99
Shelton, Dora	wbk	1934, 35
	wfh	1934, 35
Shepard, Teri	wtr	1981, 82, 83, 84
Shephard, Henry	rif	1956
Shephard, Julie	wgo	1989, 90, 91, 92
Shepherd, Barry	mtr	1967, 68, 69, 70
Shepherd, Rob	mgy	1980, 82
Sheppard, Merry	warc	1967
Sher, Jim	mgo	1964
Sherbeck, Eric	mtn	1978, 79
Sheridan, Susanne	wsw	1989
Sherman, Helen	wbk	1940
	wtn	1938, 39, 40, 41
Sherman, Ruth	warc	1952, 53
Sherman, Tony	ftb	1989
Sherrell, Kim	wsw	1978
Shield, Roger	wre	1985
Shiflett, Matt	bb	1987
Shiflett, Susan	wsw	1988
Shifren, Nolan	msw	1995, 96
Shill, George	mcc	1933
Shill, LeNore	warc	1932, 33
	wbk	1934
	wfh	1933, 34
Shill, Otto	bb	1914, 15
Shill, Scott	bb	1915
Shill, Scott	mtr	1987
Shimkus, Mike	ftb	1970, 71
Shiner, Susan	warc	1967, 68
Shines, Bob	wre	1967, 68, 69, 70
Shinholster, Vince	bb	1986
Shinn, Ron	bb	1960
Shinner, Doreatha	wtr	1977
Shinnick, Rich	msw	1988, 89
Shipes, Henry	mtr	1971, 72
Shipkey	mtr	1933
Shipley, D	wbk	1945
Shipley, Lee	warc	1950
Shipman, Kathy	wsw	1980, 81, 82, 83
	wvb	1979
Shipp, Jim	mtr	1979, 80, 81
Shirey, Ray	ftb	1964, 65, 66
Shirie, Don	mtr	1981, 82, 83, 84
Shirley, Greg	bb	1983
Shively, Tom	ftb	1955
Shoemaker, James	rif	1956
Shoemaker, Jim	mtn	1953
Shoemaker, Pinky	wtn	1961, 62, 63
Sholl, John	msw	1986, 87, 88, 89
Shoore, Dave	rif	1959, 60
Shoore, Joe	rif	1957
Shores, Scott	bb	1993, 94
Shorty, Larry	ftb	1971, 72, 73
Shough, James	wre	1981
Shower, Cecily	wgo	1967
Shrader, Mike	wre	1977
Shrigley, Sam	bb	1907
Shuck, Frank	ftb	1916
	bb	1917
Shudinis, Mike	wre	1983, 84
Shuey, Ray	bb	1955

In addition to being a three-time All-American (first team in 1988 and 1989, honorable mention in 1987), Pearl Sinn was the first woman golfer to win the U.S. Amateur and U.S. Public Links titles in the same year (1988).

Shuler, Don	wre	1976, 77, 78
Shulik, Wendy	wcc	1984
Shumway, Boyd	mbk	1938, 39
Shumway, Gordon	mbk	1951, 52, 53, 54
Shumway, Royd	mcc	1952, 53
	mtr	1951, 52, 53, 54
Shupe, Mark	ftb	1983, 83, 84
Shushack, Mark	mgo	1972, 73
Shute, Eugene	ftb	1904
Shute, Walter	ftb	1899, 1900, 02
Sibrie, Wali	ftb	1995
Sica, Dick	ftb	1965, 66, 67
Sicola, Mark	mtr	1986, 87
Sidler, Vic	ftb	1983
Sidoti, Becky	wvb	1999, 2000
Sidoti, Tony	wre	1974
Sie, Tonnie	mtn	1978, 79
Siebelts, Steve	mtr	1992
Sieben, Bob	mtr	1949
Siefarth, Cappi	wsw	1973, 74, 75, 76
Siegel, Jay	mgy	1982
Siegelsky, Charles	rif	1953
Sienicki, Jill	wcc	1989, 90
	wtr	1990, 91
Sieper, Tom	ftb	1974, 75
Sieras, Art	mtr	1949
Sierks, Chriss	wtn	1976
Siford, Scott	msw	1988
Sihner, Wendy	wcc	1983, 84, 85
	wtr	1984, 85, 86
Sikorski, Diane	wgo	1982, 83, 84, 85
Silcox, Rusty	bb	1990
Siler, Drew	bb	1984, 85
Silliman, Rich	mgo	1964
Silva, Manuel	mcc	1951, 52, 53
	mtr	1951, 52, 53, 54
Silva, Mike	msw	1982
Silver, Steve	msw	1973, 74, 75, 76
Silverthorn, John	mcc	1963
	mtr	1963, 64
Simkew, Ron	mtr	1973
Simkins, Bally	mbk	1925, 26, 27
Simmons, Barbara	wtn	1947
Simmons, Bob	mtn	1947, 48, 49
Simmons, Harry	mtn	1939, 40
Simmons, Hervey	mgo	1956
Simmons, Jason	ftb	1994, 95, 96, 97

Simmons, La Shawn	wtr	1991, 92
Simmons, Linton	mtn	1916
Simmons, Marianne	wsoc	1996, 97, 99, 2000
Simmons, Nicole	wtr	1999, 2000, 01
	wcc	1998
Simmons, Pam	wsb	1991
Simmons, Rick	mgo	1969, 70
Simmons, Thomas	bb	1996
	ftb	1994, 95, 96, 97
Simone, Ron	ftb	1985
Simoneau, Jeff	ftb	1989
Simonton, Mary	wgo	1933, 34
Simpkins, Ernest	bb	1925
	ftb	1924, 25, 26
	mtr	1925, 26, 27
Simpson, Aaron	wre	1995, 96, 97, 98
Simpson, Bob	ftb	1926, 27
	mtr	1927
Simpson, Danny	mtr	1991, 92, 93
Simpson, Errol	mgy	1979
Simpson, Heather	wsw	1985
Simpson, Larry	wre	1966
Sims, Jim	bb	1956, 57, 58, 59
Sims, Mike	mbk	1976, 77, 78, 79
Sims, Stan	msw	1963, 64, 65
Simson, Al	ftb	1996
Sinadinos, Jim	wre	1987, 88
Sinclair, Lillian	wfh	1948
	wsb	1951
	wvb	1948
Sinclair, Pete	mcc	1964
Sine, Melvin	bb	1927, 28, 29
Singer, Kevin	mgy	1988, 89, 90, 91
Singer, Sue	wsw	1986
Singleton, Brian	ftb	1995
Singleton, Ron	mbk	1985
Singleton, Vicki	wgo	1976, 77, 78, 79
Sinn, Carol	wsb	1979, 80
Sinn, Pearl	wgo	1986, 87, 88, 89
Sinohui, Andrea	wsb	1978, 79, 80, 81
Sinohui, Jeanette	wsb	1975
Sinovic, Dave	mtn	1965, 66
Sipe, Kathy	wtr	1977
Sirrine, Keith	mbk	1947
Siskowski, Mitch	ftb	1961, 62, 63
Sitzman, Jay	bb	1997, 98, 99

Sterling Slaughter set a school record, whiffing 22 Colorado State batters in March of 1963.

Harold Slemmer was an offensive tackle for the 1974 Sun Devils. Now he's head of the Arizona Interscholastic Association.

Sizemore, Melvin	bb	1934, 35, 36
	mbk	1934, 35, 36
Skagen, Greg	msw	1974
Skala, Mike	ftb	1986
Skarin, Neal	ftb	1972, 73
Skinner, Kim	wgy	1998, 99, 2000, 01
Skogland, Bonnie	wsw	1969
Skousen, Ana	wbk	1925
Skousen, Annis	wbm	1964
Skousen, Cecille	wbb	1936
	wbk	1935, 36, 37
	wfh	1935
Skousen, Della	wbk	1939
Skovanek, Joann	wtn	1979
Skurdall, Barbara	wtn	1972, 73
Slabinski, Paul	ftb	1991
Slade, Justin	msw	1994, 95
Slagle, Howard	bb	1948
Slater, Kristin	wsoc	1998, 99, 2000
Slaughter, Bob	bb	1952
Slaughter, Sterling	bb	1961, 62, 63
Slayton, Shannon	wbk	1993, 94, 95
Slemmer, Gerald	ftb	1972, 73
	wre	1973, 74
Slemmer, Harold	ftb	1974
Slezak, Joe	msw	1984, 85, 86, 87
Slick, Stacey	wcc	1997
	wsb	1996, 97
	wtr	1998
Sloan, Sue	wsw	1977, 78, 79, 81
Slocum, Doug	bb	1973, 74
Slonac, Steve	bb	1959, 60, 61
	ftb	1959, 60
Slonim, Marc	mgo	1969, 70
Sluka, Marie	wsw	1987, 88
Smaltz, Terri	wsw	1982
Smart, Joe	mcc	1961, 62, 63
	mtr	1963, 64
Smart, Lindsey	wsw	2001
Smart, Rocky	wre	2001
Smatana, Beckie	wbk	1984, 85
Smigel, Beth	wtn	1984, 85, 86, 87
Smiley, Janette	wtn	1983, 84
Smit, Karel	msw	1994, 95, 96
Smith, Aaron	mgy	1993
Smith, Andre	ftb	1997
Smith, Barb	wbk	1982, 83, 84, 85

Smith, Barry	mtr	1986,87	Smith, Robert	bb	1928, 29, 30, 31	
Smith, Bill	bb	1953, 54, 55, 56	Smith, Robert	msw	1994, 95, 96	
Smith, Bill	msw	1964	Smith, Roger	bb	1986	
Smith, Bob	ftb	1929, 30, 31	Smith, Ron	mtr	1978	
	mbk	1928, 29, 30, 31	Smith, Rosemary	wbk	1942, 43	
Smith, Brent	bb	1992, 93		wfh	1942, 43	
Smith, Brian	bb	1991		wsb	1942, 43	
Smith, Brian	msw	1970		wvb	1942, 43	
Smith, Carla	wvb	1950	Smith, Sandy	wtn	1960, 61, 62, 63	
Smith, Carrie	wgy	1976, 77		wvb	1961	
Smith, Cecil	ftb	1914	Smith, Scott	msw	1983	
Smith, Cecila	wcc	1979	Smith, Shawn	wbk	1981, 82	
	wtr	1980	Smith, Shera	wbm	1977	
Smith, Cheryl	wsb	1988, 89		wsb	1979	
Smith, Chris	mgy	1990, 91, 92	Smith, Sid	marc	1952	
Smith, Chuck	mtr	1993	Smith, Steve	mcc	1980	
Smith, Cliff	mtr	1972, 73		mtr	1981	
Smith, Dan	mcc	1992	Smith, Stevin	mbk	1991, 92, 93, 94	
Smith, Dan	mgy	1969, 70, 71, 72	Smith, Sumner	ftb	1956, 57	
Smith, Darice	wvb	1998, 99		mtr	1957	
Smith, Dave	mgo	1949, 51, 52	Smith, Susan	wtr	1978	
Smith, Dave	mtr	1975	Smith, Syd	bb	1962, 63	
Smith, Derek	ftb	1995, 96	Smith, Terrelle	ftb	1997, 98, 99	
Smith, Derek	mbk	1998, 99	Smith, Terri	wsb	1979, 80	
Smith, Dick	ftb	1942	Smith, Terry	wtn	1950	
Smith, Don	bb	1982	Smith, Tom	rif	1957	
Smith, Dwaine	mtn	1979	Smith, Tommy	mbk	2000, 01	
Smith, Earle	wre	1958	Smith, Vance	ftb	1991	
Smith, Ed	ftb	1970	Smith, Wilard	ftb	1931, 32	
Smith, Eldon	msw	1964	Smitheran, Horace	ftb	1928, 29, 30, 31	
Smith, Evan	msw	2001		mtr	1929, 30, 31	
Smith, Garth	mtn	1963, 64	Smitheran, Jack	bb	1964, 65, 66	
Smith, Glen	bb	1965, 66	Smorin, Norb	ftb	1953	
Smith, Harold	ftb	1991	Snapp, Elizabeth	wbk	1938, 39, 40	
Smith, Helen	wbb	1922		wfh	1938, 39	
	wbb	1923		wgo	1938, 39, 40	
Smith, Helen	wtn	1942		wsb	1940	
Smith, Holly	wsb	1997, 98, 99	Snider, Bill	marc	1980	
	wtr	2000	Snider, Eva	wsw	1983	
Smith, J.	wsw	1963	Snow, Butch	msw	1966	
Smith, James	mtr	1962	Snyder, Gayle	wgo	1968	
Smith, Jay	ftb	1951, 52, 53, 54	Snyder, Jeff	wre	1981	
Smith, Jean	warc	1950	Snyder, Jennifer	wvb	1994, 95	
	wbm	1950	Snyder, Joey	mgo	1993, 94, 95, 96	
	wtn	1950	Snyder, Kevin	ftb	1990, 91, 92	
Smith, Jean	wvb	1927	Snyder, Marie	wsw	1986, 87, 88, 89	
Smith, Jeff	mcc	1986, 87	Sodaro, Abbie	wsb	1992	
	mtr	1987, 88	Sodders, Mike	bb	1980, 81	
Smith, Jerry	ftb	1963, 64	Soeli, Joe	wre	1974	
	wre	1964	Sohlen, Erika	wsw	1995, 96, 97, 98	
Smith, Jesse	mtn	1995	Sohn, Cody	wcc	1998, 99	
Smith, Joanie	wbk	1976, 77, 78		wtr	2000, 01	
	wvb	1974, 75, 76, 77	Sollenberger, Barry	mtr	1967	
Smith, Jodi	wtr	2000, 01	Sollenberger, Jim	mgo	1967	
	wvb	2000	Sollenberger, Mark	mgo	1971, 73, 74	
Smith, Joe	bb	1925, 26, 27, 28	Solorio, Joe	wre	1980, 81	
	ftb	1925, 26	Solow, Ken	bb	1977	
	mbk	1925, 26, 27, 28	Sones, Holly	wvb	1992, 93, 94, 95	
Smith, John	mtr	1936, 37, 38	Sonkin, Allan	msw	1997, 98, 99, 2000	
Smith, Joni	wtr	2000, 01	Sontondi, Virginia	wsb	1951	
Smith, Jovonne	wbk	1990, 91, 92, 93	Soper, Bill	mgy	1982, 83, 84	
Smith, Kirby	mgy	1983, 84, 85	Sopp, Matt	msw	2000	
Smith, Larry	bb	1926	Soqui, Danita	wsb	1978	
Smith, Larry	bb	1961, 62, 63	Sorensen, Dave	mtn	1958	
Smith, Lloyd	marc	1951	Sorenson, Carol	wgo	1962, 63, 64, 65	
Smith, Mark	ftb	1988, 89	Sorenson, Carol	wgo	1967, 68, 69	
Smith, Marvel	ftb	1997, 98, 99	Sorenson, George	ftb	1924, 25	
Smith, Mary	wbb	1943		mbk	1925, 26	
Smith, Mary	wfh	1935	Sorkness, Jeff	mcc	1990, 91	
Smith, Mike	msw	1958		mtr	1991, 92, 93	
Smith, Mildred	wfh	1942	Sorrells, Dorothy	wtn	1927	
	wvb	1942	Sorrenson, Joe	bb	1952	
Smith, Pam	wsw	1970	Sosnowich, Lawrence	mcc	1964	
Smith, Raythan	ftb	1991				

Carol Sorenson captured the national collegiate women's golf individual title in 1962 and was a two-time member of the U.S. Curtis Cup team.

Sosnowski, Michele	wcc	1989, 90
	wtr	1990, 91
Souder, Dick	mtr	1972
Soulier, Percey	bb	1913
Southerland, Barbara	wtn	1955
Southerland, Rick	msw	1988
Soward, Marcus	ftb	1992, 93, 94, 96
Sowers, Ron	ftb	1979, 80, 81, 82
Soza, Bob	bb	1940, 42
	mbk	1940, 41, 42
Spagnola, Joe	ftb	1968, 69, 70
Spallina, Marc	mgy	1981, 82
Span, Pete	mcc	1969, 70, 71, 72
	mtr	1969, 70, 72, 73
Spanko, Bill	ftb	1956, 57, 58, 59
Spann, Creig	ftb	1996, 97, 98
Spann, Guy	mgy	1974, 75, 76, 77
Spann, Nick	mgy	1966, 67, 68
Spannagel, Ann	wsb	1974
Spanos, Mike	mcc	1994
	mtr	1994, 95
Spargo, Dave	mcc	1987, 88, 89
	mtr	1989
Sparks, Phillippi	ftb	1990, 91
Spehr, Tim	bb	1987, 88
Spence, Mal	mcc	1957
	mtr	1958, 59, 60, 61
Spence, Mel	mcc	1957
	mtr	1958, 59, 60, 61
Spencer, Mark	wre	1973
Spencer, Miguel	wre	1993
Spengler, Bill	mgo	1959
Spengler, Paul	mgo	1960, 61
Spenser, Kaipo	bb	1994, 95, 96
Spetman, Brian	msw	2000, 01
Spezia, Ernie	ftb	1942
Spiegler, Dave	marc	1951
Spier, Dale	bb	1966
Spikes, Albert	bb	1911, 12, 13, 14
	mbk	1912, 13, 14
	mtr	1912, 13, 14
Spikes, John	bb	1911, 12 13
	mbk	1912, 13
	mtr	1913
Spitler, Jason	mgo	1991, 92
Sprague, Marc	wre	1983, 85
Sprague, Sara	wgy	1977
Sprein, John	ftb	1980, 81

Name	Sport	Years
Spring, Bill	wre	1968
Springfield, Ron	mtr	1958
Sproul, Dennis	ftb	1974, 75, 76, 77
Spurling, Steve	ftb	1986, 87, 88
St. Clair, Jack	ftb	1969
St. John, Bob	bb	1971
St. John, Dan	wre	1987, 88, 89, 90
St. John, Steve	wre	1993, 94, 95, 96
Staab, Kim	wsw	1988
Staat, Jeremy	ftb	1996, 97
	mtr	1997, 98
Stacy, Desiree	wtn	1984
Stadler, Ray	bb	1963, 64, 65
Stah, Greg	bb	1978, 79
Stahl, Regina	wvb	1984, 85, 86, 87
Stahr, Mike	mcc	1983, 84
	mtr	1984, 85
Stair, Cecil	mtn	1961
Stalick, Peter	mtr	1996
Stallard, Ron	rif	1961
Stalman, Ria	wtr	1979, 80, 81
Stamper, Janet	wsw	1980, 81
Stamps	mtr	1932
Standage, Earl	bb	1908, 09
Stanford, Amanda	wsw	1999, 2000, 01
Stangeland, Jim	mtr	1946, 47
Stanger, Julie	wgo	1975
Stanhoff, Mike	ftb	1954, 55, 56
Stankowski, Tom	mgo	1985, 86, 87, 88
Stanley, Heather	wsoc	1996
Stanley, Israel	ftb	1988, 89, 90, 92
Stanley, Larry	mtn	1966
Stanphill, Ennis	ftb	1953, 54
Stans, Terrie	wgo	1981, 82, 83
Stansbury, Herman	bb	1918
Stansbury, Jerry	mgy	1962, 63, 64
Stanton, Craig	mbm	1980, 81
Stanton, Dennis	mgo	1966, 67
Stapley, Leona	wtn	1959
Stapley, Norman	bb	1942
Stark, Mike	mtr	1969
Starkins, Dennis	bb	1962, 63
Starks, Michi	wsw	1999
Starley, Claudine	warc	1941
Starnes, Howard	ftb	1940, 41
Stasser, Al	wre	1974, 75
Stawicki, Ray	mgo	1960, 61, 62
Steeby, John	mtr	1968
Steed, Spring	wbk	1997, 98
Steen, Greg	bb	1981, 82, 83
Steere, Howard	mgy	1988
Stefan, Kristy	warc	1984
Steiber, Debbie	wcc	1995
Steiger, Ann	wtn	1980
Stein, Glen	mtn	1973
Steinbaugh, Jim	msw	1966
Steiner, Brent	mcc	1980
	mtr	1981
Steiner, Patricia	wsoc	1996, 97
Steiner, Paul	mtr	1974
Steinkemper, Jake	bb	1993, 94, 95
Stelsriede, Jack	ftb	1899, 1900, 02
Stempien, Matt	msw	1982
Stencel, Alex	ftb	1973, 74, 75
	mtr	1972
Stensen, Jessica	wsw	2001
Stensland, Geoff	mbm	1978
Stephans, Russ	bb	1980
Stephen, Scott	ftb	1983, 84, 85, 86
Stephens, Leslie	wtr	1987, 88
Stephens, Mabel	wbk	1915
Stephens, Mandy	wvb	2000
Stephens, Margurite	wbk	1914
Stephens, Mark	msw	1981

Name	Sport	Years
Stephenson, Jean	warc	1975, 76
Stephenson, Jim	ftb	1951, 52
Stern, Tracey	wtn	1978, 79, 81
Stetzar, Chris	ftb	1961, 62
Stevens, Becky	wsb	1986, 87, 88
Stevens, Diane	wsb	1980, 81
Stevens, Don	wre	1980, 81
Stevens, Eric	wre	1974
Stevens, Mike	ftb	1994, 95
Stevenson, Anthony	ftb	1998
Stevenson, Bill	mtn	1947, 48
Stevenson, Lois	warc	1934, 35, 36
Stevenson, Ruth	wtn	1967
Stevenson, Tom	marc	1980, 81, 82, 83
Steverson, Norris	box	1933
	ftb	1928, 29, 30, 31
	mbk	1929, 30, 31
	mtr	1929, 31, 33
Steverson, Steve	bb	1930
Steverson, Todd	bb	1990, 91, 92
Stewart, Ambrose	ftb	1922, 24
	mtr	1923
Steward, Ashley	wgy	1999, 2000, 01
Stewart, Beulah	wvb	1948
Stewart, Clyde	ftb	1896, 97, 1905
Stewart, Donna	wsb	1986, 87, 88, 89
Stewart, Eric	ftb	1980
Stewart, Jack	ftb	1948, 49
	mtr	1948
Stewart, James	msw	1976
Stewart, Janine	wtn	1955
Stewart, John	ftb	1950, 51
Stewart, Leona	wtn	1938
Stewart, Leonard	mtr	1926
Stewart, Leroy	bb	1907
Stewart, Tim	mcc	1993
Stice, Cheryl	wsb	1973, 74, 75, 76
	wvb	1973, 74, 75
Stich, Geraldine	wbk	1934
Stickle, Harold	mcc	1947
	mtr	1947
Stidham, Edith	wbk	1941
	wfh	1942
Stidham, Katherine	wvb	1927
Stidham, Margie	wtf	1945
	wtn	1945
Stieber, Deborah	wtr	1995, 96
Stiefel, Val	ftb	1938
Stiffler, Bob	mcc	1964, 65
	mtr	1964, 65, 66
Stiger, Don	mgy	1974, 75
Stigmen, Clay	mtr	1980
Stiles, Donna	wgo	1971
Stiles, Tim	msw	1976, 77
Still, Gary	mtn	1963, 64
Stilson, Marci	wbk	1996, 97
Stinnett, Danny	marc	1989, 90, 91
Stiteler, Jerry	mbk	1952, 56, 57
Stitt, Jimmy	bb	1940
Stitt, Marydea	warc	1935
Stitt, Sandlin	warc	1976, 77, 78, 79
Stivers, Mike	wre	1988, 89, 90
Stocek, Darren	msw	1995, 96
Stock, Cindi	wsw	1970
Stock, Sandy	wsw	1965, 66, 67, 68
Stocker, Kirsten	wcc	1994, 95
	wtr	1995, 96
Stocker, Mel	bb	2000, 01
Stockton, Brady	mgo	2000, 01
Stoddard, Joe	bb	1993
Stokes, Eddie	ftb	1988, 89
Stokes, Ryan	mcc	1993, 94
	mtr	1993, 94, 95
Stoll, Kate	wsb	1995, 96

Name	Sport	Years
Stone, Bruce	msw	1973
Stone, Bryan	mcc	1991
Stone, Cade	mgo	1991, 92, 93, 94
Stone, Doug	wre	1979
Stone, Kim	wsb	1993
Stone, Maxine	wbk	1939
Stone, Walt	mbk	1981, 82, 83
Stonebrook, Scott	mtr	1975
Stoneman, Dan	msw	1982
Stoner, Al	wre	1957, 58
Stoner, Mike	wre	1980
Storey, Awvee	mbk	2000, 01
Stovall, Jack	ftb	1953, 54, 55, 56
Stovall, Paul	mbk	1971, 72
Stovall, Richard	mgy	1967
Stover, Rick	msw	1979
Stovland, Stian	mtn	1992
Stowe, Bill	mtr	1946
Stowe, Jesse	bb	1919
Stowe, Merle	mtr	1940
Stowicki, Tom	mgo	1959
Strachan, Eric	mcc	1991, 92, 93
	mtr	1992, 93, 94
Straehley, Doug	wre	1972
Stramiello, Ariane	wsoc	1997, 98, 99
Strand, Casey	wre	1995, 96, 97, 98
Strand, Marie	wgo	1968, 69
Strangeland, Al	ftb	1950, 51, 52
Strangia, Mike	ftb	1955
Stratton, Rick	wre	1966
Strauch, Marc	msw	1988, 89
Straughan, Ora	wbk	1916
Strauss, Michael	mgy	1991, 92
Strawn, Mike	mbk	1980
Strayhand, Tony	mtr	1975
Streeter, Sally	wgo	1947
Strickland, Jim	mgo	1986, 87, 88, 89
Stringer, Dennis	msw	1959
Stroble, Dennis	wre	1977
Strole, Aaron	mtr	1989
Strong, Brandon	mcc	1997, 98, 99, 2000
	mtr	1999, 2000, 01
Strong, Garret	bb	1973, 74, 75
Strong, Jim	mgo	1971, 72, 73, 74
Strong, Kenneth	bb	1923, 24
	ftb	1922, 23
Stroope, Billie	wfh	1950
	wsb	1949, 50, 51
Stroud, Bob	mtn	1927, 28
Stroud, Forest	mtr	1930
Strunk, Eugene	ftb	1942
Struthers, Mary	wtn	1966
Stuart, Gary	rif	1959
Stuart, Greg	msw	1977
Stuart, Howard	mtr	1980, 81
Stubbs, Sue	warc	1967
Stuck, Lisa	wbk	1983
	wvb	1980, 81, 82
Studer, Carl	marc	1968
Stufflebeam, Paula	wsb	1978, 79, 80, 81
Stuhr, Donna	wvb	1976, 77, 78
Stull, Janis	wtr	1979
Stump, Bill	mtr	1948
Stump, Pat	wfh	1948
Stupey, Nick	mtr	1969
Sturdivant, Jeff	ftb	1990
Sturgess, Jean	wtn	1923
Stutts, Chris	mgo	1993, 94
Sudol, Kathy	wsw	1977
Suehr, Jennifer	wtn	1982
Sugar, Tom	marc	1976
Suggs, Terrell	fb	2000
Sulcer, Michael	mtr	1991
Sullivan, Angela	wtr	1996

Lisa Stuck set a school single-match record of 35 kills against Santa Clara that has withstood all challenges since 1982. Stuck earned volleyball All-America honorable mention honors.

Sullivan, Brien	mtn	1984, 85, 86
Sullivan, Cindy	wsb	1983
Sullivan, Dennis	mbm	1970
Sullivan, Joe	mtr	1986
Sullivan, Larry	mcc	1951, 52, 54
Sullivan, Lee	mtn	1965, 66
Sullivan, Michael	mtr	1980, 81, 82, 83
Sullivan, Robert	ftb	1932
Sullivan, Scott	mgo	1989, 90, 91, 92
Sullivan, Timothy	mtr	1923
Sullivan, Tom	msw	1974, 75
Sullivan, Van	ftb	1922
Sullivent, Andy	wtn	1965
Summers, A.J.	msw	1989
Summers, Marilyn	wtn	1955
Summers, Mark	mgy	1989
Sund, Aaron	ftb	1905
Sundberg, Larry	marc	1952
Sunderman, Matthew	mtr	1990, 91, 92
Sureephong, Cindy	wtn	2001
Suter, Matt	wre	1995, 96, 97, 98
Sutherland, Joyce	wtn	1955
Sutter, Bob	ftb	1941
Sutter, Fay	wsw	1968
Sutter, Gwen	wsw	1964, 65, 66
Sutter, Jeff	bb	1986
Sutter, Lonna	warc	1968
Sutter, Wilbur	ftb	1926, 27, 28
	mtr	1926, 27, 28, 29
Suttle, Brandi	wsw	1986, 87
Sutton, Dorothea	warc	1952
Suzuki, Dale	wre	1986
Suzuki, Keith	mgy	1989, 90, 91, 92
Swackhammer, Robert	mgo	1938
Swagger, Nikki	wbk	2000
Swain, Chris	mcc	1990
Swan, Craig	bb	1969, 70, 71, 72
Swan, Dionne	wsb	1986
Swanberger, Jean	wtn	1949
Swanlund, Lynn	warc	1967
Swanner, Jim	ftb	1957, 58
Swanson, Andy	wre	2000, 01
Swanson, James	marc	1987, 88, 89, 90
Swanson, Lona	wtn	1972
Swanson, Nancy	wvb	1977
Swayda, Shawn	ftb	1993, 94, 95, 96

Swayze, Velma	wfh	1942
	wgo	1942
Sweeney, Chona	wbk	1916, 17, 18, 19
Sweeney, John	mgy	1986, 87
Sweeney, Kathy	wtn	1970
Sweete, Mary	wbk	1979
Swenson, Brynnar	msw	1989
Swetel, Kristin	wsb	2001
Swette, Mary	wtn	1979
Swift, Florence	wgo	1933, 34
Switlick, Dan	msw	1991, 92
Switzenberg, Don	bb	1965
	ftb	1963, 64
Switzer, Jon	bb	1999, 2000, 01
Switzer, K.	wsw	1972
Sythe, Julie	wtn	1979
Szlauko, Kimberly	wtr	1996, 97, 98, 99
Szymanski, Franz	msw	1977, 78
Szymanski, John	wre	1986

T

Taaca, Derek	wre	1987
Tabertshofer, Angela	wbk	1981
Tackett-Hicks, Kathy	wsb	1981, 82, 83
Talanoa, Ken	ftb	1993, 94
Talanoa, Shiloh	wsb	2001
Taliaferro, Bob	marc	1967, 68, 69, 72
Talley, Terrence	mtr	1969, 70
Tal-Shahar, Rottom	wre	1995
Talt, Rick	mgo	1964, 65, 66, 67
Tamarin, Carrie	warc	1971
Tamarin, Patsy	warc	1971
Tamboimo, Dorothy	wbk	1912
Tamboimo, Polly	wbk	1913
Tameron, Joe	bb	1949, 50, 51
Tang, Dorra	wsw	1994, 95, 96, 97
Tang, P.	wbm	1962
Tang, Robert	wre	1963
Tanke, Adam	ftb	1999, 2000
Tanner, Sue	wsw	1959
Tanselli, Lia	wgo	1987
Tape, Lohnnie	mbk	1999
Taplin, Justin	ftb	1998, 2000
Tapper, Richard	msw	1989, 90, 91, 92
Tarbell, Henry	bb	1947
Tarentino, Pete	wre	1956
Tarkett, Shannon	wgy	1996
Tarney, B.	ftb	1916
Tarrant, Dave	mbk	1976
Tarwater, Bob	ftb	1951, 52, 53
Tassinari, Joe	ftb	1947, 48, 49, 50
Tate, Don	mtr	1974
Tate, M.	wtf	1945
	wvb	1945
Tate, Shelby	rif	1956, 57
Tate, Tana	wtr	1982, 83, 84
Tate, Valerie	wbm	1977
Tatter	mtr	1927
Tatterson, Gary	bb	1990, 91
Tatum, Mike	bb	1960, 61
Taylor, Blake	mbk	1977, 78, 79
Taylor, Bob	mtr	1965
Taylor, Charley	ftb	1961, 62, 63
	mtr	1961
Taylor, Cheryle	wcc	1982
Taylor, Chris	mcc	1986
Taylor, Christopher	msw	1999, 2000, 01
Taylor, Elvena	wcc	1980
Taylor, G.T.	wre	1989, 90, 91, 92
Taylor, Jean	wtn	1927, 28
Taylor, Jim	bb	1997, 98

Taylor, Jon	mbk	1985, 86
Taylor, Lisa	wcc	1980, 81, 82
	wtr	1981, 82
Taylor, Nancy	wgo	1979, 81, 82, 83
Taylor, Pat	ftb	1984, 85, 86, 87
Taylor, Rhea	mbk	1971, 72
Taylor, Rick	mbk	1975, 76, 77, 78
Taylor, Ruth	warc	1950
Taylor, Tennille	wsw	1997, 98, 99, 2000
Taysom, Paul	mcc	1976, 77
	mtr	1977, 78
Telep, Mike	mgo	1950, 54
Temple, Dean	mcc	1956
Tendall, Skip	mgo	71, 72, 73, 74
Tennant, Ashley	wsb	2000
Tennell, Jim	bb	1979
Terpack, Bill	mgo	1948
Terrell, Lawrence	bb	1927
	ftb	1926, 27
	mbk	1927
Terrill, Julie	wsw	1990, 91
Terrill, Mark	wre	1986
Terry, Dale	msw	1958
Terry, Nicole	wsoc	1999
Tetford, Lori	warc	1992
Tetteh, Micchaelene	wtr	1993, 94, 95
Teychea, Fred	ftb	1936, 37
Theberge, Ron	mcc	1979
Theiler, Jeff	wre	1992, 93, 94, 95
Therrien, Claire	wsw	1972
Thevenot, Merlin	mtr	1947, 48, 49
Thiele, John	mtn	1964
Thiem, Heike	wcc	1983, 84
	wtr	1984, 85
Thoene, Yvonne	wsw	1993, 94
Thomas, Aisha	wsoc	1996, 97, 98
Thomas, Alia	wsw	1996
Thomas, Arthur	mbk	1985, 86, 87, 88
Thomas, Bob	ftb	1970
Thomas, Bruce	mbk	1980, 81
Thomas, Cassy	wtr	1977
Thomas, Dave	bb	1935, 38
	ftb	1937, 38
Thomas, Dorothy	wbm	1952
	wtn	1952
Thomas, Dwight	bb	1986, 87
Thomas, Gary	mtr	1972, 73
Thomas, Hope	wfh	1935
Thomas, Johnny	ftb	1993
Thomas, Keith	mtn	1984, 85
Thomas, Kevin	ftb	1983, 84, 85, 86
Thomas, Laura	wbm	1953
	wtn	1952, 53, 54, 55
Thomas, Mike	wre	1984
Thomas, Mitchell	ftb	1978, 80
Thomas, O'Megalyn	wtr	1987, 88
Thomas, Steve	mtr	1981
Thomas, Tammy	wsw	1978, 79
Thomas, Tomasina	mtr	1986
Thomee, Roland	mtr	1977
Thompson, Barbara	wtn	1988, 89, 90, 91
Thompson, Bill	ftb	1953
	mtr	1983
Thompson, Bobby	mbk	1984, 85, 86, 87
Thompson, Charles	ftb	1926, 27
Thompson, Craig	msw	1958, 59
Thompson, Dick	wre	1966, 67, 68, 69
Thompson, Fred	mtr	1949
Thompson, Georgia	wtn	1950
Thompson, Jancy	wsw	2001
Thompson, Jeff	msw	1973
Thompson, Kay	wgo	1966
Thompson, Linda	wsw	1982, 83
Thompson, Michelle	wsw	1988, 89, 90

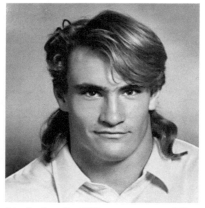

Linebacker Pat Tillman was named Pac-10 Defensive Player of the Year in 1997, one season after he helped lead the Sun Devils to the Rose Bowl.

Thompson, Mike	mtr	1993
Thompson, Nichole	wsb	1999, 2000, 01
Thompson, Nikki	wbk	1991, 92, 93, 94
Thompson, Pam	wtr	1977
Thompson, Pat	ftb	1994, 96
Thompson, Phil	mgy	1954, 55
Thompson, Sandy	wsw	1977, 78, 79, 80
Thompson, Sue	wgo	1967
Thomsen, Jeff	mgo	1973, 74, 75, 76
Thomson, Karyn	wsw	1991, 92
Thorleifson, Dane	mcc	1981
	mtr	1982
Thorn, Roger	mgo	1983, 84
Thorngren, Malyssa	wbk	1995
Thornhill, Martha	wtn	1972
Thorpe, Mike	bb	1984, 85, 86
Thorud, Mary	wsb	1951
	wvb	1948
Thul, Anne	wsb	2000
Thurston, Greg	ftb	1992, 93
Tibbets, Helen	wbm	1966, 67
Tiedeman, Lorraine	warc	1947, 48
	wgo	1948
Tiernan, Maureen	wvb	1976, 77, 78
Tietjen, Irmgard	wvb	1968
Tiffany, Ned	marc	1952
Tijoriwala, Madakvi	wbm	1985
Tillman, Kevin	bb	1997, 98, 99
Tillman, Pat	ftb	1994, 95, 96, 97
Tillotson, Willadene	wgo	1947
Tilman, Maria	wtr	1978
Timarac, Steve	ftb	1965, 66
Timmons, Mary Frances	wtn	1941
Tindle, Janice	wtn	1971, 72
Tingstad, Mark	ftb	1986, 87, 88, 89
Tinkey, Lee	marc	1982, 83, 84, 85
Tinney, Pat	mtr	1975
Tinoco, Dave	bb	1984
Tintsman, Amber	wsb	1990, 91, 92, 93
Tipton, Jim	bb	1959
Tipton, Joyce	wvb	1976
Tisdell, David	ftb	1990
Titcomb, Katie	wsw	2000, 01
Titmas, Johanne	wsw	1966
Tobert, Rick	ftb	1974, 75, 76, 77
Tobin, Marnie	wsw	1991, 92
Todare, Steve	bb	1979
Todd, Larry	ftb	1962, 64
	mtr	1962
Toft, Heidi	wsw	1992, 93, 94, 95

Togiai, Farrington	ftb	1992, 93
Tognozzi, Jim	bb	1981, 82
Tokarczyk, Diane	wtn	1971
Toland, Frances	wbk	1925
Tolbert, Lynda	wtr	1986, 88, 89, 90
Tolmie, Mike	mgo	1986
Tom, Michelle	wbk	1998, 99
Tomarelli, Nello	ftb	1966, 67, 68
Tomberg, Debbie	wsw	1969
Tombs, Tina	wgo	1981, 82, 83, 84
Tomcheck, Andy	wsb	1967
Tomco, Mike	ftb	1969, 70, 71
Tomcray, Audrey	wfh	1949
Tomei, Jeff	mtn	1980, 81
Tomes, Jack	bb	1952, 53, 54, 55
Tomilson, Catherine	wtn	1933, 34, 35
Tomilson, Evelyn	wtn	1933, 34, 35, 36
Tomlinson, Rob	mcc	1985
Tomlinson, Roger	bb	1960, 61
Tommasini, Kevin	bb	1996, 97
	ftb	1995, 96, 97
Toncray, Bob	mtr	1950, 51
Tone, Diane	warc	1974, 75
Toney, Ken	bb	1957, 58
Toney, Kim	wcc	1990, 91, 92, 93
	wtr	1991, 92, 93, 94
Toohey, Charlene	wgo	1950
Toohey, Jack	mcc	1948
Toplin, Albert	box	1935
Torok, John	bb	1963, 64
	ftb	1963, 64
Torrance, Sheri	warc	1973, 74, 75, 76
Torres, Andy	bb	2001
Torres, Brianna	wcc	1999, 2000
	wtr	2000, 01
Torrish, Mike	mgy	1961
Torti, Mike	bb	1996
Tosdal, Peggy	wsw	1975, 76, 77, 79
Toth, Rob	msw	2000
Townsend, Brooke	wsw	2001
Townsend, Frank	mtn	1947, 48, 49, 50
Townsend, Tom	msw	1975, 76, 77, 78
Townsend, Tom	mtr	1967, 68, 69
Townsend, Tommie	ftb	1999, 2000
Tracy, Ronald	ftb	1952
Traversi, James "Jiggs"	bb	1931, 32
	ftb	1930, 31
	mbk	1931, 32

Kim Toney set school records at 800 meters and 1,500 meters in 1993 and also established a school mark for 800 meters indoors.

Molly Tuter averaged 13.9 points for the women's basketball team from 1994-1997. She's third on the school's all-time scoring list.

Traylor, Manley	bb	1947
	ftb	1946
Trbovich, George	bb	1948, 49, 50, 51
Trees, James	bb	1954
Treguboff, Jim	ftb	1947, 48, 49, 50
Trejo, Gil	mbk	1949
	bb	1949
Trejo, Stephen	ftb	1997, 98, 99, 2000
Trepel, Tony	mtr	1951, 52, 53
Tresnon, Bill	mtr	1938
Tribble, Charles	wre	1965, 66
Tribioli, Shawn	wre	1987
Trick, Debbie	wsw	1980
Trimble, Lyle	ftb	1932, 33
	mtr	1934, 35
Trinidad, Andrey	msw	1997, 98, 99, 2000
Troilo, Darren	bb	1995
Trosper, Billie	wbk	1935
	wfh	1935
Troupp, Arlene	wsw	1971
True, Jane	wgo	1933, 34
Trujillo, Clyde	wre	1973
Trujillo, Kelly	wre	1971, 72
Trujillo, Maria	wcc	1981, 82
	wtr	1981, 82
Truman, Lois	wbm	1964
Trung, Mary Jane	wbm	1949, 50, 51
	warc	1950
Truter, B.H.	rif	1957
Trybus, Brian	wre	1982
Tryon, Merlin	mtr	1935
Tsosie, Andreatta	wtr	1979
Tsosie, Roxanne	wsb	1995, 96, 97, 98
Tsutsumida, Pat	wre	1972, 73
Tu'ua, Onosai	ftb	1983, 86
Tubbs, Leon	mtr	1979, 80, 81, 82
Tucker, Jim	mtr	1962
Tucker, Marquis	ftb	1991
Tucker, Myron	mgy	1970, 71, 72, 73
Tucker, Natalie	wbk	1999, 2000, 01
Tucker, Tom	mtr	1958
Tuckey, Vernon	bb	1931, 32, 33, 34
	ftb	1932, 33
	mbk	1932, 33, 34
Tudos, Jessica	wgy	1990, 91
	wsw	1989

Karli Urban was a gymnastics All-American in 1987 and 1989.

Kirsten Voak was the pitching star of the 2000 and 2001 Sun Devil softball teams.

Vizcaya, Jim	bb	1946
Voak, Kirsten	wsb	1999, 2000, 01
Voelckel, Bob	bb	1920, 21
	mtr	1921, 22
Vogel	mtr	1933, 34, 35, 36
Voght, Erich	msw	1970
Vollmer, Wayne	mgo	1966, 67
Vollstedt, Linda	wgo	1967, 68
Volney, Bruce	bb	1973
Von der Ahe, Scott	ftb	1995, 96
von Hartitzsch, Stefin	msw	1994, 95
von Heijne, Ulrika	wgo	1990, 91, 92, 93
Von Heiland, Erika	wbm	1989, 90, 91
Von Tempsky, Kim	mgo	1963
Vonderau, Kate	warc	1950
	wsb	1949
	wtn	1949, 50
VonSchoff, Scott	msw	1998, 99, 2000, 01
Vreeke, Cassidy	wgy	2000, 01
Vucichevich, John	ftb	1957, 58, 59, 60
Vukcevich, George	ftb	1941, 42
Vukcevich, Steve	ftb	1940, 41, 42
Vyskocil, Cindy	wbk	1988, 89, 90, 91

W

Waas, Orlin	mtr	1948
Wackerbarth, Merle	mtr	1950, 51, 54, 55
Waddell, Mike	fb	2000
Waddy, Denise	wtr	1978, 79
Wade, Bill	mbk	1939
Wade, Donna	wbm	1959
Wade, Judy	wbm	1959
	wsw	1958, 59
Wade, Ty	ftb	1994
Wadham, Thomas	rif	1959
Wadlington, DeAndre	mtr	1992, 93, 94
Wager, George	mtr	1933
	ftb	1933, 34
Waggoner, Patsy	wtn	1956, 57
Wagner, Albert	wre	1963
Wagner, Allison	wsw	1981
Wagner, Bob	wre	1962
Wagner, Harve	ftb	1899, 1900
Wagner, Kim	wsoc	1996, 97, 98, 99
Wagner, Larry	wre	1967, 68

Wagner, Randy	mtr	1972, 73, 74, 75
Wagner, Sharon	wsw	1981, 82
Wagoner, Fred	wre	1983
Wahab, Sinikka	wbm	1990, 91, 92, 93
Wahl, M.	warc	1962, 63
Wahlin, Marvin	ftb	1950, 51, 52
Waid, Judy	wtn	1965, 66
Wainwright, Joel	msw	1994
Waitt, Rocky	mgo	1973, 74
Wakamatsu, Don	bb	1982, 83, 84, 85
Wake, C.	wsw	1963
Walbert, Bob	ftb	1939, 40
Walbot, Erik	mcc	1991, 92
	mtr	1991, 92, 93
Walden, Bill	ftb	1977
Waldman, Alan	mtn	1978, 79
Waldram, Michelle	wgy	1999
Waldrip, Will	bb	1999, 2000
Walker, Bob	ftb	1949
Walker, Brian	marc	1983, 84
Walker, Buzz	mtr	1952
Walker, Chasity	wtr	1996, 97
Walker, Collin	msw	1995, 96
Walker, Erin	wsw	1985
Walker, Gladys	wbk	1913, 14, 15
Walker, Helen	warc	1933
Walker, Jim	mbk	1946, 47
	mtr	1946
Walker, Jim	mbk	1965, 66
Walker, Jim	wre	1965, 66
Walker, John	ftb	1984, 85
Walker, Jon	wre	1963, 64
Walker, Larry	bb	1935, 36
Walker, Larry	bb	1962
Walker, LaVerne	mtr	1951
Walker, Michael	msw	1992
Walker, Mike	mbm	1971
Walker, Rick	mtr	1974, 75, 76, 77
Walker, Rico	mtr	1988
Walker, Scott	ftb	1988, 89
Walker, Shirley	wtr	1987
Walker, Ulysee	mtr	1982
Wall, Dick	mtr	1957
Wallace	box	1929
Wallace, Anna	wgo	1942
	wtn	1942
Wallace, Bill	bb	1925
	ftb	1924, 25, 26
	mtr	1925
Wallace, C.	warc	1962
Wallace, Iorraise	wfh	1935
Wallace, Marie	wtn	1923
Wallace, Rebecca	warc	1982, 83, 84, 85
Wallace, Suzy	wsw	1984
Wallace, Wiley	msw	2001
Wallenius, Rob	msw	1981, 82, 83
Waller, Mike	mgy	1970, 71, 72
Waller, Ron	mbk	1989, 90
Wallerich, Mark	wre	1975
Wallerstedt, Brett	ftb	1989, 90, 91, 92
Wallin, Kurt	ftb	1998, 99, 2000
Walls, Carolyn	wtn	1957
Wallwork, Sierra	wtr	1980
Walser, Carolyn	wtn	1968, 69, 70
Walsh, Colleen	wsw	1982, 83
Walsh, David	ftb	1991
Walsh, Dick	ftb	1947
Walsh, Ed	mbk	1945, 46
Walsh, Nick	bb	2001
Walston, Steve	mbk	1996
Walter, Nancy	wgo	1975
Walters, Jannie	wsw	1983
Walton, Aubrey	ftb	1919
	mbk	1918

Walton, Dale	ftb	1981, 82, 83, 84
Walton, Larry	ftb	1967, 68
	mtr	1969
Walton, Robin	wgo	1975
Walton, Tika	wtr	1994, 95, 96
Walty, Larry	bb	1994
Waltz, John	mtn	1974, 75, 76, 77
Wampler, Vance	mbk	1954
Wang, Fleur Belle	wtn	1951
Wang, Gilbert	mtn	1945
Wang, Marion	wtn	1949, 50, 51
Wanless, Bill	mbk	1952, 53
Ward, Bill	mbk	1942
Ward, Bonie	wtr	1986
Ward, Doug	mgo	1971
Ward, Gary	mtr	1988
Ward, Monti	mtr	1961
Ward, Wendy	wgo	1992, 93, 94, 95
Wardein, Erin	wsb	1999, 2000, 01
Wardlow, Harold	mtn	1928
	mtr	1928, 29
Ware, Dalen	ftb	1999, 2000
Ware, Sharon	wtr	1982, 83, 84, 85
Warne, Jim	ftb	1984, 85, 86
Warren, Bill	mtr	1942
Warren, Bo	ftb	1973, 74
Warren, Kevin	mbk	1984
Warren, Mike	wre	1975, 76, 77, 78
Warren, Morrison	ftb	1946, 47
Warring, Ron	mbk	1980, 81
Was, Casey	mtn	1996, 97, 98, 99
Washburn, Greg	wre	1981
Washington, Ainslie	ftb	1974, 75
Washington, Art	mtr	1958
Washington, Marbella	wtr	1982, 83, 84, 85
Washington, Ricky	ftb	1976, 77, 79
Washington, Ron	ftb	1976, 77, 79, 80
Wasil, Alex	ftb	1983
Waters, Chris	msw	1981, 82, 83
Wathen, Dee	wsb	2000
Watkins, May	wbk	1921, 22
Watkins, Ruth	wbk	1914
Watkins, Scott	mgo	1976, 77, 78, 79
Watson, Bill	mcc	1948
	mtr	1948, 49
Watson, Hubie	mtr	1961, 62
Watson, Jim	rif	1950
Watson, Steve	bb	1975
Watson, Tom	mgy	1975
Watt, William	wre	1963
Wattier, Greg	mcc	1985
Watts, Boots	mtr	1928, 29, 30, 31
Watts, Brad	mgo	1951, 52
Watts, Buss	ftb	1936, 37
Watts, Carli	wsw	2001
Watts, Irvine	ftb	1929, 30
	mbk	1929, 30
Watts, Marcus	ftb	1977
Waugh, Rob	mcc	1972
Wax, Lisa	wgy	1982
Way, Arthur	bb	1924, 25
	ftb	1923, 24, 25
	mtr	1924, 25
Waybright, Bruce	ftb	1949
Waz, Pete	mcc	1981
Weahterly, Jim	mtr	1948
Wear, Kathy	wtn	1967, 68
Weathers, Robert	ftb	1978, 79, 80, 81
	mtr	1980
Weatherspoon, Jerome	ftb	1981, 82, 83
Weaver, Alva	bb	1922, 23
	ftb	1922
Weaver, Eddie	wre	1981
Weaver, Kent	mgy	1979, 80

Webb, C.	ftb	1903, 04, 05
Webb, Chris	mcc	1986, 87
	mtr	1987
Webb, Dee	mtn	1953
Webb, Dorothy	wfh	1942
Webb, Karen	wvb	1977
Webb, Tammy	wvb	1983, 84, 85, 86
Webber, Leslie	wsw	1970, 71
Weber, Gina	wbm	1982, 83, 84
Weber, Janie	wsw	1976
Weber, Lucas	bb	2001
Weber, Tom	mcc	1992, 93, 94, 95
	mtr	1993, 94, 95, 96
Webster, Betty	warc	1934
Webster, Paul	mgy	1982, 83, 84, 85
Webster, R.D.	mgy	1977, 79
Weddington, Mary	wvb	1928
Wedel, Grayson	wre	2000
Wedepohl, N.	mtr	1954
Weed, Jim	wre	1973, 74
Weedin, Jennie	wbk	1911
Weichens, Gary	wre	1971, 72, 73
Weigandt, Al	ftb	1974, 75, 76
Weinberger, Brett	bb	1992
Weiner, Wendy	warc	1968, 69
Weinkofsky, Corrina	wsw	1980, 81, 82, 83
Weins, Rick	bb	1998
Weintraub, Gary	msw	1978
Weir, Ben	mgo	1991, 92, 93
Weischedel, Don	mbk	1954-55
Weise, Debra	wgo	1971, 72
Weise, Ralph	mgy	1968, 69, 70
Weisel, Christina	wsw	1979
Weiskopf, Dan	mgo	1979, 80
Weiss, Ben	marc	1992, 93
Weiss, Heather	wsw	1995
Weiss, Mark	mtn	1983
Weiss, Randy	mgy	1980, 81
Weiss, Rick	wre	1981, 82
Welbourn, Graham	msw	1979, 80, 81, 82
Welchlin, Heidi	wgy	1973
Welker, Wayne	ftb	1950, 51, 52
Wellborn, Martha	wsb	1949
Welles, Robby	bb	1991
Wellington, Steve	mtn	1980
Wellman, Kristin	wcc	1990, 91, 92, 93
	wtr	1992, 93, 94
Wells, Charlie	mtr	1973, 74, 75, 76
Wells, Eddie	wre	1971, 72
Wells, George	bb	1916, 17, 18, 19
Wells, John	mgo	1963
Wells, Mike	mtr	1972
Welman, Etta	wfh	1943
Welton, Tom	bb	1969, 70, 71
Wendorf, Jaine	warc	1977
Wendorf, Jocelyn	warc	1976, 77, 78, 79
Wendorf, Kirk	ftb	1985, 86, 87, 88
Wenig, Brian	mtr	1990, 91
Wenk, Jim	mgy	1970, 71, 72, 73
Wente, John	bb	1996
Wenworth, Rob	mcc	1979, 80, 81
	mtr	1980, 81, 82
Wenzel, Pam	wgy	1976, 77, 78, 79
Wertz, John	marc	1986
Wesson, Donna	warc	1970, 71
West, Bo	msw	1999, 2000, 01
West, Dawn	wsw	1990, 91, 92
West, Geraldine	wfh	1935
West, Jeremy	bb	2001
West, Marty	wre	1998, 2000
Westbrooks, Marv	mbk	1956, 57, 58
Westby, Bob	mgo	1951, 52, 53
Westherly, Jim	mtr	1949
Westin, David	mtr	1994

Clay Westlake, who played from 1973-1976, still holds ASU career records for most at bats (935), hits (322) and doubles (88).

Westlake, Clay	bb	1973, 74, 75, 76
Westley, Doug	bb	1962, 63, 64
Westmore, Matt	ftb	1993
Westmoreland, Peggy	warc	1951
Westover, Dolly	wfh	1942
Westover, J.	ftb	1903
Wetherill, Annette	wtr	1978
Wetzel, Ron	ftb	1979, 80, 81, 82
Weyermiller, Joey	mtr	1994, 95
Weyhrauch, Tom	msw	1976, 77, 78, 79
Weymouth, Brian	bb	1980
Wheatley, Randolph	mtr	1982, 83
Wheeler, Bill	mtr	1966
Wheeler, Ken	mtr	1946
Wheeler, Sherry	wgo	1959, 60, 61, 62
Wheeler, Tarence	mbk	1988, 89, 91
Wheelock, Alicia	wsw	1999, 2000, 01
Whelan, Jeff	msw	1978
Whelen, Joe	marc	1952
Whetstine, Tom	mtr	1952, 57, 58, 59
Whipple, Flora	wsb	1940
Whistler, Randy	bb	1977, 78, 79
Whitaker, Ryan	mgo	1999, 2000, 01
White, Aaron	mtr	2001
White, Alice	wvb	1925
White, Betty	warc	1941
White, Danny	bb	1972, 73
	ftb	1971, 72, 73
White, Dave	mtr	1965
White, Don	bb	1956, 57, 58
White, Gene	mtr	1930, 31
White, Greg	mbk	1975
White, H.	box	1936
White, Jeff	bb	1986
White, Jeff	ftb	1990, 91
White, Jill	wtn	1972, 73
White, John	mtr	1981
White, Joronda	wtr	1996, 97, 98, 99
White, Kelsey	wsw	1994, 95
White, Kenton	mcc	1974
	mtr	1974, 75
White, Kisha	wbk	1998, 99
White, L.	mtr	1931
White, Lura Belle	wfh	1935
White, Marilyn	wtr	1976, 77, 78
White, Mike	ftb	1980, 82, 83
White, Mike	mtr	1987
White, Nick	mtn	1990
White, Pam	wsb	1983, 84
White, Pat	wtn	1972

White, Rudy	mbk	1973, 74, 75
White, Stephen	mtr	1994, 95, 96
White, Steve	msw	1988
White, Wilford	ftb	1947, 48, 49, 50
	mtr	1948, 49, 50, 51
Whitehead, Jim	mbk	1964, 65, 66
Whitelaw, Andrea	wsw	1976
Whitelock, Norman	mbk	1938
Whites, Bob	mtn	1948, 49, 50
Whitey, Lynn	wsb	1986
Whitham, Jeff	msw	1984, 85, 86, 87
Whitley, Gerald	bb	1948
Whitlock, Tes	mbk	1993
Whitman, Jeff	msw	1983
Whitman, Mark	msw	1977
Whitmer, Grant	ftb	1950
Whitney, Linda	warc	1969
	wbm	1970, 71
Whittaker, Pete	wre	1994
Whitten, Corey	wre	1996
Whittenburg, Ray	ftb	1986
Whittlesey, Leal	wsw	1971, 72, 73
Wholey, Linda	wsw	1977
Whuang, Peter	mtn	1923
Whyte, Jennifer	wbm	1991, 92, 93
Wickenberg, Sarah	wsw	1989, 90, 91, 92
Wicks, Bob	mtr	1987
Wicksell, Ray	mcc	1974, 75, 76
	mtr	1975, 78, 79
Widmer, Bob	ftb	1960, 61, 62
Widmer, Paul	ftb	1955, 56, 57, 58
Wiechens, Don	mbk	1945
Wiegert, Gail	wbk	1981
Wieneckke, Richard	msw	1977
Wienert, Ranz	msw	1994, 95
Wiersma, Baukje	wsw	1990, 91
Wiersum, Sue	wsw	1968
Wigent, Theo	wbm	1959
Wilbur, Carl	mtn	1952, 53
Wilbur, E.R.	ftb	1902, 03
Wilcox, Fred	wre	1964
Wilcox, Toby	msw	1995, 96
Wilde, Mary	wbk	1942
	wgo	1942
	wvb	1942
Wiley, Chuck	msw	1984, 85, 86, 87
Wiley, Jessica	wbk	1982, 83
Wiley, Tom	msw	1984, 85, 86
Wilhelm, Eric	msw	1988, 89, 90, 91
Wilhelms, Anthony	wre	1987, 88
Wilhoite, Charles	mtr	1984
Wilkening, Lisa	wtr	1979
	wvb	1976
Wilkerson, Joelle	wsb	1987, 88
Wilkinson, Celeste	wbk	1979
	wtr	1976, 78, 79, 80
Wilkinson, Charline	wfh	1947
Wilkinson, Jay	mbk	1919, 20
Wilkinson, Matt	mtr	1979
Wilkinson, Mike	mtn	1969, 70, 71, 72
Willaman, Danny	wre	1985
Willard, Brian	mgy	1977
Willard, John	mtr	1940
Willard, Mercier	ftb	1927, 28, 29, 30
	mtr	1928, 29, 30, 31
Willard, Patsy	wsw	1961, 62, 63, 64
Willard, Peggy	wsw	1958, 59, 61
Willard, Penny	wsw	1961
Willeman, Larry	wre	1974
Williams	mtr	1941
Williams	box	1933
Williams, Al	wre	1956
Williams, Alfred	ftb	1999, 2000
Williams, Bette	wvb	1967, 68

Fred Williams ranks second on ASU's all-time rushing list after leading the Sun Devils in that category in 1974, 1975 and 1976.

Williams, Bob	wre	1970
Williams, Bobby	wre	1981, 82
Williams, Brad	ftb	1989, 90
	mtn	1990
Williams, Brad	mtr	1980
Williams, Brian	ftb	1998
Williams, Channing	ftb	1983, 85, 86, 87
Williams, Charmaine	wtr	1987, 88, 89, 90
Williams, Dean	ftb	1933
Williams, Dick	mgy	1967
Williams, Don	ftb	1952
Williams, Donna	wsw	1977
Williams, Doris	wfh	1942
Williams, Ebes	ftb	1928
Williams, Eddie	mtr	1977
Williams, Eric	mcc	1969, 70, 71, 72
	mtr	1969, 72, 73
Williams, Esther	wvb	1924
Williams, Frances	wfh	1949, 50
Williams, Fred	ftb	1973, 74, 75, 76
Williams, George	wre	1990, 91
Williams, Greg	mtr	1982
Williams, Jack	mcc	1969
Williams, Jack	mgy	1966
Williams, Jeff	mtn	1999
Williams, Jim	mtr	1966
Williams, Jimmy	ftb	1981, 82, 83, 84
Williams, Katie	wsw	1994, 95, 96, 97
Williams, Kendall	ftb	1979, 80, 81
Williams, Kenny	ftb	1999, 2000
Williams, L.	ftb	1916
Williams, Lois	wgo	1948
	wsb	1947, 50
	wtn	1947, 48
	wvb	1947
Williams, Lynn	mtn	1965
Williams, Marcus	ftb	1994, 95, 96, 97
Williams, Mel	ftb	1951
Williams, Michael	ftb	1990, 91
Williams, Mike	fb	2000
Williams, Newton	ftb	1978, 79, 80, 81
	mtr	1980, 81
Williams, Norris	ftb	1976, 77, 78, 79
Williams, Paul	mbk	1980, 81, 82, 83
Williams, Penny	wbk	1987
Williams, Prentice	ftb	1967, 68, 69, 70
Williams, Randy	wre	1973, 74
Williams, Raye	ftb	1976, 77, 78
Williams, Richard	ftb	1999, 2000
Williams, Roger	msw	1983, 84

Williams, Sam	mbk	1979, 80, 81
Williams, Shante	mtr	1995, 96
Williams, Steve	mtr	1965
Williams, Steve	mtr	1974, 75, 76, 77
Williams, Ted	mtn	1976, 77
Williams, Tom	mcc	1981, 82, 83, 84
	mtr	1983, 85
Williams, Torin	mbk	1988, 89
Williams, Travis	ftb	1965, 66
Williams, Ulis	mcc	1961
	mtr	1962, 63, 64, 65
Williams, Valerie	wtr	2000, 01
Williamson, Allison	warc	1992, 93
Williamson, Antone	bb	1992, 93, 94
Williamson, Charlie	bb	1999
Williamson, Kenneth	ftb	1999, 2000
Williamson, Kevin	bb	1984, 85
Williamson, Tee	mbk	1984
Williky, Gary	mtr	1981, 82
Willis, Arch	rif	1957
Willis, Blake	bb	1949, 50

Gary Williky set school records in the shot put (68 feet, 2 1/2 inches) and discus (203 feet, 6 inches) in 1982.

Willis, Chan	rif	1957
Willis, Chris	ftb	1979
Willis, Darren	ftb	1983, 84, 85
Willis, Debbie	wvb	1975
Willis, Denise	wvb	1973, 74, 75, 76
Willis, Joanie	wgo	1958
Willis, Roy	mbk	1944
Willis, Steve	bb	1988, 89
Wills, Elliot "Bump"	bb	1972, 73, 74
Wilsen, Rex	mgo	1959, 60, 61
Wilson, Chris	marc	1976
Wilson, Christie	wvb	1973
Wilson, Don	bb	1959, 60
Wilson, Garth	mbk	1956, 57, 58
Wilson, Howard	mbk	1953, 54
Wilson, James	ftb	1905
Wilson, Jimmie	ftb	1977, 78, 79, 80
Wilson, Jo	wvb	1961
Wilson, Kelly	wsw	1996, 97, 98
Wilson, Kevin	mtr	1981
Wilson, Mike	wre	1975
Wilson, Nate	ftb	1975
Wilson, Patrick	ftb	1999, 2000
Wilson, Ralph	ftb	1949, 50
Wilson, Ric	bb	1981
Wilson, Sarah	wbk	1914
Wilson, Shamus	wre	1996
Wilson, Shelia	wtn	1964, 65, 66, 67

Wilson, Terry	warc	1973
Wilson, Wes	mbk	1956
Wimmer, Jennifer	wsw	1988
Wimp, Les	mgo	1962
Winchell, Sheila	wsb	1985, 86, 87, 88
Winchester, Billy Joe	fb	1973, 74
	mtr	1974, 75
Winchester, Gary	ftb	1976, 77
	mtr	1975
Winder, Dale	mcc	1954, 55, 56
	mtr	1954, 55, 56, 57
Windes, Eustace	bb	1911
Windes, Harold	mcc	1929
Windes, Leldon	bb	1921
	mtn	1923, 26, 27, 29
Windsor	box	1933
	mtr	1933
Wingfield, Gladys	wbm	1959
Winkelman, Elbert	ftb	1919
	mbk	1918
	bb	1918
Winkle, Christie	wtr	1998, 99, 2000, 01
Winn, Daryl	mgo	1961
Winnale, Leslie	wcc	1981, 82, 83
	wtr	1982, 83
Winningham, Glenn	mtr	1964, 66
Winningham, Jim	ftb	1941, 46
Winski, Ben	mgy	1993
Winslett, Dax	bb	1993
Winsley, David	ftb	1988, 89, 90
Winsor, Bud	mbk	1933
Winston, Ted	mtn	1963, 64, 65
Wintaiger, Ann	wgo	1947
Winter, Illselore	warc	1950
Winters, Everett	wre	1979, 80
Wise, Maria	wbk	1983
Wisener, Tom	msw	1968, 69, 70, 71
Witham, Norm	mgy	1963, 64, 65, 66
Witherspoon, Gary	wre	1991
Witherspoon, Greg	bb	1969
Witkowski, Emma	wbk	1995, 96
Witt, Staci	wvb	1991
Wittlinger, Sally	wsw	1977
Wojciak, Margaret	wgy	2000, 01
Wolfenberg, Adam	msw	1997, 98, 99
Wolk, Nina	wbm	1985, 86, 87
Wolta, Diane	wvb	1967

Leldon Windes was the school's first tennis star. He played in 1923, 1926, 1927 and 1929.

Darren Woodson, a three-time All-Pac-10 honorable mention selection at outside linebacker, has become a mainstay in the Dallas Cowboys' secondary.

	wgo	1968
	wsb	1970
Wong, Barbara	wgy	1978, 79, 80
Wong, Cynthia	wsw	1984
Wong, Kenny	mbm	1978
Wong, Shirley	wgy	1981
Wood, Andrew	mtr	1986, 87, 89, 90
Wood, B.	mgo	1962
Wood, Bill	mgo	1987
Wood, Bill	msw	1967, 68, 69, 70
Wood, Dan	mtr	1966
Wood, David	mgo	1986, 87
Wood, David	mtr	2001
Wood, Dawn	wsb	1990, 91, 92, 93
Wood, Dorothea	warc	1941
Wood, Jeff	mtn	1986, 87, 88, 89
Wood, Ryan	ftb	1994, 95
Wood, S.	wsw	1963
Woodcock, Laurie	wsb	1982, 83, 84, 85
Woodford, Scott	ftb	1988, 89, 90
Woodring, Roland	wre	1964
Woods, Bill	rif	1953
Woods, Dennis	msw	1965, 66
Woods, G.	mbk	1933
Woods, Raja	wsb	1997, 98
Woods, Ruth	wbk	1924
Woods, Tim	mtr	1984, 85, 86, 88
Woodson, Darren	ftb	1989, 90, 91
Woolery, Rhonda	wbk	1984, 85, 86, 87
Woolf, Arthur	ftb	1899, 1900, 02, 03, 04
Woolf, Billy	ftb	1896, 97, 99, 1900, 02, 03, 04
Woolf, Bob	mgy	1985
Woolfolk, Frances	warc	1941
Woolfolk, Louise	warc	1940
Woolfolk, Phyllis	warc	1941
Woolridge, M.	wtn	1963
Wools, Robin	warc	1980, 81, 82
Wooster, Dave	msw	1971
Wootan, T.K.	ftb	1939, 40, 41
Worgull, Tania	wbk	1989
Workman, Jerry	wre	1973, 74, 75

Workman, Lori	wbk	1986
Workman, Widd	bb	1996
Worley, Beverly	wsw	1969
Wornardt, Will	bb	1986
Worsley, Roger	ftb	1955, 56, 57
Worth, Andy	msw	1981, 82
Worth, Moe	wcc	1989
	wtr	1990
Wrenn, Diane	wgo	1969
Wright	mtr	1931
Wright, Dwaine	ftb	1980, 82, 83
Wright, Fred	mgo	1950
Wright, James	mbk	1977, 78
Wright, Jeff	mgo	1984
Wright, Jonathan	mcc	1979
	mtr	1980
Wright, Ken	mbk	1975, 76
Wright, Kim	wsb	1978
Wright, Linda	wtr	1976, 77
Wright, Marietta	wtr	1978
Wright, Meagan	wgy	1995, 96, 97, 98
Wright, Pam	wgo	1986, 87, 88
Wright, Phelan	wsb	2001
Wright, Roger	mtn	1966, 67, 68
Wright, Ronnie	mtn	1955, 56
Wright, Ronnie	mgo	1961
Wright, Taleni	ftb	1983, 84, 85, 86
Wright, Tom	mtn	1955
Wrightson, Bernie	msw	1963, 64, 65, 66
Wroblewski, Dave	marc	1974
Wroten, Barbara	wtn	1969, 70, 72
Wrublik, Ray	mcc	1974, 76
Wunderly, Ron	ftb	1952, 53, 54, 55
Wyatt, Clary	ftb	1947
Wyle, Vic	mtn	1956
Wynn	mtr	1933
Wynn, Howard	ftb	1934, 35, 36
	mtr	1935, 36, 37
Wyrick, Dennis	bb	2000, 01

Y

Yancy, Quincy	ftb	1997, 98, 99, 2000
Yantzer, Missy	wsw	1989, 90
Yard, Kevin	mtr	1965
Yaughn, Kip	bb	1989, 90
Yavitt, Dale	wsw	1980
Yavitt, Dawn	wsw	1980
Ybarra, Ray	bb	1940
	ftb	1939, 40, 41
Yeats, Megan	wtn	2000, 01
Yeck, Eldon	mtn	1950
Yee, Linda	wtn	1966, 67, 68, 69
Yetman, Margie	wbm	1951
	wtn	1952, 53
Yingling, Matt	msw	1967, 68, 69
Yoder, Rich	mgy	1992, 93
Yoder, Stanley	bb	1946
Yoo, Dan	wre	1983, 84
Yoshikawa, Aki	wre	1994, 95
Yoshimitsu, Brad	mgy	1989
Young, Amy	wvb	1976
Young, Barry	mtn	1972, 73, 74, 75
Young, Barry	wre	1983
Young, Bill	bb	1950
Young, Bill	mtr	1965, 66
Young, Bobby	wre	1991

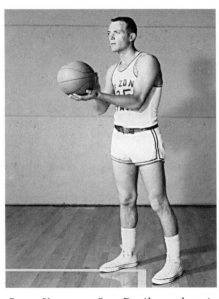

Royce Youree, a Sun Devil standout in basketball and baseball from 1956-1958, later became a legendary high school cage coach.

Young, Bruce	wre	1974, 75, 76, 77
Young, Jan	wgo	1968
	wsw	1965, 66, 67
Young, Janice	wfh	1948
Young, Joann	wtn	1951, 52, 53
Young, Larry	wre	1972, 73
Young, Meredith	warc	1938
Young, Ray	ftb	1959, 60, 62, 63
	mtr	1964
Young, Ray	mtn	1965, 66
Younis, Abbla	wsw	1998
Yountz, Ley	warc	1973
Youree, Royce	bb	1956, 57, 58
	mbk	1956, 57, 58
Yuschik, Diane	warc	1972, 73
Yuss, Fred	ftb	1959, 60

Z

Zaccaria, Jackie	wtr	1986, 87
Zache, Bob	rif	1956
Zajac, Mel	msw	1978, 79
Zakas, Harry	rif	1957, 60
Zakas, Lou	rif	1959
Zaletel, Joe	mbk	1995, 96
Zamborsky, Kathy	wsw	1991, 92, 93, 94
Zapustas, Joe	mtr	1991, 92, 93
Zazueta, Derek	ftb	1989
Zbikowski, Fran	bb	1970, 71
Zehrbach, Chris	warc	1971, 72
Zeiders, Steve	ftb	1967, 68, 69
Zeidler, Eric	wre	1984
Zeis, Lisa	wgy	1983, 84, 85, 86
Zelma, Angela	wbm	1992, 93
Zendejas, Alan	ftb	1987, 88, 89
Zendejas, Luis	ftb	1981, 82, 83, 84
Zeno, Ernie	ftb	1949
Zeno, Tony	mbk	1976, 77, 78, 79
Zerby, Bob	mcc	1976
Zerfoss, Georgann	warc	1967

Gymnast Lisa Zeis earned All-America recognition eight times during her ASU career from 1983-1986.

Sun Devil quarterback/safety Joe Zuger led the nation in punting (42.1-yard average) and interceptions (11) in 1961.

S P O R T S
H A L L O F F A M E

Junior Ah You	Football	1970-71
Gary Alexander	Gymnastics	1972-75
Danielle Ammaccapane	Golf	1984-87
Gail Amundrud	Swimming	1978-81
Kyle Arney	Track & Field	1976-77
Andy Astbury	Swimming	1979-83
Chris Bando	Baseball	1975-78
Sal Bando	Baseball	1964-65
Eddie Bane	Baseball	1971-73
Alan Bannister	Baseball	1970-71
Floyd Bannister	Baseball	1974-76
Scott Barclay	Gymnastics	1975-78
Jane Bastanchury	Golf	1966-68
Art Becker	Basketball	1962-64
Melissa Belote	Swimming	1976-79
Barry Bonds	Baseball	1983-85
George Boutell	Golf	1965-67
Bob Breunig	Football	1972-74
Jerry Bright	Track & Field	1967-69
Dr. Jim Brock	Baseball Coach	1972-1994
Hubie Brooks	Baseball	1977-78
Ron Brown	Football, Track	1979-82
Kent Brown	Gymnastics	1972-75
Jackie Brummer	Gymnastics	1983-86
Leon Burton	Football	1955-58
Joe Caldwell	Basketball	1962-64
Jeri Cameron Vanyek	Gymnastics	1980-83
Joanne Gunderson Carner	Golf	1957-61
Henry Carr	Track & Field	1962-64
Jim Carter	Golf	1981-84
Senon "Baldy" Castillo	Track & Field	
	Coach	1953-1979
Tony Cerkvenik	Basketball	1961-64
Pam Richmond Champagne	Tennis	1968-71
Carol Cheuvronot Clark	Archery	1977-80
Jon Cole	Track & Field	1963-66
Roy Coppinger	Baseball, Basketball	1951-53
Frank Covelli	Track & Field	1962-63
Curley Culp	Football, Wrestling	1964-68
Alvin Davis	Baseball	1979-82
Leslie Deniz	Track & Field	1981-83
Dan Devine	Football Coach	1955-57
Ed Doherty	Football Coach	1947-50
Bobby Douglas	Wrestling Coach	1974-92
Duffy Dyer	Baseball	1963-66
Kathy Escarcega	Softball	1984-87
Chris Evans	Gymnastics	1963-64
Dwayne Evans	Track & Field	1980-81
Heather Farr	Golf	1983-85
Dan Forsman	Golf	1979-81
Herman Frazier	Track & Field	1975-77
Ron Freeman II	Track & Field	1966-69
David Fulcher	Football	1983-85
Tom Futch	Football, Basketball,	
	Baseball	1953-56
Benny Garcia	Track & Field	1953-56
Cathy Gaughan Mant	Golf	1970-72
Gary Gentry	Baseball	1967
Cheryl Gibson	Swimming	1978-82
Bob Gilder	Golf	1972-74
Larry Gordon	Football	1972-75
Maryanne Graham-Keever	Swimming	1974-75
Dave Graybill	All-Around	1953-57
Woody Green	Football	1971-73
Larry Gura	Baseball	1967-69
Charles Haigler	Football	1896-1902
Windlan Hall	Football	1969-71
Kym Hampton	Basketball	1980-84
Al Harris	Football	1975-78
John Harris	Football	1975-77

Ben Hawkins	Football	1963-65
Jan Henne Hawkins	Swimming	1968-72
Buzz Hayes	Wrestling	1962-65
Mike Haynes	Football	1972-76
Verl Heap	Basketball	1945-48
Patsy Willard Heckel	Diving	1960-64
Alex Henderson	Track & Field	1957-60
Hascal Henshaw	Football	1938-40
J.D. Hill	Football	1967-68, 70
Steve Holden	Football	1969-72
Lionel Hollins	Basketball	1973-75
Bob Horner	Baseball	1976-78
Reggie Jackson	Baseball	1966
John Jankans	Football	1952-55
Jim Jeffcoat	Football	1980-83
John Jefferson	Football	1974-77
John Henry Johnson	Football	1952
Carol Jurn	Archery	1971-74
Bill Kajikawa	Multi-sport athlete &	
	coach	1937-79
Sue Annis Kellogg	Badminton	1970-72
Donn Kinzle	Administrator	1946-52
Margaret Klann	Badminton coach	1955-76
Bob Kohrs	Football	1976-79
Frank Kush	Football coach	1958-79
Chuck LaBenz	Track & Field	1967-70
Lerrin LaGrow	Baseball	1963-65
Luis Lagunas	Baseball	1963-65
Rudy Lavik	Coach,	
	Administrator	1933-49
Margie Wood Law	Softball	1953-56
Lafayette "Fat" Lever	Basketball	1978-82
Freddie Lewis	Basketball	1964-65
Steve Lieberman	Archery	1971-74
Alton Lister	Basketball	1978-81
Mary Littlewood	Softball, volleyball,	
	women's basketball	
	coach	1965-89
Tony Lorick	Football	1961-63
Jerry Maddox	Baseball	1973-75
Art Malone	Football	1967-69
Ben Malone	Football	1971-73
Bill Mann	Men's Golf Coach	1961-75
Vernon Maxwell	Football	1979-82
Billy Mayfair	Golf	1985-88
Randall McDaniel	Football	1984-87
Oddibe McDowell	Baseball	1983-84
Rick McKinney	Archery	1980-84
Glenn McMinn Sr.	Wrestling	1965-67
Lauri Merten	Women's Golf	1979-82
Margaret "Peggy" Michael	Tennis	1968-72
Alice Miller	Golf	1974-78
Bill Miller	Track & Field	1948-51
Dr. Fred Miller	Athletic Director	1971-80
John Mistler	Football	1977-80
Rick Monday	Baseball	1965
Jim Montgomery	Football	1946-47
Kendis Drake Moore	Swimming	1967-71
Mike Morley	Golf	1964-68
Carrie Morrison	Badminton	1977-79
Bobby Mulgado	Football	1954-58
Mark Murro	Track & Field	1968-71
Paula Miller Noel	Softball	1971-73
Kim Neal	Gymnastics	1983-85
Albert Nealey	Basketball	1957-60
Fred Nelson	Baseball	1967-68
Sheri Norris	Tennis	1983-86
Roye Oliver	Wrestling	1975-77, 79
Merle Packer	Badminton coach	1967-84
John Pavlik	Baseball	1964-66

Maurice Peoples	Track & Field	1972-73
Wayne "Ripper" Pitts	Football	1938-40
Mona Plummer	Women's	
	Swimming Coach,	
	Administrator	1957-79
Mike Pagel	Football, Baseball	1979-82
Paul Ray Powell	Baseball, Football	1967-69
Ron Pritchard	Football	1966-68
Tom Purtzer	Golf	1970-73
Lenny Randle	Baseball, Football	1968-70
Jodi Rathbun	W. Basketball,	
	Softball	1983-87
Marilyn Rau	Softball	1971-72
Sheri Torrance Rhodes	Archery	1973-76
Mike Richardson	Football	1979-82
Gerald Riggs	Football	1978-81
Don Robinson	Gymnastics coach	1969-93
Kevin Romine	Baseball	1981-82
Billy Rosado	Wrestling	1976-78
Keith Russell	Diving	1967-68
Ann Peterson Scheer	Diving	1966-68
Roger Schmuck	Baseball	1970-71
Byron Scott	Basketball	1979-83
Judy Severance	Archery	1964-67
Dan Severn	Wrestling	1977-80
Sterling Slaughter	Baseball	1961-63
Clyde Smith	Football Coach,	
	Athletic Director	1952-71
Jerry Smith	Football	1963-64
Coleen Rienstra Sommer	Track & Field	1978-81
Carol Sorenson	Golf	1960-64
Ria Stalman	Track & Field	1979-81
Jean Stephenson	Archery	1974-76
Norris Steverson	Football	1929-31
Lisa Stuck	Volleyball	1980-83
Craig Swan	Baseball	1969-72
Charley Taylor	Football	1960-63
Peggy Tosdal	Swimming	1974-79
Charlie Tribble	Wrestling	1965
Howard Twitty	Golf	1970-72
Libby Tullis	Swimming	1972-76
Sally Tuttle	Swimming	1973-76
Jeff Van Raaphorst	Football	1983-86
Eddie Urbano	Wrestling	1983-85
Rick Walker	Track & Field	1974-77
Tammy Webb	Volleyball	1983-86
Danny White	Football	1971-73
Wilford "Whizzer" White	Football	1947-50
Ulis Williams	Track & Field	1962-65
Bobby Winkles	Baseball Coach	1959-71
Bernie Wrightson	Diving	1962-66
Ned Wulk	Basketball Coach	1957-82
Royce Youree	Basketball	1955-58
Lisa Zeis	Gymnastics	1983-86
Luis Zendejas	Football	1981-84
Joe Zuger	Football	1959-61
World Record Mile		
Relay Team		
(Mike Barrick, Henry		
Carr Ron Freeman,		
Ulis Williams)	Track & Field	1963
School Record 4X400-		
Meter Relay Team		
(Gary Burl, Gerald Burl,		
Clifton McKenzie,		
Tony Darden,		
Herman Frazier)	Track & Field	1977

SUN DEVIL
OLYMPIC ATHLETES

Athlete	Country	Year	Sport
Abodo, Reema	Canada	1984	Swimming
Adams, Judi	USA	1980*/96	Archery
Adams, Lorrieann	Guyana	1996	Track and Field
Adel, Carolyn	Surinam	1996	Swimming
Akinremi, Christine	Nigeria	1996	Track and Field
Akinremi, Omolade	Nigeria	1996	Track and Field
Akinremi, Omotayo	Nigeria	1996	Track and Field
Akpan, Ime	Nigeria	1992/96	Track and Field
Amundrud, Gail	Canada	1976	Swimming
Anderson, Ross	New Zealand	1988	Swimming
Astbury, Andy	Great Britain	1980*/84	Swimming
Aumas, Francois	Switzerland	1976	Track and Field
Azvedo, Ana	Brazil	1996	Swimming
Baker, Joann	Canada	1976	Swimming
Barrs, Jay	USA	1988/92	Archery
Bartholomew, Jacinta	Grenada	1984	Track and Field
Baxter, Terri	USA	1980*	Swimming
Belote, Melissa	USA	1972/76	Swimming
Berggren, Peter	Sweden	1984	Swimming
Bera, Richard	Indonesia	1996	Swimming
Bohay, Gary	Canada	1988	Wrestling
Brown, Ron	USA	1984	Track and Field
Caldwell, Joe	USA	1964	Basketball
Carr, Henry	USA	1964	Track and Field
Cliff, Leslie	Canada	1972	Swimming
Cochran, Neil	Great Britain	1984/88	Swimming
Cook, Robert	USA	1980*	Cycling
Covelli, Frank	USA	1964/68	Track and Field
Cox, Tracy	Zimbabwe	1984/88/92	Diving
Dalby, Troy	USA	1988	Swimming
Delgado, Felipe	Ecuador	1996	Swimming
Delgado, Robert	Ecuador	1996	Swimming
Deniz, Leslie	USA	1984	Track and Field
Douglas, Bobby Coach	USA	1976/88	Wrestling
Easter, Paul	Great Britain	1984/88	Swimming
Eiter, Rob	USA	1996	Wrestling
Evans, Dwayne	USA	1976	Track and Field
Fagernes, Pal Arne	Norway	1996	Track and Field
Frazier, Herman	USA	1976/1980*	Track and Field
Freeman, Ron II	USA	1968	Track and Field
French, Linda	USA	1992/96	Badminton
Garcia, Benny	USA	1956	Track and Field
Gibson, Cheryl	Canada	1976/80*	Swimming
Graham, Maryann	USA	1976	Swimming
Gyetko, Brian	Canada	1992	Tennis
Hardy, Steve	Canada	1976	Swimming
Heber, Richard	Argentina	1956	Track and Field
Henderson, Dan	USA	1996	Wrestling
Henne, Jan	USA	1968	Swimming
Holderbach, David	France	1988/92	Swimming
Howel, Paul	Great Britain	1984/88/92	Swimming
Huish, Justin	USA	1996	Archery
Hysong, Nick	USA	2000	Track and Field
Jameson, Andrew	Great Britain	1984/88	Swimming
Jeisy, Don	USA	1964	Track and Field
Jogis, Chris	USA	1992	Badminton
Jones, Zeke	USA	1992	Wrestling
Kerston, Scott	USA	1980*	Archery
Koopman, Amy	USA	1980*	Gymnastics
Kristjansson, Logi	Iceland	1996	Swimming
Lagopatis, Panagiotis	Greece	1996	Swimming
LeBlanc, David	France	1988/92	Swimming
Lee, Benny	USA	1992	Badminton
Lincoln, Nelson	USA	1960	Shooting
Lindros, Carol	Finland	1960	Track and Field
Lister, Alton	USA	1980*	Basketball
Lundin, Therese	Sweden	1992	Swimming
Malone, Maicel	USA	1988/96	Track and Field
McDowell, Oddibe	USA	1984	Baseball
McKinney, Rick	USA	1976/84/88/92	Archery
Meyers, Glenn	USA	1984	Archery
Michelena, Christiano	Brazil	1988/92	Swimming
Miller, Bill	USA	1952	Track and Field
Moore, Kendis	USA	1968	Swimming
Moscote, Rafael	Panama	1996	Swimming
Murphy, Pat	Netherlands	2000	Baseball Coach
Murro, Mark	USA	1968	Track and Field
Nascimento, Emmanuel	Brazil	1988/92	Swimming
Nelson, Lynn	USA	1988	Track and Field
Ochs, Debbie	USA	1988	Archery
Orn, Michael	Sweden	1984	Swimming
Parker, Andrew	Jamaica	1988	Track and Field
Peoples, Maurice	USA	1972	Track and Field
Percy, Simon	New Zealand	1992	Swimming
Peterson, Anders	Sweden	1984	Swimming
Peterson, Ann	USA	1968	Swimming
Phillips, Dwight	USA	2000	Track and Field
Piccinini, Eduardo	Brazil	1992	Swimming
Ramalho, Renato	Brazil	1988/92	Swimming
Reidy, Tom	USA	1992	Badminton
Rhodes, Sheri	USA	1988	Archery Coach
Ronaldson, Tony	Australia	1996	Basketball
Rosado, Billy	USA	1976	Wrestling
Russell, Keith	USA	1968	Diving
Sanchez, Francisco	Venezuela	1996	Swimming
Sanchez, Marco	Puerto Rico	1996	Wrestling
Sargsian, Sargis	Armenia	1996	Tennis
Saunders, Townsend	USA	1992/96	Wrestling
Schad, Joelle	Dominican Republic	1996	Tennis
Scott, Louis	USA	1968	Track and Field
Senior, Mark	Jamaica	1984	Track and Field
Sloan, Sue	Canada	1976	Swimming
Sommer, Coleen	USA	1988	Track and Field
Spence, Mal	Jamaica	1956/60/64	Track and Field
Spence, Mel	Jamaica	1956/60/64	Track and Field
Stalman, Ria	Netherlands	1984	Track and Field
Tapper, Richard	New Zealand	1992	Swimming
Tolbert, Lynda	USA	1992/96	Track and Field
Tribble, Charles	USA	1964	Wrestling
Trujillo, Marie	Mexico	1984	Track and Field
Tudos, Jessica	Canada	1984	Gymnastics
Von Heiland, Erika	USA	1992/96	Badminton
Webb, Tammy	USA	1988/92/96	Volleyball
Welbourn, Graham	Canada	1980*	Swimming
Willard, Patsy	USA	1960/64	Diving
Williams, Ulis	USA	1964	Track and Field
Williamson, Alison	Great Britain	1992/96	Archery
Wrightson, Bernie	USA	1968	Diving
Zajac, Mel	Canada	1976	Swimming

*Home country boycotted the 1980 Summer Olympics in Moscow.